NEW PATHS IN JEWISH AND RELIGIOUS STUDIES

NEW PATHS IN JEWISH AND RELIGIOUS STUDIES

Essays in Honor of Professor Elliot R. Wolfson

Edited by Glenn Dynner,
Susannah Heschel, and Shaul Magid

Purdue University Press • West Lafayette, Indiana

Printed in the United States of America.

Cataloging-in-Publication Data is available from the Library of Congress.
978-1-61249-922-2 (hardback)
978-1-61249-924-6 (epub)
978-1-61249-923-9 (paperback)
978-1-61249-925-3 (epdf)

Cover: *free fall*, by Elliot Wolfson (2008)

CONTENTS

ACKNOWLEDGMENTS

THE JEWISH STUDIES PROGRAM AT DARTMOUTH COLLEGE WAS PRIVILEGED to host Professor Elliot Wolfson as our Brownstone Visiting Professor in Judaic Studies during the winter and spring terms of 2003. His presence on campus was enormously invigorating to faculty and students alike. In addition to teaching courses in Jewish studies, religion, and women's studies, Elliot delivered an inaugural address on January 8, "Unveiling the Veil: Envisioning God in Islamic and Jewish Mysticism," attended by a large audience from around the campus, including our honored donors of the chair, Clyde and Diane Brownstone.

The Brownstone Family Visiting Professorship in Judaic Culture at Dartmouth College was established by a vote of the trustees in June 1987, thanks to gifts to the college from Sylvia and Walter Brownstone (1928) and from Diane and Clyde Brownstone (1957). The professorship is intended to bring "scholars from a variety of disciplines to teach courses on Judaic history, culture, and civilization, emphasizing the historical significance of Judaic culture."

The gift of the Brownstone family established one of the foundations of our Jewish Studies Program. Thanks to the Brownstone chair, Dartmouth has been privileged to invite a series of distinguished scholars to teach here, including Grace Paley, Cyrus Gordon, Geoffrey Hartman, Sidra Ezrahi, Ruth Kark, Danny Rubinstein, Benny Morris, Jonathan and Edith Frankel, and Jonathan Karp. In the years since Elliot's visit, we have hosted Bryan Cheyette, Jonathan Boyarin, Israel Yuval, Jeremy Cohen, Shaul Magid, Marc Caplan, Francois Guesnet, Harvey Goldberg, and Sylvie Anne Goldberg. Their courses have inspired a generation of Dartmouth students and have greatly enriched the intellectual life for faculty as well. In addition to the inaugural address to the Dartmouth community, each participates actively in the lectures and seminars organized by the Jewish Studies Program.

As scholars in the field of Jewish studies with quite different disciplinary training and interests, Glenn, Shaul, and Susannah are united in our admiration for Elliot Wolfson's scholarship. His work has been inspiring to each of us in different ways, and we are grateful to have the opportunity to edit a volume of articles by our colleagues to pay tribute to Elliot's work. The articles in this volume represent just a fraction of the many scholars who have been influenced by the unique and groundbreaking nature of Elliot's work.

This project was one we enjoyed enormously, and we know it will be of great significance to scholars and students in many fields. All who read this book will join us in our enormous gratitude to Professor Marcelo Gleiser, the Appleton Professor of Natural

Philosophy and Professor of Physics and Astronomy at Dartmouth College, where he also directs the Institute for Cross-Disciplinary Engagement. One of the great stars of the Dartmouth faculty, Marcelo is a beloved teacher and renowned scholar who specializes in cosmology and high energy physics, complexity theory, and astrobiology. His work as a theoretical physicist and philosopher also brings science and religion into dialogue, addressing the major questions of our era. He is a wise and celebrated public intellectual whose impact resounds around the globe. We are deeply grateful that Marcelo Gleiser provided generous funding for the publication of this book from the Institute for Cross-Disciplinary Engagement at Dartmouth College, which he directs and which receives generous funding from the John Templeton Foundation.

We also want to thank Justin Race, editor at Purdue University Press, for his immediate and enthusiastic welcome of our proposal for this volume.

Working with the colleagues who contributed to this volume has been an enormous pleasure. We have also found it a great delight to work together as a team of three. Most of all, we are grateful for this opportunity to honor Elliot Wolfson.

INTRODUCTION

GLENN DYNNER, SUSANNAH HESCHEL,
AND SHAUL MAGID

TO READ ELLIOT WOLFSON IS TO UNDERGO AN EPISTEMOLOGICAL TRANSformation. Texts that seem familiar take on utterly new meanings, assumptions give way to startling insights, and boundaries virtually dissolve. Wolfson's engagement with primary sources sometimes becomes, itself, a primary source, for he creates his own hermeneutical tools to expose readers of texts to new ways of thinking. Wolfson is not only a great scholar but a great thinker, one of the most important Jewish thinkers of his generation who works in the Jewish tradition.

Wolfson's impact on the reader goes far beyond the attainment of knowledge. Entering through the door he has opened, we behold new hermeneutical possibilities. His ability to make the reader aware of the limitations of language while suggesting, at the same time, a new language is radically illuminating. Only by reading Wolfson do we become fully aware of the extent to which we have been trapped in our own hermeneutical straits and realize the possibility of a new kind of knowledge.

Paradigm shifts begin with affect, and for Wolfson, affect arrives through poiesis. The mood and experience of the poetic beckon readers into his realization that language points beyond itself. His poetry and paintings offer glimpses into the poiesis of his mind and coax us to escape our inherited paradigms. We might feel some regret about leaving behind scholars who have thus far shaped our thinking. But Wolfson's work explodes our scholarly provinciality. He inverts, challenges, revises. The breadth of his learning is extraordinary; some footnotes are treatises. Wolfson's writings exude a passion for and devotion to scholarship, much of which is reflected in the current collection of articles by his students and colleagues.

Wolfson's first major work, his 1994 book *Through a Speculum That Shines: Vision and Imagination in Medieval Jewish Mysticism*, revolutionized the study of Jewish mysticism and gender—indeed, the study of religion. The book presents a broad and deep analysis of rabbinic literature (and the Hebrew Bible) and proceeds to late antique Jewish mysticism and medieval Kabbalah, all the while grappling with the construction of gender through the lens of the imagination. Working with the gender theory of Luce Irigaray and others while introducing the category of "phallocentrism" to the study of Kabbalah, Wolfson was the first to deploy French literary theory and gender analysis as a lens to perceive gender as the master trope of the kabbalistic imaginary.[1] Yet in a later book, Wolfson recognizes a destabilization, if not complete overturning, of the phallocentrism of Kabbalah in the Hasidic teachings of Menachem Mendel Schneerson, the Lubavitcher Rebbe.

Speculum puts forth a thesis that virtually upends Kabbalah studies. Subverting the common assumption that Kabbalah contained a strong category of the feminine, in contrast to the patriarchal and logocentric stature of classical Judaism, Wolfson argues instead that Kabbalah actually deepens the structures of patriarchy by imagining a hierarchy whereby the independent feminine exists only as a temporary extension of the masculine (the mythological male phallus of *yesod*) that is then reabsorbed into the masculine as the culminating part of the unfolding redemptive history. Kabbalah thus not only offers the claim that the masculine is superior to the feminine; it claims that the feminine exists only as a temporal, exilic phase to be ultimately overcome in the masculine. The thesis deeply problematizes interpretations of Kabbalah that seek a proto-feminist template for Judaism.

While Wolfson's impact has perhaps been greatest in the study of Jewish mysticism, which he sees as combining intellect, imagination, mathematics, and poetry, his scholarly interests extend from classical Buddhism to Heideggerian philosophy and contemporary theories of religion yet are constantly informed by his knowledge of Jewish mystical concepts. His engagement with contemporary continental philosophy is profound, as is his revision of the historical positivism that shaped the Wissenschaft des Judentums, even while recognizing the foundational importance of historical context and philological analysis. Among the many philosophers and theorists whom he credits as influences on his thinking are Nietzsche, Husserl, Merleau-Ponty, Heidegger, Sartre, Bergson, Derrida, Levinas, Irigaray, Ricoeur, and Kristeva. To read Wolfson is to enter an era of critical-Jewish studies.

Although a radically original thinker, Wolfson emerged from an Orthodox Jewish home and received a classical Jewish education. He was born in Newark, New Jersey, the youngest of four sons. His father, Wilfred, was raised in Nova Scotia, Canada, served as Orthodox rabbi of Congregation Sha'arei Tefillah in Brooklyn, and was also a popular teacher at Yeshiva University and the Brooklyn Talmudic Academy, where Wolfson attended high school. Rabbi Wolfson attended Johns Hopkins University, where he studied the Hebrew Bible and Near Eastern languages with the renowned Bible scholar Professor William Albright, was ordained in the Ner Yisrael yeshiva in Baltimore, and subsequently received a master's degree in Semitic studies at Columbia University. Wolfson's mother, Zelda Sylvia, was born in Newark, New Jersey and, like Elliot, was the youngest of four. She initially studied German language and literature at Upsala College in New Jersey, later turning to mathematics, which she taught in the New York public high school system.

In an autobiographical reflection, Wolfson noted that his birthdate in the Hebrew calendar, the nineteenth day of the month of Kislev, was auspicious: the date when Rabbi Shneur Zalman of Liadi, founder of the Habad/Lubavitch movement within Hasidism, was released from a czarist prison and, on Habad's own account, marks the ostensible "birth of *Hasidus*." Wolfson has devoted a major study to Habad Hasidism, *Open Secret*, the largest international Jewish religious movement today. His interest in Hasidism began as a teenager, when he took classes with the famous Breslov leader in Brighton Beach, Brooklyn, Rabbi Zvi Aryeh Rosenfeld, who built Breslov in America; Rosenfeld's student, Chaim Kramer, established the Breslov Research Institute. During those years, Wolfson also began studying the works of Rav Kook, the Maharal of Prague, and the Italian mystic Moses Chaim Luzzatto (known as Ramhal).

After high school and spending some time studying in various yeshivot in Jerusalem, Wolfson studied for three semesters at Yeshiva University before transferring to a program at the Graduate Center of the City University of New York in conjunction with Queens College, where he delved into philosophy under the tutelage of Edith Wyschogrod, one of his "most important teachers." Wyschogrod, for her part, remembers Wolfson as a "precocious young undergrad interested in Jewish philosophy." Wolfson would later write a book about Wyschogrod, Susan Taubes, and Gillian Rose entitled *Nocturnal Seeing: Hopelessness of Hope and Philosophical Gnosis in Susan Taubes, Gillian Rose, and Edith Wyschogrod* (2025).

AFTER COMPLETING COLLEGE, WOLFSON SPENT A YEAR AT JOHNS HOPKINS before transferring to Brandeis University. Indeed, he simultaneously applied to the doctoral programs of the renowned Religion department at the University of California at Santa Barbara (UCSB) to study Hinduism and Buddhism and to Brandeis University for Jewish thought. Hinduism and Buddhism, or Judaism? Accepted to both programs, yet unable to choose, he signed acceptance forms for both programs, putting each one in a stamped envelope, and walked to the mailbox holding both letters, perhaps hoping for a revelatory sign. Reaching his destination, he dropped the Brandeis letter in the mailbox and discarded the letter to UCSB. Yet the UCSB path was never abandoned. One of his most lasting contributions to the study of Jewish mysticism and thought is his integration of Buddhism and Asian religions into his philosophical and phenomenological analyses, exemplified by his book *Language, Eros, Being: Kabbalistic Hermeneutics and Poetic Imagination* (2005), a work that transformed scholarly treatment of this literature. Wolfson would one day join the UCSB faculty as the Marsha and Jay Glazer Chair in Jewish Studies, where he would teach for a decade until his retirement.

At Brandeis University, which in the early 1980s possessed illustrious faculty like Nahum Sarna, Michael Fishbane, Marvin Fox, and Alexander Altmann, Wolfson wrote his dissertation under the guidance of Fox, a scholar of Maimonides and Jewish philosophy, and Alexander Altmann, who had already retired from teaching but served as a crucial influence. The dissertation, focused on Moses de Leon's *Sefer ha-Rimmon*, included, at Altmann's suggestion, an annotated critical edition and introductory study of the text. Altmann was an important mentor for Wolfson, both in guiding his interest in the nexus between philosophy and Kabbalah and connecting him to the prewar tradition of Jewish scholarship. It was Altmann who trained a small group of students as scholars of Kabbalah with an alternative approach to that being promoted at Israeli universities.[2] In some sense, Altmann embodied for Wolfson what Gershom Scholem represented for an earlier generation of Israeli scholars of Jewish mysticism. Like Altmann, Wolfson saw no inherent difference or contradiction between the philosophical and the mystical, and his scholarship moves seamlessly between the two modes of thought: he pays close attention to the philological yet frames his textual analysis broadly and eventually comparatively.

After completing his doctorate in 1986, Wolfson spent a year as a Mellon Postdoctoral Fellow at Cornell University before assuming a position in the Skirball Department of Hebrew and Judaic Studies at NYU in the fall of 1987, becoming the Abraham Lieberman Professor in 1993. For the next twenty-eight years Elliot trained many graduate students at NYU, many of whom contributed to the current volume, in subjects ranging from Kabbalah to early modern and continental philosophy to medieval and modern Jewish thought. In addition, during his tenure at NYU he taught for twelve years as an adjunct professor in the Department of Religion at Columbia University where he also mentored numerous graduate students. In 2014 he accepted the Marsha and Jay Glazer Chair in Jewish Studies at the University of California at Santa Barbara. He has also served as the Brownstone Distinguished Visiting Professor at Dartmouth College for two terms, and as visiting professor at Harvard, Rice University, the University of Toronto, the University of Notre Dame, Johns Hopkins University, the University of Chicago, the Russian State University for the Humanities in Moscow, and Shandong University in Jinan, China.

WOLFSON'S PRODUCTIVITY IS NOTHING SHORT OF EXTRAORDINARY. HE IS THE author of more than twenty academic books, including four volumes of poetry; editor of many others, as well as founding editor of the *Journal of Jewish Thought and Philosophy*; and editor of a series on Judaism with Brill Press. The author of over two hundred scholarly essays, Wolfson's intellectual reach ranges from classical studies such as *Through a Speculum That Shines* (1994), to new understandings of Hasidism and messianism in *Open Secret* (2009), to philosophically oriented works like *Giving Beyond the Gift* (2014), to works on psychoanalysis and dream interpretation like *A Dream Interpreted Within a Dream* (2011), to works on the philosophy of language like *Language, Eros, Being* (2005), to a massive work of constructive philosophy and theology, another magnum opus, *Heidegger and Kabbalah* (2019).

Many of these books won national book prizes and awards, and the significance of Wolfson's scholarship was formally recognized in the field of Jewish studies with his election to the American Academy of Jewish Research in 1998; in the study of religion with his election to the American Society for the Study of Religion in 2013; and in the humanities more generally with his election to the prestigious American Academy of Arts and Sciences in 2008. Wolfson's influence is felt deeply in the works of former students and in the hundreds of colleagues he has influenced. From this volume one can see the mark he has left in a variety of fields and across generations.

Martin Buber once said of Gershom Scholem that "he created a field," and that was surely true. But the field that Scholem created was, in turn, transformed in Wolfson's hands. His work rings dissonant to some ears, for it often exposes reigning apologetic, sanitized, romanticized, and atomized approaches to the study of Jewish mysticism. Wolfson has also confronted the darker side of that textual tradition, especially its androcentric, erotic, homoerotic, and ethnocentric aspects. With each publication, Wolfson is ahead of his time and, for the past four decades, we have been trying to catch up.

Wolfson has created a quintessentially North American school of Jewish mysticism, one that is eclectic, interdisciplinary, richly theoretical, and comparative. His thinking reflects the very architecture of North American academia, for a professor of Jewish studies at a North American university will often have an office next to a scholar of Buddhism, or Islam, or African American religion and attend talks in a variety of fields. Comparative by nature and design, religious studies in North America brings insights from other religious traditions and new methodologies to older textual traditions. Wolfson fully absorbed that ethos as a student, then as inaugural director of the newly established program in religious studies at NYU (now a department) and, most prominently, in his own scholarship and thinking. He has consequently become one of the most widely read scholars of religion today.

AFTER ASSUMING A FACULTY POSITION AT NYU AND THEN BECOMING THE ABRAham Lieberman Professor in Hebrew and Judaic Studies, Wolfson published a plethora of scholarly essays. When *Through a Speculum That Shines* appeared in 1994, his impact became more widely felt. *Speculum* was awarded both the American Academy of Religion Award for Excellence in the Study of Religion in the Category of Historical Studies and the National Jewish Book Award for Excellence in Scholarship.

Just a year after *Speculum*, Elliot published two more extraordinary studies of Kabbalah, *Circle in the Square: Studies in the Use of Gender in Kabbalistic Symbolism* (1995) and *Along the Path: Studies on Kabbalistic Myth, Symbolism, and Hermeneutics* (1995). The first further develops the gender theory Wolfson proffered in *Speculum* and expands its reach to include symbolism, the "imaginal divine body," making gender a hermeneutical trope in both the kabbalistic text and its interpreters. In *Along a Path* the focus is more specifically on hermeneutics and develops a new and profound analysis of mythology and symbolism as ways to think about the kabbalistic mind as a textual creator and textual interpreter. Wolfson's next book focused on the important medieval Kabbalist Abraham Abulafia and his relationship to the doctrine of the *sefirot*, the divine emanations, *Abraham Abulafia, Kabbalist and Prophet: Hermeneutics, Theosophy, and Theurgy* (2000). The book constitutes a major intervention not only in the existing Abulafia scholarship, but also in the history of Jewish thought.

In the next stage of Wolfson's scholarship we begin to see imagination emerge more prominently as a category that will become a more central dimension of this thinking, addressed in his books *Language, Eros, Being: Kabbalistic Hermeneutics and the Poetic Imagination* (2005; henceforth *LEB*), for which he won a second National Jewish Book Award for Excellence in Scholarship, an unusual and remarkable accomplishment, and *Dream Interpreted Within a Dream: Oneiropoiesis and the Prism of Imagination* (2011), which was awarded the American Academy of Religion Award for Excellence in the Study of Religion in the Category of Constructive and Reflective Studies. *LEB* is a tour de force in ways that extend beyond *Speculum*. In this 760-page tightly argued volume, Wolfson uses his classical and philological training to bring Kabbalah into the discourse of classical and continental philosophy and theology. Continuing his interest in hermeneutics, *LEB* broadens the discussion into theories of language, desire, and the category of being that had been the focus of philosophers from Heraclitus to Heidegger. Interweaving language, desire, and being, *LEB* exhibits a deepening engagement with Freudian psychoanalysis and Freud's theory of consciousness, revealing that philosophers have missed something crucial in ignoring Kabbalah.

In *LEB* we find a crucial development. Whereas in *Speculum* and the two books that followed Wolfson uses philosophical method and critical analysis to decode and interpret kabbalistic texts and the kabbalistic mind, in *LEB* we find kabbalistic texts themselves becoming part of the larger philosophical and theological orbit. *LEB* uses Christian, Muslim, Buddhist, and Hindu traditions comparatively—not to exhibit similitude so much as to illustrate common concerns and attitudes toward the three fundamentals of the human condition (language, desire/Eros, being) as they relate to religious expression, desire, and experience. What emerges is the category of poetics, something that will play a role in his later writing as he explores the meaning of poesis in Kabbalah (and all mystical traditions) but also its central importance in efforts of interpretation, including modern scholarship. Few contemporary works in the humanities have the breadth, depth of analysis, and command of multiple traditions and disciplines that merge in a synthetic, robust, creative, and even constructive reappraisal of the human condition as it arises from the depth of the kabbalistic imaginary. Rather than translate religion into the terminology of psychology or sociology, Wolfson studies Kabbalah on its own terms. Indeed, *LEB* is more than scholarship: It constitutes a primary text of religious thought. Wolfson's own scholarship is accordingly not only a study of Kabbalah, but an expression of kabbalistic scholarship.

The shift in trajectory that opens up Kabbalah as a source and *resource* for the basic questions of humanness in its relationship to the divine continues in Wolfson's next two books, both published in 2006. Poised to tackle the various dimensions of thought as they relate to Judaism broadly defined, Wolfson chose the categories of ethics and time: ethics in *Venturing Beyond: Law and Morality in Kabbalistic Mysticism*, and time in *Alef, Mem, Tau: Kabbalistic Musings on Time, Truth, and Death*. Introducing the possibility that Kabbalah can enrich our entire understanding of the human condition and the divine world as convened by humans, Wolfson offers a strong and complex theory of ethnocentrism and the attraction to and struggle with and against the "other" in Kabbalah. The notion of Judaism as an exemplar of "ethical monotheism" is thrown into a veritable tailspin as we behold a mythic world of demonization and sublimation of the Other in tandem with an intense attraction to that very same Other, amounting to a veritable critique of "kabbalistic Orientalism." Here, Wolfson takes on the under-researched issues of Kabbalah and the law, ethics, and nomos. The categories of law and ethics in Kabbalah, similar in their incongruity, sparked a new phase of debate about Kabbalah and law, or Kabbalah as an iteration of normative Judaism. The dramatic intensity of this and other work lies in the willingness to explore issues that most have avoided.

While Scholem has taught us about the never-ending tension between law and experience among Kabbalists, in *Venturing Beyond* Wolfson deploys the category of the "hypernomian" that is as resistant to law as antinomianism, albeit in reverse. That is, kabbalistic piety or hyperpiety can be rendered controversial from the standpoint of the normative halakhic tradition as the abrogation of the law that we see in Paul and Sabbatianism. In several essays on Sabbatianism, Wolfson deepens this point by demonstrating that the most radical critique of the law may come from *inside the law itself* when the law is rendered a vehicle for religious experience. The category of hypernomianism as deviant in *Venturing Beyond* offers a fresh reading of Kabbalah and normativity.

Alef, Mem, Tau marks Wolfson's repositioning toward the modern philosophical world, something that would inform the next period of his career. It is here we begin to see the resonances of Rosenzweig, Heidegger, Bergson, Merleau-Ponty, and Levinas become more prominent. Notions of cyclical versus linear time were certainly not foreign to the Kabbalists. They lived in the mystical world of timelessness, in a time warp, or timeswerve, and simultaneously in the corporeal world of linear time. Notions of the present or "eternally present" that exceeds time was something the Kabbalists took for granted yet did not have the language to express in a reflective, or philosophical, way. In *Alef, Mem, Tau* Wolfson attempts to unpack the various time theories of the Kabbalists by demonstrating that they are not identical yet create an orbit of cyclical returning time that contains new dimensions to other such approaches. The notion of cyclical as opposed to linear time is exemplified in philosophers such as Nietzsche, Rosenzweig, and Heidegger, who were all influences on Wolfson. But in *Alef, Mem, Tau* Wolfson exhibits how the cyclical nature of time is embedded in medieval kabbalistic texts in ways that anticipated later philosophical analysis.

At the same time, interpretation itself is not what we conventionally assume. In the essay "Occultation of the Feminine and the Body of Secrecy in Medieval Kabbalah," which was included in the volume edited by Wolfson, *Rending the Veil: Concealment and Secrecy in the History of Religions* (1997), kabbalistic texts hint that there is a hidden meaning concealed by a veil, but Wolfson argues that removing the veil does not reveal a truth other than that truth itself is a veil, that is, each interpretation brings a new veil. The kabbalistic understanding that concealment is itself disclosure anticipates

Heidegger, and Wolfson in a subsequent work would demonstrate the striking affinities of these and other kabbalistic ideas with Heidegger's. Wolfson argues that Heidegger's philosophy helps illuminate Kabbalah by recognizing that disclosure and concealment are not in opposition or in dialectic tension; rather, there is a dynamic within which all disclosure is ultimately concealment.

It is important to note here that throughout the unfolding of Wolfson's project, he continued to publish articles in scholarly journals that lay out the broad plan for the books in a highly stylized scholarly register or, in other cases, provide more detailed analyses of some of the books' subjects. This includes his growing attention to modern Jewish thinkers, specifically Franz Rosenzweig, Emmanuel Levinas, Edith Wyschogrod, and Susan Taubes, about whom he has recently completed a book, as well as Menachem Mendel Schneerson, the last Lubavitcher Rebbe.

In *Open Secret: Post-Messianic Messianism and the Mystical Revision of Menahem Mendel Schneerson* (2009), his first book to focus on a specific individual since *Abraham Abulafia*, Wolfson takes on the messianism of Schneerson, one of the most influential Jewish figures of the mid-twentieth century. Wolfson dedicates the book to Bob Dylan, "the man in the long black coat," an oblique double reference that speaks to the dual influence on his intellectual and creative life. Analyzing the enormous body of metaphysical Hasidic literature refracted through Schneerson's transformative career, Wolfson demonstrates the deep *coincidentia oppositorum* of kabbalistic teaching and argues for an extraordinary messianic revisionism: what lies at the core of Schneerson's messianism is the highly individualistic assertion that there is no Messiah in any traditional sense of a historical redeemer; that messianism is rather the consciousness that each of us possesses the capacity to actualize our own messianic potential—a redemption from the need to be redeemed. Echoing Franz Kafka, Schneerson's hidden message is that the task of the Messiah is to arrive in order to reveal a postmessianic messianism. The Messiah, in a sense, comes "on the day after he arrives." Until then, we have to wait with anticipation, an exilic posture that dissipates only when one knows that there is no one for whom to wait. Taking his reader through the vast sea of Chabad metaphysical literature, especially Schneerson's vast body of writings and teachings, Wolfson deploys a Heideggerian reading to show how Schneerson effectively undermines tradition through the inversion of the messianic *as* the messianic. Philosophers such as Jacques Derrida have entertained such a notion more generally, as did Kafka before him. Wolfson, however, does what Derrida and Kafka could not do: illustrate his theory through close readings of the entire body of a Hasidic tradition. Scholem's work on the messianic offered various models of messianism in Judaism that Moshe Idel's *Messianic Mystics* would later challenge. *Open Secret*, however, transforms the entire notion of the messianic via Schneerson, arguably the ultra-messianist, to unveil a profoundly countervailing message of postmessianic consciousness.

In *A Dream Interpreted Within a Dream: Oneiropoiesis and the Prism of Imagination* (2011), Wolfson returns to the psychoanalytic, philosophical, and comparative method of *LEB* to provide a sweeping view of human imagination. Scholars of religion have explored the importance of dreams for better understanding religious experience.

Wolfson's approach to dreams, however, is arguably as radical for the study of religion as Freud's was for the field of psychology. Wolfson adopts a decidedly Freudian lens for another foundational dimension of the Judeo/Christian/Islamic worldview: prophecy. The connection between dream and prophecy, he argues, is embedded in the Hebrew Bible, rabbinic, and kabbalistic traditions, and takes form in the Maimonidean depiction of prophecy in his *Mishneh Torah* and *Guide to the Perplexed*. Wolfson's *A Dream Interpreted Within a Dream* situates this discussion in a broader register through an analysis of how dreams function in the Gnostic, Christian, Muslim, Buddhist, neuroscientific, and philosophical traditions, and then examines the ways in which Kabbalists construct their dream/prophecy visions through mystical lenses that engage deeply with the other traditions, as well as through notions introduced by Freud in his dream work. Like *LEB*, this book is both a study of Judaism and a deep metaphysical and analytic reflection on the dream as a trope of human imaginative activity through the lens of Jewish sources. Once again, Kabbalah is offered as a template for humanistic reflection that extends beyond the sphere of the Jewish canonical corpus. Here, as in *LEB* and *Giving Beyond the Gift* (see below), Wolfson emerges as one of the most prominent living scholars in the field of religion, influencing philosophers, comparativists, literary scholars, historians, and theologians and bringing Kabbalah into the wider study of history, philosophy, and literature.

Wolfson's next work, *Giving Beyond the Gift: Apophasis and Overcoming Theomania* (2014), arguably the least kabbalistic of his works, undertakes an analysis of Cohen, Buber, Rosenzweig, Derrida, Levinas, and Wyschogrod on the understanding of "giving" and "theomania," a Buberian term that denotes obsession with God conceived theistically. Wolfson's relegation of Kabbalah to a subsidiary role here may speak to the way in which Kabbalah could and perhaps should become an integral part of humanistic studies. Wolfson seems to strive to liberate Kabbalah from Judaism so as to present it as a "gift" to the humanities. Part of Wolfson's larger project is, accordingly, to integrate those sources with a broad array of religious texts, to find a voice for Judaism within the robust conversation of the humanities more generally, that is, within the larger discourse. The work often defies "Jewish studies" by inhabiting religious philosophy in all its myriad forms. Working with Heidegger's corpus for decades, Wolfson would later produce *The Duplicity of Philosophy's Shadow*, which began as the first chapter of his more sweeping book, *Heidegger and Kabbalah*, in which Wolfson confronts Heidegger's Nazism. Written soon after the publication of Heidegger's *Black Notebooks*, where Heidegger's antisemitism is expressed in the post-Holocaust period, this book marked the beginning of Wolfson's direct grappling with the moral dilemma of reading Judaism in light of Heidegger. Wolfson argues that a fuller reckoning with Heidegger's work requires grappling with Judaism itself, since Jewish thought-worlds like Kabbalah share surprising affinities with Heidegger. Those affinities at once illuminate the greatness of both and alert us to the dangers of both.

Wolfson's most sustained reading of Heidegger and Kabbalah appears in *Heidegger and Kabbalah*, a challenging work that presents a dramatically innovative reading of each of its subjects. Here, Wolfson offers a revolutionary intervention into the very fabric of

Kabbalah, that is, its radical metaphysics (or rejection of metaphysics), in an unprecedented way. With respect to Heidegger himself, Wolfson further confronts the problematic, and tragic, elements of this thinking while nevertheless insisting that his new vision of conceiving "being" beyond ontology holds the potential for undoing its very own destructive tendencies. And he offers us another way to conceive of thinking more generally, as a tapestry that weaves through the most fundamental metaphysical questions in the history of philosophy. Heidegger is put into conversation with Kabbalah on some of the most vexing aspects of human existence, revealing similitude and convergences.

To understand Wolfson's reading of *Heidegger and Kabbalah*, one must liberate Kabbalah from its "monotheistic" orbit, Wolfson argues. To conceive *Ein Sof* as some kind of Platonic One is to miss the very undermining of the conception of *Ein Sof* as neither being nor nonbeing. Nor is *Ein Sof* the ground of transcendence, just as Heidegger's notion of Beyng is not a Schellengian "Subject" that transcends all being but rather a nullity, a *Nichts*, that exists between being and beings. Heidegger writes, "The god is neither a 'being' [*seiend*] nor a 'nonbeing' [*unseiend*] and is also not to be identified with beyng [*Seyn*]. Instead, Beyng essentially occurs in the manner of time-space as that between which can never be grounded in the god and also not in the human being, but only in *Dasein*." Heidegger speaks here of a (post)metaphysical, or meontological (the study of nonbeing) register, addressing the "last god who has come and gone" (by never coming in the first place, a futurity never realized nor realizable). Wolfson argues that *Ein Sof* serves a similar purpose. "The last god, we may infer from the kabbalistic depiction of *Ein Sof*, is the god that can never arrive except as a god that does not arrive, the end that can never stop ending, the future that is perpetually impending." *Ein Sof* is that which bestows while withdrawing; its existence can only be posited through its nonexistence, not unlike Meister Eckhart's claim that believing *in* God is itself already a disbelief *of* God. Continuing Wolfson's work on gender, as well, *Heidegger and Kabbalah* suggests that the feminine is the marker of the other in the undifferentiated oneness of the infinite. Thus, as "other" before any other, the feminine allows for *zimzum*, which brings about the very possibility of difference. *Heidegger and Kabbalah* deserves recognition as one of the most important and audacious synthetic works of kabbalistic theosophy to appear in the last seventy-five years. Its close reading of kabbalistic texts via a similarly close reading of Heidegger and the philosophical tradition he initiated will ensure its enduring legacy.

Throughout his career Wolfson has trained an impressive array of scholars in the field, some of whom have already made their own mark in Israel, in the United States, and in Europe. His work is read widely in the United States, Europe, and Israel among those in Jewish studies, in philosophy, history, literature, and the humanities more generally. His introduction of gender theory into Kabbalah studies has sparked a veritable subfield in Jewish mysticism and has profoundly influenced the study of Jewish philosophy. His use of phenomenology, psychoanalytic method, literary and critical theory, and continental philosophy to explicate kabbalistic literature has changed the way in which scholars envision Jewish mysticism. In addition, his more recent studies have bridged the field of Kabbalah studies and the humanities by introducing the Jewish mystical tradition into the broader study of religion, comparative religion, and philosophy.

Equipped with rare technical and philological skills, a wide range of languages, a deep understanding of the breadth and depth of classical Judaism (the Hebrew Bible and rabbinic literature), and a mastery of the Western philosophical tradition, Wolfson has further integrated Kabbalah into the Western canon. While this certainly may be said of scholars such as Gershom Scholem, Isaiah Tishby, Moshe Idel, and Yehuda Liebes, Wolfson's contribution is distinctive in its philosophical quality. Scholem's project, for all its depth and breadth, was essentially historiographic; he was intent on (re)writing a comprehensive history of Jewish mysticism (Scholem preferred historiosophic). Scholem, in short, believed that history was the best path to understanding a subject before one could venture beyond it. In so doing, however, Scholem often failed to acknowledge prior scholars of Kabbalah and misrepresented the efforts of the Wissenschaft des Judentums.[3]

Rather than following the philological and historiosophical paths of Scholem and his students, Wolfson turned to phenomenology yet ultimately created his own new and novel method of inquiry. His early work was shaped by the classical mold evinced by Scholem and his students, and he continues in this line of inquiry in some of his scholarly essays. Yet his books from *Speculum* onward display a unique philosophical and literary-critical sophistication. Under Wolfson, Kabbalah becomes part of the comparative exercise. Wolfson addresses a particular issue and then introduces Kabbalah into the wider array of variant textual traditions, not only to illuminate Kabbalah but to make it integral to the conversation. In this respect (as well as in many others) Wolfson's work represents the most influential specimen of what one might call "Diaspora Kabbalah studies," even as his influence in Israel remains strong among the new generation of scholars. Making Kabbalah part of the humanities in the Diaspora seems as much a goal in his work as the deep reflection and elucidation of the kabbalistic tradition. We can see the influence of this approach among many young and mid-career scholars, as well as in the ways his work is engaged in many areas of the humanities in the United States, Europe, and Israel.

Amazingly, Wolfson has also enjoyed a full artistic life, producing many abstract paintings, some of which adorn his books as well as books of other scholars, and publishing four volumes of poetry, *Pathwings* (2004), *Footdreams and Treetales* (2007), *On One Foot Dancing* (available on his website), and *Unveiling the Veil of Unveiling* (2022). Wolfson calls the broad spectrum of his poetic output "preparations for death." The term "poetics" appears throughout Wolfson's work, even in titles, and his literary style exhibits a felicity with language that borders on the poetic. As Barbara Galli notes in her foreword to *Footdreams and Treetales*, "The poems are not so much an offshoot of Wolfson's academic work but are interconnected with it. His poems, very often, speak to that which, at a particular moment, he is involved with in his scholarship, and it is safe to say that one of the contributions of this collection [*Footdreams and Treetales*] would be the application of the view that (contra Plato) there is 'convergence between philosophy and poetry.'"[4] In the future, when scholars examine Wolfson's work they will also have to engage his poetry, which can be viewed as an interpretation, perhaps an iteration, and certainly a poeticization of his scholarly arguments. Some contributors to this volume fittingly engage Wolfson's poems. Several appear in this volume, selected by Wolfson himself.

Elliot Wolfson has built a mountain of scholarly and philosophical reflection that is currently being scaled by new generations of scholars. As a truly worthwhile project is not one that exhausts the topic but rather one that opens it up to new insight, Wolfson's projects are unquestionably "worthwhile." They also offer provocative and unsettling theses, arguments that are at once dissonant and rooted in traditional sources, for Wolfson unsettles the world he inherits with a message that is at once explosive, disturbing, and exhilarating. He has occasionally generated controversy yet, as the sages teach, those disputes engaged in for the sake of heaven endure and propel us forward. Those that are not engaged for the sake of heaven will fade away. In the essays of this volume, we can feel Wolfson's work in multiple disciplines leading us along paths to new discoveries. The contributors to this volume include both his students and his colleagues in a wide range of fields. All have been influenced and inspired by his prodigious scholarship and all were delighted to accept our invitation to contribute to this Festschrift. Indeed, we anticipate that this will be the first of several publications to discuss aspects of Wolfson's scholarship.

NOTES

1. It has always been curious that with all the facets of Kabbalah Gershom Scholem explored, he never paid much attention to questions of gender in a critical way.
2. Alexander Altmann, "The God of Religion, the God of Metaphysics and Wittgenstein's 'Language-Games,'" *Zeitschrift für Religions und Geistesgeschichte* 39 (1987): 289–306.
3. George Y. Kohler, *Kabbalah Research in the Wissenschaft des Judentums (1820–1880): The Foundation of an Academic Discipline* (Walter de Gruyter, 2019).
4. Barbara Galli, preface to Elliot R. Wolfson, *Footdreams and Treetales: 92 Poems* (New York: Fordham University Press, 2007), xiii.

לאליוט וולפסון

הַדַּפִּים זְרוּעֵי הָאוֹתִיּוֹת מִסְתַּחְרְרִים בְּמָחוֹל
בַּמָּחוֹל הֵם נִהְיִים כּוֹכָבִים וְרוֹדְפִים זֶה אֶת זֶה בִּצְחוֹק וּבְקוֹל
נוֹשְׁרִים עַל מִישׁוֹרֵי הַתְּבוּאָה נוֹצְצִים בִּשְׂדוֹת הַקָּמָה
וְהַשֶּׁמֶשׁ בָּם בּוֹעֵר בַּזֹּהַר חַמָּה
הַזְּמַן נוֹהֵר דֶּרֶךְ עַמּוּד אֶחָד הָאֶמְצָעִי וְנִשְׁבַּר לְאַלְפֵי רְסִיסִים
בְּטַל בֹּקֶר שֶׁל פֶּרַח אֶחָד לָבָן הַמִּסְתַּחְרֵר בִּצְבָעָיו
וְעוֹלֶה אֶל הַמֶּרְחָב
וְאוֹרוֹ אוֹר זֹהַר
אוֹר הַמֵּאִיר בְּזֹהַר נִרְדּוּת רַךְ שֶׁל אַיֶּלֶת הַשַּׁחַר
אוֹר הַמִּסְתַּחְרֵר כָּתֹם בִּשְׁקִיעַת הַחַמָּה
אֹדֶם רַךְ הָעוֹלֶה
אוֹר לָבָן בְּיִפְעָה יַסְמִינִית דַּק מִן הַדַּק
לְאַחַר שֶׁהַלְּבָנָה הִלָּתָהּ עוֹלָה מִתּוֹךְ עָנָן
וּמִשְׁתַּבְּרִים הַצְּבָעִים עַל פְּנֵי הַמַּיִם
כִּצְחוֹקָן שֶׁל אֶלֶף מַרְאוֹת מַרְאָה בְּתוֹךְ מַרְאָה זוֹהֶרֶת

שׁוּרוֹת שׁוּרוֹת וַעֲרוּגוֹת עֲרוּגוֹת
הַזְּרִיעָה בְּדִמְעָה וּבְהִתְעַמְּקוּת נִכְתֶּבֶת
כִּי הָלוֹךְ יֵלֵךְ וּבָכֹה נֹשֵׂא מֶשֶׁךְ הַזָּרַע
הִסְתַּחְרְרוּיוֹת וְהִשְׁתַּבְּרוּיוֹת שֶׁל אוֹר
הָאָסִיף וְהַפֶּרַח וְהַפְּרִי

אַתָּה נוֹשֵׂא אֶת הָאֲלֻמּוֹת הָאִלְּמוֹת
וּמִתּוֹךְ שְׂדוֹת נִיר וּרְחוֹבוֹת מֻדְפָּסִים
הָגוּת חֲקִירָה וּתְמוּנָה רָצִים וּמִתְנוֹצְצִים
אַתָּה הוֹפְכָם לְטַלְלֵי אוֹרוֹת וּלְפִרְחֵי טַל רְסִיסִים

בֹּא יָבוֹא בְרִנָּה נֹשֵׂא אֲלֻמֹּתָיו
עד 120

For Elliot Wolfson

The pages strewn with letters dizzy in a dance,
In dance they become stars and chase each other, laugh out loud
Then fall on plains of harvest and shine in the fields of wheat
But sun burns them with its illumination, heat.
Time surges through the single central column—and shatters in a thousand stars
In morning's dew a single white flower dizzies with its shades
And rises to the spaciousness
But its light is luminous,
Light lighting in the soft rose luminescence of the doe of dawn
Light that dizzies orange at the setting of the sun
A gentle blush that rises
White light in the glory of jasmine more refined than fine
after the moon's corona has ascended from the cloud
and colors break upon the water's surface
like the giggle of a thousand mirrors showing in a luminescent glass.

Lines upon lines and beds upon beds
The sowing in tears and investigation noted
For he that goes forth weepeth, bearing previous seed,
Dizziness and brokenness of light,
The ingathering and flower and the yield.

You bear the sheaves on sheaves
And from ploughed fields and avenues of print
Reflected questions and impressions run and glint,
You turn them to shards of light and flowers of dewy tears
He shall doubtless come rejoicing bringing his sheaves with him
To live until a hundred and twenty.

—*Haviva Pedaya* (tr. Aubrey Glazer)

PART I

Studies on Religion

cloud of witnesses, by Elliot Wolfson. (Reprinted with permission from the artist.)

ELLIOT WOLFSON'S PHILOSOPHICAL THEOLOGY (A HYPOTHESIS)

MARTIN KAVKA

I HAVE BEEN OBSESSED WITH ELLIOT WOLFSON'S WRITING FOR MANY YEARS now, ever since I was an undergraduate student of his in the spring of 1992. Some aspects of that obsession are, I believe, shared among the scholarly community. Every time I read one of his books or articles, it is impossible for me to imagine anyone *not* asking themselves how Wolfson came to know so much, how he manages to write so much, and how he has continually managed to be compelling in the more than thirty-five years that he has been publishing. Yet perhaps some other aspects of that obsession are simply my own. For example, I am constantly struck by Wolfson's regular use of phrases with a chiastic structure, in which two concepts switch structural places over the course of a sentence. Take, for example, the following three phrases from a central chapter on language in Wolfson's recent *Heidegger and Kabbalah*: God is "only present because absent and absent because present"; "Rosenzweig, and I believe Scholem, would have agreed with Heidegger that enlightenment in the inherently unredeemable world consists of casting light on the shadow so that the shadow is illumined as light"; and Wolfson's interpretation of this shadow/light dynamic in the language of "what is finally disclosed [in this dark light] is the concealment that conceals itself in its disclosure."[1] What do such phrases mean, in which one pole seems to be both like and unlike its opposite? Why is their use justified?

These are the questions to which I want to offer an answer in this essay. The reader will note two aspects of this answer from my title. First, I give this answer as a hypothesis, with "fear and trembling," as my teacher (and Wolfson's teacher) Edith Wyschogrod would routinely say in her seminar room. (That room was a place of kindness to those of us who were fearful and trembling in our responses to her. That meant that we knew that our answers to her provocations were un-Pauline. She was not the path by which we were "working out our salvation," to use Paul's phrase from Philippians 2:12, the same verse that Søren Kierkegaard quoted in the title to *Fear and Trembling*.) Even though I will argue in this essay that there are good reasons for scholars to use chiastic language such as Wolfson's in describing the relation between God and the world in some Jewish texts—both because that language crystallizes a good exegesis of those texts and because there are good philosophical arguments for privileging this view over others—I do so warily, as someone who still sees himself as a student. Perhaps other commenters will have more acute readings; perhaps Wolfson himself would judge my interpretation to be a tad off. The second aspect I want to highlight is that my hypothesis involves drawing the broad contours of a philosophical theology of Wolfson's own, which he has synthesized from the texts with which he has shown so much expertise over the course of his career; these texts contain views that he endorses. This means both that Wolfson is a *constructive* thinker—he is not only commenting on the texts, but telling his readers why they should value them, why they carry the ring of truth—and that he is offering his readers a constructive *theology* that he argues is simply better (more philosophically defensible) than much of what goes by the name "Jewish theology."[2]

Part of the reason why I offer this answer as a hypothesis is that the method for giving an answer is not an easy one. It would be best to go through much of Wolfson's work in a systematic and chronological manner. But that would end up being a book of its own. So I will start near the beginning of Wolfson's scholarly career with the first appearance of that chiastic structure in Wolfson's scholarship, a paragraph near the end of his 1987 essay "Circumcision, Vision of God, and Textual Interpretation: From Midrashic Trope to Mystical Symbol," the second scholarly article that Wolfson ever published.[3] Starting here is not necessarily the wisest strategy. Origins are not necessarily the site of pristine truth; later articulations might be better and clearer. In addition, scholars might change their views over the course of several decades, as they get smarter. So returning to Wolfson's relatively youthful writings might miss opportunities present in more recent writings. Nonetheless, I make this decision for two reasons. One is that the 1987 essay contains only one sentence with this chiastic structure, and so it can be analyzed at length. The other is that it was published in some temporal proximity to one of Wolfson's most sustained treatments of a figure in the canon of modern Jewish philosophy, "The Problem of the Unity in the Thought of Martin Buber." As I understand it, this essay was originally drafted when Wolfson was a student at Queens College (where he earned bachelor's and master's degrees in the late 1970s), as a paper for Edith Wyschogrod, and was revised for eventual publication during the following decade, finally seeing print in 1989.[4] The treatment of Buber will serve as my clue for the answer of why readers of Wolfson should *endorse* the use of chiastic structure. I will argue, in effect, that whenever a reader finds a chiasm in Wolfson, it is a Buberian argument that is bubbling underneath the page. This may be surprising to some readers, who might readily think that Wolfson's chiastic phrases are adaptations of arguments from Martin Heidegger or from Jacques Derrida, whose work he has been citing for many years. And this may be true! Yet the appearance of Wolfson's article on Buber in 1989 suggests that a different interpretation may be justified, and highlights my point that whatever the immediate influence(s) on Wolfson's chiastic phrases might be, chiasms for Wolfson are a solution to a philosophical-theological problem.[5] This solution is Wolfson's, in my hypothesis; I make no claims about whether Buber's texts might be fairly described as zoharic, or whether the Zohar might be described as broadly Buberian. My hypothesis only entails that Buber was a resource for problem-solving for Wolfson early in his career. I turn now to Wolfson's 1987 article on circumcision.

"Circumcision, Vision of God, and Textual Interpretation" had been assigned to me in the class of Wolfson's in which I enrolled as a twenty-year-old student. I remember being so *stymied* by the essay, in part because of what struck me then as its explicitness, and in part because it marked an intersection of thinking and embodiment which I was then (and perhaps still am now) unable to appropriate in my own life. Wolfson here gives a brief history of the idea in Jewish texts that a Jewish male's being circumcised allows him to see God. In rabbinic literature, the proximity of the narrative of Abraham being circumcised (Genesis 17:26) and God appearing to Abraham at the terebinths of Mamre (Genesis 18:1) suggests a causal connection between the two. In Genesis Rabbah (48:1), God appears to Abraham because Abraham circumcised himself and Ishmael and his household as God commanded. In Numbers Rabbah (12:8), the foreskin is described as a block to this kind of spiritual vision.

The Zohar finds a problem with this argument and tries to solve it. For God also appeared to Abraham before he was circumcised (Genesis 15:1). So the Zohar classifies the appearance in Genesis 15 and the appearance in Genesis 18 as two different kinds of appearances. In Genesis 15, when God appears to Abraham in a vision (*bamaḥazeh*), this refers to an interaction only with the lowest of the *sefirot*, *Shekhinah*, an interaction that the Zohar describes as *Shekhinah*'s speech to Abraham.[6] (The Zohar links the vision to *Shekhinah* through a citation of Numbers 24:4, which uses the noun *maḥazeh* as a symbol of the divine name *Shaddai*, a name that is linked with *Shekhinah* in other zoharic texts.[7]) In Genesis 18, when God appears to Abraham outside of the confines of the *maḥazeh*, after Abraham is circumcised, various passages from the Zohar make clear that Abraham interacts with all the *sefirot* and has a fuller interaction with the divine as a result. For readers adept in the symbolic associations of the Zohar, this interaction is clearly sexualized.

> This is rather a hidden secret. "And the Lord appeared to him," i.e. to that gradation that spoke with him [Abraham], which did not take place before he was circumcised. For now voice was revealed and united with speech when the latter spoke to Abraham. "And he sat in the opening of the tent [Genesis 18:1]. "And he": the verse does not reveal who. [The Torah] here revealed wisdom, for all the gradations [the *sefirot*] rested upon that lower gradation [*Shekhinah*] after Abraham was circumcised.[8]

Once Abraham has been circumcised, this action engenders a complementary action in the sefirotic realm as the central *sefirah* of *Tif'eret* (linked with the patriarch Jacob, and thus "voice" per Genesis 27:22) unites with the feminine *Shekhinah* that has already spoken to Abraham (and thus represented as "speech"), allowing the upper *sefirot* to flow into *Shekhinah* for Abraham to receive at the opening of the tent. This sexual union within God is paralleled by a motif of union between Abraham and the divine: the circumcised Abraham "enters the name and is united to it."[9]

In going through these passages and some others in the first two-thirds of the 1987 article, Wolfson shows the parallels between the disclosure of the glans as a result of circumcision and the disclosure of the divine, all captured tersely in the following line from the Zohar: "he who is marked with the holy seal of this sign [of circumcision], from it [the sign] he sees the Holy One, blessed be He, from it itself [*minneh mamash*]."[10] The movement of Wolfson's argument seems to be clear: "that which is hidden must be brought to light, and the medium of the disclosure is the seal of the covenant [i.e., circumcision]."[11] In other words, there is nothing in these passages of the Zohar that suggests anything less than the complete disclosure of the divine to the mystic. Circumcision is the precondition of that disclosure. Nevertheless, Wolfson also in this same sentence describes this dynamic as a "play of closure-openness." That language suggests either an oscillation between openness and closure, or a partial openness that still deserves to be described as (partially) closed. In this play, disclosure would never *fully* manifest itself. Something would always remain hidden; the vision that circumcision affords would not be complete. This language continues in the article, reaching its peak in the sentence where Wolfson for the first time used chiastic rhetoric.

> Textual interpretation, like circumcision, involves the dynamic of closure/openness: as the one who is circumcised stands in relation to the *Shekhinah*, so the exegete—through interpretation—enters into an intimate relation with the *Shekhinah*. The duplicity of the text as that which simultaneously conceals and reveals—indeed conceals as that which reveals and reveals as that which conceals—is a thoroughly appropriate metaphor to convey the erotic quality of the hermeneutical stance.[12]

This is puzzling. Nothing in the first two-thirds of the article suggests that this is how the zoharic text works. It would seem to the reader—say, the onetime student of Wolfson!—that concealment appears on the scene where it should not. In addition, it is important to note here that Wolfson is not quite saying that the text both hides and reveals. That might suggest that the text is engaging in two different moves at the same time, or hiding at some moments and revealing at others. To say that the text "conceals as that which reveals and reveals as that which conceals" is to imply that there is *one* movement that the text makes, in which perhaps differing perspectives on the text would judge it as either revealing or concealing. But regardless of how one should read these sentences, it remains the case that as soon as Wolfson invokes "play," he is describing something more complex than the bringing of something hidden to light, or a simple movement from concealment to disclosure. Nonetheless, there are two reasons why judging Wolfson negatively, as if he had surreptitiously smuggled concealment into his analysis, would be a poor reading.

One is that the Zohar on at least one occasion describes the divine phallus as both hidden and revealed. Wolfson cites this passage in the 1987 essay, although he does not analyze it at length. In commenting on the fruit of *hadar* trees commanded to be used as part of the rejoicing before God on the first day of Sukkot, the Zohar links this to another use of *hadar* ("majestic") in Psalms 96, and then states:

> Who is majestic? Righteous One. Why is He called "majestic," when it is a concealed place, which is not to be revealed and must always be covered, whereas "majestic" applies only to one who is revealed and seen? Well, although it is a concealed gradation, it is the majesty of the whole body, and there is no majesty to the body except for this. Why? One who lacks this gradation lacks the majesty to associate with people: he lacks a masculine voice, and the majesty of voice has been seized from him; he lacks a beard and the majesty of a beard. So although that gradation is covered, all majesty of the body depends on it; it is covered and revealed.[13]

In this analysis of the *sefirah Yesod* (the divine phallus, represented as the "righteous one") we have an account that majesty signifies itself through other traits—what we would now call "secondary sexual characteristics" such as the deepening voice and facial hair that we find on some people who were assigned male at birth—that conceal the actual ground of majesty itself, the penis that is not visible to others in everyday life. The text states that this majesty is "covered and revealed," but this seems not to be sophisticated enough. There is reason to say that *Yesod* is covered. There is reason to say that it is revealed. But to say that it is simultaneously concealed and revealed seems wrong, in my view. Rather, it is the *performance* of majesty—its revealing in the entirety of the masculine body—that, in the view of the author(s) of the Zohar, signifies the genitalia that are underneath the garments. We have a right to imagine *Yesod* on the basis of its empirical signs, to see it in our minds and not in real life, even if we do not "actually" see it. In this way, *Yesod* only reveals itself by signifying its presence in other forms, keeping itself hidden. This is what it means to "conceal as that which reveals and reveals as that which conceals." What is really the case can only be acknowledged in the realm of the imagination; I have to picture to myself what might be underneath the clothing that I do actually see. The male genitalia, associated with *Yesod* in the kabbalistic imaginary, cannot come to presence. They remain shrouded.

As a result, the Zohar portrays a somewhat counterintuitive structure. For the ground of the world to be acknowledged *as* the ground of the world, it must other itself; it must signify itself through the appearance of something else. For Wolfson, this is simply part of the structure of zoharic thinking. In *Through a Speculum That Shines*, he briefly analyzes a zoharic commentary on Proverbs 31:23 ("Her husband is known in the gates") that deploys a pun on the noun *sha'ar* ("gate") and the verb *mesha'er* ("to imagine") to say that "God is known and comprehended according to what one imagines in one's heart . . . according to what one imagines in one's heart, so [God] is known in one's heart." God (the husband of the "woman of valor" in Proverbs 31) is known in the gates/imagination only. Any unfiltered or pure knowledge of God—knowledge of God Godself or knowledge of God's essence—remains impossible, as the passage goes on to say.[14] In Wolfson's commentary, "simply put, imagination provides the vehicle through which one can have access to God. In the absence of imagination there is no form, and without form there is no vision and hence no knowledge."[15] Transcendence cannot be imaged and cannot be talked about; the imagination gives language and shape and reality to that which transcends. These are powers that ratiocination lacks when it comes to that which is beyond concepts.

I now move to the second reason why it would be wrong to judge Wolfson negatively for smuggling talk of concealment into a series of texts that seem to be purely about disclosure as the *end* of concealment. Directly before the paragraph containing Wolfson's chiastic sentence, Wolfson interprets another passage from the section of the Zohar known as the *Idra Rabba*.

> R. Simeon opened and said, "A base fellow reveals secrets, but a trustworthy soul conceals the matter" (Proverbs 11). Concerning he who is not settled in his spirit and who is not faithful, the word that he hears goes inside him like that which revolves in water until it is cast outside. Why? Because his spirit is not a firm spirit (*ruḥa' de-qiyyuma'*). But he whose spirit is a firm one, concerning him it is written, "a trustworthy soul conceals the matter." "A trustworthy soul" (*ve-ne'eman ruḥa*), one whose spirit is faithful (*qiyyuma' de-ruḥa'*), as [it is written], "I will fix him as a peg (*yated*) in a firm place (*be-maqom ne'eman*)" (Isaiah 22:23). The matter is dependent on the secret (*be-raza' talya' milta'*). It is written, "Don't let your mouth cause your flesh to sin" (Ecclesiastes 5:5). The world only exists through the secret (*be-raza'*).[16]

The immediate context here is one about R. Simeon warning his students that they must not learn from others besides him. This scenario is described in a fashion that continues the sexual line of interpretation invoked earlier in Wolfson's article. If *qiyyuma'* is broadly a phallic symbol in the Zohar ("firmness," "pillar," something that sustains and erects), then the adept who does not share secrets is imagined in this passage as a tumescent phallus—a firm (*ne'eman*) peg in the lingo of Isaiah 22:23—who is therefore able to unite with the divine and produce a parallel union in the sefirotic realm.

But why is this passage about concealment? In part, this must be because the *Idra Rabba* is itself concerned about secrecy. R. Simeon, at the beginning of that section of the Zohar, exclaims, "Woe if I reveal! Woe if I do not reveal!" about the truths that he is about to share with his companions. This anxiety over revealing, over whether people might improperly learn truths and use them for wicked ends, also occurs at other places in the Zohar and builds on a concern expressed in the Talmud by R. Yoḥanan ben Zakkai about teaching various halakhot about buying and selling.[17] But if the world only comes about through the secret—since "secret" is associated with *Yesod*/phallus in other parts of the Zohar[18]—then we once again have a claim that the world only signifies its ground by *occluding* it. In other words, if the world comes about as the result of a secret, and if it is maintained *through* a secret or *in* a secret (depending on how one wants to translate the prefix "be-" in *be-raza'*), then it would seem that for the secret to no longer be secret would destabilize that world, or place it at risk. Maintaining the secrecy of the secret is necessary, if the world is to be sustained. Here, we have a claim that is slightly different from the claim found in the passage from Zohar 2:186b, the passage about "majesty," namely that clothes signify the genitalia underneath them. Here, the claim seems to be that the phallus is *more* generative or powerful when it is hidden by garments. This is why Wolfson glosses "the world exists only through the secret" by saying that "it is sustained by means of that foundation of pillar (*Yesod*) that must be concealed."[19] And yet, this very claim about concealment is also a revelation of *Yesod*, the circulation of a secret *as* the secret that it is. Hence, Wolfson is being precise when he says that for the circle of authors and readers of the Zohar, the text "reveals as that which conceals and conceals as that which reveals."

Nevertheless, it is one thing to say that passages from the Zohar exhibit this structure. It is another thing to make an argument as to why any contemporary reader should be invested in this structure, for any reasons more significant than the knowledge of historical facts. Why should we find this structure interesting, over and above its complexity? What makes it true? Here, I think that Wolfson's early Buber essay can be of assistance. That essay is, on its surface, an account of how the rhetoric of unity changes in the work of Martin Buber from his early book *Ecstatic Confessions* (1909) up through one of his last essays, "Distance and Relation" (1951). The shift here is from one in which the early Buber believed that the distinction between subject and object (or self and world, or self and other) could be erased through mystical experience, and toward a dialogical model in which relation "can occur only between beings who stand at a distance from one another."[20] Yet it seems that Wolfson also reads this shift as a movement of *progress* or improvement. It is this dialogical model in which Wolfson finds that "Buber's thought reaches the quintessence of paradox," since "man is unified with God . . . when he sets himself at a distance from God."[21] Here, Wolfson pays Buber a compliment. For one might restate Wolfson's claim by saying that God reveals as that which conceals itself (places itself at a distance) and conceals as that which reveals.

It is worth briefly recapping the argument from within Buber's works. (Here I will not always use the same books and articles that Wolfson does in his essay.) In his introduction to *Ecstatic Confessions*, a collection of mystical texts from various religious traditions, Buber wanted to highlight the phenomenon of an experience in which the experience of the pure undifferentiated I, who "has submerged itself entirely into itself . . . plunged down to the very ground of itself," is also experienced as an experience of God.[22] But by the early 1910s, this had changed somewhat. If unity was going to be felt, it was going to be felt not as an immediate presence, but one would be conscious of a *desire* for unity that one would seek to realize through acts of human religious creativity. Think of Buber's important 1911 essay on "Jewish Religiosity." Near the end of that essay, Buber writes that "multiplicity is given into our hands, to be transformed into unity; a vast formless mass is to be stamped by us with the Divine."[23] Here and in other essays from around this year, Buber imagined that Jews could just willy-nilly decide to desire such transformation and work to realize the divine in the world, thereby conquering the "dualism" that he associated with the Jews' alienation both from the non-Jewish world and from God. By the end of World War I, Buber had rethought the issue of what motivates that desire. No longer did he think that a subject could just decide to strive for unity. Now it needed prompting from some kind of encounter. In the 1919 essay "Herut: On Youth and Religion," Buber gave a new account of experience of that which transcends: the "human mind [*Menschengeist*] thus experiences the unconditional as that great something that is counterposed against it [*das große Gegenüber*], as the Thou as such."[24] The striving for unity was now not the result of an independent decision, but was the "response [*Antwort*]" to the unconditioned divine.[25] Buber's clearest argument for this shift came in the introduction he wrote when several of his essays on Judaism were republished in a single volume in 1923. To say that an individual or a group of individuals could simply decide to "realize" God

> induces the hopelessly wrong conception that God is not, but that He becomes—either within the human individual or within humankind. I call such a theory, manifest today in a variety of guises, hopelessly wrong, not because I am not certain of a divine becoming in immanence, but because only a primal certainty [*Urgewißheit*] of divine being enables us to touch on the secret meaning of divine becoming.[26]

It is the last clause that is most helpful here. How might we know that the decisions we make for unity—decisions that make us feel less alienated in our lives—are actually the decisions that we *should* make? How do we know that we're getting it right? In essays such as "Jewish Religiosity," there was no way to distinguish between a good decision and one that might be simply the result of an ego taking itself as the measure of all things. But if that decision is a response to some preexisting being that grounds the decision, then a kind of criterion of coherence emerges that would allow us to say that some decisions are better than others.

Nevertheless, with what should my decision cohere? If the answer to this question were to be my solely inner experience of the divine, I would once again be the only guarantor for that coherence, and my decision would be considered untrustworthy by others in my community. Therefore, the texts of tradition matter—for example, in "Herut," the epigram from *Pirkei Avot* that links *ḥarut* (engraved) and *ḥerut* (freedom). But more importantly, what mattered for Buber was the distance between the ground and its response, the ground being "counterposed" against the ego in a way that confronts it and cuts it down to its appropriate size. That distance famously also appears in Buber's descriptions of the dialogical scene between persons (and occasionally between persons and nonhuman things). To be in relation with someone is *not* to see them in terms of the conceptual categories in my mind, by which I usually understand the objects of my experience. To be in relation with someone is to authorize the breakdown of those categories and to acknowledge the gap between those mental categories (that are, because they are in mind, nearest to me) and the persons in the world who therefore always remain far: "Whoever says You has no something, has nothing. But she stands in relation."[27]

This story of Buber's development is in many ways a story that ends at a highly intuitive point: dialogue, like any relation, requires distance and difference. As Wolfson writes, "Though absolute distinctness [between two relata] would make relation as such impossible, it is also the case that absolute identification would make it equally impossible."[28] Nonetheless, this intuitive point is indeed as paradoxical as Wolfson insists it must be at that moment when he describes Buber's position as reaching the "quintessence of paradox." To assume that relation produces likeness or identification as its result is to say that relation must come to an end, due to its very success. Why do I need to relate to someone with whom I identify closely? Our thought processes would be the same, our instincts would be the same, and there would be no gap across which we could possibly relate. Therefore, nearness and distance must coexist in relation. As a result, any theology that involves an account of God speaking to humans, as is the case in most Jewish accounts of revelation, must admit that revelation does not cancel the distance between God and humans. God must always remain Other; whatever humans might know as a result of revelation must be only partial, or must be somehow other than divine truth in itself.[29] As soon as humans begin to think that their own conceptual categories can exhaust what God says, God is no longer relatable, and humans cross the boundary into a theology that is centered on idolatry.[30]

For Wolfson to say that the text "conceals as that which reveals and reveals as that which conceals" and thus requires the risk of interpretation is for Wolfson to affirm this necessary distance between God and humans, alongside revelation—the position that Buber had arrived at by 1919. The chiastic sentences that are common in Wolfson's prose are similar affirmations. To say that God is "only present because absent and absent because present," to repeat the first of the examples that appear in the opening paragraph of this essay, is to say that God in Wolfson's writings always remains outside of the conceptual schemes that we humans might develop, even if those conceptual schemes are rooted in texts that we claim to be revealed. The paradox of the chiasm is Wolfson's point; the locution keeps God safe from language that might make God too accessible, too ordinary, too open for idolatrous appropriation. I leave it to scholars who are greater experts in Kabbalah than I am to decide whether Wolfson, in these early essays and his later writings, has in effect shown that Buber made a broadly kabbalistic point in the account of God that appears in his dialogical writings. But we can at least say that Wolfson's readings of kabbalistic texts in this 1987 essay bear the marks of an argument that would appear in an essay that he would soon publish (but had already written in a preliminary form) about Buber's philosophical theology.

Indeed, it seems to me that we could go one step further and show that Wolfson holds Buber to account, ensuring that we apply the most coherent form of Buber's thought to philosophical and theological thinking. In a previous paragraph, I mentioned that in a relatively early book of Wolfson's, *Through a Speculum That Shines*, Wolfson describes the relation of otherness between God and humans in terms of a relation between knowledge and imagination. Because God is beyond the conceptual categories of the human mind, God cannot be known. Therefore, for "God" to be a meaningful word, it must be imaged; this image both gives shape to God, making God accessible and acknowledgeable, and others God. This is also a Buberian point, although it is not one that Wolfson brings up explicitly in his early essay on Buber. When Wolfson, in his

1989 essay on Buber, brings up the point that distance always remains unbridgeable in a dialogical (and thus also revelatory) encounter, he turns to Buber's 1951 essay "Distance and Relation," where Buber updates his view from *I and Thou* of the two primal ways of objectification (I-It) and relation (I-You) that humans take in the world. Buber's argument in that essay for what he there called "the twofold principle of human life" goes as follows. For humans to take the world as a world, other than humans themselves or individually, the world must be detached from the self, "set at a distance and given over to itself." It must become an "independent opposite [*selbständiges Gegenüber*]."[31] Yet it is only toward this "pushed-away [*abgerückten*] structure of being" that relation is possible.[32] These movements are equiprimordial for Buber: the "act of setting at a distance is no more to be understood than the act of relation which is bound up with it."[33] Yet in the last pages of this essay, Buber took on the question of how relation starts. How might I know that I am actually relating to You, as opposed to simply creating new categories in my mind by which I shall just compartmentalize you anew? His answer involves the human capacity that he called "imagining the real": "I imagine to myself what another person is at this very moment wishing, feeling, perceiving, thinking, and not as a detached content, but in that person's very reality, that is, as a life-process in that person."[34] Buber thought that an effective solidarity results from this sort of imagining, since I am imagining you in your specificity at that point. His example here of solidarity is feeling another's pain (I feel "this particular pain as the pain of the other"[35]), and even hypothesized some kind of perfect imagining in which I might feel the very pain that I inflict upon you.

As important as imagining is, Buber seems to me to have gone somewhat astray here.[36] He was correct to say that I can do nothing but imagine the real; this is a simple corollary of the distance between mind and world. Concepts are not things. Nonetheless, he made this imagining seem much easier than it seems to me actually to be. In Buber's account of the meeting of self and other where there is fulfilled relation, there is mutual "acceptance, affirmation, and confirmation [*Bestätigung*]."[37] This implies that the other person always reserves the right to refuse confirmation and tell me to try again, that I have privileged myself in my attempt at solidarity and ignored her, that I have imagined *poorly*. Buber said very little of this, only briefly discussing what might make some imaginings of the real better than others and never opining about the difficulty of the process. As a result, fulfilled relation seems to be just around the corner if only I try hard enough; the voice of the other person is silenced, and I seem to be the only arbiter of whether I have successfully imagined reality. (How could I even know if I feel your pain as you feel it?) There is too much of the artificial aroma of some of Buber's earlier claims about images and symbols—for example, the claim in "Herut" that "by creating symbols, the mind comprehends [*faßt*] what is in itself incomprehensible."[38] The image too often in Buber exists as a kind of distance that exists to be transcended; as an entry-point but never an obstacle. But everything necessary for correcting Buber on this point is already there in his own words. The necessity of distance that Wolfson rightly brought out in his 1989 article is not only an endorsement of Buber, but also a correction that makes Buber cohere with himself. In that coherence, the answer to the question "What do I know when I imagine the real?" can only be a chiastic one: "the reality of the image." Yet it is only through the image that I can say anything about reality at all; the reality of the image is still the image *of* the real. Reality can only reveal itself as that which conceals itself. And if Buber ended "Distance and Relation" by saying that "it is from one person to another that the bread of heaven of selfhood is passed," well, then that is only to say that the person only reveals the heavenly/divine ground of our imaginings by concealing it.[39]

NOTES

1. Elliot R. Wolfson, *Heidegger and Kabbalah: Hidden Gnosis and the Path of Poiēsis* (Bloomington: Indiana University Press, 2019), 317, 321.
2. My title is somewhat inspired by Kevin Schilbrack, "Bruce Lincoln's Philosophy," *Method & Theory in the Study of Religion* 17, no. 1 (2005): 44–58. But while Schilbrack's essay is polemical, I do not intend to read Wolfson against the common grain in this essay.
3. This essay originally appeared as Elliot R. Wolfson, "Circumcision, Vision of God, and Textual Interpretation: From Midrashic Trope to Mystical Symbol," *History of Religions* 27 (1987): 189–215. I will be citing from the essay's later appearance in Elliot R. Wolfson, *Circle in the Square: Studies in the Use of Gender in Kabbalistic Symbolism* (Albany: State University of New York Press, 1995), 29–48.
4. Elliot R. Wolfson, "The Problem of Unity in the Thought of Martin Buber," *Journal of the History of Philosophy* 27, no. 3 (1989): 423–44.
5. If one were to make a judgment about the figure in the modern Jewish philosophical canon that has influenced Wolfson the most, one might instinctively name Franz Rosenzweig (1886–1929). To date, Wolfson has published four articles on Rosenzweig: "Facing the Effaced: Mystical Eschatology and the Idealistic Orientation in the Thought of Franz Rosenzweig," *Zeitschrift für neuere Theologiegeschichte* 4 (1997): 39–81; "Light Does Not Talk But Shines: Apophasis and Vision in Rosenzweig's Theopoetic Temporality," in *New Directions in Jewish Philosophy*, ed. Aaron W. Hughes and Elliot R. Wolfson (Bloomington: Indiana University Press, 2010), 87–148; "Configuration of Untruth in the Mirror of God's Truth: Rethinking Rosenzweig in Light of Heidegger's Alētheia," in *Die Denkfigur des Systems in Ausgang von Franz Rosenzweigs "Stern der Erlösung,"* ed. Hartwig Wiedebach (Berlin: Duncker & Humblot, 2013), 141–62; "Rosenzweig on Human Redemption: Neither Nothing nor Everything, But Something," *Journal of Jewish Thought and Philosophy* 29, no. 1 (2021): 121–50. In addition, the second chapter of Wolfson's *Giving Beyond the Gift: Apophasis and Overcoming Theomania* (New York: Fordham University Press, 2014) also treats Rosenzweig at length. There is less attention to Buber's writings. After 1989, Wolfson has treated the work of Martin Buber at *Giving Beyond the Gift*, 25–29, and the important final footnote of *Heidegger and Kabbalah* (381n241), in addition to the important article "Theolatry and the Making-Present of the Nonrepresentable: Undoing (A)Theism in Eckhart and Buber," originally published in *Journal of Jewish Thought and Philosophy* 25 (2017): 5–35, and revised in *Martin Buber: His Intellectual*

and Scholarly Legacy, ed. Sam Berrin Shonkoff (Leiden: Brill, 2018), 3–32. Given the lesser attention to Buber, readers may find my construction of a Buberian strand in Wolfson's work puzzling as a result. Nevertheless, while I may be reading Wolfson's career against the grain, I do want to stress that I am not making grand claims about Wolfson as a "Buberian" (whatever that might mean); I am making a somewhat narrower claim that Wolfson's own take on Buber explains the purpose of the chiastic language that appears frequently in Wolfson's writing.

6. Zohar 1:88b–89a. See also *The Zohar: Pritzker Edition*, trans. Daniel C. Matt (Stanford, CA: Stanford University Press, 2004), 2:64.
7. See the references to both Zohar 2:256b–257a, and the section of Joseph Gikatilla's *Sha'arei Tzedeq* that explicitly equates *Shekhinah* and *Shaddai*, in Ellen Davina Haskell, *Suckling at My Mother's Breasts: The Image of a Nursing God in Jewish Mysticism* (Albany: State University of New York Press, 2012), 83–85.
8. Zohar 1:98b. I have used most of Wolfson's translation here, from "Circumcision, Vision of God, and Textual Interpretation," 39.
9. Zohar 1:89a; see also 1:95a, in which the divine name and circumcision are linked, following earlier rabbinic texts that link the *yod* of the divine name with the mark of circumcision. See *Midrash Tanḥuma*, Tzav 14: "What is the name and the seal that He has placed in them [circumcised Israelites]? It is *Shaddai*: the shin He has placed in the nose; the dalet in the hand, and the yod in the circumcision."
10. Zohar 1:94a.
11. Wolfson, "Circumcision," 42.
12. Wolfson, "Circumcision," 44.
13. Zohar 2:186b. Translation taken from *The Zohar: Pritzker Edition*, 6:49–50. See also the brief discussion of this passage in Yehuda Liebes's 1982 Hebrew article "The Messiah of the Zohar: On R. Simeon b. Yoḥai as a Messianic Figure," which appeared in English a decade later in *Studies in the Zohar*, trans. Arnold Schwartz, Stephanie Nakache, and Penina Peli (Albany: State University of New York Press, 1993), 27–28.
14. Zohar 1:103b.
15. Elliot R. Wolfson, *Through a Speculum That Shines: Vision and Imagination in Medieval Jewish Mysticism* (Princeton: Princeton University Press, 1994), 280. See also the important use of this quotation in T. M. Luhrmann, *When God Talks Back: Understanding the American Evangelical Relationship with God* (New York: Knopf, 2012), 185–86. I have spent some years trying to figure out whether Luhrmann's invocation of Wolfson is illegitimate or not, and have reached the tentative conclusion that much hangs on whether the author(s) of the *Zohar* and related texts would agree that the intent of prayerful practices is, as Luhrmann puts it, "to allow what must be imagined (God has no material form) to be experienced as more than mere imagination," and what the difference might be between imagination in Wolfson and "mere imagination" in Luhrmann.
16. Zohar 3:128a. The translation is from Wolfson, "Circumcision," 43; not all manuscripts contain the citation of Isaiah 22:23; some manuscripts read *be-ruḥa* (i.e., "the matter is dependent on the spirit") where Wolfson is following those manuscripts that read *be-raza'*. See also the discussion of this passage at Liebes, "Messiah of the Zohar," 26–27.

17. See Zohar 1:11b; Zohar 2:100b; B. Baba Bathra 89b.
18. Most notably, Zohar 1:236b.
19. Wolfson, *Circle in the Square*, 44.
20. Wolfson, "The Problem of Unity," 441.
21. Wolfson, "The Problem of Unity," 444.
22. Martin Buber, *Ekstatische Confessionen* (Heidelberg: Lambert Schneider, 1984), xxv; Buber, *Ecstatic Confessions*, trans. Esther Cameron (San Francisco: Harper & Row, 1985), 2. I have silently emended existing English translations, sometimes to correct them, and sometimes to render them in gender-neutral language.
23. Buber, "Jüdische Religiosität," in *Der Jude und Sein Judentum* (Gerlingen: Lambert Schneider, 1993), 75; Buber, "Jewish Religiosity," trans. Eva Jospe, in *On Judaism* (New York: Schocken, 1967), 94.
24. Buber, "Cheruth: Eine Rede über Jugend und Religion," in *Der Jude und Sein Judentum*, 120; Buber, "Herut: On Youth and Religion," trans. Eva Jospe, in *On Judaism*, 150.
25. Buber, "Cheruth," 126; Buber, "Herut," 158.
26. Buber, "Vorrede" to *Reden über das Judentum*, in *Der Jude und Sein Judentum*, 7–8; Buber, *On Judaism*, 8–9.
27. Buber, *Ich und Du*, in *Werke* (Munich: Kösel Verlag, 1962), 80; Buber, *I and Thou*, trans. Walter Kaufmann (New York: Charles Scribner's Sons, 1970), 1:55.
28. Wolfson, "The Problem of Unity," 441.
29. It is worth pointing out that this claim, which I believe Wolfson endorses, is a standard claim of feminist theology. See, for example, Judith Plaskow's remarks on "partial Torah" at *Standing Again at Sinai* (San Francisco: HarperCollins, 1990), 32–34, and her reference to Martin Buber at 244n23.
30. This is a point that Wolfson makes later in his career, for example when he defines theomania in *Giving Beyond the Gift* (25), with explicit reference to Buber's *I and Thou*: "the theomaniac (*gottsüchtige Mensch*) is so obsessed with the deity that he turns the Thou of revelatory meeting into an It in the realm of experienced objects and thereby fails to grasp the nature of either the giver or the gift."
31. Buber, "Urdistanz und Beziehung," in *Werke* 1:413; Buber, "Distance and Relation," trans. Ronald Gregor Smith, in *The Knowledge of Man: Selected Essays* (Atlantic Highlands, NJ: Humanities Press, 1988), 51.
32. Buber, "Urdistanz und Beziehung," 1:414; Buber, "Distance and Relation," 52.
33. Buber, "Urdistanz und Beziehung," 1:415; Buber, "Distance and Relation," 53.
34. Buber, "Urdistanz und Beziehung," 1:422; Buber, "Distance and Relation," 60.
35. Buber, "Urdistanz und Beziehung," 1:422; Buber, "Distance and Relation," 60.
36. It is for this reason that I hesitate to offer any hypotheses about the relationship between Buber's work and the Zohar. Wolfson's turn to Buber to solve issues in reading the Zohar may very well also solve issues in reading Buber!
37. Buber, "Urdistanz und Beziehung," 1:423; Buber, "Distance and Relation," 61. The use of *Bestätigung* instead of *Bewährung* (verification) is of note here. For more on the latter word in Buber, see Martin Kavka, "Verification (*Bewährung*) in Martin Buber," *Journal of Jewish Thought and Philosophy* 20, no. 1 (2012): 71–98.

38. Buber, "Cheruth," 120; Buber, "Herut," 150.
39. Buber, "Urdistanz und Beziehung," 1:423; Buber, "Distance and Relation," 61. I am indebted to Bob Erlewine and Shaul Magid for comments on earlier drafts of this essay. And I am deeply grateful to Elliot Wolfson for being far better than I have been at acknowledging that it is no longer 1992, and that the seminar tables of Princeton have receded into the mists of the past.

"WHAT WE ARE TO REMEMBER IN THE FUTURE"

Thoughts on Elliot Wolfson's Book on Dreams

ELISABETH WEBER

ELLIOT WOLFSON'S MAGNIFICENT BOOK *A DREAM INTERPRETED WITHIN A Dream* not only offers its readers rich and deep insight into the author's encyclopedic knowledge of the research and literature on dreams, but, drawing on sources from antiquity to kabbalistic texts, to psychoanalysis, philosophy, and neuroscience, it also reevaluates dreams in their reach beyond the purposes Sigmund Freud assigned to them: protecting sleep, working through past experiences, and offering hallucinatory wish fulfillment.

With Ludwig Binswanger via Michel Foucault, Wolfson understands the dream as "the retrieval of the 'originative movement of the imagination'—the 'bringing forth' of that 'which in *Existenz* is most irreducible to history,'" otherwise put, as "a way of freely being-in-the-world that is constituted necessarily as the eventual that transcends the confines of an immanent subjectivism," and as the paradoxical disclosure of "the point of origin from which freedom makes itself world."[1]

Of the language of such "bringing forth," the "language of oneiropoiesis," Wolfson writes that it "is both private and shared, doggedly peculiar and eerily common, [and thereby] uniquely suited to express the intensiveness of our spatiotemporal distension in the world, the genuine iteration that fosters the perpetuation of self in the eventfulness of its ongoing extinction."[2]

This essay will reflect on the paradoxes of dream language this sentence captures, and sound its depth for two dreams, two nightmares, to be precise.

The first dream occurs in the eleventh episode of the second series of the wildly popular Israeli TV show *Shtisel*, which, as its spectators know, is rich in visions and dreams, especially those dreamed by Shulem and Akiva Shtisel, father and son, the son being considered, at age 26 or 27, an "aging bachelor" whom his father is "eager to marry off." Akiva is also known for being "a *ba'al chaloymes*," a daydreamer, or, literally, a "master of dreams," who would "rather sketch lemurs at the zoo than do anything useful like study

Talmud or take a job at the cheder where Shulem teaches [and where] Akiva reluctantly agrees to freelance as a substitute."[3]

In the episode, Akiva has agreed to his uncle's condition for marrying his daughter Libbi: to give up painting for good in spite of his genuine talent that has started to receive public recognition. However, to appease Izzi Kaufmann, the art dealer who successfully nominated him for a coveted artist's prize, Akiva has also agreed to follow through with an exhibition already promised to the prestigious Israel Museum in Jerusalem. The compromise reached with Kaufmann stipulates that the exhibition will be shown under a pseudonym. Instead of working in the artist's studio, for which Akiva is paid a regular stipend as part of the prize money, he is working one day in his uncle's newly opened travel agency. Without customers and bored out of his mind, Akiva falls asleep on his desk.[4]

While the camera zooms in on him, the viewers hear the buzzing of a sewing machine in the office, through which they enter the dream: Akiva's mother, who died a couple years ago, is sewing at the family table. Akiva walks into the living room, and, surprised to see his mother, says "*Imma?*" "Mom?" [34:52]. The mother, interrupting her work, turns to look, but not recognizing her youngest son, turns back to the sewing machine. Akiva comes closer and repeats, "*Imma!*" [35:00], smiling expectantly. Looking "up at her son with total non-recognition,"[5] the mother pronounces the devastating question: "Do I know you?" "*Imma . . . zeh ani!*" "Mom, it's me!"—or, literally translated: "it's I!" He smiles at her, incredulous that she doesn't recognize him, but then, alarmed, can only repeat "*ani*," "I." His mother asks: "I? What's your name?" thereby exposing the "alienable" and thus uncertain nature of the "I" linguists and psychoanalysts refer to as "shifter."[6] As Roman Jakobson notes, "If we observe that even linguistic scientists had difficulties in defining the general meaning of the term *I* (or you), which signifies the same intermittent function of different subjects, it is quite obvious that the child who has learned to identify himself with his proper name will not easily become accustomed to such alienable terms as the personal pronouns."[7]

On the dark velvet spread over the base of the sewing machine, below the embroidery on which the mother is working, the Hebrew letters "טלית" indicate that she is decorating a pouch dedicated to hold a prayer shawl, the *tallit gadol*.[8]

In response to his mother's unsettling questions and with growing panic in his face, Akiva stammers: "*Ani . . . eh, Imma . . . ani . . .*": "I . . . eh, Mom . . . I . . .": As little as she recognizes her own son, as little can he remember his own name, and the repetition of the indexical pronoun only deepens his alienation. After the mother turns back to her embroidery work, the camera zooms in on the letters she has just finished stitching onto the velvet: ע (*Ayin*) and ש (*Shin*) [35:36], Akiva Shtisel's initials.

That evening, Akiva and his fiancée Libbi compare nightmares. Libbi too has dreamed a nightmare the night before: a high-speed train perilously traveling not on rails but on the open sea, with terrified passengers and crying children, her father speaking into a microphone to inform the passengers that to lighten the train, some people would have to be tossed into the waves. To Akiva's comment "That's not a dream, that's a movie! My dream doesn't sound scary at all compared to yours," Libbi replies: "No, forgetting your name is so scary. I mean it. Seriously." What Libbi doesn't know yet in this instant is that upon waking from his afternoon dream, Akiva called Kaufmann, the gallery owner, to declare that instead of a pseudonym, he will use his own name for the upcoming exhibition: "Akiva, Akiva Shtisel."

To get a deeper sense of this dream than the obvious interpretation the show hands the viewer—an alarming self-alienation, even self-betrayal, caused by the decision to no longer paint, ironically restored to a renewed self-affirmation through a ritually and emotionally charged garment that symbolizes Akiva's belonging to his observant community—consider Wolfson's reflection on a distinction made by the Greek diviner Artemidorus, whose treatise on dream-divination and dream-interpretations is quoted in Foucault's *History of Sexuality*: "'Dreams of desire' (*enypnia*) disclose the 'soul's reality in its present state,' whereas 'dreams of being' (*oneiroi*) 'tell the future of the event in the order of the world.'" Wolfson shows how this second-century text resonates with recent neurological studies:

> Whereas non-REM dreams are limited to reliving past experiences, REM dreams are expansive appropriations and quirky combinations of sense memories that *test possible scenarios of the future* and thus help a person to prepare for what is to come based on what has been. From the standpoint of biological evolution, dreams are a coping mechanism for human survival. In some respects, this corresponds to the distinction made in the 13th ct by Gershon ben Solomon, *Sha'ar ha-Shamayim*, 68b, between the dream in which the imagination conjures images based on previous sense experiences and the dream in which the imagination conjures images that are *not* based on what has been experienced in waking hours, which he tellingly refers to as what "we are to remember in the future" (*she-anu attidim lizkor*).[9]

Dreams that are not based on waking experience are instances of such "*prospective memory*": The "promise we customarily associate with the dream, an association that doubtless underlies the archaic alliance of dream and prognostication, is veritably a call to reminiscence, or what may be termed *prospective memory*. In this regard, the retroactive and imminent are not to be positioned dyadically. The example of ancient Israelite prophecy is instructive: the prophet is so certain of the truth of the vision that the forecast of what is to come seems to him as if it has already taken place, and thus the future prediction is expressed in the past tense."[10]

While biblical Hebrew understands the imperfect past tense as indicating an action not yet completed, and therefore open to the future, Wolfson refers here to the use of the perfect past tense characteristic of prophetic speech, the *perfectum propheticum*, in which, as Wilhelm Gesenius writes, the "prophet so transports himself in imagination into the future that he describes the future event as if it had been already seen or heard by him." "Not infrequently," Gesenius continues, "the imperfect interchanges with such perfects either in the parallel member or further on in the narrative."[11]

The dream that conjures "what we are to remember in the future" anticipates, as Wolfson quotes Foucault, "'the moment of liberation. It is a prefiguring of history even more than an obligatory repetition of the traumatic past.'" Therefore, the subject of the dream "cannot be limited to a past history, for its 'constituting moment' is an 'existence which makes itself through time,' a 'movement toward the future.'"[12]

Akiva's nightmare makes the liberating "promise" of such "prospective memory" manifest. While the dead mother, alive in the dream, doesn't recognize her living son, and her questions "Do I know you?" and "What is your name?" cause Akiva to forget who he is, her embroidering the tallit pouch with his initials makes her the guardian of her son's name. Upon waking, Akiva reclaims not only his name, but also, as he tells Libbi a bit later, something that is "inside [his] soul": "This (is) a part of me, this (is) who I (am) [*zeh mi sheh-ani* (זה מי שאני—literally: 'this who that I')], this (is) inside my soul, deep inside."[13] "This": painting. In this quote, I have put the verb forms in parentheses to indicate their absence in the original: in Modern Hebrew, the verb "to be" is not commonly conjugated in the present tense. The resulting nominal sentence reflects well the outcome of the dream's "cosmogony," which Foucault describes as "the origination itself of existence" and as "movement of solitude and of originative responsibility [*mouvement de la solitude et de la responsabilité originaire*]," as the "absolute disclosure of the ethical content, the heart shown naked."[14] Therefore, Akiva's dream can be described as one of those *oneiroi* that "tell the future of the event in the order of the world," a "dream of being" in which "being" materializes as "movement toward the future," insofar as it "projects itself toward a world which constitutes itself as the setting of its history."[15] Otherwise put, as Foucault underlines, the "dream world is not the inner garden of fantasy. If the dreamer meets there a world of his own, this is because he can recognize there the fact of his own destiny: he finds there the original movement of his existence and his freedom, in its achievement or in its alienation."[16]

Akiva's dream anticipates the moment of his liberation, precipitating his decision to reverse his acquiescence to his uncle's demand to abandon painting, and to sign his exhibition in his name. The language of Akiva's dream is indeed, to quote Elliot Wolfson's formulation again, "uniquely suited to express the intensiveness of [his] spatiotemporal distension in the world," as the painter who he understands he was (meant to be); uniquely suited also to express the "genuine iteration that fosters the perpetuation of self in the eventfulness of its ongoing extinction." In Akiva's case the "extinction" of "self" is not only "ongoing," occurring and recurring in dreams (as is the case for all dreamers), but is also threatened in the repeated attempts by his father and uncle to turn him away from his calling, to deny who he was in his soul. By contrast, with her probing questions and embroidery work, the mother reminds the son of his obligation to free himself of his father's and uncle's expectations. As Judith Shulevitz observes, in *Shtisel*, "the dead help the living push back against unreasonable demands."[17]

The second nightmare is arguably one of the most excruciating dreams in twentieth-century European literature. It is told in Primo Levi's *If This Is a Man*, the account of his life in the Auschwitz annihilation camp. Occurring in the chapter "Our Nights," the nightmare is preceded by a lucid dream, dreamed in sleep that "is very light," just a "veil" that Levi "will [. . .] tear" to "get off the railway track" on which an "engine" is "panting": his sleeping neighbor, a much stronger and menacing stranger with whom he has to share a bunk, is breathing heavily. In this lucid dream, Levi keeps his eyes closed, "lest my sleep escape me, but I can register noises: I am sure this distant whistle is real, it does not come from an engine in a dream, it can be heard objectively." The entire quote is important:

> It is the whistle of a small-gauge track, it comes from the yard where they work at night as well. A long, firm note, then another one a semitone lower, then again the first, but short and cut off. This whistle is an important thing and in some ways essential: we have heard it so often associated with the suffering of the work and the camp that it has become a symbol and immediately evokes its image like certain music or smells.

At this juncture, the sleeper slips from his lucid dream into another one:

> This is my sister here, with some unidentifiable friend and many other people. They are all listening to me and it is this very story that I am telling: the whistle of three notes, the hard bed, my neighbour whom I would like to move, but whom I am afraid to wake as he is stronger than me. I also speak diffusely (*diffusamente*) of our hunger and of the lice-control, and of the Kapo who hit me on the nose and then sent me to wash myself as I was bleeding. It is an intense pleasure, physical, inexpressible, to be at home, among friendly people and to have so many things to recount.[18]

At first, this dream also appears to contain the deeply liberating "prospective memory," "what we are to remember in the future," after a future liberation from the camp and the return to the dreamer's beloved Italy. However, while in Akiva's nightmare the dead mother's lack of recognition, paired with her guardianship of Akiva's name, is a warning that results in his liberation from his future father-in-law's "unreasonable demand," Levi's dream turns into a nightmare of dark foreboding:

> It is an intense pleasure, physical, inexpressible, to be at home, among friendly people and to have so many things to recount: but I cannot help noticing that my listeners do not follow me. In fact, they are completely indifferent: they speak confusedly (*confusamente*) of other things among themselves, as if I was not there. My sister looks at me, gets up and goes away without a word.
>
> A desolating grief is now born in me, like certain barely remembered pains of one's early infancy (*prima infanzia*). It is pain in its pure state, not tempered by a sense of reality and by the intrusion of extraneous circumstances (*è dolore allo stato puro, non temperato dal senso della realtà e dalla intrusione di circostanze estranee*) [...]; and it is better for me to swim once again up to the surface, but this time I deliberately open my eyes to have a guarantee in front of me of being effectively awake.[19]

It remains unclear whether the entire dream or only its first part is lucid. In any case, the intense pain results in waking up the dreamer: "pain in its pure state, not tempered by a sense of reality." Does the narrator imply that "pain in its pure state" is felt *outside* of reality, that is, only in the imagined irreality of a dream? While wish fulfillment clearly pervades the first part of the dream, the concept is not sufficient to decipher the nightmarish second part. But with Wolfson's explanation of a "conception well attested in, but hardly unique to, medieval kabbalistic sources," a path toward its legibility is opened: "'It must be asked why does a man suffer more concerning something that happens in a dream than if he saw it while awake? This is because when he is awake, the soul is clad in the body, and he does not feel the intensity [. . .] as much, for the body is protective; but in a dream, it is naked, and the damage inflicts him and he suffers more.'"[20]

Indeed, in Levi's dream, the soul is as naked and vulnerable as a newborn, which Levi invokes when he likens the "desolating grief" to the "barely remembered pains of one's early infancy": of the time in one's life, that is, in which the absolute dependency on physical care and loving recognition from others is most defenselessly lived and most shatteringly experienced in its absence. While, as Wolfson writes, "kabbalists [. . .] widely believed that nocturnal dreams could be explained by the fact that in sleep the spirit is stripped of it[s] *corporeal armor* and ascends to the divine pleroma in accord with its earthly demeanor,"[21] in Levi's dream such an ascension is not possible. Nonetheless, through Wolfson's reading, the kabbalistic speculations resonate eerily. Recalling the "ancient conceptions of the dream as the means by which the soul makes contact with the incorporeal realm, such as we find in Pythagorean, Stoic, and Neoplatonic philosophies," Wolfson describes sleep "as a partial simulation of the separation of body and soul, an idea that expanded the rabbinic tradition that sleep is one-sixtieth of death."[22] In the death camp, on "planet Auschwitz," as the writer and Auschwitz survivor Yehiel Dinoor called it under his chosen name Ka-Zetnik, because everything, from the cycle of time, to dress, names, life and death, even to breathing, "was regulated by the laws of another nature" rather than "in accordance with the laws of this world,"[23] the "one-sixtieth of death" that sleep is actually provides a better, albeit extremely fragile protection against the waking world that harbors much greater parts of death. For in the waking hours at the death camps, the body no longer provides an "armor" of protection, weakened beyond recognition as it was by violence, malnutrition, forced labor, and overall ferocious survival conditions. On the contrary, Levi refers to "the thin armour of sleep" that, however, with the "daily condemnation" to get up, "drops to pieces around us, and we find ourselves mercilessly awake, exposed to insult, atrociously naked and vulnerable": "'*Aufstehen*,' or more often in Polish '*Wstavać*' [. . .] Like a stone the foreign word falls to the bottom of every soul. 'Get up.'" Upon waking, the soul is not protectively clothed by the body, it is assaulted in continuous and countless ways, which is why in spite of the near absolute exhaustion, "very few sleep on till the *Wstavać*: it is a moment of too acute pain for even the deepest sleep not to dissolve as it approaches."[24]

Levi reports of his nightmare that he dreams it with tormenting regularity, "with hardly any variations of environment or details." What is more, he remembers having recounted it to Alberto, his closest friend; and "he confided to me, to my amazement, that it is also his dream and the dream of many others, perhaps of everyone (*di molti altri, forse di tutti*)." How can this happen? Why, Levi asks, "is the pain of every day translated so constantly into our dreams, in the ever-repeated scene of the unlistened-to story?"[25] Here, the dream language is indeed, to return to Wolfson's formulation, "doggedly peculiar and eerily common," literally and cruelly expressing the "perpetuation of self in the eventfulness of its ongoing extinction."[26]

The repetition of the nightmare on the individual level might to a certain degree be decipherable with Freud's concept of repetition compulsion as an irredeemably belated attempt to paradoxically prepare the psychic apparatus after the fact for the missed encounter of the traumatic assault (whose unanticipated occurrence constitutes precisely its traumatic quality), a concept that moved Freud to qualify his previously categorical assertion that dreams are hallucinatory wish fulfillments. The collective repetition is, however, harder to grasp. Freud's development of a collectively enacted repetition compulsion in *Totem and Taboo*, *Beyond the Pleasure Principle*, and *Moses and Monotheism* requires the *longue durée* of a generation of collective repression, centuries of latency, and a tradition transmitted and surviving in secret, all conditions not given here.

In Levi's account, the collective dimension is asserted over and over again, including in the chapter entitled "Our Nights, *Le Nostre Notti.*" Toward the end of this chapter, Levi returns to the collective dream, describing how, just like the dream of Tantalus, which during his lifetime would certainly have been a collectively shared myth, the nightmare is "woven into a texture of more indistinct images: the suffering of the day, composed of hunger, blows, cold, exhaustion, fear and promiscuity, turns at night-time into shapeless nightmares of unheard-of violence, which in free life would only occur during a fever."[27]

In the description that follows, the Italian original uses the reflexive pronoun reserved specifically for the impersonal form: "*Ci si sveglia . . .* " which is further emphasized by the adjective in the plural *gelidi* ("frozen"), required in absence of a specific subject for the verb: "*gelidi di terrore*": "One wakes up at every moment, frozen with terror, shaking in every limb, under the impression of an order shouted out by a voice full of anger in a language not understood."[28] In the next sentence, the impersonal "one" has morphed into an equally anonymous first person plural without any differentiations between those of whom it is composed:

> The procession to the bucket and the thud of bare heels on the wooden floor turns into another symbolic procession: it is us again, grey and identical, small as ants, yet so huge as to reach up to the stars, bound one against the other (*serrati uno contro l'altro*), countless, covering the plain as far as the horizon; sometimes melting into a single substance, a sorrowful turmoil in which we all feel ourselves trapped and suffocated; sometimes marching in a circle, without beginning or end, with a blinding giddiness and a sea of nausea rising from the preacordia to the gullet; until hunger or cold or the fullness of our bladders (*la pienezza della vescica*) turn our dreams [*i sogni*] into their customary form. We try in vain, when the nightmare itself [*il incubo stesso*: also: *the same nightmare*] or the discomforts wake us, to extricate the

> various elements and drive them back, separately, out of the field of our present attention, so as to defend our sleep (*il sonno*) from their intrusion: but as soon as we close our eyes, once again we feel our brain (*il nostro cervello*) start up, beyond our control; it knocks and hums, incapable of rest, it fabricates phantasms and terrible symbols, and without rest projects and shapes their images, as a grey fog, on to the screen of our dreams (*dei sogni*).[29]

The English translation reflects the morphing into a collective entity by assigning the possessive pronoun of the first person plural to the bladder, to the dreams, and to sleep, whereas in Italian, these nouns are accompanied simply by their article. It is therefore all the more remarkable that Levi does assign the possessive pronoun to the brain in the plural: "*il nostro cervello*": "our brain." There is only one collective brain belonging to all the sleepers, and thus, sleep and dreams have become collective too, just like the "grey and identical" bodies "bound," or locked "one against the other." Bodies and minds that, "grey and identical," are tightly crammed into an undifferentiated mass don't generate dreams able to retrieve "the 'originative movement of the imagination.'" The ceaselessly and collectively repeated nightmare does not disclose "the point of origin from which freedom makes itself world,"[30] because its dreamers have been robbed of their world, past, present, and future, to the point of being "outside this world."[31]

If Freud's repetition compulsion does not help decipher the repeated, collective nightmare, can Foucault's reflection on repetitive dreams be more useful?

> If the dream is the bearer of the deepest human meanings, this is not insofar as it betrays their hidden mechanisms or shows their inhuman cogs and wheels, but on the contrary, insofar as it brings to light the freedom of man in its most original form. And when, in ceaseless repetition, it declares some destiny, it is bewailing a freedom which has lost itself, an ineradicable past, and an existence fallen of its own motion into a definite determination.[32]

The answer to the above question is "no": this nightmare cannot "declare some destiny," because it does not bewail "an existence fallen *of its own motion* into a definite determination." Rather, just as shortly after their arrival at Auschwitz, the Italian deportees "for the first time [. . .] became aware that our language lacks words to express this offence, the demolition of a man [*per la prima volta ci siamo accorti che la nostra lingua manca di parole per esprimere questa offesa, la demolizione di un uomo*],"[33] language lacks words to name this demolition of the dream. What is true for the word "hunger," for the words "fear," "pain," and "winter," applies here as well:

> Just as our hunger is not that feeling of missing a meal, so our way of being cold has need of a new word. We say "hunger," we say "tiredness," "fear," "pain," we say "winter" and they are different things. They are free words, created and used by free men who lived in comfort and suffering in their homes. If the Lagers had lasted longer a

> new, harsh language would have been born [*un nuovo aspro linguaggio sarebbe nato*]; and only this language could express what it means to toil the whole day in the wind, with the temperature below freezing, wearing only a shirt, underpants, cloth jacket and trousers, and in one's body nothing but weakness, hunger and knowledge of the end drawing nearer.[34]

In the case of the death camp's nightmare, collectively shared, the "language of oneiropoiesis" is indeed "both private and shared, doggedly peculiar and eerily common," but the "ongoing extinction" is a literal and brutal one, in which "the perpetuation of self"[35] is eradicated continuously. Therefore, the nightmare, incessantly repeated and collectively shared, should no longer be called a dream or, for that matter, a nightmare, because the words "dream" and "nightmare" are two of those "free words [*parole libere*]," as Levi writes, "created and used by free men [*create e usate da uomini liberi*]." And just as "our way of being cold has need of a new word" [*così il nostro modo di aver freddo esigerebbe un nome particolare*]," more precisely: "would require a particular name," what visits and haunts the tormented sleepers over and over again would be in need of a particular name in an as yet unheard, harsh language.

NOTES

1. Michel Foucault quoted in Elliot R. Wolfson, *A Dream Interpreted Within a Dream: Oneiropoiesis and the Prism of Imagination* (Brooklyn: Zone Books, 2011), 57, 108. The quotes within the quote stem from Ludwig Binswanger, on whose work on dreams Foucault is commenting.
2. Wolfson, *A Dream*, 14.
3. Judith Shulevitz, "Streaming Sacred: The achievement of Shtisel," *Commentary*, June 2019, https://www.commentary.org/articles/judith-shulevitz/streaming-sacred/.
4. Ori Elon and Yehonatan Indursky, *Shtisel*, Season 2, Episode 11, 34th and 35th minutes. From here on, the numbers in brackets refer to the time-mark in the episode.
5. Shulevitz, "Streaming Sacred."
6. Roman Jakobson defined the shifter as an "indexical symbol" and Jacques Lacan as an "indexical signifier": "Shifters, verbal categories, and the Russian verb," in Roman Jakobson, *Selected Writings, II* (The Hague: Mouton, 1971), 132; Jacques Lacan, *The Seminar. Book XI, The Four Fundamental Concepts of Psychoanalysis,* trans. Alan Sheridan (London: Hogarth Press and Institute of Psycho-Analysis, 1977), 138f.
7. Jakobson, *Selected Writings*, 132.
8. In addition to the daily use for morning prayer and during Yom Kippur, it is noteworthy that in many Ashkenazi circles men wear the *tallit gadol* only after marriage, that it is often used as a *chuppa*, and that his owner is wrapped in it after death. It thus symbolizes more than the appearance in Akiva's dreamlife of the familial anxiety over his unmarried status.
9. Wolfson, *A Dream*, 108, endnote 314, 352–53, emphasis added other than words in Hebrew.
10. Wolfson, *A Dream*, 223.

11. Wilhelm Gesenius, *Hebrew Grammar* (1909), § 106: Use of the Perfect, https://en.wikisource.org/wiki/Gesenius%27_Hebrew_Grammar/106._Use_of_the_Perfect (accessed August 17, 2021). I thank Aryeh Amihay for this reference and his explanations.
12. Wolfson, *A Dream*, 138.
13. *Shtisel*, Season 2, Episode 11, 45th minute and following. I thank Ofra Amihay for her translation of this scene and for her precious grammar explanations.
14. Michel Foucault, "Dream, Imagination, and Existence," trans. Forrest Williams, in Michel Foucault and Ludwig Binswanger, *Dream and Existence*, ed. Keith Hoeller (Seattle: Review of Existential Psychology & Psychiatry, 1986), 51, 52; Michel Foucault, *Dits et Écrits I*, 1954–1969 (Paris: Gallimard, 1994), 91–92.
15. Foucault, *Dream, Imagination*, 51.
16. Foucault, *Dream, Imagination*, 54.
17. Shulevitz, "Streaming Sacred."
18. Primo Levi, *Survival in Auschwitz*, trans. Stuart Woolf (New York: Touchstone Books, 1996), 59–60. The first English edition's title, since abandoned without explanation, was more faithful to the Italian: *If This Is a Man*. Primo Levi, *Se questo è un uomo* (Torino: Einaudi, 1989), 103. Susan Derwin has offered a highly original analysis of Levi's dream and of the neighbor as Levi's alter ego: Susan Derwin, *Rage Is the Subtext: Readings in Holocaust Literature and Film* (Columbus: Ohio State University Press, 2012), 33–45.
19. Levi, *Survival*, 59f; *Se questo*, 104.
20. Joseph Karo, Safedian Kabbalist, sixteenth century, quoted in Wolfson, *A Dream*, 50f.
21. Wolfson, *A Dream*, 51.
22. Wolfson, *A Dream*, 51.
23. Yehiel Dinoor, testimony during the trial of Adolf Eichmann in Jerusalem, session 68, June 7, 1961, quoted in Shoshana Felman, "A Ghost in the House of Justice," in Shoshana Felman, *The Juridical Unconscious. Trials and Traumas in the Twentieth Century* (Cambridge: Harvard University Press, 2002), 136. That other laws than the laws of "this" world governed Auschwitz is also voiced by one of the Kapos, quoted by Levi: "*Hier ist kein Warum*": "There is no 'why' here."
24. Levi, *Survival*, 63.
25. Levi, *Survival*, 60; *Se questo*, 104.
26. Wolfson, *A Dream*, 14.
27. Levi, *Survival*, 62; *Se questo*, 106f.
28. Levi, *Survival*, 62; *Se questo*, 107. I thank Valentina Padula for her grammar explanation.
29. Levi, *Survival*, 62–63; *Se questo*, 107.
30. Foucault, quoted in Wolfson, *A Dream*, 57, 108.
31. Levi, *Survival*, 23; *Se questo*, 36.
32. Foucault, *Dream, Imagination*, 53.
33. Levi, *Survival*, 26; *Se questo*, 41–42.
34. Levi, *Survival*, 123; *Se questo*, 203–4.
35. Wolfson, *A Dream*, 14. See p. 31 in this chapter for the longer quote.

DEMONOLOGY BEYOND DUALISMS

ANNETTE YOSHIKO REED

WHAT MEANINGS DOES A BINARY MAKE, AND WHAT MEANINGS DOES it hide? Together with his celebrated contributions to the study of Kabbalah and Jewish thought, Elliot Wolfson has modeled innovative scholarly approaches that challenge us to rethink the binary frames that often strike us as most natural for reading religious literature more broadly. To bring attention to gender, as Wolfson has shown, is not merely to recover the feminine in a manner stably contrasted to the masculine.[1] To ponder embodiment is not just to raise a point of contrast with mystical transcendence; it is rather radically to reconfigure it.[2] To take forgetting seriously is to rethink remembrance.[3] And so too for darkness and light, good and evil.[4] Speech and silence.[5] Christian and Jew.[6]

In what follows, I take inspiration from Wolfson to reflect upon a topic that might seem, at first sight, to make meaning only by means of binary thinking—namely: demons. Demons are commonly contrasted to angels, read as markers of cosmic dualism, and thought to emblematize supernatural evil. In this essay, I ask whether and how discourses of demonology might draw their own lines of distinction, before and beyond the dualisms through which scholars habitually analyze the demonic. To do so, I first make the case for premodern demonology as one potent site for unsettling the modern bifurcation of human from nonhuman. In this, I draw especially on Mel Chen's articulation of "animacies" as a rubric that might help to "trouble and undo stubborn binary systems of difference" by drawing our attention to the instabilities in the distribution of agency and sentience within our speech about ourselves and our worlds.[7] Then I turn to ancient Jewish examples from the Aramaic Enoch literature and related Dead Sea Scrolls, asking what we might gain by resisting the retrojection of our own defining dichotomies and attending instead to how some premodern sources quite differently frame difference—with and about demons.

TO MANY TODAY, IT MAY SEEM WHOLLY OBVIOUS, IF NOT SIMPLY NATURAL, TO distinguish the human from the nonhuman as distinct domains. Not only does such a division inform much everyday talk about the world, but it is embedded in the defining structures of some of the main institutional engines of modern knowledge-making. Central to the emergence and structuring of the secular university, for instance, was the demarcation of academic disciplines dedicated to the animal, natural, and physical worlds (i.e., biology, chemistry, physics) and their distinction from those disciplines dedicated to human cultural, historical, and literary production.[8] The late eighteenth- and nineteenth-century development of academic disciplines—institutionalized through the spread of scientific societies and academic journals, and instantiated in the professionalization of the professoriate—thus pivoted on the bifurcation of human and nonhuman as if naturally distinct domains of study. In turn, the naturalization of this divide has arguably shaped perceptions and practices of knowledge, particularly within professional academic research where the bifurcation of "the sciences" from "the humanities" is now commonly taken for granted.[9]

Recently, however, feminist and other theorists have begun to recognize that—in the words of Elizabeth A. Wilson—"the Human and the Nonhuman are not two separate spheres that may or may not overlap," but rather permeable, intertwined, imbricated, interpenetrating, and mutually constituting.[10] Or, as Jane Bennett puts it: "There was never a time when human agency was anything other than an interfolding network of humanity and nonhumanity."[11] Variations of this point have been made especially by theorists in the interlocking subfields of new materialism, feminist criticism, queer theory, and animal studies as well as by sociologists of knowledge who have historicized the now-common bifurcation of human from nonhuman in the European Enlightenment, revealing this seemingly "natural" binary to be far from essential, stable, timeless, or universal.

The bifurcation of human from nonhuman is predicated on an ostensible human exceptionalism that is achieved through the bundling-together of all nonhuman animals and all nonanimal matter on the other side of the divide—*as if* we as human beings are more different from horses, for instance, than horses are from rocks, and *as if* we are not also both animal and material as well. Much, however, is hidden in the seemingly obviousness of the human/nonhuman distinction—including the anxiousness of the energy expended to maintain it.[12]

This is among the dynamics that Chen has richly explored in their analysis of what they term "animacy." In their 2014 book of that name, Chen calls us to attend to its configuration "*via* its ostensible opposite: the Inanimate, deadness, lowness, nonhuman animals (rendered as insensate), the abject, the object."[13] Far from self-evident, "the fragile division between animate and inanimate—that is, beyond human and animal—is relentlessly produced and policed."[14]

One of Chen's key points concerns the naturalization of the binary of human/nonhuman in conventional habits of language whereby the rhetoric of "objectification" is used more often of women and the rhetoric of "dehumanization" is used more often of racialized and foreign others, who can thus be readily likened to animals, insects, toxins, pollution, and viruses.[15] Simply to condemn such cases of gendered "objectification" or racialized "dehumanization," thus, is to risk reinscribing the very "hierarchies of sentience" upon which these stereotypes depend, which are far from natural or universal but which have specific histories as well as functions embedded in language, politics, and power.

Among the results of the "animacy hierarchies" that set the human categorically above the nonhuman—Chen further suggests—is to undergird social "hierarchies of sentience in which only some privileged humans are granted the status of thinking subject."[16] As with "objectification," thus, perhaps so too for "objectivity": it draws its rhetorical power (and roots its ostensible obviousness) in part from the overlapping binaries of human and nonhuman, culture and nature, male and female, spirit and matter, and so on, and the naturalization of these binaries also naturalizes the illusion that any human knowledge-making can be divorced from the materiality of human bodies and the nonhuman worlds that constitute us.

In this, Chen's insights bring us back to Donna Haraway's classic critique of modern disembodied ideals of "objectivity," including their tacit exclusion from scholarly knowledge-making of "those who are not allowed not to have a body" (e.g., women, children, people of color, those who are ill or aged, those who do not fit particular normative ideals of gendered difference).[17] When we return to Haraway's reminder of epistemological embodiment with the framework of Chen's concept of animacies, we are challenged to attend to the often invisible epistemological work done by the bifurcation of human and nonhuman and the "hierarchies of sentience" that depend upon it. It is the ranking of the human categorically above the nonhuman, for instance, that partly undergirds the association of men with "culture," history, agency, and rational analysis, whereby a feminized "nature" is placed in closer connection to animality and emotion. Yet even as this binary may be commonly treated *as if* a natural divide, it is also—in practice—constantly and anxiously blurred so to maintain a hierarchy of what (and who) counts as *most* human and what (and who) can thus be credited with sense and sentience, agency and autonomy, and the rational positionality of one who makes knowledge, makes history, and stands far enough apart from the materiality of the nonhuman world to be able to analyze it.

Theorists like Haraway and Chen have done much to expose the cultural contingency and invisible workings of fundamental modern dualisms, undercutting the claims to neutrality and universality typically associated with Enlightenment-era European ideals of "objectivity."[18] As a result, however, I would suggest that their insights might prove especially useful for scholars of ancient literature, opening the way for us to reconsider our sources apart from the particularistic assumptions of modern frameworks of analysis. In turn, attention to premodern sources might aid in the project of revisiting, relativizing, reassessing, and revising some of the core assumptions bequeathed to us from the specific eighteenth- and nineteenth-century European settings in which our own disciplines first took form.

For this task, I suggest that demonology might prove especially potent, opening up alternative vistas and drawing our attention to premodern precedents for what some theorists now seek to articulate as "relational ontologies" interconnecting human with nonhuman. That new materialism might prove useful for the study of demons has been suggested by scholars of early Christianity such as Denise Kimber Buell and Travis Proctor. Buell notes how such theories challenge us to "reframe our understanding of subjectivity and agency, and thus also how 'we' as humans are not only the result of ongoing material encounters but also that, in our being human, we are not separable from the environment, other animals, or technologies."[19] Accordingly, Buell has called for attention to the "continuous process of materializing differences" when interpreting early Christian texts and material culture.[20] She points to our data for exorcism as exemplary in this regard.[21] More recently, Travis Proctor has extended Buell's insights to speak further to demons, embodiment, and the environment.[22] In what follows, I build upon their insights but turn instead to focus on ancient Jewish knowledge-making about demons.

AT FIRST SIGHT, ONE MIGHT BE TEMPTED TO TREAT DEMONS SIMPLY AS AN IMAGined species or subset of the nonhuman. In many ancient cultural contexts, however, the very making of knowledge about demons—their naming and narration, and the practices of textualizing and systemizing traditions about them—cuts across the lines of any simple divide between human/nonhuman, natural/supernatural, and even good/evil. At times, as Bruce Lincoln observes, demons could function "quite literally like the black holes of a premodern cosmology, where physics, metaphysics, and ethics remain inextricably intertwined."[23] Such dynamics have been largely ignored, in Lincoln's estimation, inasmuch as "the claims made by demonological discourse having been conclusively discredited in the European Enlightenment," but as a result, "our understanding of many religions is impoverished, for some of the most serious issues of ethics, cosmology, anthropology, and soteriology were—and still are—regularly engaged via demonology."[24] In pre-Islamic Persia, for instance, demonology could even "constitute something like a unified field theory of what we treat separately under the rubrics of bacteriology, epidemiology, toxicology, teratology, criminology, Marxism, psychoanalysis, and others."[25]

Among the most common activities cross-culturally attributed to demons, moreover, is the breach of the very bounds that we now take for granted as "naturally" separating us, as if autonomous, individuated, and self-contained beings, from what we experience as the external material environment in which we dwell—that is, spirit possession.[26] Even in cases when demons too are claimed to have bodies, individuation, and personalized agency of their own, part of their power is their potential to indwell within and co-mingle with the human. Whereas modern germ theory and "discourse of immunity . . . instantiates a notion of the human as vulnerable but ideally contained," Buell thus notes how ancient amulets and narratives about exorcism presume that "the human is not simply permeable but is constituted from and continually interactive with forces that may provisionally be inside or outside of a human."[27]

In many ancient cultures, the materiality and spirituality of the demon are arguably no less inseparable. What we now call "demons" in Greek, Hebrew, and Aramaic literatures (*shedim, daimones*, etc.), for instance, are not yet categorically distinguished from "angels"; more often, in fact, both are described as "spirits" (*ruḥot, ruḥin, pneumata*, etc.).[28] Nevertheless, as Proctor has shown, the demons of the ancient Mediterranean imagination are decisively embodied—and if anything, marked by a "trans-corporality" akin to that associated with humans as well.[29]

In addition, the very act of naming the demonic can function to distribute agency and animacy no less to landscapes, objects, and animals. David Frankfurter, for instance, notes how ancient demon-beliefs often begin as a process of "informal . . . mapping onto the environment" whereby parts of the lived and local landscape—such as "points of mystery (crags, corries), danger (ponds), expanse (fields), secrecy (caves)"—come to be experienced as "a topography of catastrophe, as place and passage become correlated to misfortune through the stories of local demons" and "avoidance of misfortune is expressed through the conscious avoidance or ritual attention to places in the landscape."[30] As a result, demon and demonized place can seem inseparable.[31]

Nor is the practice of naming demons limited to landscape. As Frankfurter further shows, "demons also gain specific characters through being attached to weather, to stars, to sins or impurities (like lust or menstruation), to parts of the body, and to specific maladies."[32] Animals, too, form a prominent part of the lexicon of demonic naming in local knowledge-making: the demonic is often imagined "not only in terms of animals but also as having an intrinsic affiliation to the animal world," and in many cases, one finds a "slippage between demon and animal."[33]

It can be tempting to explain away such slippages with appeal to the demonic as hybrid. Yet it might be worth wondering whether premodern uses of demons for knowledge-making, always and everywhere, necessarily reflected our sense of the essential differences between the domains that we imagine to be so distinct so as only to be able to connect through hybridization. Did ancient discourses about demons breach an otherwise unbridgeable divide between human and nonhuman? Or might they reflect cultural worlds not necessarily shaped by the particular binaries that now strike us as so natural? Or perhaps attention to demonologies might open windows onto worlds divided along other dualisms and distinctions instead, distributing animacies along other lines?

As noted above, ancient demonologies often cut across the lines of post-Enlightenment orders of knowledge that bifurcate natural from supernatural.[34] In addition, it is striking that some even resist reduction to the dualism of good and evil. This is clearly the case, for instance, in the Hebrew Bible—as Anne Marie Kitz has recently noted, stressing that "demons as *inherently* evil subordinates did not exist in the ancient Near East."[35] Modern scholars have tended to read biblical references to "spirits," and so on (e.g., 1 Sam 16:15), by "start[ing] with the *presumption* that a demon is an intrinsically evil supernatural being and an angel is an intrinsically good supernatural being."[36] This habit, however, may say more about our own assumptions than those of our sources. Even when one finds "references to subordinate supernatural beings that engage in destructive activities" in biblical literature, as Kitz shows, they are described foremost in terms of the functions with which God charges them: their destructiveness pertains to "mission and not moral standing."[37] Or, in other words: "it is the character of the assigned tasks of these רוחות that might be considered evil or good, not the רוחות themselves."[38]

The same pattern holds even into the Second Temple period—the very period that scholars have typically credited with the rise of dualism within Judaism and the polarization of the supernatural world into "demons" and "angels." In his recent survey of these developments, Bennie Reynolds suggests that "demigods" may remain more apt to describe the range of transmundane powers in the Jewish literature of this period, further noting that "there are good reasons not to make substantive distinctions between malevolent and beneficent gods and demi-gods during most stages of Israelite/Jewish religion, even during Hellenistic times."[39] During this period, we begin to see some Jewish sources exhibit concerns with dualism (e.g., *Visions of Amram*; 1QM), concurrent with an increased interest in demons (e.g., Tobit; *Book of the Watchers*). Nevertheless, the demonology of the period still resists any simple reduction to dualism.

As much as scholars habitually sort the transmundane powers mentioned in our sources into "angels" and "demons," and speculate about their "polarization" in Second Temple Judaism, our sources use other categories, marked by moral indeterminacy and more akin to biblical precedents than later Christian ideas of cosmic dualism. Even despite the trend toward dualism within later sectarian Dead Sea Scrolls, for instance, P. S. Alexander thus stresses how "the generic term for a demon in the Scrolls is a spirit (רוח)"—a term that is quite explicitly "not exclusive to demons" but also includes angels.[40] The wickedness of "wicked spirits" is not intrinsic, but rather describes how they "cause harm and mischief to humans in a variety of ways."[41]

So too with *daimones* and related terms in Greek: despite the etymological connection to our English term "demon," such terms retain the moral indeterminacy of their traditional usage even in Greek Jewish writings.[42] In fact, Giovanni Bazzana has recently shown how even the evidence of the New Testament "runs counter to the often-repeated assumption that the Jesus movement introduced a significant polarization in demonology."[43] This is in keeping with the dynamic that Frankfurter sees as continuing into late antiquity: even after the articulation of more dualistic notions of the demonic, the Christian concept of *daimones* still "involves a perpetual oscillation between the terrifying and the protective."[44] Spirits may be tasked with actions that harm humankind, but this does not necessarily equate to their perception as evil in an intrinsic or even stable sense (and hence, the same figures sometimes slip from angel to demon and back again).

WE MISS MUCH WHEN WE PRESUME THAT ALL REFERENCES TO "DEMONS" NECESSARILY form part of a stable binary system of cosmic dualism or necessarily hew to the lines of post-Enlightenment notions of the "supernatural" as distinct from the "natural." Might something similar be said for demonology across the divide of human and nonhuman? And what might we see when we set aside our own binary frames and attend instead to how our ancient sources have theorized both demons and difference?

Such questions, I suggest, might aid us in understanding one particular set of data for ancient Judaism—that is, the earliest known examples of ancient Jewish demonology and related "magical" and other materials. It is often noted that systematic Jewish reflection about demons is not attested until around the third century BCE, when it appears with a seemingly sudden explosion of explicit exuberance, exemplified by the Aramaic Enoch literature.[45] The Enochic *Book of the Watchers*, composed in Aramaic and preserved also in Greek and Ethiopic (4Q201–206; *1 Enoch* 1–36), is famous as the first known Jewish text to include an explanation of the origins, nature, and fate of "wicked spirits" (Gr. πνεύματα πονηρὰ; Eth. *manfasa 'ekuya'*). As such, it is often hailed as marking the beginnings of the explicit and systematic interest in demons among Jews in the Second Temple period.

This systemization is achieved with a focus on angelic transgression and its consequences for the origin and spread of demons, and it is explored along both temporal and spatial axes. Temporally, the *Book of the Watchers* appeals to the antediluvian past, recounting the earthly descent of 200 angels from the class "Watcher" (Aram. עיר; Eth. *teguh*), their desire for human women, their teachings of corrupting and civilizing arts, and their paternity of monstrous giants who tormented humankind and polluted the earth—in flesh until the purification of the Flood and as "wicked spirits" thereafter (*1 Enoch* 6–8; 15:8–16:1; 19:1). Spatially, it is marked by Enoch's claim to know the places of angelic descent, imprisonment, judgment, and punishment (*1 Enoch* 18–21) no less than God's heavenly abode (*1 Enoch* 14), the structure of the cosmos and its partitioning into archangelic domains (*1 Enoch* 20), and the sites of the postmortem and eschatological fates of humankind (*1 Enoch* 22–27). The *Book of the Watchers'* much-discussed etiology of "wicked spirits" thus forms part of a sophisticated and systematic account of "spirits" that includes their association with the distant past but also their spatial mapping onto the present and future.

Despite the celebrated place of the *Book of the Watchers* within the history of Jewish demonology, past research had tended to focus on what might lie behind its concern for fallen angels, giants, and demons—either debating which human historical figures or events they might symbolize or speculating about what they might figure of a theological position within some posited reconstructed debate.[46] It has been largely taken for granted, for instance, that discussions of demons must either be metaphorical in character or answer abstract theological concerns about the problem of evil. The tendency, in other words, has been to reduce the richly detailed treatment of transmundane powers in the *Book of the Watchers* to some sense of significance situated, instead, in what *we* distinguish as human historical experience and the challenges of the human condition.

But what happens when we take seriously the *Book of the Watchers'* claims to knowledge about demons as actually claims to knowledge about demons? This is among the questions that I address in my 2020 book on *Demons, Angels, and Writing in Ancient Judaism*, and what I suggested there is that its demonology is framed less in terms of theology or theodicy than in terms of cosmology and knowledge. The concern with the cosmos and knowledge, for instance, comes clear in its correlation to an angelology that is coterminous with astronomy, uranography, and geography, extending the Enochic *Astronomical Book* (4Q208–211; cf. *1 Enoch* 72–82).[47] In the *Book of the Watchers*, fallen angels, giants, evil spirits, and archangels are presented as components of the cosmos, participants in human history, and elements of lived experience—with no sense that they must be read merely or mainly as metaphors. Their concreteness, in fact, is what gives power to the claim of Jewish scribal authority over the true knowledge of their names, origins, functions, and fates.

For the purposes of the present essay, what proves significant is that the innovation of the *Book of the Watchers* is not the advent of Jewish belief in demons per se. This Hellenistic-era apocalypse, rather, provides our earliest extant evidence for Jewish engagement in the more abstractified, second-tier practices of theorizing with and about demons—or, in other words: what Frankfurter describes as the "collection, classification, and integration" of demon-beliefs into demonology.[48] As such, the *Book of the Watchers* offers us an opportunity to follow one ancient Jewish example of the theorization of the demons and difference, attending to its concerns and distinctions as they might differ from our own.

Thanks to the Dead Sea Scrolls, moreover, we are now able to compare the approach in the Aramaic Enoch literature to ancient Jewish "magical" materials that discuss demons in a more practical context. In 4Q560, for instance, we find examples of direct first-person speech to a "spirit" (רוח) as the subject of adjuration (4Q560 1 II). In addition, it includes mention of other different types of demons, including male and female shudder-demons (לחלחיא דכרא ותלתלית נקבתא) and male and female crumble-demons (פרכית, פרך; 4Q560 1 I).[49] The danger of the demonic is here linked in part to their ability to foster iniquity and transgression (I 4). Yet their power to infect is associated foremost with bodily ailments: not only do demons pose a threat to women during childbirth (4Q560 I 1), but they enter the teeth and body, and they can cause "fever, chills and heart fever" (I 3–5). Although highly fragmentary, 4Q560 thus conveys a poignant sense of the variety of Jewish beliefs about demons that circulated before and beyond scribal attempts to systematize them.[50]

Some of the dynamics of this process become more clear when we consider 11Q11. Among the Hebrew incantations there preserved in fragmentary form is one "in the Name of the Lord" (11Q11 V 4; cf. 8Q5 frg. 1), which alludes to one demon's mixed parentage as the product of the mingling of humankind and "holy ones" (i.e., angels). A number of scholars have noted the parallel to the *Book of the Watchers'* claim that "wicked spirits" arose from the sexual union of the fallen angels and their human wives.[51] Such parallels make clear that the *Book of the Watchers'* understanding of demons did not simply spring from theological debate but also (and perhaps primarily) from an acutely felt and lived sense of malevolent forces as active and experienced in everyday life.

But the differences are notable as well. In 11Q11, we find the specific setting of a written script for direct speech to one particular demon: "Who are you [the one who was born of] man and seed of the ho[ly ones]?" (V 6–8). In the *Book of the Watchers*, this knowledge of the angelic truth of demonic parentage becomes universalized into an etiology of all demons (*1 Enoch* 15:9) and integrated into a narrative about the early history of the cosmos and humankind (i.e., *1 Enoch* 6–16). Whereas 11Q11 gives us a sense of demon-belief in the sense that Frankfurter describes as the "rudimentary systematizing of demons [that] belongs to the oral, interactive domain of popular discussion, legend-telling, and the recommendation (or composition) of protective spells," wherein "it is neither relevant nor conceivable to contemplate the entire range of potentially malignant spirits,"[52] the *Book of the Watchers* makes far more totalizing claims.

In the *Book of the Watchers*, moreover, such claims to knowledge about demons also serve to ground broader claims to knowledge, contributing to the articulation of a newly totalizing vision of Jewish scribal expertise. It is in this sense that the *Book of the Watchers* takes up the intellectual project that we see already in the Enochic *Astronomical Book*, even while extending its claims about astronomy and cosmology into an even more expansive vision of Enoch as Jewish scribal exemplar and culture-hero—perhaps mirroring and answering the expansive scope of those forms of Greek *paideia* that were gaining prominence and prestige in the early Hellenistic age.[53]

The vision of knowledge in the *Book of the Watchers* thus fits well with the broader cultural trends of the early Hellenistic period, consolidating and anthologizing received knowledge in new textualized forms with a newly totalizing horizon. In the process, it activates and appropriates—for Jewish scribes—what Frankfurter has observed across the ancient Mediterranean world as a major technology of demonology, namely, "writing, as a technology allowing both abstraction from local experience and the magical force of the inscribed name."[54] Works like 4Q560 and 11Q11 claim expertise about demons to prescribe context-specific rites for individuals to counteract specific demons among a multiplicity assumed to be active on the earth—writing scripts meant for speaking. The scribes responsible for the *Book of the Watchers*, by contrast, use scribal strategies of textualization and narrative to theorize at a level of abstraction, leaving the realm of lived practice to opine instead on the cosmos and the distant past. Their acts of writing invoke the power of speech, but they also impose textualized order on the demonic by distinguishing and filiating different types of transmundane powers through both demonological and scribal strategies of systemization—such as listing, naming, etiology, lineage, and hierarchy.

This is part of why it proves so difficult to make *their* demons speak to *our* assumptions about the human and the nonhuman. The Jewish scribes who shaped the Aramaic Enoch literature are quite actively engaged in *their own* theorization of difference and *their own* construction of totalizing taxonomic distinctions—and precisely in an era in which such tasks were particularly pressing across the Hellenistic world. The *Book of the Watchers* does not adhere to the pattern that Michael Mach posits for the Septuagint, wherein a variety of early biblical creatures become subsumed into the umbrella category of *angeloi*.[55] But it does achieve something similar through its use of the term "spirits"—an umbrella category delineated with reference to the status of those beings contained therein, which spans what we would call "angels," what we would call "demons," and what we would call "winds," as well as the "spirits of the human dead." Like earlier Hebrew uses of *ruaḥ*, this category cuts across what modern thinkers tend to distinguish as "natural" and "supernatural"—encompassing the invisible but felt presence of winds, but also the invisible population of the cosmos, angelic and demonic and dead. What is notable about this sense of "spirit," then, is that it is a category that touches upon many of the topics that are newly textualized in the *Book of the Watchers* and other Aramaic Jewish literature of the early Hellenistic age, including the movement of winds through heavenly gates, the histories and fates of various angelic and demonic powers, and what happens to humankind both directly after individual death and after the end of history.

There is certainly binary thinking here at play. But it is not between human and nonhuman per se. Rather, in the *Book of the Watchers*, the meaning of "spirit" is articulated through a developed contrast with "flesh," categorically distinguishing the duties and domains proper to angels and men respectively. Human is here figured as "flesh"—more akin to animals and the other matter upon the earth, all of which are as distinct from "angels" as the heaven is from the earth.

This distinction of "spirit" and "flesh" is explicitly developed through a first-person speech attributed to God in *1 Enoch* 15. The assertion of the difference between the two is occasioned by the problem of fallen angels—a problem here identified as the choice of some "Watchers of heaven," to follow their desire to possess prerogatives not intended for "spirits" but rather particular to "flesh." With respect to these Watchers, God thus stresses that "you were holy ones and spirits, living forever" (15:4) and that "you originally existed as spirits, living forever, and not dying for all the generations of eternity" (15:6). A contrast is thereby drawn with men, who are "flesh and blood, who die and perish" and to whom "therefore I gave . . . women, so that they might cast seed into them, and thus beget children by them, that nothing fail them upon the earth" (15:4–5). The distinction between two types of continuance—immortality and reproduction—is underlined with a spatial distinction as well: "the spirits of heaven, in heaven is their dwelling" (15:7).

Even while telling of a case of transgression, the *Book of the Watchers* thus theorizes the boundaries that mark what it maps as an essential difference of "spirit" and "flesh"—thereby defining the human condition in contrast to that of the angel. It is precisely in this context, moreover, that we find its famous account of the origins of demons—that is, as the "spirits" that issued forth from the children born from the sexual union of fallen angels and human women, the giants, after the destruction of their bodies in the Flood. Demons, in other words, are here framed as the dire consequences of the wrongful crossing of the divinely set boundaries between "spirit" and "flesh" and heaven and earth—but also as an exception to what might otherwise seem to be an essential bifurcation: demons are "spirits" bound to the earth, to hunger without "flesh," and to struggle throughout history with humans, from whom they sprung.

Just as the *Book of the Watchers* reveals the secret of the origins of demons in the crossing of this divide of "flesh" and "spirit," so it also destabilizes its own binary distinctions through its image of the ideal human. The majority of the *Book of the Watchers*, in fact, is taken up by the tale of how the antediluvian "scribe of righteousness" Enoch was taken up from the proper human domain of the earth to ascend up to the heavens (*1 Enoch* 14), and from there to travel to the ends of the earth with angels (*1 Enoch* 17–36). In the process, Enoch learns and tells that even though humans are "flesh," we too have "spirits" that survive after the death of our bodies, huddled in the caves within mountains at the edges of the earth, awaiting end-time resurrection (*1 Enoch* 22). It is not just that the fates of demons and humans are intertwined. If the demon is hybrid, so too the human—and perhaps particularly the scribe, an earthly creature of flesh invested with the cosmic knowledge of the angels and the power to bridge heaven and earth with writing.

In contrast to the "animacy hierarchies" presumed in post-Enlightenment orders of knowledge, premodern demonologies can potentially function otherwise—precisely because of their distribution of animacy across the full spectrum of the nonhuman, including landscape, object, and animal alike. And the example of ancient Jewish sources further shows how demonologies sometimes make knowledge at the very points at which humans are the most permeable, least autonomous, most hybridized ourselves, not only flesh and not only spirit, and thus also human in ways perhaps only made possible by the nonhuman.

AMONG ELLIOT WOLFSON'S MAJOR INTERDISCIPLINARY INTERVENTIONS, IN MY view, has been his demonstration of the analytical power of feminist criticism to aid us in recovering neglected dynamics within premodern religious literature—in a manner not limited to writings that focus on women.[56] To his challenging of the binaries noted above, we might thus add his challenging of polarizing habits all too common in scholarly practice. Even today, it remains far too common in Jewish studies to compartmentalize gender. Even more trenchant is the presumption that a scholar's choice to engage with feminist or other recent forms of theory must be in contrast with—if not at the expense of—the rigor of the philologist and the historian's quest to avoid anachronism. But in this too, Wolfson has shown how what appears to be a binary is actually not: his work models how theoretical engagement can richly enhance our analyses of premodern sources.

As much as modern historians of religion might wish to read premodern demonologies in terms of binaries like human/nonhuman, natural/supernatural, good/evil, and so on, much of our premodern evidence resists such tidy reduction. This makes it a natural fit for theoretical projects that aim to "trouble and undo stubborn binary systems of difference."[57] In fact, to examine ancient demonologies is sometimes to reveal quite different "relational ontologies," which do not cohere to clear-cut and ranked divisions between human, animal, and object that were experienced and imagined, instead, in a manner more fluid and connected—perhaps less akin to a ranked hierarchy than to a continuum, constellation, or circulatory system.

In that spirit, I have forestalled until now what might seem like the more obvious question for an essay dealing with demons in relation to feminist criticism and related theoretical conversations: what does the unsettling of a human/nonhuman binary mean for our understanding of the demonization of people? As noted above, modern scholars are notably skittish with how seriously many of our ancient sources discuss demons—and even more so when our sources engage in demonology, making knowledge *with* and *about* demons. Interestingly, however, scholars tend to be far more comfortable discussing demonization in the sense of the rhetorical appeal to demons to denigrate human individuals and groups. The long history of associating demons with both women and Jews, for instance, has been richly catalogued, not least in condemnation of rhetorics of dehumanization that justify violence.

Our analysis above, however, suggests that even demonization might be more complex than it seems at first sight.[58] Following Chen, moreover, we might wish to look beyond the presumption of "dehumanization" in the sense of the demotion of certain people to a lower category in a clear-cut and stable hierarchy. When we set aside this seemingly self-evident function, our attention is drawn to other effects of such demonizing rhetoric: to the degree that demonologies distribute animacy across landscapes, objects, and bodies, for instance, they also distribute fear—including in memories of past catastrophe but also in the claim that some of what (and who) appears to be ordinary or harmless might be direly dangerous. Among the potential dynamics of demonizing people, thus, is to flip what appear to be the power relations within a society, casting minoritized and otherwise less powerless people as those actually secretly in power.[59] To demonize women, in patriarchal societies, is in part to claim that—despite all appearances—we pose a threat to men. And so too Jews to Christians. Blacks to whites. Like the demonological distribution of animacy to landscapes or objects, the demonization of people affects the distribution of agency, power, and fear.

Haraway has famously suggested that the cyborg offers us "a way out of the maze of dualisms in which we have explained our bodies and our tools to ourselves."[60] Perhaps much the same might be said of the demon—a much more ancient example of a seeming hybrid that can serve to reveal that some of what seems different is actually not so distinct as to need to be hybridized at all, but sometimes is already in overlap or combination or indwelling or interpenetration. At the very least, perhaps our understanding of human and nonhuman alike—including the limits of this and other seemingly self-evident dualisms for understanding ourselves and our past—might be enriched by attention to demons.

NOTES

1. An earlier form of this essay was presented at Florida State University on February 22, 2019.

To cite just a few classic examples: Elliot R. Wolfson, "Woman—The Feminine as Other in Theosophic Kabbalah: Some Philosophical Observations on the Divine Androgyne," in *The Other in Jewish Thought and History: Constructions of Jewish Culture and Identity*, ed. Laurence J. Silberstein and Robert L. Cohn (New York: NYU Press, 1994), 166–204; Elliot R. Wolfson, *Circle in the Square: Studies in the Use of Gender in Kabbalistic Symbolism* (Albany:

SUNY Press, 1995), 79–121; Elliot R. Wolfson, "*Tiqqun ha-Shekhinah*: Redemption and the Overcoming of Gender Dimorphism in the Messianic Kabbalah of Moses Hayyim Luzzatto," *HR* 36 (1997): 289–332.

2. E.g., Elliot R. Wolfson, "Images of God's Feet: Some Observations on the Divine Body in Judaism," in *People of the Body: Jews and Judaism from an Embodied Perspective*, ed. Howard Eilberg-Schwartz (Albany: SUNY Press, 1992), 143–81; Elliot R. Wolfson, "The Body in the Text: A Kabbalistic Theory of Embodiment," *JQR* 95 (2005): 479–500.
3. E.g., Elliot R. Wolfson, "Re/membering the Covenant: Memory, Forgetfulness, and the Construction of History in the Zohar," in *Jewish History and Jewish Memory*, ed. Elisheva Carlebach, John M. Efron, and David N. Myers (Hanover: University of New England Press, 1998), 214–46.
4. E.g., Elliot R. Wolfson, "Light Through Darkness: The Ideal of Human Perfection in the Zohar," *HTR* 81 (1988): 73–95; Elliot R. Wolfson, "Beyond Good and Evil: Hypernomianism, Transmorality, and Kabbalistic Ethics," in *Crossing Boundaries: Essays on the Ethical Status of Mysticism*, ed. G. William Barnard and Jeffrey J. Kripal (New York: Seven Bridges, 2001), 103–56.
5. E.g., Elliot R. Wolfson, "Negative Theology and Positive Assertion in Early Kabbalah," *Da'at* 32–33 (1994): v–xxii.
6. Especially richly, in my view, in Elliot R. Wolfson, "Inscribed in the Book of the Living: Gospel of Truth and Jewish Christology," *JSJ* 38 (2007): 234–71—on the ramifications of which, see my discussion in "Rethinking (Jewish-)Christian Evidence for Jewish Mysticism," in *Hekhalot Literature in Context: Between Byzantium and Babylonia*, ed. Ra'anan Boustan, Martha Himmelfarb, and Peter Schäfer (Tübingen: Mohr Siebeck, 2013), 349–77.
7. Mel Chen, *Animacies: Biopolitics, Racial Mattering, and Queer Affect* (Durham: Duke University Press, 2012), 3; on their use of the term, including the theoretical utility of its slipperiness, see pp. 2–12.
8. See already David R. Shumway and Ellen Messer-Davidow, "Disciplinarity: An Introduction," *Poetics Today* 12 (1991): 201–25, there tracing the emergence of new sciences, first within the old rubric of "Natural Philosophy" but at the end of the eighteenth century, specialized into "independent natural sciences" of physics, chemistry, and biology, after which "moral philosophy broke up somewhat later into the social sciences," and "while modern philosophy was defined by what was removed from it in the creation of the sciences, the other modern Humanities emerged first in the form of classical philology, which produced history, modern languages, and even art history as descendants" (p. 204).
9. Notably, as Shumway and Messer-Davidow remind us, "'the Humanities' is a 20th-century term of convenience for those disciplines excluded from the natural and social sciences"; "Disciplinarity," 204.
10. "Feminist Conversations with Vicki Kirby and Elizabeth A. Wilson," *Feminist Theory* 12 (2011): 227–34 at 228.
11. Jane Bennett, *Vibrant Matter: A Political Ecology of Things* (Durham: Duke University Press, 2010), 31. Compare also Donna Haraway's assertion, against both "grumpy human-exceptionalist Heideggerian worlding" and "post-human(ism)," that "Critters—human and not—become-with each other, compose and decompose each other, in every scale and register of time and stuff in sympoietic tangling, in ecological evolutionary developmental earthy

worlding and unworlding"; *Staying with the Trouble: Making Kin in the Chthulucene* (Durham: Duke University Press, 2016), 11, 97.

12. So already Georges Bataille on animality, e.g., in *Theory of Religion*, trans. Robert Hurley (New York: Zone, 1992).
13. Chen, *Animacies,* 2.
14. Chen, *Animacies,* 2.
15. Chen, *Animacies*, 44–50.
16. Chen, *Animacies*, 43.
17. So already Donna Haraway, "Situated Knowledges," *Feminist Studies* 14 (1988): 575–97.
18. On the parallel point made by Sylvia Wynter see also now Katherine McKittrick, ed., *Sylvia Wynter: On Being Human as Praxis* (Durham: Duke University Press, 2015).
19. Denise K. Buell, "The Microbes and Pneuma That Therefore I Am," in *Divinanimality*, ed. Stephen D. Moore (New York: Fordham University Press, 2014), 460–61. See also Buell, "Hauntology meets Post-Humanism: Some Payoffs for Biblical Studies," in *The Bible and Posthumanism*, ed. Jennifer L. Koosed (Atlanta: SBL, 2014), 29–56.
20. Buell, "Microbes and Pneuma," 460.
21. Buell, "Microbes and Pneuma," 455–56; cf. Dale Martin, *The Corinthian Body* (New Haven: Yale University Press, 1999), 160–61; Giovanni Bazzana, *Having the Spirit of Christ* (New Haven: Yale University Press, 2020), esp. 4–21.
22. Travis Proctor, *Demonic Bodies and the Dark Ecologies of Early Christian Culture* (Oxford: Oxford University Press, 2022).
23. Bruce Lincoln, "Cesmag, the Lie, and the Logic of Zoroastrian Demonology," *JAOS* 129 (2009): 45–55 at 55.
24. Lincoln, "Cesmag, the Lie," 45.
25. Lincoln, *Gods and Demons, Priests and Scholars* (Chicago: University of Chicago Press, 2012), 31.
26. See further Bazzana, *Having the Spirit*, esp. 9–14.
27. Buell, "Microbes and Pneuma," 455–56. On the demonic beyond the binary of internal/external see also Ishay Rosen-Zvi, *Demonic Desires: Yetzer Hara and the Problem of Evil in Late Antiquity* (Philadelphia: University of Pennsylvania Press, 2011).
28. On this point, see further below and also Annette Yoshiko Reed, "When Did Daimones Become Demons: Revisiting Septuagintal Data for Ancient Jewish Demonology," *HTR* 116:3 (2023): 340–75.
29. Proctor, *Demonic Bodies.* Proctor there uses the rubric of the "trans-corporeality" in conversation with Stacy Alaimo, *Bodily Natures: Science, Environment, and the Material Self* (Bloomington: Indiana University Press, 2010). See also Gregory A. Smith, "How Thin Is a Demon?" *JECS* 16 (2008): 479–512.
30. David Frankfurter, *Evil Incarnate: Rumors of Demonic Conspiracy and Satanic Abuse in History* (Princeton: Princeton University Press, 2006), 14.
31. On the locative dimension of demonology see already Jonathan Z. Smith, "Towards Interpreting Demonic Powers in Hellenistic and Roman Antiquity," *ANRW* 2.16.1 (1978): 425–29.
32. Frankfurter, *Evil Incarnate*, 14. The ramifications for understanding ancient Jewish demonol-

ogy are notable. In the case of Leviticus 16, for instance, modern scholars may debate whether "Azazel" is meant to be understood as a demonic personage or merely a place, but the blurring that seems strange to us may have seemed quite far from paradoxical for ancient Israelites/Jews, among whom the desert was often mapped as a domain of the demonic; see further Annette Yoshiko Reed, *Demons, Angels, and Writing in Ancient Judaism* (Cambridge: Cambridge University Press, 2020), 72–73.

33. Frankfurter, *Evil Incarnate*, 14, 21. So too with biblical references to שעירים, בנות יענה, עיים, ציים etc., which can be read as animalized demons and/or demonized animals and/or inhabitants of a demonized landscape—perhaps with more simultaneity than many modern readers readily imagine. For examples from Isaiah 13 and 34 and their reception, see Judit Blair, *De-Demonizing the Old Testament: An Investigation of Azazel, Lilith, Deber, Qeteb and Reshef in the Hebrew Bible* (Tübingen: Mohr, 2009), 77–80; Reed, "When Did *Daimones*."
34. See further Lincoln, "Cesmag, the Lie," 45; Reed, *Demons*, esp. 13, 310–11.
35. Anne Marie Kitz, "Demons in the Hebrew Bible and Ancient Near East," *JBL* 135 (2016): 447–64 at 447; emphasis mine.
36. Kitz, "Demons in the Hebrew Bible," 463; emphasis mine.
37. Kitz, "Demons in the Hebrew Bible," 447.
38. Kitz, "Demons in the Hebrew Bible," 464. See also Esther Hamori, "The Spirit of Falsehood," *CBQ* 72 (2010): 15–30.
39. Bennie Reynolds III, "A Dwelling Place of Demons: Demonology and Apocalypticism in the Dead Sea Scrolls," in *Apocalyptic Thinking in Early Judaism*, ed. Cecilia Wassen and Sidnie White Crawford (Leiden: Brill, 2018), 23–54 at 26.
40. Philip S. Alexander, "The Demonology of the Dead Sea Scrolls," in *The Dead Sea Scrolls after Fifty Years*, ed. Peter Flint and James C. VanderKam, 2 vols. (Leiden: Brill, 1999), 2.331–53 at 331.
41. Alexander, "Demonology," 331–32.
42. The parade example is Philo, *De Gigantibus* II.6. On LXX texts see Reed, "When Did *Daimones*."
43. Bazzana, *Having the Spirit*, 26.
44. David Frankfurter, "Master-Demons, Local Spirits, and Demonology in the Roman Mediterranean World," *JANES* 11 (2011): 126–31 at 131.
45. See further Reed, *Demons*; Reynolds, "Dwelling Place," 30–31.
46. See further Reed, *Demons*, 189–246.
47. Reed, *Demons*, 132–88.
48. On this distinction see Frankfurter, *Evil Incarnate*, 13–15.
49. Douglas L. Penney and Michael O. Wise, "By the Power of Beelzebub: An Aramaic Incantation Formula from Qumran (4Q560)," *JBL* 113 (1994): 627–50; Esther Eshel, "Genres of Magical Texts in the Dead Sea Scrolls," in *Die Dämonen: Die Dämonologie der israelitisch-jüdischen und frühchristlichen Literatur im Kontext ihrer*, ed. Armin Lange and Hermann Lichtenberger (Tübingen, 2003), 394–415 at 396–98.
50. That 4Q560 is in Aramaic proves especially intriguing inasmuch as much of the initial Jewish interest in demons clusters in Jewish writings of the early Hellenistic age written specifically in Aramaic. The two earliest known Jewish narratives about exorcism, for instance, appear in other Aramaic Jewish texts from the same era: the Book of Tobit from the third century

BCE and *Genesis Apocryphon* from the second century BCE. See further Reed, *Demons*, esp. 90–101; Reed, "Scribes, Scrolls, and Stars in the Aramaic Dead Sea Scrolls," forthcoming.

51. Eshel, "Genres of Magical Texts," 404; Philip S. Alexander, "Wrestling against Wickedness in High Places: Magic in the Worldview of the Qumran Community," in *The Scrolls and the Scriptures: Qumran Fifty Years After*, ed. Stanley E. Porter and Craig A. Evans (Sheffield: Sheffield Academic Press, 1997), 318–37; Gideon Bohak, *Ancient Jewish Magic: A History* (Cambridge: Cambridge University Press, 2008), 109.
52. Frankfurter, *Evil Incarnate*, 15.
53. See further Reed, *Demons*, 132–88.
54. Frankfurter, *Evil Incarnate*, 21.
55. Michael Mach, *Entwicklungsstadien des jüdischen Engelglaubens in vorrabbinischer Zeit* (TSAJ 34; Tübingen: Mohr, 1992).
56. See, e.g., his reflections in Wolfson, "Body in the Text," 497—there including a laudably sharp critique against those scholars of Jewish studies who react to feminist scholarship with "ignorance laced with outright hostility, a posture that seems to me far worse and morally reprehensible than simple resistance."
57. Chen, *Animacies*, 3.
58. See Frankfurter, *Evil Incarnate* on the social dynamics of demonization and its self-claimed expert agents.
59. I discuss this dynamic in relation to anti-Blackness in "Knowing our Demons," *The Immanent Frame*, January 25, 2018, https://tif.ssrc.org/2018/01/25/knowing-our-demons/.
60. Donna Haraway, *Simians, Cyborgs and Women: The Reinvention of Nature* (New York: Routledge, 1991), 181. Or, alternately, perhaps demons can function in a sense akin to how Haraway, more recently, speaks of "demon familiars" (e.g., *Staying with the Trouble*, 31).

THE HISTORY OF OUR PRESENT DISASTER

Apocalyptic Time, Buber, and 4 Ezra

DUSTIN ATLAS

And the world shall be turned back to primeval silence for seven days, as it was at the first beginnings; so that no one shall be left.
4 EZRA 7:30[1]

The disaster, whose blackness should be attenuated—through emphasis—exposes us to a certain idea of passivity. We are passive with respect to the disaster, but the disaster is perhaps passivity, and thus past, always past, even in the past, out of date.
MAURICE BLANCHOT, *THE WRITING OF THE DISASTER*[2]

THE FOLLOWING REFLECTIONS ON APOCALYPTIC TEMPORALITY EMERGED from a class I taught on Judaism and ecology, which ended with Elliot Wolfson's "Mirror of Nature." On our way to this text we worked through several apocalypses and several notions of time and image. The thoughts below began to crystallize mid-semester on the way to Wolfson's work. As is so often the case, I am not sure which of them are "mine," which I should credit to the class, and which to Elliot.[3]

BEFORE THE BEGINNING

Here is another way to think about apocalypse.[4] We can think of it as a history of the present. This history of the present can also be seen as a prediction of the present—in other words, under apocalyptic time, the present is both predicted and already part of history.[5] This has several consequences for how we think about apocalyptic time. Rather than a determinism where everything is decided at the beginning of time,[6] we can think of apocalyptic time as the historical project taken to an extreme. Read as such, for the apocalyptic person all time—the beginning, middle, and end, both natural and human events—is included in history.[7] There is neither prehistory nor posthistory—instead we have the creation and the eschaton, and both are placed within the historical fold. Everything is included in a single image of time.

I will focus upon the history of the present, which I see (literally) as a central element of apocalyptic temporality. As alienating as this bizarre formulation—the history of the present—may be, it is an enlightening way to consider our own "apocalypse": the ecological disaster we are living in.[8] This disaster was neither determined at the moment of creation, nor is it a motive force at the end of human time. But it is now part of historical time, even if the details of its unfolding are obscure.

This philosophical study of apocalypse will begin by exploring the justification for viewing apocalyptic time in this manner, and to attempt to understand how it is possible. This will be followed by a reading and critique of Martin Buber's typological distinction between the prophetic and the apocalyptic, as well as 4 Ezra, the text he takes as exemplary of the apocalyptic.[9] I suggest the apocalyptic type and texts are a more fruitful way of thinking about our disaster than the prophetic type, which has become something of an ethical cliché ill-suited to disasters that cannot be approached by a "decision," but rather require a constant monitoring and intervening in feedback loops.[10] The paper will end with a brief foray into Zupančič's "The Apocalypse Is (Still) Disappointing," to examine ways apocalyptic time can help us think about the ecological disaster and better explain our present than invoking, once again, a prophetic figure. Arguably, the apocalyptic suits the present moment better than the prophetic does, this present where managing a disaster has supplanted attempts at prevention, and where collective action is more important than individual righteousness. Zupančič removes any trace of romance from apocalyptic thought by showing that in a basic sense, in the end, nothing really happens; in so doing she helps us see how apocalyptic annihilation reveals the very thing it threatens to destroy: it is only when we are in danger of finally losing the world that we can really see it. The apocalyptic history of the present is the time of this loss.

APOCALYPSE AS A HISTORICAL PROJECT

Before an analysis of Buber's typology and understanding of the apocalyptic and the concomitant exploration of 4 Ezra, I would like to quickly sketch out in very abstract terms what it means to say that the apocalypse predicts the past and tells the history of the future. Once I have assembled this skeleton, I will hook some meat onto these bones.

In nuce, my basic claim is that if we provisionally accept that apocalyptic temporality is not primarily about "predicting" the present and the future, but rather about placing them into historical time, then the apocalyptic writer is telling the history of the present even as they are predicting it. In many of the pseudepigraphical writings, this occurs quite literally. As the apocalyptic author uses an older figure (such as Ezra) as a pseudonym, this "Ezra" uses *ex eventu* prophecy to predict the actual author's present, as well as their past (with 4 Ezra, the time of Roman occupation).

One way to think about the notion of the history of the present is to accept the following set of positions: apocalyptic writers think in terms of a historical project; this project ends in the development of an image of history, which can *in theory* be seen; but this image is only seen partially and from a position within it; supernatural assistance can expand the scope of the vision, usually by changing the seer's position (through an elevation or suchlike). Once these are granted, the idea of a "history of a present" follows naturally. Let us work through these suppositions in order, with the ancient apocalypses in the background to curb excess speculation.

The Time of Apocalypse Is History

We can, and perhaps should, see the apocalypse as "historical" and not "mythic." The form of history embraced by apocalyptic writers differs from our own, and we are right to note the presence of myth and not believe its claims, but there is ample reason to assume that the ancient apocalypses were meant to be seen as a history.[11] Applying the term "history" to an ancient text presents problems, but this application is conventional with several even older texts—such as the common claim that Kings or Herodotus are meant to be historical in some deep structural sense—and the apocalypses are at least as engaged with the historical project as these others are, if not more so. There is a cliché that ancient Israelite religion, and the Judaism that grows out of it, are historical religions, in the sense that history is a fundamental ingredient in their theology and mythology—God acts in history, and so on—and while this cliché may require refinement, it is accurate in broad outline. However, I suggest the apocalypses are even more extravagantly historical, at points absurdly so. Apocalyptic temporality is what happens when *all* time, the entirety of the past, the enormity of the present, and the disasters of the future, is included in historical time.

A milder claim is made by John Hall, who holds that history and apocalypse are connected at birth, with apocalypse being an intensification of the historical genre to encompass crisis.[12] I suggest we be wary of any claim that apocalypses are "caused" by crisis (as countless crises do not issue in apocalypses), but the notion that apocalypse is meant to take historical account of crises, past, present, and future, seems right. In a sense this is nothing more than the old claim that the Israelite relationship to God is a social relationship that occurs in historical time.[13]

Thus we need not see apocalypses as history proper, only that they are at least as historical as the prophetic writings (if not more). Hence Grabbe: "No one can doubt the importance of myth for the apocalyptic worldview. The problem is the supposition that prophecy has a historical worldview but that apocalyptic has a mythical one."[14] This leads us to the second premise.

The Apocalypse Is a *Vision* of History, an Imagining of Time

While we would rightly be loath to consider apocalypse as history proper, it is nonetheless a historical project: to articulate the past, present, and future in images. The visual nature of the apocalypses is easily seen.[15] It is not just that apocalyptic history is *expressed* in images: an image of history exists because in some strong sense history is image-like.[16]

History is revealed as images, and the apocalyptic type is able to see and understand them, because history is something *seen*, meaning there is something fundamentally visual about historical time.[17] This is more sensible than it might appear. It is commonplace to think of history as a straight line, or a circle, implying one can "see" the historical picture. That a stronger version of this applies to the apocalyptic is unsurprising.[18]

The Image of History Is Seen by Humans from a Point in the Image

If history is an image, and all time is captured in history, then any perception of the image of history takes place from within the image: one part of the image imaging the rest. I, a piece of an image, look out and see a slight bit of the image of history which contains me. The apocalyptic revelation occurs when an angel, God—or in 4 Ezra, both—reveals more of the image than would normally be accessible.

If all events—*including natural events*—are subsumed under history, then history is a whole (however broken), but this whole can only be seen either from a privileged position (God or some sort of angel) or after an ascent/descent. This expanded vision, or the increase of scope that comes with the encounter with heavenly beings (from the rather literal ascent, to the interpretive dialogues in 4 Ezra) is a revelation of a secret: the veil is stripped from time itself, and more of its image can be seen than the meagre amount granted in our mundane lives.[19] But this secret vision is undisclosed when the visionary returns to their starting point, and from there, can only be expressed either as a secret, or as images that require reinterpretation.

It is of utmost importance that this is not a vision *sub specie aeternitatis*: it remains thoroughly temporal (often as moving and metamorphizing images in need of interpretation). Humans are shown these images from a position within the picture—for instance in 4 Ezra, "Ezra" sees visions of ever-increasing scope, but remains stuck in his historical time. Even in cases of ascent, seemingly an escape from history, the seer presumably returns to their original place after seeing a larger picture. In the *Apocalypse of Abraham* this happens quite literally: Abraham ascends high into the air, at one point during the revelation is told to "look at the picture," and then presumably returns to where he began once analysis of the moving picture is complete.[20] After the return, past and future separate again and the seer's scope of vision returns to normal.[21]

All of this is meant quite literally: the seer is raised (or lowered—these are effectively the same in a universe of concentric spheres) and from this new position sees more of time than they did while "on the ground," much as you would see more if you were plucked from your seat and raised high into the air.

You Can Think the History of the Future and the Present

The impulse to write a history of the present and the future has been long lived. In an article about nineteenth-century British apocalyptic discourse, Andrew Mein wrote: "The interpreters of [biblical] prophecy undoubtedly thought of themselves not as marginal fanatics but as rational, scholarly historians of the future and passionate supporters of an orderly and paternal establishment."[22] While the ancient apocalypses may not be so orderly, it is fair to say that they too were part of this project.

To iterate: the ancient texts literally predict their present. "Ezra" lived long before the writer of 4 Ezra and so the text's predictions concern events that lie in the actual writer's past and present. Rather than dismiss this as a literary conceit to garner authority, I suggest we take it seriously: the text predicts the author's past and present. But these are abnormal predictions, as the author already knows them to be the case—and there is no reason to think they entertained many doubts about their future. Thus the point is not prediction in the banal sense (where prophets predict the best lottery number, etc.) so much as to develop an image of history that can be seen from multiple locations (before, after, above, below). In other words: the predicted but historical present is a function of a zealous historical project.

The present is a favored point of prediction, not only because it is of existential import for the writer, but because the project collapses if the present is exempted from the historical. The present of 4 Ezra's writer is the time of the eagle (4 Ezra 11:1–36), meaning Roman domination; 4 Ezra's prediction of the present is presented as a correction of the fourth beast in Daniel (4 Ezra 12:11–12; Daniel 7:2–8).[23] As Himmelfarb notes, this is an explicit updating of the older apocalypse.[24] I suggest we also read this as an explicit correction of the image of history.

BUBER: APOCALYPSE THOU

The apocalyptic type is often seen as a debased form of the prophetic type, and the apocalypses themselves as deterministic fever dreams adopted by victims and losers. Martin Buber's work provides a learned but standard reproduction of this perspective, and so provides a clear and strong reading of the conventional apocalyptic/prophetic binary. An analysis of his work helps us see what is at stake both in popular and general academic discourse, and provides an opportunity to use the temporal form sketched above to defend the apocalyptic from this derision. After this reading and concomitant defense, I will suggest ways the apocalyptic is perhaps better suited to the present moment than the prophetic, if only because the prophetic type is better suited to individual decision than collective action.

In *Paths in Utopia* (1949), Buber first engages the apocalyptic type as a counter-type to the prophetic.[25] Here Buber's position, despite his extraordinary erudition, replicates and sustains several cultural clichés. His image of the ethical prophet—the brave and solitary man speaking truth to power—is still unthinkingly adopted by a great deal of Jewish and Christian thought and culture. It is seemingly a given that any ethical or political quandary is well served by a brave and friendless man yelling at people. That this man may have mistreated his family merely for the sake of developing an allegory does not disqualify him.[26]

Buber's typology is historical insofar as it concerns the role of human decision in history: what is important for him is that the prophetic supposedly allows for decisions made by individuals to change history, and the apocalyptic does not.[27] The prophet is an individual who stands and acts during an event, whereas the apocalyptic type is less of an "individual." Indeed, we have a universally agreed upon name for the heroes of the prophecies ("prophets") but no corresponding name for the apocalypses (one could call them "apocalyptics," but the spell-checker disagrees; scholars have agreed on "seer," but the very need to establish a name for this figure speaks to my point). This concern with decision and apocalypse is not of mere antiquarian interest for Buber. Apocalypticism lives on in Marxism because (under Buber's reading) Marx's notion of history is one of inexorable process where human decision in the moment is of little to no importance.[28]

For Buber, the Jewish eschatological project, both prophetic and apocalyptic, is fundamentally concerned with pictures, what we might call real fantasies: images generated by the "longing for that *rightness* . . . which of its very nature cannot be realized in the individual, but only in human community." This process of image making is both "deeply rooted" in the human being, and yet "supra-personal," with these utopic pictures modeling "what should be."[29] Prophetic and apocalyptic eschatology are both little more than this image of what should be "realized in the picture of a perfect time."[30] The eschatological process is the story of how these pictures are realized.

Despite sharing these characteristics, the apocalyptic differs from the prophetic as a bad copy does from an original. The "elemental," prophetic eschatology "gives man a significant and active share in the coming redemption." The apocalyptic, a derivative form, which Buber attempts to discount as a foreign import from "ancient Persia," allows no such freedom.[31] The first is a decision addressed to "every person" to participate in it; the latter is "immutably fixed, and people are mere tools of the process."[32]

Buber: Decision and Time

While Buber's schema is set up to malign Marxism and to favor voluntarist socialisms, its importance is not exhausted in political polemic.[33] Indeed, as Taubes notes on Buber's later essay "Prophecy, Apocalyptic, and the Historical Hour" (1954): "Buber's typology, concerning the prophetic and apocalyptic spirit is fundamental for his understanding of history," and here I think Taubes is correct.[34] As with *Utopia*, the dichotomy between the prophetic and apocalyptic is posited, and again the apocalyptic genre is impugned as a product of a time in decline (although here he has the decency to not blame the Persians).[35] Again, these types concern not so much historical events as the place of human action within them.[36] On the one hand, you have the prophetic person, an orator invested in the present moment of decision, and on the other the apocalyptic type, an anxious and writerly person taking refuge in determinism.

Buber's distinction is nuanced in this later work: "Do I dare the definitely impossible or do I adapt myself to the unavoidable?" The difference is between a decision in the moment that I gamble will affect the course of historical time, and the supposed apocalyptic position that "no possibility of a change in the direction of historical destiny that could proceed from man, or be effected or coeffected by man."[37] This seems slightly fairer than the older implication that apocalypses are driven by something like efficient causation. As Himmelfarb notes, "The idea that the course of history was determined long ago is a central theme of the book of Daniel and other apocalypses as well."[38] But a number of questions remain: Does Buber correctly understand apocalyptic temporality and history? No. Does he adequately distinguish between the prophetic and apocalyptic type with this distinction? Also no.[39]

Taubes's affectionate critique of Buber speaks to the latter. In his "Martin Buber and the Philosophy of History" he takes Buber to task for his claim that the prophetic type allows for historical decision, noting both apocalyptic and prophetic types posit "the inscrutable and hidden God as the prime agent in history."[40] Buber's aggressive response to this reasonable critique reveals as much as it conceals:

> Taubes reproaches me because I "stress man's action as an agent of redemption"; to this it is rejoined that for the prophet "the inscrutable and hidden God was the prime agent in history." *As if the two were not compatible with each other in the reality of prophetic faith as I have sought to present it!* It goes without saying that . . . the decisions are in God's hands. But in the prophetic proclamation future actions of God are time after time bound with an "if," . . . : if the people turn to him, he will turn to them.[41]

This is a common case of "paradox for me, but not for thee": the prophetic texts are read with nuance that allows for productive paradox, whereas the apocalypses are allowed no such depth. But it does get at the distinction between Taubes and Buber rather nicely: for Buber the prophetic implies a God who is willing to change things if humans turn toward "him," while the apocalyptic permits no choice at all.

For Taubes the apocalyptic does allow a choice, it's just a different kind of choice:

> [In] apocalyptic literature, ancient or modern, a set of alternatives arises on an entirely new level that carries an appeal to the individual and to the communities. . . . The apocalyptic seer confronts us with the alternative *whether we perceive the change, the new beginning in history, or whether we are blind to the new day that is actually dawning*. . . . The brazen necessity in the course of history as all historians can attest—*has not in the slightest paralysed the efficacy of individual or communal resolutions* and actions, but strengthened the will of the apocalyptic messianists to overcome all obstacles on the way to the consummation of history.[42]

Here Taubes suggests something Buber misses: the apocalyptic does allow for a decision, and this decision leads to an intensification of historical time.[43] The apocalyptic revelation is not of a song playing from beginning to end, but an image of time in which all is included. The apocalyptic question, if there is one, is: Do you see what is happening? The apocalyptic decision does not occur outside of time, but in a present that has both been predicted and has a history. It is a commitment to the inevitabilities of time, rather than an attempt to shift its course.

Of course, as Taubes notes at the end of the above quote: this commitment to time paradoxically allows people and communities to act. According to Taubes, the apocalyptic community is galvanized by the image of time to act outside the logic of the social order, or what we might normally think of as possible.[44] Indeed, the notion that we "can" change things (in some future) often leads to our not bothering to change them now.

Buber Reads 4 Ezra

Let us move from the above rather abstract observations to a case study, that being Buber's reading of 4 Ezra, where he attempts to provide a textual basis to his typology. He chooses 4 Ezra as exemplary of the apocalyptic genre because it is "one of its . . . most mature late works . . . [and] affords a fuller insight into the relationship of the speaker to contemporary history" than does the *Revelation of John* (which is the other text he briefly considers).[45]

In taking on 4 Ezra Buber is intentionally choosing a difficult opponent, if only because 4 Ezra is arguably the most dialogical of the ancient apocalypses, at least in terms of form. It is the only apocalypse, other than the very closely related 2 Baruch, to extensively use a dialogue form (between Ezra and an angel).[46] This is particularly odd because Buber uses the text's formal literary characteristics to develop his critique of the apocalyptic type: the literary devices the text employs are symptoms of its sickness.

Against the Pseudonym

The formal role of the visionary in the text, specifically the fact that the narrator is a pseudonym, is for Buber evidence the apocalyptic type is disengaged. I would suggest instead that it is a device intended to develop a particular model of history where the past is in the present (as something recalled) and the present already part of the past (as that which is predicted). Buber instead holds that the problem with pseudonymity is far more basic: it is a distraction from the actual moment in which decision is to take place. As Buber reads the text:

> The book, whose constituent parts probably originated around the middle of the first Christian century, obviously received its final form only decades after the destruction of Jerusalem by the Romans. Yet the speaker *pretends* to be living as a member of the king's house in exile just after the destruction of Jerusalem by the Chaldeans. Such a literary fiction, common to most of the apocalyptic writers, is by no means a secondary phenomenon; the actual historical-biographical situation of the speaker is deliberately replaced by an alien scene taken over as analogous to his own.[47]

Why is this a problem?[48] Because, by placing the narrator's present in the past, this sort of text formally militates against decision in the moment. And in a basic sense, this is true: no reader of the text in the first century CE can be called to act against the

Chaldeans. This is perhaps a bizarre concern for a man so indebted to Kierkegaard (a master of the pseudonymous) and it is easy to dismiss Buber here: it seems to presume the prophetic texts were written by the prophets themselves, that they were written in the time of their supposed authors, and that the decision they call for cannot be repeated over vast swaths of time, or in analogous situations.

But let us hope Buber was not so naïve, and instead focus on the philosophical problem he has with this form of narrative: "In the world of the apocalyptic this present historical-biographical hour hardly ever exists, precisely because a decision by men constituting a factor in the historical-suprahistorical decision is not in question here."[49] In this sense the new problem is the same as the old problem: pseudonymity seemingly means that the hearer of the apocalyptic call cannot make a decision, in a specific moment, that affects history.[50] Buber, by focusing on this literary conceit, demonstrates his problem is not exclusively with determinism but with the vision of historical time the apocalyptic posits, where the present can be viewed from the past as part of an already existing future. And in this sense, he is absolutely correct: there is no prophetic call "to stand up right now and change the future" in the apocalyptic mode of time I am suggesting.

The authors' game of "pretend" is, for Buber, further proof of their distance from the prophets, who are apparently playing no such games. I would suggest the use of pseudonyms allows the apocalyptic author to create a complicated notion of history where the present is told from the position of the past and is part of a historical image that already includes the future, and further, suggests a form of humility on the part of the author, where one person cannot address collective problems as an individual.

Pseudonymity is hardly Buber's only literary issue. Indeed, the literariness of the texts is also a significant issue for him. The prophet, both in Buber and in popular culture, is a speaker, whereas the apocalyptic is a writer, lost in his books. One may "speak truth to power," but one may not "write truth to power." Oratory is greater than print, as it speaks to the moment and the active. "The apocalyptic writer has no audience turned towards him; he speaks into his notebook. He does not really speak, he only writes; he does not write down the speech, he just writes his thoughts, he writes a book."[51]

I will not dwell on the way this privileging of orality is naïve and historically questionable.[52] It suffices that for Buber the text is damned by its pseudonymous claim to authorship rather than oratory.

Against the Womb

The manly prophet calls for decision, while the effete and anxious apocalyptic dictates the future with their pen.

> Nowhere in the book does there stir the prophetic *breath*. . . . Everything here is predetermined, all human decisions are only sham struggles. The future does not come to pass; the future is already present in heaven, as it were, present from the beginning.[53]

Buber suggests the future is in heaven ("as it were"), but it is unclear that this is an apt reading of 4 Ezra, where history is not a scroll up in heaven, waiting to be unrolled. Heaven is not the metaphor for historical time, the womb is.

We can see this in the fact that the womb is used by Uriel to explain to Ezra how history works.[54] Two examples will suffice here. When Ezra asks Uriel about the timing of the end, Uriel suggests the end is inevitable, but of unknowable date:

> "Go and ask a woman who is with child if, when her nine months have been completed, her womb can keep the child within her any longer." And I said, "No, lord, it cannot." And he said to me, "The underworld and the treasuries of the souls are like the womb. For just as a woman who is in travail makes haste to escape the pangs of birth, so also do these [places] hasten to give back those things that were committed to them from the beginning."[55]

Here there is a strange logic of reversibility and irreversibility: it seems time is as irreversible and decisive as birth, and yet the births are things that were committed to the underworld and the "treasuries" (presumably in heaven). History is not stored in heaven, though: souls are. And there is no determinism here any more than there is in the very fact of existing. To argue this implies a world without decision is much like saying "all my decisions are moot, because I had no choice in being born."

This series of births is the heartbeat of historical time, and in this sense is a forward-moving force which can neither be quickened or slowed down. So when Ezra asks if we could not have just had everyone around at the same time, and gotten this whole mess over with, he receives the following reply:

> He said to me, "Ask a woman's womb, and say to it, 'If you bear ten children, why one after another?' Request it therefore to produce ten at one time." I said, "Of course it cannot, but only each in its own time." He said to me, "Even so have I made the earth a womb for those who from time to time come forth on it. For as an infant does not bring forth, and a woman who has become old does not bring forth any longer, so I have organized the world that I created."[56]

Again, time is irreversible and ordered, but in the same manner as a series of births, not a set of determined events.[57] Surely the writer could have employed countless other metaphors, or indeed, have just stated it, if their intention was to argue all events are absolutely determined, and there is no place for the human in them. A birth, even if it is a birth that "gives back" something stored, begins a process (and is in this sense done without decision on the part of the birthed) as open as any other.

This, again, is not to deny there are elements of determinism here. Indeed, the set number of births, which metronomically set the beat of historical time, do determine that there will be a past, present, and future, and the bounds of this image are set in a manner that hardly accords with contemporary sensibilities. It is only to claim this image is hardly more determined than prophetic (or indeed, most scientific) notions of time. Where it seems to broadly differ from prophetic history is in the role of the narrator (the manly vocal prophet, versus the scribal writerly apocalyptic) and the emphasis upon the disaster that is the end.

In Sum

Buber has been employed here both because he represents a standard position in modern Jewish thought (and indeed, in other forms of thought as well) and because he highlights very clearly, through his critique, the standard opposition between the prophetic and apocalyptic types. This has allowed me the space to better articulate my claim that apocalyptic temporality allows us to think of the history of the future, but also lay the ground for my final claim: the apocalyptic (both the temporality and the type) is more "useful" for thinking through our own disaster, the ecological collapse. While the prophetic type may be what one wants when there is a disaster to be averted, we are already in the midst of one. The apocalyptic is better suited to a moment where we are dealing with a disaster, rather than preventing one, and where we need collective action, rather than individual prophets.

DISAPPOINTING TIME

There is a danger in thinking ecological disaster lies in the future, to be averted perhaps by innovation or a change in values. If this were true, we would want something like a prophet, someone to inspire fear in us to change our behavior and avert the disaster, as with Nineveh. But this is to misread the time we are in: the disaster is here, visible in both our collective anxiety and callous disavowals.

These final comments are unabashedly contemporary, and I have no illusions ancient apocalyptic writers would see themselves in them.[58] I will suggest ways the apocalyptic type and temporality may be of use in confronting our disaster—more useful than the prophetic. The goal is entirely pragmatic: to see what can be explained when we adopt these ideas and images to think through ecological problems. I am guided by Zupančič's "The Apocalypse Is (Still) Disappointing," itself a revisiting of Blanchot's similarly named piece, itself a riposte to Jasper's *The Atom Bomb and the Future of Man*.[59]

Zupančič identifies the apocalypse, or revealing of the hitherto secret image of time, with the disaster that occurs at time's end.[60] This is not a bad thing: popular employment of technical terms can be productive, and the link between the disaster and the apocalypse nicely illuminates Taubes's claim that the eschaton is what makes history possible as a directional enterprise;[61] if the apocalypse is a *directed* historical image, then the end gives cogency to all the preceding moments, even in its reversal of the irreversible (where birth is a return, and death is undone).[62]

Why Is the Apocalypse Disappointing?

Zupančič's chief conceptual addition to the apocalypse is seemingly basic: despite the heady mixture of images that compose apocalypse, it is fundamentally empty, even boring. Our first impressions, fueled either by Hollywood or *Revelation*, suggest a thickness to calamity that is undone by the "event" itself—because in a strict sense, the disaster is not an event. When asking why thought of disaster usually encourages nihilism or hedonism, Zupančič notes:

> The problem is not that . . . death looks so final and irreversible; the problem is that it looks so full (of itself), so dense and substantial. Ours is a society of death, yet one that does not accept death for what it is: an enormous event (for us), but also enormously empty, "insignificance itself." Yes, like the apocalypse, death is disappointing: nothing really happens there.[63]

The end point is "primeval silence," that is, nothingness, a non-event with no participants. The entertainment and stimulation of apocalyptic texts often obscures this other claim they make: there is nothing human at the end. Similarly, those who think of the ecological collapse as a mad happening, a violent conflagration, or a stimulant to action will be disappointed by the actual process of tedious unending loss as we "adapt" to a series of situations, each more dismal and restrictive than the last.

And indeed, this is inevitable: if not this disaster the next, or the next, or one in the chain after, will destroy everything human, and in time, all terrestrial life. This brutal fact (earthly life as a whole is finite, not merely each individual life) is easily swabbed away by platitudes ("that will happen long after I'm gone"). This is why the disaster in apocalyptic texts is more chilling than Noah's biocide. The disaster at the end has no ark—there is no postapocalyptic.

The history of the present is more responsive to the disaster than several other forms of temporality, from the liberal hope for endless improvement to the prophetic call to the present. This is not to denigrate either liberalism or the decision or the moment, only to note the disaster that reveals the present is already part of a history where the end is already written (even if the details of that end have yet to be decided—much like a life). Prophetic exhortation may make us feel good, and liberalism may help us live well, but the future disaster forces us to think the present as part of its past.

When Buber derisively notes that "wherever man shudders before the menace of his own work and longs to flee from the radically demanding historical hour, there he finds himself near to the apocalyptic vision of a process that cannot be arrested," he unwittingly argues for the defendant. Who doesn't occasionally long to leave this historical hour? Who feels addressed by this disaster? Who feels they can change its course?

Buber's prophetic call works best when there is "still time," or time seems still. Whereas Zupančič notes:

> Today, the most lucid analysts do not warn against what will happen if we press the wrong buttons; they rather insist that the wrong button has already been pressed. The apocalypse has already started and is becoming an active part of our life and our world, such as it is. It is not waiting for us somewhere in the future, but is dictating our social, economic, environmental conditions as we speak.[64]

Which brings us to the notion of fear and what it can do for us. For a long time ecologists have argued over the place of fear in environmentalism: should we use fear to get people to act, or does fear paralyze them?[65] Now it seems clear this "fear of god" has failed—fear will not prevent the disaster; again, as Zupančič notes, it seems we would rather die than have the "shit scared out of us."[66]

The apocalyptic is not without fear, but it is a fear of an entirely different temporality. It is a fear not *of* the disaster, which is unavoidable, but a fear for what will be lost. And here is the final apocalyptic revelation (in the contemporary sense): it reveals what is to be destroyed. In this sense apocalypse, in a very specific way, reveals what it negates: "We could also say: the final result of the apocalypse (total extinction) is insignificance itself. The problem is that apocalypse is not so much the end of the world as it is itself first and foremost the revelation of a new world."[67] But what is meant by this? Is this some sort of nihilistic "critical theory flourish," where the apocalypse reveals life beyond life, or some other ephemera we are to pin our literary hopes onto?

If this is the case, then the apocalypse has nothing for us. But this is not the case: if the prophetic calls to a moment of decision, the apocalyptic calls to the history of the disaster—a different present entirely, not a present to be changed, but a present that only now appears: it reveals the thing to be destroyed. As Zupančič's Blanchot suggests,

> the threat of the Bomb and its destructive potential made appear, for the first time, the idea of a whole (of the world)—a whole, precisely, that can be lost, or disappear forever. We can lose it all; but the idea of the whole (of an all that can be lost) only appears through a negation.[68]

But the difference between the Bomb (which is "in the future") and the ecological collapse is that the ecological collapse is both here and inevitable. The world is being revealed now, as it is being lost to history in that same moment: but what is revealed was not apparent until it was under threat of destruction. This from the most banal sense, where we appreciate what is of value when it is under threat, to the phenomenological sense that the collectively shared world—easily ignored in our private and continuous struggle to keep afloat—is revealed only when we are already slipping away in the midst of a disaster. The apocalyptic call is to attend to the disaster and to save what is only now seen as past, because it is worth saving in and of itself, even knowing it is already done.

I have no idea how this is to be done. What I do know is that if we require a spiritual transformation in the moment, something to avert the end, we are doomed.

A call to attend to the disaster as here, and to see the present as past, is perhaps a more hopeful place.

NOTES

1. M. E. Stone and M. Henze, *4 Ezra and 2 Baruch: Translations, Introductions, and Notes* (Fortress Press, 2013).
2. Maurice Blanchot, *The Writing of the Disaster*, trans. A. Smock (University of Nebraska Press, 2015), 3.
3. It is an honor to write a work for Elliot Wolfson's festschrift. Indeed, his work has affected my own so deeply it is difficult to properly cite him, as to credit him fully would overwhelm the page. This paper follows Wolfson in both making temporality the object of the reading and allowing it to inform my method. That Wolfson is a thinker of time and difference goes without saying: it is no secret he grounds his method in his ontology of time, such that while many of his arguments stand without the ontology, it is the ontology that organizes, creates, and mobilizes them. The temporality that is theorized here is not nearly as complex as the phenomenological-kabbalistic time dealt with by Wolfson, but my reading remains indebted to his work as a whole. This paper is what happens when a philosopher without the proper expertise reads apocalypses. In this I depart from Wolfson's work, but very few can claim to simultaneously possess the combination of philosophical and philological expertise he has. My interest is not in the people who wrote but the stereotypes and archetypes of the apocalyptic that prevail both in modern Jewish thought and ordinary language and culture. These reflections would be impossible without discussions with Meghan Henning, Sharday Mosurinjohn, Lutz Greisiger, Zak Braiterman, Robert Erlewine, and of course Elliot. For a wonderful collection of Wolfson's works on time (heavily revised) see: Elliot R. Wolfson, *Suffering Time: Philosophical, Kabbalistic, and Ḥasidic Reflections on Temporality* (Brill, 2021).
4. The following will treat the apocalyptic as a type or a figure, one inclusive of texts, persons, cultural and rhetorical forms, and something like a "philosophy." For instance, while it will fairly strike a philologist as wildly inappropriate to use the term "apocalyptic" to refer to disaster as well as revelation, this is the sense it has in much modern Jewish thought as well as popular culture. This paper leans heavily on the insights of those who have explored the relation between the apocalypse and social movements (Hall, Collins, Henning, Watts-Belser, Faubion, Henze) to try to understand the past, the present, or to use present millenarian/apocalyptic movements to understand the past (Grabbe).
5. We can also think of it as a history of the future and a prediction of the past: in this sense the present is much like the "collision" of these two inversions. But I am going to focus on the history of the present both for reasons of brevity, and because my own interest in disaster is best seen here.
6. Apocalyptic temporality has often been read as a kind of crass determinism, a crude popular literature, or, in the twentieth century, as a banal proto-Marxism. For Buber, Marxism is very much the wrong kind of socialism (he hews closer to anarchism). For the best analysis of

Buber's theopolitics see Samuel Haim Brody, *Martin Buber's Theopolitics* (Indiana University Press, 2018). This is hardly the only instance of Buber using an ancient figure for contemporary political polemic. As Erlewine has noted, his animosity toward "Gnosticism" was in fact a polemic against Harnack and the attempt to strip Christianity of any Jewish influence. R. Erlewine, *Judaism and the West: From Hermann Cohen to Joseph Soloveitchik* (Indiana University Press, 2016), 45, 63; S. Heschel, *The Aryan Jesus: Christian Theologians and the Bible in Nazi Germany* (Princeton University Press, 2010). I unfortunately must leave unaddressed the question of whether or not Marxism is intrinsically apocalyptic.

7. The apocalypse integrates the natural world: apocalyptically, what we call "natural history" (meaning, not really history) is as historical as the French Revolution.
8. Of course the word "apocalypse" refers to a revelation via an unveiling, and not to the disaster. As Wolfson notes: "The Greek apokalpysis means unveiling, from the verb apokalypto, to uncover, as in stripping the veil to reveal the face of the virgin. To speak meaningfully of the unveiling, one must presume the existence of the veil and what is beneath the veil. . . . Disclosure of the mystery, therefore, is not discovery of something for the first time, but rather uncovering what had been concealed." However, both in popular discourse and indeed, in most of the ancient apocalypses, the unveiling reveals the concealed disaster. It is in this sense we can read the aporias of Blanchot's disaster. Elliot R. Wolfson, "Gazing Beneath the Veil: Apocalyptic Envisioning the End," in *Reinterpreting Revelation and Tradition: Jews and Christians in Conversation*, ed. Hayim Goren Perelmuter and John Pawlikowski (London: Sheed & Ward, 2000).
9. Following Buber, for this paper I will treat the apocalyptic as a substantive *type* encompassing rhetoric, literature, movements, and an implicit set of philosophical positions (see fn. 4). I understand that the philosophical habit of using an adjective (apocalyptic) as a noun might be stylistically awkward, but it allows me to treat this entire complex of forms, ideas, and historical actualities as a single concept—which in turn allows me to build a bridge between academic definition games and popular discourse (see the final section).
10. Hans Jonas, *The Imperative of Responsibility: In Search of an Ethics for the Technological Age* (Chicago: University of Chicago Press, 1984), 32.
11. Grabbe summarizes this nicely when he says: "To the apocalypticist the events he describes are no less real than those of 'real history'—these events are 'real history.' There is of course no reason why we as modern twenty-first-century people should not distinguish between myth and history. There is no reason why we should not reject the apocalyptic worldview as a historicizing of myth. We rightly view the fundamentalist interpretation of Daniel, Revelation and history as incompatible with a modern scientific worldview. Where we go wrong, though, is trying to impose this distinction on an ancient literature whose writers would not have understood it at all." Following Wolfson, we can say our attempt to view the apocalypse as (literally) anachronistic is itself an anachronism. Meghan Henning, *Educating Early Christians through the Rhetoric of Hell* (Tübingen: Mohr Siebeck, 2014), 47–51; Lester L. Grabbe, "Prophetic and Apocalyptic: Time for New Definitions, and New Thinking," in *Knowing the End from the Beginning: The Prophetic, Apocalyptic, and Their Relationship*, ed. L. L. Grabbe and R. D. Haak (Bloomsbury, 2004); Elliot R. Wolfson, "Hyperphilology and the Anachronism of

Anachronism," in *Los Angeles Review of Books* (2019), https://marginalia.lareviewofbooks.org/hyperphilology-anachronism-anachronism/.

12. John R. Hall, *Apocalypse: From Antiquity to the Empire of Modernity* (Wiley, 2009), 18–42. Hall uses an expansive definition of apocalypse because his goal is social theory, and so the term is expanded such that it can take account of many social events and forms; it is thus looser than I would prefer, and this is why I am not adopting it, but for those interested in sociology it would perhaps be preferred.
13. Hall, *Apocalypse*, 20.
14. Grabbe, "Prophetic and Apocalyptic," 112, 114.
15. Henning suggests that the primary distinction between the prophetic texts and the apocalyptic texts is that the latter aggressively accentuate the visual. Meghan Henning, "Apocalyptic Literature," in *The Cambridge Companion to the Bible and Literature*, ed. Calum Carmichael (Cambridge: Cambridge University Press, 2020).
16. In this my project again approaches Wolfson's, however effetely. Wolfson's most famous study of the image is his *Speculum* but the claim that a great deal of Jewish thought and writing is concerned with the intersection between time and the image—in particular, the ways Jewish thought offers alternatives to the image of time as a straight line—occurs throughout his work. Elliot R. Wolfson, *Through a Speculum That Shines: Vision and Imagination in Medieval Jewish Mysticism* (Princeton: Princeton University Press, 1994). See also Elliot R. Wolfson, "Iconic Visualization and the Imaginal Body of God: The Role of Intention in the Rabbinic Conception of Prayer," in *Elliot R. Wolfson: Poetic Thinking*, ed. Hava Tirosh-Samuelson and Aaron W. Hughes (Brill, 2015).
17. It is important to note I am only looking at one "side" of the apocalyptic vision: the temporal/historical that concerns "eschatological salvation" and not the "supernatural realm," as delineated by Wolfson. Wolfson, "Gazing Beneath the Veil," 79.
18. The primary distinction is that we might see these "shapes" as forms of history, whereas the apocalyptic also sees the content.
19. For a treatment of the apocalyptic secret, see Wolfson, "Gazing Beneath the Veil."
20. "The Apocalypse of Abraham," trans. R. Rubinkiewicz, in *The Old Testament Pseudepigrapha*, ed. J. H. Charlesworth (Hendrickson, 2010), 22, 23.
21. To wit, Koselleck: the question of history is "how, in a given present, are the temporal dimensions of past and future related? This query involves the hypothesis that in differentiating past and future, or (in anthropological terms) experience and expectation, it is possible to grasp something like historical time." For the apocalyptic writer, this is done at the point of the pseudonym. Koselleck is therefore incorrect when he says: "Prognosis produces the time within which and out of which it weaves, whereas apocalyptic prophecy destroys time through its fixation on the End." Reinhart Koselleck, *Futures Past: On the Semantics of Historical Time*, trans. K. Tribe (Columbia University Press, 2004), 3, 19.
22. Andrew Mein, "The Armies of Gog, the Merchants of Tarshish, and the British Empire," in *In the Name of God: The Bible in the Colonial Discourse of Empire*, ed. C. L. Crouch and Jonathan Stökl (Brill, 2014), 136.
23. 4 Ezra (12:11): "The eagle which you saw coming up from the sea is the fourth kingdom which

appeared in a vision to your brother [Daniel 12:12]. *But it was not explained to him as I now explain it to you*" (emphasis added).

24. Martha Himmelfarb, *The Apocalypse: A Brief History* (Wiley, 2010), 61. See also the informative Lorenzo DiTommaso, "Dating the Eagle Vision of 4 Ezra: A New Look at an Old Theory," *Journal for the Study of the Pseudepigrapha* 10, no. 20 (1999).
25. Here we see the transposition of a philological argument over genre (what is the difference between prophetic and apocalyptic texts) into a typological key—although the philological argument was likely never far from this concern with types. Much of the philological debate is concerned with genre: what makes a text an apocalypse, and how do we distinguish the apocalyptic from the prophetic? Since the 1830s it has been assumed there is something called an apocalypse, related to, but distinct from, the prophetic. But the tenability of this distinction has been questioned since the '70s. See John J. Collins, *The Apocalyptic Imagination: An Introduction to Jewish Apocalyptic Literature* (William B. Eerdmans, 2016), 3–55. Collins, rather than looking for the characteristics of a genre, focuses instead on the way a genre and the forms of thinking it evinces develop a "self consciousness." Grabbe instead looks at characteristics or attributes of each type of text (and, unsurprisingly, finds no principled way to distinguish them): "Our terms 'prophecy', 'mantic wisdom', 'apocalyptic' and so on are abstractions. They do not exist by themselves in nature. They are a way of understanding common features found in individual writings. Ultimately, a 'prophecy', an 'apocalypse' and the like is what we agree to call it." Grabbe's nominalism is thus less useful than Collins for the present typological project. Grabbe, "Prophetic and Apocalyptic," 110.
26. T. Drorah Setel, "Prophets and Pornography: Female Sexual Imagery in Hosea," in *Feminist Interpretation of the Bible*, ed. Letty M. Russell (Philadelphia: Westminster Press, 1985), 86–95.
27. Cassirer would call Buber's engagement with the apocalyptic figure in *Paths* "mythic," rather than historical, but they are the mythic component of historical thought—in other words, types or figures that allow for his theory of history, even if they themselves aren't historically actual. Ernst Cassirer, *Language and Myth* (Dover Publications, 2012), 33, 57.
28. Asher Wycoff helpfully notes: "Buber's prophecy–apocalypse distinction refracts Engels's distinction between utopian and scientific socialisms through a theological lens, inverting the value judgment to favor the former over the latter. If 'prophetic' socialist projects often fail, at least their failures are less catastrophic and their achievements less ambiguous than those of 'apocalyptic' socialism"; it is in this sense that Buber identifies the apocalyptic with Moscow and the prophetic with Jerusalem. Asher Wycoff, "Between Prophecy and Apocalypse: Buber, Benjamin, and Socialist Eschatology," *Political Theory* 49, no. 3 (2021): 355.
29. Martin Buber, *Paths in Utopia*, The Martin Buber Library (Syracuse: Syracuse University Press, 1996), 7 (emphasis in original); for a later articulation of the image-making drive, see *Martin Buber, The Knowledge of Man*, trans. Maurice S. Friedman (New York: Harper & Row, 1965); Zachary Braiterman, *The Shape of Revelation: Aesthetics and Modern Jewish Thought* (Stanford: Stanford University Press, 2007); and also, Dustin Atlas, "How to Do Things with Things: Craft at the Edge of Buber's Philosophical Anthropology," *IMAGES* 12, no. 1 (Oct. 24, 2019).
30. Buber, *Paths in Utopia*, 8. Contrariwise, a utopia is revelation realized in *space* and for this

reason the eschatological can afford to think outside of the social, whereas the utopic is bound by it.

31. Buber's obnoxious use of Persia, from this text to *Images of Evil and Good,* as both a competitor and contaminator of Israel, deserves treatment. Here he unthinkingly adopts a colonialist rejection of the apocalypses as a foreign "banal popular literature" favored by nineteenth- and early twentieth-century Bible scholars. Collins, *Apocalyptic Imagination*, 1–2; Meghan R. Henning, *Hell Hath No Fury: Gender, Disability, and the Invention of Damned Bodies in Early Christian Literature* (Yale University Press, 2021), 13.
32. Buber, *Paths in Utopia*, 10.
33. This is not to say Marx disappears from the later essay, only that Buber engages an actual apocalypse, giving textual grounding to his typology (rather than relying on anti-Marxist fulmination).
34. Jacob Taubes, "Martin Buber and the Philosophy of History," in *From Cult to Culture: Fragments Toward a Critique of Historical Reason* (Stanford University Press, 2010), 13.
35. Martin Buber, "Prophecy, Apocalyptic, and the Historical Hour," in *Pointing the Way: Collected Essays*, trans. Maurice S. Friedman (New York: Schocken Books, 1974), 174.
36. Nahum Glatzer unironically replicates this ahistorical cliché with obvious approval: "It is the rejection of the ahistoric, world-denying, time-denying, transcendent philosophy of the apocalyptic that deepens in Buber affirmation of prophecy. . . . The two opposing views are not issues of the past but perennial interpretations of the human condition. . . . Theories such as those pounded by Karl Marx and Lasalle are modern expressions of the apocalyptic. . . . Here 'necessity' rules and the efficacy of individual resolutions actions is passed over and obliterated." Nahum N. Glatzer, "Aspects of Martin Buber's Thought," *Modern Judaism* 1, no. 1 (1981).
37. Buber, "Prophecy, Apocalyptic, and the Historical Hour," 202.
38. Himmelfarb, *The Apocalypse: A Brief History*, 36.
39. I take as given that any contemporary account of freedom must deal with the paradox that, from most scientific standpoints, as well as many theological and rationalist ones, we are in some sense "determined," and yet appear to be "free." I cannot believe Buber—no stranger to paradox—was opposed to the apocalyptic because of its determinism; his issue is with its seeming denigration of *historical decision*. Elliot Wolfson suggests a better way of distinguishing between the prophetic and apocalyptic where history is concerned: "History no longer was viewed as containing within itself the possibility for its own redemption. Apocalyptic salvation is predicated on the recognition of the temporal domain as the great abyss, an awareness that wells from the existentialist encounter of the soul with the looming end of the historical epoch." Wolfson, "Gazing Beneath the Veil," 91.
40. And further, "What use is a typology concerning the prophetic and apocalyptic experience of history if Deutero-Isaiah, whom Buber rightly calls 'the originator of a theology of world-history' has to be exempt from the rule? Among the prophets he was the man who had to announce world history . . . as divinely predestined." Taubes, "Martin Buber and the Philosophy of History," 19.
41. Martin Buber, *The Philosophy of Martin Buber* (La Salle: Open Court, 1967), 721 (emphasis added).

42. Taubes, "Martin Buber and the Philosophy of History," 21 (emphasis added).
43. Taubes, however, still thinks of time in far too linear a manner. For him the center of the apocalyptic is the eschaton, which is what makes history possible as a directional enterprise. In this sense the apocalyptic is, for him, a limit of thinking that creates a space in which the arrow of history can fly forward. Jacob Taubes, *Occidental Eschatology*, trans. David Ratmoko (Stanford: Stanford University Press, 2009), 4.
44. This accords with Taubes's conviction that the apocalyptic break does not come from on high, but is firmly on the side of those who are left outside the established order. Taubes, *Occidental Eschatology*, 39.
45. Buber, "Prophecy, Apocalyptic, and the Historical Hour," 199.
46. Himmelfarb, *The Apocalypse: A Brief History*, 57, 58. Collins notes that not only do the first few "revelations" take the form of a dialogue, Ezra seems to stand in for the covenantal project, while Uriel employs extensive nature analogies that stress individuals. Both are washed away by the dense visions at the end. Collins, *Apocalyptic Imagination*, 246.
47. Martin Buber, *Pointing the Way: Collected Essays*, trans. Maurice S. Friedman (New York: Schocken Books, 1974), 195 (emphasis added).
48. Note that for Wolfson this pseudonymous concealment of history is a statement about the nature of history, suggesting "history" has value only after it has gone through an interpretive process: "hiding one's identity behind the veil of a figure from the past bespeaks an act of utmost piety. Nevertheless, the use of pseudonym may strike the ear as a curious dimension to find in a literary tradition concerned with unveiling secrets hidden beneath the surface. In spite of—or perhaps on account of—the insistence in apocalypticism on seeing what is unseen, there is a tendency to mask, to conceal, the historical moment in the garb of fictional narrative. This does not diminish the sense of history, however, but simply highlights the fact that the latter can only be expressed in symbolic language predicated on the assumption that the value of the historical datum lies in its narratological retelling." Wolfson, "Gazing Beneath the Veil," 92.
49. Buber, "Prophecy, Apocalyptic, and the Historical Hour," 200.
50. For a man whose dialogical philosophy hinges on our ability to say "here I am," and be present, it is odd Buber misses the following: "14:1 And it came to pass, on the third day, while I was sitting under an oak, behold, a voice came out of a bush opposite me and said, 'Ezra, Ezra.' 14:2 And I said, 'Here I am, Lord,' and I rose to my feet."
51. "At the beginning of his book the speaker . . . lies on his bed and, visited by a great anxiety over the fate of Israel and that of the human race, laments to heaven and complains." Here anxiety is a deficit, the vice of an artist, and utterly unlike the manly voice of the prophets. Buber, "Prophecy, Apocalyptic, and the Historical Hour," 200.
52. As Wolfson notes, "These sources render problematic the tendency to posit a rigid dichotomy between textual interpretation and visionary experience" and so it is hermeneutically questionable. Wolfson, "Gazing Beneath the Veil," 87, 92–93. Historically speaking, see Grabbe: "Both prophetic and apocalyptic literature are scribal products." Grabbe, "Prophetic and Apocalyptic," 129.
53. Buber, "Prophecy, Apocalyptic, and the Historical Hour," 200.
54. "In the first half of the narrative, the characters Ezra and Uriel juxtapose their conceptions

of time and the purpose of creation with the pregnant bodies of women in order to communicate their ideas." Alexis Lee Felder, "Birthing the Apocalypse: Images of Pregnancy and Childbirth in First Century Apocalyptic Literature" (PhD diss., Boston University, 2018), 198–204.

55. 4 Ezra 4:40–42.
56. 4 Ezra 5:46–49.
57. And to iterate: neither is it *sub specie aeternitatis.*
58. Here I do not at all intend to say "what the tradition entails," or retread the tedious claim that Jewish sources, properly interpreted, will avert the ecological disaster. I am far from the opinion that religion will save us. I am only saying that there are *elements* in the apocalyptic texts, figures, and concepts that can help us with our thinking here. But the text's authors would no doubt view my prescinding as an act of ignorance or impiety.
59. Alenka Zupančič, "The Apocalypse Is (Still) Disappointing," *S: Journal of the Circle for Lacanian Ideology Critique* 11 (2018); Maurice Blanchot, *Friendship*, trans. E. Rottenberg (Stanford University Press, 1997); Karl Jaspers, *The Atom Bomb and the Future of Man* (University of Chicago Press, 1963).
60. One could argue ecological collapse is closer to Noah's biocide than an actual apocalypse. However, apocalyptic concern with the end of historical time is as much invested in the destruction of the natural world as the human.
61. Taubes, *Occidental Eschatology*, 4.
62. Meghan Henning, "Narrating the Future," in *Narrating Religion*, ed. Sarah Iles Johnston (Macmillan Reference, 2016). Wolfson makes an even stronger case for thinking of the end as an essential element of the apocalypse, noting the end and secrecy must be thought together such that the telling itself is impossible otherwise: "From beginning to end, the end is the mystery that marks the horizon of our envisioning and delineates the limit of our language." Wolfson, "Gazing Beneath the Veil," 83.
63. Zupančič, "The Apocalypse Is (Still) Disappointing," 23.
64. Zupančič, "The Apocalypse Is (Still) Disappointing," 24.
65. Jonas, *The Imperative of Responsibility*, 26.
66. Zupančič, "The Apocalypse Is (Still) Disappointing," 29.
67. Zupančič, "The Apocalypse Is (Still) Disappointing," 24.
68. Zupančič, "The Apocalypse Is (Still) Disappointing," 17.

BAD FAITH; OR, WHY THE JEWS AREN'T A RELIGION

DANIEL BOYARIN

IN HONOR OF ELLIOT WOLFSON, MY INTELLECTUAL COLLEAGUE AND DEEP friend these many years, *inter alia* important Rosenzweig interpreter נר״י who may very well disagree.[1]

Until quite recently, it has commonly been held that every human group has a "religion." It has been notoriously difficult to define the word "religion" and thus to delineate the concept, although myriad attempts have been made. Notwithstanding this stumbling block, it seems fair to say that in modern usage, we have had a pretty good idea what we mean when we call something a religion, even without being in absolute agreement with what is in and what is out of the category. At the same time, however, it is increasingly recognized that the concept of "religion" as an autonomous sphere of human activity, separate or separable from other spheres of activity named as the realm of the secular, such as law, politics, kinship, and economics, is itself as modern (and as "Western") as is the usage of the word "religion" to denote that sphere. Because, as is now recognized by many scholars, "religion" as a concept and category emerged out of the very forces that defined it, during the time of the Enlightenment, it becomes very difficult to imagine how a Jewish religion could possibly exist as such before any religion did—that is, before one aspect of the things humans do is separated out, isolated from cultural activity in general, and named, however it is defined, "religion." "Judaism," as a "religion," as the term is commonly understood today, emerged only as a product of modernity.[2] This point can be sharpened even further, for the forces that historically produced the category of "religion" as a distinct entity from the "secular" during the seventeenth century in Europe are precisely the same forces that raised the "Jewish Question" to the center of attention that in one way or another it has occupied since then.[3] As Aamir Mufti has pointed out, the "projects of secularism," citizenship, separation of church and state, national language, national literature and culture, "have circled around the question of the Jews."[4]

EXISTENTIALIST *JUDAITE*: FRANZ ROSENZWEIG

The most important philosopher of Jewishness (hereafter *Judaite*[5]) in the first half of the twentieth century, Franz Rosenzweig[6] denies that *Judentum* (comprising English "Judaism," "Jewishness," and "Jewry") is a religion, claiming it as rather a complete *Kulturvolk* in the sense used by Wilhelm von Humboldt referring to Germans (German speakers) or Zunz with Jews. The very fact of his engagement in this question, through this denial (shared with Martin Buber),[7] however, indicates that he is already embedded in an episteme that recognizes "religion" as an autonomous concept—as does my own querying as well. It is nearly inevitable that we do so. And Rosenzweig, at least, seems to have understood this clearly, as he declared to Gerhard [Gershom] Scholem: "In a sense we are ourselves guests at our own table, we ourselves, I myself. So long as we speak German (or even if we speak Hebrew, modern Hebrew, the Hebrew of '1921') we cannot avoid this detour that again and again leads us the hard way from what is alien back to our own."[8] Rosenzweig's own ascription to himself of alienation from Jewish language involves the usage of such words as *Judentum*, *Jüdischer Glaube* (the Jewish faith) to refer to ourselves. In the past, in the Hebrew of before 1921 and in Yiddish, such usages are not to be found. There was no separate Jewish faith at all.

So that was then, but what about now? Aren't the Jews a religion now?[9] Not in any normative or prescriptive sense. There are myriad Jews, myriads of myriads of Jews, who do not profess any religion and yet are deeply engaged with the Jewish enigma, producing literature and other culture in Jewish idioms, whether in Hebrew or in Yiddish or in both and in other Jewish languages, as well. Sigmund Freud provides an explicit and excellent example, writing as he did that he is free of religion, a "godless Jew," but "very much a Jew."[10] And he/they are recognized as Jews by other Jews. Manifestly, one does not have to be a part of a "religion" in order to be Jewish.[11]

Michael Walzer of the Institute for Advanced Studies in Princeton, one of the most distinguished American political theorists, in a strenuous defense of Zionism, demonstrates, nonetheless, that claiming that the Jews are not a nation but only a "faith" is a fallacy. For all his defense of Zionism, that is, Walzer argues that anti-Zionism is *not antisemitism*. Walzer notes that the Jews share many characteristics of a nationality, a national group, or even a nation, even (or especially) in Ernst Renan's sense that the "essence of a nation is that all individuals have many things in common, and also that they have forgotten many things."[12] The forgotten things are the discreditable actions of the nation in the past, viz. slavery in the United States. Walzer also makes it clear why anti-Zionism is *not* tantamount to antisemitism. As he puts it, the problem he has with anti-Zionism is that it is anti-Zionism—and, according to him, wrong—and not that it is covert or overt antisemitism. After all, as recently as one hundred years ago, the vast majority of Jews in the world and an overwhelming majority of Orthodox (and Reform) rabbis were bitterly opposed to Zionism, just about as bitterly as today they might be bitterly opposed to anti-Zionism and brand it antisemitism. This compelling argument is, in essence, Walzer's reason for denying that the Jews constitute a religion. This point can be unpacked further than Walzer does: merely professing the tenets of or even practicing the practices of the Torah does not qualify one as a member of the Jews—a fellow traveler perhaps, but not quite a Jew, yet.

Here's a second reason for why it's not a good idea to exchange the historical visions of the Jews as a nation for a claim that they are a church. If the Jews wish to take advantage of laws that depend on Christian definitions of "religion," which are essentially all the definitions there are, we will end up with a "Judaism" that looks very much like Christianity, that is, belonging defined by belief, "the Jewish faith," "*jüdischer Glaube*," something we might call—with no offense intended—Jewtheranism.[13] As Gil Anidjar has remarked, wittily summing up Edward Said's thinking, "*Wo es war*—where Christianity was, there is now religion."[14] "Religion" is Christian, and if a so-called "Judaism" is a religion, then it is a variant form of Christianity: if you believe this way, you are a Christian, and if you believe that way, you are a Jew.

These beliefs, moreover, are normatively of no interest whatsoever to the public sphere. As Aamir Mufti has concisely stated, "This is the Jewish emancipation that liberalism promises from its very inception. Enlightenment . . . thus requires the privatization of religious affiliation, that is, its confinement to the (patriarchal) realm of the (bourgeois) family under the rubric of practice and belief. The signs of religious affiliation and community must cease to have a public existence."[15] To which I would add: unless they are properly Christian and even Protestant signs. One reason that certain versions of a "religion" named *Judentum* has been so successful in postwar Germany is precisely that it looks exactly like Protestantism from a broadly cultural point of view, thus effectively eliminating the *Judaite* that incorporates way more than *Glaube* (faith). And Max Weinreich pointed out with reference to an earlier scholar's identification of "religion," *Judaite* (*Yiddishkayt*) is what joins Jews world over:

> Today many Jews and Christians live in essentially the same fashion, and the difference all year is merely that [the] former attend (or can attend) services on Saturday and the latter on Sunday. In relation to the rise of language, one should not speak of the Jewish religion, but of Jewishness [*Yiddishkeit* (*sic*)]. In the traditional Jewishness of diverse culture areas there are many variants and even contradictions; and yet Jewishness has linked all Jews over time and space in a community of historical fate and in a consciousness of this fate.[16]

In former times, Jews were a whole (by this I don't mean simplex) culture-nation, speaking their own way, worshiping their own way, dressing, eating, marrying, rearing children, their own ways. All of this and more and more were deeply informed by the Talmud, not just the worship and all of its appliances, but all of it, and all of it imbricated and intertwined. Impossible to pull one thread and say this is the "religion" of the Jews without the entire fabric unraveling and disintegrating.

"FREEDOM OF RELIGION" AND THE OFFENSE OF CIRCUMCISION

The result of defining something called "Judaism" as a religion is seemingly a grotesque mismatch in which the Christian "faith" always comes out on top. This point has been made most recently by legal scholars Lena Salaymeh and Shai Lavi, who also make clear how the notion of secularism also implicates Protestant thinking:[17] "First, modern states synthesize Protestant Christian traditions and new, emerging interests of the state, such that secular states are neither purely Christian nor purely nonreligious. One implication of the Protestant Christian genealogy of the modern secular state . . . is that (late antique) Christian criticisms of Judaism linger in the state's construction of religion."

Salaymeh and Lavi explicate how the assignment of "religion" to a separate and defined sphere is what clears out the space of the secular.[18] What renders such secular clearing and construction of religion Christian, and perhaps especially Protestant, is the focus on the individual and his or her "faith," his or her ostensibly free choice to be saved through belief or not.[19] This privatization of "religion," taking it out of the public (or at any rate, the political) sphere empowers discourses on the model of being a Jew at home and a German in public, for example.

What makes the essay of Salaymeh and Lavi particularly relevant here is their specific application to the fraught issue of circumcision. For example: a German court quite recently wanted to ban infant circumcision as a violation of the child's "self-determination," that is, his religious freedom. By circumcising the child, he is allegedly prevented from choosing to be or to become a Christian or an unbeliever when he grows up.[20] They show how European state discourses about male circumcision are dependent on the production of "religion" by the secular state and the construction of circumcision as a matter of "private belief." This results in discrimination against so-called "religious minorities," paradoxically "under the doctrine of religious freedom."[21] The result in the United States is what Will Herberg defined decades ago as the three forms of American Protestantism: Catholic Protestantism, Protestant Protestantism, and Jewish Protestantism. (By now we should add Muslim and Buddhist Protestantism—or maybe not.) My issue here is not, of course with Protestantism itself, but in the way that, as amply shown by scholars, it ends up defining "religion" and thus "religious freedom" on the model of Protestantism, which places individual private faith and "salvation" over corporate identity and places inner movements of the psyche over communal practices or "doings." As Salaymeh and Lavi point out, when this becomes the publicly promulgated version of "religion," it is inherently discriminatory vis-à-vis Jews and Muslims, as opposed to Christians.

The Cologne court is imagining the human subject as a monad with no history and completely autonomous in defining their identity, "beliefs," practices, and affiliations, while the Jews stand precisely against such notions of the "self." We Jews purvey the sources of the nonself of the person who is already, without willing, thrown or inscribed into a bond with others not of their own "free" choice.[22] In other words, the Cologne court, like all colonial powers, is making judgments on the basis of theological/

philosophical bases that it claims are universal, but are, in fact, highly culturally specific. Thinking of Jewry as being a "religion" inevitably involves the imposition—even the willing imposition—of the West on a people not of the West, however much in it.[23]

Thus, when Jews claim that Judaism is a religion, we're inevitably falling into a trap, since religion is understood quite differently than Jewish belonging. We ought no longer to reject Immanuel Kant's notorious observation that "Judaism is really not a religion at all but merely a union of a number of people who, because they belonged to a single stock, formed themselves into a commonwealth under purely political laws, and not into a church."[24] The rejection of "faith" is precisely signified, as Kant understood well, in the preconscious marking of the penis; the sign is only for men, of course, but the demand is to men and women alike (this is meant as a descriptive, not normative nor apologetic, claim on my part). A testimony: In 1795, in a letter to the writer David Veit, Berlin salon Jewess [*sic*] Rahel Varnhagen confessed that she imagined that at her birth, "some supramundane being . . . plunged these words with a dagger into my heart: 'Yes, have sensibility, see the world as few see it, be great and noble, nor can I deprive you of restless, incessant thought. But with one reservation: Be a Jewess!' She goes on to say, "now, my life is one long bleeding," and declares defiantly, "I shall never accept that I am a schlemiel and a Jewess." A dagger in the heart; a knife to the penis. The claim of Jewishness is also a theoretical and rhetorical claim, a command to the child: "Be a Jew!" Varnhagen's confession is a perfect example of the experience of interpellation ["the process by which ideology, embodied in major social and political institutions . . . , constitutes the very nature of individual subjects' identities through the process of 'hailing' them in social interactions."]. Varnhagen was unhappy at this constitution of her subjectivity as a "Jew" against her will; Rosenzweig, implicitly manifesting the same sense, was happy with it, experiencing, as many of us do, an affect that in my wild youth I called *Jewissance*. And here, of course, one might claim that gender is one possible differentiating factor, although by no means an ineluctable one, even in earlier modern Europe.[25]

I repeat that I am not making here a feminist point nor an apology for anything—feminist critique remains valid and is not answered here. This being thrown, as it were, into the world as a Jew is experienced differently, obviously, by different individuals and even classes of individuals, especially in this circumstance genders, but it has its power. Even when we reject, later on—and we are free to do so—the tradition into which we are born, that rejection shapes us also. Only the powerful symbolic marker of that existential givenness, the mark of the covenant, remains to remind us that Jewishness for men and for women is not chosen. We are thrown into the world as Jews, to make of that what we will. It is this thrownness or interpellation that the Cologne court wishes to cancel.

With the entry into the modern, "enlightened" world, there is an entrance fee, a fairly steep one. As W. J. T. Mitchell once remarked wittily and in another context: "There is no representation without taxation." This movement into modernity constitutes a total paradigm shift in German Jewish self-consciousness, a shift that extended itself ultimately far beyond German lands. It is owing to the shock waves released by that earthquake that in the present, by and large, there is the nearly perfect binary and mutually exclusive opposition in conceptions of what "the Jews" denotes, a religion or a nation/ethnicity, with seemingly no other options.[26]

BLOOD AS PERFORMANCE

In a provocative declaration that seems at first (and perhaps even second) glance to blow a staggeringly racist dog-whistle, Rosenzweig, contrasting the Jew with the Christian, says:

> Only he belongs to Christianity who knows his own life to be on the way which leads from Christ come to Christ coming. This knowledge is belief. It is belief as the content of a testimony. It is belief in something [*Glaube an etwas*]. That is exactly the opposite of the belief of the Jew. His belief is not the content of a testimony, but rather the product of a reproduction. The Jew, engendered a Jew, attests his belief by continuing to procreate the Jewish people. His belief is not in something: he is himself the belief.[27]

This claim has been interpreted as a bare confession of "racial" superiority. (One recent reader even interpreted it to mean that "the Jew" is meant to worship himself.) But Rosenzweig's claim here is the very opposite of racism. It stands in opposition to racism precisely because it attributes no superior character to the Jews, indeed attributes to them no character at all, surely nothing innate, other than the sheer existential fact of being genealogically a Jew.[28] The Jew is pure existence as a Jew; this existence is prior to any essence whatever.

Aamir Mufti has, however, challenged this very existentialist claim: "In Enlightened society, that is, the Jew cannot simply be a sign of himself in his difference."[29] What's at issue is how to signify that difference today. In the antinomies whose impasses I'm trying to suggest we should and can escape, the alternative to signifying Jewishness as a religion has seemed sometimes to be only to represent it as constituted by race. This is borne out, it would seem, by the recent actions of the Israeli rabbinate—or at any rate, some of it—in declaring folks Jews on the basis of their mitochondrial DNA—mitochondrial, of course, since Jewishness is determined through the maternal line.

But is it so? Has this been the historical self-conception of the Jews (as opposed to the Nazis, for instance)? Do practices of genealogy and endogamy (marrying "in" and not "out") constitute the Jews as a race, or, even more troubling, as necessarily racist? Have the Jews imagined themselves as biologically different from other peoples of the earth?

For the vast most part, the answer to these questions is no: racialized Jewish self-fashioning is, I think, something of an anomaly, although to my horror less and less so. In the stories Jews tell about themselves and each other, their shared narrative, the narrative of the Jewish collective, the model for thinking about Jewish corporate existence is and has been that of family. Selah Boyarin had gotten it by the age of four:

Selah Hanna Boyarin: Are you Jewish, Zaidie?
Zaidie: Yes, I sure am.
Selah: Because you're in the family! I'm Jewish too, because I'm in our family.

We are Jews owing to the fact that we are a family. And you don't choose your family nor are you part of it owing to its particular character for better or worse.

While families can and do incorporate much violence, this is a superior way of thinking of the genealogical component of the existence of the Jews to racial thinking. Insistence on family intimacy and shared interest does not imply anything essentialistic about the particular family, just that it is a family, and certainly not that it is superior in essence to all other families.

Consanguinity, the fact of being descended from the same ancestor, shared "blood," is one of the most powerful of symbols for human connection and disconnection, motivator of extraordinary acts of self-sacrifice and kindness, as well as the most extraordinary acts of cruelty, violence, and even attempted genocide: "Ties of blood"; "Blood is thicker than water"; "Blood and soil."[30] I want to reclaim here that power for peaceful ends while at the same time tempering it with the claims of affinity—affines are the people with whom we *choose* to be in social groups (typically relatives by marriage), the opposite of consanguinity. Moreover, I wish to insist that the use of this symbol need not imply racist claims. If a black Jew is related to me by ties of common ancestry, then it is clear that it is not "race" in the ordinary sense of which we are speaking when we speak of Jewish blood, but something else. Words of legal theorist Patricia Williams explain this better than I could. It is worth an extended quotation:

> I cannot help but see the bodies of my near ancestors in the current caravans of desperate souls fleeing from place to place, chased by famine, war and toxins. "The bodies of my ancestors" may sound romantic, but I take the idea seriously. I am not speaking here of biologized inheritance: my epigenetics, my predispositions for depression or resilience. Instead, I mean the inheritance of linguistically and rhetorically embedded traditions passed on in habits of speech. I am composed of the voices of those who bred me. We are talked into the world by our forebears: by how they parsed words or not. . . . Their emotional inflections and instincts for fight or flights inhabit us, inhabit me. Their accented soundscape is the familiarity through which we filter all experience. It is an idea of home, even when groundless, or unsupported by structure, or bereft of actual landscape.[31]

If the black Jew has inherited such "linguistically and rhetorically embedded traditions passed on in habits of speech," then they are composed of those voices who bred them, who are their ancestors (which is not to deny the possibility of multiple sets of such voices). The consanguinity of Jews is not racial but linguistic.

But if not race, of what are we speaking when we speak of "Jewish blood"?

We can answer by looking at how consanguinity has been figured in traditional Jewish texts. While common descent is a very powerful topos in the Hebrew Bible, "blood" is not generally used to denote it. This is not to deny the significance of "blood" as a powerful symbol, but it is not a symbol of race or even of kinship or the ties that bind and divide within the classical Hebrew concept world. As Gil Anidjar has noted: "There is little room . . . to doubt that, for the Bible more than for classical Greece, blood is a symbol of life, of mere life, and indeed of the flesh."[32] He goes on:

> Indeed, neither law nor politics, neither science nor kinship, nor theology or literature are universally or naturally determined by or predicated on blood, on a figuration or an understanding of blood. It makes as little sense, in other words, to claim that blood is a universal than to say, after Foucault, that sexuality is a universal. At stake is rather the peculiar way in which blood circulates, the way it speaks and is spoken, the way it governs and rules over us—beginning perhaps with the very fact that the conception of a collective body, whether familial, tribal, national, or racial, is, in the Christian West and its historical avatars, massively conceived or figured as consanguinity by way of blood.[33]

Blood is actually a terrible symbol for "race," in its modern sense—of a collection of biological characteristics—since everyone (or nearly everyone) understands very well that genetics has virtually nothing to do with blood.

But more broadly, as a symbol, "blood" does not involve essences of any kind at all. As Anidjar has argued, "Blood . . . is a word. It is merely a name here, a figure, a metonymy," the figure of part for whole. "It is only the name we give to something else, and for some other thing. What is that thing, then?"[34] It clearly isn't some particular characteristic feature. Let's not forget, after all, that "family resemblance" is Wittgenstein's name for groups that are formed without even one particular characteristic feature. The only thing that joins the members of a family (say, "the Jews") is their membership itself, however that has been defined within the collective.

Consider the following statement by Rosenzweig. Once again, at first, it sounds grotesquely and egregiously racist:

> There is only one community in which such a linked sequence of everlasting life goes from grandfather to grandson, only one which cannot utter the "we" of its unity without hearing deep within a voice that adds: "are eternal." It must be a blood community, because only blood gives present warrant to the hope for a future. . . . Only a community based on common blood feels the warrant of eternity warm in its veins even now. . . . Among the peoples of the earth, the Jewish people is "the one people," as it calls itself on the high rung of its life, which it ascends Sabbath after Sabbath. . . . We were the only ones who trusted in blood and abandoned the land; and so, we preserved the priceless sap of life which pledged us that it would be eternal.

> Among the peoples of the world, we were the only ones who separated what lived within us from all community with what is dead.[35]

This paragraph demands some earnest interpretation. First of all, we must attend to the catachresis in Rosenzweig's use of "blood" here, since as I have already mentioned, this is *not* a usage found in premodern Jewish texts, which are wont to refer to "seed" or "flesh" (flesh of my flesh), or even "bone."[36] As Anidjar points out, "Although there may be a deep link between sacrifice and kinship, indeed, between blood and covenant, it is simply a fact that for the Old Testament, flesh and bone—never flesh and blood—signify the basis of the elementary communal bond."[37]

Second, we must attend to the crux whereby Rosenzweig bases the eternality of "blood" precisely and necessarily on renunciation of the land. It is only by renouncing temporal power that any claims for a particular Jewish pith can be posited at all. The intimacy of Jewish genealogical interconnection—as "thick" as that of siblings or lovers, *pace* Appiah—can only be sustained ethically in the renunciation of sovereignty over a particular piece of land. Hence Rosenzweig's absolute rejection of Zionism, "abandoning the land."[38] This is a deep ethical and theological commitment on his part, and not a matter of taste or distaste for power per se. An example may help to see the point. East and Central European Jews have traditionally, at least since the early modern period, made gestures of contempt when passing churches (if no one was looking), a sort of Jewish rebellion. This can be understood as a kind of weapon of the weak but only for the weak, not the strong.[39] Gestures of contempt for non-Jewish places of worship in a Jewish state are, themselves, contemptible and not at all the same thing. In a so-called "Jewish state," paradoxically the performances of Jewish solidarity and intimacy, indeed *Jewissance* itself, must needs be foregone, and we see the bloody results when they are not. Neither Rosenzweig nor Boyarin desire such an end.

On this background, we can begin to understand the difficult passage in Rosenzweig better. Rosenzweig is saying that the substitution of genealogy for compatriotism enables a kind of eternality, precisely because it enables existence without prior essence: a Jew is a Jew is a Jew, not one who believes this or does that, but simply one who is born to a certain people anywhere or has become naturalized into that people. The basis of this existence without prior essence is the withdrawal from a land in favor of a genealogy: for Jews, where you are born does not matter, only to whom.[40] In other words, I argue that for Rosenzweig, the *fact* of genealogy is what confers *Judaite*; all the rest is representation, but the representation must be nurtured to perdure. Another way to say this would be that for Rosenzweig, the Jewishness of a person is determined *on a theological level* by genealogy but *Judaitude* in the sense of content/representations is produced in history.

Benedict Anderson has movingly written of the human desire for continuity, expressed in "links between the dead and the yet unborn," and adding that "the disadvantage of evolutionary/progressive thought is an almost Heraclitean hostility to any idea of continuity." He continues by pointing out that with the sunset of religious modes of thought, other modes of "transformation of fatality into continuity, contingency into meaning" became almost necessary. And Anderson concludes these reflections by declaring that "few things were (are) better suited to this end than an idea of nation."[41] A Jew is not asked whether or not they wish to be a Jew; they are thrown into that condition simply by being born and by bearing. There's no way to stop being Jewish, no escape from Jewishness. No one born Jewish is given a choice not to be Jewish; that is what marks off Jewishness theoretically from Christianness and the very reason that the statement "My parents were Jewish, but I'm not" is so much more startling than "My parents were Christians, but I'm not." There may be various means of getting into a family, including marriage and adoption, but it is very hard to get out of one. The most common way of entering a family is to be born into one, thrown into the world, as it were, always already with these connections that Rosenzweig is noting as being characteristic of Jewishness, marking its difference from Christian thinking in which the infant is an autonomous monad. Rosenzweig scholar Haggai Dagan has compellingly argued that for Rosenzweig, discourse is not rational in the Hegelian sense but narrative/mythic, "paint[ing] a picture," and thus, "according to such interpretation, terms like 'blood' and 'procreation' are part of a picturesque image, an image of self enfolded, a religious, enthusiastic existence."[42] This is what renders Jewry eternal and that at the same time guarantees there is nothing in the essence of Jewish life; phenomenologically (by which I mean as a matter of lived experience), of course Jews can be as bad as other folks sometimes are and as good as the best of humanity without it changing their status as Jews. The Talmud already said this: "An Israelite, even were they to sin, remains an Israelite." Rosenzweig draws this out to a philosophical limit point, writing famously (or infamously), "It [the people of Israel] does not have to hire the services of the spirit; the natural propagation of the body guarantees its eternity," correctly glossed by Dagan as "the Jewish people does not rely upon the spirit [in the Hegelian sense], nor upon intellectual or ethical uniqueness, nor upon one or another mental quality, but upon blood ties and natural procreation alone."[43]

TROUBLE IN PARADIGM

This is not to say that the relocation of the Jews from a place-based to a generation-based, genealogical belonging does not pose problems at the same time that it is powerfully liberating from other kinds of problems. Oppression can shift from external "others" to internal others—for example to "women."[44] The most obvious site where that occurs is exactly the mark of circumcision. That "covenant placed into our flesh," insofar as "flesh" is penises, surely seems to exclude women. The very fact that Jewishness can *only* be conferred by a Jewish mother—only the son of a Jewish mother is to be circumcised, not the son of a Jewish father—carries some powerful counterforce, but, this hardly seems a sufficient response on its own: "This community rooted in blood, is first and foremost the responsibility of the woman, who gives birth, who gives life"[45] is not, of course, any kind of a feminist message or even amelioration. Circumcision, like matrilineal genealogy, is a cultural inscription, a representation, not itself a fact of being, of being "engendered," or even a fact of gender, but that which represents such differences. One who is born a Jew also is born into the community of Jews, the Jewish nation.

Benedict Anderson famously defined nations as imagined communities, but he imagined his imagined communities in space: a family, their neighbors, then the people of the next valley, and then all the valleys all the way to Paris are part of such a community. The Jewish nation is a community imagined in time, not space. It is formed from my connection with my grandmother, to her mother, and hers until I have included all the generations in my imagined community in time all the way back to Mother Sarah (and her consort, Abraham, of course). Unlike a community that is formed in space, which can retain its identity while changing over time, expanding or contracting, what is formed in time exists and retains its identity only by repetition. As anthropologist Engseng Ho puts it, "What matters is that the dispersed understand themselves to be linked by bonds, usually those of kinship. Such bonds exist and endure, rather than atrophying, only so long as people continue to speak, sing, recite, read, write, narrate, and otherwise represent them."[46] For Ho, as for Rosenzweig, as for nearly everyone—the bonds of kinship are taken somehow as the foundations, the object of the representations, more or less as for most who think about it at all, sexual dimorphism (or multimorphism) has been taken as the "biological" ground for gender. Even Rosenzweig's radical and nonracist existentialism is based on the same fundamental structure—the bonds are primary and the representations secondary, almost superstructural.[47] So even though I am with Rosenzweig until this point, I am arguing against Michaels that bonds of kinship need not be racist nor even racialized, even when these bonds are incredibly powerful, for sure in the case of Jews, but also acknowledging that there is a grave difficulty, a rupture in the heart of Rosenzweig's work. This obtains because, as articulated lucidly by Rosenzweig scholar Haggai Dagan: "Rosenzweig attributes great significance to culture and tradition, to ritual and to ways of thinking, even in the case of the uniqueness of the Jewish people. But this does not detract from the definitive nature of what was said above [namely the absolute absence of essence or content in Jewish identity, DB]. Hence, one needs to ask, finally, on the assumption that he was not guided by racism, why Rosenzweig saw fit to emphasize the matter of blood so strongly."[48]

To gloss this, on the one hand Dagan writes compellingly:

> In the context in which these things are stated, blood serves as a metaphor for stability, non-dependence, being gathered in upon oneself. The people are gathered within their own existence. The meaning of redemption for Rosenzweig is that the Jew is cut off from the world that surrounds him. He lives practically within history, but essentially outside of it.[49]

But, on the other hand, as he just confessed as well, Rosenzweig is very devoted to content as well. It may not "detract" from Rosenzweig's insight and insistence that *Judaite* is empty of essence but the two kinds of descriptions do need to be read together, if not reconciled, and the danger—not the necessity but the danger—of falling into racism is always present, especially when one speaks of blood. It is necessary, then, to take our analysis further beyond Rosenzweig and, in the light of some of the most exciting theorization of sex/gender of the last three decades, begin to move into a new direction of theorizing about kinship, generation, and diaspora.

JUDAITE AS PERFORMANCE; OR, *JUDAITUDE*

I want then to move beyond even the radically correct insights of both Rosenzweig and Ho and treat representations as the primary force generating diasporic identities, including the representation that constitutes the imagined community in time, namely kinship. Rather than some kind of biological relationship of consanguinity, I propose that consanguinity is itself the product of representations, keeping well in mind, as anthropologist Paul Rabinow put it so pellucidly now a quarter-century ago, "representations are social facts."[50] Ho himself hints that the very bonds of which he has spoken are depictions—"understand themselves"—but nonetheless seems to imagine a hierarchy between the bonds and the narratives and so forth that sustain them and enliven them, almost as if the bonds are a real thing distinct from the representations. Paralleling or tracking, perhaps, the classic move that Judith Butler made vis-à-vis sex and gender, I suggest that the bonds themselves are always already (as we used to speak) a representation;[51] the ties of kinship that produce the imagined community of the diasporic nation are part and parcel of the representations, produced by the representations and not productive of them. This does not make them fake or invalid, because let us remind again, once more with feeling: representations are social facts.

After introducing the concept in her now-classic *Gender Trouble*,[52] Butler has returned to it frequently, refining and complicating and ramifying the concept. In one fairly recent iteration, she has written helpfully. In one sense, she explains:

> it seems possible to conclude first, that performativity seeks to counter a certain kind of positivism according to which we might begin with already delimited understandings of what gender, the state, and the economy are. Secondly, performativity works, when it works, to counter a certain metaphysical presumption about culturally constructed categories and to draw our attention to the diverse mechanisms of that construction. Thirdly, performativity starts to describe a set of processes that produce ontological effects, that is, that work to bring into being certain kinds of realities or, fourthly, that lead to certain kinds of socially binding consequences.[53]

Unpacking and expounding each of these four points will be, I reckon, quite sufficient—more than sufficient—to lay out the uses of performativity I am making in my move beyond Rosenzweig's "blood and procreation," a move that I mean as a kind of sublimation and not of erasure.

Butler's points one and two challenge the physical, real, or factual existence of a given cultural category, such as gender, and argue for (not demonstrate) their constructedness by human actors. Points three and four, on the other hand, assert that it is the process of repeated performance of certain practices that constitutes the internal sense of belonging to a category and of constructing it socially as a shared and given identity "with binding social consequences." Performativity thus delineates a theory and a process. Following the same analysis, I want to claim here that it is repeated and reiterated performance that produces the internal sense of being a Jew and thus connected particularly (not exclusively) with other Jews and thus constitutes a Jewish diasporic nation. As mentioned before, this move solves—or so I reckon—problems in both Rosenzweig and Engseng Ho. For both of these theorists, we explain now in a different manner how representations (practices) are tied to bonds (of kinship), understanding that the representations produce the bonds and not merely sustain or vivify them. The ties that bind are not lies that bind (although they can be, of course) but rather powerful effects of representations and performances that give rise to the internal—and very powerful—sense of kinship and identity. Kinship and identity themselves function something like the internal movements that, deriving their power from performance, construct gendered senses of selves as well according to Butler.

Encore Butler:

> The point is not simply that such an "effect" is compounded through repetition, but that reiteration is the means through which that effect is established anew, time and again. To understand how this happens more specifically, one would have to, with adequate time, consider the relation between processes of reiteration, re-establishment, and sedimentation in order to sort out the paradox of a process that achieves its effects in both regenerative and accumulative ways.[54]

Precisely. The practices that constitute Jewish identity—and perhaps more broadly ethnic or national identities in general *mutatis mutandis*—consist of the speaking of Jewish languages or the use of markedly Jewish forms of language (Throw Mama from the train—a kiss), modes of walking, body language, telling stories, singing songs, as well as the study of Talmud, practicing the rituals of the holidays, eating this food and not that. The sharing of these repetitious performances are what produces kinship bonds. (In this fashion, once blood is determined as a representation, Jewish kinship bears comparing with or thinking with queer kinship and even queer nationhood.) None of these apply to all Jews, nor need they. At the very beating heart of such narratives, practices, representations, scripts, doings, all the performances that produce *Judaite* and *Judaitude*, is Torah, primarily but not necessarily or only, the study of the Talmud (with all of its ramifications for forms of Jewish speech and speech practices),[55] and the *performance* of the Jewish doings whether or not they are conceived of as divine commandments. As that very Torah itself reminds us: "Forever let a person study the Torah even not for its own sake, for from such study, they will come to study for its own sake."[56]

NOTES

1. This article will appear *mersesem* in suitably expanded form as a chapter in my forthcoming *The No-State Solution: A Jewish Manifesto.* For Wolfson as Rosenzweig-scholar, see Elliot R. Wolfson, *The Duplicity of Philosophy's Shadow: Heidegger, Nazism, and the Jewish Other* (New York: Columbia University Press, 2018), chapter 2; and most recently Elliot R. Wolfson, "Rosenzweig on Human Redemption: Neither Nothing nor Everything, but Only Something," *Journal of Jewish Thought and Philosophy* 29 (2021): 121–50. And there is so much more, so much more, on Heidegger and Hasidism, Kabbalah and kenotic atheology (Elliot R. Wolfson, "Apotheosis of the Nothing in Altizer's Kenotic Atheology," *Journal for Cultural and Religious Theory* 19, no. 1 [2019–20]: 52–84)—and the list of fields in which Wolfson is a grandmaster goes on.
2. This and what follows immediately below has been drawn and quartered from my own recent work arguing these historical points at length: Daniel Boyarin, *Judaism: The Genealogy of a Modern Notion*, Key Words for Jewish Studies (New Brunswick, NJ: Rutgers University Press, 2018).
3. Aamir R. Mufti, *Enlightenment in the Colony: The Jewish Question and the Crisis of Postcolonial Culture* (Princeton, NJ: Princeton University Press, 2007), 10.
4. Mufti, *Enlightenment in the Colony*, 7–8.
5. This usage is not a gesture toward a Miss Piggy–like pretentiousness ("Pretentious? Moi?") but an attempt to coin a non Ashkenazocentric term for *Yiddishkayt,* and there is no word that I know of other than *Yiddishkayt* that carries the sense of all the content and practices of corporate Jewish identity that I need here.
6. For an excellent succinct account of Rosenzweig's unique contribution to a philosophy of "Jewish identity," see Haggai Dagan, "Blood and Myth in the Thought of Franz Rosenzweig," in *Jewish Blood: Reality and Metaphor in History, Religion, and Culture*, ed. Mitchell B. Hart (London and New York: Routledge, 2009), 152–53.
7. "The difference between the two was Zionism. Buber sought to set the people in the space of its land, whereas Rosenzweig sought to plant that blood in the temporal rhythm of a ritual calendar." Zachary Braiterman, cited in Elliot R. Wolfson, *Heidegger and Kabbalah: Hidden Gnosis and the Path of Poiēsis*, New Jewish Thought and Philosophy (Bloomington: Indiana University Press, 2019), 376, n. 152.
8. Cited in Leora Batnitzky, *How Judaism Became a Religion: An Introduction to Modern Jewish Thought* (Princeton, NJ: Princeton University Press, 2011), 3. For more on Scholem and Rosenzweig on language, see Wolfson, *Heidegger and Kabbalah*, 330–33 and especially notes there.
9. For a description of the effects of that self-definition in modernity, see Amnon Raz-Krakotzkin,

"Exile Within Sovereignty: Critique of 'The Negation of Exile' in Israeli Culture," in *The Scaffolding of Sovereignty: Global and Aesthetic Perspectives on the History of a Concept*, ed. Zvi Ben-Dor Benite, Stefanos Geroulanos, and Nicole Jerr (New York: Columbia University Press, 2017), 400–401; and for a fuller (Hebrew) version of his argument, Amnon Raz-Krakotzkin, "Exile Within Sovereignty: Toward a Critique of the 'Negation of Exile' in Israeli Culture," *Theory and Criticism: An Israeli Forum* 4 (Autumn 1993): 23–56; 184–86 (English summary), in Hebrew.

10. For discussion of this point, see now Joel Whitebook, *Freud: An Intellectual Biography* (Cambridge: Cambridge University Press, 2017), 377–80, esp. 380.
11. Ilan Pappe, with whom I am in agreement on so many things, defines "the Jews" as a "religion" with hardly a bit of reflection on that claim and seems, indeed, to believe that the Czechs, Poles, Greeks, as well as the Jews, are either ethnic groups or religions striving to be nations in the nineteenth century (Ilan Pappe, *Ten Myths About Israel* [London: Verso, 2017], 23). He is totally collapsing nation with nation-state, of course. Many of these national groups were seeking cultural autonomy and dignity for their languages, literature, and cultures way before they even imagined, as did the Jewish nation, a nation-state.
12. Ernst Renan, "What Is a Nation," in *Nation and Narration*, ed. Homi K. Bhabha (London and New York: Routledge, 1990), 11.
13. See Gil Anidjar, "Secularism," *Critical Inquiry* 33 (2006): 59, 62.
14. Anidjar, "Secularism," 74.
15. Mufti, *Enlightenment in the Colony*, 51.
16. Max Weinreich, *History of the Yiddish Language*, trans. Shlomo Noble, with the assistance of Joshua A. Fishman, and the editorial assistance of Paul Glasser. Yale Language Series (New Haven: Yale University Press, 2008), 164.
17. Lena Salaymeh and Shai Lavi, "Religion Is Secularized Tradition: The Case of Jewish and Muslim Circumcisions in Germany," unpublished paper (Tel Aviv, 2019). I wish to thank the authors of this paper for providing me access prior to its publication and also to thank them deeply for the paper and its bibliographical references and discussions, which have helped me tremendously in working out the argument of this chapter. For a concise and helpful account of "Judaism" becoming a "religion" in the early modern period, see Batnitzky, *How Judaism* and now Eliyahu Stern, *Jewish Materialism: The Intellectual Revolution of the 1870s* (New Haven: Yale University Press, 2018), 9–10.
18. Even more sharply, they state their objective—which matches mine—"to refine the existing legal-analytical tools for evaluating *how* states discriminate against religious minorities under the doctrine of religious freedom."
19. It should be pointed out for the record that the authors of the essay are careful not to essentialize Protestantism nor to assign it as the only cause for the developments; I would suggest that Protestant thought is the enabling condition rather than cause of the process of secular production of "religion." See the very important essay by Samuel Moyn, which nuances and complexifies these formulas without, I think, discrediting them (Samuel Moyn, "From Communist to Muslim: European Human Rights, the Cold War, and Religious Liberty," *South Atlantic Quarterly* 131 [2014]: 63–86).

20. Opines the court: "The circumcision changes the child's body permanently and irreparably. This change runs contrary to the interests of the child in deciding his religious affiliation later in life" (Alexander Aumüller, "Unofficial Translation of 151 Ns 169/11." https://www.dur.ac.uk/resources/ilm/CircumcisionJudgmentLGCologne7May20121.pdf.) This is factually erroneous, owing to the empirical fact that over the centuries quite large numbers of Jews circumcised on the eighth day have chosen Christianity without let or hindrance. One could, in fact, argue that the sort of religious indoctrination certainly allowed by the Cologne court is a more powerful hindrance to the free choice of religion than circumcision.
21. Salaymeh and Lavi, "Religion Is Secularized Tradition." See the claim made by Saba Mahmood (ךורב הרכז) and Peter Danchin, who argue that "in all modern states we can see a consistent pattern of protecting state-sanctioned traditions or dominant religions and a corresponding insensitivity to and denial of the claims of minority, nontraditional, or unpopular religious groups" (Saba Mahmood and Peter G. Danchin, "Immunity or Regulation? Antinomies of Religious Freedom," *South Atlantic Quarterly* 113, no. 1 [2014]: 154).
22. Of course, at the same time, I would defend the "right" of the grown individual to choose to respond to that thrownness in their own fashion, including the right to convert to Christianity, despite their (when male) circumcised state and even the lack of recognition of such conversion from the (theoretical) Jewish perspective. Interestingly, this seems to be the correct interpretation of *German* law itself, notwithstanding the perverse reasoning of the Cologne court (Bijan Fateh-Maghadam, "Criminalizing Male Circumcision? Case Note: Landgerich Cologne, Judgement of 7 May 2012—No. 151 Ns 169//," *German Law Journal* 13, no. 92012 [2012]: 1131–45.)
23. Cf. Nicholas B. Dirks, "The Policing of Tradition: Colonialism and Anthropology in Southern India," *Comparative Studies in Society and History* 39, no. 1 (1997): 182–212.
24. Immanuel Kant, "Religion Within the Bounds of Bare Reason," 69. https://www.earlymoderntexts.com/assets/pdfs/kant1793.pdf. Kant, of course, operates under the modern and European notion that "political laws" and a church are mutually exclusive entities, the opposition rejected here, a necessary rejection for the further delineation of the Jews as a nation.
25. Daniel Boyarin, "Anna O(Rthodox): Bertha Pappenheim and the Making of Jewish Feminism," *Bulletin of the John Rylands Library,* Special Issue on *Experience, Representation, and Gender* 83, no. 3 (Autumn 1998): 65–87.
26. Zvi Gitelman, ed., *Religion or Ethnicity?: Jewish Identities in Evolution* (New Brunswick, NJ: Rutgers University Press, 2009). For more extended discussion of this issue than I can provide here, see Boyarin, *Judaism.*
27. Franz Rosenzweig, *The Star of Redemption. Translated from the 2d Ed. of 1930 by William W. Hallo* (New York: Holt, Rinehart and Winston, 1971), 342. Prof. Manuel d'Olivera, from whom I learned of this quotation, I think, misreads it when he writes: "There is but a small step between the identification of oneself as the contents of one's belief and the integration of the divine nature intrinsic to that contents that initiates the process of 'self-deification.'" But more on this anon.
28. In support of this reading, see Haggai Dagan who writes, "Rosenzweig does not attempt to conceal this aspect of his thought in his book: 'It [the people of Israel] does not have to hire

the services of the spirit; the natural propagation of the body guarantees it eternity.' All this is stated explicitly: The Jewish people does not rely upon the spirit, or upon its intellectual or ethical uniqueness, or upon one or another mental quality, or even upon tradition or culture, but only upon blood ties and natural procreation" (Haggai Dagan, "The Motif of Blood and Procreation in Franz Rosenzweig," *AJS Review* 26, no. 2 [November 2002]: 244). This is somehow structurally similar to the conclusion of another existentialist that Jews would not exist at all were it not for the hostility of others, antisemitism in short (Jean-Paul Sartre, *Anti-Semite and Jew* [New York: Schocken Books, 1946]). And yet somehow it carries the opposite effect and affect.

29. Mufti, *Enlightenment in the Colony*, 47.
30. Gil Anidjar has tied the blood symbol at its point of origin to war: "War was a consequence of blood and its logical end. It was conducted for blood motives (family and tribe, lust and revenge). It maintained and reproduced itself as the culmination of innumerable and massive instances of blood feuds" (Gil Anidjar, *Blood: A Critique of Christianity*, Religion, Culture, and Public Life [New York: Columbia University Press, 2014], 3).
31. Patricia Williams, "To the North: Race, Migration and Violence in the United States of America," *TLS* 6160 (April 23, 2021): 8.
32. Anidjar, *Blood*, 7.
33. Anidjar, *Blood*, 25–26.
34. Both cites Gil Anidjar, "We Have Never Been Jewish: An Essay in Asymmetric Hematology," in *Jewish Blood: Reality and Metaphor in History, Religion, and Culture*, ed. Mitchell B. Hart, Routledge Jewish Studies Series (London and New York: Routledge, 2009), 37.
35. Rosenzweig, *Star of Redemption*, 298.
36. Anidjar, *Blood*, 44–49.
37. Anidjar, *Blood*, 45.
38. This point was made already in Daniel Boyarin and Jonathan Boyarin, "Diaspora: Generation and the Ground of Jewish Identity," *Critical Inquiry* 19, no. 4 (Summer 1993): 693–725, oddly, or so it seems now, without reference to Rosenzweig.
39. James C. Scott, *Weapons of the Weak: The Everyday Forms of Peasant Resistance* (New Haven: Yale University Press, 1985).
40. Boyarin and Boyarin, "Diaspora."
41. Benedict Anderson, *Imagined Communities: Reflections on the Origin and Spread of Nationalism* (London: Verso, 1983), 11. He, moreover, draws clear distinctions between the nation and the nation-state, writing there as well, "If nation-states are widely conceded to be 'new' and 'historical,' the nations to which they give political expression always loom out of an immemorial past, and, still more important, glide into a limitless future. It is the magic of nationalism to turn chance into destiny." On this distinction I shall have much to say in other parts of the essay cum manifesto in which the present piece will eventually find a home.
42. Dagan, "Blood and Myth," 153.
43. Dagan, "Blood and Myth," 153.
44. Boyarin and Boyarin, "Diaspora."
45. Dagan, "Blood and Myth," 153.

46. Engseng Ho, *The Graves of Tarim: Genealogy and Mobility Across the Indian Ocean*, The California World History Library (Berkeley: University of California Press, 2006), xxii.
47. See, however, Wolfson's arguably more sensitive and nuanced account of Rosenzweig (Wolfson, *Duplicity of Philosophy's Shadow*, 71–73). I believe that our two readings are compatible and surely converge in our judgment that Rosenzweig is not making a racist argument or claim.
48. Dagan, "Motif of Blood," 242.
49. Dagan, "Blood and Myth," 153.
50. Paul Rabinow, "Representations Are Social Facts: Modernity and Post-Modernity in Anthropology," in *Writing Culture: The Poetics and Politics of Ethnography: A School of American Research Advanced Seminar*, ed. James Clifford and George E. Marcus (Berkeley: University of California Press, 1986), 234–61.
51. I want to acknowledge here Dr. Elad Lapidot who has been singularly helpful to me in thinking through these claims as well as much else.
52. Judith Butler, *Gender Trouble: Feminism and the Subversion of Identity*, Thinking Gender (London: Routledge, 1990).
53. Judith Butler, "Performative Agency," *Journal of Cultural Economy* 3, no. 2 (2010): 147–61, https://doi.org/10.1080/17530350.2010.494117.
54. Butler, "Performative Agency," 149.
55. Daniel Boyarin, *A Traveling Homeland: The Babylonian Talmud as Diaspora*, Divinations (Philadelphia: University of Pennsylvania Press, 2015), to be further developed in later chapters of the present manifesto from which this essay has been excerpted.
56. See BT Pesachim 50b. In a sense, then, the convert (or rather the act of conversion) is the "ideal type"—in the Weberian sense—of *Judaite*, because, and only because, it manifests the performativity of Jewish identity explicitly and openly, even celebratorily. The right practices are practiced and the right words said by the right person and the person becomes a Jew by *fait accompli*, by birth and blood, as all us Jews are.

DIVINE ECONOMY

Notes on the Religious Apparatus

HENT DE VRIES

THIS IS THE PROPER PLACE TO ACKNOWLEDGE THE ENORMOUS DEBT OWED to Elliot R. Wolfson by all those who have long been interested in philosophical matters at the intersection of theological traditions, in addition to being steeped in metaphysical and pragmatic questions of both the Continental and analytic variety, while making excursions into critical, cultural, and literary theory; readers whose paths of inquiry have, in many cases, touched upon the immense archives of heterodox or antinomian traditions of mystical thought, the biblical ban on images and idolatry, early Christian clashes regarding iconoclasm, and the negative theology or apophaticism its legacies have continued to inspire. All those who have tried indefatigably to search for the dialectical—or, more fundamentally, economic—resolution of the presumed ineffability of the divine have found resources to draw from in Wolfson's compelling writings. Whether pursued with conceptual (i.e., philosophical), political (i.e., messianic), or aesthetic (e.g., imagistic or rhetorical) means, the resulting aporia is always and everywhere the same, namely a predicament of all predication (discursive and other); a predicament for which not even silence offers a solution per se. For the interested student and scholar, Wolfson's numerous thoughtful books and essays raise as many speculative quandaries as they suggest theoretical, practical, and experiential modes and moods for receiving, addressing, and, perhaps, even answering them. In the following I will claim that this is nowhere clearer than in the way his oeuvre sheds light on the age-old and apt terminology of *oikonomia* (οἰκονομία). The latter might help us to revisit and rethink some of Wolfson's guiding philosophical and ethical concerns, which, if I am not mistaken, revolve around the central challenge of what he sees as the flip side—or shadow—of apophaticism, namely *theomania*.

Literally, theomania connotes the belief—now often considered a mental illness, long after the positive use that Socrates, in Plato's *Phaedros*, had for the term mania—that one is either a god oneself or possessed by an indwelling god. For this syndrome Wolfson sees two potential dangers and simultaneous remedies. The first difficulty or aporia is that theomania, all by itself, is unsustainable and, hence, unstable. In its volatility, it further yields more negative, not to mention nihilistic, than positive tendencies and affects that affect and fundamentally undermine its purity and, hence, the very possibility of its manifestation. The second problem is that theomania by its own all too stringent logic reverts into the equal divinization of its putative opposite, that is, not so much to sacralization but to profanization, so to speak.

Theomania, all by itself, may thus lead to an astounding conclusion, which Wolfson, with reference to the teachings of Rav Kook, calls "the atheistic relativization of theistic belief," while adding:

> If one follows the *via negativa* to its logical conclusion, we come to the paradox of needing to believe categorically in the relative truth of what we know to be untrue. Belief, on this score, would not only encompass unbelief but, paradoxically, would be most fully instantiated as unbelief.[1]

Wolfson goes on to recall a striking passage from Henri Atlan's magnum opus, a diptych entitled *Les étincelles de hazard* (*The Sparks of Randomness*), whose second volume, *The Atheism of Scripture*, rightly observed that the "'personal god' of monotheistic theology is, strictly speaking, the 'ultimate idol' and consequently claimed that 'the only discourse about God that is not idolatrous is necessarily an atheistic discourse. Alternatively, whatever the discourse, the only God who is not an idol is a God who is not a God.'"[2]

Paradoxical, not to say aporetic, as such statements must sound, they correspond to a precise figure of thought that captures a mode of existence and corresponding form of life.

Whether we can speak here of religion and mysticism, theology and ethics, politics or aesthetics—or, instead, choose to use these words with more caution and reluctantly (relegating them, perhaps, to a time when an unquestioned, all too restrictive metaphysics of presence and absence, actuality and potentiality, cause and effect, still held sway over their respective definitions)—the difference matters little. I, for one, prefer to speak here of *a thinking and living in contradictions*, a spiritual practice or exercise of sorts, which espouses an idea of *inexistence* and *impotentiality*, whose unfathomable *virtual* resources and unexpected—and, as Walter Benjamin quipped, "weak messianic"—*force* we would do well not to underestimate, even or especially under so-called modern secular and global postsecular conditions (designations that themselves become increasingly questionable in light of the notions discussed here).[3]

One way of understanding and practicing such paradoxical or aporetic thought and life is by seeing and experiencing it not so much as a direct consequence, but as a reminder or an echo of the Jewish mystical, more precisely Lurianic, "myth" of divine contraction. Known as the *Tzimtzum* (or, in Wolfson's spelling, *Ṣimṣum*), this notion resembles the contours of the New Testament, Christian doctrine of divine *kenosis* and is often cited in conjunction with it. Yet more than suggesting a historical continuity between these distinct motifs, it is important to emphasize their formal similarity and systematic as much as pragmatic relevance. Each of these theologoumena, it seems, serves as a rationale, if not downright explanation, for our freedom to think and to act (and to do so in contradictions, as we said); a freedom that puts limits upon the absoluteness of apophaticism and the resoluteness of theomania, just as it allows us to disavow and distance ourselves from the brute naturalness of things as they are or from the presumed justification of the powers that be, while negotiating a provisional and pragmatic balance and compromise between the extremes these two poles of our experience present. *Tzimtsum* and *kenosis*, then, form part and parcel of the *economy*, which is premised on the divine's self-restraint and self-diminution or self-emptying, which opens onto a quasi-providential but in essence unpredictable, contingent and occasionalist, messianic and miraculous, eschatological and apocalyptic—and, hence, by and large ungovernable—logic or illogic of history as we know it or as it appears to us *prima facie*. Such alternative account contrasts with, in other words, dialectically negates and normatively invalidates the straightforward conceptions of History (with a capital "H") that pretend to offer grand narratives, ideologies based on larger metaphysical and theologico-political schemes of things, appealing *either* to the teleology, linear progression, and asymptotic approximation of a providential or Promethean endgame *or* resigning in defeatist and quietist cyclical or also dualist—that is, gnostic and Manichean—conceptions and practices that provide no way out, no matter what happens. By contrast, a largely negatively operating metaphysical critique, accompanied by a deep and resolute pragmatics, revolutionizes the scene and not just in the spirit. Seeing and setting all things aright, it snaps out of a fateful return and repetition of the self-same. Instead, the alternative vision and practice lets "a hundred flowers blossom and a hundred schools of thought contend," and this well beyond the original meaning and intention behind the Maoist mantra. The reason is that—as a life in contradictions—it cannot presume to be conclusive, much less to resolve all things by one stroke or without ambiguity or without remaining paradox, indeed, aporia. If any such salutary result or eventual outcome there is (which, for metaphysical and pragmatic reasons, we cannot and ought not exclude), it will be unplanned and quite certainly undeserved.

In the spiritual experience thus conceived and exercised, a simple, if difficult to conceptualize "truth" (in Martin Heidegger's lingo, an "unconcealment [*Unverborgenheit*]") is surreptitiously at work. When and where it is expressed and realized, such "truth" is not merely conveyed (i.e., witnessed and testified to) but also distorted (i.e., inevitably misunderstood and falsely idolized). What results is the paradoxical or, again, aporetic impression rather than clear and distinct insight that "concealment is the cause of disclosure and disclosure the cause of concealment."[4] It is an intuition that Wolfson renders as follows in rigorous philosophical terms, drawn in large part from Heidegger but veering also significantly beyond the ontology and phenomenology, metaphysics and method that the latter borrowed from Edmund Husserl and radically renewed, starting with *Sein und Zeit* (*Being and Time*) and ending with the later "thought of Being," whose "gift" may have been less generous and more limited than its author pretended:

> Translated phenomenologically, every appearance of the infinite is a nonappearance—the nonapparent cannot appear except as inapparent—whence it follows that

> the infinite is present in the world to the degree that it is absent from the world; indeed, the infinite light is present precisely as that which is absent, not as a presence presently absent nor as an absence absently present, but as the absent presence that continuously withdraws in the spectacle of its present absence.[5]

One need not necessarily agree with the language of "cause" here (as in "the cause of disclosure" and "the cause of concealment")[6] to fully appreciate the deeply metaphysical insight and pragmatic realization that "the infinite" does not *translate* and, hence, in a double sense of that term, also *betray* itself otherwise. What is important to note is that the divine, in its very revelation or also dissimulation—and, as we will see, fundamental as well as political economy—de facto and de jure proves itself to "be" a potentially poisonous no less than salutary or unambiguous gift or mode of giving. As Wolfson observes, Heidegger may have inadvertently signaled as much since his later thought is premised on "giving the gift ungiven," thus hesitating to go all the way and limiting his original ontological intuition and its revealing potentiality in a restrictive economy of sorts. Yet in saying as much, we also acknowledge the incontrovertible fact that the actual status of all things nowhere acquires the ontological stability that would so much as allow us to identify it as such. As a consequence, not merely ontic and empirical or historical matters, but also metaphysical questions regarding existence and essence—to the very extent that they claim fixity and structural constants or features (categories, existentials [*Existenzialien*]), respectively—are thereby rendered moot. To resort to their concepts and reasonings is, from here on, hypothetical and pragmatic, rhetorical and strategic. Whatever their nominal worth or currency, they have no *fundamentum in re*.

What emerges, on Wolfson's account is a "meta-ontological" thought and practice of "abandonment," whose further explication he undertakes with the help and, in part, against the tradition to which not only the mystical treatises of Kabbalah, but also, more indirectly, Heidegger's pathways belong, each in their singular, incomparable manner. Indeed, each, on Wolfson's extensive reading, serves as a compelling as much as contested model of inquiry not just of "infinity" and its divine economy, but also and, perhaps, more importantly of the "nihility" that surrounds, pervades, and exceeds their messianico-mystical and theopolitical archives and references, thereby circumventing, destabilizing, and "overcoming" their respective tendencies toward "theomania" and its dangers.

BETWEEN AND BEYOND UNRESTRICTIVE UNIVERSALISM AND EXCLUSIONARY PARTICULARISM

Against this background and, it should be said, with far more philological rigor and historical erudition than many illustrious predecessors engaging the tortuous subject in question (Otto Pöggeler, Marlène Zarader, Jacques Derrida, Jean-François Lyotard, Giorgio Agamben, and Donatella di Cesare, to mention just a few), Wolfson has cast new light on the relationship between Heidegger's ontology, phenomenology, hermeneutics, and "thinking of Being" (genetivus subjectivus and objectivus), on the one hand, and the intricate legacy of the Hebrew tradition—and, hence, not merely Christian scriptures—on the other. More specifically, he has expanded this ongoing elucidation—a genuine *Auseinandersetzung*, in Heidegger's jargon, if ever there was one—deep into the domain of the Jewish messianicio-mystical and esoteric tradition, notably Kabbalah.

This further exploration and extrapolation is all the more urgent and no less fraught with difficulty, compared to Heidegger's own—at times profound and extensive, then more opportunistic and episodic—engagements with so-called originary Christianity, medieval scholasticism, Lutheran Protestantism, even Daoism and Buddhism, precisely because of this author's undeniable, deliberate, and active involvement with the ideology and movement of National Socialism. The difficulty in question has been aggravated even more by the latter's more isolated, if blatant, antisemitic remarks, which are as shocking and have come to light nowhere more painfully than in the posthumous publication, ordered by Heidegger himself, of the *Schwarze Hefte* or *Black Notebooks*, which have eradicated much of the remaining goodwill in terms of ethical and political judgments regarding this author, and this even among his most ardent readers and sympathetic interpreters.

Wolfson's *The Duplicity of Philosophy's Shadow*: *Heidegger, Nazism, and the Jewish Other*, next to his magnum opus *Heidegger and Kabbalah*: *Hidden Gnosis and the Path of Poiesis*, and *Giving Beyond the Gift*: *Apophasis and Overcoming Theomania* are, in my view, among the very best treatments of the inescapable and painstaking task of contemporary thinking as it pursues a principally unlimited, *unrestrictive universalism* vis-à-vis the absolute or absolutes, on the one hand, while avoiding, indeed, combating the spiritual and political dangers of a limiting and de facto *exclusionary particularism*, on the other. In Wolfson's words, it is the "ethnolinguistic enrootedness" underlying the "invocation of historical destiny" tied to a land and soil, if not blood—moreover, in Heidegger's peculiar case, a form of relentless "Germanism"—which has proven fatal, indeed, lethal in the intellectual and political legacy of the West.[7]

Yet this stern and fair judgment should not seduce us to choose complacency and ignore the undiminished lessons to be learned from Heidegger's thought altogether. The latter, on Wolfson's careful reading, is in most of its basic concepts and phenomenological descriptions, which prepare an "enlightenment" and "elucidation" not just of thought but of existence and agency, strictly speaking, "neither defensible nor disposable."[8] In this, it should be noted, it shares the fate and no less lethal legacy of much of the broader and, at times, deeper *metaphysical* archive of Western (and that means, for Heidegger, Greek and to a lesser extent Roman or Latin) thought. The latter tradition has been the resource and repository that made Heidegger's own thinking—like that of so many others before, besides, and after him—possible and, perhaps, necessary or unavoidable to begin with.

An equally undeniable aspect and potentially pernicious element of this same fatefulness is this Western tradition's seemingly intractable *religious* and *theological* signature, not to say nature or essence. This signature registers and imprints the immemorial echoes and effects of an inexhaustible, indeed unfathomable archive, whose even deeper hold over us may—or may not—lose its tenacious grip over our captive minds one fine, if also terrible, day. When and where this happens, its guiding axioms and concepts, figures and common places will have become "optional" and no longer be our "default," while, at the same time, bestowing on us even more daunting responsibilities and political challenges than we thought we must meet and master already.

SEEING AND SEEING THINGS ARIGHT

In the remainder of this contribution, I would like to expand—and, perhaps unwisely, double down—on this, at first glance, somewhat counterintuitive and, come to think of it, massive, perhaps excessive claim. I mean the contention that virtually every theoretical and critical term we have been using in scholarly as well as political and everyday discourse, even or especially under so-called modern and presumably secular conditions is *deep down* or *ultimately* of a theological or theologico-political nature. To claim as much is to imply that "religion" and, up to a point, as we will see, the "sacred" and its accompanying notion of "sacrifice" continue to cast their light and shadow on the thinkable and doable. Yet, that they do this to such an extent that even our intentional negation, denial, or resolute destruction of its most entrenched traditions and legacies still, unwittingly, continues to stand under their very aegis. This is one of the reasons why the designation "postsecular" holds as little promise in establishing clarity as its counterpart, "the secular."

The presumed "overcoming" of the theological or the religious—and, notably, their inherent tendency toward "theomania"—is, on this view, *still* or *yet again* theological and religious in its very nature, concept, and strategy (and, perhaps, even more so). Fighting off the violence of the sacred, exposing it not merely to enlightened (if, historically and intellectually, largely failed) forms of secularization but to a more relentless "profanation," as has been advocated by a host of contemporary thinkers, therefore, necessarily fails to do the trick (i.e., liberate all from superstition and the like). In fact, the very act of "overcoming," like that of "mediation" or even "mitigation," perpetuates and indirectly justifies what it aims to put into question and out of business (bringing thought and practices, subjects and objects, back into greater or renewed circulation, ending their fixation and separation, as it were). Indeed, even the purportedly radical and critical move directed against the historical legacies of theology and religion leaves much, even most, just as it is: a torn, internally split, divided, and unequal world. Yet the latter is only *seen for what it is* and *set aright* if it is, at once, abstractly theorized in resolute and largely negative metaphysical terms and practically as well as pragmatically engaged. Under present conditions, at least (if this was not, in fact always, the case), such theorization and pragmatics must intuit and broach the phenomenal appearance of all things under two aspects or from two angles *at a minimum*. For, paradoxically, only a dual optics and ditto orientation will allow thought and action to take a *maximal* effect on "life" and, it is hoped, on "fate."

I would now like to make that clear by briefly discussing an author, Giorgio Agamben, whose work I have long held at bay, even though many traits of his thinking touch upon unresolved questions that resemble my own. Agamben, incidentally, is also an occasional reference for Wolfson in his magnum opus,[9] notably at the very juncture at which the *nameless infinite* in the medieval and modern Jewish mystical tradition as well as in more recent articulations of thinking and practice—that is, under the Kabbalistic name of *Ein Sof* or, for that matter, that of the later Heidegger's construct of *Seyn*—is postulated as an elusive, counterfactual, and near-virtual being.

Speaking of "being" is problematic enough, as in these mystical and philosophical pursuits the legacy of traditional metaphysical language and thought is deeply contested, such that the spiritual inquiry and practice, in its very "thinking of Being," ventures "outside the ontological economy,"[10] as Wolfson says. Yet thinking of "being" and doing so "beyond the ontological economy" boils down to postulating and, perhaps, experiencing an *inexistence*, so to speak. Assuming this is possible and can be pursued as a theoretical and practical, indeed spiritual exercise of sorts, at what *price* does it come (conceptually and normatively, that is, discursively and pragmatically speaking)? A preliminary matter to resolve in so much as raising this broader question is the problem of definition, namely: how to conceive "economy" (as in: divine or ontological economy) and this not only in philological and philosophical terms, but also and especially in view of its wider ethical and political ramifications?

Now, economy can be seen as a *category* and *apparatus*, an element and a device, for language and thought, agency and judgment, structures and systems, whose inevitably discursive mediations, social adaptations as well as communicative mediatizations require a stringent and replicable form or format. The latter alone allows them to give *actual* presence to the—in principle, if not de facto—infinite variety of modes and moments, modalities and moods without which the *virtual* archive (resource and repository) of all we may yet aspire to would not come to life. Unless the *inexistent* is betrayed, that is, conveyed, translated, and thereby transformed, it cannot enter into our individual and collective ways of existence or living.

What, then, might lie beyond and remain "outside" this broadly defined—"ontological"—economy, if not the *divine* economy, that is, the undelimited, if indelible, ways in which it *economizes* (i.e., gives as much as it withholds) *itself*? After all, the divine, in this view, exceeds and retreats behind the very "bounds of sense" that it, economically—must impose to begin with. This, nothing else, is the predicament of its predication, discursive and other, without which it could not so much as even enter, let alone steer, create, and redeem this world, phenomenologically, materially, and spiritually speaking.

A GENEALOGY OF ECONOMY

Agamben's essay "*Che cos'è un dispositivo*?" or "What Is an Apparatus?," in the brief span of some twenty sparsely filled pages, presents itself as a quasi-philological footnote to a central concept and idea widely *used*, if, as we will see, not exactly coined or introduced, by the later Michel Foucault, namely that of *le dispositif* (meaning "apparatus" or also "construction," "machinery," "device," and "deployment"). Yet the essay is programmatic in the context of Agamben's own extensive body of work and, in my eyes, highly instructive beyond the presumed direct and indirect theoretical aims formulated in the writings of Foucault with which it takes issue here, if only to *deepen* and *broaden* or *generalize* them to an extent that the latter might not have endorsed. Moreover, it is in and through Agamben's own extrapolation *in extremis* of Foucault's concept of apparatus that the historical and contemporary concept and practice of "religion"—taken here as the very first and, perhaps, last mediation or medium of tradition and, indeed, all ontology—enters the fray unexpectedly. To the extent that the concept of religion is encountered here, first of all, in theological terms, one suspects that the short text offers nothing short of a theologico-political rather than, say, bio-political rethinking of the intellectual, normative, and governmental justifications, institutions, and organizations with which the West has shored up the powers that be (offering them a categorical and instrumental backup and ideological imaginary, as it were).

The apparatus, for all purposes, is seen, just as it serves as, a religious or, in Agamben's characterization, "sacred" and "sacrificial" category, whose eventual undoing—in his terms, its "profanation"—is never fully assured, perhaps not even possible. With Wolfson's suspicion of theomania firmly in mind, one might wonder whether "profanation's" ultimate goal, namely the relentless eradication of religion's tendency to set itself aside and apart, is not merely the flip side of the sacred and of sacrifice thus defined. The pure act of profanation and the purity of a world "without religion" toward which it tends would be a form of theomania *in reverse*, the postulation and celebration of a transcendental signified, of sorts, which eludes further drift and contamination of its meaning and use.

While religion reveals itself, on Agamben's reading, as epitomizing and itself caught in the very *predicament of all predication*, discursive and other, indeed, as the *organon of all organization*, through the ways in which it not just conveys but ipso facto betrays or reframes the meaning and force of all "life," including "bare life" itself, this fate and determination does not mark its end. For this reason, Agamben's insistence on "profanation" does not have the last word. On the contrary, when all is said and done and his archaeology of power as well as genealogy of economy has taken its course, some sort and *form*, if not content, of religion—a "true religion [*vera religio*]," in his own words—may well be the sole salutary remedy for and *way out* of the captivity of all thought. And the latter regards not only speaking and writing, but also the very agency and judgment that it instructs or imposes and that impresses itself upon concepts and words, in turn. Not even silence, much less so-called performative gestures and perlocutionary effects, ever truly escape this *economic* regimen.

Yet neither the Foucauldian understanding of the "apparatus" nor that of the "archive" and its "archaeology" (developed in the third and fourth chapters of the latter's *L'archéologie du savoir* [*The Archaeology of Knowledge*])—nor, for that matter, Agamben's sympathetic retrieval of these historically and philologically related concepts—fully exhaust the *near-metaphysical depth* as well as *deep pragmatic* relevance of the virtual repository of the absolute, immemorial and, so far, irretrievable past. By the same token, these authors, I would claim, do not fully fathom the thus far irreducibly torn, that is, divided and unequal, nature of the present. As a consequence, they also leave the existence—or, rather, *inexistence*—of, as of yet, imaginable possibilities, challenges, and opportunities of the future undiscussed.

The argument in "What Is an Apparatus?" and its surrounding and supporting texts seems straightforward. If all religion is mediation, which implies mediatization; moreover, if, conversely, all mediation is, in its essence or formal nature, also religious (as Agamben will claim, identifying religion with "sacralization" and "sacrifice" or setting apart, first and foremost), then to *think* and *act* beyond such mediation, mediatization, and their inherent pitfalls—seeking to avoid or mollify the very predicament of their predication (discursive and other)—comes down to *secularizing* or, rather, *profaning* all speech and action, judgment and imagining, organizing and administering (or, indeed, governing). But can we ever pretend or so much as hope to succeed in doing so, overcoming the apparatus's religious and theologico-political underpinnings and, instead, be "absolutely modern" (as Arthur Rimbaud mused) or, at least, "contemporary" (as Agamben claims for his part)? Should we try as much, if we could? Or is "religion" the name not merely for the very *first* but also for the very *last* mediation and as such a "mediation" (concept or figure or gesture) that presumably does away with the medium and mediatization—that is, the apparatus—altogether, once and for all? The latter ambition, it seems, would restore once more a form of theomania, to cite again Wolfson's term.

POSITIVE RELIGION

Agamben's short text revolves around his understanding of Foucault's apparent rediscovery of the historical term and idea of *le dispositif* or *apparatus*, a "decisive technical term in the strategy of Foucault's thought,"[11] as he calls it, and a term that emerges notably in his writings and lectures on "governmentality" from the mid- and late 1970s onward. In a philological tour de force, Agamben relates this concept not only back to the original use of the word "positivity [*Positivität*]" in G. W. F. Hegel's earliest theological writings, notably *Die Positivität der christlichen Religion*. Interestingly, he also inscribes this technical term into a much older Christian theological and ecclesial archive—or, more in particular, Trinitarian idiom—of which Foucault may or may not have been fully aware when he first introduced the technical term (*dispositif*, apparatus) in his aforementioned writings and lectures. The term and concept would soon receive a defining and regulatory place in his archaeology of the human sciences as well as in the general method of genealogy he devised for it. In fact, the term encapsulates at a minimum what Foucault's guiding concepts of *episteme* and *historical a priori* intend and engage far more broadly. Or so it seems. In fact, as I will show, the Christian Trinitarian theologoumenon in question, premised as it is on an incarnational and a providential logic—regarding the creation, revelation, and redemption—of all things, may well hold sway over the mention and use of Foucault's and, in his footsteps, Agamben's fundamentally philosophical categories.

The reference to Hegel, Agamben suspects, comes via Jean Hyppolite, who, by Foucault's own admission, was his "master" during his studies at the École Normale Supérieure, rue d'Ulm, in the 1940s and 1950s, and whose chair at the Collège de France he would eventually inherit in 1969.[12] The motif, Agamben further adds, may have been drawn from Hyppolite's *Introduction à la philosophie de l'histoire de Hegel* (Part Three, entitled "*Raison et histoire: Les idées de positivité et de destin*").[13] If this is correct, a direct and indirect reference to the early fathers of the Christian church enters Foucault's texts from an even greater historical distance, more precisely from what is, in fact, a long forgotten, repressed, and fundamentally misunderstood past and archive that Agamben begins to unearth and revisit here and elsewhere. As he explains, at the time of writing *The Archeology of Knowledge*, published in 1969, Foucault still used the Hegelian terminology of "*positivité*"—"an etymological neighbor of *dispositif*"[14]—albeit without providing much of a definition. We would have to wait until a much later interview, published in 1977 under the title "The Confession of the Flesh," which was republished in the volume *Power and Knowledge*, to find a somewhat concise response to the question as to what the terminology of *dispositif* or "apparatus" actually means. More specifically, Foucault here also addresses what methodological function the term might actually fulfill within the context of the larger project of an archaeology of the human sciences that he had begun to undertake. In Foucault's words:

> What I am trying to single out with this term [i.e., *dispositif*] is, first and foremost, a thoroughly heterogeneous *set* consisting of discourses, institutions, architectural forms, regulatory decisions, laws, administrative measures, scientific statements, philosophical, moral, and philanthropic propositions—in short, the said as much as the unsaid. Such are the elements of the apparatus. The apparatus itself is the *network* that can be established between these elements.[15]

In other words, although this distinction is not always made in full rigor, the "elements" of the apparatus are not the apparatus itself, the relation between them—that is, their mediation, mediatization, even medium; more specifically, their "thoroughly heterogeneous set" or "network"—is!

This broad definitional characteristic does not prevent Agamben's reading of Foucault from making a much broader (if, in my view, also weaker) claim, which is that every apparatus is both de jure and de facto a quid pro quo. Every individual apparatus is, as it were, a nonsynonymous substitution for—an instantiation as well as obfuscation of—a more original relation, whose "set" or "network" it not only continues and strengthens but also makes us forget and no longer question. Fundamentally, then, the apparatus is a *setting apart* or *separating out* of a putative singular, unique, and unified meaning, intent, and purport; a "separation," whose fetishization and commodification, representation and repetition, and eventual generalization and universalization Agamben associates with an act of "sacralization." Paradoxically, it is this very act and gesture of sacralization that deemphasizes, indeed, *sacrifices* everything else. Only the counteracting gesture of "profanation," as we saw, corrects or undoes that trend.

For Hegel, in Agamben's rendition, "positivity"—as in "positive religion" and distinguished from so-called "natural religion" (which, he recalls, expresses "the immediate and general relation of human reason with the divine")—had designated "the set of beliefs, rules, and rites that in a certain society and at a certain historical moment are imposed on individuals."[16] Positivity connoted "the historical element—loaded as it is with rules, rites, and institutions that are imposed on the individual by an external power, but that become, so to speak, internalized in the systems of beliefs and feelings."[17] As Hyppolite had noted, for Hegel, what was central was the dialectic between "pure reason" and "the historical element." After all, the latter *constrains* and (in the dialectical idiom) *negates* the former, but, more significantly, thereby also *robs it of its mere abstraction*, in the process of which Spirit "adapts to the concrete richness of life."[18] This, one might say, is precisely how the divine economy of Spirit, in Hegel's conception, "overcomes" the tendentially empty formalism and existential as well as political risk of theomania (given with religion or, perhaps, "natural religion" as such).

In Hegel's own view, the positivity of religion emerged and gained prominence only "in modern times [*in neuern Zeiten*]." As opposed to natural religion, which is presumed to be "one," because there is only one "human nature," the concept of positive religion implies multiplicity. Moreover, positive religion can be "counter- or supra-natural" and contains notions that exceed the understanding and reason, just as it summons feelings and actions that are not according to human nature, but rooted in fixtures that are violently produced and conducive to actions that follow a structure of command and obedience, not that of "proper interest [*eigenes Interesse*]."[19]

Positivity, thus defined, stands *opposed to vain subjectivity*, with which Agamben will precisely come to associate it, while taking exception only with the "larval," if "indestructible" remnant of subjectivity whose "humbler, simpler form of life" and "vital experience—which is always and simultaneously corporeal *and* spiritual"—is under constant attack. As he puts it, subjectivity, in the historical process, has been "broken into a purely biological entity, on the one hand, and a social, cultural, and political existence, on the other."[20] One is tempted to hear in this diagnosis of a alienating split—a separation, which Agamben will come to identify as nothing short of a "schizophrenia" under modern conditions—a distant echo of Hegel's earlier differentiation between "natural" and "positive" religion (without any nostalgia for the "pure" or "bare" form of "life" that presumably and inevitably has been lost).

In adopting the Hegelian motif and understanding of "positivity," on Agamben's reading, Foucault gained deeper insight into a problem that had become very much his own, namely "the relation between individuals as living beings and the historical element"; a relation expressed through "processes of subjectivation," that is, through "rules" and "institutions" in which "power relations" acquire "concrete modes."[21] For Foucault,

Agamben goes on to explain, the term "*dispositif*"—translating Hegel's and Hyppolite's sense of "positivity"—replaced the reference to abstract "universals [*les universaux*]," notably of state and law, sovereignty and power. Yet the term continued to hint at a decisive *enabling* and *structuring* role, which its ultimate referent, if one can say so, played as part of a broader series of different processes, captured by other "operative concepts with a general character" equally distinct from abstract generality (the "historical a priori" and "episteme" figuring prominently among them):

> Apparatuses [Agamben writes] are, in point of fact, what take the place of the universals in the Foucauldian strategy: not simply this or that police measure, this or that technology or power, and not even the generality obtained by their abstraction. Instead, . . . an apparatus is "the network that can be established between these elements."[22]

According to "What Is an Apparatus?" and, more extensively, his *The Kingdom and the Glory*, we cannot theorize or rethink the *dispositif* without acknowledging the *historical continuity*—perhaps the *structural analogy* and *formal equivalence* or, rather, *resemblance*—between the archaeological and genealogical approach to knowledge and power that Foucault proposes, on the one hand, and the unmistakable, minimally *religious, theological,* and one is tempted to add, *metaphysical* register, on the other. The latter's "weak" and "modal" ontological aspects and "potentialities"—as forms of *inexistence* rather than present actuality—can nonetheless not be ignored.[23]

The *pragmatic* significance of the term "apparatus" becomes especially clear, Agamben argues, if we look into one of its further historical *philosophical* precursors, which is the Greek word and concept of *oikonomia* (οἰκονομία), next to the subsequent *theological* appropriation and reinterpretation of its meaning in the early Christian church. For *oikonomia* connotes not only the "administration" or "management" of the "*oikos*" (the household) but also—witness Aristotle's *Politics* (1255 b21)—a "praxis" or "a practical activity that must face a problem and a particular situation each and every time."[24] This said, this pragmatic use of the concept was given a theological or theologico-political backup and reorientation by early Christian theologians. Agamben mentions Tertullian, Irenaeus, Hippolytus, and Clement of Alexandria and goes on to note that they "slowly got accustomed to distinguishing a 'discourse—or *logos*—of theology' and a '*logos* of economy.' *Oikonomia* became thereafter an apparatus through which the Trinitarian dogma and the idea of a divine providential governance of the world were introduced into the Christian faith."[25]

In fact, although Agamben doesn't say so in "What Is an Apparatus?," this historical differentiation and, it seems, bifurcation between "theology" and "economy" may well have echoed, accompanied, and reinforced an even earlier distinction within the Aristotelian corpus and notably his *Metaphysics* itself. The distinction in question is that between "potency/in-potency" (or *dunamis*/*dunameis*) and "act/in-act" (or *energeia*/*energeiai*) that would give way, in medieval theology and early modern political theory, to a fundamental understanding of divine sovereignty as divided—and, one might say, held out—between God's absolute power (or *potestas absoluta*) and His delegated or ordained power (or *potestas ordinata*);[26] an at once radical and subtle differentiation that withholds full or unreserved divine identification and justification just as much as it transmits and transposes, diffuses and disseminates the latter, thus at once invalidating and validating all that exists and the powers that be with a double gesture, a dual optics (i.e., giving abstractly and also concretely, with a "giving beyond the gift" that withholds even more than it dispenses already).

In sum, the *dispositif* would be nothing less than the mediation and negotiation between absolute and delegated or ordained power, between *potestas absoluta* and *potestas ordinata*, the two key concepts and separate, if analogically, related realms that informed and, more importantly, formed the early modern understanding of sovereignty, of nations and states as well as the subjects and citizens of (and by) which they are made up.[27] Interestingly, this distinction between the two concepts of power echoes the differentiation between *God as He is in and for Himself* (i.e., absolutely), on the one hand, and *God as He governs the world* in a vicarious (i.e., indirect) manner, on the other.

THE SCHISM BETWEEN BEING AND ACTION

With this established, Agamben's essay has sketched out the first conceptual part of a much larger philological and archaeological, philosophical and political project whose original type of inquiry and interpretative method is described as "a theological genealogy of economy and government."[28] "For a Theological Genealogy of Economy and Government" is the subtitle of *The Kingdom and the Glory* and captures an agenda of research continued in works such as *Opus Dei: An Archaeology of Duty* and *The Use of Bodies: Homo Sacer IV, 2*. The extremely complex details of and theological reasons for this "divine economy" need not occupy us here. They concern the internal relationship of the persons making up the Trinity, namely God the Father, God the Son, and God the Holy Spirit. But they also entail the relationship between creation, redemption, and salvation and, hence, lay out the whole gamut of an at once "divine providential" and "redemptive governance,"[29] enabled, first of all, by Christ's incarnation and the union of his two natures, as codified by the famous councils of the early church (notably in Nicaea in 325 CE and in Chalcedon in 451 CE) and reaffirmed throughout much of the medieval and early modern periods of Scholasticism and the Protestant Reformation. Yet traces of it can also be found in by now classical studies as diverse as Ernst Kantorowicz's *The King's Two Bodies*, Carl Schmitt's *Politische Theologie I & II*, Erik Peterson's *Theological Tractates*, and, lest we forget, Karl Marx's *Das Kapital.*

Suffice it to note here that the Greek *oikonomia* was rendered by the Latin fathers of the church as *dispositio* or *dispensatio* and that, for Agamben, this translation inaugurates a crucial distinction—nothing short of a certain "fraction, "caesura," and, indeed, "schizophrenia"—between *God's "being" in and for Himself* (i.e., in His "nature" or "essence"), on the one hand, and His *"action" in the phenomenal world* (i.e., in His "operation," that is, "governance" and "administration" of creaturely affairs), on the other.[30] Again, this differentiation, if not separation (itself the most religious, theological, and theologico-political aspect of *oikonomia* thus defined and translated) reflects or comes down to that between *potestas absoluta* and *potestas ordinata*.

Against this historiographical and philological background, it is important to further add that term *oikonomia* and then also *dispositio* and *dispensatio* (which, again, in Hyppolite's and Foucault's hands will become the *dispositif* or apparatus) highlights the (at a minimum) analytical distinction between "ontology" (here: the logics or ideality and potentiality of God's "being") and "praxis" (here: the normative aspect or actuality and pragmatic reality of His "agency"). The divine economy and the transposition of its formal schema onto the modern apparatus, on this account, thus regulate the separation as well as relation between, say, *mystic disengagement*, on the one hand, and *active engagement*, on the other. In a more technical idiom, they cover the respective *exitus* and *redditus* or, in my preferred idiom, they qualify the subsequent moments and modalities of *snapping out* and *zooming in*, whose conceptual distinction and separation, but also alternation and imbrication, has animated and haunted much Western intellectual and political culture. It has done so ever since religious scriptures, including the mystico-theological edifices built upon them, intuited and spelled out the open-ended dialectic between openness and closure, dynamism and statics, to use Henri Bergson's terminology in his *Les deux sources de la morale et de la religion* (*The Two Sources of Morality and Religion*). The initial form or format that mediation and mediatization took is that of *oikonomia* in the Greek and more specifically Patristic sense of the word, but, as said, more recent, even contemporary adaptations and transformations of the model abound and offer a key to understanding and evaluating how meaning- and world-making cannot but operate or, indeed, must be recast and reimagined or revolutionized such that the ancient-modern logic and law of "operativity" loses its—historically, institutionally, and politically—ever tightening grip, its repetition of the same and of the force of immanence (with its particularistic and generalized myths and built-in inequalities, injustices, and the like).

With Hegel, Agamben recognizes the dangers of enshrining the mediation between heaven and earth in one instant or instance—notably, the nature and person of Christ—alone. The one first and last mediation, for Agamben as for Hegel, is, therefore, not so much the individual Christ the Son, nor for that matter God the Father, or even Holy Spirit, but "religion," seen now under its dual aspect or even caesura of its positive and natural features (i.e., *religio* or, as Spinoza would have added, *superstitio*), on the one hand, and true religion (i.e., again, in Spinoza's idiom, *vera religio*), on the other. The metaphysical and pragmatic mediation—paradoxical and aporetic as it must remain, at least as long as History, as we know it, runs its nightmarish course—is that of *oikonomia*. The latter, we may extrapolate, keeps the unattractive alternatives of mythical immanence and theomanic transcendence—each of them individually and together in their sought after, if potentially fatal, communion—*in* and *off* balance.

And yet, if the ontotheological basis of the divine economy, its *providential* order and, by simple extension, the modern secular or Promethean version of this Patristic apparatus is to be found, as Agamben also claims, in a vaguely *analogical* continuity (rather than strict opposition, "caesura," schism or "schizophrenia") between the three registers of Trinitarian logic and everything they have since come to stand for, what then is the exact ground for his deeply pessimistic—near-Gnostic or Manichean—diagnosis of the apparatus's totalitarian grip on nearly every form of life, if not "life" or "bare life" as such?

There is a silent axiom that informs Agamben's text and that finds no analogy in (indeed, on his reading seems completely absent from) Trinitarian thinking. It is the assumption that, unlike the differentiation between God the Father and God the Son, in divine *oikonomia*, the posttheological, secular, or modern apparatus "designates that in which, and through which, one realizes a pure activity of governance devoid of any foundation in being."[31]

The broadly economic activity of government and administration is "pure," one presumes, because there is nothing that carries, justifies, or warrants its process and outcome. It is, in other words, not merely phenomenal; it is the essence, the metaphysical techne of all that there is, without any further, original or ulterior metaphysical backup that could give us any founded—necessary or so-called sufficient—reason to put it in question and "out of business," bring it to a halt, as we somehow sense or feel we must.

Earlier, Agamben had spoken of a "fracture that the theologians had sought to avoid by removing it from the plane of God's being."[32] Call it the fracture between God as creator and His creation as fallen and finite, which the doctrine of divine providence and, hence, economy aimed to put back into one single frame, as part of one operation, the operation of the One. Yet the fracture, Agamben continues, "reappeared in the form of a caesura that separated in Him [i.e., God] being and action, ontology and praxis,"[33] even as the medieval, early modern, late modern, and contemporary results of this partition were simply the same: "Action (economy, but also politics) has no foundation in being: this is the schizophrenia that the theological doctrine of *oikonomia* left as its legacy to Western culture."[34]

In passing we should note that Christian theology centrally based its *oikonomia* on the doctrine of the *homousion*, that is, of the *consubstantiality*, the being one of essence or substance of God in two or three persons or hypostases "*without confusion, without change, without division, without separation*" (as the Council of Chalcedon decided in 451). Nor should we forget the more peripheral, if not necessarily marginal, but resolutely heterodox, mystical, and apophatic conceptions of God that may seem to come much closer to what Agamben has here precisely in mind (and that have, perhaps, more clearly laid out their premises and arguments well before him); conceptions that were as much part of Christianity's fractured history as the prevailing paradigm he seeks to question, but in so doing, strangely, also inherits.

But then, these conceptions are less important and relevant for Agamben's purposes and ours, in this context, than the one he mentions explicitly in *The Coming*

Community, drawing on Gershom Scholem, Walter Benjamin, and Ernst Bloch, while discussing the nature of the kingdom of the Messiah and the *how* rather than *when* of its possible arrival. These authors summarize different versions of the "tiny displacement" that the messianic redemption is deemed to entail, such that, in Agamben's rendition, "everything will be as it is now, just a little different."[35] For Agamben, the difference in question "does not refer to a state of things" but rather to "their sense and their limits," thus faintly echoing the early Wittgenstein's *Tractatus Logico-Philosophicus* and suggesting that the state of perfection or of redemption is a virtual "halo" (the term is Thomas Aquinas's) surrounding all things at their "periphery."[36] Bloch puts the matter succinctly in his volume *Spuren* (*Traces*), which invokes a rabbi, a true "cabalist," who claimed the following:

> To bring about the kingdom of freedom, it is not necessary that everything be destroyed, and a new world begin; rather, this cup, or that bush, or that stone, and so all things must only be shifted a little. Because this "a little" is hard to do, and its measure hard to find, humanity cannot do it in this world; instead, this is why the Messiah comes.[37]

For Agamben, by contrast, redemption, like the beatitude of the chosen according to Thomas Aquinas, is to be understood as an accidental supplement, a potential surplus to a necessary state of perfection in immanence, if also "the imperceptible trembling of the finite that makes its limits indeterminate."[38] Adorno, who draws on this very same tradition, puts it more aptly in ways that are more systematically astute and downright concrete: "In the right condition, as in the Jewish *theologoumenon*, all things would differ only a little from the way they are; but not the least lets itself conceive how things would be then."[39] This suggests that in the redeemed situation material elements, conditions and facts, may indeed shift around—minimally, albeit to maximal effect—such that things are distributed equally and justly. Yet the important proviso to make, the eschatological caveat, as it were, is that nothing in the facts, whether of nature or history, themselves can all by itself offer any guidance, much less provide guarantees as to *how* and *when* or *where* this will come about, *if at all*. Adding a halo to perfection (i.e., what, presumably, could not be other than it is, according to the age-old metaphysics of immanentism) does not suffice: a resolutely nonethereal, if "nonfactual"—or, as Adorno will say, "spiritual"—element in and of "facticity" alone might do the trick and, in this, unlock reality, lifting its "ban."

CONCLUSION

This much is clear: for Agamben, there is no firm ontological basis to the *oikonomia* of *dispositifs* or apparatuses per se. For one thing, according to Agamben, the "being" or *aseitas* and *potestas absoluta* of God-in-and-for-Himself, in other words, of God the Father, does not translate itself immediately—directly or fully—into the incarnated and visible as well as phenomenal and invisible realm of the Son and the Holy Spirit, respectively. For another, there is even in God Himself, he notes, a irremediable "fracture," namely between His being (i.e., to be understood in ontological terms) and action (i.e., praxis, to be exerted in terms of a normative register), that is, between "nature or essence," on the one hand, and "operation," on the other. Indeed, this differentiation follows (or lies at the origin of) that between the "logos" of "theology," on the one hand, and that of "economy," on the other. The upshot of these divisions, as said, comes down to the same fundamental insight:

> Action (economy, but also politics) has no foundation in being: this is the schizophrenia that the theological doctrine of *oikonomia* left as its legacy to Western culture.[40]

More precisely, the operativity and efficacy of *oikonomia* does not find the ground of its apparent "being"—the very order of its appearance, dialectically and phenomenologically speaking—in itself, first or foremost. But also further: not even the very ground of its being, which is, presumably, God in His very being, oneness as *aseitas*, is itself without "fracture" and, therefore, not really one (or, indeed, One).

One is tempted to say, then, that Agamben's theological genealogy of economy and government does not so much take its point of departure in a theology of creation, much less in that of emanation, but rather in one of original "fraction": a motif that comes closest to that of *retraction* or *contraction*, both of which, in "What Is an Apparatus?" and *The Kingdom and the Glory*, may have borrowed as much from the later Heidegger as from the Jewish mystical, more precisely, kabbalistic motif of *Tzimtsum*. Uncovered and interpreted by Gershom Scholem and, more recently, Christoph Schulte, this doctrine's legacy can be discerned in thinkers as diverse as Jürgen Habermas in his early work on Schelling, in Odo Marquard's philological and "transcendental-belletristic" accounts of the origins of the modern philosophy of history, and in Jacob Taubes's reconstruction of occidental messianism and eschatology.[41] But its reverberations and implications, while still very much in the dark, reach no doubt further. They affect the very integrity and integrality of the divine conceived as One and indivisible, *alpha* and *omega*, all in all, that is, of a Being called at once highest, most perfect, and infinite.

These silent and explicit *onto*-theological axioms, as much as they may have determined the concept of God *in and for Himself* in the long tradition of Western religion and metaphysics, might have to be dropped as soon as we fully conceive of ourselves as existing historically and empirically, that is, as finite and contingent. But then again, these latter presumably postmetaphysical notions are themselves, first of all, *conceptual schemes* based on what we have experienced and come to know thus far, in and on those very terms. When taken as absolutes, in isolation and separate, they become ipso facto the reverse image of the standpoint of theomania and cause the same damage. Hence, their meaning and use is merely nominal and pragmatic, without *fundamentum in re*. To either claim or, for that matter, deny them abstractly is to fall prey to theomania all over again, even if in so doing the word or reference of "God" does not even enter our discourse.

NOTES

1. Elliot R. Wolfson, "Secrecy, Apophasis, and Atheistic Faith in the Teachings of Rav Kook," in *Negative Theology as Jewish Modernity*, ed. Michael Fagenblatt (Bloomington and Indianapolis: University of Indiana Press, 2017), 131–60, 131; and Elliot R. Wolfson, *Giving Beyond the Gift: Apophasis and Overcoming Theomania* (New York: Fordham University Press, 2014), xvii. The citation is from Henri Atlan, *The Sparks of Randomness*, Vol. 2: *The Atheism of Scripture*, trans. Lenn J. Schramm (Stanford: Stanford University Press, 2013), 346–47.
2. Wolfson, "Secrecy, Apophasis, and Atheistic Faith," 131. The citation is from Atlan, *Sparks of Randomness*, Vol. 2: *Atheism of Scripture*, 346–47.
3. See my "On Inexistence, Divine and Other," in Tarek R. Dika and Martin Shuster, eds., *Religion in Reason: Metaphysics, Ethics, and Politics in Hent de Vries* (London and New York: Routledge, 2022).
4. Elliot R. Wolfson, *Heidegger and Kabbalah: Hidden Gnosis and the Path of Poiesis* (Bloomington: Indiana University Press, 2019), 5.
5. Wolfson, *Heidegger and Kabbalah*, 5. See also Wolfson, *Giving Beyond the Gift*, 236 ff.
6. A concept more fully developed and critically inverted in later pages of Wolfson, *Heidegger and Kabbalah*, cf. 67–68.
7. Wolfson, *Heidegger and Kabbalah*, 337.
8. Elliot R. Wolfson, *The Duplicity of Philosophy's Shadow: Heidegger, Nazism, and the Jewish Other* (New York: Columbia University Press, 2018), xv.
9. For the reference to Agamben, see Wolfson, *Heidegger and Kabbalah*, 67, 345, 365.
10. Wolfson, *Heidegger and Kabbalah*, 66.
11. Giorgio Agamben, "What Is an Apparatus?," in Agamben, *What Is an Apparatus? And Other Essays*, trans. David Kishik and Stefan Pedatella (Stanford: Stanford University Press, 2009), 1–24, 1. The lemma devoted to "*Dispositif* (Apparatus)," included in Leonard Lawlor and John Nale, eds., *The Cambridge Foucault Lexicon* (Cambridge: Cambridge University Press, 2014), 126–32, is by Gilles Deleuze.
12. Leonard Lawlor, "Jean Hyppolite (1907–1968)," in Lawlor and Nale, *Cambridge Foucault Lexicon*, 639–40.
13. Jean Hyppolite, *Introduction à la philosophie de l'histoire de Hegel* (Paris: Éditions du Seuil, [1948] 1983); *Introduction to Hegel's Philosophy of History*, trans. Bond Harris and Jacqueline Bouchard Spurlick, with a Foreword by Arkady Plotnitsky (Gainesville: University Press of Florida, 1996).
14. Agamben, "What Is an Apparatus?," 3.
15. Michel Foucault, *Power/Knowledge: Selected Interviews and Other Writings, 1972–1977*, ed. C. Gordon (New York: Pantheon Books, 1980), 194–96; cited after Agamben, "What Is an Apparatus?," 2. Emphasis added.
16. Agamben, "What Is an Apparatus?," 4.
17. Agamben, "What Is an Apparatus?," 5–6. In *The Kingdom and the Glory: For a Theological Genealogy of Economy and Government* (Homo Sacer *II*, 2o), trans. Lorenzo Chiesa with Matteo Mandarini (Stanford: Stanford University Press, 2011), 2, Agamben refers to the

Tridentine canons that discuss "oikonomia" in "just a few lines under the rubric *De dispensatione et mysterio adventus Christi*" and recalls that "*dispensatio* is with *dispositio*, the Latin translation of *oikonomia*" (ibid.).

18. Hyppolite, *Introduction to Hegel's Philosophy of History*, 23, cited after Agamben, "What Is an Apparatus?," 5.
19. Georg Wilhelm Friedrich Hegel, "Zum Begriff der Positivität . . . ," in Hegel, *Frühe Schriften: Frankfurter Manuskripte und Druckschriften*. Mit einer Einleitung und Anmerkungen versehen von Walter Jaeschke (Hamburg: Meiner Verlag, 2020), 219.
20. Giorgio Agamben, *Where Are We Now? The Epidemic as Politics*, trans. Valeria Dani (Lanham, Boulder, New York, London: Rowman & Littlefield, 2021), 63.
21. Agamben, "What Is an Apparatus?," 6.
22. Agamben, "What Is an Apparatus?," 7.
23. That the question regarding the concept and nature of the apparatus has a deeply ontological dimension is clear to Agamben. See his "An Archeology of Ontology" and "Ontological Apparatus" in Part II of his *The Use of Bodies*, trans. Adam Kotsko (Stanford: Stanford University Press, 2016), 111–34. On the notion of potentialities, see Giorgio Agamben, *Potentialities: Collected Essays in Philosophy*, trans. Daniel Heller-Roazen (Stanford: Stanford University Press, 2000).
24. Agamben, "What Is an Apparatus," 9.
25. Agamben, "What Is an Apparatus," 10, cf. 9, 11.
26. Cf. Gwenaëlle Aubry, "Miracle, Mystery, and Authority: A Deconstruction of the Christian Theology of Omnipotence," in *Modern Language Notes* 132, no. 5 (December 2017): 1327–50. See also Aubry, *Dieu sans la puissance.* Dunamis *et* Energeia *chez Aristote et chez Plotin* (Paris: Vrin, 2006) and *Genèse du Dieu souverain. Archéologie de la puissance* II (Paris: Vrin, 2018) as well as the special issue of *Revue Philosophique de la France et de l'Étranger* no. 3 (juillet–septembre 2010), ed. Gwenaëlle Aubry, on "L'impuissance de Dieu," and notably her "Présentation," ibid., 307–20.
27. Cf. William J. Courtnay, *Capacity and Volition: A History of the Distinction of Absolute and Ordained Power* (Bergamo: Pierluigi Lubrina Editore, 1990).
28. Agamben, "What Is an Apparatus," 8. Martin Rueff's translation, *Que'est-ce qu'un dispositif?* (Paris: Éditions Payot & Rivages, 2007), 21, which I follow here, adds "*et du gouvernement*."
29. Agamben, "What Is an Apparatus?," 10, 11.
30. Agamben, "What Is an Apparatus?," 10, cf. 16.
31. Agamben, "What Is an Apparatus?," 11.
32. Agamben, "What Is an Apparatus?," 10.
33. Agamben, "What Is an Apparatus?," 10.
34. Agamben, "What Is an Apparatus?," 10.
35. Giorgio Agamben, *The Coming Community*, trans. Michael Hardt (Minneapolis: University of Minnesota Press, 2007), 53.
36. Agamben, *The Coming Community*, 54.
37. Cf. Agamben, *The Coming Community*, but cited above after Ernst Bloch, *Traces*, trans. Anthony A. Nasser (Stanford: Stanford University Press, 2006), 158.

38. Agamben, *The Coming Community*, 56.
39. Theodor W. Adorno, *Negative Dialektik*, GS 6, ed., Rolf Tiedemann, Gretel Adorno, Susan Buck-Morss, and Klaus Schultz (Frankfurt am Main: Suhrkamp, 1997), 294; Adorno, *Negative Dialectics*, trans. E. B. Ashton (New York: Continuum, 2000), 299, trans. modified.
40. Agamben, "What Is an Apparatus?," 10, 11.
41. Cf. Christoph Schulte, *Zimzum. Gott und Weltursprung* (Berlin: Suhrkamp, 2014).

IN THE NAME OF TIME

Marcel Proust, the Zohar, and Elliot Wolfson's Notion of Timeswerve

CLÉMENCE BOULOUQUE

FOR WALTER BENJAMIN—PHILOSOPHER AND LITERARY CRITIC, DECIPHERER of Jewish messianism, as well as of Kafkaesque and Proustian metaphors—Marcel Proust's writing reflected "the absorption of a mystic, the art of a prose writer, the verve of a satirist, the erudition of a scholar, and the self-consciousness of a monomaniac."[1] This characterization of Proust as a mystic captures a man dedicated to his art who would venture out in the world of French fin de siècle high society, only to retreat into his creative solitude and seclude himself in his cork-lined bedroom where he articulated—and reflected on—the alchemy of time and writing. But the quote also conveys the possibility of a deep Proustian connection with mysticism—a mysticism of time into which Elliot Wolfson's kabbalistic hermeneutics offer unparalleled insights.

Proust's mother, Jeanne Weil, was Jewish, but his father, the doctor Adrien Proust, was Catholic, and Proust did not receive a traditional Jewish education.[2] In a letter to his cousin and confidante, Lionel Hauser, he opened up about his spiritual unrest: "even though I do not have Faith . . . religious concerns are never absent, every day of my life. I deny nothing, I believe in the possibility of everything; objections to belief based on the existence of Evil etc are absurd, since Suffering alone seems to me to have raised and continue to raise man above the status of a savage."[3]

Elements of Judaism, sometimes labeled marranism,[4] are nevertheless deeply embedded in his work. Shortly after his death, he was reclaimed by young Jewish intellectuals, and even the budding Zionist movement, as Antoine Compagnon has shown in a study provocatively titled "Proust, Zionist."[5]

The Proust scholar Juliette Hassine, who has probed the many aspects of the novelist's Judaism, sees it as having three facets: "Judaism as a religion, Jewishness [*judéité*] as a cultural identity, and Jewdom [*judaïcité*] as a human community."[6] Proust's Jewishness has certainly been examined through the lens of his descriptions of the Dreyfus affair and of the manner in which the wrongful conviction that agitated France's fin de siècle reverberated through its most refined salons.[7] In *In Search of Lost Time*, a central character, Charles Swann, returned to Judaism after the affair. His religious divided self stood as but one among several excuses he used that enabled him to avoid his true calling, that of art—and thus of eternity. On the other hand, the figure of Bloch, the narrator's arrogant friend turned successful playwright,[8] has fueled questions about Proust's dubious category of the self-hating Jew.[9] The Jewdom dimension comes across as an implicit cultural language: the distinct use of Talmudic discussions and of a principle of uncertainty.[10] Proust's style, with its nested sentences and discursiveness, was called "the style of a rabbi commenting the scriptures," leading to comparisons with the polyphony of Talmudic worldview and syntax—in which possibilities were pondered, opinions collected, and dissents registered (even within oneself).[11]

As for his knowledge of the scriptures, the translation Proust made of Ruskin's *Bible of Amiens* from 1900 to 1904 led him to write a preface in which he claimed, "The Bible is something real, present, and we have to find in it something else besides the flavor of its archaism and the entertainment of our curiosity."[12]

His relation to esotericism and interest in the Zohar, the mystical commentary on the Pentateuch, may have been merely a product of his time but, with the exception of one monograph by Juliette Hassine,[13] it has received little more than passing mentions. When they have probed the presence of mystical elements, most critics have concerned themselves with the treatment of metempsychosis, as well as with gender fluidity and homoeroticism—and rightly so.[14] Elliot Wolfson's trailblazing work on gender and homoeroticism in the Zohar might illuminate these two aspects. But it is to Wolfson's thinking on time that I wish to turn here.

Studies of Proustian time would indeed benefit from examining it through a mystical lens.[15] In a letter to Henry Bordeaux dated March 1914, Proust made a double confession, that he had withdrawn into solitude, and that he was in search of time in its "esoteric sense," which he would capture in the last volume of his grand oeuvre: "My solitary life helps me somewhat 'to regain' (not in the esoteric sense that the last volume of my novel will unveil) lost time."[16] *Esoteric* is an interesting word for Proust to choose here. Whereas mysticism is, according to Gershom Scholem, "a kind of knowledge which is by its very nature incommunicable. It cannot be directly transmitted; it can be made visible only indirectly, because its substance cannot be expressed in human language. Esoteric knowledge, on the other hand, means a kind of knowledge that may be communicable and might be communicated, but whose communication is forbidden,"[17] and is thus limited to initiates. The term *unveil*, meanwhile, conveys both revelation and secrecy—and furthers asserts the esoteric nature of his work on time.

Among his many contributions, Elliot Wolfson has introduced the figure of the *timeswerve* to capture kabbalistic temporality and hermeneutics. In a recent monograph, *Suffering Time*, a collection of his reflections on time, Wolfson outlined his conception of the geometry of time: "To capture this sense of the timeswerve, I have coined the expressions *linear circularity* or *circular linearity* to avoid the conventional split between the two temporal modalities of the line and the circle."[18]

Wolfson explains that the timeswerve is a "temporalization of the spatial," which also leads to "hermeneutic reversibility."[19] This "calls into question the linear model of aligning events chronometrically in a noetic sequence of now-points stretched invariably between the retention of the before that is no more and the protention of the after that is not yet."[20] If the usual model of temporality is no longer relevant, a whole interpretation system based on the deployment of a linear, unidirectional reasoning must also be revisited, or complemented with dream, imagination, or memory-like modes of perception. Wolfson rightly claims that "the imaginary fusion of presence and absence, visible and invisible imparts to us the key to understanding linear circularity."[21]

Such a multifaceted vision accords exceptionally well with the work of Proust. The timeswerve is the conceptual and visual equivalent of the narrator's magic lantern, understood by critics to be a metaphor for Proust's vision.[22] I would argue that the timeswerve is not only the proper understanding of time; it also silently conjures up previous instantiations of swerves in literature and philosophy. Swerve is, indeed, the translation of Lucretius's Latin term *clinamen* in *The Nature of Things* (*De Rerum Natura)*, the first-century poem describing the natural order of the world based on Epicurus's philosophy and physics. The clinamen is the deviation of atoms falling down through the void: rather than falling straight down, they swerve, which explains why they collide. Their collisions then account for the creation of the universe.[23] In *The Birth of Physics*, Michel Serres reflects on the deviation in the fall of the atom and on the fact that this deviation is nevertheless not a rogue phenomenon but one that conveys indeterminacy—it is the opposite of necessity.[24] Over time, the term has become synonymous with inclination and the antithesis of necessity—or the course of necessity reversed, which is one of the possible accounts of modernity.[25] Wolfson's "hermeneutics of reversibility" thus accords with the possibility of deviation, a central concept of Proust's temporality, and its concept of involuntary memory. The present brims with hidden possibilities of remembrance, but one stumbles upon them only accidentally in Proust's novels. Yet it is through this deviation, this aleatory happenstance, that one gets to the substance of time. Benjamin's reading of Proust centers on time and involuntary memory—a disruption that could also describe messianic time.

I contend that Elliot Wolfson's hermeneutics, and particularly the timeswerve, shed new light on previous Proustian scholarship and that kabbalistic studies expand the field of Proustian studies. I will then first examine a distinct locus of the "temporalization of the spatial": the city of Venice, in which Proust saw a reflection of the Zohar, and then probe the Wolfsonian concept of timeswerve in light of Proust's temporality and of the previous instances of swerve from the inception of the notion with Lucretius's *clinamen* and the deviation of free-falling atoms as the possibility for collision and creation. Finally, I will show how Elliot Wolfson's hermeneutics complement Benjamin's reading of Proust and thus open new avenues for literary studies.

"TEMPORALIZATION OF THE SPATIAL" AND THE HERMENEUTICS OF REVERSIBILITY: VENICE AND THE ZOHAR

Venice occupies a distinctive place in Proust's work, at its very beginning and end.[26] Its first mention, in his early, unpublished novel *Jean Santeuil*, symbolizes the possibility of a union, albeit a secret one. It is a place of revelation in the final volume of *In Search of Lost Time*. The two appearances thus bookend the novelist's oeuvre. It might seem ironic to take such a bio-bibliographical approach, still inscribed in a linear understanding of time. Indeed, the city, described in light of the Zohar, served the author as a catalyst for upending that very notion of linearity, as he conflated the city and the book, time and place—a conflation best illuminated by Wolfson's understanding of kabbalistic hermeneutics. But focusing on Venice also illustrates this disruption of linearity so central to Proust's work.

Jean Santeuil, begun in 1895 and left unfinished, is often understood as a trial run for *In Search of Lost Time*, but it is a more straightforward chronicle of his era. In it, the high-strung narrator, Jean, breaks a Venetian glass during a fit of hysterics and tries to hide the news from his mother:

> Running to her, he flung his arms about her neck, burst into tears, and held her in a prolonged hug. But she, happy in the knowledge that she was loved, but not wishing that he should love her with an excess of passion which one day might cause him pain, said gently, in a tone of blessed common sense, and ceasing to smile: "Now, don't be a little silly: go back to your place, and let us get on with dinner." He could not bring himself to leave her, and told her in a low voice that he had broken the Venetian glass. He expected that she would scold him, and so revive in his mind the memory of their quarrel. But there was no cloud upon her tenderness. She gave him a kiss, and whispered in his ear: "It shall be, as in the Temple, the symbol of an indestructible union."[27]

It is by breaking the glass, a remembrance of the destruction of the Temple, that the union can come to fruition, through an altered state of brokenness, with the feminine other. But here, with the Venetian glass, the feminine is that of the mother and is thus sameness. Further, the alliance is marked by secrecy—the mother whispers in her son's ear.

Around the same time, Proust contemplated translating John Ruskin's *Stones of Venice*, the art critic's three-volume study of the art and architecture of the city, published between 1851 and 1853. In the book, the English writer and esthete associates Venice with divine Wisdom.[28] In his *Cahiers*, Proust likewise described the Palais des Doges as "one of the pillars of the gate to the ineffable" ("l'un des piliers de la porte de l'Ineffable"). The esoteric aspect of Venice coincides with the identification of Venice and the Zohar.

Juliette Hassine has also explained Proust's fascination with the Venetian palaces as indicating the likelihood that the author had discovered the *heikhalot* literature, the literature of the palaces, a whole corpus of Jewish esoteric tradition and narratives of mystical ascents and glimpses into the dwelling of the divine.[29] The allure of Venetian palaces might have fueled Proust's esoteric imagination. But I would argue that the city commanded a deeper sense of mysticism, one that structures the entire work—a mysticism of time. Venice is where time and place merge, and this warrants the use of Wolfson's hermeneutics. In this "temporalization of the spatial" of kabbalistic temporality, Wolfson claims, time-space as "the Fourth Dimension"[30] is the extension of a three-dimensional space, and the continuum of one temporal and three spatial coordinates in which any event or physical object is located—a break from Newtonian physics and a central tenet of Einstein's theory of relativity.[31]

> "Zohar"—This name has remained entangled in my hopes of yesteryear. It recreates all around itself the atmosphere in which I lived then, its bright wind, the idea I had formed of Ruskin and Italy. Italy contains less of my former dream than the name that lived within it. Here are the names, things are not names, [names] as soon as we think about them become thoughts, they take place in the sequence of former thoughts and mix with them and this is why the Zohar has become something analogous to the thought I was having before reading it, as I gazed at the stormy sky, thinking that I was going to see Venice.[32]

> "Zohar"—Ce nom est resté pris entre mes espérances d'alors, il recrée autour de lui l'atmosphère où je vivais alors, le vent ensoleillé qu'il faisait, l'idée que je me faisais de Ruskin et de l'Italie. L'Italie contient moins de mon rêve d'alors que le nom qui y a vécu. Voici les noms, les choses ne sont pas des noms, [les noms], dès que nous les pensons, ils deviennent des pensées, ils prennent rang dans la série des pensées d'alors en se mêlant à elles, et voici pourquoi Zohar est devenu quelque chose d'analogue à la pensée que j'avais avant de le lire, en regardant le ciel tourmenté, en pensant que j'allais voir Venise.[33]

These notes—taken in 1908—conjure up the time preceding Proust's journey to Venice in the months of January or February 1900 when he had just abandoned *Jean Santeuil* and, in the grip of a depression, was contemplating giving up writing.

This is a moment that would prove crucial for his new project, and his understanding of "the sense of time," in the words of Julia Kristeva or the experience of time embodied. Kristeva did not ponder the question of mysticism in her *Proust and the Sense of Time*, but she subsequently acknowledged the importance of mysticism and its occurrences.[34] The Zohar merges with Venice because it is part of Proust's new vision of time—that fourth dimension in which time is inscribed and, indeed, embodied. It is a recreation of a bygone time in which the senses—here feeling the "bright wind," but also the sight of a "stormy sky"—are part of the reminiscence.

The Zohar is an object as much as an event: "The Zohar has become something analogous to the thought I was having before reading it, as I watched the stormy sky, thinking that I was going to see Venice." It is the anticipation of a trace and thus that which has already happened before happening—a retrospective futurity. Once again, Elliot Wolfson's characterization of the triangulation of past, present, and future—leading, in fact, to their sublation—is fitting: "we should readily speak of every actual present becoming an expectation of a past that induces the repetition of a future. In the contours of imagination, we affirm the coming to be of what is always yet to come. This inversion is at the heart of the hermeneutical process that has informed the variegated nature of textual reasoning at play in rabbinic and kabbalistic sources, and, I would add, in scholarly analyses of these sources as well."[35]

Whether Proust did read the Zohar may be disputed.[36] His familiarity with Jewish mystical sources, at least on a cursory or intuitive level, should not be surprising given some of the novelist's early writings, including pastiches of the towering figure in religious studies, Ernest Renan,[37] and the fin de siècle attraction to mysticism. Among Proust's acquaintances, Adolphe Franck, an exemplary representative of French Judaism (as was the maternal branch of the Proust family) and the first Jewish holder of a chair at the Sorbonne, published an influential work on Kabbalah[38] and was part of the literary circle around Geneviève Straus-Halévy that Proust, too, frequented.[39] Less rigorous scholarly works on Kabbalah flourished in the late nineteenth century.[40] The first French translation of the Zohar was published between 1906 and 1912, and it constituted a literary event that gripped a number of artists and intellectuals.[41] Around the time of Proust's references to the Zohar in his notebooks, two volumes out of six had been published by Jean de Pauly, who died in 1903 and whose identity is obscure. A self-proclaimed Albanian aristocrat, he was most likely a converted Jew named Paul Meyer. It also is believed that the library of Proust's brother contained the *Kabbalah denudata*,[42] a Latin digest of kabbalistic key texts by the seventeenth-century Christian Hebraist and Kabbalist Christian Knorr von Rosenroth, published in 1677, which he had inherited from Marcel. Baudelaire claimed to have detected its influence on Victor Hugo, thus indicating that the book held a degree of influence in literary circles.[43] To be sure, Proust's reverie on the name of the Zohar, quoted above, could be but one of his musings on proper names found throughout *In Search of Lost Time*, as Roland Barthes suggested: "Proper names are the linguistic form of the act of reminiscing."[44] In the passage, Proust had not gone to Venice yet, and he is reminiscing about what had not happened yet. Names can thus be a vessel of multiple temporalities, which is the case for both the city and the Zohar.

It was in the first decade of the century, during the years when the volumes of the de Pauly translation were being published, that Proust's new, specific temporality emerged. In the 1908 *Carnet*, the retrospective mention of his anticipation of his time in Venice, the temporal flash in which he remembers his presence in the city (and more broadly in Italy) is captured by the name of the Zohar, which suggests a specific temporalization of the spatial. In addition, other notebooks at that time further the connection:

> Only what has appeared in the *depths* is worth expressing, and these depths are normally hidden, except when lit up *by a flash of lightning*, or in weather that is exceptionally clear and refreshing. These *depths*, this inaccessibility to us is the only mark of value, and thus perhaps also of a certain *joy*. It does not matter what it is about. A bell tower—even if it is indiscernible for a few days—is more valuable than an entire theory of the world. See in my large notebook the description of the arrival in front of the Campanile and Zohar also.[45]

> Seul mérite / d'être exprimé ce qui / est apparu dans les profondeurs / et habituellement sauf / dans l'illumination / d'un éclair, ou par / des temps exceptionnellement / clairs, animants, ces / profondeurs sont obscures. Cette / profondeur, cette inaccessibilité / pour nous-même est la / seule marque de la / valeur—ainsi peut' / être qu'une certaine / joie. Peu importe de / quoi il s'agit. Un / clocher s'il est insaisissable / pendant des jours a plus / de valeur qu'une / théorie complète du / monde.
>
> Voir dans le gros / cahier l'arrivée / devant le Campanile— / et aussi Zohar.[46]

This entry sees Proust expressing his conception of the arts, which has religious overtones. The mystical and the artistic share a similar effort of extraction from darkness to light: "That which presents itself obscurely, deep within our consciousness, before being realized in a work of art . . . must be made to cross an intermediary region / between our / hidden self and the exterior, our intelligence."[47] The region Proust alludes to here might be the unconscious or the mystery of creation, which he seemed to conflate.

The movement of descent into the depths is matched by an implicit ascent back into the light, a clarity whose potential violence and brevity is conveyed by the image of lightning. Being able to get a glimpse of the inaccessible, or even knowing of the existence of this inaccessible abyss, is already evidence of being an initiate, which explains the "worth" and the joy derived from it. Expressing what is concealed in the opposite forces of darkness and light can only be achieved through an experiential knowledge of what is hidden. This aligns the Zohar with artistic inspiration, thus establishing writing as a mystical experience.

But how could the sight of an "indiscernible bell tower" be "more valuable than an entire theory of the world"? The depth of the abyss is symmetrical with the height of the tower, and the inaccessibility of the former matches the indiscernibility of the latter. This equivalence suggests a cosmological principle: as above, so below. This is another instance of reversibility. Hermeneutic reversibility is the essence of Proustian meaning and of time, and of the meaning of time, and also—in Wolfson's approach—of what is concealed and revealed: "The manifestation of the nonmanifest, the exposure of what is hidden that perforce must be a hiding of what is exposed. From this vantage point, the spatial and the temporal are threads that cannot be disentangled; I would contend nevertheless that the former is an offshoot of the latter."[48]

In *Le Temps retrouvé*, the final volume of Proust's heptalogy, the narrator stumbles on an uneven paving stone as he heads to a party at the home of the Guermantes, the aristocratic family whose chateau was the destination of some of the walks in Combray, the rural town where the narrator's family also owned a home and where most of his childhood recollections take place. Being invited to a Guermantes party at their Parisian home with the chosen few meshes past and present together. But the paving stone brings back another layer of the past, the memory of Saint Mark's Basilica in Venice, which the distraught narrator had visited with his mother, and where he tried—and eventually succeeded—to free himself from the memory of his unfaithful lover, Albertine.[49] It is through these deviations, these *swerves*, that the narrator understands what his calling as an artist may be.

The Basilica's pavements are located in the baptistery, a place that lends itself to purification—rebirth if not resurrection—which inflects the text with Christian overtones. But Wolfson's hermeneutics—he argues that "the exposure of what is hidden that perforce must be a hiding of what is exposed"[50]—would nuance such a straightforward reading. This recollection may also represent a counterpoint to the scene of the broken Venetian glass in *Jean Santeuil*; this may be part of the structure of the work that is destined to remain silent.[51]

In any case, a distance has to be maintained in order to let memory submerge the narrator: Saint Mark's Basilica is reflected in Saint-Hilaire, Combray's church, a sight the narrator observes from his hotel room:

> I received there impressions analogous to those which I had felt so often in the past at Combray, but transposed into a wholly different and far richer key. When, at ten o'clock in the morning, my shutters were thrown open, I saw blazing there, instead of the gleaming black marble into which the slates of Saint-Hilaire used to turn, the golden angel of the Campanile of Saint Mark's.[52]

> J'y goûtais des impressions analogues à celles que j'avais si souvent ressenties autrefois à Combray, mais transposées selon un mode entièrement différent et plus riche. Quand à 10 heures du matin on venait ouvrir mes volets, je voyais flamboyer, au lieu du marbre noir que devenaient en resplendissant les ardoises de Saint-Hilaire, l'Ange d'or du campanile de Saint-Marc.[53]

The Basilica reflects a range of influences, exhibiting multiple strata of time and identity, Gothic and Byzantine, and offers a bridge between Orient and Occident; it invites the narrator to return to Combray but cannot be confused with Combray itself.[54]

READING THE TIMESWERVE

The horizontality of Venice and the description of the shining angel atop Saint Mark's Campanile can be set against the circular depiction of the countryside village of Combray, but this opposition is actually an apposition, which leads to the motif of the swerve described by Elliot Wolfson as zoharic temporality.

Many of Proust's depictions of Combray present it as a perfect circle, and a picturesque one—lending to the village in Normandy the characteristics of primitive painting, widely associated at the turn of the century with fourteenth- and fifteenth-century Flemish or Italian painting, foreshadowing a possible merging of the two. One of them is found in the opening pages of *In Search of Lost Time*, when it anchors the novel in what seems to be a repetitive, circular life of habits or family rituals.

> Combray at a distance, from a twenty-mile radius, as we used to see it from the railway when we arrived there in the week before Easter, was no more than a church epitomizing the town, representing it, speaking of it and for it to the horizon, and as one drew near, gathering close about its long dark cloak, sheltering from the wind, on the open plain, as a shepherdess gathers her sheep, the wooly gray backs of its huddled houses, which the remains of its medieval ramparts enclosed, here and there, in an outline as scrupulously circular as that of a little town in a primitive painting.[55]

> Combray, de loin, à dix lieues à la ronde, vu du chemin de fer quand nous y arrivions la dernière semaine avant Pâques, ce n'était qu'une église résumant la ville, la représentant, parlant d'elle et pour elle aux lointains, et, quand on approchait, tenant serrés autour de sa haute mante sombre en plein champ, contre le vent, comme une pastoure ses brebis, les dos laineux et gris des maisons rassemblées qu'un reste de remparts du Moyen Âge cernait çà et là d'un trait aussi parfaitement circulaire qu'une petite ville dans un tableau de primitif.[56]

The circularity of Combray is subtly countervailed by the verticality of the steeple, which foreshadows the verticality and upward lines of Venice where the narrator will later receive his revelation about the nature of art and time—breaking the circularity of nefarious relations and habits, and the need to forget in order to find the essence of time and start writing.

Combray is ultimately illuminated by Venice, in a retrospective glance, making sense of what was here all along—namely the bell tower of Saint-Hilaire. Following Wolfson's temporal markers, "we can reverse the timeline: the end precedes the beginning, and yet, the beginning overtakes the end."[57] Venice is already in Combray and Combray is in Venice; the beginning of the novel and its ending merge—the revelation that was yet to come has happened, or had always already happened. This proximity of differences illustrates Wolfson's use of the timeswerve as an operative concept

> in which line and circle meet in the sameness of their difference. The convergence of line and circle can be thought from the vantage point of the confluence of the three modes of time in the moment: the present is determined by the past of the future that is yet to come as what has already been and by the future of the past that has already been what is yet to come.[58]

Such a nexus of similarities and distinctiveness is only accentuated in dream and memory. The circularity of the dream is key in the narrator's experience of Combray, which is signaled from the very first page with the ordeal of the narrator's bed ritual, the separation from his mother, his falling asleep before waking up again and contemplating his previous thoughts as from a past life, invoking metempsychosis—which is another conflation of sameness and difference.

> When a man is asleep, he has in a circle round him the chain of the hours, the sequence of the years, the order of heavenly bodies. Instinctively he consults them when he awakes, and in an instant reads off his own position on the earth's surface and the time that has elapsed during his slumbers; but this ordered procession is apt to grow confused, and to break its ranks.[59]

> Un homme qui dort tient en cercle autour de lui le fil des heures, l'ordre des années et des mondes. Il les consulte d'instinct en s'éveillant et y lit en une seconde le point de la terre qu'il occupe, le temps qui s'est écoulé jusqu'à son réveil; mais leurs rangs peuvent se mêler, se rompre.[60]

Here the circularity is not only one of landscape but is also an internalized circularity—a cosmological one. And this is where Proust is best understood at the confluence of Wolfson and Benjamin in that questioning of sameness and difference. For Benjamin, "the similarity of one thing with another which we rely on, which occupies our waking state, only plays on the sort of similarity in the dream world, where whatever emerges in a form that is never identical but similar to itself."[61] This parallels the sameness and difference of the swerve. As Wolfson writes in his study of oneiropoesis, *A Dream Interpreted Within a Dream*, the nocturnal dream actually takes place within the dream that is reality "in a uroboric state that puts into question the logic of a linear reason."[62]

Such a stance accords with the philosophy of Henri Bergson (who married into Proust's family in 1891). In 1908, the year of Proust's entry on the Zohar in his notebooks, Bergson wrote the following assessment of the nature of reality and memory:

> Let us set aside this preconceived idea, and the dream-state will then be seen, on the contrary, to be the substratum of our normal state. The dream is not something fantastic hovering above and additional to the reality of being awake; on the contrary, that reality of the waking state is gained by limitation, by concentration and by tension of a diffuse psychical life, which is the dream-life. In a sense, the perception and memory we exercise in the dream-state are more natural than those in the waking state . . . it is the awake-state, rather than the dream-state, which requires explanation.[63]

For Bergson, consciousness was a dream constrained by concentration, whereas sleep was the basic unit, the true possibility of psychic life. And inducing dream-states is key in order to retrieve memory in its natural state.

In Proust's work, the crucial transitional object near the bed, the object capable of inducing a dream state, is the magic lantern: it leads from night to dream, and from dream to memory, and it offers a curvature of time and vision. The lantern produces a physical swerve—a scene contained in the shapes of the cutout figures projected against the wall and distorted in the process—that leads to a timeswerve of its own: it bends the linear view of perception but also of memory. The narrator professes: "my memory [was like] the curve of the projections of my magic lantern."[64]

Swerve, as I noted earlier, is also a translation of Lucretius's *clinamen* in *De Rerum Natura*. The nineteenth century saw the rediscovery of the *clinamen*, notably by the young Karl Marx in his doctoral dissertation[65] and by Bergson, who published an *Extraits de Lucrèce*.[66] The autonomy of the atom turns geometry into ethics—the swerve, the change of trajectory, leads to life—as an instance of freedom and for this reason Stephen Greenblatt took it as a metaphor for modernity.[67] It has also come to take on the broader meaning of *chance* in twentieth-century literature.[68]

If one understands *swerve* as the locus of reversibility—of that which could have not happened, or of indeterminacy, it can capture the Proustian experience of involuntary memory that disturbs the linearity of our existences. As Wolfson writes: "the reversibility of the circular linearity implies no closure but an ever-changing fluctuation, an indeterminacy that destabilizes the model of an irreversible succession proceeding unidirectionally from start to finish."[69]

In "Small Talk on Proust, Held on My Fortieth Birthday" (July 1932), Benjamin captures this motif of circularity in a linearity: "On the knowledge of the *mémoire involontaire*: not only do its images come unsummoned, but it is a matter of images we never saw before remembering them." Indeed, in the words of Proust, the past is "hidden . . . in some material object (or the sensation that such an object arouses in us) but we have no suspicion which one it could be. It depends entirely on chance whether we come upon that object before we die or whether we never encounter it."[70] (Le passé "est caché hors de son domaine et de sa portée, en quelque objet matériel (en la sensation que nous donnerait cet objet matériel) que nous ne soupçonnons pas. Cet objet, il dépend du hasard que nous le rencontrions avant de mourir ou que nous ne le rencontrions pas."[71])

The awareness of the deviation, of this moment in time in which the time experienced is actually made up of other layers of time, should lead to greater attention to every passing moment and is not equivalent to atemporality derived from such "fragments of existence withdrawn from the world."[72] Benjamin rightly objected to this characterization.[73] Wolfson offers a more satisfactory and more capacious conception, one that triangulates Proust and Benjamin: "Bolstering the opposition of the temporal and the eternal is the paradox of sameness and difference that underlies the notion of time as the linear circle or the circular line."[74]

Wolfson's hermeneutics applies to the commandments in Jewish life but captures the logic of involuntary memory: "on the one hand, each moment a commandment is fulfilled reflects the moment the commandment was first given, but, on the other hand, each moment that commandment is fulfilled is a retrieval of the unprecedented, a genuine duplication of the same that is always the same in virtue of always being different."[75]

Involuntary memory can be compared to an irruption akin to the messianic moment in which the course of history is upended by the figure of redemption and where traditional temporality is disrupted and abolished. For Benjamin, messianic time is also spatial: "For every second of time was the strait gate through which the Messiah might enter."[76] In Benjamin's "Theses on the Philosophy of History," each moment is a moment in which the messianic can arrive—and it is always a delayed arrival. And the tension of the delay, the tardiness, is perceptible in the lengthy, revised sentences, by the sudden appearance of the delayed final element that produces a sense of long-awaited closure, while still destabilizing the meaning of closure. And, more than the so-called Talmudic sentence, the Proustian sentence could be called messianic.[77]

In *Proust and Signs*, Deleuze argues that "the Search is oriented to the future, not to the past," and that the past is not the deepest structure of time.[78] It is the "narrative of an apprenticeship, more precisely of an apprenticeship of a man of letters."[79] We have seen, however, that futurity misses the point—that future is past and past future. This reversibility is indeed the premise of zoharic hermeneutics, and it is also at the core of Walter Benjamin's understanding of the creative process as one of the first interpreters of Franz Kafka, Proust's quasi-contemporary: "Reversal is the direction of learning which transforms existence into writing."[80] But his lines about Kafka can equally be applied to Proust, who is less traditionally associated with the mysteries of the Jewish tradition but whose interpretation opens new paths for interpreting his work.[81] Proustian reversals are anchored in time, and it is with this final word, *Time*, that Proust's work concludes—the space of time it takes for the novel to be written and for the apprentice to become an author.

CONCLUSION

The concluding pages of *In Search of Lost Time* represent the dizzying culmination of embodied time: "A feeling of vertigo seized me as I looked down beneath me, yet within me, as though from a height, which was my own height, of many leagues, at the long series of the years."[82] The space (above, inside) is actually temporal, and the time spatial. The narrator's vertigo indicates the depth of the time. Yet time is indeed no longer an abyss, the bottomless measure of despair that seized him as a child during the nights in Guermantes described in the opening of the book—or, rather, it is an abyss into which he is now able to look.

In 1913, as he was embarking on the first volume of *In Search of Lost Time*, Proust expressed his pleasure in a letter that his correspondent had "guessed that my book is a dogmatic work and a construct."[83] Yet Proust's dogma cannot be separated from its construct, nor from his style, an ever-delayed closure that questions the very possibility of closure, which is precisely where creation lies. This echoes Gérard Genette's description of Proust as "the illustration of a doctrine, the demonstration, or at least the progressive unveiling of a Truth,"[84] which Genette also calls a palimpsest; it bears a striking resemblance to the notion of progressive revelation that emerged in the nineteenth century in an effort to reconcile faith and science.[85] Applying Wolfson's zoharic hermeneutics thus casts a unique light on Proust's edifices—and, in the wake of Wolfson's scholarship, it should open new paths for a much-needed cross-pollination between Kabbalah studies, literature, philosophy, and critical theory—as well as for venturing beyond. Indeed, as Proust wrote a few months before his death, "One should never fear venturing too far because the truth is always beyond."[86]

NOTES

1. Walter Benjamin, "The Image of Proust," in *Illuminations* (New York: Schocken, 2007), 201–15.
2. "Though I am a Catholic like my father and brother, my mother is Jewish." Marcel Proust, letter to Montesquiou, May 19, 1896 (estimated date), *Selected Letters, 1880–1903*, ed. Philip Kolb; trans. Ralph Manheim (New York: Oxford University Press, 1989), letter 92, p. 121; Maurice Samuels, *Inventing the Israelite: Jewish Fiction in Nineteenth-Century France* (Stanford: Stanford University Press, 2009).
3. *Correspondance*, vol. 14, 218, as translated in Margaret Topping, "Religion," in *Marcel Proust in Context*, ed. Adam Watt (New York: Cambridge University Press, 2013), 138.
4. Juliette Hassine, *Marranisme et hébraïsme dans l'œuvre de Proust* (Paris: Minard, 1994); Perrine Simon-Nahoum, "Marcel Proust et la vocation du narrateur: Un marranisme littéraire," in *Les Marranismes: De la religiosité cachée à la société ouverte*, ed. J. Ehrenfreund and J.-Ph. Schreiber (Paris: Demopolis, 2014), 229–51.
5. Antoine Compagnon, *Proust sioniste*, Collège de France, accessed October 2, 2021, https://www.college-de-france.fr/site/antoine-compagnon/Proust-sioniste.htm.
6. Hassine, *Marranisme et hébraïsme*, 139.
7. For Hannah Arendt, for example, the Dreyfus affair was "an example of the Jew in non-Jewish society and . . . a truthful record of it." Arendt, *The Origins of Totalitarianism* (New York: Harcourt, 1973), 80. See also Juliette Hassine, "The Dreyfus Affair in the Work of Marcel Proust: A Critique of Hannah Arendt and Julia Kristeva," *Shofar* 14, no. 3 (1996): 107–24.
8. André Spire, *Quelques Juifs* (Paris: Mercure de France, 1913); Spire, *Quelques Juifs et demi-Juifs* (Paris: Grasset, 1928); Jonathan Freedman, "Coming Out of the Jewish Closet with Marcel Proust," in *Queer Theory and the Jewish Question*, ed. Daniel Boyarin, Daniel Itzkovitz, and Ann Pellegrin (New York: Columbia University Press, 2003), 340; Patrick Mimouni, *Les mémoires maudites: Juifs et homosexuels dans l'œuvre et la vie de Marcel Proust* (Paris: Grasset, 2018); Maurice Samuels, "Proust, Jews, and the Arts," in *Proust and the Arts*, ed. Christie McDonald and François Proulx (Cambridge: Cambridge University Press, 2015), 223–31.
9. Alessandro Piperno, *Proust anti-ebreo* (Milano: F. Angeli, 2000); Seth L. Wolitz, *The Proustian Community* (New York: New York University Press, 1971); H. David, "Marcel Proust et ses amis antisémites," *Revue d'Histoire Littéraire de La France* 71, no. 5/6 (1971): 909–20.
10. Saul Friedlander, *Proustian Uncertainties* (New York: The Other Press, 2020); Jack Jordan, *Marcel Proust's* A la recherche du temps perdu: *A Search for Certainty* (Birmingham, NY: Summa Publications, 1993).
11. Quotation from Denis Saurat, "Le Judaïsme de Proust," *Les Marges,* October 15, 1925, 83–87

(also excerpted in *La Revue juive*, no. 6, November 1925, 792–95). See also Marisa Verna, *Proust, une langue étrangère* (Paris: Classiques Garnier, 2020), 63–79. The comparison between the Proustian sentence and Talmudic style first appeared only three years after his death. See Compagnon, *Proust sioniste*, "Episode 6: 'Le style du rabbin.'" Léon-Pierre Quint specifically zeroed in on the syntax of "soit que" in *Marcel Proust, sa vie, son œuvre* (Paris: Sagittaire, Simon Kra, 1925), 133; The term "Talmudic minds," a staple of antisemitic rhetoric, was used by the novelist Louis-Ferdinand Céline. See Céline's letter to Lucien Combelle, dated December 2, 1943, in Pascal Alain Infri, *Céline et Proust: Correspondances proustiennes dans l'œuvre de L.-F. Céline* (Birmingham, AL: Summa, 1996), 11–12. "Proustian poetry, conforming in style, in origins, to Semitism!" Such ramblings about the "judaizing" of literature were mocked by the novelist Patrick Modiano in his first book, *La Place de l'Étoile* (Paris: Gallimard, 1968). More recently, Julia Kristeva has started addressing the place of Judaism in Proust's work. Kristeva, "Conference: Question of Identity: The 'Talmudic' Experience of Marcel Proust," November 25, 2018, http://www.kristeva.fr/proust-question-of-identity.html.

12. Marcel Proust, preface to *La Bible d'Amiens* (Paris: Mercure de France, 1904). As translated in Marcel Proust, *On Reading Ruskin: Prefaces to* La Bible d'Amiens *and* Sésame et les Lys *with Selections from the Notes to the Translated Texts*, trans. and ed. Jean Autret, William Burford, and Phillip J. Wolfe (New Haven: Yale University Press, 1987), 20.
13. Juliette Hassine, *Esotérisme et écriture dans l'œuvre de Proust* (Paris: Minard, 1990).
14. Mimouni, *Les Mémoires maudites*.
15. Unsurprisingly, the only study to do this is Hassine's chapter, "Temps proustien et temps zoharique," in *Ésotérisme et écriture*, 28–37.
16. Proust, *Correspondence*, vol. 13, 105. "Ma vie solitaire m'aide un peu 'à retrouver' (pas dans le sens ésotérique que dévoilera le dernier volume de mon roman) le temps perdu."
17. Gershom Scholem, *Jewish Mysticism in the Middle Ages: The 1964 Allan Bronfman Lecture* (New York, 1964), 3–4.
18. Elliot R. Wolfson, *Suffering Time: Philosophical, Kabbalistic, and Hasidic Reflections on Temporality* (Leiden: Brill, 2021), x.
19. See also the prologue "Timeswerve/Hermeneutic Reversibility," in Elliot R. Wolfson, *Language, Eros, Being: Kabbalistic Hermeneutics and Poetic Imagination* (New York: Fordham University Press, 2005), xv–xxxi.
20. Wolfson, *Suffering Time*, 354.
21. Wolfson, *Suffering Time*, 354.
22. Emily Zants, "Proust's Magic Lantern," *Modern Fiction Studies* 19, no. 2 (1973): 211–16; Theodore Johnson, "'La Lanterne Magique': Proust's Metaphorical Toy," *L'Esprit Créateur* 11, no. 1 (1971): 17–31.
23. Lucretius, *De Rerum Natura* (New York: Loeb Classical Library, 2006), 2.216.
24. Michel Serres, *The Birth of Physics* (London: Rowman & Littlefield, 2018).
25. Stephen Greenblatt makes a case for the swerve as the essence of modernity in *The Swerve: How the World Became Modern* (New York: Norton, 2012). Vesperini has criticized this approach for its historicism and he shows how the reception of Lucretius offers a more multifaceted approach of the uses of the classic.

26. Peter Collier, *Proust and Venice* (Cambridge: Cambridge University Press, 2004); D. R. Ellison, "Proust's 'Venice': The Reinscription of Textual Sources," *Style* 22, no. 3 (1988): 432–49.
27. Marcel Proust, *Jean Santeuil*, trans. Gerard Hopkins (New York: Simon and Schuster, 1955), 218. In the original, the final line, spoken by the mother, is "ce sera comme au temple le symbole de l'indestructible union." Marcel Proust, *Jean Santeuil* (Paris: Gallimard, 1952), 423.
28. John Ruskin, *Stones of Venice* (New York: John Wiley, 1880), vol. 2, chap. 32.
29. Hassine, *Esotérisme et écriture*, 20–27.
30. Compagnon, *Proust sioniste*, "Episode 6: 'Le style du rabbin.'"
31. Proust's musings on time coincide with Einstein's first paper on relativity, which dates back to 1905, building on the work of Max Planck, who had coined the term. The final exposition of the theory of relativity was published in 1916. On the early reception of the theory and what could have transpired, see Arthur I. Miller, *Albert Einstein's Special Theory of Relativity: Emergence (1905) and Early Interpretation (1905–1911)* (Reading, UK: Addison-Wesley, 1981).
32. Fonds Marcel Proust—II, *À la recherche du temps perdu* [henceforth RTP], Bibliothèque Nationale de France, Département des manuscrits, NAF 16670 [cahier 5], fol. 53v, https://gallica.bnf.fr/ark:/12148/btv1b6000472j/f57.item.r=NAF%2016645. My translation.
33. Fonds Marcel Proust, cited in previous note.
34. "Proust would see the light of the Zohar projecting itself on Saint Mark's Campanile." Julia Kristeva and Sergio Benvenuto, "Le temps et l'expérience littéraire: Proust. Une conversation," *European Journal of Psychoanalysis*, May 12, 1994, https://www.psychomedia.it/isap/recenti/kristeva-fr.htm.
35. Wolfson, *Suffering Time*, 354.
36. Antoine Compagnon has expressed doubts, whereas Patrick Mimouni has questioned the rationale for dismissing something he considers very likely.
37. Proust wrote a pastiche of Renan. See Jean Milly, *Les Pastiches de Proust* (Paris: Librairie Armand Colin, 1970), 197–225.
38. Adolphe Franck, *La Kabbale ou la Philosophie religieuse des Hébreux* (Paris: Librairie Hachette, 1843).
39. Joyce Block Lazarus, *Geneviève Straus: A Parisian Life* (Leiden: Brill, 2017).
40. Examples include Alexandre Weill, *Mystères de la création* (Paris: Dentu, 1855); Papus (Eliphas Lévi), *Livre des splendeurs* (Paris: Charconac, 1894).
41. Paul Vulliaud, *La Kabbale juive: Histoire et doctrine (essai critique)* (Paris: É. Nourry, 1923), 192; Paul B. Fenton, "La cabale et l'académie: l'étude historique de l'ésotérisme juif en France," *Pardès*, no. 19–20 (1994), 219–23; Charles Mopsik, "Les formes multiples de la cabale en France au XXe siècle," *Journal des études de la cabale* 1 (1997): 255–82. On the flaws in de Pauly's translation, see Gershom Scholem, *Major Trends in Jewish Mysticism* (New York: Schocken, 1995), 212; Henri-Charles Puech, analysis of *La Cabbale: Pages classées du Zohar*, trad. J. Pauly, in *Revue de l'histoire des religions* 132, no. 1–3 (1946): 222–23.
42. Mimouni, *Les mémoires maudites*, 15.
43. This is why Patrick Mimouni regards the *Kabbala denudata* as a more serious possibility for Proust's deeper knowledge than the de Pauly translation of the Zohar. Charles Baudelaire,

"Notice sur Hugo," in *Oeuvres Complètes*, vol. 2 (Paris: Gallimard, Bibliothèque de la Pléiade, 1973), 103.

44. Roland Barthes, "Proust et les noms," in *Œuvres completes*, vol. 4 (Paris: Seuil, 2002), 69.
45. In this version of this translation, the grammar gets rearranged for the English, and this renders the line breaks nonsensical or fictional, so they were not included.
46. Marcel Proust, *Le Carnet de 1908* (Paris: Gallimard, 1976), 102. Emphasis added. ("Ce qui se présente ainsi obscurément au fond de notre conscience avant de le réaliser en oeuvre . . . il faut lui faire traverser une region intermédiaire entre notre moi obscur, et l'extérieur, notre intelligence.")
47. Proust, *Le Carnet de 1908*, 102.
48. Wolfson, *Suffering Time*, 116.
49. Marcel Proust, *In Search of Lost Time* (hereinafter *ISLT*) (New York: Modern Library, 1992), 3:346; Peter Collier, *Proust and Venice*, 117.
50. Wolfson, *Suffering Time*, 410.
51. André Benhaïm, "Unveiling the Synagogue beyond Proust's Cathedral," *Contemporary French and Francophone Studies* 9, no. 1 (2005): 73–86.
52. Proust, *ISLT*, 3:637.
53. Marcel Proust, *RTP*, 202.
54. Elliot R. Wolfson, "Novelty and Repetition of the Altogether Otherwise," in *Heidegger and Kabbalah: Hidden Gnosis and the Path of Poiesis* (Bloomington: Indiana University Press, 2019), 35–40.
55. Proust, *ISLT*, 1:39.
56. Proust, *RTP*, 1:47.
57. Wolfson, *Suffering Time*, 71.
58. Wolfson, *Suffering Time*, 255.
59. Proust, *ISLT*, 1:3–4.
60. Proust, *RTP*, 1:5.
61. Walter Benjamin, *Illuminations*, 204.
62. Elliot R. Wolfson, *A Dream Interpreted Within a Dream: Oneiropoiesis and the Prism of Imagination* (New York: Zone Books, 2011), 16.
63. Henri Bergson, "Memory of the Present and False Recognition" (1908), in *Mind-Energy Lectures* (New York: Henri Holt, 1920), 155. On Bergson's pure memory and Proust's involuntary memory, see David Gross, "Bergson, Proust, and the Revaluation of Memory," *International Philosophical Quarterly* 25, no. 4 (1985): 369–80.
64. Proust, *ISLT*, 5:605. ("ma mémoire [était] comme la courbure des projections de ma lanterne magique." Proust, *RTP*, 3:529.)
65. Peter Fenves, "Marx's Doctoral Thesis on Two Greek Atomists and the Post-Kantian Interpretations," *Journal of the History of Ideas* 47, no. 3 (1986): 433–52.
66. Henri Bergson, *Extraits de Lucrèce* (Paris: Librairie Delagrave, 1884), xiv–xv; Pierre Vesperini, *Lucrèce: Archéologie d'un classique européen* (Paris: Fayard, 2017); Marcel Conche, *Lucrèce et l'expérience* (Paris: PUF, 1967).
67. Greenblatt, *The Swerve*.

68. For an interpretation of *clinamen* as *chance* in contemporary literature, see Morgane Cadieu, *Marcher au hasard: Clinamen et création dans la prose du XXe siècle* (Paris: Classiques Garnier, 2019). See also Alison Calhoun, "Montaigne's Swerve: The Geometry of Parallels in the Essays and Other Writings," *Neophilologus* 101 (2017): 351–65.
69. Wolfson, *Suffering Time*, 71.
70. Proust, *ISLT*, 1:34.
71. Proust, *RTP*, 1:44.
72. Proust, *RTP*, 3:908.
73. On this discussion of the timeless and its occurrence in other works of Benjamin (such as "On Some Motifs of Baudelaire," 1940, or "On the Concept of History," 1940), see John McCole, *Walter Benjamin and the Antinomies of Tradition* (Ithaca: Cornell University Press, 2018). In *The Cities of Passage* (*Sodome et Gomorrhe*), the narrator questions this notion of immortality in any case: "On avait l'impression de cette équivoque qui fait qu'une religion parle d'immortalité mais entend par là quelque chose qui n'exclut pas le néant." *RTP*, 2:1081.
74. Wolfson, *Suffering Time,* 405.
75. Wolfson, *Suffering Time*, 405.
76. Benjamin, "Theses on the Philosophy of History," in *Illuminations*, 264.
77. Françoise Leriche, "Proust: An Art Nouveau Writer?" in *Proust in Context*, ed. Armine Kotin Mortimer and Katherine Kolb (University of Illinois Press, 2002), 189–212; Luz Aurora Pimentel, *Metaphoric Narration: Paranarrative Dimensions in À la recherche du temps perdu* (Toronto: University of Toronto Press, 1990), 83–113.
78. Gilles Deleuze, *Proust and Signs* (Minneapolis: University of Minnesota Press, 2000), 4.
79. Deleuze, *Proust and Signs*, 4.
80. Walter Benjamin, "Franz Kafka: On the Tenth Anniversary of His Death," in *Illuminations*, 138.
81. Peter Szondi, *Walter Benjamin and the Antinomies of Tradition* (Ithaca: Cornell University Press, 2018).
82. Proust, *ISLT*, vol. 4. ("J'avais le vertige de voir au-dessous de moi, en moi pourtant, comme si j'avais des lieux de hauteur, tant d'années." Proust, *RTP*, 4:624.)
83. "Enfin je trouve un lecteur qui devine que mon livre est un ouvrage dogmatique et une construction." Marcel Proust, letter to Jacques Rivière, February 7, 1913, *Correspondance*, vol. 12 (Paris: Plon, 1984)—this is in regard to *Swann's Way.*
84. Gérard Genette, "Proust palimpseste," in *Figures* (Paris: Seuil, 1966), 66.
85. On the concept of progressive revelation that emerged in the nineteenth century, see Norman Solomon, *Torah from Heaven: The Reconstruction of Faith* (Portland: Littman Library of Jewish Civilization, 2012), 212–14.
86. Marcel Proust, letter to Curtius, September 17, 1922, in *Correspondance* (Paris: Plon, 1993), vol. 11, note 324, 478–79. ("Il ne faut jamais avoir peur d'aller trop loin car la vérité est au-delà.")

THE TIMESWERVE

Reading Elliot Wolfson in a Block Universe

JEFFREY KRIPAL

> *My argument rests on taking seriously an alternative understanding of time as a reversible swerve, a scientific perspective that conflicts with the commonsensical view of time's irreversible linearity. . . . Methodologically, the appeal is to apply a natural scientific model of time to the humanist effort to understand historical experience.*
>
> ELLIOT WOLFSON, "TIMESWERVE/HERMENEUTIC REVERSIBILITY," PROLOGUE TO *LANGUAGE, EROS, BEING*

IT HAS BEEN A LONG TIME. IT WAS THE LATE 1990S AND THEN THE TURN OF the millennium. I was writing what would become my second book, *Roads of Excess, Palaces of Wisdom*, a study of the mystical experiences of scholars of mysticism and how these altered states of consciousness and erotic energy secretly shaped the public scholarship and so the different intellectual lineages of five major scholars of religion. The first four figures were, in this order: the early proponent of Christian "mysticism" and British Episcopalian spiritual guide Evelyn Underhill, the French Islamicist and biographer of the crucified Sufi ecstatic al-Hallaj Louis Massignon, the British Oxford Zoroastrian scholar and Sanskritist R. C. Zaehner, and the Austrian American anthropologist turned countercultural Hindu monk and mystic Agehananda Bharati.

All four had passed at the time of my writing. The early work of Elliot Wolfson on the theophanic envisioning of the body of God in medieval Kabbalah, the identity of mystical experience and scriptural interpretation in the theory-practices of the kabbalists, and the homoerotic structures of their ecstatic visions constituted my fifth case study.[1] That final chapter thus brought the conversation about the mystical experiences of scholars of mysticism into the then present. The present essay brings it into our own present, which is now the future of that past.

It was the spring of 2001. I was proofreading the galleys of this same book when Elliot came up to Cambridge from New York City to help me teach a seminar at Harvard Divinity School on "Method as Path." It was *Roads* in pedagogical form. I was teaching Elliot's work that week. We were both young. For some reason, I most remember the hat he was wearing on a crisp New England day: one of those flat wool caps often called "Ivy." Was this some stylish nod to his Jewish identity, a way of covering the male head that was not obviously Jewish? Such visual paradoxes are certainly Wolfsonian enough. But I may be overreading my memory. Maybe he was just cold and needed a hat.

I do know that Elliot was happy. So was I. And why not? What we were envisioning in our respective bodies of work seemed possible, thinkable, doable—a profound hermeneutical engagement with the full history of religions that embraced and celebrated all of the critical and historical methods of the humanities, particularly the gender and sexual theories so prominent in the humanities at that time, but also recognized the potential gnostic or esoteric effects such a study could have on the scholars themselves and their careful readers. We saw a new world.

Then it all seemed to disappear, vanish, before our eyes, partly, it turned out, via Logan Airport, the very airport I was using to commute back and forth between Boston and Pittsburgh every other week. I would take my last flight home in the middle of June 2001, after a beautiful Harvard graduation where the German Continental philosopher and hermeneut Hans-Georg Gadamer was present and honored. A few months later, everything would seem to collapse in fire, smoke, and leaping, choking, and crushed bodies.

I know perfectly well that there were one or two other major engagements with Wolfson's early work in circulation at the turn of the millennium, but I believe my long chapter essay on his hermeneutical mysticism and imaginal theory of visionary experience in his first major monograph, *Through a Speculum That Shines* (1994), was probably the longest engagement with the young intellectual's body of work at that particular historical moment. In any case, a quarter of a century ago (we are getting old!), in the mid- and late 1990s, it was already patently obvious to me that Elliot Wolfson would become a major voice not only in the study of medieval Kabbalah and Jewish studies, but in the larger field of the comparative study of religion.

Allow me to begin there. It is my own long held opinion, which I have shared with Elliot on many an occasion (to his own considerable doubts and discomfort), that, although it is perfectly true that his body of work has been mostly ignored by scholars outside Jewish studies, his seemingly endless stream of essays, monographs, and collections of essays carry tremendous if as yet unassimilated implications for the study of religion, indeed, for the future order of knowledge itself (and, yes, I really mean that). To call Elliot Wolfson "ahead of his time" is something of a grotesque understatement, although, as we shall see here, it may also be literally true.

Having said as much, I do think of Elliot's paradoxical thought somewhat differently today than I did back in the 1990s. I would not change anything about that initial chapter essay of 2001, but I would say something else, which is what I want at least to gesture toward here. The point is worth underlining. My engagement with the books and essays of Elliot Wolfson has been anything but exhaustive. It has been selective and partial. That, of course, is how life and scholarship generally work, this life and this scholarship, anyway. If there is anything I possess in great measure, it is finitude. I certainly claim no complete knowledge, total reading, or adequate comprehension of the Wolfsonian oeuvre, and I will pretend none here.

Part of the problem is, obviously, the sheer scope and length of Elliot's body of work. Who can read all of these dense essays and exquisite books, with Talmudic notes that constitute more mini-essays and other directions, no less? And even if one *could* read all of this, pursue all of these directions, how exactly can one really understand it all, unless one happens to be professionally trained in ancient and medieval Hebrew, the history of Judaism, kabbalistic hermeneutics, biblical scholarship (Torah and New Testament), Continental philosophy, the histories of Gnosticism, Neoplatonism, and Western esotericism, *and* the contemporary comparative study of religion?

Where in that list did *you* stop? I personally possess an adequate knowledge of only the last subject and, on my best days, a smattering of some of the others. I do not read Hebrew, and I possess no adequate knowledge of the history and hermeneutics of kabbalistic literature, much less Jewish studies. I am a goy, a gentile, a voice from outside the tradition.

Okay, but then why *was* I so drawn, and still am, to Elliot's work? What was it that so attracts this most inadequate reader?

I think I know.

EROS, GNOSIS, HERMES

That uncanny attraction has in fact morphed over the decades. In the 1990s, our initial conversations orbited around the exoteric heterosexual practices and symbolisms and esoteric sublimated homoeroticisms and autoeroticisms of male mystical traditions around the world. We had arrived at the same fundamental conclusion—the orthodox prominence of a kind of esoteric or sublimated male homoeroticism—with completely different cultural materials: he with medieval kabbalistic texts, I with Roman Catholic mystical literature and then the Bengali texts surrounding the Shakta Hindu saint Ramakrishna (1836–1886).[2] There was a kind of shock of realizing that the two of us, completely independently and with historically unrelated traditions, had come to more or less identical conclusions about any number of things, from the intensely erotic nature of male ascetic practice, to the homoerotic underpinnings of two ostensibly heterosexual symbolisms, to the deeply androcentric nature of apparently feminine religious imaginaries.

Related here was the fact that I saw mirrored in Wolfson's corpus one of my own deepest methodological convictions, namely, that psychoanalytic theory and traditional forms of mystical thought display any number of analogous structures and insights, and that this correspondence or resonance renders psychoanalytic theory a particularly apt tool with which to explore the comparative erotics of mystical literature. Such a shock was further deepened and personalized when both of our works became the objects of severe criticisms by individuals who missed, completely, the dialectical nature of our psychoanalytic theorizing, that is, who mistook our dialectical gnosis for a grossly simplistic reductionism or culturally naïve psychologism.

As our conversations grew and deepened, however, I became more and more convinced that a big part of the resonance worked on another plane. I began to intuit something comparative in nature. Allow me to explain. I have been struck over the years by how Elliot refuses what every other scholar of religion seems simply to assume or wish: a historical positivism or absolute contextualism, a total immanence with not a whiff of transcendence, a kind of intellectual bowing down to absolute multiplicity, complete difference, and, frankly, ultimate meaninglessness.

Not here. As far as I can tell, Elliot Wolfson has done as much as anyone to emphasize and explore historical differences, even when such differences are anything but congratulatory and positive. Think of his extensive explorations of Jewish phallomorphism and the ontological subsumption of the female into the male in *Speculum*, his long meditations on medieval Jewish exclusivism and essentialism in *Language, Eros, Being*, or his radical critique of theism, or what he calls theomania, in *Giving Beyond the Gift*.

But, at the same time, Wolfson has also identified and refigured profound transtraditional themes, like the double mirroring of humanity and divinity in both medieval Kabbalah and Christian mystical sources, what he calls "the specular entwinning of anthropomorphism and theomorphism: envisioning the divine as human mirrors envisioning the human as divine."[3] More radically still, he has always insisted on a kind of transhistorical unity or even identity among the religions at their most radical and most sophisticated, an empty not-one but also a shimmering not-two at the heart of global mystical literature, especially in these literatures' more apophatic modes.[4]

Such a paradoxical thinking that emphasizes both radical historical particularity and ontic emptiness-fullness is extremely familiar to the historian of Asian religions. And it is no accident at all, I think, that so much that Elliot writes looks a good deal like some kind of postmodern fusion of the medieval Kabbalah's *Ayn Sof* or Infinite and some of the most sophisticated streams of Buddhist and Hindu thought. If I may, there is a certain Zen-like or Mahayana Buddhist quality here. Elliot Wolfson reads like a Jewish Nagarjuna. If I had to describe Elliot Wolfson in a few words, I would say that he is a postmodern kabbalist with strong Buddhist convictions in the "emptiness" and apophatic "nothingness" of a shared and universal Godhead, which, very much in line with the ancient Jewish and Christian Gnostics, is *not* the "God" of the Bible that we are always asked to believe (as if it were not so natural or obvious to do so).

On this same comparative mystics (as in "physics"), consider especially his second big book on the poetics and ontologies of the kabbalistic imagination, *Language, Eros, Being* (2005). I will in fact focus the essay around this particular text. It had been just a little over a decade since *Speculum* (1994), and Wolfson had seemingly read, well, almost everything. He thus cites scholarship on Sahajiya Vaisnavaism, the *yin* and *yang* of Taoist symbolism, various schools of Buddhism, Hindu Tantrism, Neoplatonism, and Valentinian Gnosticism.[5] He also invokes, again in a comparative mode, Lacanian psychoanalysis, the poetry of William Blake, Jungian archetypal psychology, even contemporary scientific speculations on space-time and string theory, to which we will soon return.[6] Obviously, this is a mind that does not feel bound to a single time period, culture, discourse, or ethnic identity.

From a strictly Indological perspective, I could cite many striking comparative moments in the book. Wolfson's comparative pattern of the male androgyne in Valentinian Gnosticism and medieval Kabbalah, for example, whereby the feminine is ontologically assimilated into the masculine, fits powerfully with many Indic materials, including the famous figure of Ardhanarisvara, that classical androgynous deity of the Hindu pantheon whose name means literally "the Lord Who Is Half Woman" (and not "the Goddess Who Is Half Man"). One might also recall here the central Indic icon of the *lingam*, Siva's symbolic phallus that—very much like the Lacanian phallus—both is and is not a penis and whose Sanskrit name literally means "signifying mark" (*lingam*). Lacan might as well have been writing in Sanskrit.

But perhaps one of the most striking comparative moments of the book is Wolfson's explication of the theme of the erotic eunuch and what he describes as "the ascetic practice of retaining the discharge of semen from the corona of the penis (*ateret berit*) and elevating the sexual energy to the top of the head, whence it is transformed into the crown of royalty (*keter malkhut*)." In his typical dialectical fashion, Wolfson notes that this process is "at once the crowning object of visualization, the subject who is crowned and thereby empowered to see, and the medium by which the former is envisioned and the latter envisions." He recognizes, in other words, that mystical visionary experience is often a nondual erotic event. He also recognizes that this particular aspect of Kabbalah "bears close phenomenological resemblance to Tantric practice."[7]

The correspondences here with various Kaula and Shakta subtle physiologies are indeed striking. Indeed, they are uncanny. I can only wonder, out loud, whether such comparative resonances across space and time do not witness to something well beyond the social constructions and historical relativisms of our present methodologies, that is, whether we cannot begin to speak of a certain *corpus mysticum*, that is, of the human body in *all* its global modes—"even the invisible astral body, *corpus sidereum*"[8]—as the gnostic ground of our comparative speculations.

Like Wolfson, I must issue a series of warnings and denials here. I am not suggesting an ahistorical essentialism, nor am I calling for a return to some naïve perennialism. I am, however, suggesting, very much with Wolfson, that "matters pertaining to the spiritual have repeatedly been depicted in erotic images."[9] I am also suggesting that this strong comparative pattern can be explained by the physiological facticity and—dare I say—universality of the human body.

Which is not at all to claim either a cross-cultural homogeneity nor a "simply sexual" reductionism. How could such moves possibly be adequate, when each culture attributes different and multiple symbolic meanings and ontological resonances to what we today call sexuality, masculinity, femininity, the body, desire, and so on? Rather, the hermeneutical challenge consists in trying to understand other ontological conceptions of human sexuality—many of them quite astonishing—which are in turn embedded in elaborate webs of cultural practices and emotional fields, and allowing these to define and guide, at least initially, our interpretations. Something like erotic forms of mysticism, in other words, cannot be discussed comparatively, as if they were all minor variations on the exact same thing. Behind such a discourse lies the unspoken assumption that every time and culture has more or less agreed on the ontological natures of spiritual *and* sexual experience *and* on the manner in which they do or do not intersect.

Along related lines, I also know of *no one* who has done more to advance a remotely adequate theory of the religious imagination, an understanding of the "veilings" of the religious imagination that also constitute a series of genuine "revealings." Deeply indebted but by no means restricted to earlier (Heideggerian) theorists like Henry Corbin, such a theory of ecstasy and vision understands the imagination as a potential organ of cognition that displays forms that are both fundamentally true and literally false. Such a theory of the religious imagination balances and embraces both difference and sameness, even as it recognizes both the tricks and the truths, *even the truths within the tricks*, of the history of religions. Who else today still speaks and writes of the "symbol" in anything but superficially social or cognitive psychological terms? The Platonic symbol has become nothing but an Aristotelian metaphor, a "representation," a "discourse," always doing more or less bad things, of course.

Very much a part of this same theory of the poetics and hermeneutics of the imagination is Wolfson's keen sense that hermeneutical activity and mystical practice were more or less identical in medieval Kabbalah, that reading sacred scripture and interpreting it—often through elaborate techniques that can only be described as creative (mis) readings—constituted an effective contemplative practice for these reading communities. Trained in the Benedictine monastic discipline of *lectio divina* or "divine reading" and a general Christian mystical and liturgical context within which the *logos* or word was believed to have literally become flesh, this was always an implicit understanding for me, but never had I seen it so fully explained and explored.

Elliot's insistence on the double mirror of the human and the divine forms in *Language, Eros, Being* did little to dissuade this reader and much to pull him in further. Wolfson gave me a way to understand my own Christian tradition as Jewish and, in the double mirror of his hermeneutics, the Jewish tradition as Christian. He gave us all a way to think in between and, frankly, beyond.[10]

MORE MIRRORS

Looking back from today, I would say now that there is something deeper still in the Wolfsonian oeuvre that attracted me so, a particular structure of thought that it is difficult to name but that is nevertheless easily recognizable. One might name this structure with any number of inadequate words: paradoxical, circular, hermeneutical, reflexive, specular. It is this that I most want to say, even if it cannot quite be said.

Consider the reflecting image of the mirror again. The specular image of the mirror shines throughout Elliot Wolfson's corpus, of course. There is a certain optics here, which also encodes both a hermeneutics and a kind of postmodern gnosis that is, by definition, not restricted to any particular tradition or culture. That gnosis is rigorously dialectical and self-reflexive. It continuously bends back on itself, very much, as Wolfson himself recognizes, like the ancient *ouroboros* biting its own tail (the image, as we shall see below, is more than metaphor). This serpentine or tail-biting movement (which is also somehow vaguely autoerotic) doubles throughout the body of work, determining in the process some of that work's most basic paradoxical insights.

Consider, in particular, Wolfson's consistent reflections on the epistemological paradox of the veil, that is, the previously mentioned theoretical notion that the religious symbol reveals only through concealing and conceals only by revealing, that the imaginal world mediated by the mystical organ of the imagination may be both metaphysically true and literally false. Hence also Wolfson's insistence that it is entirely traditional to subvert the tradition, that heterodoxy and orthodoxy are symbiotic, that the greatest respect one can show a religious tradition is to engage it in a radically critical fashion and thereby to change *and* preserve it. And why not? In my own terms, tradition is always a trick and a truth, or, better, a truth through a trick.

I think we can also place here Wolfson's consistent embrace of Nicholas of Cusa's *coincidentia oppositorum* or "coincidence of opposites" as a model of kabbalistic thought and as a forerunner or fulfillment of postmodern theory today. This coincidence of opposites or identity of opposites, which violates and *transcends* the Aristotelian logic that presently defines pretty much the entire academy, is perhaps the deepest structure of all Wolfson's cognitive structures, the firmest bite of the serpent's own tail in his looping, doubling, and doubled texts. Here is how Wolfson describes that structure early on in *Language, Eros, Being*:

> To savor the mystical intuition of the divine as the coincidence of being and nothing—what may be considered for the kabbalist, as his counterpart in medieval Islamic and Christian mystical speculation, the primary ontological binary that comprises other binary constructions, the binary of binaries, we might say—one must reclaim the middle excluded by the logic of the excluded middle, for it is only by positioning oneself in that middle between extremes that one can appreciate the identity of opposites in the opposition of their identity: that a thing is not only both itself and its opposite, but neither itself nor its opposite.[11]

The reflections of the Wolfsonian mirror do not, however, stop here. Each reading into its reflective surface evokes another series of reflections, another envisioning. Accordingly, I have been struck over the years how the Wolfsonian corpus reflects, in an almost occult manner, my own thought and writing. I am not exaggerating. There is something uncanny about this man's words, something that finally escapes and overflows reason, something that makes me actually believe in a *kabbalah*, that is, a received tradition—not of a purely Jewish wisdom, of course, although that is part of it too, but of our own modern and now postmodern comparative gnosis.

The "our" of my expression is carefully chosen, and deliberately open-ended. I include myself in it and have, indeed, self-identified as a gnostic intellectual many times over the years.[12] I also include, with care, the texts of Elliot Wolfson, although Elliot, of course, is free to reject or qualify my appropriation of his own mirroring thought. As readers, you too are free to extend this comparative gnosis to yourself, or to reject it as inappropriate. Still, *these texts are mirrors*.

THE REALIST IMPULSE

And they mirror more than ourselves. Indeed, what is so remarkable about the Wolfsonian mirror is that it means to make a claim on reality, on *physical reality*, on space-time and causality themselves. They mirror the real. Wolfson thus instantiates what I have elsewhere called the "realist impulse of the cosmic humanities."[13]

Wolfson enacts this realist impulse quite explicitly in *A Dream Interpreted Within a Dream*, where he puts kabbalistic dream interpretation into conversation with the speculative reaches of quantum mechanics in order to demonstrate how the construal of meaning in the dream is brought into being or actualized through attention, consciousness, and the act of dream interpretation itself, much as the act of observation is said to "collapse the wave function" in one interpretation of the quantum mechanical experiment. It is simply not possible to extricate the presence of consciousness from the behavior of reality in either context: to perceive is to be.[14]

But Wolfson also enacts this realist impulse in the prologue to *Language, Eros, Being*, and it is there that I most want to go in this essay. Before I do, however, it is worth pointing out that there is a particular intellectual lineage at work in such moments. Most substantively for our own academic practices in the humanities, such a realist impulse goes at least as far back as the ecstatic nineteenth-century figure of Friedrich Nietzsche. More immediately, however, it goes back to the Romanian historian of religions Ioan Couliano.

Before he was murdered in a bathroom stall in the spring of 1991, Couliano was teaching and writing about the history of mystical literature and paranormal experience and their likely relationships to quantum physics, hyperdimensional geometry, and modern cosmology. Ioan was asking, in so many words, why historians were writing about "history," as if time really were a simple linear causal process, when we know, since Einstein, that this is simply not so, that time does not work like this at all. In effect, Couliano was asking the bracing question: How should we think and write about the history of religions, and in particularly about mystical experiences and paranormal events, in a post-Einsteinian universe?

Hence his bizarrely beautiful introduction to *The Tree of Gnosis*, where Couliano begins to explore what is essentially a Platonic model of historiography, with hyperdimensional idealist forms interacting in three-dimensional historical time with different actors and movements as these forms play out their different cognitive possibilities.[15] Hence also his little potent essay, "A Historian's Kit for the Fourth Dimension."[16]

I ask all my PhD students to read two essays: Couliano's "A Historian's Kit for the Fourth Dimension" and Wolfson's "Prologue: Timeswerve/Hermeneutic Reversibility." I think of both constantly. It is my own conviction that these few pages contain some of the most provocative lines ever written in the modern study of religion. I have written about Couliano's toolkit and how it reflects and draws on various Spiritualist and psychical research currents elsewhere. For his part, Wolfson takes up the question of Einsteinian space-time in order to answer a most obvious and common criticism of his work: that there is something anachronistic or inappropriate about employing nineteenth- and twentieth-century Continental philosophy to medieval kabbalistic literature.

Not if space-time is curved, not if time is both linear and circular, not if the future can reach back to the past in order to change or reveal its meaning, Wolfson answers back. Listen:

> Without delving into the thicket of theoretic grappling that this subject demands, I pose the rhetorical question: What would be the consequences if a historian were to take seriously the conclusion reached on the basis of Einstein's General Theory of Relativity that spacetime—the "mathematical structure" that "serves as a unifying causal background for phenomena"—is to be regarded as a curve? Does this not at least entail the possibility that the past is as much determined by the present as the present by the past?[17]

This, of course, is Couliano's question. Wolfson pushes the point further, into the heart of matter, by invoking and quoting the German mathematician and physicist Hermann Weyl: "The possibility of future connecting with past, of time moving backwards, 'arises because a gravitational field implies that spacetime is curved, and the curvature might be great enough and extended enough to join a spacetime to itself in novel ways.'" What we end up with here is "a closed loop figuratively depicting the object/subject becoming its own past." Hence Einstein's famous remark in a letter he wrote after receiving the news of the death of his friend Michele Basso, that the distinctions between past, present, and future are ultimately illusory, that time itself is "a stubbornly persistent illusion."[18]

One can begin to see why historians would not look too kindly on Einsteinian spacetime, why they might want to ignore the advances of theoretical physics, pretend, in effect, they never happened. Reality has fundamentally changed beneath their feet, but best not to look. Just keep walking on the surface of things. This new reality, after all, presumes the final illusory status of their discipline and, presumably, of themselves. It implies that space-time is, to quote the physicists themselves again, one immense "block," and that causal influence can move both forward *and* backward within such a block universe.

Such a model is speculative, like all cosmological hypotheses, but it is seriously maintained by numerous physicists and cosmologists, is supported by Einstein's relativity theory, and has received major philosophical attention.[19] In the block universe cosmology, developed after the work of Einstein and his teacher Hermann Minkowski, all of time or history—past, present, and future—already exists within an immense cosmic "block" or space-time continuum that extends from the Big Bang to however the cosmos finally ends (or "bounces" back). Temporality or our sense of linear time (and so all of "history") is, in effect, a neurological illusion that our brains produce as we experience ourselves "moving" through this eternal and unchanging spatiotemporal block.

We are not really moving, of course. What we experience as our present bodies and specious selves are merely phenomenological snapshots or single frames along the running film of a "long self" or a "long body" that can be imagined as a decades-long, four-dimensional space-time worm wiggling out from conception to death.[20] Here is such a block universe as described by the scholar of mysticism and philosopher of religion Paul Marshall:

> The special theory of relativity has led some thinkers to speculate that past, present and future events coexist in a unit of space and time called "space-time." Likewise, mystical experiences sometimes give the impression that past, present and future exist together in an "Eternal Now." This was certainly true in my own experience.[21]

Marshall is careful and qualified here, perhaps because he writes with significant training in special relativity. But he also writes of this particular comparison through his own mystical experience, as his last line makes clear. Like countless mystical philosophers before him, Marshall will argue, in great detail and with great care, that such a universe not only exists as such, but can be directly known as such.[22] This all, of course, implies the very real possibility of retrocausation within the block universe, to speak in the terms of the physicists. It implies "willing backwards," to speak in the terms of Nietzsche.

Yes, Friedrich Nietzsche.

THE RETURN OF THE ETERNAL RETURN

It is well known that one of Nietzsche's most important teachings, indeed what Michael Allen Gillespie has called his "final teaching," was the "eternal recurrence of the same" (*ewige Wiederkunft des Gleichen*), also known more simply as the eternal return.[23] The teaching was about the circularity of time and how everything and each of us will be repeated, in our tiniest details, over and over again, not in some serial fashion but in a circular one. Much as someone traveling on the equator might think that they are traveling in a straight flat line, they are not, and they will see the exact same landscapes and coastlines repeat themselves soon enough. They are, after all, in fact traveling on the surface of a sphere. If we extended this global circling to space *and* time, we would have something approaching the ecstatic vision of Nietzsche's eternal return.

It is important to understand that, at least since George Simmel famously rejected Nietzsche's central teaching in 1907, commentators on Nietzsche have generally followed suit and widely dismissed the eternal recurrence of the same as incoherent and indefensible, as just a little, or a lot, crazy. When they are feeling more generous, they read eternal recurrence as an "idea" to which the philosopher reasoned or thought and that we can now play with and "think" in our heads, as if it were nothing more than a cognitive act of neurons and education, or some moral experiment designed to get us to accept the unchangeable details and directions of our lives.

It simply is not so. As recent Nietzschean scholars like Paul S. Loeb have taught us, such a safe metaphorical reading is not reflective of Nietzsche's fierce conviction that, in the words of Loeb, "he had discovered a fundamental truth about the nature of the cosmos that would change his life and the history of humankind."[24] Indeed, Nietzsche clearly thought of eternal recurrence as the most scientific of truths and whispered its awesome truths to his closest disciples as some kind of transgressive, almost unspeakable secret.[25]

That's because it was. And it came with equally awesome implications, including physical immortality (since these bodies always return exactly as they are) and a kind of retrocausal influence. In Loeb's reading again, one of the central claims of *Thus Spoke Zarathustra*, woven right into the narrative arc of the book that Nietzsche himself considered his most important, is the claim of "willing-backwards" (*Zurückwollen*), in other words, the power to influence the meaning and import of the past, if never to change the physical events of that past. This, of course, constitutes a kind of occult hermeneutics, a willed interpretation of the past from the future that changes the meaning of that past, much, I dare point out, as Elliot Wolfson's philosophical readings of medieval Kabbalah change and transform the meanings of those kabbalistic texts. Hence his use of twentieth-century figures like Husserl, Merleau-Ponty, and Heidegger to read texts from the medieval period.

Unsurprisingly, numerous commentators on Nietzsche's philosophy of time have noted and emphasized a clear correlation with Einstein's (later) theory of relativity.[26] In lay terms, this is the notion that there is no absolute space-time through which all things are moving—space-time is relative to the observer; what is past, present, or future is not laid out on a single linear arrow; tense is entirely relative to the position of the observer. Put more colloquially still, time and space are not "out there" as a universal container in which all things flow in a single direction.

I must quickly add that Nietzsche did not understand his eternal return in block universe terms. He did not have that particular cosmology available to him. He thus interpreted the eternal recurrence of the same *in numerical terms*, that is, he argued that the same things repeat themselves over and over again eternally within a numerical series of cycles. With the simplest "click" from the modern lens of the block universe cosmology, however, Nietzsche's implausible claim immediately becomes plausible, if also admittedly different (I want to own my own backward-willing or future-reading here). This is *not* what Nietzsche thought, but I cannot shake the idea that the two ideas—eternal recurrence and the block cosmology of space-time—are somehow related, somehow two human attempts to get at the same superhuman reality from a genuine Archimedean point outside space and time altogether.

In any case, with this new block cosmological click, things come into quick focus now. In the block cosmology, after all, every moment *is* happening again and again, right now, within the same, that is, within the block universe. So is every past moment. So is every future moment. It is all there, at once, simultaneously, happening "over and over again" not in a linear but in a block eternal sense. It is all one immense Now, one gigantic *déjà vu* universe.

IT'S ABOUT TIME

I began this essay by quoting Wolfson describing his project as taking seriously a scientific model of time as a "reversible swerve," as an effort "to apply a natural scientific model of time to the humanist effort to understand historical experience."[27] What I would like to add here is that, much more often than we imagine, the humanist's "historical experience" does not work "historically" at all and looks *a lot* like the natural scientific model that allows for retrocausal influences, particularly as we find it in the block cosmology. Put a bit differently, I think the most extraordinary moments of historical experience, singular life events that the individuals *never forget* and so are by definition "set apart," confirm a natural scientific model of time, including and especially the ability of the future to reach back to the past or present.

I find such a block cosmology so satisfying and so necessary for a very simple reason: because it does not deny, because it does not make impossible, because it in fact makes very good sense of my own texts, which are *filled* with individuals precognizing or dreaming a future that shows every sign of already existing. Such texts even include numerous instances of individuals seeing themselves visiting themselves from the future, in effect influencing (or haunting) the present from the future, more or less exactly as Nietzsche claimed is possible in Loeb's provocative reading.

Clearly, if we take these reports seriously (and, please tell me, why should we not?), then such events can hardly be whisked away as instances of "luck," "coincidence," or "anecdote." This kind of hand-waiving strikes me as a shameless intellectual cop-out. Is it not more honest to admit that precognition and visits from a future self simply *happen*; that these are only "impossible" in the framework of our present, obviously fallible and relative present understandings of space and time; and that we can make such events possible again if we simply imagine ourselves living in a block universe in which the future has already happened and sometimes flows back into the present as a kind of apparitional self-guiding or spectral adjustment of history?

Perhaps such information does not really "flow" at all within such a universe. Perhaps, as the mystical literature claims again and again, *it is all one thing*. If so, reality is just communicating with itself as One, instantly and immediately, altogether in and as the block universe, from "eternity," as we say in religious terms.

In this specific reading back, we can now say that human beings can know, or dream, or, in some cases, literally "see" in a vision or apparition what is about to happen, not because they are guessing well or getting lucky in some cosmic poker game, not because they are "intuitive" (another cop-out), but because the event has in fact *already happened* and they themselves are *already physically connected* to it, really *are* it within the world block in that same future. There is not the slightest physical separation. It is all One.

Allow me to list a few examples of this shared space-time block to give the reader a felt sense of what is at stake. I leave the authors, dates, and places in the footnotes to emphasize that such experiences, being outside space and time as we normally think of these, cannot be reduced to these historical or contextual notions. Listen:

> As one comes suddenly out of darkness, I perceived the full meaning of the doctrine of immutability and said: "Now I can believe that fundamentally all things neither come nor go." I got up from my meditation bed, prostrated myself before the Buddha shrine and did not have the perception of anything in motion. I lifted the blind and stood in front of the stone steps. Suddenly the wind blew through the trees in the courtyard, and the air was filled with flying leaves which, however, looked motionless. . . . When I went to the back yard to make water, the urine seemed not to be running. I said: "That is why the river pours but does not flow." Thereafter all my doubts about birth and death vanished.[28]
>
> What happened to me between 12:30 and 4 o'clock on Friday, December 2, 1955? After brooding about it for several months, I still think my first, astonishing conviction was right—that on many occasions that . . . afternoon I existed outside time. I don't mean this metaphorically, but literally. I mean that the essential part of me (the part that thinks to itself "This is me") had an existence, quite conscious of itself, enjoying itself, reflecting on its strange experience, in a timeless order of reality outside the world as we know it. I count this experience . . . as the most astounding and thought-provoking experience of my life. . . . From my peculiar disembodied standpoint, all the events in my drawing-room between one-thirty and four existed together at the same time. . . . When we take off from an airport at night, we are aware of individual runway lights flashing past in succession. But when [we] look down a little later, we see them all existing together motionless. It is not self-contradictory to say that the lights flashed past in succession and also that they exist together motionless. Everything depends on the standpoint of the observer.[29]
>
> [In this frame of being] everything that has ever happened, as well as everything that will ever happen, all have an equal temporal status. In a certain sense, they are all there and one only has to look at them. . . . A perspective is taken by which all that will have happened at all times is co-present. In this limit situation, the temporal may, in a fashion, be reduced to the spatial.[30]
>
> Time didn't run linearly the way we experience it here. It's as though our earthly minds convert what happens around us into a sequence; but in actuality, when we're not expressing through our bodies, everything occurs simultaneously, whether past, present, or future.[31]
>
> And then it all made sense. In that unsettling, parallel reality . . . Dinah arrived at the realization that "birth and death actually don't have any meaning." When forced to clarify, she adds, "It's more of a state of always being. . . . Always being. So being now and always. There's no beginning or end. Every moment is an eternity of its own."[32]

The above are all experiences of the block universe of past, present, and future. Here is one on willing-backward, on an actual lived timeswerve, on the future reaching back to the past to "interpret" and so make bearable its specific suffering. It comes from an email dated March 9, 2020, from a PhD student of mine, John Allison. It is best simply to quote John's own words. He had told me this story before, and I had asked him to write it down. This is what he wrote:

> Late one night in early September 2013, I am sitting alone in my basement apartment in Princeton, NJ, after having had a few new friends over to play cards. As I sit there musing happily over the day's events, I suddenly notice a pair of flipflopped male feet and legs (with red shorts down to the knee), walking towards the basement window to my right. I am surprised by this, but even more so when a voice in my head materializes and begins repeating the same words over and over: "You're going to be OK, you're going to be OK, you're going to be OK."
>
> Rather than feeling frightened by this voice or the unknown person standing outside my basement window late at night, I inexplicably begin to sense a strange, loving energy moving through my whole body, and I begin to cry uncontrollably. After about a minute or so, the figure outside the window vanishes. I then rush out my backdoor to see where he has gone, but there is no one in sight. I write down the incident in my journal. Eventually, I will forget about it completely.
>
> The next three years were the absolute worst of my life. I suffered through terrifying bouts of heart arrhythmias, tachycardia, hypertension, and frequent visits to the ER, which led to chronic anxiety and depression. I often wondered if I was going to die. However, by 2016, I had made a turn for the better, and was getting happier and healthier.
>
> Cut to May 2017. I am out on a quiet, late night walk, thinking about nothing in particular. As I am returning home, I unexpectedly get this sense that something important is about to happen, and then I notice that the light is on in my front room (which surprises me because I know I had not left it on). But in a moment, I am not just surprised, but stunned as I perceive that there is a man sitting in the basement room, and that man is *me*, except younger. The hairs on my arms stood up on end. My heart began racing. I felt a surge of adrenaline in my body. And then, suddenly, a voice in my head said, "Now is the time." And somehow, I knew what I was going to do.
>
> I rushed up to the basement window and I then put my forehead against the house, closed my eyes, and just "sent" this feeling of love and comfort to my younger self with the whole of my being. I don't know how long I stood there doing this, but when I was done "sending" this message, I looked down, and the basement lights were off.
>
> I then ran inside, turned on the lights, and things were as I left them before my walk. And I fell upon the basement floor, weeping in joy, clutching my flip flops to my chest, and feeling like I had just been given some unthinkably tremendous gift. I often now wonder what would have happened if I had *not* somehow sent a message to myself during my years in crisis.

> This was easily one of the most important events of my entire life. I have hardly told anyone about it. Since this event, I have felt a deep assurance that all moments in time somehow exist simultaneously, and that, for whatever reason, sometimes two moments in time not *directly* connected to each other in linear causality still somehow "bleed" into and affect each other.

An "unthinkably tremendous gift." "This was easily one of the most important events of my entire life." Sit with those phrases, and then try to ignore them. Try to pretend that such events do not matter, do not possess historical agency, cannot be a very special and important part of what we so confidently call "history." Obviously, I do not read such claims with the usual dismissive categories of the humanities, that is, I do not read them as discourses, representations, or metaphors. I read them as honest and relatively accurate phenomenological descriptions of actual encounters with the physical cosmos of a warped or swerved spacetime.

And Elliot Wolfson? I personally cannot imagine such an intellectual writing so eloquently and extensively about the timeswerve and its hermeneutics without having some experience of the same, but I also know that Elliot is extremely reticent to speak or write of his own experiences. I do not expect him to do so, then, or even to find out if there have been such experiences. In some profound sense, it simply does not matter, *even when it matters.*

Let me explain.

As I signaled in the first lines of this little essay, it has long been my argument that some of the most canonical authors of the humanities—take Nietzsche, again, but there are literally hundreds of others—derived their ideas from the inspirations of altered states of consciousness and energy. The core ideas of the humanities are superhuman ideas in the sense that they emerged from "above" or "beyond" (super-) the ordinary human and historical condition. They arose from ecstatic epiphanies of mind. They were *not* the result of simple cognitive processes or logical syllogisms. They just *appeared.* I have been saying this simple truth for decades, at least since *Roads* (2001), but I have enacted this fundamental argument again in my forthcoming book on *The Superhumanities* (2022), which tries to call attention again to the esoteric and ecstatic roots of the humanities and some of their most influential texts and critical theories.[33]

Unsurprisingly, Wolfson makes a related argument at the very beginning of *Language, Eros, Being,* translating my focus on phenomenological experience into a more careful "direct or indirect connection with kabbalah." And why not? From the very beginning, from *Speculum* on, he has shown us how direct mystical experience and indirect textual interpretation have implicated one another, have become one another in this particular Jewish mystical tradition:

> Whether or not any of the thinkers to be discussed in chapter one has had direct or indirect connection with kabbalah is not a necessary condition to justify the employment of their insights in decoding this singularly complex expression of the Jewish religious imagination. Nonetheless, one cannot by any means rule out such links.

> On this score, it is of interest to ponder the possibility that Western esoteric speculation, which is greatly indebted to kabbalistic tradition, has had an impact on the history of linguistics, especially evident in the period of Romanticism and its aftermath, including Heidegger, well versed in the theosophy of Böhme and its reverberations in the idealist philosophy of Schelling.[34]

Others have made resonant observations about the esoteric roots of other major humanist thinkers, for example, Glenn Alexander Magee on the Hermetic structure of Hegel's thought or Jonathan Bricklin on the psychedelic and psychical inspirations of William James.[35] One could go on for a very long time here. I know. I have.

My point here? That, from where I sit and stand in the fall of 2021, this is why I think I have been so struck by the work of Elliot Wolfson over these years and decades, why his work has always felt so uncanny to me, so familiar and yet so other. Elliot not only understands what I have variously called the mystical experiences of scholars of mysticism, the gnostic dimensions of the study of religion, or, now, the superhumanities. He theorizes, lyricizes, performs them in erudite ways that stun and astonish. I do not know many things with certainty, but I know this: I know that Elliot Wolfson is one of my generation's most gifted and most far-seeing intellectuals, theorists, and poets. Time, I am convinced, will show our future selves as much, wherever and whoever we are. There will be a future of this past in the block universe and its looping, swooping timeswerves.

NOTES

A version of this chapter was originally published as "The Timeswerve: Theorizing in a Block Universe," in Jeffrey J. Kripal, *How to Think Impossibly: About Souls, UFOs, Time, Belief, and Everything Else* (Chicago: University of Chicago Press, 2024).

1. See "The Mystical Mirror of Hermeneutics: Gazing into Elliot Wolfson's *Speculum* (1994)," in Jeffrey J. Kripal, *Roads of Excess, Palaces of Wisdom: Eroticism and Reflexivity in the Study of Mysticism* (Chicago: University of Chicago Press, 2001). I apologize beforehand for citing so much of my own work in relationship to Elliot's throughout this essay, but that is, in the end, what this essay is really about: a relationship, a friendship, a most profound intellectual and spiritual debt. I make no apologies there.
2. Jeffrey J. Kripal, *Kali's Child: The Mystical and the Erotic in the Life and Teachings of Ramakrishna* (Chicago: University of Chicago Press, 1995/1998).
3. Elliot R. Wolfson, *Language, Eros, Being: Kabbalistic Hermeneutics and Poetic Imagination* (New York: Fordham University Press, 2005), xiii.
4. I really want to emphasize this apophatic universalism. I have attempted much the same balance between difference and sameness in my own work, most recently in "The Future of the Human(ities): Mystical Literature, Paranormal Phenomena, and the Politics of Knowledge," for Edward F. Kelly and Paul Marshall, eds., *Consciousness Unbound: Liberating Mind from the Tyranny of Materialism* (Lanham, MD: Rowman & Littlefield, 2021).

5. These citations are, in order of my listing of the traditions: Wolfson, *Language, Eros, Being*, 262; 107–8; xvi, 56–58, 441–42; 79–80, 234, 262, 271; 212–24; 155–56. I am positive such a list is not exhaustive.
6. Again, in order: Wolfson, *Language, Eros, Being*, 128–36; 142, 177, 190; 67, 105, 126–27, 141, 272; xvi–xxii, xxiv, 49, 201, 393–94.
7. Wolfson, *Language, Eros, Being*, 271.
8. Wolfson, *Language, Eros, Being*, xiv.
9. Wolfson, *Language, Eros, Being*, 261.
10. I would later have the honor of directing a dissertation on this mystical humanism, largely in Wolfson's body of work. See Gregory Perron, O.S.B., "Open Secret: Henry Corbin, Elliot Wolfson, and the Mystical Poetics of Deification," PhD dissertation, Rice University, 2020.
11. Wolfson, *Language, Eros, Being*, 27. The final phrase is indebted to the early Mahayana Buddhist philosopher Nagarjuna (ca. 150–250).
12. For the latest such self-description, see Jeffrey J. Kripal, "Reflections of an American Gnostic," *Gnosis: Journal of Gnostic Studies* 5 (2020): 121–25; reprinted with minor changes in *Gnostic Afterlives in American Religion and Culture*, ed. April D. DeConick and Jeffrey J. Kripal (Leiden: E. J. Brill, 2021).
13. This is one of the twenty gnomons I identify and explore in my memoir/manifesto: Jeffrey J. Kripal, *Secret Body: Erotic and Esoteric Currents in the History of Religions* (Chicago: University of Chicago Press, 2017).
14. Elliot R. Wolfson, *A Dream Interpreted Within a Dream: Oneiropoeisis and the Prism of Imagination* (Zone Books, MIT Press, 2011). Does anyone other than me think that the image of the sleeping man on the cover of this book looks more or less exactly like Elliot?
15. Ioan P. Couliano, *The Tree of Gnosis: Gnostic Mythology from Ancient Gnosticism to Modern Nihilism* (New York: HarperCollins, 1992).
16. This essay originally appeared in the defunct and especially rare journal *Incognita* (which Couliano edited), but later was happily employed as the opening chapter of Ioan P. Coulianu, *Out of This World: Otherworldly Journeys from Gilgamesh to Albert Einstein* (New York: Shambalah, 2001).
17. Wolfson, *Language, Eros, Being*, xvii.
18. Wolfson, *Language, Eros, Being*, xvii.
19. For a philosophical discussion, see Huw Price, *Time's Arrow and Archimedes' Point: New Directions for the Physics of Time* (New York: Oxford University Press, 1996). Contrary to the dogmas of the present humanities, it turns out that there may well be such a thing as an aperspectival position, the much abused (or much feared) "Archimedean point."
20. My understanding and use of these two phrases—"long body" and "long self"—are indebted to the work of the graphic novelists Grant Morrison and Alan Moore and the anthropologist and theorist of precognition Eric Wargo. See Eric Wargo, *Time Loops: Precognition, Retrocausation, and the Unconscious* (Anomalist Books, 2018); and *Precognitive Dreamwork and the Long Self: Interpreting Messages from Your Future* (Rochester: Inner Traditions, 2021).
21. Paul Marshall, *The Living Mirror: Images of Reality in Science and Mysticism*, 2nd ed. (London: Samphire Press, 2006), viii.
22. Note in particular the subtitle of his most recent book: Paul Marshall, *The Shape of the Soul:*

What Mystical Experience Tells Us about Ourselves and Reality (Lanham, MD: Rowman & Littlefield, 2019). Here is a near-perfect expression of the realist impulse of the cosmic humanities.

23. Michael Allen Gillespie, *Nietzsche's Final Teaching* (Chicago: University of Chicago Press, 2019).
24. Paul S. Loeb, *The Death of Nietzsche's Zarathustra* (Cambridge: Cambridge University Press, 2010), 11.
25. This is no doubt why at one point he seriously considered studying physics and mathematics at the University of Vienna or the University of Paris. See Gillespie, *Nietzsche's Final Teaching*, 183.
26. See Loeb, *The Death*, 26, n. 22.
27. Wolfson, *Language, Eros, Being*, xviii, xxi.
28. This is the Buddhist hermit-poet Han Shan or Cold Mountain. He is usually placed in the eighth or ninth century of the Western calendar. I am relying for this text on Peter Kingsley's use of it in his *Reality* (The Golden Sufi Center, 2004), 203.
29. This is British parliamentarian Christopher Mayhew, friend of Aldous Huxley, in Benny Shanon's chapter on "Time" in *The Antipodes of the Mind: Charting the Phenomenology of the Ayahuasca Experience* (Oxford: Oxford University Press, 2002), 227–28. Jonathan Bricklin fills in more details. He tells us that Mayhew's experience was on mescaline, which he took for a British documentary that was never aired, lest it offend the religious. Bricklin also points out that Mircea Eliade called this same account a "prodigious document" and confessed that he "trembled with joy" when he read it, since he had long worked on "the possibility of abolishing time, and of putting oneself into a trans-temporal condition" (Jonathan Bricklin, *The Illusion of Will, Self, and Time: William James's Reluctant Guide to Enlightenment* [Albany: State University of New York Press, 2016], 235–36). Eliade is, of course, well known for his insistence on a version of the eternal return and endlessly bashed for his so-called "anti-history." That is what happens to someone who tries to write about time in ways outside the positivist order of knowledge.
30. This is the Israeli psychologist Benny Shanon on the general phenomenology of the ayahuasca experience, in *The Antipodes of the Mind: Charting the Phenomenology of the Ayahuasca Experience* (New York: Oxford University Press, 2003), 47.
31. This is a near-death experience of the contemporary writer Anita Moorjani in *Dying to Be Me: My Journey from Cancer, to Near Death, to True Healing* (Carlsbad, CA: Hay House, 2014), 67.
32. This is the New York grandmother, atheist, and cancer survivor Dina Bazar after she was given psilocybin during a clinical trial at Johns Hopkins University, in Brian Muraresku, *The Immortality Key: The Secret History of the Religion with No Name* (New York: St. Martin's Press, 2020), v.
33. Jeffrey J. Kripal, *The Superhumanities: Historical Precedents, Moral Objections, New Realities* (Chicago: University of Chicago Press, 2022).
34. Wolfson, *Language, Eros, Being*, xv–xvi.
35. See, for example, Glenn Alexander Magee, *Hegel and the Hermetic Tradition* (Cornell: Cornell University Press, 2008); and Bricklin, *The Illusion of Will, Self, and Time.*

SEE UNDER

Erich Neumann's Typologies of the Great Mother and the Kabbalistic Lexical Tradition

PINCHAS GILLER

CARL GUSTAV JUNG'S CONCEPTION OF "THE ARCHETYPES OF THE COLLECTive Unconscious" is often applied to the analysis of religious symbolism. The writings of Jung and his immediate disciples revel in the employment of a seemingly encyclopedic understanding of religious symbolism to make their psychological points. Images from the world's religions are isolated, compared, and, most importantly, portrayed and analyzed in the writings of Jung, Erich Neumann, Joseph Campbell, Sheila Moon, and subsequent Jungian theorists. And yet, as will be discussed later, the avowed focus of Jungian psychology is clinical. The application of its ideas to religion and culture is a side-product of the methodology, popular as such studies have become.

Along with Sigmund Hurvitz, Erich Neumann was senior among Jung's Jewish students, and he maintained a good relationship with Jung through the war years until his death in 1960 in Tel Aviv.[1] For Neumann, as with all the Jungians, the interpretation of symbols, whether in dreams or in the happenstance of daily life, was a device to derive meaning from experience, to provide a window into the processes of the unconscious mind. Neumann saw his work as reflected in various elements of the mystical canon, particularly in his portrayal of Hasidism as an expression of Jung's goal of individuation, that is, developing a stable personality, in a Jewish context. In fact, the contemporary reader will discover that his understanding of Hasidism was well refracted through the lens of his contemporary German Jewish redactors Martin Buber and Gershom Scholem.

More original was Neumann's work on the mother archetype, which, in its use of artistic images and archaeological relics, expanded on Jung's early treatises and forecast later popularizers of the form such as Joseph Campbell. In his major study, *The Great Mother*, Neumann portrayed the mother archetype as a recurrent theme in the development of civilization, moving from primitive images of fecundity and the demonic into more sophisticated expressions of individuated wholeness. The archetype originated in the animating fears and insecurities of primitive society, from the "elementary" expressions of the feminine, both negative and positive, into the more complex, "transformative" portrayals of the "Great Mother." His typologies of the recurrence and parallel expressions of the theme in world mythology and culture created a compelling narrative of the role of the feminine archetype in the evolution of human consciousness. In Kabbalah, of course, these impulses took shape in the image of the Shekhinah,[2] a subject that has been plumbed exhaustively in the academy.

Religious structures and lore provided an apt source of symbols, serving to achieve individuation, self-understanding, and the attainment of religious and personal consciousness. Mythic and image-laden religious systems, such as alchemy, Gnosticism, orthodox Christianity, Vedic traditions, and Tantra were also apt sources of archetypal symbolism. The symbolic content of classical Kabbalah is also a ready corpus for Jungian analysis. The Jungian enterprise, identifying the transpersonal symbols and analyzing their significance for the purposes of therapy, is comparable to the isolation of the symbol in classical Kabbalah, and in the symbolic lexicons that constitute a significant literary genre.

In the case of Kabbalah, as with other spiritual systems and canons, Jungian symbols exist mainly in the unconscious, yet they are windows into transcendence. In practice, the classical Jewish mystic moves through a phenomenal world in which the tropes of the law and the canon, the symbols and imagery of religious practice, and the phenomena of the natural world are all shuffled into one set of insights into the shifting nature of reality. In this reshuffling of the imagery of the Jewish canon, the archetypal feminine coalesces and asserts itself. Within the palate of symbols, cross-cultural commonalities emerge, so that the vicissitudes of the Shekhinah come to resemble the lore of other religious systems. This paper will examine the possible overlap between the two systems, the isolation of symbols of the feminine in Neumann's work and in the kabbalistic lexical tradition. The feminine archetype permeates the Hebrew canon, from the Bible through the Talmud, into the zoharic and Lurianic systems of Kabbalah. Neumann's typologies of the mother archetype are common throughout Jewish literature, in its symbolism and textual imagery.

THE SYMBOLIC LEXICONS

In applying psychological ideas to the lexical tradition, the material to be analyzed is not what, say, a patient might involuntarily blurt out but what the compiler chose to see. In this regard, the early Kabbalah chose to see a symbolic universe inside of the general Jewish canon. As Daniel Abrams has observed with regard to the "Commentary to the Ten Sefirot" genre,

> what are conceived today as literary works functionally served in the Middle Ages as literary invitations to revise such structures such that the physical manuscripts were the material sites for discussion of those who participated in the textual communities of kabbalists that reproduced and engendered textual variation and similar discussions on paper and parchment. In other words, the textual practice of the

> kabbalists, from the thirteenth century and on through modern times, refashioned such works by expanding, editing, and revising the text with countless forms of revisions, from the altering of a single word to the interpolation of a marginal gloss and the creation of recognizable different version.[3]

The symbolic lexicons are very much the result of the vagaries of circulation and publishing, as Andrea Gondos has stressed in her recent studies.[4] Their development and circulation came about as the result of a number of factors. Kabbalists wanted to record their notes and observations for posterity outside of the context of a commentary or monograph. The public was anxious to acquire the wisdom and publishers, importantly, were on the lookout for content. Kabbalistic lexicons were circulated as the result of these impulses on the kabbalistic street of early modernity.

Theosophical Kabbalah has always been a mysticism of language, in which all its components, its consonants, vowels, and cantillation, control metaphysical energies and specific powers.[5] The Zohar is written in an interpretive code, based in often archetypal symbolism,[6] portraying the interplay of divine processes. Andrea Gondos, in her recent surveys of lexicological literature of Kabbalah, has addressed the problems of interpreting the Zohar literature according to its most simple meaning.[7] Lexicons of all sorts were employed to decipher that Zohar's idiosyncratic and fanciful use of Aramaic. Another set of lexicons, however, was developed to analyze the Zohar's symbolic content.

Throughout the literature of Kabbalah, symbolism was self-consciously employed to invoke ideas deemed too arcane and transcendent to portray as they truly are. The need to properly interpret these symbols led to a particular type of interpretive literature, including, through the generations, a series of symbolic lexicons.[8] Historically and geographically, this literary genre extends from the period contemporary with the Zohar's circulation to the present, from Ottoman Galilee and Tripoli to Galicia and Lithuania to contemporary Israel, over the course of several centuries. In all of these schools of thought, the symbolic exegesis of the canon, including the Zohar, remains important and, as a rule, one needed a program to know the players and understand the game.[9] As explained by Hartley Lachter, the intent of a lexicon, as with the earlier commentary form, is that "when (one) reads a biblical verse, or Rabbinic dictum, or a matter described in a kabbalistic composition, that he will understand the intention of that verse or dictum."[10]

The symbolic lexicons that will serve as source material for this study were generated over a period of nearly eight hundred years, from the earliest stirrings of the Kabbalah in Provence and Gerona, through the Safed renaissance and into Hasidic and non-Hasidic compendiums. This process has continued into modernity, from the traditional compendia of Asher Zelig Margoliot and Natan Tzvi Kenig,[11] to the academic efforts of Gershom Scholem, Yehudah Liebes, and Elyahu Peretz. The earliest of them, the work *Sha'arei Orah*, or "Gates of Light," by Joseph Gikatilla of thirteenth-century Castile, properly belongs in the voluminous genre of "Commentaries to the Ten Sefirot."[12] Such commentaries were among the earliest systematic presentations of early Kabbalah.

What distinguishes a symbolic lexicon, as defined here, from the earlier "Commentaries to the Ten Sefirot" that flourished from the thirteenth century onward to the later lexicons as defined by Boaz Huss, Andrea Gondos, and Yehudah Liebes? The latter works were generated, to begin with, by the arcane nature of the Zohar's Aramaic, so that the language itself requires a guide for its understanding, especially the numerous neologisms coined by the author(s). Gondos has described an entire genre of lexicons developed to help with the difficulty of the Zohar's language. And yet, the symbolic lexicon is not like either the earlier *sefirot* commentaries or the later lexicons.[13]

A "Commentary to the Ten Sefirot," for example, from the earliest examples to Gikatilla, may be ordered according to the *sefirot* themselves, with the *kinnuyim* or euphemisms presented with the given *sefirah*. Daniel Abrams, in fact, has suggested that in the earliest examples of the genre, the guide was merely the prescriptive notation or the ecstatic result of performative kabbalistic speculation.[14] It may be said, then, that there is only one "Commentary to the Ten Sefirot," in multiple editions.

The later symbolic lexicons were also defined by the marketing strategies that came about through mass printing. Hartley Lachter has addressed the vagaries of publishing and circulation of such works in the following terms:

> The choices made by printers and kabbalists in the early modern period have also impacted the academic study of Kabbalah and the choices that scholars have made in terms of which texts are most deserving of academic analysis. . . . The history of publishing has created a skewed lens through which the history of Kabbalah is viewed, in that scholarship has tended to focus more heavily on printed texts, while other compositions that did not have the good fortune of attracting the attention of printers have been relatively neglected.[15]

Clearly, the influence of kabbalistic works was limited by reticence over their publication. The moment of transition from the terse format of the "Commentaries to the Ten Sefirot," predating the printing press, to the more expansive lexicon format will have to await another study. Once this bridge was crossed, however, the printed page was the impetus for the lexical tradition and the lexicons themselves developed as printed books swept through the Jewish world.

A symbolic lexicon is not intended to elucidate difficult words and terms due to the obscure Aramaicisms of the Zohar, as are the lexicons described in the work of Andrea Gondos[16] and Boaz Huss.[17] Like a dictionary, it is structured around the words themselves, presented alphabetically.[18] The level of understanding that is communicated, however, is the symbolic association of the word as it appears in context, understood according to the earlier or later systems of the theosophical Kabbalists, through the multiple systems of the Kabbalists of sixteenth-century Galilee and their European and Middle Eastern interpreters. The composer of the lexicon was faced with the questions of incorporating ideas that even predated the ideas of the classical Kabbalah, such as materials from the *Iyyun* circles or the independent teachings of the German pietists, which did not dovetail with the traditions of Castilian theosophical Kabbalah in its excelsis.

Moshe Cordovero's lexicon, *Sha'ar 'Erkhei Kinnuyim*, is foundational for the form of the symbolic lexicon, being a series of alphabetical *'arakhim* or entries. This format would dominate the subsequent examples of the genre. In Cordovero's lexicon, symbols were listed alphabetically, or under the headings of a particular *sefirah*, with explanations of the possible content that they might signify.[19] At the same time, Cordovero relied on the metaphysical systems of the Zohar. Subsequent collections would incorporate, to a greater or lesser extent, the ideas of Isaac Luria, which swept the Jewish world in the seventeenth century and were based on the imagery of the penultimate sections of the Zohar, commonly called the *Idra* literature. Later authors had to deal with the question of crossing into "Lurianic" ideas, which arise when the ideas of the penultimate sections of the Zohar, the *Idra* literature, are addressed.[20] Some later lexicons strive for completeness at the expense of incorporating disparate materials, as in Jacob Tzvi Yellish's *Kehillat Ya'akov*.[21] Even the Sabbatian heresy imposed strictures on the methodology of some compilers, such as Ya'akov Emden.[22] Others maintain a certain rigor with regard to Lurianic orthodoxy, as is Eliezer Tzvi Safrin's *Or 'Einayyim*[23] or, to a lesser extent, Meir Poppers's *Meorei Or*.[24] Yet others are idiosyncratic, moving across genres and even out of Kabbalah entirely, as in Yechiel ben Solomon Heilprin's *Erkhei Kinnuyim*.[25] The Hasidic movement fostered an unselfconscious embrace of Lurianic ideas, so that lexicons that originate under the Hasidic aegis freely draw on the Lurianic theories and materials that were available.[26]

THE MOTHER ARCHETYPE

In *The Great Mother*, Neumann set up his typologies of the feminine along several axes in his schematic interpretation of symbols of the feminine (see figure). At one end of the spectrum are transformative figures of the divine feminine, which would include the Tibetan goddess Tara, the Virgin Mary, the goddess Athena, and other exemplars of the healing, nurturing, enlightening feminine. Neumann referred to this aspect of the feminine as the "Transformative Positive Character." The "Elementary Positive Character" represents the eroticized, mothering, and poignant dimension of the feminine.

In kabbalistic terms, this femininity was paradigmatized in two images. The elementary character is exemplified in the eroticized Shekhinah, weeping for her children like the foremother Rachel (Jeremiah 31:15), who is posited at the bottom of the sefirotic hierarchy in the realm of Malkhut, a parallel, perhaps to the Vedic Shakti. Neumann referred to this quality as the "Elementary Positive Character." Besides this "lower" Shekhinah, there is the quality of Binah, or understanding, that sits at the apex of the sefirotic tree and represents the transformative feminine, the engendering womb for the seed of Wisdom, itself Ḥokhmah. This role is parallel to the transformative archetypes of the Tibetan goddess Tara, the Virgin Mary, the goddess Athena, or other aspects of the divinized feminine.

Neumann also posited a "Negative Elementary Character" of the feminine, invoked through images of the "grave" and of course Ashera, Ashtoret, or Astarte, the pagan

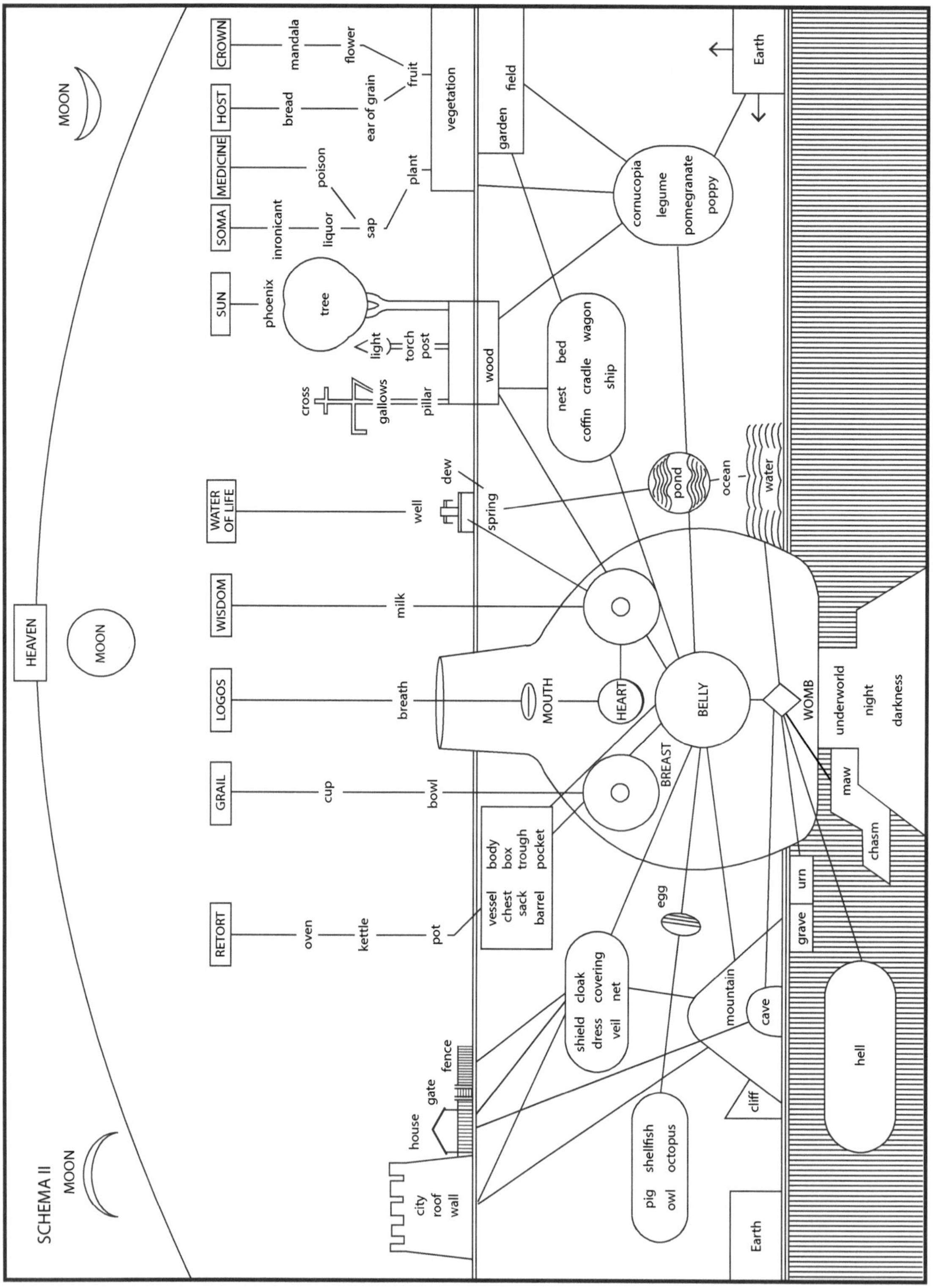

Erich Neumann's typologies of the mother archetype. (Used with permission of Princeton/Bollingen, from *The Great Mother*, Erich Neumann, p. 45, 1963; permission conveyed through Copyright Clearance Center, Inc.)

NEUMANN'S TYPOLOGIES OF THE MOTHER ARCHETYPE

The Fortress (Redoubt): city, roof, wall, house, gate, fence
Creatures: pig, shellfish, owl, octopus
Protectors: shield, cloak, dress, covering, veil, net
Mountain: cliff, mountain, cave
Hell: the underworld, night, darkness, chasm, maw, grave, urn
Retort: oven, kettle, pot, vessel, body, chest, box, sack, trough, barrel, pocket, belly
Grail: cup, bowl, breast, belly
Logos: breath, mouth, heart, womb
Wisdom: milk, breast, belly
Water of Life: well, spring, dew, breast, belly, womb, pond, ocean, water
Sun: phoenix, tree, light, torch, post, cross, gallows, pillar, wood, nest, bed, coffin, cradle, wagon, ship
Soma (Medicine): intoxicant, liquor, sap, plant, poison, vegetation, garden, field, cornucopia, legume, pomegranate, poppy
Host: bread, ear of grain, garden, field, earth, fruit
Crown: mandala, flower, fruit

goddess figures of the Canaanites.[27] The negative archetype is exemplified in the primordial fear of the raging demonesses such as Medusa, or in human form, Medea, the devouring Hindu goddess Kali, and other symbols and exemplars of the raging, devouring womb of the feminine. The elementary character of the feminine is also invoked in images of the grave and, in the Canaanite milieu, the pagan goddesses Ashera, Ashtoret, or Astarte, with their attendant fertility rites.[28] In the Jewish folkloric panoply, this would include Lillith, often referred to in the Zohar as the "first wife."[29] Lillith is the devouring demoness of crib death and nocturnal emission, and the various paradigms of the lascivious, promiscuous woman described in the book of Proverbs, Ben Sira, and, of course, the people of Israel itself, in the form of the adulterous wife described in the books of Hosea and Isaiah. According to the nineteenth-century Lublin lexicographer Jacob Tzvi Yellish, she is transformatively destructive, as he avers "Lillit is *Binah* of the realm of *kelipah*."[30]

The *Bahir*, the first "kabbalistic" text, crossed a certain conceptual line by portraying the Shekhinah in terms of four feminine roles: the bride, the princess, the sister, and the mother. The *Bahir* also began the process of portraying the Shekhinah conceptually, in terms of natural imagery that nonetheless conveyed archetypal femininity: the field, land, date, and hazelnut. Later, the Shekhinah came to be symbolized by other feminine images in the phenomenal world: the pomegranate, dove, well, cave, moon, rose, and other archetypal symbols of femininity.[31] The *Bahir*'s paradigm for the relationship of God and the Shekhinah was the paradigm of the father and the daughter,[32] while the

Zohar emphasized the sexual union of the divine and the corporeal. This set of values was laid out in forthright terms by the Kabbalist Jacob Tzvi Yellish:

> *Em* is Binah the Higher Mother. One might say that she is the *sefirah* of Raḥamim and the *dinnim* spring from her, therefore it includes the qualities of Ḥesed and of Din. This is the secret of the qualities of truth which embody the qualities of Ḥesed and Din.[33]

Hence the symbolism of classical Kabbalah evolved into archetypal paradigms that were in accord with other spiritual traditions. The values of classical Judaism, particularly the unruly traditions of the Aggadah, or Talmudic lore, had come into conformity with the mythic structures of other, admittedly pagan, religious traditions.

NEUMANN'S ARCHETYPES

Neumann's "Schema II" (see figure) in his work *The Great Mother* is a conceptual chart of the interrelationship of dream images, totems, and religious themes as they emerge. As such, it is multipurpose in its employment in the Jungian system. In searching for examples of the appearance of archetypal symbols in yet another corpus, in this case the kabbalistic lexical tradition, one inevitably reviews each lexicographer's private obsessions. Symbolism of the Shekhinah asserted itself in the mind of Moshe Cordovero in one way, and to R. Eliezer Safrin of Komarno in rather another. In particular, the eroticized Shekhinah of the zoharic traditions that are the basis for Cordovero's thought are very different from the Lurianic interest in the matriarch *Imma* and the cypher-like consort *Nukvah* that are the foundation of the Lurianic system, drawing, as it does, from the penultimate texts in the Zohar, the *Idra* literature.[34] Kabbalists from the sixteenth century found themselves influenced by one set of images over another, hence they will see these images in different ways throughout the Jewish canon. Hence, one will find overlapping schools of thought in the appearance of the mother archetype in these various symbolic lexicons. In comparing them, one may also summarize the overlap of one religious psyche onto another.

Let us structure the review according to Neumann's chart. The moon, obviously, is the archetypal symbols of the feminine, not least because its waxing and waning relates to the menstrual cycle, which was a subject of fascination in the (originally patriarchal) rabbinic and kabbalistic canons. The Zohar repeated, frequently, the rabbinic view, which saw the messianic age in terms of the rabbinic trope "that the light of the moon will again be as great as that of the sun."[35] In Neumann's schematic, he portrayed the various phases of the moon as the linear umbrella for the structure of the other archetypes.

A recurrent theme in Neumann's typologies is the image of a box or container, pointing, inevitably, to images or nascent memories of the womb. Similarly, buildings that convey shelter or sanctuary, such as the images of "fortress" and "redoubt," *migdal*, or tower, evoke the elementary and transformative *sefirot* of *Malkhut* and *Binah*.[36] The kabbalistic portrayal of the biblical "Tent of Meeting" and the marital canopy, as well as the canopy of heaven itself all contribute to the image of the chamber[37] as evoked, as well, in the myth of Osiris, itself a frequent touchstone of Jungian theorists.[38] Another "chamber" image in the Jewish subconscious is that of the ark, whether the Ark of the Covenant, the synagogue ark, or the ritual hut of the Sukkot holiday.[39] The walled city of Jerusalem is a symbol of *Malkhut* as well, according to Cordovero.[40] The various images of city, itself a feminine word in Hebrew (*'ir*, pl. *'ayarot*), reinforce the image of womb/sanctuary. This includes "house" and the womb of the cave, both of which are explicit in the early and late strata of the Zohar.[41]

Jerusalem, similarly, is the "Heart of the World" in an important zoharic passage.[42] The subsets of the fortress motif, "shield," "cloak," and even "crown" are representations of the *sefirah Malkhut* in the Zohar, although the term "crown" is applied throughout the sefirotic system.[43] Hence the Zohar's well-known reference to the gazebo or *apiryon* of King Solomon, with its erotic mosaic floor, represents the realm of *Malkhut*,[44] while, with the addition of the round letter *samekh* (ס) it becomes *afarsimon*, "persimmon," the realm, of *Binah*.[45] Ohel, or "tent," is interpreted as the *yesod* or sexual foundation of the feminine *sefirah Binah*.[46]

Heikhal, palace, according to the Hasidic lexicographer Yellish,[47] references all the *sefirot* because everything can be hidden in a palace. And yet, the same may be true of the *sefirah Binah*, as everything may be sequestered in it, even all the other *sefirot*. The pivotal compiler of the Lurianic canon, Meir Poppers, portrays *Heikhal* as "the *Malkhut* of the primordial Adam, including all of the worlds."[48] The four banners in the camps represent the four abodes of the Shekhinah.[49]

The earth itself, *areẓ*, or *Ereẓ Yisrael*, "the land of Israel," or *adamah*, "Adam-stuff,"[50] are similarly feminine archetypes. The images of the garden and field represent the *sefirah Malkhut* in the early and later strata of the Zohar.[51] This identification is evident as early as the *Bahir*. *Areẓ* serves as a universal, protean representation of the Shekinah in all sources.[52] To that end, according to the *Bahir*,[53] the field itself is one of the elemental figurative symbols of the Shekhinah. Thus, work in the field can be a spiritual practice itself, a form of intercourse with the divine that will survive into the vocabulary of early Zionism. The corner of the field, left for the poor to glean, is also a symbol of *Malkhut*.[54] In later movements of Kabbalah, such as the Safed renaissance and Hasidism, adherents viewed wandering the roads of Israel or even Eastern Europe as a form of sexual intercourse with the Shekhinah.[55] The recovery and appropriation of the land was multifaceted; it was being recovered in concrete terms, yet its appropriation was like the betrothing of the Shekhinah herself, so that "Eretz Yisrael (the land of Israel) is *Malkhut* of *Malkhut* of the world of *'Assiyah*,"[56] the most protean level of the Cordoverean tree of existence. For Yellish and Poppers, the many definitions of *Eretz* are all variations of the gradations of Binah and *Malkhut* in the zoharic and Lurianic systems.[57]

A recurrent theme from Jung to Neumann to the popular works of Joseph Campbell is that of "The Great Round," evoking a primordial theme in the individual's view of the feminine, the womb itself. While the lexical tradition, for obvious reasons, elides the continuum of "pig-shellfish-owl-octopus," given that they are unclean animals in Jewish legal parlance, the egg and the womb-belly do figure as kabbalistic symbols. Hence, all the imagery of the enclosed chamber, namely the pot, vessel, body, and box necessarily lead to the womb. In mainstream Kabbalah, the egg is male, being linked to the male principle of Wisdom, *Ḥokhmah*.[58]

Beten, "stomach" or "womb" in the *Song of Songs*, also falls into this category,[59] as does the image of the "rounded goblet," *agan sahar*, which has particular resonance in the Hasidic lexicons of the nineteenth century.[60] Yellish frankly links *beten* to *Imma*, mother,[61] and Cordovero links it to *Binah*.[62] Similarly *gaḥon*, "belly," has the numerical coefficient of ADN"Y, the sacred name that corresponds to *Malkhut*.[63] In ancient society, women were both chattelized and otherwise objectified and, in the bluntest terms, the womb itself was acquired in the acts of betrothal and marriage. Hence, the associations "oven-kettle-vessel," wherein the woman's body is reduced to its role as an engendering container for progeny.

Neumann began a continuum of images with the image of the spring and the life-giving water associated with it, placing, at the base of it, the trope "water of life" and beginning with the image of the spring. Robert Alter has described the spring as an erotic or fertility hint in biblical narrative, as the spring is accepted as a meeting place for biblical heroes. The image recurs in the accounts of the betrothal of Isaac and Rebecca, Jacob and Rachel, Moses and Zipporah, and other biblical figures,[64] as well as the Song of Songs' Shunamite who becomes, upon stimulation, "a well of living waters (Song of Songs 4:15)." In Kabbalah, wells, particularly in their construct form, such as "well of living water" and "spring of gardens," are interpreted as references to the transformative feminine *sefirah Binah*.[65]

Images of water are a ubiquitous invocation of the feminine, and the image of the sea, *yam*, is a symbol of *Malkhut* in the Zohar, Moshe De Leon's *Shekel ha-Kodesh*, and Yosef Gikatilla's *Sha'arei Orah*, but *Binah* elsewhere in the *Tiqqunei ha-Zohar*, a later work.[66] Plain water represents the middle *sefirah Ḥesed*, loving-kindness, across the canon but mainly in construct forms, "waters of life," "waters of the heart," "great waters," and so forth.[67] Caves and pools are often combined, particularly the most sacred pools, the *mikveh* or pool of purification. These are often to be found in hewn caves, the product of mountain pools. The most ancient of these still extant is the tunnel of Hezekiah beneath the City of David in Jerusalem. The *mikveh* associated with the kabbalist Isaac Luria in Safed in the northern Galilee is another such pool. Oddly, Cordovero understands *mikveh* itself as most often the male *sefirah Tiferet*.[68] Yellish[69] refers to a discussion in Zohar I 33a as to whether the *mikveh* symbolizes *Malkhut* or the erotic realm of *Yesod*. He concludes that the proper role of *mikveh* is at the level of *Binah*.

The central continuum of Neumann's diagram begins with the ephemeral *Logos*. This concept is not directly present in kabbalistic iconography, although similar abstractions enter the pantheon from philosophical sources, such as the philosophical "active intellect" or the Maimonidean "First Cause." Further on the continuum, however, one enters the realm of the breath, feminized as the *neshamah*, which is, as Robert Alter might call it, "soul breath" as his *ruaḥ* is "spirit wind."

The next continuum begins with grail, in this case sacred cup, mirroring a teaching showcased in the Mantua editions of the Zohar,[70] in which the blessing cup on the Sabbath is an overt invocation of the Shekhinah, which is then compared to the rose image of the Song of Songs. Hence, the Mantua edition of the Zohar begins with an examination of the "grail-rose-Shekhinah." The Song of Songs' "as a rose among thorns" is portrayed in the very posture of the benediction rite, as the fingers cup the chalice like the proverbial rose supported by the "thorns" of the fingers.[71] In the Grail continuum, "cup" appears in the Zohar as *Malkhut*.[72]

Neumann portrays "Wisdom" as a continuum that runs to images of the "breast" and suckling. This image as it appears in the Zohar has been thoroughly reviewed by Ellen Haskell.[73]

The most primordial passages of the Torah portray God as the construct composed of the Canaanite deities *El Shaddai*. The Hebrew "*Shaddai*," meaning literally "my breast," is part of a compound name for God in Genesis.[74] Hence the breast is a numinous symbol from the earliest parts of the canon, while "milk" is the *sefirah* of *Ḥesed* or loving-kindness. In this, as in other cases, the Zohar's symbolism does not necessarily parallel that of the transpersonal and the symbolism of Lurianic Kabbalah will depart from the archetypal even further. Yellish defines *dad*, or teat, being doubled, as the *Neẓaḥ* and *Hod* of *Tevunah*, a gradation of *Binah*, so they are an instrumental aspect of *Binah*.[75] This leads to various images in which the feminine is perceived as a vessel from which one draws sustenance, the *kad*, or jug.[76] The very image of suckling, or *yenika*, is widespread, particularly in various forms of Lurianic Kabbalah.[77]

Similarly, "mountain" is invariably a symbol for the mediating *sefirah Tiferet*, although, as Moshe Cordovero pointed out, "there are many mountains."[78] The heart, *lev*, a grammatically irregular word that is inflected in feminine form but modified in the masculine, is indicated in the Zohar's description "Binah-Heart and through it the heart understands."[79] However, there is a discrepancy between texts as to which level of the feminine, the elementary or the transformative, the heart represents. It is the feminine *sefirah Malkhut* in the Zohar and the late composition *Ra'aya Meheimna*, "Faithful Shepherd," but *Binah* in the *Tiqqunei ha-Zohar*, a rare discrepancy between these two late texts, which are ostensibly by the same author.[80]

The "underworld-night-darkness" continuum at the bottom of the chart is linked to the elementary negative feminine and thence to primordial fears of death and the grave. Caves retain a mystique, also linked to the feminine and often linked to the ancient *mikvehs* that were so often hewed out of underground streams such as those associated with Isaac Luria or the medieval sage Rashi. In those instances, the cave is associated with the cleansing waters deep within it and is itself an agent of transformation. Hence, there are also benign caves that are pilgrimage sites, such as the cave of Makhpelah in Hebron, burial place of the patriarchs according to Judaism and Islam.[81] For Yellish, the cave of Makhpelah is the combination and conduit of the feminine *sefirot* of *Malkhut* and *Binah*.[82] Hence, in the lexicons, *bor*[83] or "pit" or "well" are uniformly in the feminine, whether *Binah*, Shekhinah, *Malkhut*, or, in the Lurianic reading, *Nukvah*.[84]

The continuum that leads from the sun to the tree is intrinsic to Judaism, though slightly less so in kabbalistic terms. The sun itself is the male *sefirah Tiferet*, and trees that are nurtured by it are foundational images of the Bible. The Tree of Life and the Tree of Knowledge of Good and Evil, from the account in the Garden of Eden, came to represent the central and earthly realms of the kabbalistic system from its earliest manifestations.[85] The Tree of Life represents the entire sefirotic system, which itself is portrayed as male. The Tree of Knowledge of Good and Evil, with its binary qualities, is viewed as feminine. The sap of either tree represents the dynamism of the internal elements inside the sefirotic system. Otherwise, "fruit," in the Zohar, is synonymous with the Shekhinah in all its construct forms,[86] including the sacred citron of the Sukkot holiday, the etrog.[87]

The soma-intoxicant-liquor continuum manifests in kabbalistic symbolism in the interplay of the middle *sefirot* of judgment (*Din* or *Gevurah*) and loving-kindness (*Ḥesed*). In this way, all intoxicants are seen as having a double side, for good or for evil, indicated in the interplay of red wine versus white wine. In the Zohar "grape" or "vine" is almost always a representation of the *sefirah Malkhut*, although their primary quality is not necessarily as somatic intoxicants.[88] The grape cluster, or *eshkol*, is likened to *Binah*, the "High Mother" (*Immah Ila'ah*) according to Safrin.[89] In fact, grapes are identified as one of the seven species of produce that have particular liturgical significance, along with wheat, barley, figs, pomegranates, honey, and dates (Deuteronomy 8:8). Safrin calls the shofar, or ram's horn, "Shekhinah," which may be relevant to Neumann's inclusion of "cornucopia" in the continuum.[90]

Vegetation itself proffers many associations with the archetypal feminine, as is clear from the work of Georgia O'Keeffe and others. The Jewish tradition had various traditions for the fruit of the Tree of Knowledge, which was not an apple (although apples had their own career as a male symbol) but rather a grain of wheat or a date,[91] or, especially, the hazelnut (*egoz*),[92] each a representation of the vulva. Wheat is therefore a feminine symbol in the Zohar, as is *ḥallah*, the dough offering.[93] If the Edenic fruit was a grain of wheat, then the breadmaking process parallels the development of civilization in Middle East. Neumann also groups the pomegranate and the legume together in his construction, along with the intoxicating poppy, invoking the progression of the Song of Songs (4:12–16), which commences a seduction narrative with the declaration that the female protagonist is a "locked garden, a sealed spring," which then leads to "a garden of pomegranates, a spring of flowing waters."[94]

The lexicons contain many conceptual archetypes that Neumann doesn't address. The end of things, *aḥarit*, is also commonly interpreted as *Binah*.[95] King David's harp is also symbolic of *Malkhut*, although no musical instruments are presented in Neumann's chart.[96] Neumann also seemed to ignore the bestiary in his presentation of the feminine archetype, while Judaism, from the lions of the Galilean synagogue floors to the fructifying gazelle of the Zohar, has a strong tradition of zoological imagery.[97] The *ayelet*, or gazelle–Earth Mother, is absent here,[98] as is the stork (*ḥasidah*), which is widely considered a symbol of the *sefirah Binah* in most kabbalistic texts.[99]

KABBALAH AND THE SYMBOLIC LIFE

Although it is certainly a rich enterprise to apply the symbolic repertoire of Jungian religious analysis to a given religious tradition, transpersonal psychology was not invented to analyze the world's religions and cultures. That has been a lucrative side-industry of the Jungian enterprise. This paper has argued that there is a similarity between the categorizing of symbols in Jungian psychology and in the kabbalistic lexical tradition. Did kabbalistic lexicographers and Jungian theorists "read" their sources in similar ways?

In popular, classical Kabbalah, there were two stages in the fashioning of the lexical tradition. Initially, the Zohar's theosophical understanding of the symbolism of the Jewish canon applied the meanings based on the basic sefirotic system, toggling between the elementary character of the *sefirah Malkhut*, the eroticized Shekhinah, with her shadow side in the demonic elements of the negative elementary character, and the transformative image of the *sefirah Binah*. In the second stage of the kabbalistic lexical tradition, the worldview both expanded and contracted. The Lurianic system offered an expanded palette of symbols, perhaps grounded in the traumas and anxieties of his own psychological makeup, if not his political milieu. At the same time, some of its lexicographers restricted their purview only to the kabbalistic classics, beginning with the Zohar and passing to the Lurianic canon, putting aside the Bible and the Talmud; hence, a very orthodox Lurianist such as Eliezer Safrin of Komarno mainly provided a guide to the imagery of the newly published Lurianic oeuvre. In the lexical tradition, every compilation remains a window into what the compiler sees on their own journey though the canon.

Finally, the methodological preferences for the study and expression of Kabbalah had an influence on each lexicographer's outlook, but something of their own psychological contents may have come into play as well, as it clearly did in their other, more systematic kabbalistic works. The Kabbalists were readers and interpreters, but the inclusion of a symbol in each one's lexicon was based on their own associations and the images that particularly snagged their attention, based on their various sensibilities.

This little study has reviewed a Jungian methodology, but it is possible that Lurianic Kabbalah is based on more of a Freudian wound. The Zohar's impulse was to continue the worldview of opposites, such as the knight and his lady, the scoundrel and the whore. This symbolization, which is so redolent of the Wisdom literature,[100] gives way to the helpless pathos of Isaac Luria's reading of the *Idra* texts, the sundered parents with their backs to each other, defending their child from a world in social collapse, under the ambivalent benevolence of the uber Lord and the empty, cypher-like nature of the feminine consort.

If there is any tool to measure the quality of these lexicons, it is in the richness of expression and the broadness of selection and in that regard, Yellish's *Kehillat Ya'akov* is certainly the strongest collection. The measure of this study is the extent to which the kabbalistic lexicons mirror the collecting of symbols in Jungian practice. Does the literary nature of a given lexicon mirror the psyche of the compiler? As for the raw materials of the symbolic systems, different readers are going to project different things because of their variant psychologies. As the therapist reads the text proffered by the patient, different lexicographers read the canon and saw what they saw, based on their own insights and the limits of their imaginations.

NOTES

1. Implementing Jungian ideas in the analysis of Jewish content can be a fraught enterprise, due to Jung's support for Nazism in the years leading up to the Second World War. With regard to Jung's own antisemitism, which seems to have persisted in the works of his student Joseph Campbell, Gershom Scholem was untroubled enough by Jung's activities that he lectured for some years at the Eranos Institute. Later in his life, as well, Jung embraced Gershom Scholem's research and welcomed Scholem to his Eranos Institute, perhaps hungry for validation as Jung's long and complex relationship with Nazism came under examination. On Jung's acquiescence to Nazi antisemitism, see Dierdre Bair, *Jung: A Biography* (New York: Little, Brown, 2003), 115, 133, 434–35, 437, 440, 442, 443, 449, 459–60, 469, 510, 689 note 44; Micha Neumann, *The Relationship Between C. G. Jung and Erich Neumann Based on Their Correspondence* (Asheville: Chiron, 2015), 6–9. On the Eranos Institute, see Steven Wasserstrom, *Religion after Religion* (Princeton: Princeton University Press, 1999), 20–36.
2. There are many studies of the Shekhinah in contemporary scholarship. Recently, there have been distinguished studies by Merav Carmieli, "This Stone Which I Have Set Up as a Pillar: The Feminine and Its Evocation in the Zohar," in *The Zoharic Story*, vols. 1 & 2, ed. Yehudah Liebes, Yonatan Benarroch, and Melilah Hellner-Eshed (Jerusalem: Ben Tzvi, 2017), 307–53; Biti Roi, *Love of the Shekhina: Mysticism and Poetics in Tiqqunei ha-Zohar* (Ramat Gan: Bar Ilan, 2017); Ruth Kara-Ivanov Kaniel, *Holiness and Transgression: Mothers of the Messiah in the Jewish Myth* (Tel Aviv: Kibbutz ha-Meuchad, 2014); Elliot R. Wolfson, "*Tiqqun ha-Shekhinah*: Redemption and the Overcoming of Gender Dimorphism in the Messianic Kabbalah of Moshe Ḥayyim Luzzatto," *History of Religions* 36, no. 4 (1997): 1; Elliot R. Wolfson, *Luminal Darkness: Imaginal Gleanings from the Zohar* (Oxford: One World, 2007), 258–94. See also Gershom Scholem, *Origins of the Kabbalah* (Princeton: Jewish Publication Society and Princeton University Press, 1987), 162–80.
3. Daniel Abrams, "A Commentary to the Ten Sefirot from Early Thirteenth-Century Catalonia," *Kabbalah* 30 (2013): 8.
4. Andrea Gondos, "Decoding the Language of the Zohar: Lexicons to Kabbalah in Early Modernity," *AJS Review* 45, no. 1 (2021): 25–27, 33, 36; Gondos, *Kabbalah in Print: The Study and Popularization of Jewish Mysticism in Early Modernity* Albany: State University of New York Press 2020), 25–58; Zeev Gries, *The Book in the Jewish World 1700–1900* (Portland: Littman Library, 2007), 75–87.
5. The use of symbols in Kabbalah is addressed in Joseph Dan, "Midrash and the Dawn of Kabbalah," in *Midrash and Literature*, ed. Geoffrey H. Hartman and Sanford Budick (New Haven: Yale

University Press, 1986), 127–39; Pinchas Giller, *The Enlightened Will Shine: Symbolization and Theurgy in the Later Strata of the Zohar* (Albany: State University of New York Press, 1993). 7–20; Moshe Idel, *Kabbalah: New Perspectives* (New Haven: Yale University Press, 1988), 173–249; Idel, "Infinities of Torah in the Kabbalah," in *Midrash and Literature*, ed. Geoffrey H. Hartman and Sanford Budick (New Haven: Yale University Press, 1986), 141–57; Idel, "Reification of Language in Jewish Mysticism" in *Mysticism and Language*, ed. Steven Katz (Oxford: Oxford University Press, 1992), 42–79; Ronit Meroz, "Redemption in the Lurianic Teaching" (PhD thesis, Hebrew University, 1988), 33–35; Mikhal Oron, "Place Me for a Sign upon Your Heart: Studies in the Poetics of the Zohar's Author in *Sabba de-Mishpatim*," in *Massuot: Studies in Kabbalistic Literature and Jewish Thought Presented in Memory of Professor Ephraim Gottlieb* [Hebrew] (Jerusalem: Mossad Bialik, 1994), 8–13; Gershom Scholem, "The Meaning of the Torah in Jewish Mysticism," in *On the Kabbalah and Its Symbolism* (New York: Schocken, 1965), 32–86; Scholem, "The Name of God and Linguistic Theory of the Kabbalah," *Diogenes* 79–80 (1972): 59–80, 164–94; Elliot Wolfson, "By Way of Truth: Aspects of Nachmanides' Kabbalistic Hermeneutic," *AJS Review* 14 (1989): 116–17, note 43; Elliot Wolfson, "Female Imaging of the Torah: From Literary Metaphor to Religious Symbol," in *From Ancient Israel to Modern Judaism: Intellect in Quest of Understanding: Essays in Honor of Marvin Fox*, vol. 2 (Atlanta: Scholars Press, 1990), 271–307; Elliot R. Wolfson, "The Hermeneutics of Visionary Experience: Revelation and Interpretation in the *Zohar*," *Religion* 18 (1988): 311–45, Elliot R. Wolfson, *Language, Eros, and Being* (New York: Fordham University Press, 2005), 261–70; "Light Does Not Talk but Shines: Apophasis and Vision in Rosenzweig's Theopoetic Temporality," in *New Directions in Jewish Philosophy*, ed. A. Hughes and E. R. Wolfson (Bloomington: Indiana University Press, 2010), 93–107; Elliot R. Wolfson, *Through a Speculum That Shines: Vision and Imagination in Medieval Jewish Mysticism* (Princeton: Princeton University Press, 1994), 283–85, 298, 356–92.

6. Recent scholarly activity has shed particular light on the Zohar's literary structure. Such studies include Yonatan Benarroch, *Sava and Yanuka: God, the Son and the Messiah in Zoharic Narratives* [Hebrew] (Jerusalem: Magnes, 2018); Eitan Fishbane, *The Art of Mystical Narrative: A Poetics of the Zohar* (Oxford University Press, 2018); Melilah Hellner-Eshed, *The Secrets of the Face: The Secrets of the Idra-Rabba (Great Assembly) in the Zohar* (Rishon Le-Tzion: Yediot Acharonot, 2017); Kaniel, *Holiness and Transgression*; Yehudah Liebes, Yonatan Benarroch, and Melilah Hellner-Eshed, eds., *The Zoharic Story*, vols. . . . (Jerusalem: Ben Tzvi: 2017); Ronit Meroz, *The Spiritual Biography of Rabbi Simeon Bar Yochay: An Analysis of the Zohar's Textual Components* [Hebrew] (Jerusalem: Mossad Bialik, 2018); Meroz, *Headwaters of the Zohar* [Hebrew] (Tel Aviv: University of Tel Aviv, 2019); Roi, *Love of the Shekhina*; Oded Yisraeli, *Temple Portals: Studies in Aggadah and Midrash in the Zohar* (Jerusalem: Magnes, 2013).
7. Gondos, *Kabbalah in Print*, 131, 153–73; Gondos, "Decoding the Language of the Zohar," 27–32.
8. Gershom Scholem, *Bibliographia Kabbalistica* (Berlin: Schocken Verlag, 1933), 185–210.
9. The rationale for this hermeneutic lies in the linguistic possibilities of the Hebrew Bible, its convoluted order, and even the shape of its letters. See Boaz Huss, "Ketem Paz—The Kabbalistic Doctrine of Rabbi Simeon Lavi . . . in His Commentary to the Zohar" [Hebrew] (PhD

dissertation, Hebrew University, 1992), 153, 170n; Yehudah Liebes, *Some Chapters in a Zohar Lexicon* [Hebrew] (PhD dissertation, Hebrew University, 1976, Jerusalem: Hebrew University, 1982), 174–75; Liebes, *Studies in the Zohar*, trans. Arnold Schwartz, Stephanie Nakache, and Penina Peli (Albany: State University of New York Press, 1993), 56–57; Elliot Wolfson, "Biblical Accentuation in a Mystical Key: Kabbalistic Interpretation of the Ta'amim," *Journal of Jewish Music and Liturgy* 11 (1988): 1–13; cf. *Tiqqunei Zohar Hadash* 101a; *Tiqqunei ha-Zohar* 20b, 39b, 40b, 45a–51b, 104b, 105a,108a; *Ra'aya Meheimna* III 247b.

10. Hartley Lachter, "An Anonymous Commentary on the Ten Sefirot: Text and Translation," in *To Fix Torah in Their Hearts: Essays on Biblical Interpretation and Jewish Studies in Honor of B. Barry Levy*, ed. Jaqueline S. du Toit, Jason Kalman, Hartley Lachter, and Vanessa R. Sasson (New York: Hebrew Union College Press, 2018), 33. See Lachter, *Kabbalistic Revolution: Reimagining Judaism in Medieval Spain* (New Brunswick, NJ: Rutgers University Press, 2014), 42.
11. In the twentieth century, the influential Jerusalem kabbalist Yeshayahu Asher Zelig Margoliot (1894–1969) compiled a modest work, *Kol ha-Nikra be-Shmi* (Jerusalem: Yarid ha-Sefarim, 1995), at the age of 22 or 23, one of his many works of annotation and textual correction. Margoliot's general activity merits greater scrutiny than it has received to date, as he was an important figure in the development of Kabbalah in the twentieth century. A denizen of the Bucharian quarter and its neighboring Beit Yisrael neighborhood, he was a student of the Syrian Kabbalist Ḥaim Shaul Dweck at his yeshiva Rehovot HaNahar (see Pinchas Giller, *Shalom Shar'abi and the Kabbalists of Beit El* (New York: Oxford University Press, 2008, 87–89). In 1925, on business for Dweck, he traveled to Damascus and prostrated himself on the grave of Ḥayyim Vital. He became a disciple of Shlomo Eliezer Alfandari and R. Avraham Yeshaya Karelitz, the Ḥazon Ish. He published Alfandari's responsa and halakhic works. He maintained correspondences with Karelitz and R. Yoel Teitelbaum of Satmar. During his life, he annotated and commented on many works, which are widely circulated among kabbalists.
12. Avinoam J. Stillman has recently reviewed the circulation of *Sha'arei Orah* and its influence, cf. Stillman, "A Printed Primer of Kabbalistic Knowledge: *Sha'arei Orah* in East Central Europe," *European Journal of Jewish Studies* 16 (2022): 16.
13. On this genre of writing, see Gershom Scholem, "A Key to Commentaries on the Ten Sefirot" [Hebrew], *Kiryat Sefer* 10, no. 4 (1933); Abrams, "Commentary to the Ten Sefirot"; Na'ama Ben Shachar and Tzahi Weiss, "An Anonymous Geronese Kabbalistic Commentary on the Ten Sefirot," *Kabbalah* 38 (2017); Elliot Wolfson, "The Anonymous Chapters of the Elderly Master of Secrets: New Evidence for the Early Activity of the Zoharic Circle," *Kabbalah* 19 (2009); Elliot R. Wolfson, "Anonymity and the Kabbalistic Ethos: A Fourteenth-Century Supercommentary on the Commentary on the Sefirot," *Kabbalah* 35 (2016); Yehudah Liebes, "The Zoharic Story in General and the Development of the Ideas of 'Hormanuta' and Semitra," in *The Zoharic Story*, 49–53.
14. See Abrams, "Commentary to the Ten Sefirot," 7–8.
15. Lachter, "Anonymous Commentary on the Ten Sefirot," 331, 333.
16. A brief review of lexicons in general Jewish parlance from their medieval origins is provided in Gondos, *Kabbalah in Print*, 217–18, note 24.

17. Boaz Huss, "A Dictionary of Foreign Terms in the *Zohar*," in *Kabbalah: Journal for the Study of Jewish Mystical Texts*, ed. Daniel Abrams and Avraham Elqayam (Los Angeles: Cherub Press, vol. 1, 1996), 167–204; Gondos, *Kabbalah in Print*, 135–36.
18. Yissakhar Baer's *Imrei Binah* is arranged according to the order of the Torah readings, but that is an anomaly. See Gondos, *Kabbalah in Print*, 149.
19. Gondos, "Decoding the Language of the Zohar," 35–36, 41–42; Gondos, *Kabbalah in Print*, 93–94.
20. Aaron Meir Altshuler's *Kelalei Hatḥalat ha-Ḥokhmah* [Hebrew] (Warsaw, 1893) was compiled by a student of the Vilna Gaon, with a significant influence of the systems of Moshe Hayyim Luzzatto. This little manual is Cordoverean, "in the breach," as both the Gaon and Luzzatto evinced a zoharic emphasis in their systems, with implications for their use of the mother archetype.
21. Jacob Tzvi Yellish's *Kehillat Ya'aqov* (Lemberg, 1870) reflects the understandings of the charismatic circles that surrounded and emanated from the court of the Seer of Lublin in southeastern Poland.
22. Another small collection, compiled posthumously, is the work *Ẓiẓim U-Praḥim* (Jerusalem: Yarid ha-Sefarim, 1995, first published in 1768 in Altuna by R. Natan Neta Duner of Kalniel) from the fiery Bohemian polemicist Ya'akov Emden. Among his many traditionalistic elements in Emden's teaching is his cleaving, as well, to the Cordoverean system, as opposed to the Lurianic. Emden's avowed intent is to "give eyes to the beautiful maiden who has not eyes," a reference to the courtly love imagery of the Zohar's composition *Sabba de-Mishpatim* (cf. Zohar II 94a; *Kehillat Ya'akov II* 21d).
23. Eliezer Tzvi Safrin's *Or 'Einayyim* (Premishlan, 1882) is but one volume of the prodigious literary output of the Komarno line of Hasidism, which concentrated its efforts in formal, Lurianic Kabbalah as well as a strong impulse to control the Hasidic narrative. *Or 'Einayyim* is, therefore, an enormous work that overflows its banks somewhat and goes beyond the role of lexicon to be a general work of Lurianic Kabbalah. With regard to the very purpose of this enormous work, the author's descendant, R. Netanel Safrin, wrote in 1999: "Essentially it is clear that his intention in this holy composition, (was to provide) a key to concepts, numbers and *gematriot*, according to the wisdom of Kabbalah, to ease the path of those who in this holy true path the seven days, the spirit (breathed into) our nostrils, the anointed of God, our Rabbi Yisrael son of Eliezer, the *Besh"t*, that the essence of our practice is to intend and to unify and to sanctify everything in the world" (Safrin, *Or 'Einayyim I*, introduction to 1999 edition).
24. Meir Poppers was the last editor of the Lurianic canon, producing the enormous works *Eẓ Ḥayyim* and *Pri Eẓ Ḥayyim*. His lexicon *Meorei Or* (Jerusalem, 1868) makes use of both Lurianic imagery as well as the more protean aspects of *sefirot* and worlds that typify Cordovero's influence. The commentary to Poppers's lexicon, *Ya'ir Nativ* by R. Natan Neta' Manheim, locates many of Poppers's sources in the Lurianic canon, although Poppers avers that he had based his analysis on the earlier analyses of Moshe Cordovero (see introduction, *Meorei Or*). Manheim himself was a Jerusalem Kabbalist of the seventeenth century who was part of the circle that came to Israel under the leadership of R. Yehudah he-Hasid. Manheim came to

Israel in the year 1701 with R. Yehudah he-Hasid and R. Jacob of Vilna. They were students of R. Avraham Revigo, himself a student of R. Moshe Zakhut, the *RaMa"Z*. The work was first published in Frankfurt on Main in 1709, then in 1867 in Warsaw.

25. Yechiel Heilprin, the author of *Seder ha-Dorot*, an influential social history of the Jewish tradition, also composed a lexicon, *Erkhei Kinnuyim*, which was published in 1806. Heilprin's employment of Kabbalah is idiosyncratic and largely Cordoverean.
26. Moshe Idel, *Hasidism: Between Ecstasy and Magic* (Albany: State University of New York Press, 1995), 41–43, 66–71; Roee Horen, *The Ba'al Shem Tov and the Lurianic Kabbalah: Intentions and Unifications for Sweetening the Judgments, Delivered by the Founder of Hasidism to His Disciples* (Ramat Gan: Bar Ilan, 2021), 23–32.
27. Cordovero, *Sefer Pardes Rimmonim, Sha'ar Erkhei ha-Kinnuyim* [Hebrew] (Munkacz, 1872), henceforth *SPR, EhK* 8d.
28. Cordovero, *SPR, EhK*.
29. Giller, *The Enlightened Will Shine*, 36–37, 47, 49, 75, 89, 102.
30. Yellish, *Kehillat Ya'akov I* (b) 48b.
31. Yellish, *Kehillat Ya'akov I* 41a; Scholem, *Origins of the Kabbalah*, 63.
32. Cordovero, *SPR, EhK* 10c–d.
33. Yellish, *Kehillat Ya'akov I* 13a; Poppers, *Meorei Or* 8a.
34. Pinchas Giller, *Reading the Zohar: The Sacred Text of the Kabbalah* (New York: Oxford University Press, 2001), 133–38.
35. Isaiah 30:26, Cordovero, *SPR, EhK* 22a; Elliot R. Wolfson, *Open Secret: Postmessianic Messianism and the Mystical Revision of Menahem Mendel Schneerson* (New York: Columbia University Press, 2009), 200–223.
36. Cordovero, *SPR, EhK* 25d.
37. Cordovero, *SPR, EhK* 16d.
38. Joseph Campbell, *Oriental Mythology: The Masks of God*, vol. 3 (New York: Viking, 1963) 47–48, 98–100; Erich Neumann, *The Origin and History of Consciousness* (Princeton: Bollingen, 1954), 63–72.
39. Cordovero, *SPR, EhK* 7d, 32b.; Yellish, *Kehillat Ya'akov II* 15d.
40. Cordovero, *SPR, EhK* 22a.
41. Cordovero, *SPR, EhK* 9c–d; Poppers, *Meorei Or* 5a, 14b.
42. Zohar III 161a.
43. Cordovero, *SPR, EhK* 34a.
44. Poppers, *Meorei Or* 12b.
45. Safrin, *Or 'Einayyim I* 28c; cf. Zohar II 122b–123b; Giller, *Reading the Zohar*, 222.
46. Poppers, *Meorei Or* 4a.
47. Yellish, *Kehillat Ya'akov* 11b–c.
48. Poppers, *Meorei Or* 25b.
49. Yellish, *Kehillat Ya'akov I* (b) 4c–d.
50. Cordovero, *SPR, EhK* 2b.
51. Cordovero, *SPR, EhK* 12c.
52. Cordovero, *SPR, EhK* 8a–b.

53. Scholem, *Origins of the Kabbalah*, 163, 168.
54. Safrin, *Or 'Einayyim I* 196d.
55. Elliot R. Wolfson, "Images of God's Feet: Some Observations on the Divine Body in Judaism," in *People of the Body: Jews and Judaism from an Embodied Perspective*, ed. Howard Eilberg-Schwartz (Albany: State University of New York Press, 1992), 143–91; Elliot R. Wolfson, "Walking as a Sacred Duty: Theological Transformation of Social Reality in Early Chasidism," in *Hasidism Reappraised,* ed. Ada Rapoport-Albert (London: Littman Library, 1996), 225–50.
56. Safrin, *Or 'Einayyim I* 30a; although he also cites a view that "The Land of Israel" represents the world of *Yeẓirah*, based on the Lurianic text *Liqqutei Torah* 13b.
57. Yellish, *Kehillat Ya'akov I* 16c–d; Poppers, *Meorei Or* 10a.
58. Poppers, *Meorei Or* 9d.
59. Cf. Song of Songs, 7:2; Cordovero, *SPR, EhK* 9c.
60. Safrin, *Or 'Einayyim I* 8d; Yellish, *Kehillat Ya'akov I* 4b; Poppers, *Meorei Or* 1b.
61. Yellish, *Kehillat Ya'akov I* 21a.
62. Cordovero, *SPR, EhK* 9c.
63. Safrin, *Or 'Einayyim 1* 47c.
64. Robert Alter, *The Art of Biblical Narrative* (New York: Basic Books, 1981), 52–54, 60–61.
65. Cordovero, *SPR, EhK* 29a, 31b. *Nahar*, or "river light," is variously *Ḥokhmah* or *Tiferet*. For Yellish, it is the "secret of *Binah*." Yellish, *Kehillat Ya'akov* II 9d, 10d.
66. Elyahu Peretz, *Ma'alot ha-Zohar* (Jerusalem, 1987), 23.
67. Cordovero, *SPR, EhK* 26b.
68. Cordovero, *SPR, EhK*; 29c; Safrin, *Or 'Einayyim* 1 153d.
69. Yellish, *Kehilat Ya'akov* 2 5c; cf. Heilprin, *'Erkhei Kinnuyim* 45a,
70. Zohar I 2a.
71. Zohar I 1a.
72. Peretz, *Ma'alot ha-Zohar* 24.
73. Ellen Haskell, *Suckling at My Mother's Breast* (Albany: State University of New York Press, 2011), 55–88.
74. Genesis 17:1.
75. Yellish, *Kehillat Ya'akov I* (b) 5a,
76. Yellish, *Kehillat Ya'akov I* (b) 40c.
77. Safrin, *Or 'Einayyim I* 111b.
78. Cordovero, *SPR, EhK* 14b.
79. *Tiqqunei ha-Zohar* 15a.
80. Cordovero, *SPR, EhK* 4b, 24a.
81. Cordovero, *SPR, EhK* 28a.
82. Yellish, *Kehillat Ya'akov II* 2a.
83. Poppers, *Meorei Or* 14a; Yellish, *Kehillat Ya'akov I* 20c.
84. Poppers, *Meorei Or* 14b; Yellish, *Kehillat Ya'akov I* 19b.
85. Elliot Wolfson, "The Tree That Is All: Jewish-Christian Root of a Kabbalistic Symbol in Sefer ha-Bahir," *Journal of Jewish Thought and Philosophy* 3 (1): 31–76.
86. Cordovero, *SPR, EhK* 4b, 4b.

87. Cordovero, SPR, EhK 9a–b; Yellish, *Kehillat Ya'akov I* 18c; Poppers, *Meorei Or* 13b; Roi, *Love of the Shekhinah*, 70–73.
88. Cordovero, *SPR, EhK* 12a.
89. Safrin, *Or 'Einayyim II* 27c.
90. Safrin, *Or 'Einayyim I* 243b.
91. Cordovero, *SPR, EhK* 44d.
92. Cordovero, *SPR, EhK* 1d.
93. Cordovero, *SPR, EhK* 17d.
94. The eroticism of the Bible is very olfactory, so that as the dry garden becomes "water" and fructified, as the sealed garden becomes the garden of pomegranates, all manner of spices assault the system, myrrh, aloes, sacred and secular spices. Unlike the airbrushed eroticism promulgated in the last century, the eros of the Song of Songs is full of smell.
95. Cordovero, *SPR, EhK* 4a.
96. Cordovero, *SPR, EhK* 23c.
97. Cf. Barbara Hannah, *The Archetypal Symbolism of Animals* (Willamette: Chiron, 2006).
98. Cordovero, *SPR, EhK* 4b.
99. Cordovero, *SPR, EhK* 18b.
100. See Ronit Meroz, "Between Sefer Yezira and the Wisdom Literature: Three Binitarian Approaches in Sefer Yezira," *Journal for the Study of Religions and Ideologies* 6, no. 17 (2007).

THE BEING OF INSTITUTIONAL LOGICS?

Notes for a Religious Institutionalism Without God

ROGER FRIEDLAND

It is the constellation of being that is uttering itself to us.
MARTIN HEIDEGGER, "THE TURNING"[1]

INSTITUTION BECKONS AS A WAY FOR SOCIAL THEORISTS TO CONFIGURE society without assuming an ordered, coherent, consensual whole, a bounded collective entity. Institution beckoned to me as a religious phenomenon. In my own approach I had formulated the concept of institutional logic, a network of acts and actors, both human and nonhuman, which sustain and are sustained by linked modes of being and doing, and thus of forming subjects and objects. I first figured institutional logics as polytheistic phenomena while working in Jerusalem in 1983–1984. Within its crenelated stone walls, the Israelite Temple once stood, with its veiled and heavily gilded cubic "Holy of Holies," one of the fullest empty spaces in the world. I am not an observant Jew, but wherever I walked in the city, that razed platform on which the al-Aqsa mosque and the Dome of the Rock now stand, that no-longer and not-yet there, was my point of orientation. For the Israelites the Temple had not been a representation of divinity; it was a site, a dwelling-place, for its absent presence to be available as invisible, unspeakable, unmeasurable, inaccessible in an empty stone box of possibility, uniquely filled with divine being. Pilgrims claimed they could see His fibrillating light there. In the main, if they could, people listened to liturgy. They saw nothing. The Holy of Holies, into which only the high priest was allowed to enter once a year on Yom Kippur, the "day of atonement," the day Jews asked God for forgiveness for their personal sins, was kept in darkness, just as Moses encountered God in a dark smoky cloud that blanketed Mt. Sinai. As the earliest Kabbalist Iyyun sources from the thirteenth century declared: "infinite light lies hidden within the mysterious darkness."[2] One can never know the oneness of God without seeing the unseeable blackness.

It was here in Jerusalem that I first focused on a new institutional project forming around us, and not just here around this rocky redoubt. The assemblage of a set of practices was steadily creating a new kind of worldhood: religious nationalism, a hybrid of largely theist religions and exclusionary and expansive nation-states, whose righteous violence, patriarchalism, particularism, and derivation of national identity, state authority, and law from sacred—typically revealed—texts was just starting to shake the world order, in my country too.[3]

The modern nations of Israel and Palestine had both been imagined and assembled into collective form in the early twentieth century through their historical and imaginary relation to this central site.[4] More and more, it was through the sight of that platform that each people would see themselves and each other. In Israel, the Gush Emunim, "the bloc of the faithful," fused messianic Judaism and Zionism, seeing the settlement and annexation of all the lands conquered in the 1967 war as divinely obligated collective actions that would speed the coming of the Messiah and the rebuilding of the Temple .[5] Two decades later, founded in 1987 during the first intifada, or "shaking off," growing out of younger members of the Muslim Brotherhood in Gaza, Hamas, "the Islamic resistance movement," fused Palestinian nationalism and radical Islam, seeing all Mandatory Palestine as sacred lands that could not be ceded and jihad as a religious duty, the primary vehicle to defeat and drive out the Zionist aggressors.[6] Hamas, indeed all devout Palestinian Muslims, consider Jerusalem the first *qibla*, or prayer direction, and the Haram-al-sharif, known by Muslims as the noble sanctuary, as a site from which the Prophet, traveling from Mecca in the seventh century, rode on his magical steed Buraq to the Seventh Heaven where he met many, including Moses and God himself.

Nobody has an adequate explanation for the growing force and reach of this religious nationalist form, and those on offer tend to do hermeneutic violence to the sense of being of those who sustain it, reducing religion either to a political tool for mobilization, or to a cosmological enactment done for its own sake.[7] And nobody knows what to do about it. While I was working on a historical ethnography of Jerusalem with Richard Hecht, a historian of religions, I was trying to fashion the practices we observed in this multiply sacred city into a template, what my mentor Robert Alford and I would later term institutional logics, constellations of subjects, practices, and objects whose choreography of space, time, and bodies was both practical and meaningful, instrumental and value rational.[8]

It was against this background that I was dissecting Max Weber's essay on value spheres as heterogeneous directions of worldly rejection, which Weber posed as a polytheism.[9] Weber's was a brilliant, even beautiful piece of work; for me it was also a provocation to imagine that the likes of Jerusalem, a multiply sacred center of warring gods, might be everywhere, and not some aberrant site where the laws of social physics did not apply. It was then, in 2013, that Elliot Wolfson entered my life at a recruitment lecture for an endowed chair in Jewish studies at the Department of Religious Studies at UC Santa Barbara. The department was an expanding academic parliament of the gods, the communities of each tradition wanting to be represented through their own academic delegates. One by one they funded their own chairs. Wolfson would be the Jewish totem at the table, the Marsha and Jay Glazer Endowed Chair in Jewish Studies.

Wolfson, too, was working in Jerusalem's shadow, conjoining his lifelong study of Judaism, and kabbalistic Judaism in particular, with continental philosophy, specifically that of the philosopher Martin Heidegger. At UCSB he would begin toiling on two books: *Heidegger and Kabbalah* (2019), on the unexpected parallels between the Nazi Heidegger's philosophy and the thinking of Jewish mysticism that flowered in southern France and northern Spain in the twelfth and thirteenth centuries, and *The Duplicity of Philosophy's Shadow* (2018), a text on Heidegger's Nazism and antisemitism. It was clear that Wolfson is drawn, following Heidegger, to undoing apparent oppositions by holding sameness and difference together. Wolfson daringly applies what he terms "juxtaposition," his rendering of what Heidegger calls *Zusammengehörigkeit*, to explore how Heidegger and the Kabbalists in this way "belong to each other."[10]

When Elliot lectured, his words periodically doubled back on themselves or folded into chiasmus, so you had no idea where you were standing. I strained to listen. He spoke of the nothingness of God within the mystical tradition of Kabbalah and the atheism that implied.[11] The God of the Kabbalah was without will, without Other, yet the "Cause of causes." When he quoted Azriel of Gerona, the thirteenth-century Kabbalist thinker, on *Ein Sof*, the figure for God before his self-manifestation in the production of the world, it was as if a roadside device had exploded next to me:

> The One who brings forth something out of nothing is not depleted, for the something is in the nothing in the manner of the nothing, and the nothing is in the something in the manner of something. . . . The Creator is the principle of identity for every way of faith and way of heresy, for they are identical in the place of the conjunction of his nothing in his something.[12]

As Wolfson put it, the One must "embrace its own other in a unity of opposition that is opposed to any opposition to itself." The distance between transcendence and immanence is undone. "Simply put," Elliot concluded, "*Ein Sof* is outside everything because it is inside everything as that which is outside everything." The parallels were extraordinary; the genealogical goat-tracks between them sparse.

I have not recovered from this beautiful wound. I did not fully understand what was being said, but I glimpsed another way to religious institutionalism, an atheological institutionalism without God. Through Wolfson's studies of mysticism and his apophatic, or negative theological, readings of Heidegger, whose texts are unexpectedly peppered with gods, I began to sense that I could abandon the frame of an anthropomorphic transcendent god and still fashion a religious sociology of institutional practice, mysterious and magisterial, yet prosaic and practical.[13] I offer this essay as a first crude assay of the possibility that people like me might use Heidegger's language to fabricate a house for institutional being.

I did not expect to discover that this unapologetic, antisemitic Nazi, almost completely ignored by Anglo-American sociologists, is great for thinking the institutional.[14] For Heidegger, thinking in values was anathema. Heidegger thought that "things 'invested with value'" was a useless understanding, ontic attributes that revealed nothing about the being of the thing, the value, or the "good," which would be reduced to worldless things present-at-hand.[15] I did not understand why this had to be so. Heidegger didn't miss an opportunity to denigrate the vulgarity, the "impurities," and the inauthentic ground of an ontic sociology.[16] In his discussion of the "dictatorship" of the "they" in *Being and Time*, Heidegger's master narrative of the public realm, he took pains to insist that it "in no way means to furnish an incidental contribution to sociology."[17] As I explored this new place questions rose all around me, zigging like flies in a kitchen whose door has been left open to let in uncertain breezes. Had Heidegger, through his existential phenomenology, provided elements for institutional logics of practice? Could we think the institutional constitution of being?

In this short and speculative text I can only offer glimpses of how I might appropriate, translate, or transpose some of Wolfson's engagements with religious mysticism, phenomenology, and especially with Heidegger's vast corpus as frames by which to reconsider the mystery of institutional life. As a scholar of Kabbalah Wolfson is comfortable with fiery celestial thrones and chariots that bespeak awesome, unspeakable powers that appear incommensurable with the offices, organizations, and groups that have been the primary elements of my intellectual infrastructure.[18] I spent my academic life looking to glean something from the correlation of attributes of entities. I was trained to explain. Now after Wolfson, I struggle to understand how I might apprehend "nothing."

THE LOGIC OF INSTITUTIONS

This question of institution is not arcane. We are living it in increasingly fraught and uncivil conflicts, where facts and values have become ammunition that doesn't work, where a critical few committed to institutional meanings have—so far—saved our republic from collapse, a new force field where fellow citizens face off as friends and enemies, where you can buy guns but the stores have run out of ammo, where truth is not only relative, but unreal, like a childhood fairy tale. Our institutional worlding is up for grabs. In the face of all this, I had imagined, following Weber, that we're in the midst of a war of the gods, that conflicts between institutional "value spheres" should be likened to "an unceasing struggle of these gods with one another," an image that shows up in Heidegger as well when he posits that conflict between gods as the source of their "divinization."[19]

My starting point now is institution not as an entity or sphere dependent on or animated by gods on the one hand, nor on a subjective belief that attaches compelling absolute values to material arrangements and practices on the other. My question is whether and in what way the logic of institutions, as regular constellations of practices grounded in groundless institutional substances, can be thought of as godless but nonetheless religious, in the sense that visible practices and invisible substances are co-constitutive, immanently dependent on belief and faith.

In the social sciences the concept of institution has lost its identification with bounded entities like the state, the army, or the church. The focus has shifted from entities to relations, from organizations with hierarchical forms and neat boundaries seeking to buffer themselves from external uncertainties, to distributed action and practice, from agents to agency, from a realist materialism to a constructivist worlding.

The very category of institution is under erasure. The most significant displacement has been toward the relational field in which "social objects," argues John Levi Martin, America's most theoretically sophisticated field theorist, are "sets [or 'tangles' or 'constellations'] of social relations"—whether the IRS or a sexual partner—that we experience as entities or unities able to bear qualities, qualities that "tell us what we are to do."[20] A female "date," for example, is a social object. In field theory a woman's desirability, the quality that impels men to "date" her, derives from her desirability as ranked by others, her "popularity as a date."[21] This process, Martin and George claim, is what "underlies the 'sexual capital' that is equivalent to a consensus regarding desirability."[22] A woman's attractiveness neither inheres in the attributes of the object, nor the independent subjective preferences of individual men, but is endogenous to the field itself in men's agonistic relations to each other in their competition for women as potential partners.

Institutions, Martin asserts, are not real entities, but misrecognized second-order refractions of agonistic relations between occupants of differentially powerful positions within a field who maneuver to improve their access to mutually recognized, qualified "social objects." In his view value is a retrospective "folk theory" of why we are doing something, while institution plays the same role—an "intersubjectively valid representation of the patternings of regulated conduct"—for *what* we are doing.[23] Institutions are shadows on the wall. It is the network of social relations that constitutes social objects.

In sociology institutions are now variously figured as spheres of valued activity, competitive fields characterized by regular repertoires of acts whose premises and promises are a common sense consonantly incorporated and objectified,[24] or as taken-for-granted, rationalized myths immanent in rules and consonantly constituted in couplings of types of actor and action .[25]

Institutional logics are none of these. Institutional logics are neither organizational entities, nor spheres, nor a structure of differentially powerful positions constituting a field.[26] They are networks of practices, not positions. Nor, despite a kinship with Foucault's power/knowledge, are they properly apparatuses, in the genealogical sense Agamben backtracks to the Christian *oikonomia* from Foucault's *dispositif,* a "set of strategies of the relation of forces," as that in and through which "one realizes a pure activity of governance devoid of any foundation in being."[27] Institutional logics are not devoid in the way that Agamben claims, but it is what counts as or works as "being" that is crucial to their identification and specification, what they are and how they work. Institutional rationalities, as Heidegger bitingly accused any kind of practice grounded in the Western metaphysics of presence, are not without content.

Institutional logics are regular constellations of meaningful, material practices, always open, indeterminate, incomplete, self-organizing and thus ever-generative.[28] These constellations, and the relational networks of practices that comprise them, afford and depend upon certain modes of bodily being and equipped doing, regimes of affect and effect. The material organization of that practice is afforded and constrained by the

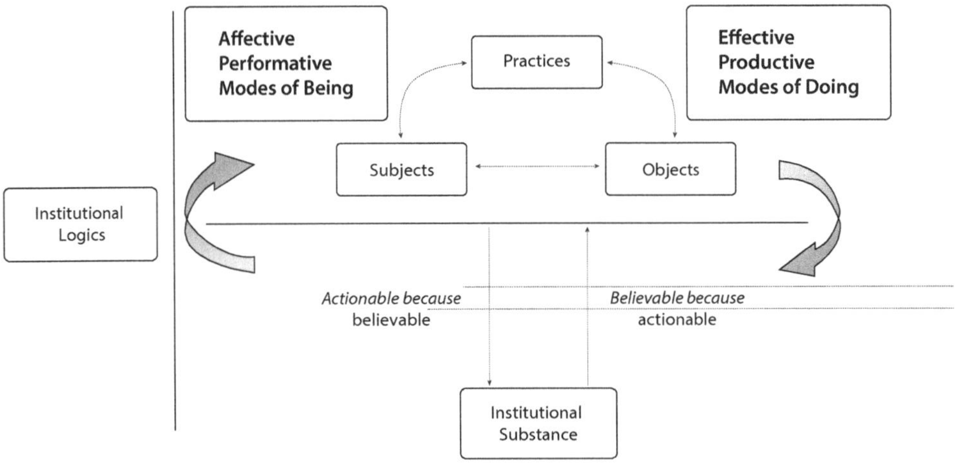

Institutional logics.

corporeality of subjects and by formatted equipment—whether devices or instruments, rules, accounts, codes, sites, languages. In an institutional logic subjects and objects are not external to each other, independent entities that interact; they are active elements gathered intra-actively.[29] As Wolfson puts it, they belong to each other. Institutional logics have an immanent intent, an internal telos. They are logics of practice in the sense not of rules of inference, the classical understanding of logic, but in terms of the reproductive regularities of production or enactment of nonphenomenal goods. I call these nonphenomenal goods institutional substances, drawing from Aristotle's later understanding of the term, not from the Cartesian notion of substantiality as an extended thing.[30]

It was Aristotle and his preoccupation with the analogical unity of being, of is-ness and as-ness, that early on set Heidegger on his way to a phenomenological rereading of his work.[31] Substance, his translation of *ousia,* or being, was central to Aristotle's lexicon. Heidegger rather understood the "substance" of man as existence, as standing out "in the openness of being"[32] For Aristotle a substance is a "principle" that sustains a kind of determinate being over time, without which it would not continue to exist. That principle is "the primary cause of being" of something.[33] The substance is what enables a thing to persist as that thing even as its attributes change. Unlike Plato, a substance is not an independent idea, hence a being, nor an ideal form; it is an actuality, not a potentiality; and it does not exist independently of that which it is the substance, a form eternally enfolded somewhere in an untouchable hyperspace.[34] For Aristotle substance is not a being, but a beingness, both the basis of something's thisness, that a thing can be identified as a particular, separable individual, and its whatness, such that it qualifies as a kind of being.[35]

Aristotle understands substances as immaterial principles that are "sources of movement," that initiate causal structures that "produce . . . unity" over time.[36] Substance is primordially actuality, not potentiality; form, not matter. As actuality substance is *energeia* and *entelecheia*, the latter a word he coined himself.[37] These two terms refer respectively to being at work in the world and to ends-oriented activity or completion.[38]

Entelecheia's literal meaning is "intrinsic possession of the end."[39] Substance thus joins what we conventionally divide: means and ends. It conjoins the two as actualization of a potential and the realization of an end. The end, the for-sake-of-which, is internal to the organization of its production and its product. What a thing is is integrally related to its end, that for the sake of which its activity is done, linking ontology to telos.[40] Substances are the source of practical movement toward ends, movements that already contain those ends within them.

Institutional substances, onto-teleological fusions, are not transcendent beings, nor transcendental ideas, nor what Heidegger, drawing on Plato, terms the look, the *eidos*, of their whatness.[41] Institutional substances do, and must have, causal force, but not in Heidegger's sense when he writes of being as "not brought about by anything else nor does it itself bring anything about. Being never at any time runs its course within a cause-effect coherence."[42] Institutional substances do run their course within the coherent movements of practice that they afford and are afforded by them. Institutional substances are causes of causes, of the directional movements of practice that constitute worldhood. Institutional substances are, as the Kabbalists say of infinity, the "nothing of *Ein Sof*," the cause of causes, constitutive of the productive gathering of subjects, practices, and objects.[43] Institutional substances afford the gathering of institutional logics. Although I do not think of them as gods, they have a structural kinship with the polytheistic thought of Proclus, a fifth-century neo-Platonist, who wrote: "In each order or causal chain there exists a unique monad prior to the multiplicity, which determines for the entities ranged within it their unique relation to one another and to the whole. Admittedly, among members of the same series, one may be cause of another. But that which is the cause of the series as a unity must be prior to them all."[44] Institutional substances unify practices; they afford constellations.

Institutional substances make institutional practices doubly objective—as objectives to be actualized and as actual objects. Institutional logics are grounded in and ground these institutional substances, invisible goods that can never be present, absent presences that are nonetheless preconditions for the appearance, the coherence, and the productivity of the constellations. In Heideggerian terms, the elements of an institutional logic cohere because they belong to each other.[45] Institutional substances are integral to that belonging. Like the neo-Platonic god they "participate" in the constitution of the constellations. These constellations of practices are intentional movements that create kinds of places, or as Heidegger puts it, "clearings" in which humans with their concerns stand and in which their practices are both intelligible and actionable.[46]

When Heidegger analyzes regional ontologies, his understanding of their practice can have much in common with institutional logics. One example is the ontologically and teleologically specific ways Heidegger discerns the way modern technology "brings what presences into appearance."[47] Modern technology, he affirms, is no longer a poiesis, a "bringing-forth" out of their earthly concealedness, but a "challenging-forth" in which the "energy concealed in nature is unlocked" and "everything is ordered to stand by."[48] In this quantitative Enframing, like the nature whose energies we seek to extract, store, and mobilize, we, too, become "standing reserve," a "calculable coherence of forces."[49]

Although Heidegger does not use institutional concepts, he here identifies modern technology's practices as tied to a specific teleo-ontology, simultaneously a final cause and an ontology of matter. That teleo-ontology depends on and affords a co-constitutive subjectification and objectification.

Institutional logics create institutional worlds, or what Heidegger understood as a "referential totality which constitute significance."[50] Human concerns and purposive things, the institutionally specific potentialities for human being and the affordances of institutional entities, conjointly make the worlds to which we belong and belong to us. Institutional logics are mechanisms of world-formation, paralleled and propelled by intra-active objectification and subjectification that make them ours and place us there. Institutional substances are both the teloi and the ontologies of those practices, both the good the practices are understood to produce and the good both immanent in and transcendent to the constellation of practices that presume and produce them, practices that keep that world open to those goods and conceal their presence within them.

Institutional logics are grounded in nonphenomenal goods—like justice, sovereignty, democratic representation, nation, race, love, beauty, knowledge, market value, nature, transparency, information, personality, and, of course, God.[51] These goods are not entities, nor essences, nor just ideas. They are virtual realities immanent in, yet excessive to, institutional practices. Each good has a concealed infinitude, a plenitude of the unknown, the unthought, the unspoken, and the undone, kinds of possibility excessive to its manifold manifestations, a no-thing and a no-body, that which can neither be observed nor touched.[52] In practice institutional substances open clearings in which an unknown multiplicity of possibilities might be effected. Institutional substances are like the zero, as the mathematician Robert Kaplan titles his book, each *The Nothing That Is*, or as Wolfson puts it, "actual but nonexistent," real and imaginary.[53] They are the immeasurable bases of measuring. They are indivisible bases of multiplicitous division. Their incalculability affords the possibility of calculation.

Institutional substances are bases of world-making. The constellations of practices that compose institutional logics manifest the goods; they are not their ground. Institutional logics depend on their substances, typically invoked when the logic forms or fails, when it is challenged by practices premised on another, when what was in darkness casts another kind of light. It is at these points that institutional substances reveal themselves as "nothings," to play with, pluralize, and transpose Heidegger's concept of the "nothingness" of being that bestows being by withdrawing from beings.[54] These are goods that can never be present, but whose absent presence is responsible for the logic of the logic, that it both means and does something. We know them by our common participation in that doing, by what it does to and for us.

An institutional substance does not fit the Humean division of fact and value, of what and why: it is both an ontological assertion of what is or can be and a valuation, a good toward or around which one can organize some segment of life. By comparison to the presence of things, an institutional substance is an absent presence toward and around which practice incessantly moves, known only through this movement. This is the mysterious core of an institutional logic, the marvel of our doing, that we can recognize and say that this is that, that institutional substances, the basis of institutional being, give us the is-ness of life that we can take for granted and depend upon to get on with just about everything. In practice, institutional substances are laden with unknown possibilities, including unexpected extensions (that a corporation can be modeled on a legal person; a worker an independent contractor; a chromosome a commodity), as well as the dangers of getting locked into practical, and particularly procedural, idolatry, mistaking the practice of beings for the institutional being of practice.

Institutional practice and substance depend on, but cannot be reduced to, each other. As Gunther Teubner, the German legal theorist, has pointed out, the law depends as much on justice as justice depends on the law. As Teubner writes, "No philosophical theory of justice or other external authority can dictate the normative content of law. It is law itself that puts the law on trial."[55] The practice of law, through the substance of justice, is always outside itself. Institutional logics are teleo-ontological enactments, a why-what done through a how, popular sovereignty through democratic election, justice through juridical practices that classify actions according to the binary of legal and illegal, divinity through pilgrimage, prayer and sacrifice, romantic love through intimate exchange of body and word. Institutional substances give institutional logics the modes of being appropriate to the presence and productivity of its practices, the real and the good that are immanent in their actualization, the conjunction of the what and why that are fitting to them.

Institutional logics are grounded in the absent presence of a good that affords and is afforded by the space of practice, a kind of there through which bodies become kinds of subject and things kinds of object. That there houses our institutional being; we "are" that there. A particular kind of object, which I term institutional objects, are central to these formations. Institutional objects are good-dependent: accounts, money, property, corporations, economic models, territorial borders, capitals, censuses, information, offices, taxes, passports, parliaments, votes and ballot boxes, altars, sacred centers, communion wafers, revealed texts, altars, experimental results, artworks, and family homes. These are material symbols, not signs. It is through good-dependent objects that the practices manifesting the absent presence of those goods form into constellations. While objects can be institutionalized as to their properties and their uses, most objects are not themselves institutional. Institutional objects are intentional; they have an intrinsic relation to practices through which they become objective, objects intending a good. Institutional objects are like classical icons in that we are seen by them, or more precisely, that our subjectivity is an imaginary site, an invisibility, formed in the relation between us and them, by their invisible sight.[56] Institutional objects touch us; they move us and we move through the pathways they make possible. The Edenic parable of eating the apple is perhaps a figuration of the first institutional object, through which we looked at ourselves and realized that we are naked. It is the knowing of the good that makes us understand that we can be raw data. Our flesh was the first taboo, the sacred, the set apart that could not be eaten. As subjects we are dual with the apple; lacking it, we are just beasts.

Institutional objects, unlike things or ordinary equipment, are conspicuous, bringing attention to their nature and the look of their substantiality. This is the way Heidegger writes about "works," like the three Doric temples at Paestum to Poseidon, Hera, and Ceres built in the fifth century BCE.[57] Such works, unlike ordinary objects of use, are set up to create worlds; they hold open the Open of that world; they are consequently consecrated; and "the god is present" within them.[58] Worlding, in Heidegger's example, is bound to the whole cycle of existence of a historical people; the work gathers the worldhood of a people and its gods. He writes:

> It is the temple work that first fits together and at the same time gathers around itself the unity of those paths and relations in which birth and death, disaster and blessing, victory and disgrace, endurance and decline acquire the shape of destiny for human being. The all-governing expanse of this open relational context is the world of this historical people. Only from and in this expanse does the nation first return to itself for the fulfillment of its vocation.[59]

At one level Heidegger's things and works can be read as institutional objects: here they gather the practices that constitute a nation, an institutional substance. At another level they gather the universal relationality of world-making.[60] Like works, institutional objects are essential to what we might call the "gathering" of the components of an institutional logic. For Heidegger a gathering that worlds is a building site for the willed collective choreography of existential conditions, not for the play of culturally and practically distinctive institutional substances. Heidegger's gatherings are existential and relational, but not, by and large, institutional. In his late work, in what he calls "the fourfold" Heidegger speaks of the bridge as a "thing" that gathers the "fourfold"—earth, sky, divinities, and mortals—into the "primal oneness of dwelling."[61] It is striking that dwelling "preserves the fourfold by bringing the presencing of the fourfold into things."[62] In this "mirror-play of the betrothed, each to the other in simple oneness. The fouring presences as the worlding of the world."[63]

Being and meaning are tightly linked for Heidegger.[64] While Heidegger's divinities in the fourfold are messengers of meaningfulness, no particular meaning is specified.[65] The problematics are universal existentials, reducing all to a fundamental ontology.[66] Substantive goods, produced and preserved by institutional practice, are nowhere to be found. It is through particular goods that institutional objects are objective, that they can produce the goods. And it is through these objects that goods are objectified, a signified "this" that is both teleological and ontological, objective in the double sense.

WHAT GIVES?

The dominant sociological understanding of institution is the taken-for-granted "repetitive social behavior that is underpinned by normative systems and cognitive understandings."[67] Institutional theorists took the "taken-for-granted" to be the essence of, indeed synonymous with, an institution, referring to conventionally accepted types of actor and action.[68] In the terms used here institutionalization would be indicated by institutional substances that ground particular networked sequences of practice becoming so obvious you no longer invoke them or even notice that they are their presuppositions.

The term "granted" offers a conceptual boundary object to interface institutional logics and the worlds of beyng. Central to the way Heidegger understands being is as that which gives; playing on the double meaning of *es gibt*, "there is/it gives."[69] That givenness, this letting be, this gift of un-concealing, is the mysterious "being of being."[70] Being, unlike beings, is not an entity.[71] Beyond representation, it is rather a no-thing, the *Nichts*, "that which is altogether other than all beings, being is that which is not. . . . the pervasive expanse of that which gives every being the warrant to be."[72] It is not that it is not; it does not "is."[73] Being bestows being by withdrawing from beings, a "fullness of the nothingness of beyng that withdraws from all beings."[74]

The strangest thing happens in Heidegger's philosophical progression: gods, and even God, make increasingly central appearances in the organization of worlding. In his view, Christianity was integral to robbing beings of being. Heidegger mocked the uncreated creator God of Christianity, "the being-est of beings."[75] This "creator is the most certain and all beings are the effect of this most extant cause."[76] In Heidegger's eyes this Christian idea of God as highest being, ultimate cause, and dispenser of being led to a hegemonic understanding of the human as a created being, *ens creatum*, a being who can be treated as if he were a presence, simply "there," a rational animal or a generic "life."[77] In *Contributions to Philosophy* he explained the result:

> *Abandonment of beings by being* means that be-ing has withdrawn from beings and that beings have become initially (in terms of Christianity) only beings made by an other being. The highest being as cause of all beings took over what is ownmost to be-ing. These beings, once made by the creator god, then became of human making, insofar as now beings are taken and controlled only in their objectness.[78]

Nonetheless Heidegger's texts are peppered with Christian terms, especially his invocation of god and gods. In his *Beitrage, Contributions to Philosophy*, written in 1936–1938, he writes, "A people is a people *only* if it receives its history as allotted to it through finding its god, the god that compels this people beyond itself and thus places the people back amid beings."[79] This was written when Heidegger's beloved German nation was then unmaking another people.

God, for Aristotle, is the highest being, the highest good, and the primary cause of all entities. Heidegger's invocation of gods is a question mark, not an assertion. It is certainly not a good, a category he did not use, nor a purpose, a category he abjured.[80] It is not clear what role gods play in Heidegger's approach, or why he even needs them. He refuses the metaphysical absolute, transcendent, self-sufficient concept of God, the highest and most-being One. Unlike the One who is the source of being, Heidegger's gods are needful; they do not give being; they seem to borrow it. Heidegger insists that gods are not to be "identified with beyng."[81] Being, or beyng, is the beyond beings that grants being to beings and gods from the space-time between them.[82] Being is grounded in Dasein, not the gods. "'Gods' need be-ing in order through be-ing—which does not belong to gods—nevertheless to belong to themselves."[83] Gods are here antisocial forces that "tear humans away from 'beings' and that compel beyng as the 'between' [*das Zwischen*] for themselves and for humans."[84]

How to locate institutional substances? There are, as I have tried to show, elements shared with Heidegger's beyng. Institutional substances are absent presences that open a space and grant institutional being to and through practice. Admittedly I have pushed hard on the comparison when, in fact, it is difficult within Heidegger's philosophy to commensurate institutional logics into privileged sites for particular kinds, or modes, of being. Heidegger didn't consider goods to be that which is "ownmost to a being (as work, tool, thing, deed, view, and word)."[85] At the end of his life he opined that human action and philosophy would be impotent to counter our steady machination by the technological world. "Only a God can save us," he famously declared.[86] But which god? What good? How? He really had no answers, other than an elitist vanguard willing to jump into the abyss of nothingness to see whether they might become friends once again with the gods. His own life had been a celebration of will. He saw no reason to atone for his murderous choices; he never actually left the Nazi Party. He never considered the ways in which particular goods might afford different constellations of practice that would afford more habitable worldhoods. His project remained the pathetic same: a second beginning to re-form his nation's power.

You take institutional substances for granted because they are granted, or given, to you, and they give you the kind of being that is essential to the operability of that practice. These meanings are the invisible bases of their visibility. Institutional substances are taken for granted not just because they are presumed to be based on what everybody does or knows, the way sociology understands conventions and existential phenomenology understands everyday existence, but also because they are what grants or gives us institutional being, a mode of being that is specific to the practices grounded in that institutional substance. We take them for granted because they participate in what we do and who we are. We are not just social beings thrown into normativity and the functional exigencies of practice; we are institutional beings beyond ourselves grounded in institutional substances, substances that are made manifest in practice that gather us together as kinds of "we" bonded as such through implicit and explicit belief in the invisible substance. We are unified by the common good, or substance, that undergirds the practices that generate our otherwise contentious differential worth.[87] We are gathered by our common participation in the gatherings institutional logics compose. This is the institutional basis of our truth, the truth of our being.

Institutional substances are the invisible, infinite, incalculable ground of institutional logics. Institutional logics thus both refract and conceal what is beyond saying and their elusive referents. Institutional substances cannot be seen but are the condition of visibility. They will never be objects, but are the condition of objectivity. Although they are categorical, they evoke a collective, institutional counterpart to Heidegger's beyng, as a giving of an institutional mode of being to beings, which helps make the institutionally logical constellations of subjects, practices, and objects intelligible and accessible. Heidegger referred to the giving of beyng, "something which, to be sure, is not but which must be given if we are to experience and understand beings at all."[88] It is out of the not that beying both gives and withholds. Although that giving is manifest in beings and their practices, those manifestations necessarily conceal not only the beyng, but its concealment in their revelatory giving, covered up in the uncovering. Wolfson puts it this way:

> Beyng conceals itself in the manifestness of beings—hence, beyng is present in the very beings from which it is absent, not as an objective thing that is occluded—the invisible—but as the inapparent that can appear only as not appearing, the mystery that is bestowed in the refusal of bestowal.[89]

This kind of story is a plausible account of many institutional genealogies, that money, for example, can successively be cut away from commodities, state authority as fiat money, or banks and financial institutions as blockchain-based cryptocurrencies, and still be understood as measures, media and stores of market value. Or that the Israelite Temple, where God abided, could be destroyed by the Roman legions and the Israelites forced into exile and yet the rites, many of them modeled as transcriptions of Temple practice, would still be understood as enactments of the same religion grounded in the same God.

Institutional substances do not exclude, but exceed objectification, invariant rules, calculability, causal determination. These substances are not phenomenal; the practices that host them, however, are. People, both scholars and ordinary folks, believe that one can get behind their apparent manifestations, reduce them, for instance, to interests and powers. Whether they can or cannot is immaterial; we cannot seem to accept that there are only appearances at work. Institutional substances are always at risk of withholding or withdrawing from existent practices into an abyss, a void, the ab-ground, whose emptiness is both a potential source of anxiety and inexhaustible possibility, with what is to become and what will never become.[90] Institutional substances, as Heidegger notes of the "refusal" of being, "*this* not-character of be-ing itself" is part of the "nothing" that beyng is.[91] The immanent tendencies of beyng to manifest itself in beings as Dasein conceal the fact that our most important institutions are grounded in nothing, not only in that which can wither and die, be displaced by others, but most primordially are grounded in a nothing filled with possibility upon which being and non-being both stand.[92] That gap, that space between, not only injects a wanting and a waiting into making, a love story, a passion to world that impassions us, but also allows those who sense the nothing that grounds their conventions to anxiously feel the threat to worldhood, for others that their making will always be deficient, that exemplarity is forever something to be aimed at, and for a select few the inceptual intimation of something that can not only be intuited or dreamed, but fought for through practical reengagement with the substance. The withholding, the never arriving, is not only a functional structure of desire, for maintaining the sameness in difference, as Wolfson puts it. It works well because the nonphenomenal substance, the ground of institutional being, kept and keeps us waiting forever, beckoning on the horizon of countless practitioners, thereby allowing institutional logics to perdure and to change and to "maintain the sameness of their difference."[93]

THE SUM OF INCOMMENSURABILITIES

Institutional logics are concerned with the nonapparent conditions of appearance, with the inceptual formation of new worlds, with the instituting and organizing force of what is not phenomenal. They put practices at the center of human existence and being. They too are centrally concerned with the relations of meaning, which finds its basis in a kind of being, which cannot be present to present beings whose essence is existence. They, too, posit an atheistic and atheological religious constitution of worlds. They, too, are dependent on yet exceed language, testifying to its foundation in silence, in namelessness, in nothing. In thinking institutional logics there is a move away from the causality of before and after, toward a relational holism, what Wolfson calls a "relational fabric of beings."[94] Institutional logics concern the multiple meanings and practical orders of institutional being, both incommensurable and complementary, which cannot be reduced to existence, neither to subjectivity nor objectivity. Institutional logics are mechanisms of worlding, of the formation of fields. Institutional logics are gatherings. And research in institutional logics increasingly cleaves to relational techniques, looking for constellations of practices, not their net causes and consequences as independent or dependent variables.[95]

Institutional logics are effected through the conjunction of metaphysical goods and material practices, in what is beyond the seeable or the sayable on the one side, and what is doable through linguistically mediated discourse and the effects of materially equipped agency on the other. The mystery of institutional life is located in the conjunction of the invisible and the visible and in the practical coherence of the logic, the steady reproduction of these incomplete, inherently unstable alignments, with changing referentiality and changing practices, held together by the assumption of an invisible substance. That substance is located in the transom of practice, a space that affords both the mystery of socially meaningful practice and the implosive catastrophe of meaningless social construction.

Building an institutionalism based on atheistic mysticism, while homologous in many ways with an institutional logical understanding of worldhood, is markedly nonconsonant in others. Institutional logics are grounded in teleo-ontologies, their animating principles, and hence have immanent aims or goals. Beyng, its structural analogue in Heidegger's approach, has no goal, no ends. As he wrote in his "Black Notebooks":

> Beyng itself is and only beyng is—and as beyng it is without a goal. . . . The truth of beyng is to be grounded, because this truth belongs to beyng. . . . Because beyng is only the abyssal ground, it has no goals and averts every setting of a goal.[96]

Heidegger adjures values as the subjectivist slag of metaphysical thinking. Institutional logics, to the contrary, are based on four moments of valuation: institution, production, territorialization, and evaluation .[97] Institutional logics put the primacy on the production of goods. Heidegger rejects the category of production as a Greek metaphysical approach to being, particularly the production of substantial entities.[98] He also cuts the legs out from evaluation, construing calculation as a practice yoked to metaphysics, a mode of being from which the new beginning must be "imperishably withdrawn."[99] He makes the standard identification of calculation with business whose "unshielded" "assertive man lives by staking his will. He lives essentially by risking his nature in the vibration of money and the currency of values. As this constant trader and middleman, man is the 'merchant.' He weighs and measures constantly, yet does not know the real weight of things."[100] I reject the notion that the economy in general, and capitalist production and exchange in particular, should be set apart as a profane, objectified space of partible goods, instrumental and calculable, as opposed to the noninstrumental "attunement" of poetry, which takes the "mysterious measure" through which "the gauging of the dimension of dwelling" is accomplished.[101] And I am repulsed by his racial identification of calculation with the Jews, about whom he writes in his "Black Notebooks," "with their marked gift for calculation, the Jews 'live' according to the principle of race."[102] In Heidegger's eyes calculation is of a piece with the Jews' worldlessness.[103] The Jews, racially inclined to truck in calculation, neither belong to a "people," nor to themselves.[104] In contrast to Heidegger, who argues that calculability is a mark and medium of machination, of objectification, of worldlessness,[105] I understand counting and calculation—how many are good and how good is their goodness—as a practice that substantiates the good, apparently making its nothing into something. Production and evaluation cannot be neatly cleaved.

Heidegger has set things up such that goods cannot be gods, as they were for Aristotle and Proclus, for example, nor forms of beyng, nor beings, but are reduced to present-at-hand things. Heidegger is only willing to accord values the status of an ontical predicate of a thing, such that both values and goods can only be present-at-hand. Heidegger links the two. He writes: "Adding on value-predicates cannot tell us anything at all new about the Being of goods, *but would merely presuppose again that goods have pure presence-at-hand as their kind of Being*. Values would then be determinate characteristics which a Thing possesses, and they would be *present-at-hand*. They would have their sole ultimate ontological source in our previously laying down the actuality of Things as the fundamental stratum."[106] Value is part of the willing and making of the super-subject that Heidegger sees as part of our perverse inheritance of the ontotheological creator-God who makes beings who take that as a model of their own being, as producers of everything, including themselves. In his "Letter on 'Humanism,'" he declares that "thinking in values is the greatest blasphemy imaginable against Being. To think against values therefore does not mean to beat the drum for valuelessness and the nullity of being. It means rather to bring the clearing of the truth of Being before thinking, as against subjectivizing beings into mere objects."[107] Value is part of the grand stratagem to withdraw being from beings. I would argue that value's excision as a blasphemy against being robs it of its institutional sources, which are just as mysterious—and in some of the same ways—as Being.

ACKNOWLEDGMENTS

I am grateful to the editors for inviting a nonphilosopher to join an esteemed assemblage of them honoring Elliot Wolfson, and to Elliot himself who has been my teacher and my friend as I have wended my way through this strange and sometimes impenetrable territory. Many other people have helped me with this project, my friend Tom Carlson most importantly who first guided me through Heidegger's *Being and Time*, as well as Yoav Shaeffer, Ted Schatzki, John Levi Martin, Jeff Alexander, Paul DiMaggio, Sarah Friedland, Iddo Tavory, and Luke McCracken. I am grateful to them all. I particularly want to thank Glenn Dynner for his critical edits on the text.

NOTES

1. Martin Heidegger, "The Turning," in *The Question Concerning Technology and Other Essays*, trans. William Lovitt (New York: Harper Torchbooks, 1977), 36–49.
2. Ariel Evan Mayse, *From the Depth of the Well: An Anthology of Jewish Mysticism* (New York: Paulist Press, 2014), 13.
3. Roger Friedland, "Religious Nationalism and the Problem of Collective Representation," *Annual Review of Sociology* 27 (2001): 125–52; Roger Friedland and Kenneth B. Moss, "Thinking through Religious Nationalism," in *Words: Religious Language Matters*, ed. Ernst van den Hemel and Asja Szafraniec (New York: Oxford University Press, 2015).
4. Roger Friedland and Richard Hecht, "The Nebi Musa Pilgrimage and the Origins of Palestinian Nationalism," in *Pilgrims and Travelers to the Holy Land*, ed. Bryan F. Le Beau and Menachem Mor (Omaha: Creighton University Press, 1996).
5. Friedland and Hecht, "Nebi Musa Pilgrimage."
6. Shaul Mishal and Avraham Sela, *The Palestinian Hamas: Vision, Violence, and Coexistence* (New York: Columbia University Press, 2000), 183.
7. Roger Friedland, "Money, Sex and God: The Erotic Logic of Religious Nationalism," *Sociological Theory* 20, no. 3 (2002): 381–425; Friedland and Moss, "Thinking through Religious Nationalism."
8. Roger Friedland and Robert R. Alford, "Bringing Society Back In: Symbols, Practices and Institutional Contradictions," in *The New Institutionalism in Organizational Analysis*, ed. Walter W. and Paul DiMaggio Powell (Chicago: University of Chicago Press, 1991), 232–63.
9. Roger Friedland, "The Value of Institutional Logics," Princeton University, November 10, 2014; Max Weber, "Religious Rejections of the World and Their Directions," in *From Max Weber*, ed. Hans Gerth and C. Wright Mills (New York: Oxford University Press, 1958), 323–62.
10. Elliot R. Wolfson, *The Duplicity of Philosophy's Shadow: Heidegger, Nazism, and the Jewish Other* (New York: Columbia University Press, 2018), 68–69; Elliot R. Wolfson, *Heidegger*

and Kabbalah: Hidden Gnosis and the Path of Poiesis (New York: Columbia University Press, 2019), 265–67.

11. Elliot R. Wolfson, "Mystical Atheism, Idolatry, and the Nothingness of God in the Kabbalah," Santa Barbara, unpublished, 2013.
12. Wolfson, "Mystical Atheism," 11.
13. Known in Greek as the apophatic approach, a "speaking away," it is, as Wolfson describes it, "a form of speaking which is an unspeaking, not a silence of not speaking" (Elliot R. Wolfson, *Giving Beyond the Gift: Apophasis and Overcoming Theomania* [Fordham University Press, 2014, rpt. 2020], 172.)
14. Patrik Aspers and Sebastian Kohl, "Heidegger and Socio-Ontology: A Sociological Reading," *Journal of Classical Sociology* 13, no. 4 (2014): 487–508.
15. Martin Heidegger, *Being and Time*, trans. John Macquarrie and Edward Robinson (New York: Harper and Row, 1962 [1926]), 96, 132.
16. Pierre Bourdieu, *Language and Symbolic Power*, trans. Gino Raymond and Matthew Adamson (Cambridge: Polity Press, 1991), 90; Heidegger, *Being and Time*, 76.
17. Martin Heidegger, "Letter on 'Humanism,'" in *Basic Writings*, ed. David Farrell Krell (San Francisco: Harper-Perennial, 2008 [1949]), 221.
18. Elliot R. Wolfson, *Language, Eros, Being* (New York: Fordham University Press, 2005); Elliot R. Wolfson, *Through a Speculum That Shines* (Princeton: Princeton University Press, 1994).
19. Weber, "Religious Rejections of the World," 152; Wolfson, *Heidegger and Kabbalah*, 99.
20. John Levi Martin, *The Explanation of Social Action* (New York: Oxford University Press, 2011), 226–27; Martin, "The Crucial Place of Sexual Judgment for Field Theoretic Inquiries," in *Sexual Fields*, ed. Adam Isaiah Green (Chicago: University of Chicago Press, 2014), 181.
21. John Levi Martin and Matt George. "Theories of Sexual Stratification: Toward an Analytics of the Sexual Field and a Theory of Sexual Capital," *Sociological Theory* 24, no. 2 (2006): 110–11, 119; Martin, *Explanation of Social Action*, 228.
22. Martin and George, "Theories of Sexual Stratification," 124.
23. Martin, *Explanation of Social Action*, 303.
24. Pierre Bourdieu, *The Logic of Practice*, trans. Richard Nice (Stanford: Stanford University Press, 1990); Paul DiMaggio and Walter W. Powell. "The Iron Cage Revisited: Institutional Isomorphism and Collective Rationality in Organizational Fields," *American Sociological Review* 48 (1983): 147–60.
25. John W. Meyer and Brian Rowan, "Institutionalized Organization: Formal Structure as Myth and Ceremony," *American Journal of Sociology* 83, no. 2 (1977), 40–263; John Meyer, "Reflections on Institutional Theories of Organization," in *The Sage Handbook of Organizational Institutionalism*, ed. R. Greenwood, C. Oliver, R. Suddaby, and K. Sahlin (Thousand Oaks: Sage, 2008), 519–38.
26. Roger Friedland, Henk Roose, and John Mohr, *The Institutional Logics of Love: The Order of Passion in an Intimate Field*. Department of Religious Studies, University of California Santa Barbara, 2022.
27. Giorgio Agamben, "What Is an Apparatus?," in *What Is an Apparatus?*, ed. Giorgio Agamben (Stanford: Stanford University Press, 2009), 2, 11.
28. Roger Friedland, "What Good Is Practice? Ontologies, Teleologies and the Problem of In-

stitution," *M@n@gement* 21, no. 4 (2018): 1357–404. https://www.cairn-int.info/journal-management-2018-4-page-1357.htm?contenu=article.

29. Karen Barad, *Meeting the Universe Halfway: Quantum Physics and the Entanglement of Matter and Meaning* (Durham: Duke University Press, 2007).
30. Aristotle, *The Metaphysics*, trans. Hugh Lawson-Tancred (London: Penguin, 2004); Aristotle, *De Anima* (on the Soul), trans. Hugh Lawson-Tancred (New York: Penguin, 1986).
31. Thomas J. Sheehan, "Heidegger, Aristotle and Phenomenology," *Philosophy Today* 19, no. 2 (1975): 88–89.
32. Heidegger, *Being and Time*, 255; Heidegger, "Letter on 'Humanism.'"
33. Aristotle, *The Metaphysics*, 22, 1041b; 227, 1041a; 229, 1041b.
34. Aristotle, *The Metaphysics*, 34, 991b.
35. Aristotle, *The Metaphysics*, 212, 1036b.
36. Aristotle, *The Metaphysics*, 387–88, 1075b.
37. Aristotle, *The Metaphysics*, 272–77.
38. Joe Sachs, "Aristotle: Motion and Its Place in Nature," *Internet Encyclopedia of Philosophy*, https://iep.utm.edu/aris-mot/.
39. Hugh Lawson-Tancred, "Introduction," in Aristotle, *De Anima* (on the Soul) (London: Penguin, 1986), 119.
40. Aristotle, *The Metaphysics*, 13, 1097a.
41. Martin Heidegger, *Introduction to Metaphysics*, trans. Gregory Fried and Richard Polt (New Haven: Yale Nota Bene, 2000), 195–97.
42. Heidegger, "The Turning," 44.
43. Wolfson, *Heidegger and Kabbalah*, 112–14.
44. Proclus, *Elements of Theology*, trans. E. R. Dodd (Oxford, UK: Clarendon Press, 2004), 271.
45. Wolfson, *Heidegger and Kabbalah*, 12.
46. Heidegger, "Letter on 'Humanism,'" 252.
47. Martin Heidegger, "The Question Concerning Technology," in *The Question Concerning Technology and Other Essays*, trans. William Lovitt (New York: Harper Torchbooks, 1977), 10.
48. Heidegger, "Question Concerning Technology," 17.
49. Heidegger, "Question Concerning Technology," 21.
50. Heidegger, *Being and Time*, 145, 160.
51. Roger Friedland, "Toward a Religious Institutionalism: Ontologies, Teleologies and the Godding of Institution," in *On Practice and Institution: Theorizing the Interface*, ed. Michael Lounsbury, Margaret Anderson, and Paul Spree (Bingley: Emerald Publishing, 2021), 1–90.
52. Wolfson, *Giving Beyond the Gift*, 129.
53. Robert Kaplan, *The Nothing That Is: A Natural History of Zero* (Oxford: Oxford University Press, 1999); Wolfson, *Heidegger and Kabbalah*, 112.
54. Martin Heidegger, *Contributions to Philosophy (from Enowning)*, trans. Parvis Emad and Kenneth Maly (Bloomington: Indiana University Press, 1999 [1989]), 335; Wolfson, *Heidegger and Kabbalah*, 106, 138–39.
55. Guenther Teubner, "Self-Subversive Justice: Contingency or Transcendence Formula of Law?," *Modern Law Review* 72, no. 1 (2009): 14.

56. Jean-Luc Marion, *God Without Being*, trans. Thomas Carlson (Chicago: University of Chicago Press), 10–11.
57. Martin Heidegger, "The Origin of a Work of Art," in *Poetry, Language, Thought*, trans. Albert Hofstadter (New York: HarperCollins, 1971), 40.
58. Heidegger, "Origin of a Work of Art," 39–45.
59. Heidegger, "Origin of a Work of Art," 41.
60. Andrew J. Mitchell, *The Fourfold: Reading the Late Heidegger*, ed. Anthony J. Steinbock (Evanston, IL: Northwestern University Press, 2015).
61. Martin Heidegger, "Building, Dwelling, Thinking," in *Poetry, Language, Thought*, trans. Albert Hofstadter (New York: HarperCollins, 1971), 147–51.
62. Heidegger, "Building, Dwelling, Thinking," 149.
63. Martin Heidegger, "The Thing," in *Poetry, Language, Thought*, trans. Albert Hofstadter (New York: HarperCollins, 1971), 178.
64. Wolfson, *Giving Beyond the Gift*, 125.
65. Mitchell, 2015: 167, 183.
66. Wolfson, *Heidegger and Kabbalah*, 111.
67. Royston Greenwood, Christine Oliver, Roy Suddaby, and Kerstin Sahlin, *The Sage Handbook of Organizational Institutionalism* (London: Sage, 2008), 4–5.
68. Joel Gehman, "Revisiting the Foundations of Institutional Analysis: A Phenomenological Perspective," *SSRN Electronic Journal* (2009), 3–4, http://dx.doi.org/10.2139/ssrn.1327508; Gehman, "Revisiting the Foundations of Institutional Analysis: A Phenomenological Perspective," in *Macrofoundations: Exploring the Institutionally Situated Nature of Activity: Research in the Sociology of Organizations*, ed. C. W. J. Steele, T. R. Hannigan, V. L. Glaser, M. Toubiana, and J. Gehman (Bingley: Emerald Publishing, 2021), 235–59; Meyer, "Reflections on Institutional Theories of Organization," 528.
69. Wolfson, *Giving Beyond the Gift*, 125, 129, 240.
70. Wolfson, *Giving Beyond the Gift*, 239–41.
71. Martin Heidegger, "Kant's Thesis About Being," *Southwestern Journal of Philosophy* 4, no. 3 (1973 [1962]): 32.
72. Martin Heidegger, "Plato's Doctrine of Truth," trans. Thomas Sheehan, in *Pathmarks*, ed. William McNeil (Cambridge: Cambridge University Press, 1998 [1931]), 233.
73. Heidegger, *Contributions to Philosophy*, 335.
74. Wolfson, *Heidegger and Kabbalah*, 138–39.
75. Heidegger, "Plato's Doctrine of Truth," 181.
76. Heidegger, *Contributions to Philosophy*, 77.
77. Thomas A. Carlson, *The Indiscrete Image: Infinitude and Creation of the Human* (Chicago: University of Chicago Press, 2008), 11; Heidegger, *Being and Time*, 74–75.
78. Heidegger, *Contributions to Philosophy*, 77.
79. Heidegger, *Contributions to Philosophy*, 279.
80. Wolfson, *Heidegger and Kabbalah*, 153.
81. Heidegger, *Contributions to Philosophy*, cited in Wolfson, *Heidegger and Kabbalah*, 99.
82. Heidegger, *Contributions to Philosophy*, 335.

83. Heidegger, *Contributions to Philosophy*, 309.
84. Heidegger, *Ponderings*, cited in Wolfson, *Heidegger and Kabbalah*, 153.
85. Heidegger, *Contributions to Philosophy*, 290.
86. William J. Richardson, "'Only a God Can Save Us': The *Spiegel* Interview," in *Heidegger: The Man and the Thinker*, ed. Thomas Sheehan (Piscataway, NJ: Transaction, 1981), 45–67.
87. Luc Boltanski and Laurent Thévenot, *On Justification: Economies of Worth*, trans. Catherine Porter (Princeton: Princeton University Press, 2006).
88. Martin Heidegger, *The Basic Problems of Phenomenology*, trans. Albert Hofstadter (Bloomington: Indiana University Press, 1982), 10; cited in Wolfson, *Giving Beyond the Gift*, 24.
89. Wolfson, *Heidegger and Kabbalah*, 67.
90. Wolfson, *Giving Beyond the Gift*, 81.
91. Heidegger, *Contributions to Philosophy*, 174.
92. Wolfson, *Giving Beyond the Gift*.
93. Wolfson, *Heidegger and Kabbalah*, 98.
94. Friedland, Roose, and Mohr, *Institutional Logics of Love*; Wolfson, *Heidegger and Kabbalah*, 147.
95. Friedland, Roose, and Mohr, *Institutional Logics of Love*.
96. Wolfson, *Heidegger and Kabbalah*, 171.
97. Friedland, "Value of Institutional Logics"; Roger Friedland and Diane-Laure Arjaliès, "Putting Things in Place: Institutional Objects and Institutional Logics," in *On Practice and Institution: New Empirical Directions*, ed. Michael Lounsbury, Deborah A. Anderson, and Paul Spee (Bingley, UK: Emerald Publishing, 2021), 45–86.
98. Heidegger, *Being and Time*, 124–25.
99. Wolfson, *Heidegger and Kabbalah*, 73, 172.
100. Martin Heidegger, "What Are Poets For?," in *Poetry, Language, Thought*, trans. Albert Hofstadter (New York: HarperCollins, 1971), 133.
101. Heidegger, "The Thing," 223.
102. Peter Trawny, "The Universal and Annihilation: Heidegger's Being-Historical Anti-Semitism," in *Heidegger's Black Notebooks: Responses to Anti-Semitism*, ed. Andrew J. Mitchell and Peter Trawny (New York: Columbia University Press, 2017), 12.
103. Wolfson, *Duplicity of Philosophy's Shadow*, 37.
104. Heidegger, "Plato's Doctrine of Truth," 279.
105. Wolfson, *Heidegger and Kabbalah*, 144–45.
106. Heidegger, *Being and Time*, 132.
107. Heidegger, "Letter on 'Humanism,'" 251.

PART II

Studies on Kabbalah

blood tree, by Elliot Wolfson. (Reprinted with permission from the artist.)

THE TREE AND THE MINISTERING ANGELS IN *SEFER HA-BAHIR*

RONIT MEROZ

SEFER HA-BAHIR (THE BOOK OF BRIGHTNESS)[1] PROVOKES MUCH CONTROVERSY among scholars. The debates revolve around its most fundamental characteristics—when and where it was written, whether it was written by one person or multiple people, and whether it changed due to later glosses, or even intentional deletions, random omissions, and loss. These questions were bound up in the attempt to decipher the meaning of the puzzling writing of the *Bahir*, which is filled with contradictions and discontinuity. Is the author(s) of the book ignorant and illiterate, or have we not delved deeply enough into the authors' opinions or the cultural and linguistic contexts of the book? Since the *Bahir* has been considered the first kabbalistic book, the answers to these questions have implications for our perception of the history of Kabbalah.[2] In this article, which is one of a series of articles dealing with the riddle of the *Bahir*, I will try to shed light on these questions by examining only a few paragraphs from the book—paragraphs §64–65, 67.

A careful study of the details of these paragraphs supports the supposition that the *Bahir* is a patchwork of texts from different periods. This is how Gershom Scholem described the *Bahir* in his many studies, and I will attempt to use his findings as much as I can, directly or indirectly—as well as the findings of others—while delving into this text.

I will present some of the phrases of these sections as a core text and the rest of the phrases as glosses that process, interpret, and adapt it to a different way of thinking. There are some indications that this is the right path of research (though they might be indicative only of the writer's—or writers'—style, ambiguity, or of negligent copyists). For example:

A. Internal Contradictions. In phrase 16 (and again in phrase 18) it says that "the 32 are given over to the 32," while in phrase 29 it is said "the 32 are given over to the 36" (and this claim will also be repeated in §70). Phrase 17 maintains that the number of entities in question is 64, while phrase 19 determines the number is 72.

B. Inconsistencies in Terminology. Phrases 2, 3, 5, and 7 indicate that there are 36 "officials" (or ministering angels). Phrases 9–11 mention 36 powers, while phrases 15, 24, and 30 discuss "Forms," "guarding Forms," or "holy Forms"; sometimes there are 32 of them, and sometimes they are not numbered.
C. Repetition of Sentences. This phenomenon may develop when later glosses are incorporated from the margins into the body of the text or while trying to present an earlier idea in a new way. By reviewing the contradictions or inconsistencies in terms, we have already mentioned some repetitions, but we may add that phrases 6, 7, 12, and 15 repeatedly mention the number 36, while the idea of "the power of each is in the other one" appears in both phrase 9 and phrase 13.

But the main support for the possibility that we are dealing with a patchwork text is our ability to convincingly break it down into its presumed components. In this article I will try to demonstrate that at least three different layers are evident in these particular paragraphs: the oldest "Tree Stratum," the Babylonian "Luminaries' Stratum," which interprets the earlier stratum, and the "Provençal Stratum," constructed as commentary on the previous ones.

To the best of my knowledge, all scholars agree that the *Bahir* contains a textual layer that was composed in Provence, and that it describes the ten divine *sefirot*. In my research, however, I have argued that at least two additional layers can be clearly discerned, each with a different theology. The oldest layer, originating somewhere in the Middle East, presents a binitarian conception, according to which the entity assisting God is a great angel whose form is likened to a Tree. Another layer is primarily Babylonian and was probably written at the turn of the ninth and tenth centuries; I called it the "Luminaries' Stratum."[3] This layer reveals the time and place of its composition by making use of parables about the divine world that rely on the Babylonian vocalization system. By the third decade of the tenth century a debate about the legitimacy of the Babylonian vocalization system versus the Tiberian one had ended with the victory of the latter; thus the use of the first in describing the Holy would no longer have been an option.[4]

The cornerstone of the theology of this layer is based on a combination of Isaiah's words about God as the world's everlasting light (Isa. 60:20) and two well-known rabbinical myths; the myth of the Diminution of the Moon (BT Hulin 50b and elsewhere) and the myth of the Hidden Light awaiting the righteous in the world to come (BT Hagiga 12a, and more). According to the Babylonian layer in the *Bahir*, the light created by God in the beginning split in two. One part, symbolized by the sun (it is not the actual sun, though), remains hidden in heaven until the End of Times. The other, symbolized by the moon, descended to earth and serves the world in which we live. These lights are also considered to be Wisdom, and in the spirit of the beginning of *Sefer Yetzirah*, each of them is divided into 32 paths (§43, 75, 97); thus they are also symbolized as hearts, 32 being the numerical value of the Hebrew word for "heart," *lev*. This description of the two wisdoms serves as a theological anchor for messianic expectations; by properly performing the commandments, humankind will raise the lower wisdom until it unites with the higher wisdom, thereby bringing redemption to the world (§98, 131). This is why the two wisdoms are called "this world" and the "world to come" (§96, 98, 129). The two wisdoms share some of their symbols; for example: "precious stone" (§131), "fear of God" (§129, 131), and "justice" (§50, 84, 133). But there are also some differences: the upper wisdom is "radiating light" (*or mazhir*), day, sun, and sky, while the lower wisdom is "bright light" (*or bahir*), moon and earth (§23, 25, 37, 39, 49, 50, 85, 97).

This article presents my views on the multiplicity of authors of the *Bahir* and the spreading of its composition over a long period of time; here, however, I focus solely on the details of a limited number of paragraphs (§64–67). I do not intend to discuss the core of the *Bahir*, but only the core of those few paragraphs. From these paragraphs, similarly to the rest of the book, it appears that the *Bahir* reflects a multiplicity of dialogues between different authors, members of the same generation and even members of different generations. Thus, I depict the book as a puzzle of embedded texts and ideas from different periods. The gradual attachment of interpretations and glosses to the core text during the long process of the development of the text obscures its contents. Here I will try to demonstrate that a careful philological analysis has the potential to unravel the jumble of intertwined threads and clearly present the uniqueness and quality of its components.

THE FIRST SECTION: THE TEXT'S CORE

The core of the text discussed in this article is found in the first part of §64, and I suggest that it belongs to the oldest layer in the *Bahir*, the "Tree Stratum." I have divided this section into 7 phrases, including one phrase (phrase no. 4) that is a proposal of a reconstructed sentence, which seems to have been lost over the generations:

<table>
<tr>
<td>1. The Blessed Holy One has a Tree, and it has "twelve diagonal boundaries: the north-eastern line, the south-eastern line, the upper-eastern line, the lower-eastern line, the north-western line, south-western line, the upper-western line, the lower-western line, the upper-northern line, the lower-northern line, the upper-southern line, the lower-southern. And they expand continually for ever and ever and they are (Deut. 33:27)[5] 'the arms of the universe.'"[6]
And inside of them is the Tree.</td>
<td dir="rtl">[§64] 1. אילן אחד יש לו להקב"ה ובו "שנים עשר גבולי אלכסון: גבול מזרחית צפונית, גבול מזרחית דרומית, גבול מזרחית רומית, גבול מזרחית תחתית, גבול מערבית צפונית, גבול מערבית דרומית, גבול מערבית רומית, גבול מערבית תחתית, גבול צפונית רומית, גבול צפונית תחתית, גבול דרומית רומית, גבול דרומית תחתית, ומרחיבין והולכין עד עדי עד והן זרועות עולם [דב' לג כז, יצירה §47]".
ובפנים בהן הוא האילן.</td>
</tr>
</table>

2. And corresponding to all these diagonals there are functionaries, and they are twelve.	2. וכל אלה האלכסונין יש כנגדן פקידים, והם שנים עשר.
3. And also within, in the Wheel, there are twelve functionaries.	3. וגם בפנים, בגלגל, שנים עשר פקידים.
4. <And also within, in the Heart, there are twelve functionaries>.[7]	4. <וגם בפנים, בלב, שנים עשר פקידים>.
5. These are the thirty-six functionaries [who adhere to the] diagonals, and each one of them has [its] diagonal, as it is written (Ecclesiastes 5:7), *"for one higher than the high watcheth."*	5. אלה ל"ו פקידין עם האלכסונין, ולכל אחד יש אחד, דכתי' כי גבוה מעל גבוה שומר [קה' ה ז].
6. It thus comes out that the east has nine, the west has nine, the north has nine, and the south has nine.	6. נמצא לרוח מזרחית תשעה, לרוח מערבית תשעה, לרוח דרומית תשעה, לרוח צפונית תשעה.
7. And they are twelve, twelve, twelve, and they are the "functionaries in the *Teli*, the Wheel, and the Heart [*Yetzirah*, §59]." [Thus] they are thirty-six.	7. והינו שנים עשר ושנים עשר ושנים עשר, שהם "פקידים בתלי וגלגל ולב [יצירה, §59], והם לו.

As in other sections of the "Tree Stratum," here too the tree is an entity distinct from God—"The Blessed Holy One has a Tree."

The wording in this paragraph is short, technical, and direct. In the other parts of the "Tree Stratum," however, the text is more poetic. Thus, for example, in the *Bahir*, §4, one may read an allegory about "a King who wanted to build his palace among strong rocks. He crushed stones and hewed rocks. A great spring of water issued forth, [a spring of] living water. The King said: since I have flowing water, I will plant an orchard (following Genesis 2:8).[8] And I, and the whole world, will delight in it (following Proverbs 8:30)."

In phrases 1–7 discussed here, the Tree is part of the cosmic structure and is at its center. The Tree supports and stabilizes the cosmos through the twelve "diagonals," which are its "arms" or branches, and they are spread out to all the winds of heaven. Several rabbinic texts (e.g., BT Hagiga 12b) describe the arms of God ("arms of the world") in just the same role, sometimes even adjacent to a reference to the number 12. However, it seems that this role of God is most clearly presented in a Midrash of the eleventh century, *Bereshit Rabbati*:[9] "And why is God, Blessed be He, called a rock? Because, like a rock that supports all the pillars of a house, so too does the Blessed be He support all those worlds, and this world and the world to come under his great arm . . . as it is said (Deuteronomy 33:27): '*and underneath are the arms of the universe.*'"[10] The text from the *Bahir* does not relate to the verse in Deuteronomy, but bases its idea on a quotation from §47 in *Sefer Yetzirah*. According to this book, including those parts not quoted in the *Bahir*, the world's center (*Axis Mundi*) is the Holy of

Holies.[11] The discussion of the Tree in the context of this quote from *Sefer Yetzirah* positions the Tree in place of the Holy of Holies, and it follows that it receives its status as a sanctified *Axis Mundi*.

The *Bahir* borrows three terms from *Sefer Yetzirah*: the *Teli*,[12] which probably represents the cosmos' expanse; the Wheel (*galgal*), that is, the zodiac, which represents time; and a Heart (*lev*), representing the human factor in the world and a human being in general. *Sefer Yetzirah* links these terms to another term, namely the "officials" (*pekidim*), but does not tell us in what way; thus the passages discussed here in the *Bahir* are an interpretation of this matter. If indeed the "Tree Stratum" was composed in the ninth or tenth century, it is one of the earliest commentaries on *Sefer Yetzirah*. According to the *Bahir*'s interpretation, three virtual spheres, as it were, are stretched between the Tree's branches, and their common center is in the trunk. Although they are called *Teli*, Wheel, and Heart, the *Bahir* does not specify their new meaning; it is clearly not the same as that of the *Sefer Yetzirah*, if only because the Heart is no longer the representative of mankind, but rather a cosmological component. In each of the meeting points between the branches and the virtual spheres, one can find an "official" (*pakid*), and altogether 36 "officials." The "officials" must be some kind of higher beings, or ministering angels, and their exact number, as well as their connection to the concept of the Wheel, leads us to Gershom Scholem's hypothesis that they are the decans.[13] The term "decan" was coined in the Greco-Roman world, but it derives from ancient Egyptian astronomy. The Egyptians observed, at least as early as 2100 BCE, that every ten days a new constellation of stars can be seen on the eastern horizon; they can be observed for the first time at dawn, just before sunrise. The constant movement of the constellations helped to create a daily and yearly "Star Clock." And so it follows that these 36 decans, described in various personifications, form a typological year of 360 days (to which five special days are added, so that the yearly cycle is closer to the solar one).[14]

Beginning in the second century BCE, the descriptions of these Egyptian astronomical systems showed influences of Hellenistic and Mesopotamian systems. Among other things, the concept of the zodiac was incorporated into the Egyptian system, and thus three decans, or three different personifications, were incorporated into each zodiac sign, creating a link between the numbers 3, 12, and 36. These new combinations were disseminated in various versions in Europe and the Middle East, even after the rise of Islam; during this process aspects of astral magic and astrology became more dominant.[15]

The *Bahir* is very ungenerous in providing details. The *Bahir*'s attempt to connect the numbers 3 and 12 and thereby create the number 36 bolsters Scholem's proposal. Further reinforcement emerges from the interpretation found within the *Bahir* itself, namely in §70, which we cannot discuss here in detail. In this paragraph, following Abayei's statement in the Talmud (BT Sanhedrin, 97b), the number 36 is linked to the idea of the Righteous Person (the *Tzaddik*) as the foundation that sustains the world. In Scholem's opinion, Abayei's position is already based on an adaptation of the idea of decans.[16] The "Provençal Stratum" will bring in again the idea of the Righteous Person, but this will be dealt with elsewhere.

To summarize this section: The core of the text from the *Bahir* on the particular matter discussed here presents a rather simple cosmic picture: God "has" a tree, which takes the function, the status, and the place of the Holy of Holies, and operates the world through its appointed "officials." This description presents "The Tree" as an angel, or rather an archangel. Not only does this entity employ 36 assistants, who outline the specific conduct of the cosmos, but it spreads its arms, in the place of God, to give the cosmos a hermetic and stable structure. The fact that some of the functions of God are entrusted to a different entity points to a binitarian doctrine. It is likely that the cosmological picture that emerges in the *Bahir* at this stage is based on the integration of the concept of "decans" within the zodiac, as well as of ideas derived from astrology and astral magic (their specific nature is, however, not specified in the *Bahir*).

THE SECOND AND FOURTH SECTIONS: THE BABYLONIAN "LUMINARIES' STRATUM"

The Babylonian layer adds its own words as if they were a continuation of the earlier text, but in fact presents new ideas. Here is the Babylonian text, according to my division into phrases, skipping what I assume are the later Provençal glosses.

THE SECOND SECTION

8. And all [the] thirty-six are <within> [the] thirty-six.	[§64] 8. וכלן ל״ו <ב>ל״ו.[17]
9. Since the power of each is in the other one.	9. שכֹח האחד בחברו.
10. And although there are twelve in each of the three "they all adhere to each other [*Yetzirah*, §48b]."	10. ואע״פ ששנים עשר בכל אחד ואחד מהשלשה – "כלן אדוקין זה בזה [יצירה, §48ב]".
11. And all thirty-six powers are in the first, which is the *Teli*. And if you seek them in the Wheel you will find the very same ones. And if you seek them in the Heart [Vatican: in the thirty-two paths] you will find the very same ones.	11. וכל השלשים וששה כחות נמצאות בראשון, שהוא תלי. ואם תדרשם בגלגל תמצאם אותם עצמן. ואם תדרשם בלב [וטיקן: בל״ב נתיבות] תמצאם אותן עצמן.

THE FOURTH SECTION

18. And how do we know that the thirty-two were given over to the thirty-two? Because it is written (Ecclesiastes 5:7), "*for one higher than the high watcheth*."[18] We thus have sixty-four.	[§46] 18. ומנא לן דמסר ל״ב לל״ב? דכתי׳ כי גבוה מעל גבוה שומר [קה׳ ה ז]. אם כן הינו ס״ד.

19. Eight are still missing [to reach] the 72 names of the Blessed Holy One, and they are alluded to in the verse, (Ecclesiastes, ibid.) "*and there are higher ones above they*"[21] and they are the seven days of the week. [But] one is still missing. This is referred to in the verse (Ecclesiastes 5:8), "*The advantage [of the Advantage] over the Earth is in everything; it is the King of the cultivated field.*"[22]	19. חסרו[19] שמונה לשבעים ושתים שמותיו של הקב"ה, והינו דכתי' וגבוהים עליהם [שם], והם ז' ימי השבוע וחסר אחת, והינו ויתרון ארץ בכל היא מלך לשדה נעבד [קה' ה ח].[20]
20. What is "*Advantage*"? This is "There," the place from which the Earth was hewn. It has an advantage over whatever <has emerged from it>.	[§56] 20. מאי יתרון? מקום! שמשם נחצב ארץ, והוא יתרון ממה ש<נ>היה.[23]
21. And what is "*Advantage*"? "*Advantage*" is everything which people of this world are worthy to partake in its radiance.	21. ומאי נינהו יתרון? כל דבר שבעולם שכשאנשי העולם ראויין לקחת מזיוו אז הוא יתרון.
22. And what is *Earth*? Earth was carved from Heaven, and it is the Throne of the Blessed Holy One, and it is a precious stone, and it is the Sea of Wisdom. And correspondingly you find the sky-blue color in a Tallit's Tzitzit, "as Rabbi Meir would say: What is different about sky-blue from all other colors? because sky-blue is similar to the sea, and the sea is similar to the sky, and the sky is similar to the Throne of Glory, as it is stated (Exodus 24:10), '*And they saw the God of Israel; and there was under His feet*' etc. And it is written (Ezekiel 1:26), '*the likeness of a throne, as the appearance of a sapphire stone.*'"[25]	22. ומאי ניהו ארץ? דנחצבה ממנו שמים, והוא כסאו של הקב"ה, והיא אבן יקרה והיא ים החכמה, וכנגדה תכלת בטלית ציצית,[24] "דאמ' ר' מאיר: מה נשתנה תכלת מכל מיני צבעונין? מפני שהתכלת דומה לים, וים דומה לרקיע, ורקיע דומה לכסא הכבוד, שנאמר ויראו את אלהי ישראל ותחת רגליו וגו' [שמ' כד י], ואומ' כמראה אבן ספיר דמות כסא [יח' א כו; סוטה יז ע"א]."

Phrase 8 ostensibly continues the matter with which phrase 7 ended, namely the 36 entities; however, an in-depth scrutiny of this text reveals that although this matter technically connects the two sections, the later one embodies a completely different ideological world. There are a number of indications of this. Let us start with the characteristics of the number 36. In the first section these were 36 "officials"; in the second and fourth sections 36 "Forces" (phrases 9, 11) or "the names of God" (phrase 19). In the first section, the "officials" were located at 36 intersections between the "diagonals" and each of the components of the cosmos: *Teli,* Wheel, and Heart. In the second section this central feature disappears; now "the power of each is in the other one" (phrase 9 and similarly in phrases 10, 11). That is why I also suggest correcting phrase 8 and adapting it to the same spirit. In Abrams's edition it says "that all 36 [are derived] from [some other] 36 [entities]," but no paragraph in the *Bahir* provides any basis for the claim that those 36 entities are derived from any other ones. It seems that the wording required here is "And all [the] thirty-six [entities] are <within> [the other] thirty-six [entities]," just like phrases 9, 10, 11.[26]

In the first section, 36 different entities were discussed, and their nature was based on an earlier division into 12. In the second section the entities have been combined into one aggregate of 36 Forces; each of them is within the other, and all of them can be found in the *Teli*, the Wheel, and the Heart. It thus seems that the differences between the Forces have faded away; if so, the whole is now more important than the uniqueness of each entity. It might be that the nature of these "new" powers can be inferred from their connection to the concept of God's 72 names (phrase 19), that is, magical powers, which even the initiates, and not just the angels, can activate. It follows that the number 12 has lost its place and importance; the number 36 has, for the time being, been granted a more important status, and even this number is close to being swallowed up in the system of 72 names, which has a rich history in itself.[27] Through this process, the text has converted the astronomical system based on the idea of thirty-six "officials" (apparently, in the sense of decans), into a more chaotic system of angels: The first system has significant connections to the cultures of Egypt and Babylon, as mentioned above, and can also be seen as a continuation of those parts in *Sefer Yetzirah* (from which it quotes) that have a scientific focus, and in particular an astronomical one. The second system, however, is probably perceived (whatever our own understanding is) as more Jewish, and is close both to the *Heikhalot* literature and to the magic of holy names.

Once we understand that the distinctions between the 36 different Forces become blurred in the second section, we can notice that phrase 11 presents this matter in a special way by changing the meaning of the term "heart." In *Sefer Yetzirah* this term represented the human factor in the world, whereas in the "Tree Stratum" of the *Bahir* it represents a cosmological layer that houses some of the "officials." But now, as the Vatican manuscript clearly states, the Heart (*Lev* in Hebrew), having a numerical value of 32, is identified as the 32 paths of Wisdom, in the spirit of the beginning of *Sefer Yetzirah*. This matter is confirmed by the continuation of the text; already in phrase 18 there are hints of two Wisdoms in the mention of the existence of two entities called "32." This is the cornerstone of the Babylonian "Luminaries' Stratum." In the beginning there was a great light, and it was Wisdom, with 32 paths. And Wisdom split in two—32 paths of the "radiating light" (*or mazhir*), hidden and awaiting the future, and 32 paths of the "bright light" (*or bahir*), which serve this world. As long as we have not reached the End of Times, the lower Wisdom will be subject to the upper one, since it was created by the diminishing of the first light and its descent. That is why the wording of phrase 18 that "the thirty-two [paths of lower Wisdom] were given over to the thirty-two [paths of higher Wisdom]" makes sense. Alternatively, it is also described through a verse from Ecclesiastes (5:7)—"*for one higher than the high watcheth*."

Despite Arabic influence (especially in syntax), which introduces some roughness to the text, phrases 19–22 disclose the common symbols of the two Wisdoms, according to the Babylonian layer. The lower Wisdom is earth and a cultivated field (i.e., a field cultivated through the commandments; compare to the *Bahir* §98, 131); it is the throne of God (compare to §25), a precious stone (compare to §131), and a sea (similarly to §34). The Supreme Wisdom, on the other hand, is referred to as "There" (*Sham*; compare to §61, 129, 133), and also as "King" and "Advantage," since it is the highest in the chain of entities in this world.

The astronomical system, with the Tree at its center, was first transformed into a system that focused on two Wisdoms. Now the text goes one step further and determines that it is identical to another system, which is quite different, namely the system of the 72 holy names of God (probably representing 72 angels). This is the calculation that is supposed to prove this point: since each Wisdom is equivalent to 32 paths, both add up to 64.[28] To this 7 should be added as a corollary to the number of days in a week, or to the number of entities (*sefirot*) that are actually formed in the process of separating the two Wisdoms (see for example §129). To this the number 1 is added, representing the advantage of the "Advantage," that is the higher Wisdom, thus reaching 72. Moshe Idel has already pointed out the artificiality and strangeness of this calculation; he suggested that its origin was in an ancient Gnostic text and raised the possibility that there was an unknown historical connection between these two texts.[29]

It is quite interesting to note that, in spite of the ideological shift, it seems that the "Luminaries' Stratum" attributes sufficiently high authority to the actual words of the previous stratum, and therefore adds its own redactions, instead of presenting its new ideas independently of the earlier text. The same is true with regard to the processes that will take place in Provence, in which the text continues to change.

THE THIRD AND FIFTH SECTIONS: PROVENÇAL GLOSSES

The Babylonian layer uses the term *sefirot* in the sense of archaic entities, which spread *between* God and the world when Wisdom split into two. In Provence, however, the *sefirot* are part of God Himself. Nevertheless, the Kabbalists of Provence were still interested in the world angels. This interest is expressed in the text discussed below. Here are some paragraphs that were probably written in Provence, as part of the dialogue with the earlier layers.

THE THIRD SECTION

12. Thus each has twelve. Since there are three—they are thirty-six, time and again.	[§64] 12. הילכך לכל אחד שנים עשר. נמצאו לשלשה – ל״ו, וחוזרות חלילה.
13. Therefore, the power of each is in the other one.	13. ונמצא כח כל אחד בחברו.

14. Thus each has thirty-six.	14. הילכך לכל אחד ואחד – ל״ו.
15. And all of them are no more than thirty-six Forms.	15. וכלן אינן יותר מל״ו צורות.
16 And they all get completed [when] thirty-two [thirty-two paths] is given over to <thirty-two>.	16. וכלם נשלמות בל״ב [וטיקן: ל״ב נתיבות] מסור <לל״ב>.[30]
17. And they are 64 Forms.	17. והם ס״ד[31] צורות.

THE FIFTH SECTION

23. And they [the Forms] sustain the Heart and the Heart sustains them.	[§67] 23. ומהן[32] מתפרנס הלב והלב מפרנסן.
24. And they are all holy Forms, appointed upon every nation and nation.	24. וכלן צורות קדושות ממונות על כל אומה ואומה.
25. But holy Israel[34] takes the Tree <itself> and its Heart.	25. וישראל קדושים נטלו <גוף>[33] האילן ולבו.
26. Just like <the heart is the splendor of the body> so Israel takes (Leviticus 23:40), "*the fruit of splendid trees.*"[36]	26. מה לב פרי הדר הגוף[35] < לב [הוא] הדר הגוף> אף ישראל נטלו פרי עץ הדר [וי׳ כג מ].
27. Just like the date palm is surrounded by its branches all around it and has its sprout *(Lulav)* in the center, so Israel takes the <body> of this Tree which is its heart.	27. מה אילן תמר ענפיו סביבו ולולבו באמצע אף ישראל נטלו <גוף>[37] האילן הזה שהוא לבו.
28. And corresponding to the <body> [of the Tree] is the spinal cord in a man, which is the main part of the body.	28. וכנגד <הגוף>[38] הוא חוט השדרה באדם שהוא עקר הגוף.
29. And just as the spelling of *Lulav* is *lu*[39] *lav*,[40] so the thirty-six is given over to the thirty-two.	29. ומה לולב זה כתי׳ ל״ו ל״ב, אף ללב מסור ל״ו.
30. And just as the Heart has in it thirty-two wondrous paths of Wisdom, so in each of those paths there is also a guarding Form; as it is written (Genesis 3:24), "*To guard the way to the Tree of Life.*"[42]	30. ומה לב, זה שלשים ושתים נתיבות פלאות חכמה בו, אף בכל נתיב מהם צורה שומרת,[41] שנא׳ לשמור את דרך עץ החיים [בר׳ ג כד].
31. And what are those Forms? As it is written (Genesis 3:24), "*and at the east of the garden of Eden he placed the cherubim, and a sword flaming and turning [to guard the way to the Tree of Life].*"[43]	31. ומאי נינהו צורות? דכתי׳ וישכן מקדם לגן עדן את הכרובים ואת להט החרב המתהפכת [שם].

In the third and fifth sections, a new term, "forms," replaces the term "forces," which had previously replaced the term "officials." The third section opens with three phrases (12–15) that repeat, in a similar but not identical language, what has been said earlier at the end of the second section ("The Luminaries' Stratum," phrases 9–11). The same is probably true for phrases 16–17, which repeat phrase 18 ("The Luminaries' Stratum"). Such repetitions are characteristic of glosses originally written in the margins and later inserted into the text, not necessarily in the right place. But in phrase 15 the change in language is significant. Here we learn that the "forces" are now called "Forms," and thus "36 Forms" are being discussed and not "36 Forces."

From the linkage (in phrases 30–32) between the Forms and the Cherubs we learn about their nature and their function in guarding the way (according to Genesis 3:24)—and its paths—to the Tree of Life. It might be that this identification between the Forms and the Cherubs led to an indication of the number 64 (instead of 72, which appears in phrase 19) because in Targum Jonathan to Ezekiel 1:6 the total number of Cherubs' faces is 64.

The Tree of Life seems to be the palm tree, discussed in phrases 25–30. Its branches are the "holy Forms" that "are appointed upon every nation and nation" (phrase 24). The number of the nations, and thus the number of ministering angels, is typologically 70 to 72, rather than 64, as mentioned in the preceding words. The most beautiful and tender branches, that is, the *lulav* (לולב), are reserved for the people of Israel (phrase 25).

The image of the *lulav* opens up, for the Kabbalists, the possibility of reading phrase 16 in a different way from the above (that is, not as a repetition of the words of "the Luminaries' Stratum"). They read it as a Midrash on the word *lulav* (לולב) by "correcting" its text so that the "thirty-six is given over to the thirty-two" (phrase 29; and compare to phrase 16). This Midrash splits the Hebrew word into two by noticing that the numerical value of its first half—*lu*—is 36, and that of its second half—*lv*—is 32, but also means "heart." This argument appears both in §67 and in §70.

The Provençal layer presents a new theological-cosmological system in these paragraphs. Just like the "Tree Stratum," so now the Tree is again in metaphorically the heart of the world (probably at the spatial midpoint). But in that earlier stratum, the Tree was but God's helper, whereas now it is God himself, the Tree of the *sefirot* (following *Vaykra Raba* [30,9], which compares palm fronds to God). The identification with God is not openly stated in the paragraphs quoted here from the *Bahir*, but appears again in other paragraphs (for example 85§) and became one of the basic tenets of Kabbalah in general. According to the *Bahir*, there are many nations in the world, but Israel is likened to the heart of the nations and their essence (phrases 24–27). This specific image of the heart is taken from R. Yehuda Halevi's Kuzari (2:36), as Scholem has already commented.[44] Thus, these Provençal passages must have been written after the year 1167, when this book was translated from Arabic to Hebrew.[45]

CONCLUSION

Three layers of thought within the *Bahir* have been identified in the short text discussed here (paragraphs 64–65; 67): the "Tree Stratum," and the "Luminaries' Stratum," both apparently from the Middle East in the ninth or tenth centuries, and a Provençal Stratum, written at least partially after 1167.

It seems to me that following the term "Heart" and the shifts in its meanings will be illuminating, giving us a general overview of the transformation that the text underwent.

In the present context, the term "Heart" begins its career in *Sefer Yetzirah* as a representative of the human element in the world, alongside the cosmological terms, the *Teli* and the Wheel. The spatial center of this cosmos was in the Holy of Holies. It should also be noted that the motif of the letters, which is generally perceived as the main characteristic of *Sefer Yetzirah*, is not mentioned at all in the group of paragraphs discussed in this article.

The core of the paragraphs that construct the "Tree Stratum" in the *Bahir* cites these matters from *Sefer Yetzirah*, but integrates the "Heart" into a binitarian-astronomical system. The Tree, God's assistant, occupies the center of the cosmos in place of the Holy of Holies, while the "Heart" becomes the seat of part of the array of "officials" that surround it (apparently, decans within an astral or astrological system). We might conjecture that this layer inherited from *Sefer Yetzirah* the connection between the concept of "Heart" and the human world, and that what characterizes the officials of the "Heart" is that they are in charge of the human world (and likewise with the officials of the *Teli* and the Wheel).

There is no doubt that in the paragraphs added to this nucleus as part of the "Luminaries' Stratum," the concept of the "Heart" has completely detached from its meanings in the human world and has taken on new meaning (taken from the first section of *Sefer Yetzirah*). Now it is the numerical value of the Hebrew word for "heart"—32, לב, *lev*—that plays a role; and it points to the 32 paths of each of the two Wisdoms from which the rest of the world originates.[46]

If these two layers of the *Bahir* were indeed written in the ninth or tenth centuries, then they should be counted among the earliest interpretations of *Book Yetzirah*.

In the paragraphs added to these layers in Provence, the Heart is identified with the Tree. Now the Tree is God, the Tree of the *sefirot*, the heart of the world. Israel is directly connected to God, while the rest of the nations are indirectly connected to Him through the branches of the Tree.

One technique is common to the various writers of these texts, and through it they cast their different opinions into one composition and hide the transformations of the text and its history:[47] they make use of the words of their predecessors and do not expose the disagreements. They expropriate the text by giving new meanings to existing terms. The term "Heart" is a good example for this; it is difficult to feel how the various writers glide between its meaning as an organ in the human body, literally or figuratively, as a comprehensive cosmic concept, or as a representative of Wisdom on its 32 paths.

This article demonstrates the structure and nature of the *Bahir*'s text in the scientific edition used by us today, and probably also in the similar editions used by thousands of Kabbalists since the late Middle Ages: the text is a patchwork of writings from different eras, a text that includes its own elaborations, commentaries, and various glosses that have been integrated into it. Each layer is aware of its predecessor, borrows terms or ideas from it, re-kneads them, and creates a new theology. And yet, at the same time, we should be aware of the fact that, had not the astral text presented at the beginning of §64 been given new meaning, it is doubtful whether it would have been preserved. The same is true with regard to the world of concepts of the "Luminaries' Stratum," which apparently lost their charm with the passage of time. Only the Provençal dynamic theurgy survives in the generations to come and colors in its shades all parts of the passages discussed here, as well as those of the rest of the *Bahir*.

NOTES

1. The text presented in this article follows the Abrams edition (Los Angeles, 1994), and so does the numbering of the paragraphs. The inner text is given in the same edition, according to Ms. Munich 209, of 1298. Some variants are given according to Ms. Vatican, Or. Barb. 110, of 1397. I usually adhered to the inner text; sometimes I preferred the Vatican wording, and if so, I noted it in a footnote. Translation and punctuation marks are my own and are meant to support my commentary. Suggestions for reconstructing the text appear in angle brackets; additions to the Hebrew text were brought in square brackets.
2. Here is a short selection of the many studies that have been devoted to the *Bahir*: D. Abrams, *Kabbalistic Manuscripts and Textual Theory: Methodologies of Textual Scholarship and Editorial Practice in the Study of Jewish Mysticism* (Jerusalem & Los Angeles, 2013), especially 122–98; A. Bar-Asher, "Historiographia bi-Tna'e Ma'abada: Meḳorotayha-Medumim shel 'Sefer ha-Bahir' ve Shiḥzur Toldoteha shel 'Reshit' ha-Ḳabbala," *Tarbiz* 84 (2019): 489–522; R. Ben-Shalom, *Yehude Provence—Rennesans be-Tsel ha-Knesiya* (Ra'anana, 2017), 565–631; Y. Dan, *Toldot Torat ha-Sod ha-'vrit*, 7 (Jerusalem, 2012), 106–299; M. Idel, "Le-Be'ayat Ḥeker Meḳorotav shel Sefer ha-Bahir," *Meḥḳare Yerushalayim be-Maḥshevet Yisrael*, 6 (1987): 52–77; M. Idel, "Ha-Tfila be-Ḳabbalat Provence," *Tarbiz* 62 (1993): 265–86; M. Idel, *Kabbalah—New Perspectives* (New Haven & London, 1988) (by the index) and many other later publications; Y. Knohl, "Ha-Merkava, ha-Tzadiḳve ha-Satan: le-Fitron Ḥidat Sefer ha-Bahir," *Mada'e ha-Yahadut* 52 (2017): 47–76; Y. Liebes, "Berekha u-Male be-Sefer ha-Bahir, Iyun Meḥadash," *Kabbalah* 21 (2011): 121–42; R. Meroz, "Or Bahir hu ba-Mizraḥ—'al Zmano u-Meḳomo shel Sefer ha-Bahir," *Da'at* 49 (2002): 137–80; Meroz, "Ha-Ilan she-Hu Mal'akh—'al Tfisa Binetarit ha-Nikeret be-Sefer ha-Bahir," *Maḥshevet Yisrael* 2 (2021): 218–49; Ḳ. Pedaya, "Shikhvat ha-'Arikha ha-Provensalit be-Sefer ha-Bahir," *Sefer ha-Yovel le-Shlomo Pines, Meḥḳare Yerushala'm be-Maḥshevet Yisrael* 9 (1990): 139–64; Ḳ. Pedaya, *Ha-Ramban—Hit'alut, Zman Maḥzori ve-Teḳst Ḳadosh* (Tel Aviv, 2003), 362–64; P. Schäfer, *Mirror of His Beauty—Feminine Images of God from the Bible to the Early Kabbalah* (Princeton & Oxford, 2002), 118–34; M. Shneider,

"Mitos ha-Satan be-Sefer ha-Bahir," *Kabbalah* 20 (2009): 287–344; Scholem (many studies, but I shall limit myself to three): G. Scholem, *Das Buch Bahir* (Leipzig, 1923); G. Scholem, *Reshit Hakabbalah (115–1250)* (Jerusalem & Tel-Aviv, 1948), chap. II; G. Scholem, *Origins of the Kabbalah*, ed. R. J. Zwi Werblowsly, trans. A. Arkush (Philadelphia, 1987), chap. 2; E. R. Wolfson, "The Tree That Is All: Jewish-Christian Roots of a Kabbalistic Symbol in *Sefer ha-Bahir*," *Journal of Jewish Thought and Philosophy* 3 (1993): 31–76; E. Wolfson, "Hebraic and Hellenistic Conceptions of Wisdom in *Sefer ha-Bahir*," *Poetics Today* 19 (1998): 147–76; E. Wolfson, "Biblical Accentuation in a Mystical Key: Kabbalistic Interpretation of the Te'amim," *Journal of Jewish Music and Liturgy* 11 (1988–1989): 1–16; (1989–1990): 1–13. In addition see the extended bibliographical list at the end of the Abrams edition.

3. These matters were described in my above-mentioned articles (note 2), in my lecture at the Tel-Aviv Forum (March 16, 2021), and in some of my other forthcoming publications.
4. B. Chiesa, *The Emergence of Hebrew Biblical Pointing* (FaM, 1979), especially 44–45; I. Yevin, *Masoret ha-Lashon ha-'Ivrit ha-Mishtaḳefet ba-Niḳud ha-Bavli* (Jerusalem, 1985), esp. 22–23; R. Drori, *Reshit ha-Maga'im shel ha-Sifrut ha-Yehudit 'im ha-Sifrut ha-'Aravit ba-Me'a ha-'Asirit* (Tel Aviv, 1988), 135–39.
5. My translation follows the context; the common translation, however, is "*the everlasting arms*."
6. Yetzira, §47. All quotations from Yetzira were taken from: A. P. Hayman, *Sefer Yesira: Edition, Translation and Text-Critical Commentary* (Tübingen, 2004).
7. According to phrase 7 (and following *Sefer Yetzira*) the "officials" are divided between a *Teli*, a Wheel, and a Heart. Phrase 3 describes the Wheel's officials and states that they are "within," "inside" something else. This implies that the previous phrase dealt with *Teli*, without explicitly stating that it was the external one and the first to be counted. Hence, there are two possibilities. The first one is that the Heart is the same as the Tree. This is probably how the Provençal §67 understood this matter (as quoted below), for according to that paragraph the Tree's trunk is its heart. But the end of phrase 1 implies that the Tree is "inside them [all diagonals]," at their point of departure; that is, the trunk of the Tree is the center of the branches and also of all the 36 "officials" and not one of them. The other possibility is that some sentences, which originally described the third being, the Heart, were lost. I have preferred the second option and thus added the fourth phrase.
8. This translation accords with the New English Translation (NET) and this paragraph's context in the *Bahir*.
9. Bereshit Rabbati on Gen. 1:1, Albeck's edition (Jerusalem, 1967), 48.
10. See note 5 above.
11. This is an adaptation of some rabbinic ideas; see especially what is said about the foundation stone in BT Yoma 54b and Tanhuma, Pekudei 3.
12. The meaning of the term "*Teli*" in *Sefer Yezira* might have been the cosmic "Weaving Beam" on which all the stars hang, that is, the Milky Way. A large variety of additional meanings of this term in different periods are mentioned in the following studies (which include many references to other studies): P. Mancuso, *Shabbatai Donnolo's Sefer Ḥakhmoni: Introduction, Critical Text, and Annotated English Translation* (Boston, 2010), especially 25, 70–74; R. Meroz, "Merkavat Yeḥezḳel—Perush Zohari Bilti Yadu'a," *Te'uda* 16–17 (2001), esp. 574–80.

13. Scholem, *Origins*, 77 (and more).
14. On the origins of the concept of decans in Egyptian astronomy see, for example: J. F. Quack, "Astronomy in Ancient Egypt," in P. T. Keyser, *The Oxford Handbook of Science and Medicine in the Classical World* (Oxford, 2018), 61–70; S. L. Symons, R. Cockcroft, J. Bettencourt, and C. Koykka, *Ancient Egyptian Astronomy* (2013). [Online database]. Available at: http://aea.physics.mcmaster.ca/.
15. On the general interest in and practice of different types of astrology and astral magic in the Middle East, as well as on the integration of the concept of decans in these teachings after the rise of Islam, see, for example, Quack, in the previous note and in the following studies (the advantage of Panaino's articles is that they supply a general historical view, and not only of the Iranian ideas): T. M. Green, *The City of the Moon God—Religious Traditions of Harran* (Leiden, New York, & Koln, 1992), especially 40–43, 159–60, 175–80; J. Hameen-Antilla, *The Last Pagans of Iraq—Ibn Wahshiyya and His Nabatean Agriculture* (Leiden & Boston, 2006), especially 188–93; D. Pingree, "From Alexandria to Baghdād to Byzantium—The Transmission of Astrology," *International Journal of the Classical Tradition* 8 (2001): 3–37; A. Panaino, "The Decans in Iranian Astrology," *East and West* 37 (1987): 131–37; A. Panaino, "The Conceptual Image of the Planets in Ancient Iran and the Process of Their Demonization: Visual Materials and Models of Inclusion and Exclusion in Iranian History of Knowledge," *Naturwissenschaften, Technik und Medizin* 28 (2020): 359–89.
16. G. Scholem, *Od Davar* (Tel Aviv, 1989), II, 199–200.
17. <ב>ל״ו] מינכן: מל״ו. וראו את ההסבר להלן, בסמוך להערה 26.
18. Following the translation of JPS (1917).
19. חסרו] כך בוטיקן; מינכן: חסר.
20. לשדה נעבד] כך במסורה וגם בגיליון כ״י מינכן, ע״פ עיון בתצלומו בתוכנת כתיב הנגישה מתוך אתר הספרייה הלאומית של ישראל; מהדורת אברמס: לשד״ה כנגד (קריאה שגויה).
21. Following the translation of JPS (1917).
22. This is a notoriously difficult verse. See, i.e., the NRSV translation: "this is an advantage for a land: a king for a plowed field."
23. נהיה] התוספת של האות הראשונה היא בחזקת פירוש למובנו של משפט זה; ה'יתרון' הוא בעל יתרון לעומת כל מה שנהיה ונוצר ממנו.
24. טלית ציצית] צירוף זה עשוי לנבוע מתיקון סופרים.
25. BT, Sota 17a; Davidson's translation.
26. See next to note 17.
27. The *Bahir* expresses intense interest in the concept of God's 72 names. See, for example, paragraphs 63, 76–82.
28. See notes 29, 31.
29. See Idel, "Ḥeker" (see note 2, above). For more on the possibility that the text originally referred to the number 64 and not 72, see notes 28, 31.
30. לל״ב] מינכן: לל״ב ל״ב, אולם נראה שהתיבה השנייה מיותרת, ומקורה בטעות סופרים.
31. והם ס״ד] כך בוטיקן; מינכן: ונשארו ארבעה והם ס״ד.
32. מהן] כך בוטיקן; מינכן: מהם.
33. <גוף>] מינכן: נוף; והתיקון הוא בעקבות שלום, מקורות, עמ' 78, הע' 50.

34. The coin of words "holy Israel" appears already in BT Hulin 7b (and more). See G. Scholem, *Origins* (see note 2 above), 79, n. 51.
35. פרי הדר הגוף] כך בנוסח המתוקן על ידי סופר מינכן עצמו; מינכן לפני התיקון וכן וטיקן] הדר פרי הגוף.
36. Following the ES translation.
37. ראו הערה 33.
38. ראו הערה 33.
39. Meaning—*to him*, pronounced according to this Bahiric Midrash *lo*; its numerical value being thirty-six.
40. Meaning—*heart*, and pronounced according to this Bahiric Midrash *lev;* its numerical value being thirty-two.
41. שומרת] כך במינכן אחרי שהסופר תיקן את דבריו וכן בוטיקן; מינכן, לפני התיקון: שמורת; מהדורת אברמס: שמורה/שומרה (קריאה שגויה).
42. Following the NRS translation.
43. Following the NRS translation.
44. Scholem, *Origins* (see note 2, above), 78.
45. These paragraphs in the *Bahir* tend to emphasize the androgynous aspects of divine sexuality. See: E. R. Wolfson, *Through the Speculum That Shines: Vision and Imagination in Medieval Jewish Mysticism* (Princeton, 1994), especially 363–64; E. R. Wolfson, *Circle in the Square: Studies in the Zohar* (Albany, 1993).
46. And it should be emphasized that *Sefer Yezirah* itself does not directly and openly link the "heart," as a term representing a human being, to the concept of the 32 paths.
47. Except for those remaining contradictions that are concealed in the text but serve as a silent testimony to that history, as presented at the beginning of the article and then over and over again throughout.

GENDER AND VISION IN *OTZAR HAYYIM/HEIKHAL HA-BRAKHA* BY R. ITZHAK EIZIK SAFRIN OF KOMARNO

JONATHAN GARB

> *You must keep in mind that cabala is made to be confounding, and your utter bewilderment will be no reflection on you, but on the nature of the material. Knowledge comes sometimes only through the struggle to comprehend the incomprehensible.*
>
> DAVID LISS, *THE TWELFTH ENCHANTMENT*

INTRODUCTION

The voluminous writings of R. Itzhak Eizek Yehuda Yehiel Safrin of Komarno (1806–1874) can be safely described as one of the more kabbalistic corpuses of Hasidic writing and one of the more mystical corpuses of Kabbalah. Despite this, there has been little academic discussion of these texts, and especially not of his magnum opus, the combined commentary on the commandments *Otzar Hayyim*, and on the Bible, *Heikhal ha- Brakha.*[1] R. Safrin began to write *Otzar Hayyim* around 1842 and completed it in 1854–1855. He published part of it in 1848 and another part in 1858. The full edition was serially published between 1864 and 1874, together with *Heikhal ha-Brakha.*[2]

Elliot Wolfson has addressed some locutions by R. Itzhak Eizek Safrin within wider contexts in various locations in his own monumental oeuvre.[3] However, Safrin's masterpiece significantly influenced the third-generation leader of a school close to the heart of Wolfson's writing: Habad-Lubavitch. As we learn from a recently published and relatively direct testimony, *Heikhal ha-Brakha* was constantly pursued by R. Menahem Mendel Schneerson (1789–1866, known as the *Tzemakh Tzedek*), and hence it may well have influenced subsequent generations, including his namesake R. Menahem Mendel Schneerson (1902–1994), the subject of Wolfson's *Open Secret: Postmessianic Messianism and the Mystical Revision of Menahem Mendel Schneerson.*[4]

In the present article, I shall examine the nexus between two of Elliot Wolfson's most central concerns: gender and vision, through close readings of texts from Safrin's main work. The methodological premise guiding this study is simple: due to the far-reaching and revolutionary nature and implications of Wolfson's arguments, they are best examined with regard to a single work, though preferably a large one. Likewise, one should focus on the thought found within a couple of Wolfson's larger works. I believe that the patient and steady accumulation of such in-depth examinations will yield a far different picture than that offered by generalizations concerning Wolfson's contribution, or its validation within the vast and often puzzling literature of Kabbalah.

GENDER, REDEMPTION, AND VISION

In *Heikhal ha-Brakha* (on pericope *Shmot*), Safrin differentiates between the redemption from Egypt, which was "from the feminine side," and the future redemption "from the masculine side, *Yesod*, the righteous." While the earlier redemption was famously incomplete, not reaching the fiftieth gate of understanding (and thus not rectifying the fiftieth gate of impurity), the future redemption will amend this lack.[5] Safrin, as is his wont, psychologizes this distinction: The earlier redemption, the exodus, exited the negative character traits related to the "passions of this world," starting with "adultery and such like."[6] The later and final redemption will be from heresy (*minut*).[7] It is clear from a parallel in *Otzar ha-Hayyim* (on pericope *Yitro*), that Safrin is addressing what he perceives as the current situation of the Jewish people: "and now the *Shekhinah* has entered the heels, 'her steps lead straight to the grave' [Prov. 5, 5 and note bene the first part of the verse: "her feet go down to death"] and hence now is the full force of exile, that there has not been alike, and heresy rises and succeeds."[8]

In other words, the incompleteness of the redemption of the feminine in the Exodus leads to the present predicament of the *Shekhinah*, descending to lower realms and thus besieged by heresy. Based on various parallels within this corpus, it is highly plausible that heresy here denotes the *Haskalah* movement or secularization in general. It is the male, phallic aspect that will complete the redemption. It is not far-fetched, given the profoundly autobiographical and self-messianic nature of Safrin's writings (stressed in previous scholarship), that he himself is the *tzaddiq*, the righteous, who leads this process.[9] In this context, it is important to note that both here and in further texts marshaled in this section, Safrin departs from his customary mode (as in his volumes on the Zohar) of anchoring himself in zoharic or Lurianic precedents (though as we shall see, Luria is mentioned as a visionary exemplar).

The mystical-visionary nature of Safrin's self-consciousness as the redeeming *tzaddik* is clarified in a much longer discourse (on pericope *ki-Tavo)*:[10]

> . . . the matter of the exile in Egypt was that they [the people of Israel] lacked the knowledge [*da'at*] to decide that there is a Creator who renews the act of creation

> every moment . . . until Moses came, the aspect of *da'at*. . . . But the aspects of this *da'at* that was revealed in Egypt was that of the feminine . . . for they were recessed in forty-nine gates of impurity . . . and there the light of His *Shekhinah* was revealed upon them with feeling and pleasantness and the light of the *Shekhinah* and wonderful vitality . . . and through this they knew that there is no reality besides God . . . and all this is literally the daily exodus . . . for every day a person descends into several aspects of concealments and darkness . . . and the righteous lives in his faith [Hab. 2, 4], that he believes that there is no reality that he sees or hears besides God . . . and literally becomes a new creation . . . and all this is only the revelation of the Holy Spirit and of *da'at* of the feminine world, that the hearts shall be filled with light and adherence [*dvekut*] and divine vitality in the study of Torah with great feeling, and all this is from the feminine world.[11]

This passionate text merges ontology and psychology: The redemption from Egypt, reenacted on a daily basis, was through sensation and feeling, leading to a strong and vitalizing faith in the a-cosmic truth of God as the sole true reality. Yet all this is merely the feminine aspect, paradoxically facilitated through the figure of Moses. Safrin now ventures beyond:

> But the male *da'at*, 'and in all the great awe, which Moses did' [Deut. 34, 12], uplifting Israel from the feminine world in order to reveal divinity, the male *da'at*, as it will be revealed in the future in the days of the Messiah . . . and this in the future they will see [alluding to Ex. 20, 15] the letters of the Torah and prayer that they learn and pray will be before their eyes . . . and shades of blazing fire, and they will see chambers [*heikhalot*] and worlds above, and this is male *da'at*, literal seeing and not merely feeling . . . and truly there are chosen few who refined themselves to the utmost, and merited real vision, seeing the lights with their eyes, such as our master the ARI [R. Itzhak Luria] and our master the Besht, Rashi and the Ra'abad and R. Hai Gaon and all of the Geonim.

In other words, the feminine knowledge rendered by the exodus is that of feeling and faith, greatly superseded by the male capacity for vision, in the midst of study and prayer (and thus leading from the letters to the worlds and the strongly visual manifestation of colors, rendering the more generalized vision of light more complex and rich).[12] Due to the nature of some of the current writing on gender and Kabbalah (in the popular, academic, and popular-academic genres), I am obliged to note some basic items of sociohistorical context: This is a text written by a man, for men, dealing with practices almost entirely reserved for men at his time, extolling male figures from various periods. Is it then a wonder that the view of the feminine realm found here confirms to gender stereotypes?[13] It is also important to note that only in the feminine mode is the *Shekhinah* an object of vision, while the male visionary (who in the previous texts rescues the *Shekhinah* from her plight) obtains a vision of forms that do not appear to have an engendered identity.[14] However, as always, recourse to the theoretical framework developed by Wolfson enables going far beyond the obvious, as I shall now essay.

A WOLFSONIAN READING

Following the method described above, I now turn to locutions found in what are widely regarded as two of Wolfson's most central works (and that he himself has juxtapositioned, as we shall see): the early *Through a Speculum That Shines: Vision and Imagination in Medieval Jewish Mysticism*, and the later *Language, Eros, Being: Kabbalistic Hermeneutics and Poetic Imagination*. Close to the outset of the former work, Wolfson points at both the ocular-centrism of various Jewish mystical traditions and to its association with androcentric and phallocentric eroticism.[15] However Wolfson very soon takes great care to stipulate that this general finding needs to be situated in specific contexts. As he puts it, one cannot reduce different forms of mystical vision to one typology, and therefore one must pay attention to the theoretical assumptions shaping visionary experience and, at the same time, assume unity through diversity.[16]

Let us pause to relate these insights to the texts that we have just examined: First, Safrin clearly belongs to the type described by Wolfson as "cognitive." In other words, for him spiritual knowledge (described by him with the term *da'at*, in turn one of the *sefirot*) "comes by way of revelation, intuition or illumination." As Wolfson goes on to say, this entails sensory imagery, quite vivid in Safrin's case, as he stresses the possibility of real vision.[17] It is true that here, unlike numerous instances throughout the corpus (discussed in previous scholarship, and also addressed in a study of my own under review), Safrin is not speaking in the first person and yet the autobiographical background is quite transparent. And as the specific sense employed here is vision, it is predictable (though by no means an a priori must) that his texts reflect what Wolfson has termed an "ontology of light," which "gives shapes to and generates the mystic experience, which is essentially a state and process of illumination."[18] In other words, despite the emphasis on the letters (that in my reading is a first stage leading to a vision of the worlds), the leading representational system here is visual rather than auditory (and hence the culmination with a vision of colors and fire).[19]

In the sixth chapter of Wolfson's book, in this very context of luminosity, one can discern a shift from more general discussions of vision to the nexus between vision and gender. While the very connection between the two is of great portent and utility, one can also note more specific parallels (as well as subtle differentiations) between Wolfson's analysis and what we have learned from the texts: In the medieval sources discussed by Wolfson the hidden male is visually apprehended through the prism of the feminine.[20] On the other hand, for Safrin the feminine form of knowledge predictably grants vision of the feminine, while the masculine vision is that of a genderless, yet more visually compelling set of spatial domains, "chambers" and "worlds." At the same time, the structural hierarchy is similar.[21]

The concern with gender increases in Wolfson's 2005 *Language, Eros, and Being*, explicitly delving deeper into "gender signification, based on a strong expansion of the thesis of the earlier book: there is no form . . . that is not embodied . . . and there is no embodiment that is not engendered."[22] Yet this exposition is not only deeper but far wider, both in sheer scope and in the theoretical apparatus that is marshaled here. One expression of this transition is a definite shift in focus from the visual representational system to the auditory one (hence the L of *Language, Eros, and Being*, or language). Furthermore, the historical range is greatly extended, moving from the erstwhile focus on antiquity and the middle ages well into modernity (thus drawing closer to the texts discussed here). Thus, it behooves us to focus on two themes, the first of which is discussed here and the second below, after presenting another text.

Wolfson's discussion of the role of the letters is fruitful in its profound appreciation of their role in the last text cited from Safrin: following the fourteenth-century R. Shem Tov ibn Gaon, who describes the letters as "signposts" on the way to the revealed and to the concealed, Wolfson poetically employs the image of "planks on a bridge connecting matters open and hidden."[23] Similarly, for Safrin it is visual engagement with the letters that leads male knowledge ("the letters of the Torah and prayer that they learn and pray will be before their eyes") toward vision of the higher worlds ("above"), while the chosen few (presumably including Safrin himself) can "see the lights with their eyes," granting access to a realm concealed to all but these select few.[24] In my reading, the linguistic, and hence ultimately auditory (even in a visionary mode) dimension of the letters is transitional, the goal being the "real vision" of pure or "clear" light (as the Asian texts espoused by Wolfson often term it).[25]

When gleaning the fruits of returning to Wolfson's by now classic formulations, it is important to note one realm that was especially central in our first text, yet is not addressed at least in these two studies: emotion. One can say that Wolfson's psychology, informed by psychoanalytic theory, is cognitive/imaginal rather than emotive.[26] With these insights and caveats in mind, let us turn to one more text.

WHISPERING DROPS

Our first text here reverts to Safrin's above-mentioned practice of working off a Lurianic text: in this case, we are dealing with the discussion of the festival of Sukkot in the manual of *kavvanot*, or meditative intentions, *Pri 'Etz Hayyim*.[27] Deciphering the verse "I have more understanding than all my teachers, for Thy testimonies are my meditation" (Ps. 119:99), Luria (possibly via his main disciple R. Hayyim Vital) explains that "I" here refers to the traditionally ascribed author of Psalms—King David, and in kabbalistic terms to the "aspect" of *Malkhut*. He then reads the word *mi-kol* hyper-literally, not as "than all" but "from all."[28] Predictably for those versed in sefirotic symbolism, *kol* refers to *Yesod*. In other words, the feminine *Malkhut* (though initially cast as a male figure), "teaches her" Torah. This is accomplished by drawing down the seminal "drop" from the higher configurations (*partzufim*) of *Abba* and *Imma*. Thus, gaining understanding, *hiskalti*, refers to this influx obtained from these two higher "teachers," whose own phallic subaspects, or *yesodot*, are the source of the lower *Yesod*, as an entire *sefirah* in its own right, which is in immediate contact with *Malkhut*.[29] Thus, adds Luria, this lower *Yesod* itself becomes the teacher for *Malkhut*, and "it is he who reveals himself to her."

On this basis, Luria moves to the second part of the verse. The key phrase here is *asiha*, classically translated in meditative terms, yet usually connoting conversation. Yet for Vital it refers to a whisper, perhaps due to the hissing sibilants: "For *siah* is the whispering and hidden and concealed speech." In kabbalistic terms, though it is the lower *Yesod* that is overtly conversing with *Malkhut*, the higher *yesodot*, concealed within the lower *Yesod*, are secretly whispering to her.

In his commentary (found in his exegesis on pericope *Pinhas*), Safrin adds a telling gloss to his summary of the Lurianic prooftext.[30] First, the whispered communication from the supernal *yesodot* consists of the secrets of the Torah, and the secrecy is necessitated by the imperative of preventing the access of the "wicked and the husks" [*qelipot*] to this "great light." In other words, he introduces demonological and sociological dimensions to the theosophical discussion of his prooftext. Also, the theme of esotericism is reinforced through connecting it to that of evil and to demonology. One may surmise that this danger is bound up with the situation of *Malkhut*, whose vulnerability to demonic adherence is a commonplace in Lurianic writing. The importance of this formulation lies in the reflection on the position of transmitters of Kabbalah, such as Safrin himself. Indeed, esoteric locutions soon follow: "understand this well, for I have no power to expand and he who understands will understand."

Both Luria's texts and Safrin's explication are well receptive to a Wolfsonian reading: turning to the sixth chapter of his *Language, Eros, Being* book, one can readily locate rich discussions of the conjoining of rhetoric of concealment and phallocentrism with regard to the seminal influx from the higher *partzufim*, all found in key Lurianic texts.[31] More broadly, this chapter contains highly relevant formulations as to the close connection between engendered symbolism and secret modes of transmission.[32]

CONCLUSION

It is fitting that one of Elliot Wolfson's relatively recent (2014) books is entitled *Giving Beyond the Gift: Apophasis and Overcoming Theomania*. Elliot has given us all a great gift: many thousands of examples of fresh, unsettling, yet beckoning readings of texts from all periods of Jewish mysticism. Yet beyond that, he gives us clear yet elaborate theoretical frameworks, which enable us to generate general insights from these readings. As this case study shows, these frameworks are highly conducive for obtaining new visions of previously unstudied texts. These include, in the sample surveyed here, not only *Otzar Hayyim/Heikhal ha-Brakha*, but also the Lurianic *Pri 'Etz Hayyim*, interpreted by Safrin in one case.[33] What we have learned even from comparing two of his works, within a publication range of approximately a decade, is how rapidly Wolfson's thought deepens and widens. This being the case, I can look forward to being further surprised, challenged, encouraged, and instructed by Elliot along our joint path of reading Jewish mystical texts.

NOTES

1. The research for this article was supported by a grant from the Gershom Scholem Foundation.
   Overviews of scholarship (almost entirely in Hebrew) are found in the two most extensive academic texts devoted to Safrin: Yaakov Meir, "The Formation of a Hasidic Scholarship: The Bio-Bibliography of R. Yitzḥak Isaac Safrin of Komarna" [Hebrew] (MA thesis, Hebrew University of Jerusalem, 2012); Yonatan Schreiber, "A Cognitive Model for Mystical Experience Applied to the Writings of R. Yitzḥak Isaac Safrin of Komarna" [Hebrew] (MA thesis, Hebrew University of Jerusalem, 2014). These should be updated to include: Jonathan Garb, *Yearnings of the Soul: Psychological Thought in Modern Kabbalah* (Chicago University Press, 2015), 59, 84, 153; Ariel Evan Mayse, "Setting the Table Anew: Law and Spirit in a Nineteenth-Century Hasidic Code," *Journal of Jewish Thought and Philosophy* 27 (2019): 210–42; Levi Cooper, "Jewish Law in the Beit Midrash of Hasidism," *Diné Israel* 34 (2020): 51*–110* (as this list discloses, the current interest in scholarship focuses on Safrin's legal writing).
2. See in the excellent introduction to the recently published (Jerusalem, 2019) vol. I of the annotated edition, 10–12.
3. See, e.g., Elliot R. Wolfson, *Along the Path: Studies in Kabbalistic Myth, Symbolism and Hermeneutics* (Albany: SUNY Press, 1995), 100, 234n, 235n, 237n, 239n; Elliot R. Wolfson, *Venturing Beyond: Law and Morality in Kabbalistic Mysticism* (Oxford University Press, 2006), 222, n. 126; Elliot R. Wolfson, *Suffering Time: Philosophical, Kabbalistic and Hasidic Reflections on Temporality* (Leiden: Brill, 2021), 437, n. 200.
4. See the biographical introduction (by R. Yehoshu'a Safrin) to *Pri Hayyim* (Jerusalem, 2020) by his father, R. Hayyim Ya'akov Safrin, 23, based on the latter's conversation with the sixth Lubavitch rebbe (R. Yosef Yitzhak Schneerson). Clearly, the reservations with regard to the writings of Moshe Hayyim Luzzatto (1707–1746?), imbued by R. Schneerson from R. Safrin's introduction to *Otzar ha-Hayyim*, were continued by his son, R. Shmuel Schneerson (1834–1882). At the same time, a no less reliable testimony (on the part of the renowned Habad intellectual R. Hayyim Liberman) attests to the disappointment with Safrin's writings experienced by R. Shmuel's own son, R. Shalom Dov Baer Schneerson (1860–1920). See the collectively edited *Sefer Sofer Vesipur: Memorial Volume for Yehoshua Mondshine* (Jerusalem: Makhon Kramim, 2021), 739.
5. Safrin, *Heikhal ha-Brakha* (New York, 1950; reprint of Lemberg, 1872), vol. II, 16A.
6. In Hasidic writing the term *ni'uf*, literally adultery, usually refers to sexual sin in general.
7. This is a recurring theme in *Heikhal ha-Brakha*, the distinction of our texts being the engendering of the distinction. Compare to vol. V (Lemberg, 1869), 81B (pericope *re'e*).
8. Vol. II, 138A. Compare to Vol. V, 53B (pericope *va-Ethanan*).

9. Here one should especially note the sole work of Safrin's translated: Morris A. Faierstein (ed. and trans.), *Jewish Mystical Autobiographies: Book of Visions and Book of Secrets* (Mahwah, NJ: Paulist Press, 1999).
10. I follow Wolfson and others in the employment of the term mysticism, without here engaging with recent challenges to the use of the term in Kabbalah scholarship and beyond; see esp. Boaz Huss, *Mystifying Kabbalah: Academic Scholarship, National Theology and New Age Spirituality* (Oxford University Press, 2020).
11. Vol. V, 161B. Compare to vol. IV (Lemberg, 1864), 136A.
12. The play of shades and fire adds a dynamic element to the static spatial forms of chambers and worlds.
13. It is conceivable that Safrin is opposing his own visionary abilities to the "simple faith" espoused by other nineteenth-century Hasidic schools; for the broader context, see Benjamin Brown, "The Comeback of Simple Faith: The Ultra-Orthodox Concept of Faith and Its Rise in the 19th Century," in *On Faith—Studies in the Concept of Faith and Its History in the Jewish Tradition*, ed. Moshe Halbertal and Avi Sagi [Hebrew] (Jerusalem: Keter Publishing House, 2005), 403–43. Nota bene: the feminine realm (albeit associated with the predominantly male practice of Torah study) is not demeaned or denigrated. It is given positive associations such as vitality, pleasantness, even light. Yet it is clearly subordinate in the hierarchical structure constructed here. I am not claiming that for any given Hasidic writer the social construction of the feminine carries over into his view of the feminine realm, yet here this connection, though not explicit in the texts, is plausible.
14. Compare to the texts discussed in Elliot R. Wolfson, *Through a Speculum That Shines: Vision and Imagination in Medieval Jewish Mysticism* (Princeton University Press, 1994), 41–46. For Safrin's descriptions of his vision of the *Shekhinah* in distress (one of which is found in the introduction to *Otzar Hayyim*), see Moshe Idel, *Kabbalah: New Perspectives* (New Haven: Yale University Press, 1988), 83–86.
15. Wolfson, *Through a Speculum That Shines*, 5.
16. Wolfson, *Through a Speculum That Shines*, 7 (compare to the methodological caveat in 9).
17. Wolfson, *Through a Speculum That Shines*, 60. It is telling that Safrin alludes to *Heikhalot* literature, the subject of the third chapter of Wolfson's book. Compare to 145–47, 169–70, on R. Hai Gaon, one of Safrin's exemplars.
18. Wolfson, *Through a Speculum That Shines*, 270, and see also 188. It is interesting that two years after Wolfson's book was published, similar claims as to the centrality of light were developed (examining many mystical traditions, yet not the Jewish one) in Jesse B. Hollenback, *Mysticism: Experience, Response, and Empowerment* (University Park: Pennsylvania State University Press, 1996).
19. Compare to Wolfson, *Through a Speculum That Shines*, 287–88. For the relationship between the visual predilection and Torah study, another theme of our texts, see esp. 384.
20. See Wolfson, *Through a Speculum That Shines*, esp. 283, 307.
21. For the role played by the sociocultural context, see Wolfson, *Through a Speculum That Shines*, 360. While Wolfson refers to the medieval period, I would contend that in terms of gender constructs, modernization does not seem to have played a transformative role.

22. Elliot R. Wolfson, *Language, Eros, Being: Kabbalistic Hermeneutics and Poetic Imagination* (New York: Fordham University Press, 2005), xiv (compare to 127).
23. Wolfson, *Language, Eros, Being*, 198.
24. Safrin's locutions are clearly vertical, while many of the texts assembled by Wolfson in this work refer to the horizontal (left-right) axis.
25. I shall discuss Safrin's use of the language of visual clarity in a forthcoming study of my own.
26. While in Safrin's text the term "heart" refers to the center of emotion, in Wolfson's analysis (e.g., Wolfson, *Through a Speculum That Shines*, 293–94), it is the locus of imagination. Another notable difference is that although Wolfson's chosen sources do not foreground the redemptive concern of our texts, these nonetheless feature at times (see, e.g., Wolfson, *Through a Speculum That Shines*, 292–93, discussing the Exile from Egypt). Also, Wolfson's analysis centralizes the sefirotic system. While Safrin indeed refers to specific *sefirot*, it is in neither a systemic nor systematic manner (this being far from a rare phenomenon in Hasidic writing).
27. *Pri 'Etz Hayyim*, Gate of the Festival of Sukkot, chapter 2, 145A–B in the Dubrovna, 1804 edition. I cannot enter here the question of the transmission of this specific text from Luria. It suffices that for Safrin this is a Lurianic text.
28. On hyper-literal exegesis in Kabbalah, see Elliot R. Wolfson, *Luminal Darkness: Imaginal Gleanings from Zoharic Literature* (Oxford: Oneworld Publications, 2007), 70–71, 80–83.
29. What makes such texts somewhat confusing is the constant move between *sefirot* (in other words the terminology of premodern Kabbalah) and sub-*sefirot* of the *partzufim* (in other words the typical Lurianic terminology).
30. Safrin, *Heikhal ha-Brakha*, vol. IV, 189B.
31. Wolfson, *Language, Eros, Being*, 270–71 (and see also 370). These are more in the theoretical mode, while the text interpreted by Safrin (and the parallels I shall cite below) are practice-centered (or as it is at times termed, theurgical).
32. Wolfson, *Language, Eros, Being*, 294, Despite my declared intent of focusing on two of Wolfson's central works, due to the principle of "not withholding good from its owner" (Prov. 3, 27), I cannot resist referring to but one of several relevant studies: "Murmuring Secrets: Eroticism and Esotericism in Medieval Kabbalah," in *Hidden Intercourse: Eros and Sexuality in the History of Western Esotericism*, ed. Wouter J. Hanegraaff and Jeffrey J. Kripal (Leiden: Brill, 2008), 65–109.
33. To note but two closely positioned examples of texts from this work that bear out Wolfson's general argumentation and are closely related to the source interpreted by Safrin, see *Pri 'Etz Hayyim*, Gate of the New Moon, chapter 4 (on Hanukkah), 109A and chapter 5 (on Purim), 110A. When assessing Safrin's views of gender symbolism, the sources that he worked with need to be factored in.

LOVE LETTERS

The Literal Foundations of Love in the Zohar on the Song of Songs

JOEL HECKER

INTRODUCTION

In his essay "Analysis Terminable and Interminable," Sigmund Freud writes about "various methods . . . for making [an undesirable] book innocuous. One way would be for the offending passages to be thickly crossed through so that they were illegible . . . the next copyist of the book would produce a text . . . which had gaps in certain passages, and so might be unintelligible in them. Another way . . . would be . . . to proceed to distort the text. . . . Best of all, the whole passage would be erased and a new one which said exactly the opposite put in its place."[1]

Using this quotation as an epigraph for an article on the Song of Songs, Andre LaCocque characterizes Rabbi Akiva's protest against singing the Song in banquet halls as an attempt to impose an allegorical interpretation in order to facilitate the Song's admissibility to the canon. Critiquing a raft of modern readers who continue the ancient allegorizing tendency, he writes,

> To the *eros* of the poem was artificially opposed a disembodied *agape*. Because of this, the rebellious spirit of the work was tamed into a mystical and dualistic hymn where the male character is no longer a man and the female character is no longer a woman; they are asexual personae.

Rephrasing Freud, LaCocque continues, "It seems that the more a love scene is daring, the more it is likely to be interpreted mystically."[2] Daniel Boyarin formulates it as follows: "[Allegory] is a non-literal way of reading that raises a certain anxiety within a set of traditions that at regular intervals insist on different forms of literalism."[3]

Taking this statement as a prompt, I intend to show how in the Zohar's beautiful sustained commentary on the Song of Songs, eros is not sacrificed and, if the male and female characters of the Song are not read exactly as man and woman, they are decidedly masculine and feminine, with desire, longing, affection, complaint, adoration, and consummation all part of the romantic stew. This paper is intended as a modest complement to Elliot Wolfson's extended discussion of these problematics.[4] In a departure from a prevailing view that mystical allegorization of the Song of Songs has robbed the text of its erotic content, I want to claim that the Zohar re-eroticizes the Song in its treatment of the sexually animated alphabet. In its reading of the Song of Songs, the Zohar uses techniques of linguistic mysticism to elaborate the ways in which the Hebrew letters manifest intra-divine longing and erotic union.[5]

What I plan to demonstrate is the way in which the relationship of the lover and beloved in the Song of Songs is explicated by the Zohar in terms of the relationships between masculine letters and feminine letters, masculine alphabets and feminine alphabets. Inevitably, the love depicted here is similar to that between the male and female potencies of divinity (*Shekhinah* and *Tif'eret*). It is of course not surprising that the eros-charged Zohar is interested in love between masculine and feminine projections onto the alphabet, nor that letters should be an area of its interpretative investigations.[6] What interests me here is less the symbolic ontology that is expressed in the Zohar's treatment of the letters,[7] than the nature of the romantic relationship that is evinced by them. The exegetical approach of the Zohar—mystical midrash—allows for surprising readings that both confirm the Zohar's customary patriarchal, androcentric, and even phallocentric model of gender relations and subverts it, giving voice to the prominent feminine presence in the scriptural Song.[8]

The letters, like the kabbalistic *sefirot*, are designated masculine or feminine, interacting in ways that are romantically and erotically generative, and strangely evocative of the themes of love in the Song of Songs. So, even though anxiety about adolescent sexuality embedded within the canon may subconsciously have driven early allegorizing readings of the text, the libidinal energies are reinscribed, and even amplified in an idealized frame.[9]

In the course of this analysis, I will consider the following facets of love relationships:

1. Union and Plurality
2. Exclusivity of the Relationship
3. Complaint
4. Delight of Domestic Containment
5. Courtship and Erotic Union
6. Adoration

Throughout the Zohar, and other works of thirteenth-century Castilian Kabbalah, Kabbalists thought about the meanings of the letters of the Hebrew alphabet, significant in and of themselves because they were God's building blocks in creating the universe. In the Castilian rereading given to *Sefer Yetzirah, The Book of Formation*, the letters are viewed as the very stuff of Divinity, as much a part of God as the breath that uttered them in speaking, "Let there be light." As if they were subatomic particles of reality, these letters are the very foundations of supernal and even material reality. This approach lends itself to a textualization of the universe, a conception of the world as being wholly made up of letters.[10]

THE GLORY OF THE SONG OF SONGS

In ancient and medieval Jewish thought the Song of Songs has received the ultimate encomia regarding its glory, defined in terms of its provenance and authorship.[11] Most famously, Rabbi Akiva says in M *Yadayim* 3:5, "All of scripture is holy, but Song of Songs is holy of holies."[12] It is in the Zohar, however, that the praise reaches its pinnacle. The following passage about the Tabernacle extols the significance of the Song of Songs:

> The day that this song was revealed was the same day that *Shekhinah* descended to earth, as is written: *The priests could not stand and minister. . . .* Why? *For the Glory of YHVH filled the House of the Lord YHVH* (1 Kings 8:11). On that very day this praise was revealed, and by the Holy Spirit Solomon uttered the praise of this song, which is totality of the whole Torah, totality of the whole work of Creation, totality of mystery of the patriarchs, totality of the exile in Egypt—and when Israel went out of Egypt, and the praise at the Sea—totality of the Ten Commandments and standing at Mount Sinai, and Israel's wandering in the desert until they entered the Land and the Temple was built; totality of crowning the supernal Holy Name in love and joy, totality of Israel's exile among the nations and their redemption, totality of revival of the dead, until the day that is *Sabbath to the Lord* (*YHVH*) (Leviticus 25:2). Whatever was, whatever is, and whatever will eventually be . . . is all in Song of Songs. (Zohar 2:143b–144a)[13]

In this hyperbolic litany that equates the Song of Songs with the rabbinic high points of Jewish history and the temporal exhaustion of the entirety of reality, the Zohar raises the stakes for a work that already enjoyed inflated esteem.

Though the Zohar cites the Song extensively throughout its 2,000-plus pages, its thirteenth-century Castilian authorship also devoted a treatise to expounding on the Song of Songs, offering focused explications of its first eleven verses.[14] The treatise is marked by a persistently rapturous style and a recurrent interest in the theosophic implications of the letters of the Hebrew alphabet.

LOVE LETTERS

Union and Plurality

The very first teaching in the treatise explains that concealed within the first four words of the Song of Songs—*Shir ha-Shirim asher li-shelomo* (*Song of Songs of Solomon*)—are sublime mysteries, and that they signify four radiances, the four letters of the tetragrammaton, and the four *sefirot*—*Malkhut, Yesod, Tif'eret*, and *Binah*. These latter four themselves comprise the "upper chariot" with the highest *sefirot*, and possibly *Ein Sof* as well, riding upon them. The entire work of Song of Songs has now been construed as a literary projection of the letters *yod*, *he*, *vav*, and *he*, the letters of the tetragrammaton. Since the Kabbalists have an essentialist rather than nominalist approach to language, in which the tetragrammaton is not merely a label for God, but is itself a manifestation of God,[15] those first four words, in this case ironically considered by scholars to be a late superscription, indicate why Rabbi Akiva deemed the Song to be the Holy of Holies. The first line alone expresses divinity itself.

Moreover, the passage explains that while *Shekhinah* is ultimately represented by the cognomen שיר (*shir*), *Song*, She is known first as שר (*sar*), minister, until She is consummated in Her relationship with the phallic member of divinity, the *sefirah Yesod*, represented by the letter י (*yod*). *Yesod* is signified by the plural word שירים (*shirim*), *songs*, so that in their union they are now *Shir ha-Shirim*, Song of Songs.[16] *Shekhinah* is thus the ultimate expression of song, sung by the upper male *sefirot*, deriving from the plurality of songs that abound within the blessed Holy One.

In this series of moves we see how letters, in this case the letters of the divine name, are both represented by the title of the work, but also how a single letter can trigger intra-divine union.

Exclusivity

In the next passage under consideration, the letter *yod* again plays a signal role in its relationship to *Shekhinah*. The Zohar on Song of Songs gives sustained attention to fragments of verses 5–6 in the Song's first chapter: *Black am I but beautiful . . . Do not look upon me.* This verse, of course, has drawn extensive attention on account of perceived racism and the semiotics of the word *black*,[17] but the Zohar trains its focus not on skin color but on orthography, with the blackness understood as a characteristic particularly distinctive to the letter *yod*.

The tantalizing paradox of *black . . . but beautiful* leads the letter-intoxicated Kabbalists to redirect the image back from the beloved's interactions with other young women to other tensions that emerge in romantic relationships:

> When letters are engraved and inscribed on the Tree of Life, all letters ascend, inscribed in one letter—gathered in that letter. Once they are all combined within, it sends them forth.
>
> That letter—praise of them all. That letter makes no other mark beyond itself, embracing all within itself, leaving no inscription beyond concealment and hiddenness.
>
> Which is it? י (*Yod*)—single point with no other inscription. All other letters have some other mark where they are written, that mark remaining in the whiteness of that letter. י (*Yod*) is distinct, a single point, with no whiteness from elsewhere.
>
> This point, inherited by the Bride among Her array. It is a single point in the midst of Her forces and camps—designated as *Yod*, single point. Once She has ascended

> into this name and is called *Yod*, She is embellished with heavenly adornments, saying, "*Black am I*—I have no room to embrace others within Me at this time. For I have been called by the name *Yod*, in order to ascend above.
>
> "Thus, *Black am I, but beautiful*—like the preeminent embellishment, top of all rungs. I have been comprised within it, ascending upward. Right now, I have no leeway to expand, to be revealed. I am covered up, with no visibility within mystery of a single point, ascending point by point.
>
> "Since I am *black* with no latitude for expansion beyond, *you cannot look upon me*—you have no license to view me at all. You are unable to gaze upon me, for I am concealed and hidden in the mystery of a single point—no known dimensions at all." (*Zohar Ḥadash* 69d–70)[18]

Some preliminary explanation of the text is necessary before proceeding to consider the romantic relationship it depicts. When *Shekhinah* looks upward, She receives within Herself the letter י (*yod*), here symbolizing *Ḥokhmah*. As before, internalizing the letter signifies a new identity, and She is now called *yod*.[19] In this capacity, *Shekhinah* is now oriented exclusively upward, unable to embrace Her angelic retinue below. Identified with the *yod* She has only blackness, She has been rendered essentially invisible. Not only can She not be seen, *Shekhinah* is distinct from *yod* when it represents *Ḥokhmah*, since *Ḥokhmah* is the emanative source for the *sefirot* below, whereas *Shekhinah* is now defined by Her inability to project outward.

Thus, two different aspects of the letter *yod* are revealed: first, as expressive of *Ḥokhmah*, the letter *yod* is the conceptual starting point. While, in practice, the letter *yod* is not the starting place for calligraphic initiates, the Zohar speaks as if it is, on account of its graphic primacy, a dot from which one begins to inscribe any letter. Second, the letter *yod* is conceived as a point that, understood geometrically, takes up no space at all. Most letters attain their visible form through the interplay of black script and the white space within or surrounding them. In its essence, then, י (*yod*) is unique, conceived as a simple point of blackness. The paradox of ultimacy as unknowable is a hallmark of the apophasis in Neoplatonism and its beneficiaries, such as Kabbalah. Thus, *yod* is the paradigmatic kabbalistic symbol expressing the paradoxical unity of the many and the one. Its calligraphic integrity is unimpeached, while conceptually it contains all.

In terms of the romance, the passage describes the exclusivity of the relationship. Once contained within that love, *Shekhinah* has nothing for anyone else, changing the meaning of Songs 1:6 from *Do not look at me* to *You are prevented from seeing me* (or *You have no license to view me*). She is invisible on account of Her new transcendence, the transcendence of mystical romance. *Shekhinah* has thus sacrificed Her own identity in the interest of love and union above.[20] Complementing Wolfson's vast collection of sources demonstrating the absorption of the feminine into the masculine, here the narrative bestows agency upon the character *Shekhinah* who yearns for mystical absorption into the One, even as from another perspective, She sounds trapped.

The beloved's beauty in the Song is described as *black . . . but beautiful*, the interpretation of which is famously contested. The Zohar here offers an interpretation: the blackness is the self, subsumed by love, here represented as a self-compression as tiny and intense as the letter *yod*, the easiest to write, a black hole, and the most powerful initial letter of the tetragrammaton. This Self, absorbed in an Other, bears signs of both exaltation and complaint, and this erotic and emotional drama of the letters suggests an interpretation of the lovers' erotic chase in the biblical poem that comes surprisingly close to its original poetic content.

Complaint

All love relationships, or at least all that are rooted in reality, at a certain stage encompass complaint. And complain *Shekhinah* does. Commenting on Song of Songs 1:6, *My mother's sons were incensed at me*, *Shekhinah* says,

> They constricted me into this point, preventing others from gaining entry to my interior. They spread out, perfected in their configuration, fittingly. Perfected, expanding in the letter ו (*vav*) that emerged from a transcendent point, perfected in their configuration, fittingly. Perfected, expanded, and engraved in the letter ש (*shin*) that emerged from there. Perfected, engraved, and expanded in the letter ן (final *nun*). Perfected, engraved, and expanded in the letter ץ (final *tzadi*). And I—I cannot expand in any direction, nor have they left me any space to incorporate you. . . .
>
> *My own vineyard I did not guard* (ibid.) for I have neither extension nor branch, to this side or that. For if I were to spread out branches, I would grasp you within me. . . .
>
> And I, *guardian of the vineyards*—casting forth and extending branches to all letters, composed from within me. While, from My own letter, I have not extended branches. As a result, *You cannot see me*—you are unable to gaze upon Me, or enter into My midst. (*Zohar Ḥadash, Shir ha-Shirim*, 70b–c)[21]

Shekhinah contrasts herself with the expansive and relational qualities of the orthographically masculine letters *vav*, *zayin*, final *nun*, and final *tzadi*. The *mother's sons*, signifying the complex of male *sefirot* (from *Ḥesed* through *Yesod*), will only bond with *Shekhinah* when She is not attached to angels and humanity below. Those *sefirot* compress Her into the single-dimensionality of a point to prevent access to Her. She laments that they may manifest themselves fully, in sharp contrast to the limitations they have imposed on Her.

In this particular riff She gives voice to, speaking anachronistically, a kind of feminist complaint, saddened by the constraints on her freedom. All the other letters emerge from Her (*guardian of the vineyards*) even as She cannot guard Her own. While the right to complain does not stand out as the most eminent form of agency in a relationship, it is perhaps the most basic. At the very least, in this context, grievance is the mark of a character who has maintained Her individuation sufficiently to call out Her oppression. While She protests Her constraint, it is decidedly not total.

The Delight of Domestic Containment

Another passage offers this symbolic resolution explicitly:

> "*Why should I be as one veiled* (Song of Songs 1:7), self-contained, for I cannot spread out on any side at all." For She is sealed up on all sides, more than all other letters.
>
> "*If you do not know . . . go forth* (ibid., 8)—extend Yourself in all directions, gathering delights and pleasures in expansion. What is that expansion, fashioned like a hut that is built by those who guard flocks of sheep? ה (*He*).
>
> "This is also the meaning of *go for yourself* (ibid.). It is not written צאי (*tze'i*), *go*, but rather צאי לך (*tze'i lakh*), *go for yourself*, as is written: *Enlarge the site of your tent, let the curtains of your dwellings be stretched out. Do not stint!* (Isaiah 54:2). For at first, She was only a small, black point, without dimension, sealed up within Herself. Now that She has risen, bonding with Her Husband, He says to Her: '*Go for yourself.*' *Enlarge the site of your tent*—expand Yourself. Then, *graze your kids* (Song of Songs 1:8)—now You can gather delights and pleasures." (*Zohar Ḥadash, Shir ha-Shirim*, 71a–b)[22]

Here, too, *Shekhinah* carps about Her isolation and constrictions. Once *Tif'eret* has united with *Shekhinah*, however, He encourages Her to manifest the divine efflux that She has received from above and to spread out. The form of the letter ה (*he*) is itself the symbolic expression of this broadening. After *Shekhinah* has attained union with the Lover, She should spread Her blessings; Her capacity and permission to give is contingent upon the prior reinstatement of a relationship of reciprocity that exists between two lovers. *Shekhinah* should expand Herself, for Her own benefit. When *Tif'eret* instructs Her, "*graze your kids*," the intention is that She can now receive overflow from above and then transfer it to entities below. Consummation of their relationship allows *Shekhinah* to proceed from verse 7 to verse 8, and to be transformed from a *yod* into a *he*. There is a background assumption at work here as well. Her confinement is construed in terms of Her identification with the letter ד (*dalet*), relying on the association of *dalet* with the word *dal*, meaning "lowly," "thin," or "sparse." With the orthographic infusion of י (*yod*) from *Ḥokhmah* above, She metamorphoses from ד (*dalet*) into ה (*he*).[23] Notwithstanding the fact that Her completion ensues upon receiving efflux from the divine male, the Zohar can only interpret the scriptural text as it finds it, with the female beloved voicing Her plaint as an individuated entity.

This blossoming and fulfillment are expressed in the Zohar's interpretation of the phrase in the middle of the same verse: *O loveliest of women*:

> *O loveliest of women*—singular point among the letters. There would be no beauty among all the letters if not for *yod*. With this point, all letters are consummated, and She Herself is the beauty of them all. No letter stirs without this point. She is in them all and they are all in Her. She is beautiful and the loveliness of everything. For She comes from a lofty, concealed place, head of all supreme rungs, and She

> is Herself pinnacle of all lower rungs below. Consequently, *O loveliness in women* (ibid.)—beauty of all.
>
> Further, *O loveliest of women*. It is written: בנשים (*ba-nashim*), *in the women*—in the letters that are female. Who is She? ה (*He*). She is surely the expansion and elegance of all, pasturing and dividing up portions for all Her celestial troops. For this reason, צאי לך (*tze'i lakh*), *Go forth*—from this concealment, for You are contained and sealed up within Yourself. לך (*Lakh*), *For yourself*, and for your own benefit. All in the mystery of letters. (*Zohar Ḥadash*, *Shir ha-Shirim*, 71a–b)[24]

If י (*yod*) is essentially a small, black point, how can it be represented as the "*loveliest of women*"? This recalls the dilemma of Song of Songs 1:5: *I am black, but beautiful*. Here, the speaker explains that the *yod* is the very essence of all letters. Graphically, all letters begin with a point; thus, none can be written without her. Whatever beauty they have can be ascribed to her. *Yod* has its origins in the most recondite regions of divinity, in the sense that *Shekhinah* emanated from above and in the sense that it resembles the first letter of the tetragrammaton, most commonly associated with *Ḥokhmah*, called Supernal Point. It is through the expansion of *Shekhinah* from the form of *yod* to *heh* that *yod*'s beauty can be disseminated to all the letters, which are female, and then to the legions below. The phrase יפה בנשים (*yafah ba-nashim*) can now be read not as *loveliest of women*, but rather as *loveliness in women*. Even as *Shekhinah* is extolled for Her beauty, the source of that feminine beauty originates in the masculine *Ḥokhmah* by whom She has been inseminated.

At-bash—Erotic Union of Letters

The next text under consideration relies upon the technique of letter permutation called *at-bash*. In this passage, the Zohar deploys the method of *at-bash* as an exemplary performative interpretation of Song of Songs 1:4: *Draw me after you, let us run, let us delight and rejoice* בך (*bakh*), *in you*. The numerical value of the word בך (*bakh*) is twenty-two, corresponding to the number of letters in the Hebrew alphabet. Thus, the *delight* that the two letters derive is said to be from their linguistic union.

> In the joining of the letters of the Holy Name, ו (*vav*) [representing the masculine aspect of Divinity] descends, drawing ה (*he*) [representing the feminine aspect of Divinity] upward from below—becoming a single bond. Subsequently, letters of the alphabet descend and ascend. א (*Alef*) descends toward ת (*tav*), drawing her toward him, joining these within those. ב (*Bet*) ascends toward ש (*shin*), from below, upward—drawn from below—crowned by Her husband. א (*Alef*) is mystery of the [masculine] letter ו (*vav*), who longs to raise the Bride with songs that She aroused from below, when She was adorned. He extends a hand to Her, drawing Her upward toward Him—letters rejoicing, one with the other.

At the moment that She says to Him *Draw me* (Song of Songs 1:4), א (*alef*) . . . descends toward ת (*tav*) to draw Her toward him. At the moment that She says *Let us run!* (ibid.), ב (*bet*) [a feminine letter] ascends, running after [the masculine letter] ש (*shin*). . . .

At the moment that She says *Let us rejoice and delight in you* (ibid.), ג (*gimel*) comes to cleave to ר (*resh*)—then there is delight and desire within the twenty-two letters, completed by the letter *gimel*. Letter *resh* uncovers Herself before Him, to receive from Him, with no shame at all. He cleaves to Her, pouring into Her with desire. (*Zohar Ḥadash*, *Shir ha-Shirim*, 67a)[25]

This sequence of linguistic unification through the esoteric technique of *at-bash* begins with the bonding of the last two letters of the tetragrammaton, ו (*vav*), with ה (*he*). This generates the subsequent pairings of letters—letters associated with the male, such as א (*alef*) and ש (*shin*), bond with letters associated with the female, such as ת (*tav*) and ב (*bet*). Thus, in the use of *at-bash* here, the interest is not in substitution, but in the formal matching of letter pairs, with one sequence identified as masculine, the other as feminine.

The letter *gimel* signifies גומל (*gomel*), "bestowing," as in the prominent liturgical phrase *gomel ḥasadim*, "bestowing kindnesses." The letter *resh*, in turn, signifies רש (*rash*), "poor."[26] Thus, *gimel* bestows upon *resh* as the male bestows upon the female. The union of donor and recipient is marked by the proclamation of *Let us rejoice and delight* בך (*bakh*), *in you*, where the word *bakh* is written with the letters *bet* and *khaf*—whose numerical sum is twenty-two, the number of letters in the Hebrew alphabet.[27]

The gendering that we see here is typical of the medieval Kabbalists when they are expressly defining masculine and feminine roles: the masculine is active, beneficent, containing abundance, while the feminine is passive, receptive, and essentially dependent. While some have argued for a feminine sensibility in the writing of the biblical Song of Songs, and at times even in the Zohar, it is lusty mystical patriarchy that is vibrantly on display here.

Later on, the passage continues, carefully explaining the *at-bash* sequencing as an exegetical performance of Song of Songs 1:4. With each phrase that *Shekhinah* utters, She and the blessed Holy One, the masculine aspect of divinity, take on successive alphabetic forms of representation, expressed through the permutations of *at-bash*:

Here one must look closely. When She says *Draw me*, He is א (*alef*) and She is ת (*tav*). When She says *After you, let us run*, She is ב (*bet*) and He is ש (*shin*). When She says *Let us delight and rejoice in you*, He is ג (*gimel*) and She is ר (*resh*). . . . Why are all these letters exchanged from one place to another—He substituted by various letters, and She substituted by various letters?

The explanation is that when She says *Draw me*, no letter draws Her other than this—letter illuminating from the side of Primal Light, mystery of the right. For the

> right is always drawing near, strengthening Her to draw Her upward. Thus, He is א (*alef*) and She is ת (*tav*), for She is adorned by all sides to ascend upward—praising and glorifying to arouse above. (*Zohar Ḥadash, Shir ha-Shirim*, 67b)[28]

Union between masculine and feminine begins on the right side, with *Ḥesed*, the site of primal light. Thus, the beginning of illumination coincides with the initiation of language. *Shekhinah* ultimately derives light from all the upper *sefirot* and from all the letters of the alphabet, so She responds as ת (*tav*), last letter of the alphabet. This homage leads to arousal above.

> At the moment that She says *after you, we will run*, She lifts up all Her internal legions—constituting a body—toward Herself. She is a house, receiving Her troops, ushering them in before the King, as is written: *Maidens behind her, her companions, are brought to you* (Psalms 45:15). Consequently, She is ב (*bet*) and He is crowned. He opens palaces—chambers of the King—to receive Her, bringing Her toward Him.[29]

This explains the second phrase of the verse in relation to the letter-pair ב"ש (*bet-shin*). *Shekhinah* gathers Her angelic forces into Herself, as if into a "house," so that they may all run to the King. The letter ב (*bet*) is spelled out as בית (*beit*), which can be read as *bayit*, meaning "house." The three upper points of the ש (*shin*) are conceptualized as upper chambers of the King, namely *Binah*. While the King signifies *Binah*, the male partner who opens up the palaces above is constituted by the grouping of *Ḥesed* to *Yesod*.

> At the moment that She says *Let us delight and rejoice in you*—behold, delight of Righteous One, poised to bring Her delight. Thus, He is ג (*gimel*) and She is ר (*resh*). Adorned alone, She is naked before Him, deriving delight. For that place is like a wife disrobed for sexual intimacy with her husband. (*Zohar Ḥadash, Shir ha-Shirim*, 67b)[30]

To be sure, the erotic pleasure as depicted here does not exactly mirror that of the Song of Songs. In the biblical book, there is a remarkable reciprocity, mutuality, and balance between the male and female (most likely unmarried) figures. Both male and female bodies are described and admired. Here, we hear about the "wife disrobed," an erotic performance of the letters, displayed for the voyeuristic pleasure of the masculine viewer (as well, presumably, the intended male reader). "The male is ג (*gimel*), signifying a benefactor, and the female is ר (*resh*), signifying someone poor," or dispossessed, in this case dispossessed of clothing. And yet, there is tenderness and love in this model as well, a medieval reconstruction and reenactment of the biblical romantic escapades.

The pairing of masculine and feminine letters is elaborated further through interpretation of the ancient notion that the first human being was created as both male and female: "*Draw me after you, let us run!* (ibid. 1:4). It is written: *God created the human in His image; in the image of God, He created him* . . . (Genesis 1:27). When the blessed Holy One created the human . . . [they were] created with two faces, with supernal large letters and small lower letters" (*Zohar Ḥadash, Shir ha-Shirim*, 66c).[31] According to the rabbinic understanding of Genesis 1:27, the original human was created as a single being with both male and female aspects; for the Kabbalists, that creation is in turn a reflection of God's own being.[32] Here, the creation of male and female is described as a function of two groups of letters. Certain letters in a Torah scroll are written large, for example, ב (*bet*) of בראשית (*bereshit*), *In the beginning* (Genesis 1:1). Others are written small, for example, the א (*alef*) of ויקרא (*va-yiqra*), *And He called* (Leviticus 1:1). With two different sizes for letters the Kabbalists conceive of two different alphabets, one of large, supernal, and male letters, and the other of diminutive, tenuous, female letters. Moreover, they proceed in opposing directions: male letters marching forward, female letters traveling in reverse. Thus, the passage continues: "Supernal, large letters, in correct order, toward the Male—א . . . (*alef, bet, gimel, dalet*). . . . Small lower letters were inverted, in reverse order within the Female—ת . . . (*tav, shin, resh, qof*)."

To explain the phrase *The King has brought me to His chambers*, the passage introduces *Binah* as the Supernal King. Supernal King prepares *Shekhinah* for union with *Tif'eret* by setting all letters in appropriate position in the King's chambers. Then female letters arouse toward male letters, inciting bonding between them, again concluding with the coda: "*Draw me after you, let us run!* (Song of Songs 1:4). . . . All of this because of *we will delight and rejoice* בך (*bakh*), *in you* (ibid.)—twenty-two letters, supernal inscriptions. בך (*Bakh*), *In you*—mystery of *You swore to them* בך (*bakh*), *by Your Self* (Exodus 32:13)."

Here the Zohar turns to the hermeneutical technique of *gimatriyyah*, a technique involving letters and numbers to construct metaphors. The numerical equivalence of the word בך (*bakh*), *in you*, to twenty-two alludes to the twenty-two letters of the Hebrew alphabet, which in turn express the divine essence. In the second instance in this paragraph, the Zohar interprets the word בך (*bakh*) hyperliterally, reading Exodus 32:13 as: *Remember Abraham, Isaac, and Israel Your servants, to whom You swore* בך (*bakh*), *by Your Self, and said to them* . . . . When Moses pleads with God not to destroy the Israelites after the debauchery of the golden calf, he reminds God that the divine promise is vouchsafed by *bakh*, these primordial foundations of language, namely the letters of the Hebrew alphabet. Thus, when *Shekhinah* says *Draw me after you, let us run . . . we will delight and rejoice in you*, She expresses the delight that She and *Tif'eret* will enjoy in the erotic union—a mystical union of linguistic restoration.

Adoration

My final example begins with a question about the seemingly strange shift in which the beloved addresses her lover in the second person—*Draw me after you*, to third person, *The king has brought me into his chambers* (Songs 1:4). The Zohar's Rabbi Shim'on suggests, "It should say '*Bring me to your chambers*,' and then *we will delight and rejoice in you* (ibid.)! But upper and lower entities—all worlds—depend on the mystery of letters. This is the link of words—a cluster of praise toward the light above Her—that

She spoke to Her husband, center of the א (*alef*): '*Draw me* with You,' as has been said" (*Zohar Ḥadash, Shir ha-Shirim*, 65c).[33]

My argument at the beginning of this paper started with the symbolic meanings and interactions among the four words of the very first verse. Then, I proceeded to the romantic entanglements of male and female letters. In this last example, the Zohar atomizes the first letter of the alphabet, א (*alef*), which, since it signifies the number one according to the technique of *gimatriyyah*, is construed as the entirety of divinity. The central shaft of the *alef*, understood graphically as the letter ו (*vav*), comprises the central six *sefirot*—*Ḥesed* through *Yesod*. The two branches above and below are conceptualized as a *yod* above and *yod* below. The one above comprises the top three *sefirot*, called Supreme King, while the inverted, lower one signifies *Shekhinah*. In this passage, *Shekhinah*, lower י (*yod*), is speaking to Her lover, the central shaft of the א (*alef*).

> Even though She is below Him, diminished compared to the middle of the *alef*, resting beneath Him, She says: "This is negligible to me. Despite my status in relation to you, *The king has brought me into his chambers*—I am elevated and loved by the Supreme King, with no lowliness, for He *has brought me into his chambers*. Where is this place? In ה (*he*), the expansion above of the mystery of the Supernal King. Who enters there? It is I! Accordingly, I am greatly praised, in glorious exaltation, though I am common next to you. I care only to be lying under You, with You ruling over Me. Therefore, though I am lowly in relation to You, I and my legions, *we will delight and rejoice in you*. It is our delight and pleasure to be next to You, not set apart from You, for delight and pleasure are only in You. There is only delight and pleasure for a woman with her husband, mother, and father. *The king has brought me into his chambers*. I have received rapture and delight only in You." (*Zohar Ḥadash* 65c)[34]

We find here a resolution to many of the questions that have arisen before.[35] The Supernal King brings *Shekhinah* into the royal chambers, meaning into relationship with the male, the blessed Holy One. Although *Shekhinah* stands in the position of the lower branch of the *alef*, She is untroubled by Her apparently inferior position, and is actually rapturous in Her connection to the King, *Tif'eret*, opting for humility and gratitude over complaint. When *Shekhinah* says *The king has brought me into his chambers*, She exults in Her fortunate status.

Shekhinah asks rhetorically about the location of the King's chambers, answering that they are in the letter ה (*he*), meaning the second letter of the tetragrammaton, associated with *Binah*. The tetragrammaton יהוה (*yod he vav he*) represents the entire structure of the *sefirot*: the tip of the letter י (*yod*) corresponds to *Keter*; י (*yod*) itself represents *Ḥokhmah*; ה (*he*), *Binah*; ו (*vav*), *Tif'eret*, stands for the six middle *sefirot*, namely *Ḥesed* through *Yesod*; and the final ה (*he*) symbolizes *Shekhinah*. *Binah*, represented as "chambers," is the site of spatial expansion of *Ḥokhmah*, represented by *yod*. *Shekhinah* ascends to these chambers through Her relationship with *Tif'eret*, symbolized by the *vav* that is present in the tetragrammaton, as well as by the middle shaft of the letter א (*alef*). Moreover, the union with husband *Tif'eret*, mother *Binah*, and father *Ḥokhmah*, a reconstituted family, is evidenced through the unification of the tetragrammaton.

CONCLUSION

Readers have long accused the commenting tradition of robbing the Song of Songs of its erotic content by so allegorizing the relationship between the lovers that the poetic carnality all but disappears. In this paper I have argued that in its own elaborate, esoteric, and certainly arcane way, the Zohar recasts the love of the Song of Songs as a depiction of the romance between the letters of the Hebrew alphabet. The Zohar, famously erotic itself, reads the Song as a highly sexualized dance among the letters of its composition, in which the discrete, literally literal elements of God unite romantically, sexually, and creatively in a way that honors the poem's plain sense romance. In the Zohar's reading, the Song of Songs receives its ultimate exaltation in being shown to be the story of love between masculine and feminine aspects of divinity who are symbolically represented by the letters of the Hebrew alphabet. For the zoharic authorship, the Song of Songs is the holy of holies because it marks the perfection of God, attained through the perfection of language, a perfection of language conceived as the pairing of masculine and feminine letters, and masculine and feminine alphabets. To be sure, the sexual ethics of the Zohar would not condone lying in orchards, admiration of one's partner's body, nor premarital sexual relations. In many ways, the Zohar is far more chaste than the Song, even demonstrably ascetic.[36] And yet the Zohar draws on sexual energies to project the eros of the Song onto the holiest realms in a way that etherealizes human sexuality rather than eviscerating it. The spiritualizing reading offered by the Zohar simultaneously revels in and celebrates the libidinal energies it might seemingly be seeking to subvert. For the Kabbalists—how else could they imagine (and read) the meaning of love, at its depth? Elliot Wolfson captures this precisely in his analysis of the rabbinic and kabbalistic treatment of the Song of Songs: "Just as in the particular case of the Song the contextual meaning is figurative, so the hermeneutical pattern of Scripture in general is related to the poetic structure of metaphor, the *mashal* in Hebrew, which presumes an interplay of inner and outer signification, the duplicity of meaning, the secret hidden beneath the veil. . . . [T]he Song is the poem par excellence, for the contextual sense (*peshat*) overlaps with the figurative (*mashal*)."[37] In the hermeneutical circle in which they found themselves, the Song could only be fathomed at the most basic level—the level of letters, that is, the literal level.[38] And, indeed one of the aspects of the plain meaning of the zoharic text is the persistence of the scriptural substrate with its narrative of two lovers, whose consistent gendered personalities remain a present element notwithstanding the symbolic theosophic androgynizations that may be occurring simultaneously.

NOTES

1. *Standard Edition of the Complete Psychological Works of Sigmund Freud*, vol. 23, p. 236.
2. Andre LaCocque, "The Shulamite," in Andre LaCocque and Paul Ricoeur, *Thinking Biblically: Exegetical and Hermeneutical Studies*, trans. David Pellauer (University of Chicago Press: Chicago, 1998), 251–52.
3. Daniel Boyarin, "Origen as Theorist of Allegory: Alexandrian Contexts," in *The Cambridge Companion to Allegory*, ed. Rita Copeland and Peter T. Struck (Cambridge: Cambridge University Press, 2010), 39.
4. See Elliot R. Wolfson, *Language, Eros, Being: Kabbalistic Hermeneutics and Poetic Imagination* (New York: Fordham University Press, 2005), 334–71.
5. The Zohar's approach may be seen as being anticipated by Origen in his Commentary on the Song of Songs: "So, as we said at the beginning, all the things in the visible category can be related to the invisible, the corporeal to the incorporeal, and the manifest to those that are hidden; so that the creation of the world itself, fashioned in this wise as it is, can be understood through the divine wisdom, which from actual things and copies teaches us things unseen by means of those that are seen and carries us over from earthly things to heavenly." Cited in Boyarin, "Origen as Theorist of Allegory," p. 40, n. 1.

   In defense of allegorical approaches, Ilana Pardes writes, "Allegorists of the Song may seem to us utterly oblivious to the text itself but are in fact well attuned to the exhilarating metaphorical play in the Song." See Ilana Pardes, *The Song of Songs: A Biography* (Princeton University Press: Princeton, 2019), 23.
6. Scholarship on the Zohar's approach to letters includes Mikhal Oron, "Sippur ha-Ottiyot u-Mqorotav: Iyyun be-Midrash ha-Zohar al ha-Ottiyot ha-Alef-Bet," *Meḥqere Yerushalayim be-Maḥashevet Israel* 3, nos. 1–2 (1984): 97–109; Elliot R. Wolfson, "Dimmui Antropomorphi ve-ha-Symboliqah shel ha-Otiyyot," in *Sefer ha-Zohar ve-Doro* (*Meḥqerei Yerushalayim be-Maḥashevet Yisra'el* 8 [1989]), 147–81; Elliot R. Wolfson, "Letter Symbolism and *Merkavah* Imagery in the *Zohar*," in *Alei Shefer: Studies in the Literature of Jewish Thought Presented to Rabbi Dr. Alexandre Safran*, ed. Moshe Hallamish (Ramat Gan: Bar Ilan University Press, 1990), 195–236; Shifra Asulin, "Ha-Parshanut ha-Mistit le-Shir ha-Shirim be-Sefer ha-Zohar ve-Riq'ah" (PhD diss., Hebrew University, 2007), 269–77.
7. See Wolfson, *Language, Eros, Being*, 340.
8. The androcentricity and phallocentricity of Kabbalah has been a central interest of Elliot Wolfson's over the decades. See, for example, Elliot R. Wofson, "Woman—The Feminine as Other in Theosophic Kabbalah: Some Philosophical Observations on the Divine Androgyne," in *The Other in Jewish Thought and History: Constructions of Jewish Culture and Identity*, ed. Laurence J. Silberstein and Robert L. Cohn (New York: New York University Press, 1994), 166–204; Elliot R. Wolfson, "Crossing Gender Boundaries," in *Circle in the Square: Studies in the Use of Gender in Kabbalistic Symbolism* (Albany: State University of New York Press, 1995), 79–121; Elliot Wolfson, "Coronation of the Sabbath Bride: Kabbalistic Myth and the Ritual of Androgynisation," *Journal of Jewish Thought and Philosophy* 6 (1997): 301–44.
9. Addressing this phenomenon similarly but in terms of an ascetic abnegation of carnal sexuality, see Wolfson, *Language, Eros, Being*, 363–71.

10. On letters and the textualization of reality, see Wolfson, "Dimmui Antropomorphi," and Wolfson, "Letter Symbolism," cited above, n. 6.
11. See, e.g., *Shir ha-Shirim Rabbah* 1:12 (on 1:2); *Aggadat Shir ha-Shirim*, p. 5.
12. For other praises, see *Shir ha-Shirim Rabbah* 1:1:11; Rashbam; *Shir ha-Shirim Zuta* (Buber), 9 and notes 32, 34; *Shir ha-Shirim Zuta* (Schechter), 53 and notes; Abraham ibn Ezra, "Introduction to Commentary on *Shir ha-Shirim*; *Bahir* (ed. Abrams), 117; Joshua ibn Shuaib, *Drashot Yehoshu'a ibn Shuaib*, 42a; Zohar 2:18b, 98b (both *Midrash ha-Ne'lam*), 145b; *ZḤ* 47d (*Midrash ha-Ne'lam, Rut*), 61b (*Midrash ha-Ne'lam, Shir ha-Shirim*), 61d (Zohar on *Shir ha-Shirim*).
13. Translation from Daniel Matt, *The Zohar: Pritzker Edition* (Stanford: Stanford University Press, 2009), vol. 5, 314.
14. Zohar on *Shir ha-Shirim* appears in *Zohar Ḥadash*, ed. R. Margaliot (Jerusalem: Mossad ha-Rav Kook, 2002), 61d–74d.
15. On divine names in Kabbalah, see: Moshe Idel, "Defining Kabbalah: The Kabbalah of the Divine Names," in *Mystics of the Book: Themes, Topics, and Typologies*, ed. R. A. Herrera (New York: Peter Lang, 1993); Hillel Ben-Sasson, *Understanding YHWH: The Name of God in Biblical, Rabbinic, and Medieval Jewish Thought* (Switzerland: Palgrave Macmillan, 2019), 195–279.
16. In his many studies devoted to the analysis of gender in Kabbalah, most especially to its phallocentric aspects in which the feminine is absorbed within the masculine in the course of sexual union, Wolfson has shown how the letter *yod* plays a primary role, often representing *Yesod*. See above, n. 8, and on this particular passage, *Language, Eros, Being*, 362.
17. See Marvin H. Pope, *Song of Songs: A New Translation with Introduction and Commentary*. Anchor Bible, vol. 7c (Garden City, NY: Doubleday, 1977), 307–18.
18. Trans. in Joel Hecker, *The Zohar: Pritzker Edition*, vol. 11 (Stanford: Stanford University Press, 2016), 462–63.
19. The text here is ambiguous. It could be construed that since She is contained within the *yod* that designates *Ḥokhmah*, she is constituted as part of that encompassing rubric. A straightforward reading of the text, however, suggests that *Shekhinah* gains that name on account of Her situational orthography. In kabbalistic texts, the letter *yod* can also signify the mark of the covenant, that is, *Shekhinah* as emblazoned upon the masculine member, *Yesod*. *Shekhinah*'s containment within the *yod* here might lead to that reading except for the other telltale indicators in the text that point toward its signification as *Ḥokhmah*. For the various meanings of the letter *yod*, see Wolfson, *Language Eros Being*, index, s.v., *yod*.
20. As one finds in religious communities in which women are covered top-to-bottom from wig and hat to thick stockings and shoes, or wearing a form-concealing garment leaving only eyes exposed, the blackness of the *yod* marks the exclusive, and sexually proprietary, nature of the relationship.
21. Trans. in Hecker, *Zohar: Pritzker Edition*, vol. 11, 468–69.
22. Trans. in Hecker, *Zohar: Pritzker Edition*, vol. 11, 479. On this passage, see Wolfson, *Language, Eros, Being*, 357–58.
23. See above, n. 16.
24. Trans. in Hecker, *Zohar: Pritzker Edition*, vol. 11, 480.

25. Trans. in Hecker, *Zohar: Pritzker Edition*, vol. 11, 424–25.
26. Cf. the teaching in BT *Shabbat* 104a (ascribed to the children in the study hall): "*Gimel dalet*, show kindness to the poor [*gemol dallim*]. Why is the foot of the *gimel* stretched toward the *dalet*? Because it is the habit of the benevolent to run after the poor. And why is the foot of the *dalet* stretched out toward the *gimel*? To make himself available to him [the benefactor]. And why does *dalet* turn its face away from the *gimel*? So that he will give him secretly, lest he be ashamed of him." See also JT *Megillah* 1:8, 71d.
27. On gendering of letters, see *Sefer Yetzirah* 3:5–8; *Bahir* 56–58 (83–86); *Zohar Ḥadash*, *Shir ha-Shirim*, 74c–d; Elliot Wolfson, "Anthropomorphic Imagery and the Symbolism of Letters in the Zohar," *Jerusalem Studies in Jewish Thought* 8 (1989): 173–75.
28. Trans. in Hecker, *Zohar: Pritzker Edition*, vol. 11, 427–28.
29. Trans. in Hecker, *Zohar: Pritzker Edition*, vol. 11.
30. Trans. in Hecker, *Zohar: Pritzker Edition*, vol. 11, 428.
31. Trans. in Hecker, *Zohar: Pritzker Edition*, vol. 11, 417. On the alphabet imagery here, see Asulin, *Ha-Parshanut ha-Mistit*, 271–77.
32. On the androgyne in Kabbalah, see, e.g., Wolfson, *Language, Eros, Being*, 142–89.
33. Trans. in Hecker, *Zohar: Pritzker Edition*, vol. 11, 399.
34. This text is modified based on the reading in F12 141, Trinity College, Cambridge; MS heb. 780, Bibliotheque Nationale, Paris; Cod. Parm 351, Biblioteca Palatina, Parma; *Zohar Ḥadash*, Salonika (1597); and Moses Cordovero, *Or Yaqar*, vol. 17, 81a; trans. in Hecker, *Zohar: Pritzker Edition*, vol. 11, 400.
35. The depiction of *Shekhinah* as happy in Her subordinated state appears to resolve the tension between the Bible's two interpersonal instances of the term *teshuqah*, "desire": Eve's curse from Genesis 3:16, *Your desire will be for your man, and he will rule over you*; and the sentiment expressed in Song of Songs 7:11 (read according to the Zohar's understanding), *I am my beloved's, and my desire for him is upon me*.
36. On the asceticism of zoharic Kabbalah, see Elliot R. Wolfson, "Eunuchs Who Keep the Sabbath: Becoming Male and the Ascetic Ideal in Thirteenth-Century Jewish Mysticism," in *Becoming Male in the Middle Ages*, ed., Jeffrey Jerome Cohen and Bonnie Wheeler (New York: Garland, 1997), 151–85.
37. Wolfson, *Language, Eros, Being*, 336.
38. On the letter as the foundational unit in kabbalistic reading of the Torah, see Moshe Halbertal, *Nahmanides: Law & Mysticism* (New Haven: Yale University Press, 2020), 48–50.

A KING WITHOUT THE MATRONITA IS NOT CALLED "KING"

Between Queen Consort and Divine Consort in Thirteenth-Century Kabbalah

SHARON KOREN

Many scholars have noted that Alfonso the Wise's cultural Renaissance facilitated a "flowering of Kabbalistic symbolism" that encouraged the development of zoharic literature.[1] However, Alfonso was not solely a scholar; he was also a political and military leader with a lifelong ambition of becoming the Holy Roman emperor, and he marketed the monarchy to enhance his prestige and promote the ideals of the Reconquista. Locating zoharic literature within this historical context throws light on striking parallels between medieval Iberian queens and kabbalistic symbolism. The attribute of the Shekhinah in zoharic literature developed in a culture that recognized queens as political partners. As Theresa Earenfight explains, "Spanish political culture . . . created a distinctive form of queenship. . . . Spanish royal women were more likely to be active in the governance of the realm. They exercised considerable legitimate authority more often, more publicly, and more directly than queens elsewhere in Europe."[2] In particular, in this era, Alfonso's queen, Violante of Aragón, functioned prominently first as his political partner and, toward the end of his reign, as his foe. Her authority was well known among Christians, Muslims, and Jews alike. The circle of the Zohar would have been familiar with the queen, and we have evidence that Todros ben Joseph ha-Levi Abulafia, the model of the Zohar's Shimon bar Yochai, knew her personally. A section of Zohar that describes the Shekhinah as "Matronita," an Aramaicized version of the Latin matrona, lady, or doña,[3] seems to be inspired by her life.

ZOHAR 2:51A

In a section of the Zohar's commentary on the Israelites' flight from the Egyptians in front of the Sea of Reeds, God instructs Moses to raise his staff and split the sea so that the Israelites

> may come in the midst of the sea on dry land. As for me, look, I am about to toughen the heart of the Egyptians, that they come after them, and I shall gain glory through Pharaoh and through all his force, through his chariots and through his riders. And the Egyptians shall know that I am the Lord when I gain glory through Pharaoh, through his chariots and through his riders. (Exodus 14:16–18)

To bring this all to pass, God sent a messenger: "And the messenger of God that was going before the camp of Israel moved and went behind them" (Exodus 14:19). The Zohar here identifies God's messenger with the Matronita:

> Every mission that the king wishes issues from the house of the Matronita; every mission from below to the King enters the house of the Matronita first, and from there to the King. Consequently, Matronita is agent of all, from above to below and from below to above, for She is the opening to the King, way to the King and no secret is concealed from Her, from above or from below or from below to above. Thus she is agent of all, as it is written Malakh, The messenger of Elohim who was going before the camp of Israel moved (Exodus 14:19)—Israel above—Malakh, the messenger of Elohim.[4]

The Zohar ponders whether it is seemly for a woman to act as an agent of the king:

> Now is it an honor for the King that Matronita should go and wage wars and act as an agent? Well, this may be compared to a king who coupled with a lofty noble lady. The King saw how her glory surpassed all other noble ladies of the world. He said, "they are all concubines compared to my lady! She surpasses them all. What shall I do for her? Well look! My entire household will be in her hands." The King issued a proclamation: "henceforth, all the affairs of the King are entrusted to the Matronita." What did he do? The King placed in her control all his weapons, all the warriors, all those royal jewels, all the royal treasures. He said, "from now on anyone who needs me cannot speak with me until he notifies the Matronita."
>
> Similarly, the blessed Holy One, out of his great love for the assembly of Israel entrusted everything to her. . . . What shall I do for her? Well, look! my entire household will be in Her hands. He issued a proclamation: "Henceforth, all affairs of the King are entrusted to Matronita."[5]

The term "Matronita" means "married woman, wife, matron, noble woman" and is one of the many symbols of the Shekhinah. A myriad of associated symbols accrues to the Shekhinah, and each is chosen for a particular exegetical or theological context. The Shekhinah may be a bride anticipating her wedding on Friday night, the matriarch Rachel who mourns with her children in exile, or a beautiful fawn who nourishes her young. In this teaching, the term Matronita is chosen to refer to the Shekhinah in her capacity as queen.

Here the Matronita/queen is described as the perfect and trusted messenger of the king. In contrast to the many representations of the Shekhinah in other zoharic teachings as "having nothing of her own," here she is "agent of all." Rather than the Shekhinah changing gender when she is active, as Elliot Wolfson has powerfully demonstrated, here she functions actively as a queen, and her power is not subsumed by her symbolic male counterpart, King David.[6] This departure from many of the representations of the Shekhinah in other zoharic teachings strongly suggests a different model. Wolfson has also shown that Kabbalists were a product of their time and that their interpretation of gender was grounded in their historical milieu: "the theosophical myth that informs kabbalistic symbolism and ritual reflects the androcentric and patriarchal norms of medieval society in general and that of rabbinic culture in particular."[7] I would like to suggest that the description of the Matronita as queen consort, royal agent, and palace gatekeeper is also a reflection of the Kabbalists' historical milieu—medieval Iberia.

THE SOURCES OF FEMALE POWER IN IBERIA

The unique role of the Iberian queen's power in the High Middle Ages can be traced to the legacy of Visigothic hereditary law. Parents could choose to bequeath riches and property both to their male and female heirs. Women's right to inheritance became integral to Iberian Christian culture and remained the status quo among Christian kingdoms after the Muslim invasion in 711.[8] Primogeniture was unnecessary given the abundance of land, and partible inheritance enabled Iberian women to amass wealth and power. This female financial power paved the way for a mindset that permitted, if not embraced, female political power—a direct contrast to neighboring French salic law that prohibited women from inheriting or ruling. Although kings would always favor their sons, in the absence of a male heir, daughters could and did inherit the throne.[9] Women inherited the throne outright in Castile, León, Navarre, and Portugal, though few retained power independently.[10] Most of the notable exceptions were in Castile, where Urraca inherited the throne of Castile-León in 1109; Berenguela inherited the throne in 1217 but chose to bequeath the crown to her son Fernando III; and, most famously, Isabella inherited the throne in 1474.

Most medieval Iberian queens gained power through marriage rather than through direct inheritance. Queen consorts—queens by marriage—became particularly influential and prominent during the Reconquista.[11] When absent from court while engaging in battle or on diplomatic missions, Iberian kings trusted their wives to serve as their political partners.[12] In Castile, Alfonso the Wise, king of Castile and León (b. 1221, r. 1252–1284) and his wife Violante of Aragón (1236–1300/1) formed a political partnership for thirty of their forty years of marriage.[13] Violante served Castile prominently both within and outside the confines of the court, concurrent with the development of zoharic literature.[14]

VIOLANTE OF ARAGÓN, QUEEN CONSORT OF CASTILE-LEÓN[15]

Violante (r. 1252–1284) was the eldest daughter of James I of Aragón and his second wife, Violante of Hungary.[16] Betrothed at four, Violante married Alfonso when she reached adolescence in 1249. She became queen when he was crowned in 1252,[17] and they eventually had 11 children together.[18]

Violante first appeared on the political scene at Alfonso's behest. In 1256, Alfonso's brother Enrique incited nobles to revolt and approached James I (Violante's father), the king of Aragón, for support. Alfonso sent Violante, armed with two children, to beg her father to relinquish support to Enrique, and she succeeded.

Violante proved herself to be an invaluable mediator between Castile and Aragón, and her role only increased during the Mudéjar uprising in Andaluçía and Murcia in 1264. The Muslim king of Grenada roused his co-religionists living under Christian rule to rebel against Alfonso. Panic ensued throughout Castile.[19] Fearing for her life and throne, Queen Violante appealed to her father for help. Doubleday suggests that her appeal was entirely of her own volition and a sign of her growing political prominence.[20] Violante secured her father's support and, in so doing, ensured Castile's safety.[21]

Violante not only served as a mediator for Alfonso but also interceded before Alfonso on behalf of others.[22] In the same year as the Mudéjar uprising (1264), Violante pleaded to Alfonso on behalf of nobles from Extremadura struggling with their tax burden. She hosted Marie de Brienne, empress of Constantinople, who hoped Violante would mediate on her behalf with King Alfonso to secure funds to ransom her son.[23] Violante had a reputation as an effective mediator to Alfonso and was sought out to negotiate for others.[24]

Violante's independence, courage, and political savvy are most clearly manifest during the revolt of the nobility (1271–1273) in which she was far more active a participant in the negotiations and in resolution of the conflict than Alfonso.[25] Alfonso's restructuring of Castilian law and his aggressive taxation to fund his imperial ambitions angered many nobles who wanted to retain their ancient rights, inciting them to revolt. Alfonso assembled a cortes in Burgos in September 1272 to address the demands of the disgruntled nobility and appointed Violante to a commission to consider their petitions. Though Alfonso acceded to most of their requests, several rebellious magnates nonetheless left the cortes, renounced their ties to the king, and headed south to the kingdom of Grenada, where they would eventually pledge fealty to the Muslim king. Intent on restoring peace, Violante continually urged Alfonso to accede to the rebels' demands to restore order in Castile and wrote letters to the rebels in turn urging them to relent.[26] Despite her efforts, the rebels remained intransigent.

During the summer of 1272, Alfonso was faced with the continued rebellion as well as the threat of a Moroccan invasion. He also began to show symptoms of the sinus cancer that would eventually take his life.[27] He therefore dispatched his trusted partner in politics, Violante, with their seventeen-year-old son Fernando de la Cerda to Cordoba to negotiate with the king of Grenada and the insurgent nobility while he convalesced.

According to the *Chronicle of Alfonso X* (CAX),

> the king . . . considered it good to send his wife, Queen Violante, to Cordoba so that she and Prince Don Fernando could resolve the affairs of the noblemen and bring them back to the king's service. Notwithstanding that the king gave her in writing the things she had to resolve, he ordered her and pleaded with her to resolve it to his honor. . . . she resolved it better than what the king ordered her.[28]

Violante exceeded his expectations. Once she arrived in Cordoba and confronted the rebellious nobles in May 1273, Violante's intervention made the mediation of other emissaries unnecessary.[29] A year after she was dispatched, Violante independently negotiated a resolution to the conflict, which had been one of the greatest challenges of Alfonso's reign. According to the *Chronicle of Alfonso X*, Alfonso

> thanked her as much as he could because he knew how well she worked in resolving these matters, and notwithstanding that he trusted her much beforehand as a wife and as someone he had raised as a daughter, he now trusted her even more because she resolved these matters so well and so much to his service, for he was more pleased and considered it as a greater honor than if he had resolved it himself.[30]

VIOLANTE: MORE THAN QUEEN CONSORT

Violante far exceeded the responsibilities Alfonso had codified for queens in his *Siete Partidas*.[31] This code required four qualities for a queen: lineage, beauty, good habits, and wealth, and in the absence of beauty and wealth, good habits and lineage would suffice.[32] The *Partidas* legislates that a queen consort be a devoted wife and mother. Queen consorts were required to educate their daughters, who would be queens themselves one day. They were also responsible for arranging their children's marriages. But Violante of Aragón accomplished so much more. She served as a doorway to the court, interceding between her subjects and the king; she served as an ambassador for visiting foreign dignitaries; and she functioned as Alfonso's messenger and chief negotiator. Indeed, in addition to fulfilling the requirements of queen consort, she filled the description of a king's messenger as stipulated in the *Siete Partidas* as well.[33]

VIOLANTE, THE IDEAL MESSENGER[34]

The *Siete Partidas* describes two types of messengers. One functions as a postman or, in the words of the *Siete Partidas*,

> there are messengers who are the bearers of other communications in writing, and who resemble the feet of men, which move at times to their advantage without speech.[35]

The other, more trusted and important, are the king's messengers,

> whom the king sends to certain men, because he cannot declare his will to them by words, or cannot, or does not wish to communicate it to them in writing. These occupy important, and highly honorable positions, being persons whose duty it is to declare the will of the king by word of mouth. On this account Aristotle compared them to the king's tongue, for the reason that, wherever he sends them they are required to say for him what he cannot say. He also compared them to the eye and ear of the king, wherever they go for they have to see, and hear, what he does not see, or hear. Wherefore officials like these should be of good standing, loyal, intelligent, wise, fluent in speech, without covetousness, and of great secrecy.[36]

Alfonso's reference to Aristotle above is noteworthy and demonstrates his indebtedness to the Pseudo-Aristotelian *Secret of Secrets*, a book-length letter qua advice manual written by the philosopher to his most famous student, Alexander the Great. Originally in Arabic, the text became very influential in western Europe though its translations into Hebrew, Latin, and eventually Castilian as the *Poridat de las Poridades* (1256).[37] Though scholars debate which edition or translation Alfonso and his collaborators used for the *Siete Partidas*—some say Castilian while others say the Latin—all allow that the work was, as Doubleday suggests, "an inspiration, a literary muse," for Alfonso's *Siete Partidas*.[38]

The *Partidas* cites Pseudo-Aristotle's description of these two types of messengers. "Aristotle" describes ordinary messengers as "the king's feet" because they deliver the king's demands in writing, and the king's messengers are the king's "tongue, eyes and ears," conveying sensitive information orally and functioning as spies. In the Latin *Secret of Secrets* and the Castilian *Poridat de las Poridades*, "Aristotle" describes a third type of messenger:

> better than those already described, a person so intelligent and faithful that he will only need to know what the king wants to act on his behalf without necessary instructions. The messenger will always know how to react as he [the king] would in every situation—should a king be lucky enough to find one.[39]

The two descriptions of the messengers in the *Partidas* and the third in the *Poridat* correspond precisely to Violante's responsibilities as messenger for Alfonso. According to the CAX, when the queen first departed from Ávila, "she carried the king's letters for Prince Don Fernando and the masters and the nobleman who were sent on the frontier, and for Prince Felipe, Don Nuño, and Don Lope Díaz. She also carried letters for the king of Granada and for the chiefs." She is thus entrusted as the king's feet.[40]

However, in addition to transporting letters for others, Alfonso gives her a letter of authority "to accomplish all of these deeds."[41] Violante not only delivers written messages but has the authority to act *in loco regis*. Her duties exceeded those of the messengers who functioned as the king's tongue because she has the authority to act in place of the king. She may negotiate freely in real time without the limitations of other messengers, who would have to travel back and forth to Castile to receive new orders from the king. Hernández notes that after her arrival in Andalucia in 1273, no other messengers were dispatched from Castile.[42]

Violante surpasses the expectations of the role of messengers in the *Siete Partidas* and functions instead like an ideal agent—someone whom "Aristotle" states a leader "would be lucky to find" in the *Poridat*.[43] The queen is not merely a postman but rather an ambassador and arbitrator trusted to negotiate for Castile using her own discretion. And Alfonso was extremely grateful.

VIOLANTE AND THE JEWISH COMMUNITY IN CASTILE-LEÓN

Jews in Castile-León would have been aware of Violante of Aragón. A sculpture of Alfonso and Violante may have adorned the main façade of the Cathedral of Burgos[44] but is now found attached to a wall adjacent to the cloister entrance (see figure below).[45] The king and queen are represented during their wedding at the moment when the crowned king delivers a wedding ring to the queen.[46] The prominent placement of this statute made the figures' familiarity more likely.

Violante of Aragón and Alfonso the Wise, cloister exterior, Cathedral of Burgos (stone sculpture). (Album / Alamy Stock Photo.)

Moreover, the Jewish community certainly would have been aware of Queen Violante, when she unwittingly incited Alfonso to punish the Jewish community in 1281.[47] Cag de la Maleha, a Jewish tax farmer, released funds Alfonso had earmarked for the siege of Algeciras to secure Violante's return to Castile.[48] On January 19, 1281, Alfonso X imprisoned Jewish leaders in synagogues on Shabbat until they agreed to pay a daily ransom of 12,000 gold maravedís. Todros ben Joseph Abulafia, chief rabbi of the Jewish community, chastised the Jewish community in the wake of the crisis and set forth a program for religious reform.[49]

Violante's memory remained alive in Jewish texts in the fifteenth-century *Kitzur Zekher Tzaddik* by Joseph ben Tzaddik. Ben Tzaddik peppers his history of the Jewish chain of tradition with "other great events that occurred in every time period, whether for the good or the bad, and the memory of the kings of Spain and the kings of Portugal." Ben Tzaddik focuses most of his attention on Castilian history from the reign of Alfonso's father Ferdinand III to the reign of Isabella. It is noteworthy that despite Joseph ben Tzaddik's "terse style," he expatiates on the cultural legacy of Alfonso X and mentions Violante: Alfonso "married doña Violant daughter of the wise excellent King James of Aragón who received his wisdom from Nahmanides of blessed memory."[50]

JEWS IN COURT

Evidence suggests that some Jews would have not only read or seen representations of Violante but may have actually known her. Jews were an essential part of the fabric of Castilian society. Many Jews functioned as artisans and merchants while other were financiers or physicians; those who attained the highest status of courtier could serve as physicians in the court or as administrators and tax farmers in the realm.[51] Several prominent Jewish courtiers were also Kabbalists.

The Kabbalist Todros ben Joseph ha-Levi Abulafia (1220–1298 or 1220–1283)[52] was one of Alfonso and Violante's most trusted courtiers. Todros was born in the royal city of Burgos, home to the second largest Jewish community in Castile, to the illustrious Abulafia family—his uncle was Rabbi Meir ha-Levi Abulafia. Baer suggests that Alfonso appointed Don Todros as chief rabbi and justice to the Jewish community in Toledo. In accordance with his prestige, he was often referred to simply as "The Rabbi." Yehudah Liebes suggests that he was also the inspiration for the character of Rabbi Shimon bar Yochai in the narrative portions of the Zohar. Rabbi Todros was well known for his esoteric knowledge and ethical behavior and likely served as an older mentor to the kabbalistic circle of the Zohar. Both he and his son knew Moses de León, and Liebes suggests that the story of R. Simeon bar Yohai's death in the Zohar alludes to the death of Rabbi Todros ha-Levi Abulafia in 1283.[53] I would like to suggest that circumstances in Todros Abulafia's lived experience contributed to the Matronita in Zohar 2:51a quoted above.

VIOLANTE AND TODROS

Todros ben Joseph ha-Levi Abulafia was both Kabbalist and courtier; however, little attention has been paid to his role in the royal household. Both kings and queens had retinues that accompanied them at home and away. A queen's retinue included men of culture and jurists who served as her advisors, ladies in waiting and their families, a priest, her confessor, perhaps a taster, a secretary, and a physician. Americo Castro, Yitzhak Baer, and others have suggested that Todros ben Joseph may have been Violante's personal physician; he was certainly part of her household during at least two important journeys.[54]

ECIJA

The first point of contact—not widely noted—dates to 1263. After the Mudéjar Revolt, Alfonso, eager to maintain control of Andalucia and forestall any future rebellions, expelled the Muslims from their vanquished towns and resettled them with Christians and Jews. Many Jews—including Don Todros—benefited from these redistributions along the southern frontier; Todros and his sons' gifts are documented in the Repartimientos of Seville and Jerez de la Frontera.[55]

The resettlement of the town of Ecija differs from those of other Andalucian towns because Alfonso named Violante "Lord of the City." Violante and Alfonso partitioned the existing town (with the help of several soon to be expelled Mudéjars) into 32 *aldeas*[56] and redistributed the land to 198 beneficiaries from their retinues and their family, each receiving a section of an *aldea* ranging from one *yugada*[57] to thirty. The average gift was four *yugadas*. The list of beneficiaries provides us with a window into the makeup of the king and queen's households.[58] Land grants were given to two archdeacons, two abbots, four pastors, one vicar, three captains, eight squires, a tax farmer, notaries, six scribes, lawyers, and a measurer, among others.

The following is the list from one of the finest parcels, the Cabeça de Castilla:

La reyna, treynta (30) yugadas
Alfonso Royz, seys (6) yugadas
Apariçio Pérez, seys (6) yugadas
Don Todros, Seys (6) yugadas
Don Marcos, tres (3) yugadas[59]

The first beneficiary is La reyna, Queen Violante, and she receives the largest land grant; next is Alfonso Royz, Violante's notary; and Aparicio Perez, the third recipient, was Alfonso's notary.[60] Each notary received six *yugadas*, two more than the average gift of four. The fourth person named on this list is Don Todros, who also receives six *yugadas*.

In the aldea de las Choçash, eight *yugadas* were given to "Al Rabe," a title that Todros ha-Levi ben Joseph Abulafia held as well.[61] It is possible that Todros is listed twice, once by his name and once by his function, or that "Al Rabe" refers to another courtier.[62]

The Repartimiento of Ecija thus strongly suggests that Todros ben Joseph ha-Levi Abulafia was part of Violante's retinue or, at the very least, confirms that they were in the same place at the same time. Todros would have witnessed her becoming the Lady of Ecija and known about her role in resolving the Mudejar uprising. He would have traveled with her and with Alfonso's retinue and witnessed the regal pageantry of the monarchy.

PERPIGNAN

There is evidence for another point of contact in 1275. After Violante's successful resolution of the revolt of the nobility, Alfonso refocused his attention on the Holy Roman Empire. Alfonso arranged a meeting with the pope in France, and Violante accompanied Alfonso as far as Perpignan. Alfonso left Violante with their family and her retinue, including Rabbi Todros ben Joseph ha-Levi. Todros ha-Levi Abulafia and Violante remained in Perpignan for at least seven months in the king's absence. Todros may have been serving as her physician or as a trusted adviser. Abulafia writes about his sojourn to Perpignan in the poems he exchanged with the poet Abraham Bedersi.[63]

TODROS, THE QUEEN, AND THE MATRONITA

Todros ben Joseph must have seen the queen engaging in acts of diplomacy while he served in her household, and zoharic literature seems to have drawn from his experience. The Zohar's equation of the Matronita with messenger as quoted above evokes Violante's many missions for Alfonso in Reconquest Castile.

> Every mission that the king wishes issues from the house of the Matronita; every mission from below to the King enters the house of the Matronita first, and from there to the King. Consequently, Matronita is agent of all, from above to below and from below to above, for She is the opening to the King, way to the King and no secret is concealed from Her, from above or from below or from below to above. Thus she is agent of all, as it is written Malakh, The messenger of Elohim who was going before the camp of Israel moved (Exodus 14:19)—Israel above—Malakh, the messenger of Elohim.[64]

Moreover, the Zohar's description of the Matronita's retinue evokes the Reconquista world of medieval Castile in the continuation of this teaching:

> He [the king] placed in Her control of all of his weapons—lances, swords, bows, arrows, catapults, fortresses, stones, all those Warriors, as it is written, "Behold the bed of Solomon! Sixty Warriors surrounded her. . . . All of them skilled with sword" (Song of Songs 3:7–8). The King said, "from now on, my battles are in your hands, my weapons are handed over to you along with the Warriors. From now on you will guard Me," as it is written, "Guardian of Israel" (Psalms 121:4). From now on, anyone who needs me cannot speak with me until he notifies Matronita.[65]
>
> The angel of Elohim who was going before the camp of Israel moved—as has been said—and went behind them (Exodus 14:19). Why behind them? So that in front of Her would appear warriors, catapultiers, lancemen, swordsmen—reveal in front of Her—since other camps were coming to wage war against Israel from above.[66]

The Matronita as the leader of armed camps is built upon a biblical source filtered through the real experience of Reconquista Castile. The Song of Songs describes sixty sword-wielding warriors surrounding the bed of Solomon. The bed of Solomon here is another symbol for the Shekhinah; however, the Zohar does not limit her arsenal to swords. The Matronita leads warriors, catapultiers, lancers, and swordsmen—a Reconquista army![67] These many references to arms and armor evoke a life lived within Reconquest Spain. According to Teofilo Ruiz, during the Reconquista "the dynamics of victory, territorial conquest, and the long and inexorable movement of the Christians south provided a setting unlike any other in the medieval west."[68] Warfare was a quotidian aspect of medieval Castilian life. Hunting scenes, knights on horseback, falconers, lancers, and standard bearers filled the pages of the illuminated *Cantigas de Santa Maria*, the facades of Burgos Cathedral, and the windows of the Cathedral of León (see figure below). The circle of the Zohar were exposed to the pervasive images in life and in art.[69]

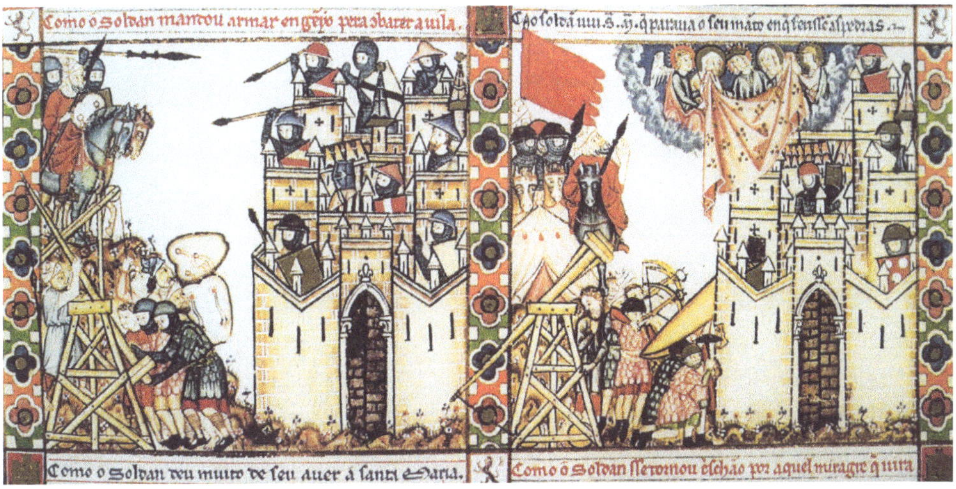

The Siege of Constantinople, Cantigas de Santa Maria, 28, Ms. T.I.I (El Escorial), fol.43r. (Album / Alamy Stock Photo.)

Queen Beatriz of Swabia and her infant daughter Berenguela on the way to Las Huelgas. *Cantigas de Santa Maria*, 122, Ms. T.I.I (El Escorial), fol.173r. (Album / Alamy Stock Photo.)

Indeed, Todros ha-Levi Abulafia must have seen standard bearers, squires, and armed soldiers who traveled with and guarded the queen. And Violante must have appeared as if sixty sword-wielding warriors surrounded the bed of Solomon when she traveled on a litter surrounded by soldiers as in the figure of Alfonso's mother Beatriz from the *Cantigas de Santa Maria* 122 (see figure above).

MATRONITA AND VIOLANTE: MESSENGERS OF THE KING

This teaching in the Zohar concludes by describing the Matronita, angel or messenger of Elohim, as filled with the radiance of the three higher *sefirot*—*Hesed*, *Gevurah*, and *Tiferet*. "On one side—crowns of *Hesed*, On the second side arrayed in lances of *Gevurah*, On the third side she was arrayed in garments of purple."[70] The Matronita is dressed as a medieval queen, crowned, protected, and wearing royal colors—a figure almost identical to the rendering of Violante in the cartulary of the Cistercian monastery of Saints Justo and Pastor, of Toxos Outos. Violante, in purple and wearing a typical medieval crown with rosettes, sits between Alfonso holding the scepter and orb on the left and her son Fernando del la Cerda on the right (see figure that follows).[71]

Tumbo de Toxosoutos, Madrid: Archivo Historico Nacional Codex n. 1002 B fol 21. (Album / Alamy Stock Photo.)

The literature of the Zohar did not emerge in a vacuum. Kabbalists were influenced by the world they inhabited. I would like to suggest that the description of the Matronita as queen consort, royal agent, and palace gatekeeper is a reflection of the Kabbalists' historical milieu—the prominence of queens in medieval Iberia.

NOTES

1. Moshe Idel, "The Kabbalah's 'Window of Opportunities,' 1270–1290," in *Me'ah She'arim: Studies in Medieval Jewish Spiritual Life in Memory of Isadore Twersky*, ed. Ezra Fleischer (Jerusalem: Hebrew University Magnes Press, 2001), 171–208.
2. Theresa Earenfight, "Partners in Politics," preface to *Queenship and Political Power in Medieval and Early Modern Spain*, ed. Theresa Earenfight (Burlington, VT: Ashgate, 2005), XIII.
3. Matt 4:252 no 197.
4. Zohar 2:51a 4:253:

   כל שליחותא דבעי מלכא מבי מטרוניתא נפקא, כל שליחותא מתתא למלכא בבי מטרוניתא עייל בקדמיתא ומתמן למלכא. אשתכח דמטרוניתא היא שליחא דכלא מעילא לתתא ומתתא לעילא בגין דאיהי פתחא למלכא ואורחא למלכא ולית רזא דאתכסיא מינה מלעילא לתתא ומתתא לעילא, ועל דא שליחא היא דכלא הה״ד ויסע מלאך האלהים ההולך לפני מחנה ישראל, ישראל דלעילא. מלאך האלהים, הה״ד ויי׳ הולך לפניהם יומם כמה דאוקימנא

5. Zohar 2:51a–b; Matt 4:252.

6. See, inter alia, Elliot Wolfson, "Coronation of the Sabbath Bride: Kabbalistic Ritual and the Myth of Androgynisation," *Journal of Jewish Thought and Philosophy* 6 (1997): 301–43; Elliot R. Wolfson, "Crossing Gender Boundaries in Kabbalistic Ritual and Myth," in *Circle in the Square* (Albany: SUNY Press, 1995); Elliot R. Wolfson, *Language, Eros, Being: Kabbalistic Hermeneutics and Poetic Imagination* (New York: Fordham University Press, 2005); Elliot Wolfson, "Woman—The Feminine as Other in Theosophic Kabbalah: Some Philosophical Observations on the Divine Androgyne," in *The Other in Jewish Thought and History*, ed. Lawrence J. Silberstein and Robert L. Cohn (New York: NYU Press, 1994); Elliot R. Wolfson, *Through a Speculum That Shines: Vision and Imagination in Medieval Jewish Mysticism* (Princeton: Princeton University Press, 1994). On King David in Kabbalah, see Ruth Kara Ivanov, "King David and Jerusalem from Psalms to the Zohar," in *Psalms in/on Jerusalem—Perspectives on Jewish Texts and Contexts* 9, ed. Ophir Muntz-Manor and Ilana Pardes (Berlin: De Gruyter, 2019), 67–107.
7. Elliot Wolfson, "Crossing Gender Boundaries in Kabbalistic Ritual and Myth," in *Ultimate Intimacy: The Psychodynamics of Jewish Mysticism*, ed. Mortimer Ostow (London: Rutledge, 1995), 321–37.
8. Lucy Pick, *Her Father's Daughter: Gender, Power, and Religion in the Early Spanish Kingdoms* (Ithaca: Cornell University Press, 2017), 32.
9. Pick, *Her Father's Daughter*, 43–55; Patricia Humphrey, "Ernessenda of Barcelóna: The Status of Her Authority," in *Queens, Regents and Potentates*, ed. Theresa Vann (Cambridge: Academia, 1993), 15–17.
10. On the many sovereign queens in Navarre, see Julia Pavón, ed., *Reinas de Navarra* (Madrid: Sílex, 2014); There was female succession in Portugal. Alfonso VI (1109) left Portugal to his illegitimate daughter Teresa and Castile, León, and Galicia to his legitimate daughter Urraca. Elena Woodacre, *The Queens Regnant of Navarre: Succession, Politics, and Partnership, 1274–1512* (United Kingdom: Palgrave Macmillan, 2013).
11. Theresa Earenfight, *Queenship in Medieval Europe* (United Kingdom: Palgrave Macmillan, 2013), 6.
12. Earenfight, "Partners in Politics," i–xxviii.
13. Violante was likely inspired by her own mother's political partnership. Yolanda of Hungary, second wife to James I of Aragón, was a savvy politician and political advisor in her own right. Queen Yolanda even mediated between James and Alfonso. *Lliber dels Feyts* 110, 109–19. Marta VanLandingham, "Royal Portraits: Representations of Queenship in Thirteenth-Century Catalan Chronicles," in *Queenship and Political Power in Medieval and Early Modern Spain*, ed. Theresa Earenfight (Burlington, VT: Ashgate, 2005), 115; Simon R. Doubleday, *The Wise King: A Christian Prince, Muslim Spain, and the Birth of the Renaissance* (New York: Basic Books, 2015), 32, 344, 347, 348.
14. To be sure, the symbolism of the Shekhinah antedated zoharic literature. Kabbalah emerged in the late twelfth and early thirteenth centuries in Provence, and many schools of kabbalistic thought first thrived in Catalonia. Moreover, the kings of the crown of Aragón—a confederation of kingdoms extending from Spain through the western Mediterranean—also entrusted their wives to govern as their lieutenants while they were away from court governing

their composite kingdom. Indeed, James I (1213–1276), Violante's own father, established the position of a king's lieutenant to meet the challenge of governing a multipart kingdom, which, by the fourteenth and fifteenth centuries, according to Earenfight, "developed into a unique form of co-rulership that became explicitly associated with Queenship." Theresa Earenfight, "Absent Kings: Queens as Political Partners in the Medieval Crown of Aragón," in *Queenship and Political Power in Medieval and Early Modern Spain*, ed. Theresa Earenfight (Burlington, VT: Ashgate, 2005), 33. However, I limit my discussion to thirteenth-century Castile for two reasons: (1) the Shekhinah in Catalonian Kabbalah functioned differently than in zoharic literature, and (2) though queens in Aragón exerted influence on their husbands—indeed, Violante's own mother advised James I—the public role of queen's lieutenant is a fourteenth- and fifteenth-century phenomenon. On the differences between the role of the Shekhinah in Catalonia and Castile, see, inter alia, Haviva Pedaya, "The Divinity as Place and Time and the Holy Place in Jewish Mysticism," in *Sacred Space—Shrine, City, Land*, ed. B. Z. Kedar and R. J. Zvi Werlowski (London: Macmillan and Jerusalem: Israel Academy of Sciences and Humanities, 1998), 84–111; Oded Yisraeli, "Honoring Father and Mother in Early Kabbalah: From Ethos to Mythos," *Jewish Quarterly Review* 99, no. 3 (2009): 396–415, http://www.jstor.org/stable/40586723; Tzahi Weiss, *Cutting the Shoots: The Worship of the Shekhinah in the World of Early Kabbalistic Literature* [Hebrew] (Jerusalem: Hebrew University Magnes Press, 2015).

15. Though there are several mentions of Violante of Aragón in Alfonsine biographies, there are only a handful of articles and one new book. Melissa R. Katz, "The Final Testament of Violante of Aragón: Agency and Empowerment of a Dowager Queen," in *Queenship in the Mediterranean: Negotiating the Role of the Queen in the Medieval and Early Modern Eras*, ed. Elana Woodacre (New York: Palgrave Macmillan, 2013), 51–71; Richard P. Kinkade, "Violante of Aragón (1236?–1300?): An Historical Overview," *Exemplaria Hispánica* 2 (1992–1993): 1–37; María Jesús Fuente Pérez, *Violante de Aragón, reina de Castilla* (Madrid: Editorial Dykinson, 2017); Joseph F. O'Callaghan, "The Many Roles of Medieval Queens: Some Examples from Castile," in *Queenship and Political Power in Medieval and Early Modern Spain*, ed. Theresa Earenfight (Burlington, VT: Ashgate, 2005), 21–32; Theresa M. Vann, "The Theory and Practice of Medieval Queenship," in *Queens, Regents and Potentates*, ed. Theresa M. Vann (Dallas: Academia, 1993), 125–47; Vann, "Violante," in *Medieval Iberia: An Encyclopedia*, ed. Michael F. Gerli (New York: Routledge, 2003), 839.
16. A note on names. Violante is the Castilian form. She was Violant in Catalan. I will anglicize the forms of monarchs' names—rendering Jaume I as James I, Pere as Peter, etc.
17. They celebrated a spousal mass in 1246; their wedding was solemnized in 1249. Joseph F. O'Callaghan, *Alfonso X, the Justinian of His Age: Law and Justice in Thirteenth-Century Castile* (Ithaca: Cornell University Press, 2019), 13.
18. The often unreliable *Chronicle of Alfonso X* (henceforth CAX) claims that Alfonso, thinking that Violante was infertile, courted a Norwegian princess. *Chronicle of Alfonso X*, trans. Shelby Thacker and José Escobar (Lexington: University Press of Kentucky, 2002), chap. 29, 109–11.
19. Even James I of Aragón, Violante's father, records the danger in his book of days: "And the king of Granada had arranged with all the castles and the towns that the king of Castile held

where there were Moors, that all would rise on a fixed day to fight with all the Christians capturing the King of Castile and his wife and recovering the towns and Castles all at one blow. And they did so. So that if the king of Castile had not discovered that Seville plot, he and his wife and children would have lost their lives. But even though he was spared the Seville plot (because the Saracens, who formed a great multitude inside did not rise), inside three weeks the king of Castile lost three hundred cities, great towns and castles." Kindle version 378 p. 282.

20. Doubleday, *The Wise King*, 109; Fuente Pérez, *Violante de Aragón*, 133; Joseph F. O'Callaghan, *The Learned King: The Reign of Alfonso X of Castile* (Philadelphia: University of Pennsylvania Press, 2016), 185.
21. Alfonso recognizes his wife's essential role in resolving the Mudéjar Revolt in his *Cantigas de Santa Maria*. Cantiga 345, written after the Mudéjar Revolt, is the sole cantiga that mentions Violante, albeit not by name. Though Alfonso had eleven children with Violante and sired others before (and possible during) his marriage, he claims to sublimate the love of all women in favor of Mary in the *Cantiga de Santa Maria* 10. Joseph F. O'Callaghan, *Alfonso X and the Cantigas de Santa Maria: A Poetic Biography* (Leiden, Boston: Brill, 1998), 16. However, after Violante saves Alfonso and Castile, Alfonso decides that both he and Violante are Mary's champions.
22. In their separate studies of English queens, John Carmi Parsons and Paul Strohm separately argue that intercession on behalf of the people was an essential part of medieval queenship. John C. Parsons, "The Queen's Intercession in Thirteenth-Century England," in *Power of the Weak: Studies on Medieval Women*, ed. Jennifer Carpenter and Sally-Beth MacLean (Urbana: University of Illinois Press, 1995); Paul Strohm, "Queens as Intercessors," in Paul Strohm, *Hochon's Arrow: The Social Imagination of Fourteenth-Century Texts* (Princeton: Princeton University Press, 1992), 95–120. Earenfight explains that "queenly intercession was part of the masculine-feminine division of labor that often reinforced cultural stereotypes of women as fickle and men as obtrusive, paternal, proud, and legalistic. Less threatening than displays of outright political control, intercession was seen as feminine pleading that made it permissible for a king to change his mind. It was socially constructed as a critique of male behavior. Ultimately it is not about women, but about men." Earenfight, *Queenship in Medieval Europe*, 12.
23. CAX 17; O'Callaghan, *The Learned King*, 204–10.
24. María Jesús Fuente Pérez, "¿Espejos de Esther? La intercesión como tarea política de la reina (León-Castilla, siglos XI–XIII)," *e-Spania* [En ligne], 20 | février 2015, mis en ligne le 13 février 2015, consulté le 29 octobre 2021. http://journals.openedition.org/e-spania/24112; https://doi.org/10.4000/e-spania.24112; Fuente Pérez, *Violante de Aragón*, 135–36; O'Callaghan, *The Learned King*, 224.
25. O'Callaghan, *The Learned King*, 218.
26. CAX, 39–40, 131–38; Fuente Pérez, *Violante de Aragón*, 137; O'Callaghan, *The Learned King*, 224–25. In fact, Violante intercepted messengers bringing news that would end further negotiations! Doubleday, *The Wise King*, 146; CAX 27, 105. On Violante's letters, CAX 41, 137.

27. Richard P. Kinkade, "Alfonso X, Cantiga 235, and the Events of 1269–1278," *Speculum* 67, no. 2 (1992): 284–323. https://doi.org/10.2307/2864374.
28. CAX 53, 173.
29. Hernández notes that after her arrival in Andalucia, no other messengers were dispatched from Castile. Francisco J. Hernández, "La reina Violante de Aragón, Jofré de Loaysa y La Crónicade Alfonso X. Un gran fragment cronístico del siglo XIII reutilizado en el XIV," *Journal of Medieval Iberian Studies* 7, no. 1 (2015): 91.
30. CAX 55, 180–81; Doubleday, *The Wise King*, 154; O'Callaghan, *The Learned King*, 227; Kinkade, "Alfonso X, Cantiga 235," 296. Alfonso thanked her in writing while he was in Cuenca meeting with James I, after he was feeling better. While negotiating with James, Alfonso shared details of his meeting with James I so that Violante could "advise him on how best to act." CAX 55, 182.
31. Alfonso recognized the queen consort as an official position and codified her role, first in the *Espéculo (Mirror of the Law)* and later revised in the *Siete Partidas.* Joseph F. O'Callaghan, *Alfonso X, the Justinian of His Age.*
32. Partida 2:6:1.
33. On Violante as an ideal messenger, see *Siete Partidas* 2:9:21 p. 326.
34. I here rely on the discussion of messengers in Hernández, "La reina Violante de Aragón," 87–111.
35. *Siete Partidas* 2:9:21 p. 326.
36. *Siete Partidas* 2:9:21 p. 326.
37. Hugo Oscar Bizzari, ed., Pseudo-Aristóteles, *Secreto de los secretos, Poridat de las poridades. Versiones castellanas del Pseudo-Aristóteles Secretum Secretorum* (València: Parnaseo, 2010), 134.
38. Doubleday, *The Wise King*, 73.
39. Hernández, "La reina Violante de Aragón," 92; Bizzari, *Secreto de los secretos*, 134.
40. CAX 53, 173.
41. CAX 53, 173–74.
42. Hernández, "La reina Violante de Aragón," 91.
43. Hernández, "La reina Violante de Aragón," 91–92; Bizzari, *Secreto de los secretos*, 134.
44. Some scholars have interpreted them as Alfonso X and Violante de Aragón, while others have identified them with Fernando III and Beatrice of Swabia, who had married in the Romanesque church of Burgos in 1219 before the existing Gothic church was erected; Alfonso and Violante married in Valladolid. On the academic debate, see E. Carrero Santa María, "CAT. 70. Pareja Real," *Maravillas de la España Medieval. Tesoro sagrado y monarquía*, ed. Isidro G. Bango Torviso, vol. I, *Estudios y catálogo* (León: Juntade Castilla y León, 2001), 150; Fuentes Pérez, *Violante de Aragón*, 68–71. For those who identify the sculpture with Violante and Alfonso, see Kinkade, "Violante de Aragón (1236?–1300?): An Historical Overview," 3–4; Frederick B. Deknatal, "The Thirteenth Century Gothic Sculpture of the Cathedrals of Burgos and Leon," *Art Bulletin* 17 (1935): 243–389, esp. 307; José María Azcárate Ristori, *Arte Gótico en España* (Madrid: Ediciones Cátedra, 1996), 159; Paul Williamson, *Gothic Sculpture, 1140–1300* (New Haven and London: Yale University Press, 1995), 341–42. Those who

identify the figures with Fernando III and Beatriz of Swabia include: Henrik Karge, *La catedral de Burgos y la arquitectura del siglo XIII en Francia y España* (Valladolid, 1995), 122; López Mata Teofilo, *La catedral de Burgos* (Burgos: Hijos de Santiago Rodríguez, 1950), 319; Francisco Javier Hernández Sánchez, "Two Weddings and a Funeral: Alfonso X's Monuments in Burgos," *Hispanic Research Journal* 13, no. 5 (2012): 407–33. On the original location, Deknatal, "Thirteenth Century Gothic Sculpture," 282.

45. Unfortunately, the original sculptures on the lower register of the west façade were badly damaged and were removed in the eighteenth century. Some are in the museum and others were moved inside different parts of the cathedral.

46. The cloister entrance lies within the Puerta de Sarmental on the south side of the cathedral. The sculptural program of the west façade, though stripped today, was likely devoted to the Queen of Heaven. Scholars imagine scenes from the coronation of the Virgin on the right doorway, the assumption of the Virgin in the middle, and Jesus's conception on the left. The only element of which we are certain is the central trumeau—Santa Maria la Blanca, Saint Mary the White Crowned, in the central trumeau of both León and Burgos. Queen culture was an essential part of thirteenth-century depictions of Mary. The Queen of Heaven would evoke Alfonso's queen who likely was originally nearby. Deknatal, "Thirteenth Century Gothic Sculpture," 282.

47. Norman Roth, "Two Jewish Courtiers of Alfonso X called Zag (Isaac)," *Sefarad* 43 (1983): 75–85; Maya Soifer Irish, *Jews and Christians in Medieval Castile* (Washington, DC: Catholic University of America Press, 2016), 163–65, 250.

48. Violante left Castile in response to Alfonso's unstable behavior in 1278. Alfonso and Violante's marriage was a casualty of his illness. As the king's health deteriorated, he experienced excruciating pain, began behaving erratically, and, several historians suggest, mistreated Violante. O'Callaghan, *Learned King*, 244–46. In response, after Alfonso declared Sancho co-ruler at the Corte of Segovia (1278), she fled Castile with her two grandsons and her widowed daughter-in-law to seek refuge with her brother King Peter III (the Great) (1240–1285, r. 1276–1285) of Aragón. To secure her return, Sancho, whether inspired by love for his mother or by his desire to disempower his rival nephews, compelled Cag de la Maleha, a prominent Jewish tax collector, to redirect funds that Alfonso had budgeted for the siege of Algeciras to pay Violante's debt in Aragón. Based on the account in CAX, Sancho needed to collect funds to settle the enormous debts that the queen had accrued while living in Aragón. Melissa R. Katz suggests "the possibility that the monies handed over by Sancho to Pere el Gran on Alfonso's behalf may have been a bribe paid to the Aragónese king to permit his sister's release. Such a prospectus is not unthinkable, given that three years later Pere III would extract financial and territorial payments from Sancho el Bravo before recognizing Sancho's claim to the throne of Castile." Melissa R, Katz, "Final Testament of Violante of Aragón," 55; Katz, "A Convent for *La Sabia*: Violante de Aragón and the *Clarisas* of Allariz," in *Culture and Society in Medieval Galicia: A Cultural Crossroads at the Edge of Europe*, ed. James D'Emilio (Leiden: Brill, 2014), 818, n. 31.

49. Yitzhak Baer, "Todros Abulafia and His Time" [Hebrew], *Tsion* 2 (1936): 19–55; Michal Kushnir-Oron, "A Sermon of Rabbi Todros Abulafia" [Hebrew], *Da'at* 11 (1983): 47–51.

50. Ram ben Shalom, *Medieval Jews and the Christian Past: Jewish Historical Consciousness in*

Spain and Southern France. (United Kingdom: Littman Library of Jewish Civilization, 2020), 186–87; on Iberian Jews' interest in the history of the monarchy, 177–90, 222.

51. Soifer Irish, *Jews and Christians in Medieval Castile*, 166–67.
52. Michal Kushnir-Oron notes there are several dates given for Abulafia's life: Graetz 1234–1304, Baer d. 1283, Scholem d. 1305. Kushnir-Oron, introduction to *Shaar ha-Razim by Todros ben Joseph Abulafia* (Jerusalem: Bialik Institute, 1998), 13 n. 1.
53. Yehudah Liebes, "How the Zohar Was Written," in *Studies in the Zohar*, trans. Stephanie Nakache (Albany: SUNY Press, 1993), 135–38.
54. Fuente Pérez, *Violante de Aragón*, 124; Yitzhak Baer, *A History of the Jews in Christian Spain*, trans. Louis Schoffman, 2 vols. (United States: Jewish Publication Society of America, 1966), 1:119; A. Castro y Quesada, *Espana en su historia, Christianos, moros, y judios* (Barcelona: Critica, 1996), 459.
55. Rab Todros also may have been listed as receiving land in the redistribution of Murcia under the name El Rab Don Todeog. Jonathan Ray, *The Sephardic Frontier: The Reconquista and the Jewish Community in Medieval Iberia* (Ithaca: Cornell University Press, 2006), 117.
56. *Aldeas* are made up of town, pasture, and farmland.
57. Spanish unit of land measurement that originated in ancient Rome based on the amount of land that two oxen can plow in a day. Approximately 32 hectares.
58. Fuentes Pérez, *Violante de Aragón*, 124–25.
59. María Josefa Sanz Fuentes, "Repartimiento de Ecija." *Historia. Instituciones. Documentos* 3 (1976): 549.
60. Hernández, "La reina Violante de Aragón," 103.
61. "Al Rabe ocho yugados," in Sanz Fuentes, "Repartimiento," 550. Manuel González Jiménez identifies Don Todros as Todros ben Joseph ha-Levi Abulafia and el Rabe as the famous wise man "Cag de Toledo," 703, n. 39. Francisco Hernández argues that the Don Todros in the Repartmiento de Ecija "is certainly the poet" Todros ben Judah ha-Levi Abulafia (b. 1247), Rabbi Todros's younger cousin; he identifies El Rabe with Cag de la Maleha (note 39, 703). Many scholars confuse the two cousins and the two Cags (Isaacs). Hernández cites Baer as proof that the Todros mentioned in Ecija is Todros the poet—but the pages that he cites (Baer 1:123) do not support his contention (n. 112 p. 103). Baer explains that Todros ben Judah's career at court began after 1270 (Baer 1:123); he would have been only 16 when Ecija was resettled in 1263. Moreover, if Todros were the poet and protégé of Cag de la Maleha described as El Rabe, wouldn't they both have received land in the same *aldea* as was customary? Why wouldn't Todros ben Judah the protégé have been awarded land in a choicer area? On the identity of Cag de la Maleha see Roth, "Two Jewish Courtiers," 75–85. Hernández identifies Don Marcos as a *rab et sobrecogedor* (tax collector) from a payroll list for Sancho IV from 1285. Hernández, "La reina Violante de Aragón," 103, n. 112.
62. In the Repartimiento of Jerez three years later in 1266, Todros is identified using both of these names. His donation is listed under the name "El Rab don Todroç." Fritz Baer, ed., *Die Juden im christlichen Spanien*, 2 vols. (Berlin: Im Schoken Verlag, 1929–1936), 1:58, note 76. Sanz Fuentes notes that the office of the awardees of the donations does not always appear next to the names in the Repartimiento de Ecija. Sanz Fuentes, "Repartimiento de Ecija," 535–51.
63. Baer, *Die Juden im christlichen Spanien*, 1:119: Abraham Bedersi, *Segullot Melakhim*, 1768, 930.

64. Zohar 2:51a, Matt 4:253:

כל שליחותא דבעי מלכא מבי מטרוניתא נפקא, כל שליחותא מתתא למלכא בבי מטרוניתא עייל בקדמיתא ומתמן למלכא. אשתכח דמטרוניתא היא שליחא דכלא מעילא לתתא ומתתא לעילא בגין דאיהי פתחא למלכא ואורחא למלכא ולית רזא דאתכסיא מינה מלעילא לתתא ומתתא לעילא, ועל דא שליחא היא דכלא הה״ד ויסע מלאך האלהים ההולך לפני מחנה ישראל, ישראל דלעילא. מלאך האלהים, הה״ד וויי׳ הולך לפניהם יומם כמה דאוקימנא

65. Zohar 2:51a, Matt 4:254.
66. Zohar 2:51b, Matt 4:255.
67. 2:51b. For other examples of the Shekhinah as Matronita leading forces, see Zohar 3:10b, 3:42b, 3:269b.
68. Teofilo Ruiz has shown that since the mid-twelfth century, Castilian and Leónese monarchs legitimized their royal authority though military might. In contrast to contemporary kings of France and England who used Christological symbols to ensure the devotion of the people, the kings of Reconquista Spain needed to appeal to a people living through a completely different historical reality in which "the dynamics of victory, territorial conquest, and the long and inexorable movement of the Christians south provided a setting unlike any other in the medieval west." This "unsacred monarchy" "was marked by symbols, ritual, and ceremonies of distinctive secular and martial flavor." Teofilo F. Ruiz, "Toward a New Concept of Power: Unsacred Monarchy," in *From Heaven to Earth: The Reordering of Castilian Society, 1150–1350* (Princeton: Princeton University Press, 2016), 134–35, 141. Pick suggests that kings' daughters and sisters "took on this sacred sphere through practices of prayer, gifts, and associations with monastic communities and who gained power from the actions they performed and the connections they developed." See also, O'Callaghan, *Alfonso X, the Justinian of His Age*, 51.
69. Doubleday, *The Wise King*, 81–83; Maximo. Gómez Rascón, *León Cathedral: The Stained Glass Windows*, 2 vols. (León: Edilesa, 2000).
70. Zohar 2:51b, Matt 4:257.
71. Tumbo de Toxosoutos, Madrid, National Historical Archive (code number CODICES, L. 1002) fol 21 (La Coruña), from 1289. This is one of the only representations that we have of Violante though it is not a portrait. Her visage is similar to those of other queens in the cartulary. Fuentes Pérez, *Violante de Aragón*, 69. Female patronage of religious institutions was a fundamental aspect of queens' piety.

ANDROCENTRIC READINGS OF KABBALISTIC TEXTS BY KABBALISTS

Delimiting the Polysemia of Kabbalistic Writings

DANIEL ABRAMS

IT IS WITH GREAT PLEASURE THAT I OFFER THIS STUDY IN HONOR OF MY teacher, Elliot Wolfson. Enrolling in his first course offered at New York University in the fall semester of 1987, I was immediately welcomed into a world in which Hebrew and Aramaic texts were read closely, without the aid of translations and without predetermined orientations offered by secondary literature. Throughout the seminars I attended on the *Book Bahir*, the Zohar, German Pietism, and the Lurianic corpus, Wolfson's stated aim was to teach us how to read texts—what I would later come to understand as learning to walk down a path. In his teaching and scholarship, Wolfson set the standard of erudition, showing us, as students, how to read and translate the literary works of Jewish esotericism, training us, step by step, how to grapple with such texts on our own. In each seminar we were asked to prepare the text and then in class, to read, translate, and explain passages.[1]

I was perhaps his first student to complete the program with a concentration on kabbalistic texts. Though I ventured far to live in Jerusalem, where I remain to this day, I took with me the charge of balancing philological detail with a greater sense of how a text's meaning can and should be constructed within the cultural context of its time, and yet also be framed in terms and concepts that participate in a wider discussion of religious studies. In the years since my graduate training, I have continued to learn from Wolfson through his many published studies, relishing the detail of his work: from his breadth of field to incorporate philosophy and the many theoretical advances of critical theory and postmodern thought in his scholarship, and to the richest bibliographic accounts in his notes, a gold mine for anyone who wishes to continue research on any particular point referenced in his work. These have served as examples of how scholarship should be conducted within and outside of any formal definition of the study of Kabbalah.

Wolfson transformed the field in many ways, one of which was the confrontation with the contextualized meanings of central rabbinic and kabbalistic traditions that were unwittingly missed or downplayed because they were unsettling for some who would wish that that which was written in the past might accord with what could or should serve the ethical expectations of Jewish life today. That is, in the years since Scholem's passing, the study of Kabbalah has been called upon by its various interpreters to answer the cultural or ideological needs of contemporary reading communities in search of authoritative rabbinic sources that might provide answers for contemporary interests. Elliot Wolfson has considered similar questions in his reading of kabbalistic sources and has, in due course, documented many of the disturbing foundations of election and androcentrism that inform the cultural worlds of rabbinic and kabbalistic texts.[2] His interpretive project has sought to explain these basic concepts, which configure "the other" in a register based on the circumcised male as the divine image created for the sake of the material world. Based on his evident love of the Jewish tradition, alongside his equally strong conviction that such texts ought to be read on their own terms, Wolfson's research draws attention to disturbing images in order to remain honest in a vocation that calls these text home. The scholarly world owes a great debt to Wolfson for having sensitized the academic community to many subjects and themes that went unnoticed in previous generations. We are richer readers because of his many studies.

It should be clear by now to any serious reader of kabbalistic manuscripts and books, and the relevant secondary literature, that the theosophic Kabbalists spoke of union between the male and the female in an androcentric key—I say this after having published a monograph many years ago that paved the way for the gynocentric reading of Kabbalah by others that followed my work, albeit with varying results.[3] Certainly to isolate either the male or female in any scholarly inquiry would be readily deemed a heretical *qitzutz ba-neityot* ("the cutting of the shoots") by the Kabbalists themselves. However, the question remains: how are the masculine or feminine to be considered together in a hierarchical structure that informs the dynamics of their relations? At issue here is both the framing of the gendered duality of the primal androgyne and the valuation of the unity later achieved in the coupling of the male and female, as the restoration and recovery of the point of departure prior to the differentiation of the sexes. This is to say, kabbalistic thinking is fundamentally predicated on the endless exploration of every variation of relations between the masculine and feminine, as it filters every biblical verse and rabbinic construction of the commandments and ritual practice through the hermeneutic processes that amount to kabbalistic discourse. That no one formulation can capture or even summarize a single kabbalistic tenet is testimony to the very tension that drives the constant revisiting of these same basic questions.

The point of a gendered duality in kabbalistic theosophy is that there is no unity unless the masculine and feminine are joined together. To be sure, the Kabbalists—even when they explicitly embraced the platonic rereading of the creation story in the rabbinic midrash of Adam and Eve, and countless other parables such as the celebrated account of the equal stature of the sun and the moon prior to her, that is, the moon's diminution—did not quantitatively assess the relative value of the sexes. The recurring theme throughout the kabbalistic revisiting of these foundational dramas is an appreciation of some sense of duality in ontological terms. Kabbalistic union is considered in metaphysical terms as the calculus of restoration that can never fully recapture the initial moment prior to separation. Statements to the contrary may be rhetorical or might mask the rupture that has occurred from the differentiation that is occasioned by the downward descent of emanation as the infinite propagates itself in a linguistically constructed theosophic order that is clearly sexualized. No doubt, some kabbalistic passages depict a messianic future that thwarts this claim. This, however, perhaps proves the point that the union, perfection, and completion that are obsessively pursued in kabbalistic writing do not amount to such a halcyonic eschaton. It is here that we must consider two major principles: the first is the status of the feminine *prior* to unification with the masculine and the second, the gendered character of the unity itself.

In his many studies, Wolfson has argued that in kabbalistic thought, feminine images are transvalued through an androcentric register.[4] It would be overly simplistic, as some would have it, to simply conclude that male authors wrote about masculine images for a male audience or to stress how it is no surprise to read such statements in this specific androcentric cultural context. While no one would challenge these facts, the question remains: what assumptions and mechanics point the way to an understanding of how these texts work on their own terms? That kabbalistic texts could be read in a modern feminist key is not to be discredited here, as it is an admirable cultural goal outside of historical concerns. Even so, it must be considered if one meaning is to be chosen over others in any interpretive exercise, particularly if certain scholarly goals are to be achieved. Kabbalistic traditions are heteronormative, which is to say that union above is predicated on identifying and joining the male and the female in sexual union below. This is not to say that the female is predominant, central, or marginal. Quite the contrary, the sexual binary that constitutes the components of union defies any clear or stable definition that would address a question formulated by modern expectations.

It is here that I would like to turn our attention to kabbalistic constructions of *completeness*, often cited by the word *shalem*, either as a verb or as an adjective that modifies the union (*ha-yiḥud ha-shalem*). To this end, I wish to discuss a passage from *Tiqqunei ha-Zohar*. The few lines to be presented here work through the four letters of the Tetragrammaton, naming their correspondence to four *sefirot*, the fourth, fifth, sixth, and tenth grades of the divine theosophy.

> The garment of the letter *yod* is Ḥesed,
> The garment of the letter *heh* is Gevurah,
> The garment of the letter *vav* is Tiferet,
> The garment of the letter *heh* is Malkhut.
> Nesaḥ, its bind [is with] Ḥesed, as it is written,
> "Delights are ever [Nesaḥ] in your right hand" (Ps. 16:11).
> Hod, its bind [is with] Gevurah,
> Sadiq, its bind [is with] the central pillar, that the body and the covenant are considered one.[5]

Malkhut is their completion.
It is the completion of the upper and lower [ones].[6]

לבושא דיו״ד חסד
לבושא דה״א גבורה
לבושא דוא״ו תפארת
לבושא דה״א מלכות
נצח קשורא דיליה חסד
הדא הוא דכתיב נעימות בימינך נצח
הוד קשורא דיליה גבורה,
צדיק קשורא דיליה עמודא דאמצעיתא
דגוף וברית חשבינן חד
מלכות שלימו דלהון,
איהי שלימו דעלאין ותתאין.

The *sefirot* are described here as garbing the letters of the divine name, giving them form or transforming them from their linguistic state into their stations above. The choice of these four *sefirot* goes back to countless older texts that map out the main limbs of the body, usually the two arms, the torso, and finally the female mate who completes the union of the male body above her, constituted herself by the first nine *sefirot*. In this brief passage from the *Tiqqunim*, Netzaḥ, Hod, and Yesod are then added to what was until this point a stock image and a stylized structure of the four basic limbs as letters of the divine name. These *sefirot*, the seventh, eighth, and ninth grades, are mentioned here to represent either the legs or the testes, as the last of the three is the phallus. In mapping out this male body from the fourth to the ninth *sefirot*, this passage is invested in showing the continuity between the powers on the right, fourth with the seventh, and those on the left, the fifth and the eighth. The presumed vertical descent of emanation or consistent identification of what is masculine on the right and feminine on the left is established with the term *qishur*, tie or bind. So too, Yesod extends as the central pillar from Tiferet to which it is bound, so that three vertical lines are depicted thus far.

Qishur does not denote coupling or some form of union, but rather a continuity. It is only when we arrive at the tenth *sefirah*, Malkhut, that we learn how she is the completion of this male structure. The text goes on, however, to indicate that the upper and lower are thereby completed, which could possibly mean that she is the axis joining the completed upper world with the lower material world. In context, however, it makes more sense to understand that the last *sefirah* is completed by her attachment to the upper *sefirot* and that they, in turn, are completed by her. So, in all, the sefirotic structure is divided into its upper and lower parts, perhaps the male body and Malkhut herself, such that each completes the other. The text is not particularly sexual in nature, but it would be difficult to escape the clear implication of union between the male body and female body, similar to the earlier enumerations of the limbs of the body in the *Book Bahir*.

We can now turn to a comment or reaction to this passage in the *Commentary on Sefer Yetzirah,* composed in sixteenth-century Safed by Solomon Turiel.[7] The commentary has survived in two manuscript witnesses, one housed in Oxford and the other in the National Library of Israel in Jerusalem. I will present the passage according to the Oxford manuscript. The comment is part of Turiel's explanation of the passage from *Tiqqunei ha-Zohar* that he cites from the Mantua edition presented above.[8]

> The left refers to the attribute of Hod as Rabbi Shimon bar Yoḥai wrote there [in the *Tiqqunim*], "Hod is bound to Gevurah." The mouth refers to the attribute of Malkhut from where speech [comes]. And one should not find difficulty with the words at the end of the passage where R. Shimon bar Yoḥai wrote that Malkhut is the one who completes them. She is the completion of the upper and lower, and it seems that this contradicts the matter [we are discussing] in saying that Malkhut is superior to them all. One should not surmise from this [that Malkhut is superior] since Tiferet, who is the trunk of the tree, is the most important of all as was explained above.
>
> שמאל רומז למדת הוד כמו שכת׳ הרשב״י שם הוד קשורא דיליה גבורה (ת״ז, מנטובה שי״ז, דף סז ע״א). הפה רומז למדת מלכות שממנה הדבור ואין להקשות מדברי סוף המאמר שכתב הרשב״י מלכות שלימו דלהון איהו שלימו דעילאין ותתאין שנראה מזה סתירת ענינינו לומר שהמלכות היא יותר מעולה מכולם אין לחוש מזה כי ת״ת שהוא גוף האילן הוא עיקר הכל כמבואר לעיל.

The passage is part of a longer discussion of the four senses in Tiqqun §70, where the four letters of the Tetragrammaton refer to Ḥesed as sight (the eyes), Paḥad as hearing (the ears), Tiferet (and Yesod) as smell (the nostrils), and Malkhut as speech (the mouth).

Indeed, this is a remarkable text if only because we have a Kabbalist interpreting an earlier kabbalistic text as he voices different possibilities of reading, namely, acknowledging that the text lends itself to multiple meanings. Turiel considers and then rejects a reading of the word *shelimo,* completion, to mean elevated or superior. He does not negate the literal meaning that Malkhut is needed to bring the theosophic structure to completion, but warns the reader not to go further in valuating Her, that is, in going beyond this basic function.

It is here that we can read with some suspicion. Is Turiel responding to a specific reading or to interpretations provided by Kabbalists he knew or texts he read? Or perhaps he is voicing his own reaction to ways he thought the text could be read? Regardless, taking this comment at face value, we see how a sixteenth-century Kabbalist entertains two modes of reading completion and how he compels his reading audience to dispense with one and read a zoharic text in light of the other.

Methodologically, I offer this text as one example of how scholarship can turn away from accepted understandings of what it means for a modern academic to read a text on its own terms and begin to construct a history of reading of Kabbalah from within the esoteric tradition. I am painfully aware that all reading is interpretation and I do not offer these remarks as proof that Turiel or any other Kabbalist grasped the Zohar's original meaning (assuming we can even speak of the Zohar's meaning, or any original intention about such a text or even use such constructs). Moreover, I am reluctant to reduce such a move to yet another chapter in the reception history of this text or any zoharic passage, for that matter. Rather, my aim here is to gradually collect reactions of how past Kabbalists read kabbalistic classics. The goal is to map out self-aware attempts to guide a readership while acknowledging the multiplicity of meanings that the text can bear. It is no coincidence that Turiel found it necessary to curtail an overly positive valuation of Malkhut and to clarify the meaning of "completion" in this context. He was adamant that the male *sefirah*, Tiferet, is the center of the sefirotic tree and is the most important. In so doing, he offered a benchmark of how to read a zoharic text. We have here therefore one clear example of this trend from within the kabbalistic tradition, a statement of how to value the gendered role of the feminine in the process of the completion of unity.

We can now turn to a second passage from this same work. Here, particularism and gender converge in a tradition that began to develop in the *Book Bahir* and reached a certain complexity or fullness in the works of Joseph Gikatilla. According to this tradition, Abraham, as the chosen one who would enter into a covenant with God, was the first to discover the Lord. While other later texts would cast this process as the discovery of monotheism, the kabbalistic tradition views Abraham's relation to God as a limited connection of intimacy: he only knew the last feminine *sefirah*. We must pause and note how the biblical tradition here collapses all of human history from Adam to Abraham, discounting all biblical figures in between in order to highlight the unique event of the covenant. Apologetic justifications of exceptions to this rule include that Adam, Enoch, or Noah were each born circumcised and so these figures could have enjoyed a close and sexualized relationship with the divine prior to the generation of Abraham; but as they did not perform the act of circumcision they did not enter the covenant willfully, or perhaps the divine did not ask for such a transformation to make such intimate contact possible. In texts belonging to similar theosophic traditions, we might also argue that Moses looms in the background of such discussions as part of a graduated hierarchy of forms of intimacy cast across the historical record of the biblical narrative. Moses, identified with the sixth *sefirah*, achieves a higher form of intimacy with the divine, and no doubt the revelation at Mount Sinai must constitute a more privileged sense of intimate knowledge. In Gikatilla's close reading of the biblical verses, Abraham knows God as El Shaddai, seen to refer to the tenth *sefirah*, while Moses knows God through the Tetragrammaton, referring to the sixth *sefirah*.

This brings us to the second passage from Turiel's *Commentary on Sefer Yetzirah*, which reads as follows:[9]

> From here on are the five Beraitot which R. Akiva, son of Joseph, composed.
>
> The first Beraita. When Abraham our father, peace be upon him, looked and saw, etc, which means that this work called *Sefer Yetzirah* was given to Abraham, our father, peace be upon him, he became wise from it and he began to see with the Holy Spirit. And he saw, that is to say, he investigated and considered. And he engraved

and carved in his mind and carved into his heart the wisdom of the book. And he acquired the wisdom of creation. And he combined the letters by combining and weighing and replacing letters according to the wisdom of this work. And he made souls, as it is written, "And the souls which they made in Haran" (Gen. 12:5).

The Second Beraita. And the master over the world was revealed to him. This means that the master is Yesod. He is the master over Malkhut which is called All, which is to say that after his forty-seventh year, which is equal to the numerical equivalence of "[The Lord appeared] to him" (Gen. 18:1; 47=אליו), he received the book [*Sefer Yetzirah*]. And with the comprehension which was granted to him when he was 52 years old and 48 years later from 52 until the time that he was 99 years old, which is 47 years, the equivalent of אליו, then Shekhinah appeared to him, included within the attribute of Yesod. And He called [Abraham] his lover, as it is written "the seed of Abraham, my friend" (Is. 41:8). And he sealed a covenant for his offspring because the foundation of circumcision (*yesod milah*) refers to Yesod and the uncovering [of the corona] to Malkhut. And Abraham did not need the uncovering [of the corona with circumcision] because the uncovering [refers to Malkhut which was already revealed to him]. And his need for [this] was only a sign that he was granted permission to enter the sefirah of Malkhut. And the attribute of Malkhut was given to him as a gift once he turned 70 years old so that he only lacked circumcision which refers to the granting of permission to enter Yesod, as is written in the *Zohar* in the appropriate place. Because prior to Abraham circumcising [himself], the attribute of Malkhut alone was revealed to him on her own, simply [as a sole entity, distinct] from the other attributes. And once he circumcised [himself] the attribute of Malkhut was revealed to him as included within Yesod. And this is what is said, the master Y(esod) of All (M)alkhut was revealed to him, as has been mentioned.

And in *Sha'arei Orah*,[10] in [the chapter about] the Attribute of Yesod in the discussion of the name covenant [of circumcision], these are his words: And this is the secret of circumcision, when pulling back the membrane. And regarding what our sages, may their memories be blessed, said, that if one cuts but does not pull back the membrane, it is as if he is not circumcised at all—that is to say, that the pulling back of the membrane is the secret [of showing the existence] of Adonai [namely the corona as the feminine, Malkhut]. And anyone who has not pulled it back lacks the first sefirah [when counting from below], through which one enters the palace of the Lord [written as the Tetragrammaton, namely the masculine, Tiferet], because through the [name] Adonai, one enters to [arrive at] El Ḥai [Yesod] and from El Ḥai, to the name of YHWH, may He be blessed. And if one has not pulled it back then even to the name of El Ḥai he cannot enter because he lacks the pulling back which is the name Adonai. End of quote.

And God established a covenant with him and his offspring, that is to say, He granted him that all his circumcised offspring would belong to the Holy One, blessed be He, and would not be subject to the rule of the Other [side] and Hell would not rule over them, as our sages, may their memories be blessed said about the verse

"[Assuredly, Sheol has opened wide its gullet] and parted its jaws in a measureless gape" (Is. 5:14). And the secret of this matter is that all who are sealed with the seal of the holy covenant which is the seal of the Holy One, blessed be He, will be [counted] amongst the sons of her Faith, that is, entrusted and considered sons of the house as has been mentioned above in the first chapter regarding the matter of establishing a covenant.

מכאן ואילך חמשה בריתות חברם ר׳ עקיבא בן יוסף.

ברייתא א׳ כשבא אברהם אבינו עליו שלום והביט וראה וכו׳ פי׳ לאחר שנתן לו לאברהם אבינו עליו השלום חבור זה הנק׳ ספר יצרה נתחכם בו וצפה ברוח הקדש. והביט וראה ר״ל חקר ועיין. וחקק וחצב במוחו וחצב בלבו חכמת הספר. ועלתה בידו חכמת הבריאה. וצירף על יד צירוף האותיות ושקל והמיר האותיות כפי חכמת החיבור הזה ועשה נפשות שנא׳ ואת הנפש אשר עשו בחרן.

ברייתא ב. ונגלה עליו אדון העולם פי׳ אדון הוא יסוד הוא אדון למלכות הנקראת כל ר״ל לאחר מ״ז שנה כמנין אלי״ו אחר שניתן לו הספר. ועם השגה שנתן לו שהיא שנת נ״ב הרי מ״ח ומשנת נ״ב עד שנת צ״ט הם מ״ז שנה כמנין אליו ואזי נראה אליו השכינה כלולה במדת יסוד. וקראו אוהבו כדכתי׳ זרע אברהם אוהבי. וכרת לו ולזרעו ברית כי סוד מילה רומז ליסוד והפריעה למלכות ואברהם לא נצטרך לפריעה כי רמז הפריעה והצטרכותו אינו אלא סימן שניתן לו רשות להכנס לספירת מלכות ומדת מלכות ניתנה לו במתנה משהיה בן שבעים שנה ולא היה חסר לו אלא המילה שהיא רמז לנתינת רשות להכנס ביסוד וכדאיתא בזוהר במקומו כי קודם שמל אברהם היתה נגלת לו מדת מלכות לבדה פשוטה משאר המדות ואחר שמל היתה נגלת לו מדת מלכות כלולה ביסוד וזהו אומרו ונגלה עליו אדון (י׳) הכל (מ׳) כנז׳.

ובספר שערי אורה במדת יסוד בכנוי ברית וז״ל וזהו סוד ברית פריעת המילה ומה שאמרו חז״ל מל ולא פרע כאלו לא מל כלו׳ שהפירעה הוא סוד אדנ״י וכל שלא פרע הרי הוא חסר הספירה הראשונה שבה יכנס להיכל יהו״ה ית׳ כי מאדנ״י יכנס לאל חי ומן אל חי לשם יהו״ה ית׳ ואחר שלא פרע אפי׳ לשם אל חי לא יכנס כי חסר הפריעה שהוא שם אדנ״י. ע״כ.

וכרת לו ברית ולזרעו ר״ל התנה עמו שכל זרעו הנמולים יהיו חלקו של הב״ה ולא תחת רשות סטרא ואין גהנם שולט עליהם כדארז״ל על פסוק ופערה פיה לבלי חק וכו׳ וסוד הענין הוא כי כל החתומים כחותם אות ברית קדש שהיא חותמו של הב״ה יהיו מבני מהימנותא דיליה ר״ל נאמניו ובני ביתו כנז׳ לעיל באומרו פ״ק ועל דבר זה נכרת ברית.

Here we have an explanation of a theme and a passage from *Sefer Yetzirah* that is built around an excerpt from Joseph Gikatilla's canonical work, *Sha'arei Orah*. And although the earlier informs the latter, we can also appreciate that here too we have a fine example of how a Kabbalist reads an earlier kabbalistic text.

In this passage, Abraham discovers God on his own, presumably the lowest rung of the ten *sefirot*. Apparently due to this revelation, he was granted access to the wisdom of creation, the tools that could be learned from *Sefer Yetzirah*, which was given to him. Following a passage at the end of chapter 6, about the "Master of All who is revealed" to him, it is apparent that the study of this book took him to higher levels of comprehension, or revelation, about the Master of All, the phallic and ninth *sefirah* of Yesod. In a third stage, Abraham circumcises himself and then is able to understand the relation between Yesod and Malkhut, by which Malkhut was revealed to him to be "included within Yesod." As explored in the passage by Gikatilla and many other kabbalistic texts, *peri'ah*, or the pulling back of the membrane, is understood as the full revelation of *'Aṭarah*, referring both to the corona of the penis and the tenth *sefirah*.[11]

One might be tempted to read this passage as focusing, in all of its stages, on Malkhut, the feminine. Indeed, the process begins with the discovery of the feminine. At the end, when she is coupled with the masculine, the passage considers her ontological placement within the masculine, again focusing on her. But the point here is that the feminine was the pathway in a process toward a higher form of revelation in approaching the Master and understanding that the feminine, which conceived on her own, is actually, or was always, contained within the masculine, *kelula be-yesod*. This text does not begin with the male king, to which is added the consort of queen, nor does it begin with the two-faced androgyne, which is split in two only in order to rejoin. Rather, this text charts a path of discovery from the feminine to the masculine in order to configure the relative ontological weight or power that defines the theosophic sense of union.

It should be apparent how Elliot Wolfson's work has informed the reading of these texts and so many others. The selection of these passages from Solomon Turiel's commentary was chosen to illustrate how we might read these texts considering some of the methodological contributions of Wolfson's scholarship. A fuller study and annotated edition of this work are certainly worthy projects for the field, and further research on this work and its period will test the limited examination offered here. Nevertheless, Turiel's work was chosen randomly, namely, these are two passages I came across when reading aimlessly in kabbalistic manuscripts; a selection of two passages from any one of countless other works could have served the same purpose. Even so, my conscious effort was to present texts in which a Kabbalist, who wrote from within the shared discourse of so many others, explained earlier esoteric sources not only by offering his own interpretation but also by acting with self-awareness, explaining why and how he arrived at his conclusions.

It is my hope that a scholarly turn inward into the views of the kabbalists themselves will help mitigate a debate about how to apply any external hermeneutic on a text and will help scholars appreciate those interpretive programs that are responsive to the inner workings of kabbalistic texts and to the ways they function on their own terms. For the skeptic who would believe that these passages have been selected precisely because they support a marginal view not representative of Kabbalah as a whole, I would say that these texts implicitly or explicitly discuss various possibilities and frame the discussion and conclusion about the primary place of the masculine in relation to the feminine. In the first passage, which interprets a zoharic text, the suggestion that the feminine might be understood as elevated or superior is rebutted. I would challenge the skeptic to find a passage that offers the opposite assertion, namely a refutation of the possibility of reading a zoharic passage in which the masculine might be considered central (*'iqqar*). In the second passage, the hierarchal and gradual discovery of the divine is narrated within the context of Abraham's life, moving from knowledge of Malkhut to

Yesod and recognizing that in the union of the two, the feminine is included within the masculine. Here too, it needs to be emphasized that such passages are commonplace, and it would be difficult to find many examples of a Kabbalist discussing the recognition of the masculine *sefirah* and moving toward its relation to the feminine, whereby the masculine is contained within the feminine.

In sum, little or no scholarly work has explored the Kabbalists' own recognition of the polysemic potential of the texts that comprise their own corpus. This move is methodologically significant for Kabbalah research only if we resist framing it as a chapter in the reception history of a work or corpus. Scholarship has enjoyed for nearly a century the layered historiography of a linear progression of ideas—structured around texts and their commentaries that were produced successively in each period, trend, or school—without considering the inner dialogue of a history of reading delimited by the hermeneutics that are specific to a particular type of thinking or textual community, when viewed across time. What I am suggesting is that, as scholars, we consider what might lie beyond the hermeneutical horizon of a group of texts in order to better appreciate the possibilities that can be found within a particular literature. So, whereas the keys to interpretation were once thought to be found within the kabbalistic texts themselves, as the voiced rejection of Kabbalah as a living tradition that was entrusted to prophets and not professors, the field has matured to the point that it now can find guides to reading from within the textual tradition that buttress the field's own interpretive efforts. The interface between a literary tradition and contemporary critical theory therefore should be respected, since the two are not mutually exclusive. As a field, we can thus move from (all) possible readings of a certain passage and quantitative assessments of a corpus based on amassing examples of any particular phenomenon to a discussion of how the Kabbalists read their own texts and how they demarcated the limits of interpretation and determined the horizons of kabbalistic hermeneutics.

NOTES

1. See Elliot Wolfson, "Lying on the Path: Translation and the Transport of Sacred Texts," *AJS Perspectives* 3 (2001): 8–13.
2. See especially Elliot R. Wolfson, *Venturing Beyond—Law and Morality in Kabbalistic Mysticism* (New York: Oxford University Press, 2006).
3. Daniel Abrams, *The Female Body of God in Kabbalistic Literature: Embodied Forms of the Love and Sexuality of the Divine Feminine* [Hebrew] (Jerusalem: Magnes, 2005). To be sure, the monograph was an exercise in what traditions could be amassed regarding this perspective. For a more recent and rather androcentric treatment of kabbalistic texts see my article, "Three Kabbalistic Secrets: Circumcision, Impurity and the Foreskin (Edition, Translation, Commentary)," *Kabbalah* 47 (2021); 7–38.
4. It would be impossible in the present context to fully discuss all of Wolfson's relevant studies on this matter. Perhaps the most succinct statement of this after Wolfson's *Language, Eros,*

Being: Kabbalistic Hermeneutics and Poetic Imagination (New York: Fordham University Press, 2005) is his article "Phallic Jewissance and the Pleasure of No Pleasure," *Talmudic Transgressions: Engaging the Work of Daniel Boyarin*, ed. C. Fonrobert et al. (Leiden, Boston: Brill, 2017), 293–335.

5. Citing the *Book Bahir*. See Daniel Abrams, *The Book Bahir: An Edition Based on the Earliest Manuscript* (Los Angeles: Cherub Press, 1994), 199, § 114.
6. *Tiqqunei ha-Zohar* (Mantua, 1558), fol. 67a (my translation). For a rationale as to why I am breaking the lines of *Tiqqunei ha-Zohar* see David Charles Solomon, "Revelation and Equivalence: A Methodology for the Translation of Sacred-Texts as applied to the Tiqqunim of the Zohar," unpublished PhD thesis, Monash University, 2018.
7. See the study by Ruth Ben-Natan, "Kabbalistic Teachings in *Eshet Ne'urim* by R. Solomon Turiel" [Hebrew] (MA thesis, The Hebrew University of Jerusalem, 1993).
8. Ms. Oxford, Christ Church College 188, fol. 63a.
9. Ms. Oxford, Christ Church College 188, fols. 75b–76a.
10. Joseph Gikatilla, *Sha'arei Orah* (Offenbach, 1715), fol. 26a.
11. See Elliot Wolfson, "Circumcision and the Divine Name: A Study in the Transmission of Esoteric Doctrine," *Jewish Quarterly Review* 78 (1987): 77–112, esp. 98 n. 63; See also the following studies by Wolfson focusing directly on circumcision: Elliot R. Wolfson, "Circumcision, Vision of God, and Textual Interpretation: From Midrashic Trope to Mystical Symbol," *History of Religions* 27 (1987): 189–215; Elliot Wolfson, "Woman—The Feminine as Other in Theosophic Kabbalah: Some Philosophic Observations on the Divine Androgyne," in *The Other in Jewish Thought and History: Constructions of Jewish Identity and Culture*, ed. L. Silberstein and R. Cohn (New York, 1994), 166–204; Elliot R. Wolfson, "Circumcision, Secrecy, and the Veiling of the Veil: Phallomorphic Exposure and Kabbalistic Esotericism," *The Covenant of Circumcision: New Perspectives on an Ancient Jewish Rite*, ed. E. W. Mark (Hanover and London: Brandeis University Press, 2003), 58–70.

SECRECY, KABBALAH, AND MAIMONIDEANISM IN THE THIRTEENTH CENTURY

JONATHAN DAUBER

I

Throughout his work, Elliot Wolfson has highlighted the interplay of medieval Kabbalah and medieval Jewish philosophy.[1] Indeed, in an interview with Hava Tirosh-Samuelson and Aaron W. Hughes, Wolfson expresses the hope that his analysis of this interplay "will be seen as one of my contributions to the field, precisely because I challenged the field in that regard." He goes on to say that "the study of kabbalistic texts should not be seen as something distinct from the study of philosophical thinking in the Middle Ages."[2] Wolfson's contention that medieval philosophy and medieval Kabbalah cannot be studied apart from one another has guided my own research.[3] My work[4] has similarly been guided by an even more central component of Wolfson's scholarship: his focus on kabbalistic esotericism. In numerous studies, he has highlighted the elaborate dynamics of revealing and concealing that animate kabbalistic literature,[5] and, as he notes, "Nothing is more important for understanding the mentality of the Kabbalist than the emphasis on esotericism."[6] In this study honoring Wolfson, I will examine a case in the early history of Kabbalah in which these two themes overlap.

My focus, here, is on how kabbalistic esotericism impacted the manner in which Samuel ben Mordekhai and Meir ben Simeon—two Talmudic scholars active in Southern France in the thirteenth century—evaluated the relationship between Kabbalah and a particular type of philosophy, that of Maimonides. These two figures were neither Kabbalists nor, in any strong sense, followers of Maimonides, and were, therefore, outside observers of this relationship. That is to say, they did not view themselves as devotees of kabbalistic ideas, and, as we will see, while both defended Maimonides in the context of the Maimonidean controversy that raged in Southern France in the first part of the thirteenth century, they were not Maimonideans, if that designation implies a commitment to the details of Maimonides's philosophy and to the Aristotelianism that underlies it.

Yet, if in other ways these two figures are ideologically and culturally parallel, they differ in their evaluations of kabbalistic thought. In Samuel's view certain kabbalistic and Maimonidean views are identical, while Meir, implicitly, sees them as standing in sharp opposition. As I will argue, their differing evaluations are the result of their differing conceptualizations of kabbalistic thought, which, in turn, are related to the type of kabbalistic views that they had access to at the time of composition. While Samuel's kabbalistic knowledge was based on an exoteric presentation of Kabbalah, Meir was privy to more esoteric kabbalistic doctrines. Both readings—or misreadings—shed light on a crucial transitional period in which access to kabbalistic literature remained uneven and knowledge of kabbalistic concepts was very much in flux.

II

Most of the little that we know of Samuel's biography has been summarized by Pinchas Roth, who set his dates as approximately 1200–1265. He seems to have lived in the town of Apt in Southern France and was thus active in the general place and period where some of the first kabbalistic works were being composed, though there is no evidence that he was aware of them. He is the author of a commentary on Maimonides's *Mishneh Torah*, which has only been partially published, as well as of a halakhic work, *Issur ve-Heter*, of which only fragments survive. We also have a number of halakhic questions in his name addressed to Shlomo ibn Aderet. For our purposes, his most interesting work is a letter to a certain Yekutiel ha-Kohen in which, among other things, he argues for the identity of the beliefs of Maimonides and certain kabbalistic ideas.[7]

While Ben-Zion Dinur and, in his wake, Ram Ben-Shalom identify Samuel as a Kabbalist,[8] the designation has no basis. He never professes to have any inside kabbalistic knowledge, and his only mention of kabbalistic ideas in his extant works appears briefly in the aforementioned letter and betrays no sign that he was a master of kabbalistic lore. Rather, as we will see, his knowledge of kabbalistic tradition was facile. Moreover, as Oded Porat astutely notes, Samuel was not aware of Kabbalah as a historical movement with a set ideology.[9] While the traditions that he refers to are, from our vantage point today and from that of Kabbalists in the thirteenth century, part of a coherent theology known as Kabbalah, there is no evidence that Samuel saw them as such. For him, they were merely received wisdom with no special status as a marker of a particular belief and practice known as Kabbalah. Accordingly, when I refer to Samuel's evaluation of kabbalistic ideas, I do so with this proviso in mind. Yet, if he had little familiarity with Kabbalah, he did have greater knowledge of philosophic sources. Nevertheless, the sources that he admired, as I will show, were often at odds with Maimonides.

Samuel's letter to Yekutiel survives in four manuscripts, none of which contain the complete letter.[10] It has been the subject of a number of brief scholarly analyses,[11] but the extant portions of the letter have never been fully published nor thoroughly examined.

While, in the letter, Samuel does attempt to align Maimonides's thought with kabbalistic ideas, his broader goal is to dissuade Yekutiel, a figure to whom I will return below, "from thinking [ill] thoughts"[12] of Maimonides. As the copyist of MS Vatican Neofiti 11, who had access to the entire letter but only copied parts of it,[13] puts it at the conclusion of the letter, "[Yekutiel] agreed with those who speak ill of Maimonides, of blessed memory, and he [Samuel] sent [the letter] to warn him and return him to the faith of Moses."[14] The "faith of Moses," of course, refers both to the faith of the biblical Moses and to that of Moses Maimonides.

Samuel's attempt to convince his addressee that Maimonides's thought is religiously proper occurs against a backdrop where, as he explains, those who fashion themselves as followers of Maimonides, erroneously (from Samuel's point of view), see, in the explanation of the reasons of the commandments given in the *Guide of the Perplexed*, an excuse not to perform commandments such as tzitzit, tefillin, and mezuzah. He adds that these misguided followers "mock those who chase after [the commandments] to perform them."[15] They further, among other things, contend that Maimonides did not believe in reward and punishment and denied the resurrection of the dead.[16]

The controversies over Maimonides's true intentions highlighted in the letter are well-known from the literature of the Maimonidean controversy, which reached its peak in 1232 and divided Jewish communities in Southern France and Catalonia, with some regarding Maimonidean thought as a heretical break with tradition and others defending him as a faithful expositor of biblical and rabbinic tradition who fully upheld religious law.[17] As previous scholars have duly noted, this fact allows us to date the letter to around the time of the controversy.[18] In his letter, Samuel is clearly on the side of Maimonides's supporters and employs various tactics to demonstrate to Yekutiel that Maimonides should be viewed as a champion of traditional Judaism. The first tactic, which I will not dwell on, involves proving, on the basis of citations from Maimonides's writings, that Maimonides did not really adhere to the radical views ascribed to him.

His second tactic is to show that Maimonides's views are in accord with those of other philosophers who Samuel presumably assumed Yekutiel would find acceptable. To understand this second tactic, we need to realize that the pro- and anti-Maimonidean camps in the Maimonidean controversy were hardly uniform. Samuel, for his part, seems to belong to the most moderate of the pro-Maimonidean camps. Indeed, I would characterize him in the same manner that Moshe Halbertal characterizes Meir ben Simeon, to whom I will return below, namely, as a Maimonidean who was not really a Maimonidean at all.[19] Samuel did adopt a number of Maimonidean viewpoints—even if they were hardly all unique to Maimonides—such as the rejection of divine corporeality,[20] the affirmation of divine unity defined as simplicity,[21] and the belief that God will not change human nature.[22] Beyond these aspects, however, he was hardly a Maimonidean at all.

Indeed, he maintained theological and religious views that are at odds with Maimonides's philosophy. I will give one striking example from his commentary on the *Mishneh Torah* before turning to the letter. In his comments on a passage in the "Laws of Torah Study" (1:10), in which Maimonides stresses the importance of studying Torah until the day that one dies, Samuel quotes a number of rabbinic passages that emphasize the need for exclusive study of Torah to the exclusion of other areas. Among these passages is one from M. Sanhedrin 10:1 according to which those who study "external works" have no place in the world to come. After first presenting the opinion stated in Y Sanhedrin 10:1 that an example of "external works" is the *Book of Sirach*,[23] Samuel offers a broader definition: "Greek wisdoms and works of logic are all external works, and one who reads them has no place in the world to come."[24] Needless to say, this statement puts Samuel completely at odds with Maimonides who, as is well known, extolled the virtue of studying precisely such works.[25] Given this view, it may seem surprising that in his letter, as we will presently see, Samuel does cite philosophical literature. The literature he cites, however, does not include purely philosophical works but is entirely composed by Jews and occupied with Jewish sources. Presumably, Samuel allowed the study of such works, including, of course, the *Guide of the Perplexed.*

Turning now to the letter, we find other views espoused by Samuel that are at odds with Maimonides's thought. In one instance, early in the letter, he conflates the positions of Maimonides and the eleventh-century Neoplatonic philosopher and poet Solomon ibn Gabirol.[26] He first presents a cosmological description of the eighth and ninth spheres, which is merely a close paraphrase of material from *Keter Malkhut*, the poem by Gabirol, even if he does not name his source.[27] He then turns to the tenth and highest sphere: "The sages called the supernal world the sphere of the intellect, which is the world of angels, which are neither bodies nor a force within bodies."[28] The notion that the highest sphere is called the "sphere of the intellect" and is the realm of the angels is also based on *Keter Malkhut*, even if this comment is not a direct paraphrase.[29] Maimonides, however, never mentions "the sphere of the intellect." His closest analogue to the "sphere of the intellect" is the active intellect, but the active intellect is associated with the lowest rather than the highest sphere. At the same time, the notion that the angels are "not bodies nor a force within bodies" is distinctly not Gabirolian since it is not in keeping with Gabirol's universal hylomorphism.[30] It is, however, a point Maimonides subscribes to as Samuel makes clear later in the letter (see below), and, indeed, Samuel's language ("not bodies nor a force within bodies," *einam gufot ve-lo' koaḥ be-gufot*) is taken from the standard medieval Hebrew translation of Maimonides's *Guide.*[31] A real Maimonidean would never undertake such a conflation.

Later on, he tries to prove the aforementioned Maimonidean view that the angels, which Maimonides identifies with the intellects of medieval cosmology, are immaterial. Yet, here again Samuel returns to the non-Maimonidean "sphere of the intellect." As a way of establishing the possibility of immaterial intellects, he compares them to the human soul, "which is emanated from the sphere of the intellect."[32] To underscore this point, he cites a poem by the twelfth-century exegete and Neoplatonic philosopher Abraham ibn Ezra, whom he refers to here and throughout the letter as "the sage," to further emphasize the point: "This is also what the sage wrote: 'from the lamp of the intellect, the soul was created.'"[33] Here again, then, Samuel assigns to Maimonides a

Neoplatonic view—the emanation of the soul from the sphere of the intellect—which Maimonides would have rejected.

Elsewhere in the letter, Samuel quotes a passage from the commentary on tractate *Berakhot* by Asher ben Meshullam, who was the son of the leading twelfth-century Talmudic scholar R. Meshullam ben Jacob of Lunel and a figure Gad Freudenthal refers to as an "amateur of neoplatonic philosophy."[34] Samuel claims that the passage "follows the path of Rabbi Moses."[35] Among the quoted material, we find:

> Although there are places where the Lord's power and His wonders are more apparent than elsewhere, like Mount Moriah, Sinai, Bethel, and similar places, nevertheless He fills the entire world. . . . And from the intellect there are unfathomably great [rational] proofs that God is immeasurable. If so, He fills everything but everything does not contain Him.[36]

In this passage which, as Freudenthal notes,[37] borrows again from Abraham ibn Ezra, Asher assumes a notion of divine immanence that is completely at odds with Maimonides's absolute commitment to divine transcendence. Samuel's understanding of the philosophical system that underlies Maimonides's *Guide* was apparently sufficiently shallow that he was unable to recognize the difference between the two views.

Significantly, these various examples are part of the aforementioned second tactic for persuading Yekutiel of Maimonides's religious acceptability. Presumably, Samuel assumed that figures such as Solomon ibn Gabirol, Abraham ibn Ezra, and Asher ben Meshullam were considered authoritative by Yekutiel (as he himself considered them), such that aligning their views with those of Maimonides would help establish Maimonides's religious bona fides. To be clear, I am not suggesting that Samuel's espousal of these views was merely tactical and that he was aware that they were not truly compatible with Maimonidean views. On the contrary, I find no reason to doubt that he genuinely believed they aligned with Maimonides's thought. My contention, rather, is that Samuel assumed that once he made this alignment clear, Yekutiel would be convinced of Maimonides's acceptability.

We know very little about Yekutiel. Porat, picking up on a suggestion by Dinur,[38] identifies him with Yekutiel of Anduze, who is the author of a very short but dense "proto-kabbalistic"[39] letter regarding the *sefirot* to a certain Yedidya of Toulouse.[40] He is also, if Porat is correct, a figure quoted in "*Sod Yedi'at ha-Metsi'ut*," a text that is part of the so-called *'Iyyun* (contemplation) literature.[41] A full exposition is not possible here, but both the short letter and the quotation are clearly of a Neoplatonic character. Indeed, the quotation in *Sod Yedi'at ha-Metsi'ut* resonates with the aforementioned notion of the emanation of the soul from the sphere of the intellect, since according to Yekutiel, "The human soul emanated from the ancient lifeforce (*ḥiyyut*)."[42] Accordingly, if the Yekutiel who is the addressee of Samuel's letter is the same Yekutiel, it is likely that he would have had an approving attitude toward such figures as Abraham ibn Ezra and Solomon ibn Gabirol.

Samuel's third tactic for persuading Yekutiel of Maimonides's acceptability is to claim that Maimonides's views are largely in accord with figures who would later be remembered as the founding fathers of Kabbalah:

> I contemplated the books of the Rabbi (Maimonides)—The *Guide* and "Book of Knowledge." I toiled and found that his words are equivalent to the traditions of the Rabbi, Rabbi Abraham, and the Nazarite.[43] There is no disagreement between them save for in small matters. And I will reveal the truth to you in an abbreviated fashion. They received an explanation of the ten sefirot. The first sefirah is called "wisdom," and it is the supernal intellect (*ha-sekhel ha-'elyon*), which is called "spirit of the living God." Regarding it, it is said, "The Lord created me at the beginning of His way" (Prov. 8:22). And all was built with wisdom and from it all of the separate intellects were emanated. They received that the tenth sefirah is that which our Rabbis in one place called the "minister of the countenance" and in another "the minister of the world," and it is he who is revealed to the prophets.[44]

Rabbi Abraham and the Nazarite are apparently Abraham ben David (Rabad) and Jacob ben Saul of Lunel (otherwise known as Jacob the Nazarite).[45] Rabad, a leading Southern French twelfth-century Talmudic scholar, wrote numerous halakhic treatises but did not leave any extended kabbalistic writings. Nevertheless, he is remembered by later Kabbalists as one of the early progenitors of Kabbalah. Various apparently authentic kabbalistic traditions survive in his name, which were either transmitted orally by Rabad or recorded by him in brief passages that were only circulated to confidants.[46] Jacob the Nazarite is a lesser known twelfth-century figure who was an exegete of the Bible and the liturgy and was the brother of Asher ben Saul, the author of *Sefer ha-Minhagot*, an important work of Southern French customs, where he is quoted. Like Rabad, he left no extended kabbalistic writings. There are, however, kabbalistic traditions preserved in his name, which likely were also transmitted orally or recorded for initiates.[47] The pairing of Rabad and the Nazarite in our passage is not surprising for they are also paired in a number of manuscripts, which present their conflicting views about proper kabbalistic intention during prayer.[48]

Both figures adhered to a code of esotericism. I have studied Rabad's esotericism elsewhere.[49] Suffice it to say here that it is seen in his choice not to include esoteric ideas in his public works and in his son Isaac's praise of his father's discretion with kabbalistic ideas.[50] The Nazarite's esotericism requires a separate study. For the time being, we may refer to Scholem's observation that while in his extant writings "there is nothing mystical," "the remnants of his commentary on prayers reveal the double aspect of esoteric and exoteric, and a closer examination shows that beneath the apparently simple meaning there lies a mystical one."[51]

In our passage, Samuel claims that according to Rabad and the Nazarite, the first *sefirah* is identical with what he refers to as the supernal intellect, which, in turn emanates the remaining *sefirot* or intellects. (It is worth noting that this is a variation of the idea seen earlier of the intellect being located at the first sphere rather than the last sphere, in contradiction to Maimonides's view.) The last *sefirah* is equivalent to the angel Metatron, also known as the "minister of the countenance" or the "minister of the world."[52] Leaving aside the particular identification of the first and last *sefirot*, the broader point he makes in this passage is that the *sefirot* are equivalent to the separate intellects. In the continuation, it becomes clear that he sees Maimonides's view that the separate intellects are identical to angels as one and the same as the view that the separate intellects are the *sefirot*. Thus he goes on to say, "And the Rabbi (Maimonides) wrote in the *Guide* that the supernal world is all forms without physicality and separate from matter, and our sages called them angels and the philosophers called them separate intellects."[53] For Samuel, therefore, the *sefirot* are identical to both angels and the separate intellects.

In the continuation, Samuel returns to kabbalistic views. After again affirming "that they all follow one path"[54]—that is, that Rabad and the Nazarite agree with Maimonides—he points to an area of disagreement. He now refers to a larger group of scholars: Abraham ben Isaac of Narbonne, Rabad again, Abraham of Bordeaux, Judah the Pious, Eleazar of Worms, Judah ibn Ziza of Toledo, and the Nazarite who received teachings from one or more (the text is unclear) of these figures. Abraham ben Isaac of Narbonne was Rabad's father-in-law and is another figure who left no kabbalistic writings but according to later traditions espoused kabbalistic ideas.[55] Judah the Pious and Eleazar of Worms were the leading exponents of German Pietism,[56] another form of Jewish esotericism that Samuel, with some basis,[57] apparently saw as linked to the kabbalistic traditions of Abraham and Rabad. Abraham of Bordeaux and Judah ibn Ziza are otherwise unknown.

Of all of these figures he states, "They all received by means of tradition alone, without philosophical demonstration or proof, analogously to a person who transmits a secret to his friend without supplying proof [of the truth of the secret]."[58] He goes on to explain that, as a result, while all of these figures affirmed divine incorporeality, some of them (*yesh mehem*), in sharp contrast to Maimonides, assigned both matter and form to the angels.[59] He does not indicate which of these figures held this view and which believed in the immaterial nature of the angels, though it is possible that the reason he only mentions Rabad and the Nazarite in the first passage, in which he stresses their general agreement with Maimonides, is because he regarded these two figures as the ones who accepted the latter belief. Whatever the case may be, it is clear that Samuel's position was that the "kabbalistic" view that the ten *sefirot* are identical to the angels is in agreement with Maimonides. Yet if Maimonides's view was based on syllogistic reasoning, the "kabbalistic view" was based on tradition. As a result, some subset of the mentioned figures believed that the *sefirot* or angels are material, in contrast to Maimonides's opinion.

Why did Samuel believe that showing Rabad and the Nazarite's agreement with Maimonides would persuade Yekutiel of Maimonides's acceptability? As mentioned earlier, Porat observes that Samuel did not see these figures as part of a new historical movement called Kabbalah. His goal, therefore, was not to persuade Yekutiel of the compatibility of Kabbalah and Maimonidean thought. It seems, rather, that Samuel himself believed, and assumed that Yekutiel would similarly believe, that these figures were avatars of correct religious belief. There is nothing surprising about this. As noted earlier, Rabad was a leading Southern French Talmudic scholar, and the Nazarite, although less famous than Rabad, was also a prominent Southern French scholar. Figures of this stature would likely have commanded Yekutiel's allegiance.

To what extent is Samuel's report that Rabad and the Nazirite identified the *sefirot* with the intellects accurate? I am not familiar with a source in either of their names where such an identification is found. There is, however, a passage in *Sefer ha-Yiḥud*, by Rabad's grandson Asher ben David, which at least approaches this view:

> The philosophers called these ten sefirot, spheres (*galgalim*), and they said that they are ten, and collectively they are called the sphere of the intellect. Each and every one has a mover who is appointed over them except for the tenth that does not need to move or to cause others to move, for everything exists by its power, and they effect their actions with the power of its primordial will, which was planted in them when they came into being. And they move unceasingly by each and every statement (*ma'amar*) that is appointed over them. And the philosophers call those things which are appointed over motion or the one thing that is appointed over the motion of them all, which is like an ax in the hands of a craftsman, for, by his hand, the motion of the spheres occurs unceasingly, and, as a result, the created and their cause will come to be. And the author of *Sefer Yetsirah*, of blessed memory, and the rabbinic Sages, of blessed memory, and the philosophers all agree that these things are ten and that the tenth cannot be apprehended and that He supports all with His primordial speech, but they have different names in the language of the Sages. Based on their apprehension and received tradition, they call them by their names.[60]

Here, Asher explains that the philosophers identify the ten *sefirot* with the ten spheres. This position is similar to the one that Samuel assigned to Rabad and the Nazarite, but not identical. As we saw, Samuel states that Rabad and the Nazarite identified the *sefirot* with the intellects that control the spheres rather than with the spheres themselves. Yet, there is some ambiguity in Asher's statement that brings it even closer to the position supposedly held by Rabad and the Nazarite. Asher goes on to describe the movers who control the ten spheres, a reference to the ten intellects. He further notes that "everything exists by the power" of the tenth sphere—that is, the highest one. While ostensibly he is talking about the sphere itself, this expression is more appropriate to the intellect that controls the sphere. The next line in the passage, which I translated as literally as possible, is garbled: "And the philosophers call those things which are appointed over motion or the one thing that is appointed over the motion of them all, which is like an ax in the hands of a craftsman, for, by his hand, the motion of the spheres occurs unceasingly, and, as a result, the created and their cause will come to be." The reference here is apparently to the intellects themselves, but it is unclear what the philosophers call them. Are they also called *sefirot*, such that the philosophers understood a *sefirah* as a combination of the sphere and the intellect that controlled it? If so, Asher's statement is even closer to the view that Samuel attributes to Rabad and the Nazarite than it initially appears. It is not inconceivable, therefore, that such a view was already being disseminated by Rabad and the Nazarite themselves.

Yet, this surely was not their actual view. It is clear from the numerous traditions in their names that both Rabad and the Nazarite had a theosophic view of the *sefirot* according to which they are aspects of God rather than elements of the cosmos. As I have shown elsewhere, while esoterically in his public writings Rabad appears to accept divine unity understood as simplicity, in esoteric traditions recorded in his name as well as in esoteric hints that he left in his own writings, he, in fact, maintained that divine unity is constituted by the conjoining of multiple *sefirot*. He did not reveal his true view as a result of a number of factors, including a growing consensus in the Jewish community that divine unity should be understood as simplicity as well as fear that his true view would seem close to the Cathar heresy and to Christian doctrine.[61] The view that Samuel attributed to Rabad, according to which the *sefirot* are identical with the intellects, is in keeping with Rabad's exoteric view, insofar as it does not challenge divine simplicity, but it is at odds with his esoteric view. Similarly, I have shown that for some of the same reasons, his grandson, Asher, in his *Sefer ha-Yiḥud*, exoterically professes to accept a version of divine simplicity while esoterically hinting that divine unity involves *sefirot* coming together.[62] In this light, the passage cited above, in which Asher equates the *sefirot* with the spheres, and thereby turns the *sefirot* into subdivine entities, is part of this same strategy. That is, it reflects Asher's exoteric view rather than his esoteric one.

We may draw a similar conclusion in the case of the Nazarite from a passage directly related to the subject of angels. As Scholem notes, according to a commentary on the prayers that derives from the German Pietists, the Nazarite interpreted a phrase from the Sabbath morning prayer service—"knowledge (*da'at*) and understanding (*u-tevunah*) surround Him"—in the following manner: "Knowledge and understanding refer to two angels, whose names are knowledge and understanding, who surround the throne of glory."[63] Yet in his aforementioned comments on the mystical intention of prayers, preserved in a number of manuscripts, he refers, as Scholem puts it, to the third *sefirah*, *binah* or *tevunah*, "in all its splendor as a divine hypostasis, as one of the *sefirot* with whose light man prays."[64] As Scholem explains, this is not because, in his comments on the morning prayer service, the Nazarite "confused the world of angels with that of the sefiroth. Rather, we seem to have before us an excellent example of the use of ambiguous terminology, one of its meanings intended for the true initiates and the other for outsiders."[65] The Nazarite's motivations for adopting this posture of dissimulation are unknown but may be similar to those of Rabad.

To be clear, neither Rabad nor the Nazarite explicitly state, in any written source of which I am aware, that the *sefirot* and the intellects are identical. My claim, rather, is that, given what we know of their esoteric tendencies, it is perfectly plausible that they did disseminate such a view as a screen for their true view. *Sefer Yetzirah*, the notoriously ambiguous text, which mentions the *sefirot*, was very much part of the public discourse, and it is not hard to imagine that Rabad and the Nazarite were asked to offer a public explanation of the *sefirot.* The explanation that they may have given is the innocuous one that they are identical with the intellects rather than their actual belief that they are aspects of God.

Samuel was not aware of the esoteric views of Rabad and the Nazarite. I would submit that insofar as he gained knowledge of their views of the *sefirot*, it was of their exoteric perspective. For this reason, he was able to claim that their views aligned with Maimonides. As noted, Samuel's Maimonideanism, such as it was, included a commitment to divine simplicity. Divine simplicity is so fundamental to Maimonidean thought that presumably if Samuel understood Rabad and the Nazarite's true explanation of the *sefirot*, he would not have been able to present their views as being in any sort of agreement with Maimonides.

III

Meir ben Simeon of Narbonne, who died sometime after 1270, was in many ways an ideological fellow traveler with Samuel even if there is no evidence that they knew each other. Meir, like Samuel, was a Talmudic scholar.[66] He is the author of the Talmudic commentary *Sefer ha-Me'orot* and of a commentary on the *Hoshanot* prayer. Reminiscent of Samuel, he also composed *Meshiv Nefesh*, a defense of the opening philosophical sections of Maimonides's *Mishneh Torah*. Like Samuel's letter, Meir presumably composed this defense in the context of the Maimonidean controversy. Again, like Samuel, he was, as Halbertal puts it, a "supporter and defender of Maimonides who was not a Maimonidean at all."[67] Indeed, as Halbertal has shown, in the midst of his very defense of Maimonides's *Mishneh Torah*, Meir explains away Maimonides's naturalistic accounts of such matters as creation and divine reward and punishment.[68] Indeed, yet again like Samuel, his allegiance to Maimonidean thought did not involve much more than an allegiance to a conception of divine unity defined as simplicity and to a rejection of divine corporeality.[69]

Meir was also the author of *Milḥemet Mitzvah*, an anti-Christian polemic consisting of various documents that Meir assembled in 1270.[70] In this work, he appended a letter on the topic of Kabbalah, which he had circulated to communities in Southern France at an earlier date. At the end of the letter Meir indicates that he wrote it with the approbation of Meshullam ben Moses. As Tzahi Weiss notes, Meshullam died around 1240. The letter, therefore, was originally composed before this time.[71] Below, I will argue that it was composed some number of years after Samuel wrote his letter, which, as noted, was around 1232. Yet unlike Samuel, he is harshly critical of Kabbalah, which he regarded as heretical.

Recently, however, Weiss has argued that Meir's polemic was not, in fact, directed at the works of the first Kabbalists. Instead, he suggests that Meir's true targets were unknown figures who espoused a binitarian view according to which prayer must be directed at intermediaries rather than God Himself. This was a view, he notes, that the first Kabbalists themselves also objected to.[72]

I find Weiss's argument that Meir was responding to a view rejected by the Kabbalists compelling. Meir does criticize this binitarian view in the letter as well as in material that follows the letter, which Meir added at a later date. Weiss also convincingly demonstrates that early Kabbalists criticized a similar view.[73] Nevertheless, in contrast to his view, it is clear to me that Meir, at least in the letter itself if not in the additional material, was *also* referring to the works of the Kabbalists, even if he did not distinguish, as the Kabbalists themselves would have, between these works and those of the unknown figures.

In the letter, Meir refers to a number of heretical works. In the case of most of them, we are not sure which works he had in mind, but the *Commentary on Song of Songs*, which he refers to, is apparently a reference to an avowedly kabbalistic work by Ezra of Gerona, a Kabbalist who received teachings from Rabad's son, Isaac the Blind. Weiss, however, argues that Meir had only heard of the works of the first kabbalists but had not actually read them.[74] Accordingly, Meir writes, "We have also *heard* that additionally [the following works] were written for them: *Commentary on Song of Songs*, *Sefer Yetzirah*, and *Heikhalot*[75]—in them matters are written in accordance with their heretical ways—as well as *Commentary on Ecclesiastes* and the remainder of the books."[76] Yet the continuation of the same passage leaves no doubt that these works were indeed in Meir's possession, as he concludes, "Inquire and investigate carefully, and if they are in your midst, burn them . . . just as we have burned those that are found in our midst."[77] Meir states explicitly that he burned *Commentary on Song of Songs*, among other books, which, of course, means that they were in his possession.

Thus, while I agree with Weiss that the letter includes attacks on binitarianism, I would argue that it also includes attacks on the Kabbalists, even if these attacks are at times conflated with attacks on binitarianism. These include attacks on the kabbalistic view that divine unity involves the conjoining of the *sefirot*, a view that was deeply at odds with Meir's moderate Maimonidean commitment to divine simplicity. This is a view that he certainly would have had access to by reading Ezra's *Commentary on Song of Songs*. Thus, for example, in the "Commentary on Reasons for the Commandments," which Ezra appended to *Commentary on Song of Songs*, he speaks of "including" within God "ten sefirot like a flame tied to a coal."[78]

Indeed, a consideration of Meir's presentation of what he regards as the heretical view of the *sefirot* makes it clear that his targets are the first Kabbalists. In one place, he argues that, in contrast to the heretical view that is the subject of his critique, God "is the true one, with a perfect unity without participation in or conjoining with the sefirot."[79] According to the view he attacks, therefore, divine unity requires the conjoining of *sefirot*. This is clearly the kabbalistic view. Again, in reference to the *sefirot* and other metaphysical entities, he notes, "It is inappropriate to combine the creation with its Creator, the material with its Former, and the emanated with the Emanator and to say His unity is incomplete, but it is only with them that all is one."[80] Here he speaks of the *sefirot*, somewhat incoherently, as both emanated and created, as he also does elsewhere in the letter.[81] This is not in keeping with the kabbalistic understanding of the *sefirot* as emanated rather than created and may be a result of the conflation of kabbalistic and binitarian views. Yet, the notion that *sefirot* are part of divine unity is very much a kabbalistic view. He again accurately depicts the kabbalistic view of divine unity when he states that "they said with their lacking intellect that all of them [i.e., the sefirot] cleave one with another, and are all one."[82]

Note, however, that his accurate understanding of the *sefirot*'s role, according to kabbalistic thought, in establishing divine unity is quite different from Samuel's understanding. Samuel, insofar as he believed that Rabad and the Nazarite identified the *sefirot* and the intellects, did not believe that their doctrines were at odds with divine simplicity and thus did not see a contradiction between their views and those of Maimonides. Meir does not explicitly compare the kabbalistic view of the *sefirot* to Maimonides's position, but, given that a major component of Meir's Maimonideanism was a commitment to divine simplicity, his attack on Kabbalah is implicitly a statement that Kabbalah and Maimonideanism are not aligned.

Interestingly, Meir, in the course of his critique of Kabbalah, also gives an indication of what he regards as an acceptable understanding of the *sefirot*. He first avers, as we have already seen, that the *sefirot* have no part in the divine economy: God "is the true one, with a perfect unity without participation in or conjoining with the sefirot." He then continues to explain that God brought the *sefirot* into existence "ex nihilo, through His will alone."[83] He goes on to say that "the spheres, the *ofanim*, and the holy creatures and everything that they call <sefirot—the heavens, the spheres and [angelic] servants are—>[84] the Holy One, blessed be He's tools . . . and through them the ancient Name, who has no beginning, may He be blessed, rules the world."[85] For Meir, then, both the spheres and the angels are identical to the *sefirot*. Thus, his view of an acceptable understanding of the *sefirot* is quite close to the view that Samuel approvingly ascribes to Rabad and Jacob, particularly if we assume that Meir followed the Maimonidean view that the angels and intellects are identical. Moreover, as the above citation shows, Meir accepts an identification of the *sefirot* with not only the angels/intellects but also the spheres. This is the position that I argued was perhaps—at least exoterically—also that of Rabad's grandson, Asher, from whom Meir may have even learned it.[86]

In all, therefore, what separates Meir's and Samuel's view of kabbalah is a different understanding of kabbalistic doctrine. I would suggest that this difference is a reflection of the different levels of access to kabbalistic teachings that each figure had. Samuel, it seems, only had access to exoteric presentations of kabbalistic doctrine according to which the *sefirot* were construed as created entities identical to the spheres. There is no evidence that he had access to or was even aware of kabbalistic writings or traditions that might betray a more esoteric understanding. This understanding of the *sefirot* presented no challenge to a moderate Maimonidean like Samuel. In contrast, Meir has access to the view—through kabbalistic texts and reports[87]—that the *sefirot* must conjoin to form divine unity. For him, therefore, Kabbalah was a theologically problematic doctrine. If Samuel had access to the same material, he likely would also have vociferously objected to Kabbalah.

I would suggest that this different level of access is a result of the fact that Meir's letter was written a number of years after Samuel's letter. It is very difficult to reconstruct a history of the early reception and spread of kabbalistic literature and thought. Perhaps, however, when Samuel wrote his letter, the more esoteric kabbalistic doctrine was not yet part of the public discourse. By the time Meir wrote his letter, however, the bounds of esotericism had been sufficiently breached that the true kabbalistic understanding of divine unity became apparent. Accordingly, if Samuel wrote his letter in around 1232, I would place Meir's letter a few years later with the terminus ad quem being 1240, as noted. The intervening years would allow sufficient time for kabbalistic ideas to spread more widely.

We can illustrate this by tracking the example of a text we know Meir had access to, Ezra's *Commentary on Song of Songs*. Like Samuel's letter, it was likely composed around the time of the Maimonidean controversy.[88] Whether it was composed shortly before, shortly after, or contemporaneously with Samuel's letter, it perhaps did not yet make its way from Catalonia, where Ezra composed it, to Southern France until some time later. By the time Meir composed his letter, however, it was already available in Southern France, thus giving him access to the esoteric view of divine unity.[89]

I would conclude with an observation that the constraints of space do not allow me to fully develop here. Key to Wolfson's understanding of the kabbalistic hermeneutic of esotericism is, as he puts it, that "the most secretive of secrets is the open secret, the secret that is so fully disclosed that it appears not to be a secret."[90] In this light, the exoteric is the esoteric, even as the esoteric is the exoteric. On the topic of divine unity, some Kabbalists took the paradoxical view that the multiplicity of the *sefirot* and divine simplicity are simultaneously true. As the thirteenth-century Kabbalist Moses de Leon puts the matter, "God is one and unique, without any change . . . although they are sefirot—speculums that are proper and right—it is one without any separation."[91] If we assume that Rabad and the Nazarite shared both this hermeneutic of esotericism and this perspective on the *sefirot*, the ostensibly exoteric view—divine simplicity—conceals the ostensibly esoteric one—unity achieved by conjoining of the *sefirot*. At the same time, the esoteric view conceals the exoteric one because one who takes the esoteric view at face value will not fathom the paradox that the multiple *sefirot* are simultaneously a perfect unity. I submit that neither Samuel nor Meir—both outsiders to the kabbalistic tradition—could have understood this point. Samuel took Rabad and the Nazarite's views of the *sefirot* literally, not realizing that it concealed the esoteric view, while Meir took the esoteric view literally, not realizing that it concealed the exoteric one.

NOTES

1. See, e.g., Elliot R. Wolfson, "Negative Theology and Positive Assertion in the Early Kabbalah," *Da'at* 32–33 (1994): v–xxii; "Hebraic and Hellenic Conceptions of Wisdom in Sefer Ha-Bahir," *Poetics Today* 19 (1998): 147–76; *Abraham Abulafia: Kabbalist and Prophet: Hermeneutics, Theosophy, and Theurgy* (Los Angeles: Cherub Press, 2000); "Beneath the Wings of the Great

Eagle: Maimonides and Thirteenth-Century Kabbalah," in *Moses Maimonides (1138–1204): His Religious, Scientific, and Philosophical "Wirkungsgeschichte" in Different Cultural Contexts*, ed. Görge K. Hasselhoff and Otfried Fraisse (Würzburg: Ergon, 2004), 209–37; "Via Negativa in Maimonides and Its Impact on Thirteenth-Century Kabbalah," *Maimonidean Studies* 5 (2008): 393–442.

2. Elliot R. Wolfson, *Elliot R. Wolfson: Poetic Thinking*, ed. Hava Tirosh-Samuelson and Aaron W. Hughes (Leiden: Brill, 2015), 213.
3. Jonathan Dauber, *Knowledge of God and the Development of Early Kabbalah* (Leiden: Brill, 2012); "Competing Approaches to Maimonides in Early Kabbalah," in *The Cultures of Maimonideanism: New Approaches to the History of Jewish Thought*, ed. James T. Robinson (Leiden: Brill, 2009), 57–88; "'Pure Thought' in R. Abraham Bar Hiyya and Early Kabbalah," *Journal of Jewish Studies* 60 (2009): 185–201; "Ezra Ben Solomon of Gerona and the Sabians," *Journal of Jewish Studies* 70 (2019): 276–97.
4. Jonathan Dauber, *Secrecy and Esoteric Writing in Kabbalistic Literature* (Philadelphia: University of Pennsylvania Press, 2022).
5. This concern animates much of Wolfson's work such that a complete bibliography is not possible here. I will suffice with a few examples: "Occultation of the Feminine and the Body of Secrecy in Medieval Kabbalah," in *Rending the Veil: Concealment and Secrecy in the History of Religions*, ed. Elliot R. Wolfson (New York: Seven Bridges Press, 1999), 113–54; *Language, Eros, Being: Kabbalistic Hermeneutics and Poetic Imagination* (New York: Fordham University Press, 2005), 128–41; "Murmuring Secrets: Eroticism and Esotericism in Medieval Kabbalah," in *Hidden Intercourse: Eros and Sexuality in the History of Western Esotericism*, ed. J. Kripal and W. Hanegraaff (Leiden: Brill, 2008), 65–109; *Open Secret: Postmessianic Messianism and the Mystical Revision of Menaḥem Mendel Schneerson* (New York: Columbia University Press, 2009); *Giving Beyond the Gift: Apophasis and Overcoming Theomania* (New York: Fordham University Press, 2014), 154–200; "Secrecy, Apophasis, and Atheistic Faith in the Teachings of Rav Kook," in *Negative Theology as Jewish Modernity*, ed. Michael Fagenblat (Bloomington: Indiana University Press, 2017), 131–60.
6. Elliot R. Wolfson, "Beyond the Spoken Word: Oral Tradition and Written Transmission in Medieval Jewish Mysticism," in *Transmitting Jewish Traditions: Orality, Textuality and Cultural Diffusion*, ed. Yaakov Elman and Israel Gershoni (New Haven and London: Yale University Press, 2000), 170.
7. Pinchas Roth, "Later Provençal Sages—Jewish Law (Halakhah) and Rabbis in Southern France" (Hebrew; Hebrew University, 2012), 81–93.
8. Ben Zion Dinur, *Israel in the Diaspora*, vol. 2 book 4 (Hebrew; Tel Aviv: Dvir, 1969), 420 n. 24; Ram Ben-Shalom, *The Jews of Provence and Languedoc: Renaissance in the Shadow of the Church* (Hebrew; Raanana, Is.: The Open University, 2017), 604–9.
9. Oded Porat, *"Who Is a Beautiful Maiden Without Eyes" and the Riddle of the Tay'a: A Chapter in the History of Kabbalah in the Second Half of the Thirteenth Century* (Hebrew; Los Angeles: Cherub Press, 2019), 257–58.
10. MS Vatican Neofiti 11, 203a–214b; MS Vat. ebr. 236, 82a–84a; MS Jewish Community of Mantua, Italy 8, 23a–b; MS Bodleian, University of Oxford, Opp. 658, 63a–65b. MS Vat. Neofiti contains the largest portion of the letter but as the copyist indicates at the beginning

and conclusion of the letter and as is clear throughout, he abbreviated the letter, leaving out material in various places. Unless otherwise noted, citations of Samuel's letter are from this manuscript.

11. Gershom Scholem, "Traces of Gabirol on the Kabbalah," in *Studies in Kabbalah 1*, ed. Yosef Ben Shelomo (Hebrew; Tel Aviv: Am Oved, 1998), 60–62; *Origins of the Kabbalah*, ed. R. J. Zwi Werblowsky, trans. Allan Arkush (Princeton, NJ: Princeton University Press, 1987), 224–27; Dinur, *Israel*, vol. 2 book 4:324–25; Roth, "Later Provençal Sages," 82–84; Ben-Shalom, *Jews of Provence*, 604–9; Porat, *"Who Is a Beautiful Maiden Without Eyes,"* 254–59; Tzahi Weiss, "The Maimonidean Controversy and the Kabbalists" [Hebrew], *Zion* 87 (2022): 475–503. Weiss's study was published after I had already completed this paper, and I regret that I was unable to incorporate his insights.
12. MS Jewish Community of Mantua, Italy 8, 23a.
13. See note 10 above.
14. 214b. Cf. 203a.
15. 204a.
16. 203b–204a.
17. The controversy has been discussed in numerous studies. For a helpful overview, see David Berger, "Judaism and General Culture in Medieval and Early Modern Times," in *Judaism's Encounter with Other Cultures: Rejection or Integration?*, ed. Jacob J. Schacter (Northvale, NJ: Jason Aronson, 1997), 85–100.
18. Roth, "Later Provençal Sages," 83; Porat, *"Who Is a Beautiful Maiden Without Eyes,"* 254. In MS Vat. Neofiti 11 206b, Eleazar of Worms, who died in 1232, is referred to as "of blessed memory." This would suggest that Samuel wrote the letter after this time. Yet "of blessed memory" is missing after Eleazar's name in the remaining manuscripts. It is quite possible, therefore, that "of blessed memory" was a late addition to the letter. See Porat, *"Who Is a Beautiful Maiden Without Eyes,"* 254 n. 1023.
19. Moshe Halbertal, *Between Torah and Wisdom: Rabbi Menahem Ha-Meiri and the Maimonidean Halakhists in Provence* (Hebrew; Jerusalem: Magnes Press, 2000), 17. See also Roth, "Later Provençal Sages," 84.
20. See, e.g., 207b, 214a.
21. See, e.g., 210a.
22. See, e.g., 211b.
23. See also B. Sanhedrin 100b.
24. MS Paris hebr. 355, 23b.
25. Shemu'el Kohen in "*Peirush rabbeinu Shemu'el be-rabbi Mordekhai le-hilkhot teshuvah meha-Ramba"m*," *Moriah* 18, 9–10 (1993): 15 notes the strangeness of Samuel's definition without elaborating.
26. 203a.
27. See Solomon ibn Gabirol, *The Crown of Kingship ("Keter Malkhuth")*, ed. Israel Levin (Hebrew; Jerusalem: Tel-Aviv University Press, 2005), ch. 21, pp. 268–69, ll. 207–9, 213; ch. 23, p. 270, ll. 229–30.
28. 203a.
29. *Crown of Kingship*, chs. 24 & 25, pp. 271–73. For an account of the place of the "sphere of the

intellect" in *Keter Malkhut*, see Adena Tanenbaum, *The Contemplative Soul: Hebrew Poetry and Philosophical Theory in Medieval Spain* (Leiden: Brill, 2002), 61–68.

30. Scholem, in "Traces," 60–62, already noted that Samuel broke with a Gabirolian view of angels in the letter. He was not, however, aware that Samuel also based part of his cosmology on Gabirol.
31. See Moses Maimonides, *Moreh ha-nevukhim*, ed. Yehuda Even-Shemuel, trans. Samuel Ibn Tibbon (Mossad Harav Kook, 2000), 2: introduction (16th premise), 208.
32. 207a.
33. 207a. It is taken from a poem titled, "*El nikra' be-shem otot*." See Israel Levin, ed., *The Religious Poems of Abraham Ibn Ezra* (Hebrew; Jerusalem: Israel Academy of Sciences and Humanities, 1975), 1:385, l. 17.
34. Gad Freudenthal, "A Twelfth-Century Provençal Amateur of Neoplatonic Philosophy in Hebrew: R. Asher b. Meshullam of Lunel," *Chora* 3–4 (2006): 161–88.
35. 208b.
36. 208a. My translation is adapted from Freudenthal, "Twelfth-Century Provençal Amateur," 173–74.
37. Freudenthal, "Twelfth-Century Provençal Amateur," 173–74 nn. 40, 44.
38. Dinur, *Israel*, vol. 2 book 4:420 n. 44.
39. Oded Porat, *"Founding the Circle": Rudiments of Esse and Linguistic Creation in "The Book of Fountain of Wisdom" and Its Related Treatises* (Hebrew: Los Angeles: Cherub Press, 2019), 110.
40. Porat, *Founding the Circle*, 104–7. Porat published the letter on p. 108.
41. Porat, *Founding the Circle*, 96–98.
42. Porat, *Founding the Circle*, 96; *The Works of Iyyun: Critical Editions* (Hebrew: Los Angeles: Cherub Press, 2013), 48.
43. MS Bodleian Opp. 658, 63a and MS. Vat. ebr 236, 82a read "Rabbi Abraham the Nazarite" as though the reference is to one figure. MS Jewish Community of Mantua, 8, 23a, in agreement with the version I cited, reads, "The Rabbi, Rabbi Abraham, of blessed memory, and the Nazarite." In view of the fact that in the continuation of the letter, according to all versions (see below), Abraham and the Nazarite are mentioned separately, the latter version seems accurate.
44. 205b.
45. Conceivably "Abraham" could refer to a different Abraham since two other Abrahams, in addition to Rabad, are mentioned in a later passage of the letter (see below). Given, though, that Rabad and Jacob the Nazarite are mentioned together in early kabbalistic traditions (see below), it is likely Rabad that is intended. This is also the conclusion of Moshe Idel, "Kabbalistic Prayer in Provence" [Hebrew], *Tarbiz* 62 (1992–1993): 287. For general background on Rabad, see Isadore Twersky, *Rabad of Posquières: A Twelfth-Century Talmudist* (1962; repr., Philadelphia: Jewish Publication Society of America, 1980). For general background on Jacob, see Abraham Ben Azriel, *Sefer 'arugat ha-bosem*, ed. Ephraim E. Urbach (Jerusalem: *Mekitsei nirdamim*, 1963), 4:118.
46. I provide a full overview of Rabad's kabbalistic traditions in Dauber, *Secrecy*, 61–104. See also Twersky, *Rabad*, 286–300; Scholem, *Origins*, 205–26; Haviva Pedaya, *Name and Sanctuary in the Teaching of R. Isaac the Blind* (Hebrew; Jerusalem: Magnes Press, 2001), 42–55.

47. On Jacob ben Saul's kabbalistic traditions, see Scholem, *Origins*, 207–9, 227–33; Idel, "Kabbalistic Prayer."
48. See Idel, "Kabbalistic Prayer."
49. Dauber, *Secrecy*, 61–104.
50. This praise appears in a letter by Isaac written to Jonah Gerondi and Nahmanides. See Gershom Scholem, "*Te'udah ḥadashah le-toldot rei'shit ha-kabbalah*," in *Studies in Kabbalah 1*, ed. Yosef Ben Shelomo (Hebrew; Tel Aviv: Am Oved, 1998), 9.
51. Scholem, *Origins*, 208.
52. "Minister of the Countenance" is a standard designation of Metatron in *heikhalot* literature. On the identification of the "Minister of the World" with Metatron, see Gershom Scholem, *Jewish Gnosticism, Merkabah Mysticism, and Talmudic Tradition* (1960; repr., New York: Jewish Theological Seminary of America, 1965), 44–50; *Origins*, 214–15 n. 26. On Rabad's use of these designations, see Dauber, *Secrecy*, 64–73.
53. 206a.
54. 206b.
55. Scholem, *Origins*, 199–205.
56. There is extensive literature on Judah and Eleazar. For an accessible overview, see Joseph Dan, *Gershom Scholem and the Mystical Dimension of Jewish History* (New York: NYU Press, 1988), 92–126.
57. See, e.g., Moshe Idel, "*Ha-kavvanah ba-tefillah be-rei'shit ha-kabbalah: bein Ashkenaz le-Provans*," in *Porat Yosef: Studies Presented to Rabbi Dr. Joseph Safran*, ed. Bezalel Safran and Eliyahu Safran (Hoboken, NJ: Ktav, 1992), 5–14 (Hebrew section); Elliot R. Wolfson, "The Image of Jacob Engraved upon the Throne: Further Reflection on the Esoteric Doctrine of the German Pietists," in *Along the Path: Studies in Kabbalistic Myth, Symbolism, and Hermeneutics* (Albany, NY: SUNY Press, 1995), 1–63, esp. 60–61.
58. 206b.
59. 206b.
60. Daniel Abrams, ed., *R. Asher ben David: His Complete Works and Studies in His Kabbalistic Thought* [Hebrew] (Los Angeles: Cherub Press, 1996), 108. My translation is based on Mark Brian Sendor, "The Emergence of Provençal Kabbalah: Rabbi Isaac the Blind's Commentary on Sefer Yeẓirah" (Harvard University, 1994), 94, n. 11.
61. Dauber, *Secrecy*, 98–103.
62. Dauber, "Competing Approaches"; *Secrecy*, 173–208.
63. Cited in Ben Azriel, *Sefer 'arugat ha-bosem*, 4:119.
64. Scholem, *Origins*, 209.
65. Scholem, *Origins*.
66. For background on his life and works, see William K. Herskowitz, "Judaeo-Christian Dialogue in Provence as Reflected in 'Milhemet Mitzva' of R. Meir Hameili" (Yeshiva University, 1974); Manoaḥ of Narbonne, *Sefer ha-menuḥah*, ed. Elazar Hurvitz (Jerusalem: Mossad Harav Kook, 1970), 16–21; Roth, "Later Provençal Sages," 74–81.
67. Halbertal, *Between Torah and Wisdom*, 117.
68. Halbertal, *Between Torah and Wisdom*, 116–33.
69. For examples of this commitment, see, e.g., Herskowitz, "Judaeo-Christian," 17, 72–73,

121–22; Tzahi Weiss, "'Their Heart Was Turned Away from the Uppermost': Rethinking the Boundaries of Kabbalistic Literature and the Opposition to Kabbalah in the First Half of the 13th Century" [Hebrew], *Da'at* 85 (2018): 334; Yehudah Hershkovits, "*Ma'amar meshiv nefesh le-R. Meir ben R. Shim'on ha-Me'ili*," *Yeshurun* 27 (2012): 80, 87; *Commentary on the Hoshanot, Sefer ha-Mikhtam*, ed. Abraham Sofer (New York, *Defus hadar*, 1958 or 1959), 151. See also my discussion in "Competing Approaches," 62–65.

70. This work is extant in a single manuscript, MS Parma 2749 (De Rossi 155), but has never been fully published. Large portions of it have, however, been published in various places. For publication details, see Roth, "Later Provençal Sages," 80 n. 64.
71. See Weiss, "Their Heart," 308. See also Scholem, *Origins*, 397.
72. Weiss, "Their Heart." See also Tzahi Weiss, "Beyond the Scope of Philosophy and Kabbalah," *Religions* 12 (2021): 6–7; "The Letter of Isaac the Blind to Nahmanides and Jonah Gerondi in Its Historical Context," *Journal of Jewish Studies* 72 (2021): 344–45.
73. Weiss, "Their Heart," 316–17, 319–23.
74. Weiss, "Their Heart," 310.
75. It is possible that the term "Commentary" applies to all three works.
76. I am using the edition of the letter provided by Weiss in "Their Heart." The above quotation is found on p. 336.
77. Weiss, "Their Heart," 336.
78. Yakov M. Travis, "Kabbalistic Foundations of Jewish Spiritual Practice: Rabbi Ezra of Gerona on the Kabbalistic Meaning of the Mizvot" (Brandeis University, 2002), 7 (Hebrew section).
79. Weiss, "Their Heart," 334.
80. Weiss, "Their Heart."
81. Weiss, "Their Heart," 334, 335.
82. Weiss, "Their Heart," 334.
83. Weiss, "Their Heart."
84. The material in angle brackets is a correction in the margins of MS Parma 2749, 230a but is implied in the text even without the correction. The word in square brackets was added for clarity.
85. Weiss, "Their Heart," 334.
86. We know that the two were in contact since in *Sefer ha-Yiḥud* (*R. Asher ben David*, 53) Asher approvingly cites a teaching that he heard "from the mouth" of Meir.
87. See the reference to oral reports in Weiss, "Their Heart," 334.
88. Dauber, *Knowledge*, 35–41.
89. My assumption is that Meir also had access to additional works that explained kabbalistic doctrine, for, as I argue in *Secrecy*, ch. 5, it is quite difficult for one without access to kabbalistic symbolism to understand Ezra's work. These additional works would include the other texts that he says he burned. See above.
90. Wolfson, *Open Secret*, 64.
91. Moses De Leon, *Sheqel Ha-Qodesh*, ed. Charles Mopsik (Los Angeles: Cherub Press, 1996), 16.

ON KABBALAH AND NATURE

Language, Being, and Poetic Thinking

HAVA TIROSH-SAMUELSON

. . . poetically man dwells . . .
FRIEDRICH HÖLDERLIN, "IN LOVELY BLUE"

KABBALAH AND JEWISH ENVIRONMENTALISM

Awareness of our massive ecological crisis has emerged as a prominent concern of contemporary Judaism. In the Diaspora and in Israel, there are numerous organizations, initiatives, and programs that offer environmental education, promote environmental activism, train Jews to cultivate a Judaic approach to farming and food systems, encourage Jews to get involved in legislation on behalf of the environment, and practice old and construct new rituals to celebrate the human rootedness in and dependence on the Earth. The various denominations of contemporary Judaism have issued official declarations about environmental concerns, ranging from global warming and climate change to hydraulic fracking and alternative energy sources. Jewish institutions have adopted a range of environmental practices (e.g., recycling, communal gardens, solarization, LEED building codes, and energy-saving technologies). Jewish environmentalism has also energized ritual life and generated a new body of scholarship.[1]

Kabbalah and its offshoot, Hasidism, have played an important role in the "greening" of Judaism. Although the environmental crisis engaged several Jewish theologians,[2] those who have attempted to articulate Jewish eco-theologies (e.g., Zalman Schachter-Shalomi, Arthur Green, David Seidenberg, and Ariel Evan Mayse) take their inspiration from Kabbalah, promoting Neo-Hasidism as "Kabbalah for the Environmental Age."[3] Inspired by Kabbalah, Jewish eco-theologians have endorsed a pantheistic or a panentheistic view that emphasizes the immanence of God, re-enchanting the world that modern science has disenchanted. In the most comprehensive attempt to bring about a dialogue between Kabbalah and environmentalism, David Seidenberg has focused on the "image of God" trope, arguing that in rabbinic sources it is not reserved exclusively to humans but is shared by nonhuman beings and by creation in its totality.[4] Moreover, in rabbinic sources the "image of God" is not equated with rationality, as Maimonides and his followers held, but rather "the structure of the body itself was the image of God."[5] This embodied understanding of the "image of God" explains why gender and sexuality are so central to kabbalistic theosophy and theurgy and why Kabbalah more than other strands of medieval Judaism coheres with contemporary ecofeminism.[6] The Kabbalists' mission was "to recover the body as the image of God,"[7] a mission Seidenberg fully endorses. The embodied and gendered image of God pertains to the notion that "every aspect of reality that represents wholeness to us can also be seen as an image of God" so that "any element of creation that represents the wholeness of Creation or the flow of energy and life between realms, and any element, species, or object that unites or ties together the heaven and earth, can be seen as an image of God."[8] If the physical world and all its inhabitants are created in the "image of God," nature is inherently sacred and must not be harmed by humans who are part of the "more-than-human world," but who have no privileged status. For Seidenberg, Kabbalah is the most suitable framework for a Jewish ecological response to the ecological crisis.

Elliot R. Wolfson, whose monumental scholarship has transformed our understanding of Kabbalah, Jewish mysticism, and Jewish philosophy, does not refer to himself as an eco-theologian nor is he involved in Jewish environmental activism. In fact, in the first conference on "Judaism and the Natural World" held in 1997 as part of the ten conferences that established the field of religion and ecology,[9] Wolfson presented a paper that problematized the use of Kabbalah to advance Jewish ecological spirituality, especially what he called "feminist ecology."[10] For starters, Kabbalah is environmentally problematic because it views nature as a linguistic construct, a text composed from the twenty-two letters of the Hebrew alphabet, the elemental building blocks of the universe. According to Kabbalah, Wolfson explained,

> there is only one ultimate reality, the divine light, which manifests itself in the garb of the twenty-two letters of the Hebrew alphabet that derive, in turn, from the four-letter name, YHWH, the root word of all language, the mystical secret of the Torah. Basic to the theosophic orientation of the kabbalists is the notion that the infinite energy of the divine is expressed in the pleroma of ten *sefirot*, which are related to the twenty-two Hebrew letters.[11]

Since nature is a linguistic construct, human interaction with nature is a linguistic act as well, an act of reading and interpreting the Book of Nature.[12] The "reading" of nature is reserved for Kabbalists, elite knowers of the semiotic rules that govern poetic nature.

The physical world we call "nature" is inherently paradoxical: what we see is not reality but only the concealment of reality garbed by linguistic veils. Although nature mirrors or reflects God, what is reflected in the mirror is only the image, and the image is not real. Wolfson clarifies the point:

> The luminous letters shine forth through the veil of the physical entities of this world. It is in this sense that the kabbalists would speak of nature as a mirror, for the corporeal world reflects the spiritual forms in the manner that a mirror reflects images.

> Just as the image is not what is real but only its appearance, so *nature is naught but the representation of that which is not real*. Yet, in the mirror of nature, the dichotomy between image and reality collapses, for here, appearance is truth and truth appearance [emphasis added].[13]

In the reflective medium of nature, the divine light is revealed because it is "garbed" by the garments of language. The hermeneutical act of ungarbing takes place in the consciousness of the Kabbalist whose soul is so "polished" that it best reflects nature/God. Through observance of the commandments and the cultivation of virtues, the human soul (or what we today call "consciousness") attains the luminosity that enables it to function as a reflecting mirror.

The inherent paradoxality of the mirror is best exemplified in the symbolism of the Shekhinah, the feminine *sefirah* that is also called "Mirror." Reflecting the nine (masculine) *sefirot* above her, the feminine Shekhinah is the "invisible surface that allows the images from above to be seen because she has no image of her own."[14] Put differently, the Shekhinah "is what she is because she is what she is not, and only in not being who she is not, is she what she is."[15] If the Shekhinah symbolism is correctly understood, Wolfson argued, it is misleading to appropriate it to construct "feminist ecology" in which the Shekhinah is worshipped as a goddess and her creative powers are venerated.[16] In truth, the Shekhinah is not an independent creative force, because in Kabbalah "the creative potency is consistently located in the phallus" (i.e., Yesod).[17] The Shekhinah functions creatively "only by virtue of the seminal fluid that she receives from the male,"[18] so that when she appears to act as a creative force, the Shekhinah is masculinized.[19] Wolfson concluded that to employ Kabbalah as the framework of feminist ecology is to misread the kabbalistic texts. In truth, Kabbalah had a rather negative view of nature, corporeality, and femininity. Nature was associated with the demonic corporeality, which the (male) Kabbalist must transcend through performance of rituals with the proper intention (*kavanah*), and femininity is never independent of male virility. Kabbalah does not venerate the natural world but seeks to spiritualize it, namely, release the hidden creative energy of the Hebrew letters, the elemental building blocks of the world, whose infinite permutations account for the multiplicity of the phenomenal world.

Ironically, Wolfson's skepticism about the usefulness of Kabbalah for Jewish environmentalism encouraged other scholars of Kabbalah to examine the vast kabbalistic corpus to offer alternative, more positive understandings of nature, embodiment, and femininity.[20] Seidenberg's *Kabbalah and Ecology* is the most elaborate example, but also relevant is the work of Melilah Hellner-Eshed who noted that "most of the Zohar's stories take place outside, in nature: while walking on roads and paths, or sitting—in the inner recesses of caves, among the shade of rocks, beside springs, and beneath the pleasant shade of trees."[21] The wandering Companions of the Zohar disclose the mysteries of the Zohar "while walking on the way,"[22] in response to all sorts of surprising encounters or in deliberate efforts to resolve textual puzzles. What does the setting of the zoharic narratives outdoors signify about nature? Does it mean the Zohar is interested in the physicality of nature as are environmentalists? I do not think so. The Zohar situates its protagonists in outdoor environments rather than in built urban settings to carry a certain message: the spiritual truths of Judaism are not to be constrained by social conventions of the Jewish community or by the oppressive measures of the Christian majority.[23] Rejecting existing social structures, the protagonists (and by implication all Kabbalists) come closest to God because they are better able to turn inward and engage in the iconic visualization of the divine.[24] This contemplative activity transports the Kabbalist to the supernal worlds, which makes the depicted natural environment but a portal through which the Kabbalist is transported to other imaginary landscapes, especially the landscape of the Holy Land.

Precisely because nature mirrors God, Kabbalah (and the Zohar in particular) enchants the world, giving it spiritual depth captured by its plethora of organic symbols (e.g., the Orchard, the Palm Tree, the Pomegranate, the Grape Cluster, the Water Spring, the River, the Rose, the Doe, the Serpent, the Rainbow, etc.). The intricate web of symbols, images, and metaphors artistically constructs a mythic reality that dematerializes nature: the symbols do not explain the function of physical objects but provide a mental map for phenomenological experiences that take place within the Kabbalist's imagination. In other words, nature is experienced symbolically within the consciousness of the Kabbalist. What makes the physical object present to the Kabbalist's consciousness is the hermeneutical act of reading Torah in which the symbols function as the code that decodes the meaning of Torah, itself a symbolic text. Thus, whether the Zohar depicts events in the earthly world or in the supernal worlds, these events exist only on the pages of the Zohar or in the consciousness of the reader/listener. Eitan Fishbane has insightfully suggested that we look at the Zohar as a particular kind of literary text, a text that belongs to the genre of magic realism and fantasy.[25] In the literary fiction of the Zohar the protagonists occupy the enchanted world in which "the veil that divides the natural and the supernatural is frequently lifted, allowing for the one to cross into the other."[26] Blending "the modes of realism and mythic fantasy" the Zohar creates an imaginative world that invites its readers/listeners to experience not the natural world they actually perceive but the fictionalized world (earthly or supernatural) generated in and by the imagination of the author and by their own imagination. In an enchanted world nature is best grasped by a fictional fantasy such as the Zohar.

Given the textualization of nature in Kabbalah, can it be useful to Jewish environmentalists who wish to respond to the environmental crisis within the framework of Judaism? I suggest that Wolfson's Heideggerian approach to Kabbalah has ecological ramifications. Heidegger's critique of modern technology, his respect for the Being of all beings, his insistence on the interdependence of "earth, sky, gods, and mortals" (i.e., "the fourfold"), and his notion that humans have an obligation to care for Being have much in common with deep ecology and have inspired environmentalists who find in Heidegger a promising path for environmental philosophy. The ecological dimension of Heidegger's philosophy of Being is pertinent to Jewish ecological spirituality that takes its cue from Kabbalah, especially if Heidegger's philosophy is complemented by ecofeminism and by feminist ethics of care.

NATURE AS A POETIC TEXT

The kabbalistic enchantment of nature is predicated on the association of language and Being: the world we know through our senses is a linguistic construct that requires language to be understood. Evolving over time, several motifs coalesced in medieval Kabbalah to bring about the textualization of nature: the notion that the world was constructed by the twenty-two letters of the Hebrew alphabet; the identification of the totality of the letters with the ineffable name of God; the correspondence between the name of God formed out of the twenty-two letters and limbs of the human body; the visualization of God's body as a mental image that the Kabbalist conjures in his imagination, and the feminization of the image. Wolfson's numerous studies explicated these motifs that intricately link the linguistic, textual, cosmological, specular, gendered, and mystical dimensions of Kabbalah.[27] The textualization of nature in medieval Kabbalah can be traced to the enigmatic *Sefer Yetzirah* whose time of composition, location, and cultural context have long been debated.[28]

Sefer Yetzirah depicts the creation of the world as an act of poiesis in which "Yah the Lord of hosts, the God of Israel, the Living God, God Almighty . . . carved out thirty wondrous paths of wisdom. He created this universe through groups of letters (*separim*): with *seper*, and *seper*, and *seper*."[29] The "thirty-two wondrous paths" consists of the twenty-two letters and the ten *sefirot*. The letters are elemental units whose combinations and permutations account for the multiplicity and diversity of the cosmos. The letters, as Tzahi Weiss put it, demarcate "the limits of human knowledge and allow for the creation of everything,"[30] and the ten *sefirot* are the structural, fractal pattern that is manifested in all levels of reality: they include six spatial dimensions as well as moral, temporal, and social dimensions. According to *Sefer Yetzirah* the physical universe manifests hidden elements whose internal structure can be expressed numerically: the number ten is foundational but so are other numbers—three, seven, and twelve—whose function is revealed through the semiotic "analysis" of the three main groups of letters. *Sefer Yetzirah,* however, is interested more in the creative power of the elemental letters than in the ten *sefirot*, and unlike rabbinic texts and the Hekhalot literature, *Sefer Yetizrah* speculates about the totality of the twenty-two letters and not only the letters of the ineffable name, YOD, HE, and WAV.

Although *Sefer Yetzirah* made no reference to Torah, when *Sefer Yetzirah* was incorporated into the rabbinic canon the association of twenty-two letters with the divine name was fused with the dominant motif in rabbinic literature: the Torah is the Name of God, and the study of the Torah is the process through which one can access the divine name and attain mystical union with God.[31] That process takes place within the imagination, a psychic function that rabbinic texts located in the human heart. Within the imagination, one conjures the semiotic body of God and orients oneself to become one with God. The rabbis, and later the medieval Kabbalists, called this "orientation" "*kavanah*" and developed contemplative techniques to cultivate it in order to achieve mystical union with God.[32] Contemplation takes place within the human imagination, the mental space wherein the incorporeal God is embodied, but embodiment is not just semiotic, it is inherently phenomenological. In Heideggerian parlance, the imaginal world is the "clearing" (*die Lichtung*) where Being is shown in all its luminosity.[33] God's poetic activity balanced saying and unsaying, expressive creativity and self-control, potentiality and actuality, infinity and finitude, nothingness and being.

Yehuda Liebes insightfully suggested that according to *Sefer Yetzirah*, "everything God creates is a literary creation."[34] Since this notion pervades the kabbalistic worldview, what are the implications? First, to view the physical world as a poetic text means that God is a poet and the divine act of poiesis is emulated by earthly poets whose literary creativity creates imaginal worlds. Poetry, as Heidegger deeply understood, has "an indispensable function for human life: it is the creative source of the humanness of the dwelling life of man."[35] Second, because the created world is a linguistic construct, a text, encountering or engaging the physical world is analogous to the act of reading, that is, a hermeneutical act. Only those who know the grammar of the language and the rules of poetic speech can correctly interpret the poetry of the universe. And third, since the encounter with nature is always linguistic, the encounter cannot escape the inherent paradoxicality of language: it simultaneously reveals and conceals, enlightens through opaqueness. This is the dialectics that the Zohar captures by the trope of "luminal darkness ("*butzina de-kardinuta*") that Wolfson unpacked in a series of essays.[36] Wolfson has insightfully grasped and clarified

> the poetic impulse stimulating the kabbalist's attempt to visualize the word as the simulacrum through which the imageless is imaged [which] coincides well with the following account of Baudelaire's notion of poetry. . . . "Poetry proclaims the primacy of language, its possible perfection, its self-sufficiency. It is in and through creative (poetic) language that duality, division, and disjunction will be resolved. The idea and the real, the abstract and the concrete will be reunited."[37]

The Kabbalists, as Wolfson further explains, are able to "speak of the unspeakable" and "envision the ineffable" because of their

> ascetic negation of the physical body [which] allows for the ocular apprehension of God's imaginal body: only the heart that is pure from carnal desire can mirror images of the invisible. In a manner consonant with Meister Eckhart, the kabbalist ideal of visual contemplation rested on a paradoxical inversion: purging the mind of images of the sensory world through a regimen of abstinence facilitated envisioning the divine in images of an erotic intimacy and intensity.[38]

In their contemplative practices, the Kabbalists become the textual embodiment and even incarnation of God.[39] Incarnation, however, is not in the flesh, but only in the mental space of the imagination, which Wolfson names, following Henry Corbin, "the imaginal world."[40] Poetic thinking is not just an apt way to capture the artistry of kabbalistic texts, especially the Zohar, it is also the phrase that best characterizes Wolfson's understanding of philosophy as a "poetic activity"[41] and the connection between his own poetic creativity and his academic scholarship.[42] Poetic thinking, of course, is mostly associated with Martin Heidegger and with the philosophy of his student, Hannah Arendt.[43] For both, poetic thinking was a radical critique of Western philosophy and a way to think "without the banisters," as Arendt called it, or as we colloquially say "outside the box" of conventional philosophy. Wolfson has forged a critical and insightful dialogue between Heidegger and Kabbalah: reading Kabbalah through the prism of Heidegger's philosophy allows for deeper understanding of the Jewish mystical tradition, while exposing its limitations (especially its misogyny and ethnocentrism); conversely, reading Heidegger through the lens of Kabbalah highlights the mystical tendencies of his philosophy, while exposing his shortcomings (especially his antisemitism and ethnocentrism). The conversation between Heidegger, Kabbalah, and Wolfson hinges on poetic thinking.

POETIC THINKING: HEIDEGGER, KABBALAH, AND WOLFSON

Heidegger is the most influential philosopher of the twentieth century, but also the most controversial.[44] Heidegger's commitment to the cause of National Socialism, as Richard Wolin has demonstrated, was not just "a temporary marriage of convenience" but a profound, albeit self-deluding, project in which Heidegger imagined he could play the role of "philosopher king" for Hitler's *Fuhrerstaat*.[45] A member of the Nazi Party, when Heidegger was appointed as rector of Freiburg University in 1933, he dutifully carried out Nazi antisemitic policies, barring Jews, including his own teacher, Edmund Husserl, and his many outstanding Jewish students, from the university. Heidegger's delusional fascination with Nazism waned in 1934 and through the mid-1930s he dissociated himself from the Nazi Party and from Nazism as a contemporary political movement. But, as Herbert Marcuse reminded Heidegger in a private letter written in 1947, "you never publicly denounced any of the actions or ideologies of the regime . . . and you are still today identified with the Nazi regime."[46] The Nazi worldview, in which ecology plays an important part,[47] remained dear to Heidegger who failed to come to terms with its horrific outcomes. Heidegger believed that "the Nazis represented a radical break from the Western tradition that begins in Greek metaphysics and culminated in environmental degradation and human dislocation in our modern technological driven societies."[48] Heidegger's now published private *Black Notebooks* (*Schwarze Hefte*) attest that he not only shared widespread antisemitic tropes, but that he also assigned to "the Jews" a significant role in his critique of Western philosophy. His denunciation of "the Jews" had much to do with his ecological critique of modern technology as well as his understanding of the history of Being, from which "the Jews" are excluded.

Wolfson addresses the controversy over Heidegger in his *The Duplicity of Philosophy's Shadow*, stating straightforwardly: "Heidegger was both a Nazi given to anti-Semitic jargon and an incisive philosopher, whose thinking not only was responding to the urgencies of his epoch but also contains the potential to unravel the thorny knots of politics and philosophy relevant for the present as much as for the past."[49] Heidegger then is "neither defensible nor disposable," and his thinking "demands reflective analysis and critical questions."[50] Heidegger's antisemitism is indeed integral to his philosophy because he refers to "Judaism" (*das Judentum*), or, to adopt Shaul Magid's suggestion, to "Jewishness," as "the 'other' that is excluded from the orbit of Dasein."[51] Wolfson rightly insists that Heidegger should not be ignored by Jewish philosophers and scholars of Kabbalah, but that his writings should be carefully read in order "to engage him critically to deconstruct his deconstructive hermeneutics."[52] Like Thomas Sheehan, one of Heidegger's leading contemporary interpreters, Wolfson "makes sense of Heidegger,"[53] but not merely as a paradigm shift within Western philosophy but also as a useful lens for the interpretation of Kabbalah. Wolfson accomplished this challenging task in his most recent book, in which he explicated the affinities between the two bodies of thought as well as their dangers and ethical limitations.[54] Wolfson's insightful analysis cannot be examined here, but to understand how his poetic thinking is relevant to environmentalism, we do need to say a bit more about Heidegger.

Heidegger's project can be defined as phenomenological ontology, that is to say, "he defined phenomenology as ontology: that kind of interpretation which allows an entity to show itself in the way appropriate to that entity itself."[55] The project was intended to critique Western philosophy, which beginning with Plato has identified Being and beings and privileged the eternal and unchanging over the temporal and the ever-changing. Greek philosophy, and consequently the entire Western philosophical tradition, went awry because it inquired about beings but overlooked or "forgot" to ask more preliminary questions: what and whenceforth Being? Heidegger's critical project was intended to "step back" from the assumptions and conventions of Western philosophy to ask more preliminary questions about what is prior to and basic for metaphysics. What matters to Heidegger the phenomenologist is not *that* things exist, but *how* and *why* things have meaningful presence (*Anwesen*) to human intelligence. To correct the mistakes of Western metaphysics, Heidegger sought to recover the philosophizing of the Pre-Socratics who experienced nature (*physis*) as self-emergence that makes things appear through concealment. By reading the Greek philosophers anew, Heidegger sought to inaugurate a postmetaphysical era in the history of Western philosophy that overcomes the binary dualism of subject and object, of mind and body, of self and world, of nature and culture.

In Heidegger's phenomenological ontology human beings are not "subjects" who stand against the "objects" in the external world. As "being-in-the-world," human existence cannot be separated from the world into which humans are "thrown." He coined the neologism "Dasein" to name the uniqueness of human existence. Translated variously as "being-there" or "there-being," the term indicates that there is always a "there" that defines how humans exist in the world. Inseparable from the world, Dasein is disposed to see the world in a particular way. This disposedness is neither something entirely subjective (i.e., it comes from the "inside") nor something entirely "objective" (i.e., imposed from the "outside"). Rather, disposedness arises out of the whole way of comporting ourselves and relating ourselves to the things and people around us. Only humans are open to the Being of beings, and they alone have the ability to encounter something that matters to them, something that they care about. While humans are in a state of mind, or mood, everything shows up as having a certain unified "tone" or "flavor" or "feel," but instead of distorting the reality of the situation, the state of mind calls us to act it a certain way. The basic mood of Dasein is anxiety (*die Angst*) that arises from Dasein's awareness of its own mortality, but anxiety is not paralyzing dread, since it generates responsible action. Since Dasein is attuned to things in the world and tuned by the things of the world, the dualism of "Man" and "Nature," so dominant in Western philosophy, disappears.

Heidegger's analysis of Dasein as being-in-the-world turns our understanding of hermeneutics from a derivative phenomenon to the central feature of human existence. Similar to the kabbalistic understanding, hermeneutics is not just a relationship between reader and text, in which the human being as a "subject" is a knower disengaged from the world and from the practical activity in the world. Rather, Dasein is coterminous with the world and therefore the human condition is trapped in the hermeneutical circle: one cannot understand the whole without understanding the parts. Radicalizing and expanding the hermeneutical circle, Heidegger claimed that "the legitimate task of achieving knowledge is a subspecies of the more general phenomenon of human understanding."[56] Understanding, however, is more than discovery of facts about particular features of the world but more primordially the disclosure of possibilities, and disclosure makes the phenomenon of discovery intelligible. Dasein's understanding of itself as possibility means that understanding has a temporal dimension.

Embedded in the world, Dasein is the "clearing," the "mental space" within which things become intelligible. The process by which things become intelligible is truth, which the Greeks named *aletheia* (or *a-letheia*), literally meaning "un-concealment," "un-hiddenness, or "dis-closure." Instead of grounding our knowledge in propositions that correspond to something in the world, Heidegger sees truth as "a way of being disposed for the world. A disposition is true, not by corresponding to the facts but by giving us a good existential grip on the world. And we only have a good existential grip on the world to the extent that the world itself has attuned us to the things we encounter in the world."[57] This is not to say that no world "exists out there," there certainly is an external world, but the only Being to which we have access is the intelligibility of things, their *aletheia*, in the sense of disclosedness to us.[58]

Truth as unconcealment is poiesis. Literally, poiesis means "making" or "producing," but poiesis "is not making in the sense of bringing something into existence for the first time but rather taking a thing that is already there and wresting it out of obscurity and into the light, in this case into the light of intelligibility. . . . To bring forth means to bring out into the light, to bring into view something which up to then, was not seen at all."[59] We do not wrest the disclosedness of a thing *from* undisclosedness but rather we wrest the thing *into* disclosedness. Poiesis is thus the "clearing" within which and whereby things become intelligible, that is, can have Being, in Heidegger's sense of the term. The revealing or bringing forth (i.e., poiesis), is what poets share with craftsmen and artists. The ancient Greek philosophers regarded making artifacts (*techne*) as poiesis, namely, production, but making artifacts is a secondary instance of poiesis. In the primary sense, poiesis belongs to nature (*physis*), the self-emerging but always self-concealing process. For humans, true poiesis means letting beings manifest themselves with the least interference and with the most cooperation. This point is crucial to Heidegger's ecological ethos that calls us to "let things be" without human control or manipulation, as we shall see below.

Language is the key feature of Dasein, but language, Heidegger famously said, "is the house of Being in which man ek-sists by dwelling, in that he belongs to the truth of being, guarding it."[60] Language shapes and guides our understanding of ourselves and the world around us "*before* we are speaking."[61] We speak because we are possessed by language that orients us by getting us in the right mood for the world. Heidegger names the thing that we are listening to "originary language," the "essence of language," or the "linguistic essence." The essence of language is the "saying that shows things." Originary language is soundless, it "says" the world without the use of words, whereas ordinary language speaks only in words. Prior to any speech, originary language makes salient particular features of the world by setting things into a certain structure. Silently and inconspicuously language says by showing us, directing us immediately to what we should say and drawing our attention to what is to be said. To quote Heidegger, language is "the saying that sets the world into motion."[62] Thus, originary language is not interested in the facts of the world but in getting us to feel the world in a particular kind of way. When we share an orientation to the world with others, we communicate using the words of ordinary language, because we are already possessed by language. Heidegger, in short, enabled us to understand the interdependence of language and being so central to Kabbalah, as Wolfson has shown in many studies.[63] Kabbalah, alas, views Hebrew as the originary language of the universe.

Wolfson, a philosopher/poet, not only explains how this type of poetic thinking is manifested in Kabbalah, but also how this type of thinking links his own academic scholarship and poetic creativity. According to Wolfson, Heidegger correctly grasped that "the essential being of language is Saying as Showing (*Das Wesende der Sprache ist die Sage also die Zeige*). Its showing character is not based on signs of any kind; rather, all signs arise from a showing within whose realm and for whose purposes they can be signs."[64] As Wolfson explains, for Heidegger "poet and thinker occupy that place where language unveils the veil of veils in the veil of their unveiling."[65] Although language and being belong together, the way in which they are so linked "remains veiled" because "not showing is intrinsic to the showing that is the saying."[66] Furthermore Wolfson notes that for Heidegger "the poetic word, therefore, is the sign that 'shows—and in showing, it makes manifest, yet in such a way that it simultaneously conceals.'"[67] The same dialectics operates in kabbalistic esotericism, justifying Wolfson's use of Heidegger's philosophy to critically explicate the link between imagination, hermeneutics, and time in kabbalistic lore.[68] Wolfson candidly attests that the same poeticizing dialectics in which "what is to be found remains entirely concealed has also informed my own path of thinking: every act of revealing is a concealing, for the truth to be revealed cannot be revealed unless it is concealed as the truth to be revealed."[69] In the light of the clearing, the shadow lurks; the "luminal darkness," as the Zohar called it, can only be captured by poetic thinking that unconceals through concealment.

FROM POETIC THINKING TO ECOLOGICAL ETHOS

In contrast to poetic thinking, the modern world is dominated by calculative thinking, which, as we saw above, Heidegger imputes to "the Jews."[70] Calculative thinking characterizes modernity, in which everything is "enframed" (*das Ge-stell*), regarded as "resource" that "stand by" ready for use by humans. In the beginning of the twentieth century, many conservative Germans took a very critical stance toward various aspects of "modernity."[71] Social theorists such as Oswald Spengler, Ludwig Klages, Ernst Jünger, and even Max Weber critiqued the markers of modernity, such as capitalism, commercialism, industrialism, urbanization, democracy, liberalism, individualism, materialism, rationalism, scientism, positivism or communism and socialism.[72] Which aspect of "modernity" was found problematic varied depending on the critic, but "the Jews" were somehow imputed in all of them. Underlying the modern worldview is the instrumental rationality (that is, calculative thinking) that has caused the "disenchantment" (*die Entzauberung*) of the world. This diagnosis is famously associated with Max Weber who lamented it but did not offer an alternative to it.[73] By contrast, Heidegger sharply critiqued the Enlightenment project and the long history of philosophy that brought it about.[74] Heidegger wished to re-enchant the world, whereas Weber acquiesced to living in a disenchanted world because he had a more positive assessment of the rationalist tendencies of the Enlightenment.

For Heidegger, modern technology is the epitome of what is wrong with modernity.[75] By "technology" Heidegger does not refer to a piece of equipment or to this or that technology, but to the essence of technology, namely, the way in which Being is disclosed in the technological age.[76] To the extent that technology is a way of disclosing, a way of bringing into appearance, technology too is a kind of poiesis, but modern technology is very different from the way that ancient or premodern craftsmen disclosed Being. Modern technology, Heidegger avers, "does not unfold into a bringing forth in the sense of *poiesis*. The revealing that rules in modern technology is a challenging [*Herausfordern*], which puts to nature the unreasonable demand that it supply energy that can be extracted and stored as such."[77] Because of the calculative thinking that undergirds it, modern technology reduces all beings and things to mere resource on standby to be optimized. Modern technology contrasts not only with premodern craftsmanship but with the way nature (*physis*) brings things forth. Bruce Foltz puts it well, saying that modern technology does not "disclose entities through an attuned responsiveness but through challenging forth, provoking, or forcing out. What is brought forth by technology is not evoked, shaped, or even forged, but rather "extracted."[78]

In the technological age, nature is assaulted by the logic of domination that characterizes modern technology. Instead of stirring us and inspiring us by its inherent mystery, "Nature becomes a gigantic gasoline station, an energy source for modern technology and industry."[79] Objectified, measured, and calculated in cost-benefit analysis, nature has been thoroughly disenchanted, and its self-emerging fullness is no longer respected or experienced. Unfolding, self-emerging nature always self-conceals, self-withholds, preserves, and shelters. For example, when a plant sprouts, emerges, and extends itself into the open, the plant simultaneously goes back into its roots wherefrom it takes its nourishment in ways that remain closed to us. But modern technology is oblivious to the poiesis of nature, to the way nature makes itself present to us. Heidegger names these aspects together "the earth" (*die Erde*).[80]

The right way of being in the world is what Heidegger, inspired by his favorite poet, Friedrich Hölderin, calls "dwelling" (*das Wohnen*).[81] Human beings "dwell" when they "stay with things," when they "let things be," when they save, conserve, and preserve rather than dominate, control, and manipulate. To "dwell" means to recognize the "oneness of the fourfold," namely the way in which "earth, sky, divinities, and mortals" belong together in interdependent oneness. As Andrew Mitchell explains, the fourfold is "a thinking of things" that names what constitutes "the thing" as a new figure of thought. The fourfold "provides an account of the thing as inherently relational."[82] Heidegger adopted "the fourfold" (*das Geviert*) from his favorite poet, Hölderlin, and "the use of the term represents a way of conceptualizing the phenomenon of existence and setting forth their simultaneous unity and separateness. No one part of the fourfold could be thought without the other three, yet we easily forget to give thought to 'the simple oneness of the four.'"[83] Dwelling entails "saving the earth," "taking under our care the fourfold in its presencing," and "always a staying with things."[84] The "fourfold," I would submit, is a Heideggerian version of what Charles Taylor called, the "immanent frame," the worldview that characterizes our secular age.[85]

Heidegger's ecological ethos of "dwelling" respects the Being of beings, understands the innate interdependence and oneness of all beings, stays with things in an act of caring that "shepherds Being" rather than controls or manipulates them as "resource." To dwell in the world is to be at home in the world and to care for the world, something that "the Jews," according to Heidegger, are incapable of because of their endemic homelessness. Poets and meditative thinkers understand what "dwelling" is because they are attuned to the mystery of Being and to the dialectics of *aletheia* as unconcealment and concealment. Susanne Claxton explains the relationship between the poet and the meditative thinker in a way that sheds light on Wolfson, the poet and meditative thinker:

> The poet's sensitivity to the divinity as the mystery of being plays an important role in ensuring our "at-home-ness" within the unified four-fold division of being. Being

> reveals itself to the Poet, the one who is closest to it. The Poet in turn reveals what she sees, and the meditative thinker elucidates the poet's revelation so as to reveal it to others. . . . Poets serve the fourfold of earth, sky, divinities, and mortals in their sensibility and openness to *aletheia* and the mystery of being that makes possible their naming of the holy. In this way, poets respond to and prepare a place for "the gods" in their absence or mystery.[86]

Poetic thinking is open to the concealment that lies at the heart of unconcealment and to the realm of the possible as such. Expressed in poetry, art, and myth, poetic thinking facilitates the right attitude toward the world: dwelling and care (*die Sorge*). In *Being and Time*, Heidegger maintained that care defines the totality of Dasein's being and is a willful concern, but in his later writings, Heidegger used care to denote "passive, faithful waiting for and guarding of Being."[87] To be the caring "shepherd of Being" requires a different posture than willful concern, a posture that Heidegger calls "*Gelassenheit*" ("releasement" or "detachment"), a term he borrowed from Meister Eckhart, the thirteen-century Dominican, German mystic.[88] By caring for the Being of beings, letting beings show themselves as they are, we acknowledge our obligations and no longer treat nature as an object ready for our use.

The relevance of Heidegger's philosophy to environmentalism was first noted and explicated by Michael E. Zimmerman in the early 1970s, and he brought Heidegger's philosophy to the attention of the leaders of the deep ecology movement, who have challenged human anthropocentrism, emphasizing the interdependence of humans and all beings.[89] Less concerned about the potential for eco-fascism, other environmental philosophers found in Heidegger's philosophy a fruitful path for environmental thought.[90] Ecofeminists in particular found Heidegger most useful because his critique of technology dismantles the logic of domination, which ecofeminists, along with all feminists, considered the roots of the oppression of women. Ecofeminists are not troubled by the potential connection between Heidegger and eco-fascism because they believe that "strategies of multiplicity, diversity, and reciprocity preclude fascism."[91]

CONCLUSION

Wolfson's penetrating studies have conclusively shown the conceptual similarity between Heidegger and Kabbalah, while exposing the limitations and moral failings of both systems of thought. Endorsing his claim that Heidegger should not be ignored by scholars of Kabbalah and Jewish philosophy, this essay pays attention to Heidegger's critique of modern technology and its ramifications for environmentalism, which Wolfson has not addressed. Wolfson's engagement of Heidegger has greatly enriched the study of Kabbalah and it can do the same for Jewish environmentalism. Heidegger's poetic thinking is indeed relevant to Jewish environmentalism, even though the role of ecology in Nazi ideology is most problematic, leading some Jewish theologians to critique environmentalism, especially deep ecology, as a worldview.[92] Hans Jonas, one of Heidegger's most influential students, was also a critic of modern technology and an ecological thinker, but he did not adopt Heidegger's poetic thinking. In fact, Jonas became a major critic of Heidegger, especially after the Second World War, because in Heidegger's philosophy he saw a revival of ancient Gnosticism that promoted the alienation from the physical world that was at the root of Nazi destructive nihilism. Instead, Jonas sought to endow the physical world with moral value that protects and preserves the preciousness of life.[93]

The relevance of Heidegger to Jewish environmentalism does not mean that Jewish environmentalists must be familiar with the intricacies of Heidegger's philosophy, but that they could benefit from the ecological ramifications of Heidegger's poetic thinking. It is also true that a Jewish theologian could articulate an eco-theology that uses the very assumptions that Heidegger has rejected: theism, transcendence, creation theology, and metaphysical dualism, as the late Jonathan Sacks has done. Heidegger's phenomenological ontology is not necessary for Jewish environmentalism, but it could inspire an ecological spirituality that calls on us to dwell on earth rather than exploiting it. Heidegger can be useful if he is read, *pace* Wolfson, noting the limitations, shortcomings, and blind spots, and complementing his thought through conversation with intellectual traditions like Kabbalah.

Heidegger's call to "dwell" and "in-habit" the earth with care and attentiveness to its richness, without enframing everything as a resource to be exploited is conducive to ecological sensibility that can and should be cultivated by all people, including Jews. The tragic irony, of course, is that no other event in the twentieth century illustrates more poignantly the horrific results of enframing than the industrialized killing of Jews in the Holocaust. It was Nazi calculative thinking that made Jewish bodies into "resource" to accomplish their dream of a Lebensraum free of Jews. Roger S. Gottlieb, a leading Jewish environmental philosopher and contributor to the discourse of religion and ecology, has shown how the genocide and ecocide are two sides of the same coin. Gottlieb further contended that because Jews have been the primary victims of the Nazis, they have a moral obligation to engage the Holocaust from an environmental perspective. Jews were not only victims of the Holocaust; their conduct and survival gifted all of us with the "spirituality of resistance," the proper response to the ecological crisis.[94] Similarly, Eric Katz has drawn out the implications of the Holocaust for environmental philosophy by considering the role of technology in the Holocaust.[95]

Although Heidegger failed to accept responsibility for the Nazi atrocities, the ecological ethos of "dwelling" does invite us to cultivate the right attitude toward the earth and all its inhabitants. Nevertheless, poetic thinking alone cannot solve the environmental crisis that threatens our future existence on Earth. Global warming, climate change, extreme weather events, acidification of oceans, soil erosion, deforestation, loss of biodiversity, rising sea levels, and many more require not only knowledge of the environmental sciences but also the use of modern technology, both of which could not have been possible without the very metaphysics that Heidegger had derided. This is the conundrum that requires us to think creatively about technology going beyond poetic thinking and the ecological spirituality it generates. We should cultivate less destructive habits of being in the world but given the depth and severity of the environmental crisis, poetic thinking and ecological spirituality inevitably fall short. Since we cannot go back to a pretechnological age, which Heidegger idealized while writing in his ski cabin, how to live with technology without it destroying us and the earth remains the challenge for the twenty-first century.

NOTES

1. For overviews of contemporary Jewish environmentalism see Hava Tirosh-Samuelson, "Judaism and the Environment," in *Oxford Bibliographies Online*, https://doi.org/10.1093/OBO/9780199840731-0118; Tirosh-Samuelson, "Judaism," in *The Routledge Handbook of Religion and Ecology*, ed. Willis Jenkins, Mary Evelyn Tucker, and John Grim (New York and London: Routledge, 2017), 60–69; Tirosh-Samuelson , *Religion and Environment: The Case of Judaism* (Kitchener, Ontario: Pandora Press, 2020).
2. See Jonathan Sacks, *The Great Partnership: God, Science and the Search for Meaning* (London: Hodder and Stoughton, 2011).
3. Arthur Green, "Kabbalah for the Environmental Age," in *Judaism and Ecology: Created World and Revealed Word*, ed. Hava Tirosh-Samuelson (Cambridge, MA: Harvard University Press, 2002), 1–15. On the relationship between Schachter-Shalomi's theological "Paradigm Shift" and Neo-Hasidism see Shaul Magid, *American Post-Judaism: Identity and Renewal in Post-Ethnic Society* (Bloomington: Indiana University Press, 2013).
4. David Seidenberg, *Kabbalah and Ecology: The Image of God and the More-Than-Human World* (Cambridge: Cambridge University Press, 2015).
5. Seidenberg, *Kabbalah and Ecology*, 176.
6. See Irene Diamond and David Seidenberg, "Sensuous Minds and the Possibilities of a Jewish Ecofeminist Practice," *Ethics and the Environment* 4, no. 2 (1999): 185–95.
7. Seidenberg, *Kabbalah and Ecology*, 177.
8. Seidenberg, *Kabbalah and Ecology*, 231.
9. On the conferences and their contribution to the field of religion and ecology see Mary Evelyn Tucker and John Grim, "The Movement of Religion and Ecology: Emerging Field and Dynamic Force," in *The Routledge Handbook of Religion and Ecology*, ed. Willis Jenkins, Mary Evelyn Tucker, and John Grim (New York and London: Routledge, 2017), 7–12.
10. Elliot R. Wolfson, "Mirror of Nature Reflected in the Symbolism of Kabbalah," in *Judaism and Ecology: Created World and Revealed Word*, ed. Hava Tirosh-Samuelson (Cambridge, MA: Harvard University Press, 2002), 305–31; the essay was reprinted in *Pathwings, Philosophical and Poetic Reflections on the Hermeneutics of Time and Language* (Barrytown, NY: Station Hill, 2004), 25–44. My references are to the first version. Wolfson's title, *Pathwings*, perhaps intentionally echoes the title of Heidegger's work, *Pathmarks*, ed. William McNeill (Cambridge: Cambridge University Press, 1998).

11. Wolfson, "Mirror of Nature," 306.
12. The "book of nature" was a common trope in medieval Christianity. For overviews see A. Vanderjagt and K. van Berkel, eds., *The Book of Nature in Antiquity and the Middle Ages* (Leuven: Peeters, 2005); J. M. Van Der Meer and S. Mandelbrote, eds., *Nature and Scripture in the Abrahamic Religions*, 2 vols. (Leiden: Brill, 2008).
13. Wolfson, "Mirror of Nature," 307–8.
14. Wolfson, "Mirror of Nature," 322.
15. Wolfson, "Mirror of Nature," 321.
16. For an extensive use of Shekhinah symbolism to articulate Jewish environmental spirituality see Lynn Gottlieb, *She Who Dwells Within: A Feminist Vision of a Renewed Judaism* (San Francisco: HarperOne, 1995). The fusion of Kabbalah and ecofeminism for Jewish feminist spirituality has been promoted by Jill Hammer, the co-founder of the Kohenet Priestess Institute. For analysis of her approach see Cara Rock-Singer, "The Kohenet Hebrew Priestess Institute and the Gendered Politics and Media of Jewish Renewal," paper delivered in *Jewish Revival(s) Inside Out: Remaking Jewishness in a Post-Secular Age*, Conference at Central European University 2019. I thank Professor Rock-Singer for sharing the paper with me.
17. Wolfson, "Mirror of Nature," 323.
18. Wolfson, "Mirror of Nature," 323.
19. Wolfson developed this analysis in numerous essays, including "Occultation of the Feminine and the Body of Secrecy," in *Rending the Veil: Concealment of Secrets in the History of Religion* (New York and London: Seven Bridges Press, 1999), 113–54, reprinted in *Elliot Wolfson: Poetic Thinking*, ed. Hava Tirosh-Samuelson and Aaron W. Hughes (Leiden: Brill, 2015), 35–68; Elliot Wolfson, "Coronation of the Sabbath Bride: Kabbalistic Myth and the Ritual of Androgynisation," *Journal of Jewish Thought and Philosophy* 6 (1997): 301–44; Elliot R. Wolfson, "On Becoming Female: Crossing Gender Boundaries in Kabbalistic Ritual and Myth," in *Gender and Judaism*, ed. T. M. Rudavsky (New York: New York University Press, 1995), 209–28.
20. For a different interpretation of gender in Shekhinah symbolism see Moshe Idel, *The Privileged Divine Feminine* (Berlin: De Gruyter, 2020). On the diverse approaches to Shekhinah symbolism in modern scholarship of Kabbalah see Hava Tirosh-Samuelson, "Gender in Jewish Mysticism," in *New Scholarship on Kabbalah and Jewish Mysticism*, ed. Frederick E. Greenspahn (New York: New York University Press, 2011), 191–230.
21. Melilah Hellner-Eshed, *A River Issues Forth from Eden: On the Language of Mystical Experience in the Zohar* (Palo Alto: Stanford University Press, 2009), 111.
22. Hellner-Eshed, *A River Issues Forth*, 113.
23. See Ellen D. Haskell, *Mystical Resistance: Uncovering the Zohar's Conversations with Christianity* (Oxford: Oxford University Press, 2016).
24. Elliot R. Wolfson, "Iconic Visualization and the Imaginal Body of God: The Role of Intention in the Rabbinic Conception of Prayer," *Modern Theology* 12 (1996): 137–62. The essay was reprinted in *Elliot R. Wolfson: Poetic Thinking*, 97–126, quote on 117. Wolfson shows that already in rabbinic circles, "mental iconography (realized in imaginal space) replaced physical geography." That is to say, the praying person invokes the iconic image within his own imagination,

but if for the rabbis that activity could happen only in "a specific space that is designated as holy," in the Zohar this intentional and contemplative activity could happen anywhere, and especially on the road and in open places. Hasidism, whose founder, Israel Baal Shem Tov, also experienced God outdoors, perpetuated that approach through hagiographic tales situated in natural settings, especially forests.

25. Eitan Fishbane, *The Art of Mystical Narrative: The Poetics of the Zohar* (New York: Oxford University Press, 2018), especially 223–79.
26. Fishbane, *Art of Mystical Narrative*, 225.
27. For example, see Elliot R. Wolfson, *Through the Speculum That Shines: Vision and Imagination in Medieval Jewish Mysticism* (Princeton: Princeton University Press, 1994); Elliot R. Wolfson, "Judaism and Incarnation: The Imaginal Body of God," in *Christianity in Jewish Terms*, ed. Tikva Frymer-Kensky, David Novak, Peter Ochs, David Fox Sandmel, and Michael A. Signer (Boulder, CO: Westview Press, 2000), 239–53; Elliot R. Wolfson, "The Body in the Text: A Kabbalistic Theology of Embodiment," *Jewish Quarterly Review* 95, no. 3 (2005): 479–500; Elliot R. Wolfson, *Language, Eros, Being: Kabbalistic Hermeneutic and Poetic Imagination* (New York: Fordham University Press, 2005), esp. 190–260, 261–95.
28. See Hava Tirosh-Samuelson, "Kabbalah and Science in the Middle Ages: Preliminary Remarks," in *Science in Medieval Jewish Communities*, ed. Gad Freudenthal (Cambridge: Cambridge University Press, 2011), 476–510, esp. 480–83.
29. A. Peter Hayman, *Sefer Yesira: Edition, Translation and Text Critical Commentary* (Tubingen: Mohr Siebek, 2004), 59.
30. Tzahi Weiss, *Sefer Yesirah and Its Contexts: Other Jewish Voices* (Philadelphia: University of Pennsylvania Press, 2018), 7.
31. Gershom Scholem, "The Name of God and the Linguistic Theory of Kabbalah," *Diogenes* 79 (1972): 59–80. The technique of letter permutation was central in the ecstatic Kabbalah of Abraham Abulafia. Moshe Idel interpreted them as "a-nomian" techniques that were disengaged from the performance of the commandments. See Moshe Idel, *Language, Torah and Hermeneutics in Abraham Abulafia* (Albany, NY: SUNY Press, 1988). By contrast, Wolfson has argued that Abulafia's techniques were "hyper-nomian, because in Jewish society of the 13th century there was no room for a-nomian position." See Elliot R. Wolfson, *Abraham Abulafia—Kabbalist and Prophet: Hermeneutics, Theosophy and Theurgy* (Los Angeles: Cherub Press, 2000), 178–228. Variously read, Abulafia's linguistic mysticism only deepened the textualization of nature.
32. See Elliot R. Wolfson, "Iconic Visualization and the Imaginal Body of God: The Role of Intention in in the Rabbinic Conception of Prayer," *Modern Theology* 12 (1996): 137–62, reprinted in *Elliot R. Wolfson: Poetic Thinking*, ed. Hava Tirosh-Samuelson and Aaron W. Hughes (Leiden: Brill, 2011), 97–126.
33. In the early writings of Heidegger, "clearing" (*die Lichtung*) was understood in the *visual* metaphor of light (*das Licht*), but in his later writings, Heidegger employed it as a *spatial* metaphor of expanse in the wood or forest. See Richard Capobianco, *Engaging Heidegger* (Toronto: University of Toronto Press, 2011), 92.

34. Yehuda Liebes, *Ars Poetica in Sefer Yetzirah* [Hebrew] (Tel Aviv: Schocken, 2000), 97.
35. Albert Hofstadter, "Introduction," in *Martin Heidegger, Poetry, Language, Thought*, trans. and ed. Albert Hofstadter (New York: HarperCollins, 1971), xv.
36. Elliot R. Wolfson, *Luminal Darkness: Imaginal Gleanings from Zoharic Literature* (Oxford: One World, 2007).
37. Wolfson, *Language, Eros, Being*, 41.
38. Wolfson, *Language, Eros, Being*, 42.
39. Wolfson, "Flesh Become Word: Textual Embodiment and Poetic Incarnation," in his *Language, Eros, Being*, 190–260.
40. See Henry Corbin, *Mundus Imaginalis: or The Imaginary and the Imaginal* (1964); Ali Shariat, "Henry Corbin and the Imaginal: A Look at the Concept and Function of the Creative Imagination in Iranian Philosophy," *Diogenes* 156 (1991): 83–114.
41. Aaron W. Hughes, "Elliot R. Wolfson: An Intellectual Portrait," in *Elliot R. Wolfson: Poetic Thinking*, ed. Hava Tirosh-Samuelson and Aaron W. Hughes (Leiden: Brill, 2011), 1–33, quote on 3.
42. Elliot R. Wolfson, *Pathwings: Philosophical & Poetic Reflections on the Hermeneutics of Time & Language* (Barrytown, NY: Station Hill, 2004); Elliot R. Wolfson, *Footdreams & Treetales: Ninety-Two Poems* (New York: Fordham University Press, 2007).
43. For analysis of Heidegger's poetic thinking see David Halliburton, *Poetic Thinking: An Approach to Heidegger* (Chicago: University of Chicago Press, 1993). On Hannah Arendt's contribution to poetic thinking and the relevance of poetic thinking to contemporary politics and ethics see Amir Eshel, *Poetic Thinking Today: An Essay* (Stanford, CA: Stanford University Press, 2020).
44. For key texts see Richard Wolin, ed., *The Heidegger Controversy: A Critical Reader* (Cambridge, MA, and London: MIT Press, 1993). On the revival of the controversy in the 1980s, especially among French and German intellectuals, see Michael E. Zimmerman, "Philosophy and Politics: The Case of Heidegger," *Philosophy Today* (Spring 1989): 3–20.
45. Wolin, *Heidegger Controversy*, 2.
46. Herbert Marcuse, "Letter from Marcuse to Heidegger of August 28, 1947," in Wolin, *Heidegger Controversy*, 161–62.
47. Boaz Neumann, *New Histories of Nazism* (in Hebrew) (Ben Shemen: Modan, 2019), esp. 166–88, 209–28.
48. Aaron James Wendland, "Heidegger's New Beginning: History, Technology and National Socialism," in *Heidegger on Technology*, ed. Aaron James Wendland, Christopher Merwin, and Christos Hadjioannou (New York and London: Routledge, 2019), 149.
49. Elliot R. Wolfson, *The Duplicity of Philosophy's Shadow: Heidegger, Nazism and the Jewish Other* (New York: Columbia University Press, 2018), xv.
50. Wolfson, *Duplicity*.
51. Shaul Magid, "Rethinking Martin Heidegger, the Jews and Judaism: Shaul Magid on Elliot Wolfson's *The Duplicity of Philosophy Shadow*: Heidegger, Nazism and the Jewish Other," Marginalia (September 28, 2018), available at https://marginalia.lareviewofbooks.org/heidegger-and-the-holocuast

52. Wolfson, *Duplicity*, xix.
53. See Thomas Sheehan, *Making Sense of Heidegger: A Paradigm Shift* (London and New York: Rowman & Littlefield, 2015).
54. Elliot R. Wolfson, *Heidegger and Kabbalah: Hidden Gnosis and the Path of Poiesis* (Bloomington: Indiana University Press, 2019). For an insightful and useful review of this remarkable book see Shaul Magid, "Heidegger and Kabbalah: Shaul Magid on Elliot Wolfson," *Marginalia* (January 29, 2021), available at https://marginalia.lareviewofbooks.org/heidegger-and-kabbalah/
55. Michael E. Zimmerman, *Heidegger's Confrontation with Modernity: Technology, Politics, Art* (Bloomington: Indiana University Press, 1990), 138.
56. David Couzens Hoy, "Heidegger and the Hermeneutic Turn," in *The Cambridge Companion to Heidegger*, 2nd ed., ed. Charles R. Guignon (Cambridge: Cambridge University Press, 2006 [1993]), 179.
57. Mark A. Wrathall, "Truth and Essence of Truth in Heidegger's Thought," in *The Cambridge Companion to Heidegger*, ed. Charles R. Guignon (Cambridge: Cambridge University Press, 2006 [1993]), 258.
58. Sheehan, *Making Sense of Heidegger*, 84.
59. Sheehan, *Making Sense of Heidegger*, 86.
60. Martin Heidegger, "Letter on Humanism," in his *Basic Writings,* ed. David Ferrell Krell, revised and expanded edition (London: HarperPerennial, 2008 [1977]), 213–66, citation on 237.
61. Mark Wrathall, *How to Read Heidegger* (New York: W. W. Norton, 1993), 89.
62. Wrathall, *How to Read Heidegger*, 94. That "language sets the world in motion" is not so different from the biblical worldview in which God spoke and the world came into existence. Although Heidegger rejected Catholicism in 1919, he was too immersed in the Christian worldview, especially its medieval mysticism, to let go of its imagery and mythic language.
63. Wolfson, *Language, Eros, Being*; Elliot R. Wolfson, *Aleph, Mem, Tau: Kabbalistic Musings on Time, Truth, and Death* (Los Angeles and Berkeley: University of California Press, 2006).
64. Elliot R. Wolfson, "Overstep/Underfoot: Envisioning the Heartland," in *Pathwings: Philosophical & Poetic Reflections on the Hermeneutics of Time & Language* (Barrytown, NY: Station Hill, 2004), 228.
65. Wolfson, "Overstep/Underfoot."
66. Wolfson, "Overstep/Underfoot."
67. Wolfson, "Overstep/Underfoot," 230.
68. Wolfson, "Overstep/Underfoot," 231.
69. Wolfson, "Overstep/Underfoot," 228.
70. Heidegger juxtaposed "calculative thinking" to "meditative thinking," another term for poetic thinking. See Capobianco, *Engaging Heidegger*, 64–66.
71. See George L. Mosse, *The Crisis of German Ideology: Intellectual Origins of the Third Reich* (New York: Grosset & Dunlap, 1964); Jeffrey Herff, *Reactionary Modernism, Technology, Culture and Politics in Weimar and the Third Reich* (New York: Cambridge University Press, 1984).
72. Heidegger's indebtedness to these critics of modernity is discussed in detail in Zimmerman, *Heidegger's Confrontation with Modernity*, 3–93.

73. Max Weber, "Science as Vocation," in *The Vocation Lectures*, ed. David Owen and Tracy B. Strong, trans. Rodney Livingstone (Indianapolis: Hackett, 2004).
74. The difference between Weber and Heidegger regarding disenchantment might reflect the fact that Heidegger came from peasant stock, grew up in a small rural town, and was emotionally tied to the landscape of the Black Forest. Heidegger composed most of his works in the ski cabin he owned and was an avid skier. In his skiing he might have experienced the oneness of "the fourfold" he theorized about. See Adam Sharr, *Heidegger's Hut* (Cambridge: MIT Press, 2006).
75. Martin Heidegger, "The Question Concerning Technology," in *The Question Concerning Technology and Other Essays*, trans. William Lovitt (New York: HarperPerennial, 2013 [1977]), 3–49.
76. Bruce V. Foltz, "On Heidegger and the Interpretation of the Environmental Crisis," *Environmental Ethics* 6, no. 4 (1984): 323–38.
77. Heidegger, "The Question Concerning Technology," 14.
78. Foltz, "On Heidegger," 328.
79. Martin Heidegger, "Memorial Address," in *Discourse on Thinking*, trans. John M. Anderson and E. Hans Freund (New York: Harper and Row, 1966), 50.
80. Foltz, "On Heidegger," 331.
81. For Heidegger's interpretation of Hölderlin's poem see Martin Heidegger, ". . . Poetically Man Dwells . . . ," in Hofstadter, *Poetry, Language, Thought*, 211–27.
82. Andrew J. Mitchell, *The Fourfold: Reading the Late Heidegger* (Evanston, IL: Northwestern University Press, 2015), 3.
83. Susanne Claxton, "Poetry and the Gods: From Gestell to Gelassenheit," in *Heidegger on Technology*, ed. Aaron James Wendland, Christopher Merwin, and Christos Hadjioannou (New York: Rutledge, 2019), 226–42, citation on 233.
84. Heidegger, "Building Dwelling Thinking," in Hofstadter, *Poetry, Language, Thought*, 149.
85. Charles Taylor, *A Secular Age* (Cambridge: MA; Harvard University Press, 2007). The "immanent frame" is the "default position," of modernity, the "unbelief" of exclusive humanism characteristic of the secular age. The literature on the "immanent frame" is too large to be cited here.
86. Claxton, "Poetry and the Gods," 234.
87. Lisa D. Campolo, "Derrida and Heidegger: The Critique of Technology and the Call to Care," *Journal of the American Academy of Religion* 53, no. 3 (1985): 431–48, citation on 442.
88. See John D. Caputo, *The Mystical Element in Heidegger's Thought* (New York: Fordham University Press, 1986 [1978]). Caputo's reading of Heidegger and Eckhart in tandem anticipated and perhaps also inspired Wolfson's reading of Heidegger and Kabbalah in tandem.
89. This story is related in detail by Michael E. Zimmerman, "From Deep Ecology to Integral Ecology: A Retrospective Study," *The Trumpeter* 30, no. 2 (2014): 247–68. As the scope of Heidegger's antisemitism became better known, Zimmerman's attitude changed from ardent support to sober critique, recognizing the potential eco-fascism of Heidegger's poetic thinking.

90. For example, see Bruce V. Foltz, *Inhabiting the Earth: Heidegger, Environmental Metaphysics and Nature* (London: Humanities Press, 1995); Ladelle McWhorter, ed., *Heidegger and the Earth: Essays in Environmental Philosophy*, 2nd expanded ed. (Toronto: University of Toronto Press, 2009); Casey Rentmeester, *Heidegger and the Environment* (London and New York: Rowman & Littlefield, 2016).
91. Trish Glazebrook, "Heidegger and Ecofeminism," in *Re-Reading the Cannon: Feminist Interpretation of Heidegger* (State College, PA: Pennsylvania State University Press, 2001), 221–51, citation on p. 242. See also Susanne Claxton, *Heidegger's Gods: An Ecofeminist Perspective* (London and New York: Rowman & Littlefield, 2017).
92. See Steven Schwarzschild, "The Unnatural Jew," *Environmental Ethics* 6, no. 4 (1984): 347–62, reprinted in *Judaism and Environmental Ethics, A Reader*, ed. Martin D. Yaffe (Lanham, MD: Lexington Books, 2001), 267–82; Michael Wyschogrod, "Judaism and the Sanctification of Nature," *Melton Journal* 24 (1991): 5–7; reprinted in *Judaism and Environmental Ethics: A Reader*, ed. Martin D. Yaffe (Lanham MD: Lexington Books, 2001), 289–96.
93. See Hava Tirosh-Samuelson, "Caring for Nature: Jonas vs. Heidegger," in *Pathways into German-Jewish Intellectual and Religious History: Studies in Conversation with Christian Wiese*, ed. Menachem Fisch, Heiko Schultz, and Stephen Vogt (Berlin: De Gruyter, forthcoming).
94. See Roger S. Gottlieb, *A Spirituality of Resistance: Finding a Peaceful Heart and Protecting the Earth* (Lanham, MD: Rowman & Littlefield, 2003).
95. See Eric Katz, *Anne Frank's Tree: Nature's Confrontation with Technology, Dominance and the Holocaust* (Winwick, UK: White Horse Press, 2015); Katz, "The Holocaust as an Environmental Problem," *Journal of Genocide Research* (2021), https://doi.org/10.1080/14623528.2021.1924588.

FEAR AND THE FEMININE

Kabbalistic Theurgy of the Negative Commandments

LEORE SACHS-SHMUELI

THIS STUDY ADDRESSES THE ROLE OF FEAR AND ITS ESSENTIAL RELATIONship with the feminine by Kabbalists as one of the predominant driving forces behind the negative cult. In analyzing the association between the feminine, fear, and prohibitions, I will build upon the presumption that guided Elliot Wolfson's pathbreaking studies of kabbalistic ethics combined with his analysis of the role of gender in kabbalistic texts. From the point of ethics, his following premise will serve as a working premise: "There is a reciprocal relationship between ethos cultivated by kabbalists and their ontology, that is, the values they hold are expressions of their understanding of the nature of being."[1] I expand this working assumption, highlighting the emotional function as an essential aspect of the rationalization of the commandments.[2] Or, as formulated by Gaston Bacherlard, "to imbue objects or actions with emotion is almost always thereby to valorize them."[3] Delineating the complex and rich history of fear as valorizing actions in kabbalistic texts and their historical context is outside the scope of the current paper. Rather, I focus solely on the connection between fear and the negative commandments, which on the one hand reveals the importance of treating prohibitions as a unique category in kabbalistic rationalizations of the commandments, but on the other hand, their inferior and temporal status. My analysis will delineate how Kabbalists associated the "terrible Feminine" archetype[4] with the divine Mothers—*Binah* and *Shekhinah*[5]—and the role they ascribed to it to secure the observance of Jewish law.

FEAR AND PROHIBITIONS

Rationalizations of prohibitions are formulated in ways that help readers navigate the internal struggle between the divine word and the evil inclination. The existing literature largely focuses on rationalizations of the commandments as encouraging the continued practice of ritual, examining the meanings that the Kabbalists attributed to ritual in order to inspire followers to continue its practice.[6] Rarely do scholars touch upon Kabbalists' active efforts to develop justifications for the negation of desire,[7] avoiding committing a transgression, the internal and external battles involved in guarding oneself against prohibitions, and the dread of the forbidden.

Elliot Wolfson discussed the key principles of the system of rationalizations expounded by the Castilian Kabbalists and examined the commandments as fulfilling a divine need, as the basis for the world's existence, and as dividing between good and evil.[8] In kabbalistic literature, this conflict is also reflected in (or projected onto) the external fight between demonic powers and the deity, transforming it into myths of cosmic battles.[9] As we shall see, fear came to be associated with the system of negative commandments and the feminine. Nevertheless, although medieval writers distinguished categorically and even essentially between the positive and negative cults, they also sought to avoid the dualism that could result from such a distinction: they emphasized the role of fear in positive observance as well as the significance of love in avoiding sin. Thus, while Kabbalists sought to accentuate the role of fear by feminizing it and attaching it to the "terrible" aspects, as a helpful tool for diminishing the desire for prohibited objects and actions, they also saw this as a transitional step and temporal stage before the containment of the left in the right, the female in the male.

Various scholars have demonstrated how Kabbalistic rationalizations of the commandments encouraged the continued practice of ritual and have examined the meanings that the Kabbalists attributed to ritual in order to inspire followers to continue its practice.[10] These studies suggest that kabbalistic texts played an edifying cultural role, enhancing social avoidance of deviant and prohibited actions.[11] I would like to add to these voices both the emphasis on the categorical difference between the negative and positive commandments, and the emotional aspect, as well as borrow the formulation offered by studies of pastoral emotions in the Middle Ages, "Hatred, fear, and cruelty on the one side, love on the other: such were the human passions that animated the masses. [. . .] Moralizing humanity by shaping its imagination and inner life, it thus contributed to the 'civilizing process' within the West."[12] Although the central category of fear in Jewish tradition has rarely been studied, the few academic studies regarding this topic usually emphasize the disparagement of fear in Jewish literature, in contrast to love, or the lower status of the fear of punishment (*yirah tata'a* or servile fear) vs. the "internal" fear unconditioned by retribution (*yirah ila'a* or filial fear).[13] Although this faithfully reflects the attitudes expressed in the various texts, it overlooks a central point: many works endeavor to preserve and foster fear by appropriating and molding it for different sectors of society.

My analysis seeks to explore the role of fear and the feminine in kabbalistic works as serving to enhance internalized discipline, but also promoting a split genderized view of emotions, in which the negative emotion of fear is inferior and associated with the Divine Feminine.

FEAR AS A MORAL ATTITUDE

Before embarking on a textual analysis of the medieval works, it is important to define the categories applied herein. I propose that the term fear (*yira'h* in Hebrew, *dehilu* in Medieval zoharic Aramaic, *ha'uf* in Arabic) designated the moral attitude toward a negative action combined with a negative emotion in the context of observing the commandments. Accordingly, when fear is used to induce obedience, this reflects not (only) a mental attitude of awe toward the metaphysical being of God but also a moral commitment to avoiding transgression. This moral attitude is oriented toward prevention—not doing evil, avoiding what is wrong.[14] It arouses the negative feelings of terror and fright associated with the consequences of sin.

The use of fear in medieval kabbalistic works followed the biblical application of this concept, as defined by B. T. Arnold in his analysis of its application in Deuteronomy: "This root yr' has a broad lexical field that includes the nuance of respectful awe or reverence, on the one hand, but also terror, on the other hand."[15] In rabbinic texts (mainly those composed before the destruction of the Temple), the designations "sin-fearing" and "God-fearing" were applied to persons who scrupulously observed the commandments and were careful to avoid transgression.[16] Furthermore, many rabbinic texts instruct their readers regarding how to attain a mental state of attention, awareness, and introspection in order to intensify the anxiety that guards against sin.[17] In kabbalistic texts, the use of this term precludes the possibility of simple awe or fidelity or the reduction of a normative commandment to mere loyalty and obedience; rather, it includes also affective and cognitive connotations of fright and dread.[18] On the lower moral level, this negative emotion can be linked to an external negative consequence of sin, namely punishment; on the higher level, an internal negative value is associated with it, for example, failing to acquire moral perfection, tainting the soul's perfection, distancing oneself from God or, in the kabbalistic framework, failing to fulfill one's responsibility toward the deity and, as a theurgic consequence, causing harm to the divine.[19] Hence, fear (*yirah*) as a moral emotion oriented toward avoiding wrong is strongly associated with the negative commandments that require the avoidance and restriction of forbidden actions, commandments that prescribe and forbid commissions. This moral attitude is intertwined with negative feelings of dread, horror, guilt, and anxiety at the defects, harm, and negative consequences deriving from sin. Psychological research concerning moral emotions (such as shame, guilt, fear, and regret) has shed light on human motivational systems and their relationship to moral standards.[20] Some have argued that moral emotions provide a motivational force to do good and to avoid doing bad. Hence, one should not perceive Jewish literature addressing moral behavior as relying solely on the intellectual discursive realm; rather, it also draws on the emotional-moral apparatus.

CATEGORICAL DIFFERENTIATION BETWEEN POSITIVE AND NEGATIVE IN MEDIEVAL LEGAL WORKS

As I argued elsewhere, in kabbalistic literature, prohibitions constitute a focal category in religious law and culture differentiated from ritual.[21] By contrast to ritual, which invites active performance and was associated by Kabbalists with the male potency, prohibitions require passivity and thus were associated with the feminine. Prohibitions restrict interactions with tempting objects, very commonly themselves associated with females, demanding avoidance and preventive steps. The term "prohibitions" here defines the system of negative commandments, framing this large corpus as a system of prohibitions that practitioners are reluctant to obey, constantly battling with the temptation to violate them.

Discerning and categorically distinguishing between positive and negative commandments is not only a sociological tool employed by scholars of religion but rather can be traced back to ancient Jewish sources. Indeed, rabbinical writings categorically distinguish between the negative and the positive commandments, as coined in Bavli Makkot 23b: "Rabbi Simlai taught: There were 613 mitzvot stated to Moses in the Torah, consisting of 365 prohibitions corresponding to the number of days in the solar year, and 248 positive mitzvot corresponding to the number of a person's limbs."[22] In the Middle Ages, beginning with Maimonides's *Book of the Commandments* (*Sefer ha-Mitzvot*), this distinction was reinforced by the literary structure employed in codifications of Jewish law: they divide the commandments into two groups—"positive" and "negative."[23] In Maimonides's legal examination, negative commandments are defined by both punishments and prohibitions, as he concludes in his discussion of the fourteenth principle in his introduction to the *Book of the Commandments* (also known as *The Fourteen Principles of Maimonides*): "Wherever the Torah says that he who commits a certain act is to be put to death, or is subject to extinction—that particular act is forbidden to be done, and constitutes a negative commandment."[24]

However, this division between negative and positive commandments was not the only organizational means utilized by Jewish scholars. Indeed, among Maimonides's predecessors we find various literary arrangements of the commandments, and he himself, in his *Code*, preferred a thematic structure. Yet in the *Book of the Commandments*, Maimonides followed the dual logic of separating negative from positive. Though medieval authors had at their disposal a range of editorial tools for arranging the Jewish legal corpus, the systematic division of the commandments into positive and negative was adopted by Kabbalists in Christian Spain, in Italy at the end of the thirteenth century, and subsequently in Byzantium. In the *Book of the Pomegranate* (*Sefer ha-Rimon*, 1287), Moses de Leon followed the structure of Maimonides's *Book of the Commandments*, arranging his book into two sections—positive and negative commandments. Joseph of Hamadan's *Rationalization of the Commandments* (*Sefer Ta'amei ha-Mizvot*), written in the late thirteenth or early fourteenth century in Castilian Spain, is likewise divided into two separate books, *The Book of Rationales of Positive Commandments*[25] and *The Book of the Rationales of Negative Commandments.*[26] The same division is found in Italian texts dating from the end of the thirteenth century and the beginning of the fourteenth century, for example the *Rationale of the Commandments* by Rabbi Menachem Recanati. The "*Piquda*," a zoharic unit,[27] similar to the slightly later *Ra'aya Meheimna*,[28] followed the categorical differentiation between positive and negative, as evidenced by the fact that both focused entirely on the positive commandments and did not conflate "prohibitions" with them. Other later compositions, such as *Sefer ha-Kannah* in the fifteenth century, Radbaz's (Rabbi David ibn Zimra) *Sefer Metsudat David: Ta'amei ha-Mizvot* (*Rationale of the Commandments*),[29] and the Lurianic works and their recensions—Rabbi Haim Vital's *Sha'ar ha-Mitzvot (The Gate of the Commandments)*[30] and *Likkutei Torah: Ta'amei ha-Mizvot*[31]—placed the rationalization of commandments at the center of their speculations yet employed alternative systems of organization.[32]

I would argue that the literary structures utilized by Kabbalists to organize their rationalizations of the commandments reflect structures of meaning and practical considerations. For example, organizing the commandments according to the sequence of the biblical portions would yield a Torah commentary focusing on practical aspects, in turn routinizing the learning by dividing it into weekly portions or making the content more easily accessible, enabling the reader to find the commandment in the related portion. The division into positive and negative cannot be explained by such practical reasons, since it does not routinize learning or make the commentary more accessible (many commandments have both positive and negative aspects, thus necessitating a separation of the related discussion into two distinctive sections). This literary structure was primarily intended to reinforce the categorical difference between the positive precepts and the prohibitions: they were understood not only as legally-formally different but also as representing two distinct, essential religious-emotional attitudes, fear and love. This difference, as we shall see, was further reinforced by medieval Kabbalists through metaphysical categories.

FEAR AND LOVE: ESSENTIALISM IN THE GERONIC VIEW OF POSITIVE AND NEGATIVE COMMANDMENTS

From the earliest systematic treatise in the genre of kabbalistic rationalization, a pivotal work composed by Rabbi Ezra of Gerona, who was active in the second quarter of the thirteenth century,[33] the distinction between negative and positive commandments was infused with an essentialist conceptualization, albeit following a more complex literary structure.[34] From this point onward, the difference between the commandments was not understood merely as a legal discernment but rather became tied to their theosophical origin in the sefirotic realm; the positive commandments were regarded as originating from the masculine and higher side, while the negative commandments originate from the feminine and lower one, the *Shekhinah*:

> And you need to know that all *mizvot* are dependent on two essential principles (*'iqarim*): the "imperative" and the "prohibitive" *mizvot*. The imperative *mizvot* issue from the attribute *Zakhor*, while the "prohibitive" *mizvot* derive from the attribute *Shamor*. It is definitively known that *Zakhor* and *Shamor* correspond to two attributes of the Holy One, blessed be He. Thus, the one who acts according to his Master's commands and fulfills them—proceeds from the attribute of Love. This is the supreme level and ultimate attribute, and [thus] it corresponds to the imperative *mizvot*. But the one who desists from doing wrong due to fear of his Master—proceeds from the attribute of Fear; which is lower than the attribute of Love, just as the prohibitive *mizvot* are on a level lower than the imperative *mizvot*.[35]

Having established this metaphysical difference between the positive and negative, Rabbi Ezra added a psychological dimension that ties the positive commandments to the attribute of Love and the negative commandments to Fear. These attributes constitute not only the essence of the law but of all people, who "by nature" are comprised of them.[36] Thus, the essential dual structure of the divine realm, the legal codification, and human nature essentially correspond with one another. Love and Fear correspond to right and left, good and bad inclinations, male and female, and the good and bad angels accompanying a person. The positive imperative reflects the good inclination, which strives to know and unite with God, while its negative counterpart seeks to nullify the bad inclination, subordinating it to the desire to do good.[37] In other words, the purpose of the positive commandments is to love and to "know the Holy one,"[38] implying not only knowledge but union, whereas the negative ones, which are considered lower, direct man to avoid "wrongdoing for fear of Him."[39] The aspect of fear may indeed constitute the essence of the difference between ritual and taboo, between the positive imperative and the prohibition. Ezra does not only associate the feminine with the negative commandments and fear, genderizing these emotions, but also highlights that the feminine is inferior to the male qualities. The temptation for crossing prohibitions is associated with the seductive Feminine, and though it is necessary, it is subordinated to the active male theurgy.

These categorical differences between positive and negative commandments were further alluded to by Nachmanides in his *Commentary on the Torah*:

> the attribute of *Zakhor* is alluded to in a positive commandment and issues forth from the attribute of Love to that of Mercy, for he who does his master's command is beloved of him and his master shows him mercy. But the attribute of *Shamor* is alluded to in a negative commandment, which goes to the attribute of Judgement (*Din*)[40] and issues forth from that of Fear, for he who guards himself from doing anything which does not please his master does so out of fear for him.[41]

Here, following Ezra of Gerona's tradition, Nachmanides further entrenched the identification of the positive commandments with the divine masculine attributes—Love (the fourth *sefirah*) and Mercy (the sixth *sefirah*)—and between the negative commandments and the feminine attributes: Fear (fifth *sefirah*) and Judgment (third or tenth *sefirah*).[42] By revealing their equivalent divine source, he differentiated between the negative and positive precepts ontologically, not only formally. Furthermore, he added a human moral-emotional state to the theosophic equation, expressed through observance of the different types of commandments.[43] When performing a positive commandment, one actively expresses the positive emotion of love of God. By contrast, when one refrains from a prohibited action and submits to a negative commandment, one acts out of fear of his master. This difference and hierarchy accounts for the different categories of punishment for disobeying each type of percept:

> It is for this reason that a positive commandment is greater than a negative commandment, just as love is greater than fear, for he who fulfills and observes the will of his master with his body and his possessions is greater than he who guards himself from doing that which is not pleasing to him. This is why the Rabbis have said that a positive commandment overrides a negative commandment.[44] And it is for this reason that punishment for violation of the negative commandment is great—the court punishing the transgressor with whipping or death—whereas no punishment at all is meted out in the case of failure to fulfill the positive commandments.[45]

Citing the legal difference formalized by the rabbis, Nahmanides concluded that, on the one hand, a positive commandment can override a negative commandment, thus its performance is of greater value; yet, on the other hand, the violation of a negative commandment is a greater sin than omitting to perform a positive percept.[46] In this, Nahmanides followed the genderized and hierarchical perspective of law and emotions formulated by Ezra of Gerona, and through his influential status as a religious leader, Kabbalist, and commentator, spread this message throughout Jewish literature. The feminine would be from now on permanently associated with the negative commandments, and the fear of punishment would overlap with the fear of death associated with the Terrible Mother.

NEGATIVE AND POSITIVE: TWO THAT BECOME ONE IN DE LEON'S RATIONALIZATION OF THE COMMANDMENTS

While the ontological differentiation between positive and negative commandments constituted the default stance espoused by kabbalistic texts, fear of the dualism suggested by the dichotomy between male and female, God and the demonic, required their theological treatment. Indeed, while further developing discussions regarding the dual essence of the precepts, some Kabbalists emphasized that the two systems serve one source and one single purpose. For example, despite the categorical differentiation between positive and negative commandments that led him to divide his *Book of Rationalizations of the Commandments* (*Sefer ha-Rimon*) into two separate parts (positive and negative), De Leon argued that the ultimate intention is the union of the divine bride and groom, *Shekhinah* and *Yesod*:

> There[47] we have been roused to decipher the matter of all the positive and negative commandments, which are the secret of *Zakhor* and *Shamor* [. . .] the secret of *Shamor*, the bride in her delights, which includes the secret of *Zakhor*, and in him she achieves her completeness, in the secret of her actions, and she divests herself of her dress of captivity. [. . .] And we have also written in the first book the secret of the positive commandments by designating them in one book, and the negative commandments in a separate one, far be it for them to be separate in the secret of knowledge (*da'at*), since the mind (*da'at*) returns to the cause of their being for them to unite and conjoin with each other, and not to be separated.[48]

Following the construction of Rabbi Ezra, de Leon identifies the negative commandments with the Bride, the *Shekhinah*. Here he develops an erotic language, to which Rabbi Ezra had alluded, further amplifying it. While the system of rationalizing positive ritual mainly focused on reparation of the godhead, uniting the *Shekhinah* and *Kudsha Brich Hu* through positive motivation, such as uniting with the divine,[49] rationalizing taboos and prohibitions explicated the anxiety caused by separation of the divine couple: "If, God forbid, one transgresses a negative commandment, it is as if he caused a divorce." The goal of the commandments is the theurgic unification of the *Shekhinah*, the bride, and her groom, the masculine divine entity.[50] Nevertheless, in these postulations, the division between negative and positive, feminine and masculine, is a temporary stage before the ultimate unification. As Wolfson argued, viewing the differentiation between male and female in these texts as only a transitory step toward its erasure challenges the eternal status of law and suggests a hypernomian stance.[51] Hence, the kabbalistic anxiety regarding separation and multiplicity led de Leon to construct the purpose of rituals and taboos as overcoming difference via the union between the divine male and female.[52]

NEGATIVE COMMANDMENTS AND THE OTHER SIDE: FEAR OF THE DEMONIC OTHER IN *TIQQUNEI ZOHAR*

The negative ontology attributed to the divine (to the left and feminine side of the *sefirot*) by Rabbi Ezra's theosophy was further demonized by later Kabbalists, who referred to the impurity outside of the Deity as a threatening force. *Tiqqunei Zohar*, Tiqqun 21, elaborates on the division between negative and positive: the fear that characterizes the negative commandments is not only fear of the left side of the Deity (the harsh divine judgment), but of the demonic Other, Satan:[53]

> And make me savory food, such as I love (Genesis 27:4), from the positive commandments. And not those I hate, from the negative commandments, that are reliant upon the fear (*dehilu*) of fear (*yirah*). And they are for banishing Satan from them, so he does not come near the Chair, which is the Heart, to prosecute the holy limbs, which are Israel, and *Shekhinah*, the Heart, between them.[54]
>
> [. . .] The positive commandments are the Holy One, Blessed Be He's, food, and the negative commandments are nourishment for Samael, when one transgresses them.[55]

Tiqqunei ha-Zohar thus adapts the theosophy advanced by Ezra of Gerona, dividing between the negative and positive commandments not only in accordance with their theosophical divine entities. Rather, according to a dualistic view, when one transgresses a negative commandment, he worships the demonic Other, Samael. This generalized the biblical idea of the sacrifices as the food of the Deity, asserting that all commandments feed supernal entities: the performance of positive commandments nourishes God, while the negative actions feed the Other side. When one avoids crossing the forbidden boundaries, it not only protects the Jewish community from demonic persecution but also guards the *Shekhinah* from the dangers of Satan. Adhering to the prohibitions guards against Satan, who threatens the body of the nation and its heart, the *Shekhinah*.[56] *Tiqqunei ha-Zohar* greatly expanded the minor dualism suggested by Ezra of Gerona's division into left and right: sin not only reveals the harsh judgment from within the divine but strengthens an external entity that threatens the Divine Feminine. In this way, *Tiqqunei Zohar* drew fear of violating prohibitions to a new climax. From a gender perspective, the fearful aspect of the negative commandment in this text is transferred to the demonic male, which is a source of horror and terror. The *Shekhinah* is in danger herself, not the source of danger. On the one hand, this could be attributed to the centrality of the *Shekhinah* as an object of worship, motivating the author to separate the demonic aspects associated with her image; on the other hand, he also reduced the power attributed to the *Shekhinah* as an object of fear by stressing her passive role in the system of theurgy dependent on human deeds.

THE PRECEDENCE AND TEMPORAL ROLE OF FEAR IN IBN GABBAI'S *AVODAT HA-QODESH*

In this concluding section, I will analyze how the previous Spanish kabbalistic traditions associating fear and prohibitions crystallized in one of the most representative works of Spanish Kabbalah bringing the theurgical power of the commandments into stark relief. Meir Ibn Gabbai, a Spanish Kabbalist who lived in the late fifteenth and early sixteenth centuries, engaged with the categorical split between negative and positive commandments. Like de Leon, while granting fear an essential status in the understanding of human struggle in observing the commandments, he was also committed to overcoming any dualistic assumptions that could logically be inferred from the split system he was illustrating:

> The secret of this matter is known to the sages of truth (the kabbalists): that the part of the Torah which is called negative commandments, that we were prohibited to commit is in order to distance ourselves from the impure side, the secret of the slag that was separated and went out, from which stem all types of human passions and pleasures, which are stumbling blocks and barriers, to be caught in the trap of temptations, to stumble in their net, and to reside in their impurity. And because the shell precedes the fruit and the darkness comes before the light, it is necessary that fear of sin take precedence.[57]

According to Ibn Gabbai, the temptations people experience stem not merely from mental or psychological causes but correspond to external impure beings and their evil reality. He adapted earlier kabbalistic terms, "shell precedes the fruit"[58] and "darkness that comes before the light,"[59] to frame their existence teleologically. One must feel fear in order to achieve this goal: "It is necessary that fear of sin take precedence."[60] The human struggle with temptation, prompted by the fear of violating the negative commandments, is part of a divine process of ontological redemption. The impurity, which originated in the Deity itself, was emitted and now rules the material world. Human adherence to the commandments fulfills a "divine need"; they participate in the divine process of eliminating the slag, illuminating the darkness.[61] When humans overcome impurity through the guidance of the negative commandments, they help the divine and the entire cosmos progress toward completeness. Nevertheless, while Ibn Gabbai illustrated the necessary role of fear in divine worship, he also emphasized, like de Leon, the unity of the negative and the positive aspects of law and the Deity, dissolving differences between them:

> [t]he positive and negative commandments are one Torah. The positive commandments stem from the attribute of *zakhor* (remember) and ascend to it, and the negative commandments stem from *shamor* (keep), the secret of *yirah* (fear, awe), and signify it through the secret of punishments [. . .] since when he says: "Fear God (Ecc. 12, 13)" he implies that the positive commandments include the negative commandments, and when he said "and keep His commandments" (idem.) he implied that the negative commandments include the positive ones, and when he said "and this is the whole of man" (idem.), since these two parts of the commandments constitute the whole man; and if one part is missing, he is not a man. And therefore, Fear which is associated with the negative commandments is a large part of man, and he needs to be crowned by it at first, since it precedes all other crowns.[62]

Ibn Gabbai here borrowed the terms used by the Spanish Kabbalists, equating the imperative of *Zakhor* to the divine male, the positive commandments and the emotion of love, on the one side; and the imperative of *Shamor*, to the divine Female, negative commandments and fear. Following the steps of de Leon, while emphasizing the distinctive and central role of fear, he also insisted on the unity of the Godhead, annulling an essential status of the feminine as other. While Ibn Gabbai preserved the lower place of fear in the hierarchy, he asserted it is the gate and first crown one should obtain in his ascent on the ladder leading to the perfection of man in his worship of God.

CONCLUSIONS

This paper discusses the role ascribed to fear by kabbalistic rationalizations of the negative commandments, and how they genderized these legal categories and emotional stances.[63] Kabbalistic rationalizations of the commandments imbued the legal category of prohibition with an essentialist theosophic worldview, in which negative commandments were associated with the Divine Terrible Feminine. Their formulations reveal that they were actively engaging with the human temptation to violate prohibitions and the anxiety this temptation awakens. Indeed, two components, desire and fear, constituted the core of the system that sought to rationalize the negative commandments. Most Kabbalists shared the genderized split of emotions, law, and theosophy, viewing fear as a feminine necessity but an inferior emotional quality associated with the Divine Terrible Feminine and prohibitions; while they were at the same time committed to overcoming the dualistic theology that could be inferred by it. In sum, fear was both understood as a degraded reason to observe the divine law, but also as necessary in stimulating social compliance with the Jewish legal code.

ACKNOWLEDGMENT

To my revered teacher, Elliot R. Wolfson, from your eager disciple, who walks in the lineage of your teachings, as a disciple of your disciple. Just as you fulfill the directive to "raise many disciples" (Avot 1:1), may your wisdom echo through the generations, with my students becoming yours, and beyond.

NOTES

1. Elliot R. Wolfson, "Beyond Good and Evil: Hypernomian Transmorality and Delimiting the Limit," in *Venturing Beyond: Law and Morality in Kabbalistic Mysticism* (New York: Oxford University Press, 2006), 186.
2. See Rob Boddice's argument in *The History of Emotions* (Manchester: Manchester University

Press, 2018), 192–93: "The *value* of experience is and has always been established by or filtered through what experience *felt* like [...] social and cultural instruments of power and influence that give meaning—in this case—punitive meaning to the code."

3. Gaston Bacherlard, "Libido et connaissance objective," *La Formationde l'esprit scientifique*, 14th ed. (Paris: Vrin, 1989), 183–209, as paraphrased and translated into English by Lorraine Datson, "The Moral Economy of Science," *Osiris* 10 (1995): 4.
4. Erich Neumann, *The Great Mother: An Analysis of the Archetype*, trans. Ralph Manheim (Princeton: Princeton University Press, 1963), 147–208; Neumann, *The Fear of the Feminine and Other Essays on Feminine Psychology*, trans. Boris Matthews et al. (Princeton: Princeton University Press, 1994), 227–80. Though Neumann's theorizing is outdated and does not fit contemporary theorizing of gender, nonetheless I found it useful in introducing the fear of the female *sefirot*, especially in a kabbalistic framework that tends to essentialism.
5. For a different stance of the mother archetype in Kabbalah see Ḥaviva Pedaya, "The Great Mother: The Struggle between Nahmanides and the Zohar Circle," in *Temps i espais de la Girona Jueva: Actes del Simposi Internacional celebrat a Girona 23, 24 i 25 de març de 2009* (Girona: Patronat Call de Girona, 2011), 311–28; Ellen Davina Haskell, *Suckling at My Mother's Breasts: The Image of a Nursing God in Jewish Mysticism* (Albany: State University of New York Press, 2012). For Wolfson's criticism of scholarly attitudes rejecting the androcentric lens for understanding the kabbalistic portrayal of feminine images, see Elliot R. Wolfson, "Patriarchy and the Motherhood of God in Zoharic Kabbalah and Meister Eckhart," in *Envisioning Judaism: Studies in Honor of Peter Schäfer on the Occasion of His Seventieth Birthday*, ed. Ra'anan S. Boustan et al. (Tübingen: Mohr Siebeck, 2013), 1058–59, n. 30.
6. In the chapter concerning ritual in his book *On the Kabbalah and Its Symbolism* (New York: Schocken Books, 1969), 118–57, Gershom Scholem discusses the sabbath, festivals, and rituals connected with marriage, death, and more, but none of these analyses entail the rationalization of a prohibition or what Durkheim calls "the negative cult." Similarly, Moshe Idel focuses on the rationalization of commandments vis-à-vis ritual in his work *Enchanted Chains: Techniques and Rituals in Jewish Mysticism* (Los Angeles: Cherub Press, 2005). Compare also Maurizio Mottolese, *Bodily Rituals in Jewish Mysticism: The Intensification of Cultic Hand Gestures by Medieval Kabbalists* (Los Angeles: Cherub Press, 2016), 100–29. An exception is the doctoral thesis by Shilo Pachter, which focuses on the preservation of the covenant but does not phrase the discussion as concerning taboo. See Shilo Pachter, "Shmirat ha-Brit: The History of the Prohibition of Wasting Seed" (PhD dissertation, Hebrew University of Jerusalem, 2006). Ruth Kara-Ivanov Kaniel, who examines the taboo of forbidden sexual relations, emphasizes mainly the positive results of breaking the taboo and antinomian approaches. On this see Ruth Kara-Ivanov Kaniel, *Holiness and Transgression: Mothers of the Messiah in the Jewish Myth*, trans. Eugene D. Matanky with Ruth Kara-Ivanov Kaniel (Brighton, MA: Academic Studies Press, 2017), 86–111. Regarding antinomianism and "the secret of incest" in the Zohar, see also Kaniel, *Holiness and Transgression*, especially 124–45.
7. For exceptions stressing the role of asceticism see Elliot R. Wolfson, "Ascetism, Mysticism and Messianism: A Reappraisal of Schechter's Portrait of Sixteenth Century Safed," *JQR* 106, no. 2 (Spring 2016): 165–77; Elliot R. Wolfson, "Eunuchs Who Keep the Sabbath: Becoming

Male and the Ascetic Ideal in Thirteenth-Century Jewish Mysticism," in *Becoming Male in the Middle Ages,* ed. J. J. Cohen and B. Wheeler (New York: Garland, 1997), 151–85 [reprinted as a chapter in his book *Language Eros, Being*, 296–33]; David Biale, *Eros and the Jews: From Biblical Israel to Contemporary America* (New York: Basic Books, 1992), 109–13.

8. Elliot R. Wolfson, "Mystical Rationalization of the Commandments in *Sefer ha-Rimmon*," *Hebrew Union College Annual* 59 (1988): 217–51.

9. Regarding the role of the left powers in Kabbalah and possible Islamic contexts, see Michel Ebstein and Tzahi Weiss, "A Drama in Heaven: 'Emanation on the Left' in Kabbalah and a Parallel Cosmogonic Myth in Ismāʿīlī Literature," *History of Religions* 55, no. 2 (2015): 148–71. For the treatment of the "Other side" in the Zohar, see Isaiah Tishby, *The Wisdom of the Zohar: An Anthology of Texts, trans. David Goldstein* (London: Littman Library, 1991), III, 890–95. See also the insights into kabbalistic illustrations of the externalized combat with the demonic other in Nethaniel Berman, *Divine and Demonic in the Poetic Mythology of the Zohar: The "Other Side" of Kabbalah* (Leiden: Brill, 2018), 229: "One thereby transforms subjective ambivalence into objective ambivalence, human anxiety into an ontological struggle between antagonistic cosmic forces."

10. See note 6. Although here I touch upon the tension between law and its transgression, most of the text by Rabbi Joseph, on which my analysis is based, does not concern breaking a taboo but rather its authorization and a description of the damage and danger that its transgression entails.

11. Studies of Western and Islamic cultures stress the central role of emotions, including fear and hope, in the culturalization processes of internalization. Concerning the roles of fear and hope in Islamic mysticism, see Sara Sviri, *Perspectives on Early Islamic Mysticism: The World of al-Ḥakīm al-Tirmidhī and His Contemporaries* (London & New York: Routledge, 2020), 139–57. Regarding the function of fear in the pedagogy of the Catholic church, see Jean Delumeau, *Sin and Fear: The Emergence of a Western Guilt Culture, 13th–19th Centuries*, trans. Eric Nicholson (New York: St. Martin Press, 1990), 491–504.

12. Damien Boquet and Piroska Nagy, *Medieval Sensibilities: A History of Emotions in the Middle Ages*, trans. Robert Shaw (Cambridge: Polity Press, 2018), 235. With regard to the role of pastoral emotions and common emotions in the civilization process in the West (considering only the Christian context), see Boquet and Nagy, *Medieval Sensibilities*, 235–44.

13. See for example, Isaiah Tishby, *Wisdom of the Zohar*, III, 974–98. For the conservative and degraded role of fear versus the vitalizing, genuine religious role of love, see Rachel Elior, "The Innovation of Polish Ḥasidism," *Tarbiz* 62, no. 3 (1993): 381–432. For exceptions, emphasizing the constructive role of fear in the mystical experience that is evident in kabbalistic texts (although not in relationship to the commandments), see Yoni Garb, "Fear and Power in Renaissance Mediterranean Kabbalah," in *Fear and Its Representations: In the Middle Ages and Renaissance,* ed. Anne Scott and Cynthia Kosso (Turnhout: Brepols, 2002), 137–51; Yehuda Liebes, *Studies in the Zohar*, trans Arnold Schwartz et al. (Albany: State University of New York, 1993), 34–37. The Jewish distinctions resemble those offered by Bede, Peter Lombard, and Thomas Aquinas between "servile fear" (*timor servilis*) and "friendly fear" (*timor amicalis*) or filial fear (*timor filialis*). About these terms and the differences between

these theologians see Robert Miner, "Thomas Aquinas's Hopeful Transformation of Peter Lombard's Four Fears," *Speculum* 92, no. 4 (October 2017): 963–75.

14. For a comprehensive analysis of the different aspects of this moral imperative in Islam, see Michael Cook, *Forbidding Wrong in Islam* (Cambridge: Cambridge University Press, 2003).
15. Bill T. Arnold, "The Love-Fear Antinomy in Deuteronomy 5–11," *Vetus Testamentum* 61 (2002): 563.
16. Ephraim E. Urbach, *The Sages: Their Concepts and Beliefs*, trans. Israel Abrahams (Jerusalem: Magnes Press, 1975), 416.
17. Jonathan Wyn Schofer, *The Making of a Sage: A Study in Rabbinic Ethics* (Madison & London: University of Wisconsin Press, 2005), 147–60.
18. On this definition of the biblical root, see Arnold, "The Love-Fear Antinomy," 562–67.
19. Regarding the negative effects on the divine ("negative theurgy"), see Moshe Idel, *Kabbalah: New Perspectives* (New Haven: Yale University Press, 1988); Jonathan Garb, *Manifestation of Power in Jewish Mysticism: From the Rabbinic Literature to Safedian Kabbalah* [Hebrew] (Jerusalem: Magnes Press, 2005), 100–104. See also Haviva Pedaya, "'Flaw' and 'Correction' in the Concept of the Godhead in the Teachings of Rabbi Isaac the Blind" [Hebrew], *Jerusalem Studies in Jewish Thought* 6 (1986): 157–285. On the concept of flaw in the Zohar, especially relating to the feminine deity, see Shifra Asulin, "The Flaw and Its Correction: Impurity, the Moon, and the Shekhinah—A Broad Inquiry into Zohar 3:79 (Ahrei Mot)" [Hebrew], *Kabbalah* 22 (2010): 193–252.
20. Jerome Kroll and Elizabeth Egan, "Psychiatry and Moral Worry, and the Moral Emotions," *Journal of Psychiatric Practice* 10 (2004): 352–60; June P. Tangney, Jeff Stuewig, and Debra J. Mashek, "Moral Emotion and Moral Behavior," *Annual Review of Psychology* 58 (2007): 345–72.
21. Leore Sachs-Shmueli, "*The Rationale of the Negative Commandments* by R. Joseph Hamadan: A Critical Edition and Study of Taboo in the Time of the Composition of the Zohar: Volume 1" [Hebrew] (PhD dissertation, Bar Ilan University, 2018), 116–83; Sachs-Shmueli, "Maimonides's Rationalization of the Incest Taboo, Its Reception in Thirteenth-Century Kabbalah, and Their Affinity to Aquinas," *HTR* 114, no. 3 (2021): 371–92.
22. Aharon Shemesh, "The Development of the Terms 'Positive' and 'Negative' Commandments," *Tarbiz* 72, nos. 1–2 (2003): 133–50.
23. For a historical survey of post-Talmudic literary organizations and listings of the 613 commandments, see Marc D. Herman, "Systematizing God's Law: Rabbanite Jurisprudence in the Islamic World from the Tenth to the Thirteenth Centuries" (PhD dissertation, University of Pennsylvania, 2016), 1–32.
24. Moses Maimonides, *The Commandments: Sefer Ha-Mizvoth of Maimonides*, trans. Charles B. Chavel (London & New York: Soncino Press, 1967), 422. See also Herman, "Systematizing God's Law," 245: "Maimonides vociferously attacked enumerators who counted 'punishments' as a category distinct from negative commandments." Concerning Maimonides's principle of identifying a scriptural warning (*azharah*) and penalty (*'onesh*) for every prohibition as following the rabbis, see Herman, "Systematizing God's Law," 184–87. About the definition and history of the term prohibitions (negative commandments) in Maimonides's code,

see Albert D. Friedberg, *Crafting the 613 Commandments: Maimonides on the Enumeration, Classification and Formulation of the Scriptural Commandments* (Boston: Academic Studies Press, 2013), 18–20, 26, 32–37, 43–46.

25. Menachem Meier, "A Critical Edition of Sefer Ta'amey Ha-Mizwoth ('Book of Reasons of the Commandments') Attributed to Isaac Ibn Farhi / Section 1—Positive Commandments, with Introduction and Notes [Portions of Text in Hebrew]" (PhD dissertation, Brandeis University, 1974).
26. Sachs-Shmueli, "*The Rationale of the Negative Commandments*: Volume 2."
27. This appears as an independent work in manuscripts but in the printed versions was scattered in various locations. For an analysis of its independent structure, see Ephraim Gottlieb, "Ma'amarey ha-Piqudin she-ba-*Zohar*," *Qiryat Sefer* 48 (1973): 499–508. Reprinted in Gottlieb, *Meḥkarim be-Sifrut ha-Kabbalah*, ed. Joseph Hacker (Tel Aviv, 1976), 215–30.
28. For a study of the rationalization of the commandments in this work, see Pinchas Giller, *The Enlightened Will Shine: Symbolization and Theurgy in the Later Strata of the Zohar* (Albany: State University of New York Press, 1993), 59–128.
29. First edition Zholkva, 1862. An edited and annotated version was printed in Jerusalem, 2003.
30. This is Shmuel Vital's edition of his father's work, printed in Salonica, 1851 and in Jerusalem, 1905. On this work see Yosef Avivi, *Kabbala Luriana, II: The Lurianic Writings after 1620* [Hebrew] (Jerusalem: Ben-Zvi Institute, 2008), 690–91.
31. This was part of Meir Popper's edition of Vital's works in *Nof Etz Haim*, printed in Zholkva, 1875. On this Lurianic edition and its manuscripts, see Avivi, *Kabbala Luriana, II*, 652–54.
32. Regarding the content and structure of the *Raya Meheimna*, see Mordechai Rozanes, "Reasoning for the Commandments According to the 'Raaya Meheymna'" [Hebrew] (MA thesis, Haifa University, 2003). Concerning that of *Sefer ha-Kanah*, see Michal Kushnir Oron, "*The Sefer Ha-Peli'ah* and *the Sefer ha-Kanah*: Their Kabbalistic Principles, Social and Religious Criticism and Literary Composition" [Hebrew] (PhD dissertation, Hebrew University of Jerusalem, 1980).
33. Yakov M. Travis, "Kabbalistic Foundation of Jewish Spiritual Practice: Rabbi Ezra of Gerona—On the Kabbalistic Meaning of the Mizvot (Introduction—Annotated translation—Critical Hebrew Edition)" (PhD dissertation, Brandeis University, 2002): 8. For the integration of halakhic and kabbalistic interests in Ezra's literary treatment of the commandments, see Jacob Katz, "Halakhah and Kabbala—First Contracts" [Hebrew], *Zion* 44 (1979): 159–67. Further discussion of this Kabbalist can be found in Isaiah Tishby, "The Kabbalists T. Ezra and R. Ezriel and Their Place in the Gerona School" [Hebrew], *Zion* 9 (1944): 178–85. Regarding Ezra's concepts of theurgy, see Charles Mopsik, *Les Grands Textes de la Cabala: Les Rites qui Font Dieu* (Lagrasse: Verdier, 1993), 115–24.
34. Travis, "Kabbalistic Foundation of Jewish Spiritual Practice," 156–59.
35. I have used Travis's translation with some adaptations. See Travis, "Kabbalistic Foundation of Jewish Spiritual Practice," 171.
36. Travis, "Kabbalistic Foundation of Jewish Spiritual Practice," 173.
37. Travis, "Kabbalistic Foundation of Jewish Spiritual Practice," 174–75. "Since these two attributes (love and fear, groom and bride, positive and negative), the good inner inclination,

corresponding to imperatives and prohibition (*'asse* and *lo ta'ase*), are imprinted in human nature, the Torah and *mizvot* were given in the form of [both] imperative *mizvot* and prohibitive *mizvot*. [This is] in order to accustom and guide him in [developing] the good character attributes (*middot*), so that the corrupt inner inclination will be drawn after the good inner inclination and be nullified before it."

38. Travis, "Kabbalistic Foundation of Jewish Spiritual Practice," 171.
39. Travis, "Kabbalistic Foundation of Jewish Spiritual Practice," 172.
40. Chavel translated *Din* as "justice," but it is more accurate in this context to translate it as "Judgment," which has a harsher connotation. Furthermore, I added capitalization since Nachmanides alludes to the name of the *Sefirah Din*, not just a simple noun.
41. *Ramban (Nachmanides) Commentary on the Torah, Exodus* 20:8, trans. and annotated by Charles B. Chavel (New York: Shilo Publishing House, 1973), 306, 309. I have used this translation with some alterations, as noted in previous footnotes.
42. For the identification of the divine feminine with judgment and the root of evil in relation to kabbalistic ethics and hypernomianism see Elliot R. Wolfson, "Heeding the Law beyond the Law: Transgendering Alterity and the Hypernomian Perimeter of the Ethical," *EJJS* 14 (2020): 230–32, 246–47.
43. For Maimonidean influences on Nachmanides's attitude toward rationalizing the commandments and motivating practitioners for their observance see Josef Stern, "Nachmanides's Conception of Ta'amei Mitzvot and Its Maimonidean Background," in *Commandment and Community: New Essays in Jewish Legal and Political Philosophy*, ed. Daniel H. Frank (Albany: SUNY Press, 1995), 141–72.
44. For the Tannaitic source of this principle see David Henshke, "A Positive Commandment Overrides a Negative One: The Tannaitic Source of This Principle and Its History" [Hebrew], *Tarbiz* 78, no. 3 (2009): 279–321.
45. Henshke, "A Positive Commandment," 309–10.
46. For a discussion of different passages in *Nahmanides's Commentary on the Torah* addressing the categorical difference between positive and negative commandments, identifying the theosophical source of the negative commandments as the attribute of fear, see Oded Yisraeli, "Taking Precedence over the Torah: Vows and Oaths, Abstinence and Celibacy in Nahmanides's Oeuvre," *Journal of Jewish Thought & Philosophy* 28 (2020): 131–32.
47. He is referring to the beginning of the first part of the book, which expounds on the positive commandments. See Moses ben Shem Tov de León, *The Book of the Pomegranate: Moses de León's Sefer ha-Rimmon*, ed. Elliot R. Wolfson (Atlanta: Scholar's Press, 1988), 14 (Hebrew section).
48. De Leon, *Book of the Pomegranate*, 256.
49. Moshe Idel, *Kabbalah: New Perspectives*, 59–73. For the latest monograph on the role of union in Jewish mysticism, which cites and discusses previous scholarship, see Adam Afterman, *"And They Shall Be One Flesh": On the Language of Mystical Union in Judaism* (Leidein: Brill, 2016). For different possibilities of reading the mystical union as an erotic union between the male Kabbalist and a divine feminine, see Daniel Abrams, "Knowing the Maiden Without Eyes: Reading the Sexual Reconstruction of the Jewish Mystic in a Zoharic Parable," *Da'at*

50–52 (2003): lix–lxxxiii. On the role of the commandments both as vehicles for personal union with the divine (*dvekut*) and as rectifying the Deity (*tiqqun*), see Moshe Hallamish, *An Introduction to the Kabbalah*, trans. Ruth Bar-Ilan and Ora Wiskind-Elper (Albany: State University of New York, 1999), 232–41.

50. There is a vast range of literature on the role of Jewish ritual as theurgic union. For example, see Isaiah Tishby, *The Wisdom of the Zohar*, 1155–71; Charles Mopsik, *Les Grands Texts de la Cabale: les rites qui font Dieu* (Paris: Verdier, 1993) (according to the index: "unification de Dieu; union théurgique; unité divine); Mopsik, *Sex of the Soul: The Vicissitudes of Sexual Difference in Kabbalah*, ed. with a foreword by Daniel Abrams (Los Angeles: Cherub Press, 2005), 128–49; Elliot R. Wolfson, "Coronation of the Sabbath Bride: Kabbalistic Myth and Ritual of Androgynization," in *Luminal Darkness: Imaginal Gleanings from Zoharic Literature* (Oxford: Oneworld, 2007), 145–84; Moshe Idel, *Kabbalah and Eros* (New Haven: Yale University Press, 2005), 1–2, 59–77, 214–17.

51. See Elliot R. Wolfson, "Beyond Good and Evil: Hypernomian Transmorality and Delimiting the Limit," in *Venturing Beyond: Law and Morality in Kabbalistic Mysticism* (New York: Oxford University Press, 2006), 186–285.

52. Joseph of Hamadan, *Rationale of Negative Commandments*, 2 commandment, Ms. Vatican heb. 177, fol.107a.

53. For a discussion of the ambivalent stance and anxiety toward the demonic other, see Berman, *Divine and Demonic*.

54. *Tiqqunei ha-Zohar*, 52a.

55. *Tiqqunei ha-Zohar*, 55a.

56. Concerning the fascination with Shekhinah in *Tiqqunei ha-Zohar* and its centrality in the text's rationales for Jewish rituals, see Biti Roi, *Love of the Shekhina: Mysticism and Poetics in Tiqqunei ha-Zohar* [Hebrew] (Ramat Gan: Bar Ilan Press, 2017).

57. Meir Ibn Gabbai, *Avodat ha-Qodesh*, I (Warsaw, 1893), Ḥelek ha-Yiḥud (The Part of Union), 25, fol. 22d.

58. On the kabbalistic idea see Asi Farber, "'The Shell Precedes the Fruit': On the Question of the Origin of Metaphysical Evil in Early Kabbalistic Thought," in *Myth and Judaism*, ed. Haviva Pedaya [Hebrew] (Jerusalem: Bialik Institute, 1996), 118–42; Bracha Zak, "Ha-Qelippah Tzorekh ha-Kedusah" [Hebrew], *Jerusalem Studies in Jewish Thought* 3 (*Studies in Jewish Mysticism Presented to Isaiah Tishby*), no. 1–2 (1994): 191–206.

59. Regarding the kabbalistic relationship between the divine and demonic implied by this term, see Elliot R. Wolfson, "Light Through Darkness: The Ideal of Human Perfection in the Zohar," in *Luminal Darkness*, 29–55.

60. Compare this imperative of fear to Ibn Gabbai's ideal of love, as discussed briefly by Morris M. Faierstein, "Meir ibn Gabbai on the Love of God," *Mekorot* 30, no. 3 (Spring 1976): 83–85. For further analysis of the Kabbalah of Ibn Gabbai, see Roland Goetschel, *Meir ibn Gabbay: Le Discours de la Kabbale Espagnole* (Leuven: Peeters, 1981).

61. Daniel C. Matt, "The Mystic and the Mizwot," in *Jewish Spirituality: From the Bible Through the Middle Ages*, ed. Arthur Green (London: Routledge & Kegan Paul, 1986), 367–404; Elliot R. Wolfson, "Mystical Rationalization of the Commandments in *Sefer ha-Rimon*," *Hebrew Union*

College Annual 59 (1988): 217–51; Seth Brody, "Human Hands Dwell in Heavenly Heights: Contemplative Ascent and Theurgic Power in Thirteenth Century Kabbalah," in *Mystics of the Book: Themes, Topics and Typologies*, ed. R. A. Herrera (New York: P. Lang, 1993), 123–58.

62. Ibn Gabbai, *Avodat ha-Qodesh*, I, Ḥelek ha-Yiḥud (The Part of Union), 25, fol. 23a.

63. Compare Hartley Lachter's interest in the social role of Kabbalah. Lachter emphasizes the role of Christian anti-Jewish missionary activity in shaping the genre of works rationalizing the commandments. Indeed, the threat that this activity posed was an important factor in kabbalistic efforts to rationalize Jewish law. See Hartley Lachter, "Kabbalah, Philosophy, and the Jewish-Christian Debate: Reconsidering the Early Works of Joseph Gikatilla," *Journal of Jewish Thought and Philosophy* 16, no. 1 (2008): 57. Lachter added another historical aspect to the formation of the theurgic system: Kabbalists responded to the Jews' misfortune, their suffering, and their lack of substantial political power in the Middle Ages by empowering them with the concept of theurgic power. See Lachter, *Kabbalistic Revolution: Reimagining Judaism in Medieval Spain* (New Brunswick: Rutgers University Press, 2014), 100–29. For a different approach to the social role of Kabbalah, which employs a sociological perspective, compare Philip Wexler, *Mystical Society: Toward Cosmic Social Theory* (New York: Peter Lang, 2013).

PART III

Studies in Jewish Thought and Philosophy

marriage, by Elliot Wolfson. (Reprinted with permission from the artist.)

MYSTICISM AND THE ONTOLOGY OF LANGUAGE IN THE POETRY OF CHAIM NACHMAN BIALIK

MICHAEL FISHBANE

INTRODUCTORY REFLECTIONS

For well over a century, since the watershed achievement of Willian James's great *Varieties of Religious Experience*,[1] the modalities of mystical consciousness have attained a privileged position of study and appreciation. In its wake, scholars have turned their attention to diverse states of mystical awareness, sensibility, and knowledge. This includes modalities of noesis in the broadest sense—grounded in both normative religious traditions as well as purely idiosyncratic conditions, when cosmic or other elements induce an ecstatic experience. This spectrum has resulted in evaluative dichotomies, like that between "sacred" and "profane" mysticisms, to employ the formulation of R. C. Zaehner.[2] But even if we characterize the second pole as "secular," to evade a tendentious binary, it remains to be determined if such evaluations are productive or adequate. It is perhaps more compelling and helpful to say that the language used by adherents of normative religions to describe their mystical states derives from a canonical literature with established or authoritative terms; whereas the terminology employed by individuals variously independent of such constraints tends to be more personal or private in nature—even if their terms may draw from a fund or residue of shared cultural discourse. Considered in their varieties, these modalities of expression help authenticate the experiences felt by the individual and collectively constitute the genre of literary testimonies of some singular moment. Traditionalists are notoriously dependent on canonical language, whereas individualists strive to state their experiences in self-authenticating ways. The personalized accounts of a Symonds or a Bucke (so precisely documented by James), or the literary ecstasies of a Tennyson or a Shelley, are specific cases in point. Accordingly, a modern poetic sensibility tends to be at an autarkic point on the spectrum of spiritual authority, and this raises the question of the status of such poetics when it tries to express states of transport through linguistic fragments or allusions drawn from a cultural canon—but significantly metamorphosed due to the posttraditional situation of the writer. Such factors raise other considerations bearing on the ontology of poetic language, especially when it seeks to recover or depict mystical states or the incipience of inspiration.

I take up these topics to honor the lifework of Elliot Wolfson whose spiritual and intellectual reach embraces all these concerns with profoundly original studies. Indeed, at the core of his labors, and a most distinctive characteristic, is their focus on the creative poesis of Jewish mystical experience, together with the ontology of language that grounds the visionary hermeneutics of its most singular expressions. Because of Wolfson's engagements with posttraditional phenomenologists and their musings on poetic language and the modes of experience revealed thereby, he has also focused on crossovers or correlates between older, religious formulations and the diverse epistemological situations of our time. Focusing on the poetry of Chaim Nachman Bialik, I shall engage these topics through the prism of mystical memories and his distinctive types of linguistic innovation.

INITIAL CONSIDERATIONS OF LINGUISTIC ONTOLOGY

The notion of linguistic ontology should not be deemed conceptually fixed or formal, and its varieties determine the authority of language in diverse cultures. The status of language—be it supernatural or natural—affects how it is presumed to express the felt truth of an experience or resonate with readers. Accordingly, a divine or divinely derived language will condition whether some textual sense is considered inherently finite or infinite, and what it means to be either a speaker or an interpreter of this language. Endemic and crucial in this regard is: who speaks for God, if God speaks or has spoken; and what is the ontological status of words, if God is not only their source but in some sense the true core of their very being? What is sound itself if, say, the intonation of "OM" is primordial but also given to ontic expressions? And what is the "Torah" if it is not merely an artifact spoken by God but a veritable modality of the divine name, itself immaterial and ineffable? Moreover, to continue in this line of reflection, what is the status of the universe if scripture portrays the divine enunciation of its creation? Such considerations are cultural bending issues—and religious "reformations" of one sort or other have impacted them and produced the fragments of our postmodern disorientation, as thinkers try to find terms to establish pivots or centers of belief. The conditions of literary fragments have served as a conceptual category since the aesthetic theories of Friedrich Schlegel, and they constitute what has been tellingly called the hazard of modern poetry. As we shall see, Bialik is a specific case in point.

Since the poetry of Chaim Nachman Bialik (1873–1934) is the main focus of this discussion,[3] and since his spiritual formation was established within the milieu of classic Jewish text study, the theological ontology of language in which he was nurtured may be epitomized through the masterwork of the founder of the academy in which he studied in his youth. R. Chaim Volozhiner (1745–1821), first rector of the Volozhin Yeshiva in Lithuania,[4] wrote *Nefesh Ha-Ḥayyim*, which articulates a religious worldview totally grounded in divine language: principally, the supernal and primordial Torah of heaven; and relatedly the revealed Torah of Moses, whose manifold esoteric dimensions are symbolically encoded in the commentaries of the Zohar; and whose exoteric aspects are recovered by the oral tradition, as classically embodied in the Talmud and its numerous explications. As "Gate Four" of Rabbi Chaim's book enunciates, a person's immersion in the language of rabbinic lore (in all its legal and homiletical iterations) is the true highway to God. And even more: it is nothing less than contact with God through God's will, as reformulated by the sacred tradition. Accordingly, study not only extends this verbal will into worldly forms and existence (since the religious world of Judaism is textually inflected at every level), but is the verbal link to the primordial Torah. As a result, perpetual study sustains the sacred sources of existence encoded in its supernal expressions. Or put more ontologically: all Being, and our universe as a concrete particular, is an infinitely formulated divine language from its supernal top to natural bottom. In truth, everything is some mode of this linguistic enunciation and thus partakes of the primordial and infinite emanations of divinity. Stated concisely, everything is resonant with divinity and there is nothing other than divine language. Inspired perception is cognizant of this linguistic manifold, and it is the desire of the adept to experience this reality. And if each worldly element is a refraction of this truth, its reception is in the eye of the beholder.

Epistemological breaks with religious tradition have ruptured this sacred syntax and resulted in the demystification of the world—to recollect Max Weber's famous locution. Hence persons born into this modern era and impacted by such a modernist sensibility must make do with their options: either to try to reform this situation from within, or experience themselves as tone-deaf to this resonance and move on to other cultural spheres. In the first instance, there is an ongoing attempt to revitalize the linguistic terms of one's religious canon; but this becomes difficult and complicated when the world to which the older language points is no longer real or revelatory—or when the canonical center of the tradition no longer holds (as Yeats poignantly said). What can one do when one can no longer engage in the exegetical projects of the normative culture? And what can one do when one feels compelled to build a new epistemic worldview from the canonical deposits found in one's deepest self? For these and other reasons the strong poet, in a teetering but lonely virtuosity, has been a spiritual hero in modernity. Aching for the renewal of a personal language, certain poets have strived to reread the demystified book of nature through the prism of their inner eye and thereby renew a vision of the external world. This was the cultural program of romanticism, in its varieties. Regenerated, language could reveal the depths of nature through sudden flashes of words that might irradiate a mystical spectrum of perception. This goal was also the center-point of Bialik's poetics. It was his ever-recursive personal longing to retrieve a lost sense of wonder—a yearning to perceive the world as an effulgence of light and to render it in verse. Because of his integrity and the circumstances of his life, this profound longing marks the rhythms of despair and ecstasy in his soul.

SOURCES OF ILLUMINATION

Toward the end of his poem *Eḥad Eḥad ube-Ein Ro'eh* ("One by One, and Without Seeing"), Bialik laments: "I know that only once does a person drink from the golden cup / and that the vision of splendor and radiance (*ziv ve-zohar*) will not happen to one twice"—as he feels the fading of this illumination into abject silence (*va-yikhlu be-yagon dumam*). And surely, it would be hard to deny that a recurrent feature of Bialik's poetry is the longing to retrieve or recoup the mystical mysteries of that time (a zone of consciousness no less than a zone of chronology) of inspired and luminous wonder. Writings about these primary moments in later years strive to recapture both the crystalline quality of light—the veritable light of creation felt as the light of consciousness itself—and its inspiring benefactions. Translucence is therefore a primary trope of the mature poet, enfolded into his deepest being prior to their linguistic refractions and recrudescence. It seems not accidental, I should say, that the previous citation speaks of the recipient of light as both *adam* and *ish* (as an adult man), since it is this later self that "knows" the cycles of inspiration and its enduring reality, ontologically embedded within nature, to be recovered through a reborn consciousness of childlike vision. And thus his poetic compositions are, in part, a waiting in hope for some "sudden" bestowal of divine "blessing (*birkat pit'om*)," when the visions of youth will again flood his soul with a silent, mystical ecstasy. I shall return to this trope, but for now we need only say that this moment is a return to a preverbal state of awareness, the ontological ground of his poetry.

Reflecting on the peregrinations of his soul, as an itinerary of consciousness, the poet depicts a dialogue with his tutelary angel. At the outset of the poem *Ve-im Yish'alekha Ha-Mal'akh* ("And if the Angel Asks"), the query is posed: "My son, where is your soul?" Note that the temporality of its whereabouts is posed in the concurrent present (*ayeha*). And to account for this temporal reality, the speaker first recalls the childhood home of the poet, overarched by a blue-luminous sky within which is a "single cloud (*'av yeḥidah*)"—to which once, at an awesome silencing of the creation, the dreaming boy was drawn in an ecstatic ascension of visual aspiration. "Drawn" upward to the luminous element, the eyes of the poet "saw" (*ha-yeḥidah, ha-zakah, ha-berurah*) (this cloud depicted respectively as "the single one, the refined one, the pure one")—and then "his soul departed (*nafsho yatze'ah*)," flying into its transcendence like a "dove" escaping its cote-cage. The overlapping soul-symbols reinforce the event of transport (the original *neshamah*, "soul," of the angel's query, now depicted as a *nefesh* and figured as a dove, joins the singular cloud, called *yeḥidah*, which word alludes to still another gradation of human soul in the Jewish mystical lexicon). At this climactic merger, the speaker says that his soul was mercifully saved by a ray of golden sunlight—whereupon it cavorted in some ecstatic dance, riding on the "wings of splendor" for days on end. With time, this supernatural transport mutated into a tear of loss that fell into the Talmudic folios of his ancestors, where it mingled with the letters of culture and the wax of ascetic nights—each a wasted remainder of prior vitality. And there it fluttered in its death throes, until the soul was revived through the metamorphosis of poetry. The speaker now significantly exclaims that these "dead letters" of the literary tradition were "suddenly visited (*heqeiru*) by the songs of life"—to the end that the cloud of his childhood and the rays of sunlight, along with the tears of loss, were "changed (*shanu*)" into verse. Poetry is therefore no mere mimesis of nature, but (per this attestation) its linguistic transfiguration—this being the transformation of the silent luminosity of creation by the revivified letters of the canonical culture, and producing something altogether other. Accordingly, if the rhapsodic words of sacred tradition could speak again, they had to be changed through the memory of the sensed, but preverbal, splendor of one's childhood. Thus the erstwhile sacred ontology of linguistic forms had to be inspired by a far more primordial ontology to be resurrected. This conjunction is the confessed revival of the poet's soul, as well, save for an inchoate yearning for love: a prayer "crying in silent inwardness (*bokhiyah be-ḥasha'i*)." Here too, as we shall see, is another source of true poetry, according to Bialik's various manifestos. But withal, the ever-new and sorrowful swerve to view a hidden light always takes pride of place. We must ponder these refractions and how they align (or realign) the physical with the metaphysical.[5]

LIGHT AND ITS VARIANTS

The poetics of light dominate Bialik's sensibility, both in their spectacular purity—giving accounts of the luminous splendor of existence, and in their radiant streams—cascading down through the formations of nature, or mirroring back their likeness in refractive dialogues. Light is therefore a medium for sight and insight.[6]

As with phenomenology generally, so also in Bialik's poetry, light is sensed as a presence before it is experienced as a specific summons or a verbal inspiration. Two typical modalities exemplify this feature. The first depicts the silent incursion of light through a window of sorts and its invasion of one's consciousness. The figure of an illumined awakening, repeatedly portrayed as the arousal of a child in bed, is most certainly also a trope for poetic arousal, since it commonly provides a segue to the flooding sensibility of awareness prior to vocalic creativity—as stated by the mature speaker of the poem. *'Im Petiḥat Ha-Ḥalon* ("At the Opening of the Window") is a case in point. The poem begins with the first shafts of the dawn as they invade the sleeping boy's bedroom, silently pronouncing to his heart "Arouse yourself . . . light has come, light has happened!"

Slowly, a gleam of splendor turns into "beams of light (*qarnei ha-or*)," and then a "billow of lights (*naḥshol orim*)" follow, manifesting a visitation of effulgence (*va-yaqeiru negohot*)—and the world is illumined like a heavenly canopy of "sapphire and splendor (*sapir ve-zohar*)"—radiant "fragments of the supernal throne (*shivrei kisei ha-kavod*)" dispersed into the "depths (*tehom*)" of existence.[7] In a mystical splendor (evocatively evinced by these images and others), the eye and heart and soul of the subject is "engorged by the light (*sovei't ha-or*)"—and the speaker exudes, in a language of the spirit: "O God of light, give (more) light!" Such is the saturation, so filled to overflowing.

Light is the source of all awakening—whose advent is the sacred expectancy of the poetic temper. The poem *Mi-Shomerim La-Boqer* ("From Those Who Await the Dawn") continues the foregoing themes but brings the speaker to another state of mind—even to the inspired cusp of song and invasion of the glow of the dawn. The poem is set in four stanzas, divided into two rhetorical structures (of query and answer) and a complex rhyme scheme repeated throughout. The dialogical nature of these queries invites the listener into a personal disclosure of the wonders of the morning glow and its impact on the close attendee (this being the imparting to the hearer of the effect of dawn's light upon the poet). The poem opens by asking: *ha-shamarta la-boqer*, "have you attended to" or "awaited the morning" when the "reddish hues of the sun" (*dimdumei shemesh*—a trope that evokes their silent glow) bursting upon the rim of earth at the outskirts of heaven extend in all directions, even before the day is "ready (*nakhon*)" to receive them. This "vision" of colored light is an awesome sight; "and like a great retinue (*sod*) of holy beings (*qedoshim*) before the disclosure" of its mystery (*sod* has this double valence), the envisioning heart is "filled with murmurings (*higayon*)." But what mouth could draw forth this sense: "call it by its name (*yiqra'ennu be-shemo*)," "speak of it (*yesiḥennu*)," or ever know "what language (*lashon*) could configure it (*kanoto*)?"

The silence of the splendor, a mysterious hiddenness, is beyond the capacity for its verbal expression—be that giving it a name, providing a simile (an imaginal likeness), or offering some epithet or figure. Evoking this imponderable reality, the poet now, somewhat repeating the opening stanza in the third, asks if one has even seen the myriads of running radiance that "burst" and "scatter" roundabout at the dawn. And also, now alluding to the "spectacle (*mar'eh*)" noted earlier, he speaks here of this "supernal vision (*maḥazeh*)" and exclaims: "Happy is the eye that has hidden (*tzafenah*) a ray of light as a remembrance (*mishmeret*)"—so that when this inner turbulence of heart gives way to speech and their lamentable tenor, this ray, transformed into a "tear" of lost splendor, "may yet be a glowing (*mazheret*)"—even a "caution" (*mazheret* evokes both senses)[8] not to confuse bland words with their primary soundings of the spirit; the silent human witness of their ontological origin is an ineffable mystery. For this reason, we may suppose that the word *mi-shomerim* also evokes those who, like Bialik, "guard" the memory (*mishmeret*) of this light as a lost truth—but who also, we may suggest, retain hope for a restored poetic inspiration. Hence, it seems quite likely that our singer chose the image of awaiting the morning light (citing Psalm 130:6) precisely because the preceding verse expresses the soul's attentive longing for the "word" of God (v. 5). Is this correlation insignificant, or a mere happenstance? We shall postpone an answer.

HIDDEN LIGHTS FOR THE EYE AND HEART

The true light of day, for the awakened soul, is more than daylight. It is a divine radiance and effulgence that emanates from every element of the external world, beckoning like glistening "sprites (*tzafririm*)"—as in the poem of the same name (*Tzafririm*)—to see everything from the inside out. To see "hair on sheaves of grain," the "rush of waves," a "sleeping child's smile," "tears," and "fractures of glass"—even, and perhaps especially, the "rhymes of song." For is this not, truly, the memory and longing of the poet, saying: "how the heart melts (*mah namog ha-lev*)" at this spectacle and exulting: "O God, light has flooded me (*Elohim, shitafani ha-'orah*)!" Who speaks, if not the poet, as if in a recovered dream: to all this radiance to enter the "depths of my eyelids (*ma'amaqei bavotai*)"—to "purify me (*haziquni*), flood me, penetrate my heart, come and descend into my soul, be there and shine (*va-'oru*)"? Surely it is the spiritual testimony of mystic inspiration rising from the ontological depths—a luminous prelude to creativity: "the heart floods (*shotef*)—overflows its banks without end, bursting like a font of streaming light (*nogah nove'a*)." The waking boy is the aroused poet, seeing with new eyes. Light is the silent source of song.

The great poem *Zohar* ("Splendor") takes us totally into this inner reality. It is an express testament of "hidden mysteries and silence (*setarim u-demamah*)" to the inwardness of light, beyond the "physicality of the world (*gufo shel 'olam*)"—where the youth who speaks envisioned supernal heights, "as if gazing into the eye (*eino*) of the world" where his companion spirits "revealed . . . their secrets (*niglu . . . razeihem*)" and "received (*qibbalti*)" and "sealed them" in the "mute silence (*ha-'ilem*)" of his heart. Here is a verbal token of an inner vision whose colors and secrets were absorbed as hidden mysteries—now disclosed in poetic song.[9] We must therefore read these words in this light: as a memorial and lament in one.

The languages of light and solicitation comprise the mystic consciousness of the poet and their innumerable refractions constitute diverse tropes within *Zohar*. There are cascading flashes and dazzling images—giving voice to the first shining or illumination of his eyes, as the summoning sprites lightened and uplifted him, purifying his vision (*qaloti, zakoti, kenaf 'or tissa'eini*). Like infinite prisms, this light blinded him (*sanverim la-'ayin*), weaving a web of golden cords around his soul. And then, suddenly, the older poet reveals not just the child's revelation but his own as well, when an "illumined youth was aroused and renewed within me (*hitna'arah, hithaddeshah bi yaldut me'irah*)"[10]—for then, suddenly, "my mouth spontaneously rejoiced, (and) in (my) heart *shemesh shirah* (a song of sun)"; and further, "from the touch of sun beams (*qarnayim*), joy and radiance—(*eqranah, enharah, eivoshah, emogah*) I was sun struck, illumined, overcome and melted." Have we not here a remarkable testament of ecstatic dying, of an overwhelming illumination, when the poet was "drunk with splendor (*shakhur zohar*)" and striated by dazzling radiance (*requmah negohot*)?

Vision within vision, the poem transports the inner eye to a pool of absolute purity (*ke-'etzem peninim la-tohar*): itself reflecting the heavens "like a polished mirror (*ke-re'i melutash*)," even "like an inverted world (*ke-'ein 'olam hafukh*)"—a visionary speculum echoing the opening stanza, when the poet spoke of attaining the source of existence.[11]

Here it is the reflecting glass of supernal realities into which the poet gazes—"so effulgent (*koh bahir*)" and "dreaming (*ḥolem*)," like his own eye, shining and bending the lights of reality into ever-new refractions. In a stunning series of episodes, the visionary not only beholds the world in new forms, but sinks into "this ocean of fiery light (*yam di-nur zeh*)," becoming saturated with it (*va-espog yam orim*), emerging like a priest from a sacred immersion "refined sevenfold (*pi sheva' mezuqaq*)." Here again, I suspect, the elder poet reveals that such light was and is the purifying agent of his language and poetic creativity (its ontological agency). For the poet has left us a telling trace of his feelings—since his language echoes Psalm 12:7, where the psalmist contrasted the false speech of dissemblers with the "pure words of God," "refined seventyfold (*mezuqaq shiv'atayim*)." And if this did not suffice, we also have the youth summoned by a "supernal splendor (*zohar 'elyon*)," by the "radiance of the *Shekhinah* (*ziv ha-shekhinah*)," declaring that they wish to "immerse you (*nitbolekha*) in the splendor . . . (and) bring you to the treasury of the hidden light (*or ganuz*) in the depths of the abyss (*be-ma'amaqei tehom*)."[12] This is a summons of ultimate experiences: an invocation to pass beyond the radiance of divine immanence, and its suffusing dimension, to a mystical light hidden, according to rabbinic and mystical tradition, at the creation of the world. It thus refers to a primordial light emanating from God's robe—an effulgence manifest when God said "Let there be light," and thus also immaterial, unlike the light of the sun.[13] But also: the speaker was summoned further, into the depths of the *tehom*—this being a truth beyond being, beyond the sensibility of light or of any natural perception. And as we shall consider later, the *tehom* is the most radically transcendent of all ontological dimensions.

Returning to the theme of immersing in this light, Bialik concludes the poem by saying that even though the primary *shirat zohar* ("song of splendor") has long since been stilled, hope against hope, "its echo is nevertheless hidden deep within his heart (*akh 'amoq be-lev kamus 'immi hed qolah*)"—and, he confesses, "I have guarded (*shamarti*) the radiance of its light under my eyelids (*bavot 'einai*)," from whose well (*'einah*) come his dreams and visions, "pure . . . and blessed from its source (*tehorim . . . u-berukhim mi-meqorah*)." This is a double hiddenness. It is the revealed luminescence of the *or ganuz*, which is itself an interior vision of true existence, itself sequestered within his mortal eyes—the regenerative source of his poetry of a pure presence, of a visionary apperception of the world. Thus the poet states that his verbal creativity reveals, when purified by light, the mystic radiance "preserved (*meshumar*)" since the creation. In this testimony, the poet gives voice to a primordial inwardness still shining (and preserved) in memory.

SILENCE AND SPIRITUAL INCEPTION

There are still other soundings from the depths, primary evocations at the cusp of language. Here, too, are the ontological sources of Bialik's poetic speech. Among the most salient are silence and sorrow, which recur both separately and in combination. Reverberating throughout are expressions of the poet's solitariness and loneliness—and, indeed, the sources of his creativity. Such poetry is language in the service of the inchoate, before words.

The confession *Yam Ha-Demamah Polet Sodot* ("The Sea of Silence That Emits Secrets") is revelatory. From the pervasive stillness of night—from this "silent (*shoteq*)" blackness, comprised of layers of shadow—a "silent (*domam*)" star fell into a "sea of silences (*yam ha-maḥashakim*)," foreboding the onset of song. Amid this quietude (*be-hishtateq*) of existence, an emergence was sensed: "I trembled (*argish*): my heart aroused and speaking (*'er u-middaber*); / I felt (*argish*) a pure fountain welling up, / slowly surging (*homeh*) in greater strength."[14] And then the speaker realized, "silently (*be-ḥashai*)," that his dreams were fulfilled and that this astral event was not his true muse: for he perceived his own star's light in the heavens above, shining in compassionate care.[15] In his contemplative gaze, he knew that the "only" true world, hidden within all the silences, was "the world in his heart (*ha-'olam she-bilvavi*)," the font of inwardness and poetic vision. In this, his inner sea of silences was the reflective impression of external stimulations—but beyond verisimilitudes for all that. The language of poetry now reveals this truth.

The fullness of inspired silence, prior to poetic speech, and the culmination of a lamented longing for the erstwhile illuminations of childhood is momentously conveyed in the extensive closing stanza of *Eḥad, Eḥad*. The trope of *'ayin* is its leitmotiv. Borne by the knowledge (*yada'ti*) that "there" the world is bathed in a radiant "splendor (*zohar*)," and that a "hidden light" illumines the blue of sky and the "color (*'ein*)" of greenish grass, and that the "eye (*'ein*)" of the child may merit this vision but once, not more—the poet also believes that "God has a blessing of suddenness (*birkat pit'om*)" reserved for those "faithful in His eyes (*'einav*)." But "no visionary can predict" its advent, and "no eye (*'ayin*) can behold its channels (*tzinoreyha*)" of inspiration.[16] Therefore, he adds, "I shall prepare (*e'erokh*) for it silently (*dumam*)"; and with his heart "strung taut (*'arukh meitarim*)" like a lyre, he will await its coming, assured that it will break upon him "suddenly (*pit'om*)" and illumine his soul with a glorious splendor—a recurrence of childhood sounds and colors and smells. And though it will last a moment "flooding me (*shetafani*)" with the wave of its sweetness, the poet knows he will "stand tremulously (*e'emod nif'am*)" again before the wondrous world of riddles and marvels upon which "no hand ever rested (*ḥalah*),[17] or any speech occurred." Overwhelmed, "my heart will be filled with overwhelming sound (*hamon*), and the bedazzlement (*timahon*) of God upon my face; / in my eyes (*'einai*) will radiate a tear, and in my soul a silent blast (*teru'ah ne'elamah*)." Wholly beyond language, the hidden splendor of being now itself becomes manifest in a poem—a verbal witness to ineffable disclosures.

Thus poetic revelation says one thing and does another: it reveals the hidden moment before language, when the poet experiences the mystery of thick silence. Among other worthy witnesses, the poem *Besorah* ("Message") conveys such an ultimate inwardness—each stanza a portent of the mystical transport of selfhood. When light breaks forth anew, cleaving the heavens and sending shafts of light to earth, each like a "golden arrow" that "speaks . . . its splendor (*millel . . . zoharo*)," the poet's eye is transported on high and, like a prophet, is transfused by radiance. "Face to face I shall speak / with the beauteous heavens; // mouth to mouth I shall open the channel (*tzinor*) of my heart: / the sky will pour forth its bounty . . . the radiance of its light." His heart will then be filled with a heavenly azure, and his heartstrings will be strummed by the play of light (*pizzuz . . . 'orot*) radiating into his soul. Transformed, the poet's "entire being will resound with new song (*kol qerovai/ shirah ḥadashah yehemayu*)"—the song of a silent, interior illumination.

BUT VISION HAS OTHER, CONTEMPLATIVE DIMENSIONS—EQUALLY FUNDAMENTAL for the poet and his inspiration. We have a personal accounting of this toward the end of the lyric *Ha-Bereikhah* ("The Pool"). In the penultimate stanza, the poet returns to the imaginal dimensions of this reflecting surface (taken up earlier in *Zohar*).[18] Bent in meditative pose and caught between the world without and its features on the water—like another mediating lens and mirror—the speaker is suddenly "aroused . . . by a silent streaming (*margish . . . nevo'a ḥeresh*)," filling his heart, sinking it deeper and deeper—and while wholly attentive to an approaching revelation (of the *Shekhinah* or Elijah), his heart "in its holy desires . . . trembled, was extinguished, (and) expired (*yaḥil, yikhleh, yigva'*)" in ecstasy—as if wholly transmuted in the very nature of his being, such that even a heavenly voice asked, within the surrounding silence (*demamah*), "where are you?" as the natural world looked on in astonishment.

As he comes to his senses in the ultimate stanza, we are given a veritable poetics of this and related matters. For we learn that there is a more primary language, one that precedes human speech. It is a "silent, divine language (*sefat elim ḥarishit*)," a "language of silences (*lashon ḥasha'im*) / without any voice or sound (*lo qol ve-lo havarah*)"; but a medley of worldly colors and shapes and spectacles. This is the language through which "God makes Himself known" to his favored ones, and from which the artist shapes "the stirring of his heart (*hagig levavo*)" and seeks solutions to "unvoiced dreams (*ḥalom lo hagui*)." Going further, we are told that this is "the language of visions (*lashon ha-mar'ot*)"—revealed in the colors of the firmament, the wings of birds, the sparkle of an eye, the shapes of human form, and the host of other phenomena on sea and land. It is thus in this very "language, the language of languages (*be-lashon zo, lashon ha-leshonot*)" that the pool conveyed its worldly, riddling truths to the speaker—reflecting in its all-seeing eye everything that may be envisioned, in all their mysterious and ever-changing diversity. The eye of the pool is thus a font of perception and projection—a veritable "visionary (*tzofeh*)" in its own right, "envisioning (*tzofiyah*)" the multiplicity of worldly sights, and even their provisionary occasions (*tzafui*), in all their great "variability (*mishtaneh*)" and variety. Through this prism (like its human counterpart), the dreamer may imagine all manner of likeness and comparison, each "as if" of the imaginal life (*li nidmetah ke'ilu*) and each speculation of awareness.[19] Arising through visual associations, human words construe the inmost figurations of consciousness.[20]

A HERMENEUTICAL INTERLUDE

We have noted that a primary source of Bialik's creativity derives from the memory of primordial visions experienced in childhood—eventually reprocessed through the canonical tradition. The first type is preverbal and sensate; the second constitutes the ancient argot of language, moribund in ancient folios and needing to be revived through the prismatic refractions of poetic speech. It is this process that changes their ontological character. The visions of the outer world—be they of its sacred, interior light, or its external images—are evocations of the creation: God's language made manifest to the human eye. The words of tradition have become, for Bialik, mere shells that no longer contain or induce sacred imaginings, despite their sacred origins and their reinterpretation over the generations.[21] What, then, is the status of a poetic argot that culls from this canon and produces a new mosaic of sound and significance? How can we understand such literary refractions—newly produced from nonverbal channels of the spirit?

Bialik's emphasis on personal and immediate experience is essential: it is the inner fire that refines older terms and melds them (or "hammers" them, as he says in his "Winter Songs") on the anvil of his heart. Absent this, the old canon is mere dross. Three suggestive examples may illustrate this vortex of creativity. The first is the reference to spiritual yearning at the beginning of *Zohar*, where the speaker says *mi gufo shel 'olam el oro 'aragti*, "I pined (from youth to go) from the body of the world to its light." This is a spiritual longing that evokes Psalm 42:2, in which the adept's soul yearns to be sated with God, like a hart seeking streams of water—for he thirsts for the living God, like a lonely pilgrim passing sacred sites with an emotional arousal of its loss (vv. 3–7). Surely Bialik has reminted the verb *'aragti* to express his lifelong yearning for the mystery of light. But what else drew him to this passage, swirling unsaid in his mind? Can we not also hear the poet's mourning for his spiritual loss of the old tradition and its capacity to inspire? For notably, the psalm goes on to depict this with the figure of waters breaking over him like "*tehom* (deep) to *tehom* at the sound of Your channels (*tzinoreykha*)"—terminology redolent with Bialik's language of inspiration (v. 8)—as we have noted earlier. Even more remarkable is that the psalmist says that during the night God's "song (*shiro*) is with me" (v. 9). Hence, quite evidently, the poet's language is more than he says with one verb—a veritable manifestation of the concealed of his soul. Thus the word is truly his, even if its full sounding goes unheard by some readers. Even so, the ontology of the psalmist's argot evokes a spiritual seeking in the contemporary guise of romantic naturalism and gives the poet's confession a liturgical character, perhaps evoking its citation in the medieval "Song of Unity," where that poet also states: "I will compose (*e'erog*) songs to God, because I pine (*e'erog*)" for His glory.[22] The impacting fusion of linguistic ontologies marks this verbal allusion and constitutes its significant hermeneutical resonance.

Of a quite different type is Bialik's use of the figure *genuvti yom* to convey his poetic revelations.[23] Literally, the phrase means "taken by stealth" and occurs in Gen. 31:39

when Jacob protests to Laban of his honesty, and that he made good any losses of the flock, be they "snatched by day" or otherwise. At first glance this image is odd, and its form requires some explanation. In fact, the "*i*-suffix" here is an old linguistic feature (see Rashi and Ibn Ezra), not a personal pronoun; and the verb is also used to indicate a divine revelation in Job 4:12 to indicate some form of unintended overhearing (a kind of spiritual stealth) of a heavenly word.[24] What does Bialik do? He takes over the verb as an innuendo of inspiration, but then also appropriates the suffix as a marker for his own private experience. The upshot is that *genuvti* now conveys "*my* purloined inspiration." Sensitive to his own all too human nature, he characterizes his poetic inspiration as a kind of stolen treasure. The complex layering of his poetics and the scriptural originals is a hermeneutical tour de force and exemplifies the convergent strata in Bialik's poetry. The ironic mixture of the patriarch Jacob's protest with his confession shows that the older, canonical authority (its divine ontology) is not obscured, but strategically elided to give the poet's innovations their remarkably striking ontological resonances. Any number of similar examples would further instantiate his personal appropriation of biblical and rabbinic tradition. Such is the template of his soul. In his view, this is the singular way to sanctify an ancient language (Hebrew) that has gone stale and secular, having been so recently employed for collective or utilitarian purposes.[25]

As a final example, we may turn to the poem *Lo Zakhiti ha-Or min ha-Hefqer* ("I Didn't Merit Light by Accident"). In it, Bialik adapts verbal elements from the legal and prophetic traditions to express personal sources of his creativity. At the outset, the poet avers that the "light" of inspiration was neither the product of happenstance or patrimony (*me-avi*), but something he "hewed" from the "rock (*sela'*)" of his "heart"—employing a series of allusions to Isa. 51:1 that refer to the ancestral rock of the "patriarch" Abraham as the source from which the nation was "hewn." Bialik then asserts that his "spark"[26] of creativity was neither "borrowed" nor "stolen" (the verb *genavtiv* here cleverly denies the theft or misappropriation of inspiration); but was rather the product of the "hammer of my sorrows (*patish tzorotai*)." Under the weight of its blows, "my heart burst (*yitpotzetz*)" and a flame entered his eye and inspired his "verse." Such imagery personalizes the language of Jer. 23:29, wherein the divine word is compared to "fire" and to a "hammer shattering a rock (*ke-patish yefotzetz sela'*)"—a figure set in contrast to the speech of those who falsely appropriate or "steal" God's word (*meganvei devari*). At the end, the poet adds a final, melancholy note. He reports that his verse also ignited the "fire (*'ur*)" of his listeners, though it disappeared from sight. In conclusion, the poet laments: "And I paid for the inflammation / with my flesh and blood (*ve-anokhi be-ḥelbi uve-dami / et ha-be'eirah ashalem*)." In this passage, the reader can hear an allusion to the forensic situation in Exod. 22:4–5, when a person ignites a fire on their own property, but the flame burns another's fields—in which case the one who causes the "fire (*ha-be'eirah*)" must "pay (*yishalem*)" requisite damages. Bialik uses the language of sacrificial offerings to indicate the personal cost and does so with another double entendre (*dam* indicates "blood" in biblical Hebrew but "money" in rabbinic parlance). It is a further testimony to the poet's strategic adaptation of canonical features to convey private truth and exemplify the power of linguistic renewal. The convergence of diverse ontologies is a subject in itself.

THE ONTOLOGY OF LANGUAGE AS SUCH

For Bialik, personal immediacy and primary experiences (emotive and preverbal) are at the core of language. He articulates this linguistic anthropology (and more) in his essay *Gillui ve-Khisui ba-Lashon* ("Revealment and Concealment").[27] Adam is paradigmatic, as first speaker and first artist. Responding to the unknown terrors of existence—its shuddering sounds and sights—the primal creature emits sounds that echo the phenomena of nature, sounds both inchoate and inarticulate, and expressive gestures. Such enunciations are reactive and onomatopoetic, and they are only subsequently formulated into designated meanings (the sound "r-r" before the word "roar" is emblematic). These articulations arise from the primary terror of existence and the emergence of a self-aware "I." The result is the development of verbal remedies to displace and name the nameless *tehom*, or depths of unknown being. Social language reinforces this remedy and dulls the wounds of experience. Only suddenly is this plaster cracked, be it impending death or sorrow or even joy; but then new balms are spread to heal the terrified soul and enable all the formal tasks of life to be continued without disruption. Poetry is one of the verbal types that may hover close to the abyss—for it is not a product of semantic symmetries and set phrases, designed to answer soluble issues, as is prose; but rather, it is a creative efflux that reacts to deep feelings, which throb in their uniqueness and require new words and phrases to respond to the issues and reflect their rawness. Thus poetry and true speaking must sense the unsayable depths and dimensions of language, its need to bespeak the wonders of existence as well as its fundamentally inarticulate core. For Bialik, the query *mah* ("what?") symbolizes this truth; and for its part, the word *tehom* names the primal upsurge of mysteries from the most abyssal depths (the dark unnamable source of primacies of every kind, swirling unnamed since the beginning of creation). It is from this font that we feel sorrow or emit a reactive cry; that we feel the surge of happiness and then laugh; or sense the play of melody and sing. These are preverbal modalities that Bialik deems "languages without words (*leshonot be-lo millim*)," but which the human speaker (*medabber*) can reformulate in ever-new responsive ways. They are, says Bialik, the inveterate words of God (citing Elihu in the book of Job) and derive from the *tehom*—capable of driving a person mad, but nevertheless rife with the essential sensibilities necessary for anyone who would be culturally creative in any way.

Surely Bialik speaks from experience. Every word he uttered needed to be a shaping of these primary experiences—be they the laughter expressed through the cavorting sprites and youth in the sunlight; in the dance of imps in the dark, who are embodiments of the moonlight upon the world; the glistening of illuminations from the icy roofs in winter, the pure snow untrammeled by feet; or the butterfly alighting upon a girl's locks in springtime. Even so, and so often, these primal sensibilities stream in tears to overflowing in poems of personal poverty and bread soaked with his mother's tears (the veritable source of his poetry, he says); or in the whirlwind of woes that stormed his lonely soul, emptied of light, or filled with the ravages of historical terrors. In this sense, his poetry is a long "scroll of fire (*megillat esh*)," whose flames curl up as lost love; as an inconsolable mourning for his now desiccated tradition; and, indeed, as his own perception of the ultimate abyss beyond meaning. It is this dimension that brings Bialik to a certain silence, to a shattering groan at the climax of perception. Thus *Hetzitz ve-Nifga'* ("He Glimpsed and Died") is a climactic formulation of his lifelong attempts to see truly. But this is no seeing into the inner light of a newly revealed world. It is a pilgrimage into the wholly dark abyss of the "nihil" of which nothing can be said, not even "what? (*mah*)." It is the incomprehensible no-thing, the absence of *mah*, a mystic dimension, if one can say this, called *beli-mah*—since even this word is a negation of a conceptual category. As the pilgrim-poet slowly proceeds past every cognitive marker in the mystical vocabulary (past the union of opposites and the capacity to think), he sinks to the borderland that is marked by this term and groans, having merely glimpsed at a state beyond Being. No one can return whole from this perception, the wound of such awareness being a death to normal seeing. There is no similitude or likeness for this; it is the very end of imagination, its dark hole.[28]

Whether linked to this epistemological event or not, Bialik wrote a poem in that same year (1915) wherein he speaks of the snapped chords of his voice; and, echoing similar images, depicted this reduction to a punishing silence. In acutest language, he portrays the impurity of his words. Repeatedly, in the poem *Ḥalefah 'al Panai* ("There Passed over Me"), the poet laments his stained, polluted words, seemingly beyond refinement,[29] and therefore determines to "go out" to hear the pure speech of children and the chirping of birds in the morning. To catch these tones we can best turn to his childhood jingles, modulating babbles of rhyme and echoing joy.[30] Perhaps none of these "songs of innocence" so purely evokes these tonalities as *Nadnedah* ("The Seesaw"). Within the brief compass of an apparently simple chant, the poet conveys a profound metaphysical insight. Tongue in cheek, he has the children sing as they cavort up and down: *mah le-ma'alah? / mah le-matah— / raq ani,/ ani ve-attah* ("What is above? What is below—Only me (I), me and you").[31] With a barely disguised irony, the word *mah* marks both a query and an assertion. Above and below, there is only *mah*—only wonder and the certitude of "I and thou" in simple dialogue. Metaphysical angst is replaced by the pleasures of shared human experience.

MY END IS MY BEGINNING, WHERE I SPOKE OF HOW THE ONTOLOGICAL LANGUAGE of older religious tradition was ruptured by modernity, and how contemporary poetry has tried to become a filter or mosaic of previous forms projected into the world of nature and natural experiences, with a palpable "romantic sensibility." After the fracture of a divine language that unites heaven and earth, the modern seeker is left with verbal fragments and various attempts at their revitalization. Such attempts at spiritual transfusion are the hazard of modern poetry. During the past century, the poetic achievements of Rilke and others are emblematic of the struggle to recover a lost spirituality of experience, and thereby the renewal of pure vision. We initially portrayed Bialik in this light; and this alignment cannot be gainsaid. But is there more? Can we integrate such a portrayal with the "silent language" of God that is, as he explicitly says, the external world of appearances? And further: can we even relate this to the divine "language without words" that pulsates within the abyssal depth of being? If so, are we not perhaps compelled to regard everything as divine language—as a divine evocation in some palpable mode or respect? May we even say that the true poet is an inspired witness to all this—trembling before emptiness and fullness, and perceiving the beckoning of the transcendent mystery in his heart before it coalesces in the imagination as figures of a sudden spiritual sensation? So understood, all poetic speaking emerges at the border of sound, where God's word may be heard anew. And thus to think with poetry is to sense the nascent creativity of speech and the ineffable divine voice at its base. This is a mystic cognizance of revelatory significance, a noetic awareness at the verge of language.

NOTES

1. Based on the Gifford Lectures on Natural Religion, 1901–1902, the book was first published by Longmans, Green and Company and frequently reprinted. It deserves note that the subtitle is "A Study in Human Nature."
2. See his *Mysticism: Sacred and Profane* (Oxford: Clarendon Press, 1957). His subtitle is: "An Inquiry into Varieties of Praeternatural Experience." I doubt that this allusion to James's work is altogether unintentional.
3. I shall cite from the classic anthology of his literary works, *Kol Kitvei Ḥayim Naḥman Bialik* (Tel Aviv: Devir, 1938). References to oral talks will be annotated accordingly.
4. See the striking memoir by a fellow student, A. Blosher, *Ḥayim Naḥman Bialik be-Volozhin, u-Volozhin be-Bialik* (Kaunas, 1935). Bialik's immortal rendition appears in the poem *Ha-Matmid* ("The Talmud-Student").
5. This latter conjunction is one of the great tasks of poetry. See the concise formulation of John Crowe Ransom, "Poetry: A Note on Ontology," in his *The World's Body* (Baton Rouge: Louisiana State University Press, 1968).
6. The primacy of light as a constitutive metaphor was articulated by Hans Blumenberg in his classic (1957) essay, "Light as a Metaphor for Truth," in *Modernity and the Hegemony of Vision*, ed. D. M. Levin (Berkeley: University of California Press, 1993), 30–86. A valuable conspectus of light in world religions can be found in *The Presence of Light: Divine Radiance and Religious Experience*, ed. M. Kapstein (Chicago: University of Chicago Press, 2004). Chapter 5 contains Elliot Wolfson's excellent statement of light in medieval Kabbalah.
7. I shall return to the hermeneutical import of such language below. Here it suffices to note the panoply of mystical allusions that pervade the terminology like fragments of dispersed light, so redolent in Lurianic Kabbalah; but also the reference to sapphire, to the *'arpelei tohar*

("clouds of purity"), and even the "ivory (*shayish*)" seeming splendor, whose impression could bedazzle the mystical adept from Talmudic episodes on (cf. *B. Ḥagiga* 14a).

8. Cf. Psalm 19:12, where the worshipper is "warned" or "illumined (*nizhar*)" by the teachings of Torah, and all those who "keep" or "observe" its teachings will find great treasure. V. 15 refers to *hegyon libbi*, "my heart-speak."
9. Nearly every word of this first stanza is drawn from Jewish mystical language: the poet speaks of the "inner essence (*'etzem*)" of his "solitary" youthful soul (*yeḥidi*); of the disclosed "mysteries (*setarim; razeihem*)" of visionary sights (*nistalkalti; tzofeh*). Notably, too, the "eye" of the world is its "font" and "color" (recurrent puns and allusions in mystical texts); and most especially the "reception" of the mysteries (*qibbalti*). Among the most salient of the biblical allusions are Isa. 29:11; Jer. 32:11; Dan. 12:9; and, suggestively, Song of Songs 4:12.
10. The verb *hitna'arah* coveys the dual sense of "arousal" and "becoming youthful."
11. The topos of prophets "seeing" God through a visionary mirror of water is classically enunciated in *Midrash Vayiqra Rabba* 1.14, ed. M. Margulies (Jerusalem: Wahrmann Books, 1972), I, 30–32. Note the pun on Ezekiel's vision (*mar'eh*) as a mirror (*mar'ah*) at the waters of Chebar (Ezek. 43:3).
12. There are many examples of mystical visions of light and the symbolism of water and sinking. A classic instance is in R. Isaac de-min Akko's *Otzar Ḥayim*, MS. Moscow-Günzberg 775, folio 161b.
13. The light of God's garment is first mentioned in Ps. 104:2; the theme is taken up in *Midrash Bereshit Rabba*, ed. J. Theodor and Ch. Albeck (Jerusalem: Wahrmann Books, 1965), 3.7 (I, pp. 19–20); the light "separated" for the righteous at the creation is specified in *Midrash Bereshit Rabba*, 3.6 (I, p. 22). This same light is first deemed "hidden" (*ganaz*) in B. *Ḥagiga* 12a, and subsequently in numerous mystical sources. For a wide-ranging exploration of this theme, see A. Altmann, "A Note on the Rabbinic Doctrine of Creation," *Journal of Jewish Studies* 7 (1956): 195–206.
14. The verbal stem *r-g-sh* thus conveys both a shuddering tremor and an inward sensibility; and *h-m-h* conveys both the swelling of sea waves and the vibrations of the heart and mind—as innumerable biblical references fully attest.
15. The image of a star conveying compassion to the poet, grieving over memories and dreams and ever longing for redemptive inspiration (the star being a heavenly semblance of childhood radiance), also occurs in *Kokhav Nidaḥ.*
16. These channels (*tzinorot*) import mystical revelations. A similar sequence of language is at the end of *Tzafririm.*
17. Deftly, the poet conveys this primordial moment of pure happening (the verb *ḥalah* also conveys, by suggestion, the absence of desecration).
18. *Zohar* is dated to 1901; *Ha-Bereikhah*, to 1908.
19. The poet himself is thus included in this "seeing," as he says at the onset of *Zohar* that in his youth he was "like a *tzofeh* at the *'ein* of the world" where primal mysteries were revealed (*niglu*). This verb has recurrent iterations.

    Bialik's use of *ke'ilu* marks his acute consciousness of the role of similes to convey imaginal effects. He also uses *kemo* in the second stanza of *Mi-Shomerim La-Boqer* to indicate the near-ineffability of mystical experience. His use of this form is a remarkable stylistic enjambment. For this and other reasons, I believe that Hillel Zeitlin greatly misspeaks his critique of Bialik's use of similes. See his "*'Al Bialik*," *Ha-Tequfah* 17 (1918): 430–42.

20. The imagery of mirrored worlds with diverse refractions is a fundamental feature of kabbalistic hermeneutics and is a topos employed by E. Wolfson to articulate mystical poesis in his illuminating chapter, "Showing the Saying: Laying Interpretative Ground," in *Language, Eros, Being: Kabbalistic Hermeneutics and Poetic Imagination* (New York: Fordham University Press, 2005), 1–45. Visionary hermeneutics has been a major feature of his scholarship.
21. See the poignant lines in *Lifnei Aron Ha-Sefarim* ("Before the Bookcase").
22. A stimulating linguistic discussion of the verb *'arag* in Bialik's oeuvre appears in D. Sadan, *Ḥayim Naḥman Bialik ve-Darko bi-Leshono ve-Leshonoteyha* (Tel Aviv: Ha-Kibbutz Ha-Me'uḥad, 1989), 15–34. The "Song of Unity" (*Shir Ha-Yiḥud*) is recited each Sabbath according to the Ashkenazi rite.
23. See near the end of *Razei Laylah* ("Mysteries of the Night"), where it is paired with a *bat qol* (divine voice).
24. The verb was also employed to give an ironic echo to the words of Laban, Rachel, and Jacob himself in Gen. 31:19–20, 26–27. The term conveys plagiaristic or false prophecy; see below.
25. Cf. Bialik's lecture, "*'Al Qodesh ve-Ḥol be-Lashon*," in Ḥ. N. Bialik, *Devarim She-Be'al Peh* (Tel Aviv: Devir, 1935), II, pp. 128–30 (delivered in 1927).
26. The mystic innuendo of *nitzotz* (soul spark) here is freighted with significance.
27. It was published in 1917. There have been various attempts to correlate Bialik's linguistic theories with Russian symbolists, German romantics, and others. See Ḥ. Bar-Yosef, "*'Al Andrei Biely, Ha-Simbolizm ha-Rusi ve-Bialik*," discussed and translated in *Miqarov* 10 (2003): 44–57; R. Cartun-Blum, "Diesendruck ve-Bialik," *Moznayim* 41, no. 2 (1965), 90–97. See Diesendruk's "*Ḥiyuv ve-Shlilah ba-Vitui*," *Revivim* 3–4 (1913): 5–18. Both he and Bialik were influenced by G. Herder's *Abhandlungen über den Ursprung der Sprache* (1770; Stuttgart: Reclam, 1966).
28. It would surely not have been lost on Bialik that the image of the world suspended over *belimah* in Job 26:7 is preceded by the figure of the north (*tzafon*) stretched out over *tohu*. Might *tzafun* (the hidden) also be intoned here?
29. The poem marks this verbal desecration through numerous inversions of old sacrificial terminology.
30. See his *Shirim u-Fizmonim LiYladim* (1933; reprinted Tel Aviv: Devir, 2008).
31. Cf. *Shirim u-Fizmonim LiYladim*, p. 19. For a full-scale study, see D. Marom, "*Bialik 'al ha-Nadnedah*," *Dor le-Dor* 53 (2017): 33–72.

UNIVERSAL SINGULARITIES

Elliot R. Wolfson on Jewish Ethnocentrism

HARTLEY LACHTER

In his first monograph, a critical edition and study of Moses de Leon's *Sefer ha-Rimmon* published in 1988, Elliot Wolfson discussed what he considered to be the "essential teaching" of de Leon regarding the unification of the masculine and feminine in the divine realm. He remarked that "by 'essential teaching' I have in mind a particular usage of Martin Heidegger. In his masterful work on Friedrich Nietzsche, Heidegger wrote that the great nineteenth-century German philosopher belonged to the class of 'essential thinkers' by which he meant 'those exceptional human beings who are destined to think one single thought, a thought that is always about *beings as a whole*. Each thinker thinks only one single thought . . . around which . . . all beings turn.'"[1] Elliot Wolfson is undoubtedly himself an "essential thinker." From his earliest publications, he has employed a comparative and philosophical approach in order to explore nonbinary forms of thought. Wolfson's attentiveness to the paradoxical nature of kabbalistic speculation through the lens of various modern continental philosophers, most notably Heidegger, has enabled him to produce unique and penetrating insights on a wide range of topics, including gender, time, language, esotericism, eros, the role of the imagination, eschatology, and other questions.

Wolfson's many rich studies, drawing upon a broad historical sweep of texts from the kabbalistic tradition, as well as sources drawn from Buddhism, Taoism, Islam, and others, have returned time and again to the irresolvable tensions that reside at the core of language and being. With each new examination of an additional text, layers are added to the endless possibilities that Wolfson's hermeneutic opens for his readers. Wolfson continues to unpack the implications of his own essential thinking regarding the simultaneous unity and difference of opposites. This has enabled scholars in many fields to gain a new appreciation of the value that can be gained by reading diverse corpora in light of one another. Using tools from modern philosophy, Wolfson has brought into view the nonbinary modes of thought at the heart of kabbalistic discussions of, for example, the nature of time and the confluence of past and future in the present, or the disclosure of the kabbalistic secret by means of its concealment. Wolfson has shown how opposites in these texts neither fully converge nor completely disentangle.

In a diary entry from January 16, 1922, Franz Kafka described his own work as "an assault on the border" that "might have developed quite easily into a new esoteric doctrine, a Kabbala." Wolfson cites this passage with approval, observing that Kafka's "image of assaulting the border" is helpful in seeking "to understand the phenomenological texture and hermeneutical presuppositions of the kabbalah."[2] I would suggest that Wolfson's work is itself an assault upon the border, unsettling the easy dichotomies of being and nonbeing, speech and silence, secrecy and disclosure, male and female, exile and redemption, past and future, self and other.

In what follows I offer a brief discussion of Wolfson's extensive engagement with the subject of Jewish ethnocentrism. This is an important domain for considering the ways that his thought enables an honest evaluation of primary sources and remains attentive to the self-deconstructing nature of the binaries that the texts construct. Wolfson's thinking on this particular subject is not confined to Judaism alone, in the sense that the tensions he exposes in Jewish sources regarding the converging dichotomy of self and other reflects striking affinities to other modes of thought. Philological, philosophical, and comparative questions are always intimately intertwined in Wolfson's thinking. As he has noted on a number of occasions, "the deeper one digs into one path, the greater the chance one will find the way to other paths. I embrace a universalism rooted in the singularity of each tradition."[3] The question of Jewish ethnocentrism in Wolfson's work provides an instructive example of his ability to reveal the many paths that intersect when examining one tradition in granular detail. Wolfson's work provides meticulous textual analysis, as well as insightful philosophical engagement and constructive observations regarding fundamental aspects of the human condition and pressing social challenges.

JEWISH CONSTRUCTIONS OF SELF AND OTHER

In a monograph published in 2006 dealing extensively with premodern Jewish and kabbalistic ethnocentrism, *Venturing Beyond: Law and Morality in Kabbalistic Mysticism*, Wolfson acknowledges at the outset the thorny ethical problems facing the scholar seeking to explore this important question. He observes:

> What is noteworthy is that the rhetoric of hatred forged in the crucible of medieval animosity continues to be used in the service of a present-day political program. . . . The task of responsible scholarship is to acknowledge the reverberations of these ideas in contemporary compositions, which undoubtedly have an influence on the current socio-political scene, even though we want to avoid ethical condemnation

of a tradition shaped in a different time. In short, we need to navigate between the extremes of pious apologetic and moral dogmatism.[4]

Wolfson's work demonstrates a balance between a frank assessment of the at times radically ethnocentric trends in premodern Jewish sources, along with their ongoing echoes in modern and contemporary thinkers, and an attempt to consider ways that the tradition points beyond itself. The possibilities for imagining a more ethical engagement with the other encoded within these sources, especially kabbalistic texts, cannot be properly understood, according to Wolfson, without first understanding the full range of discourses of alterity evident in the extant compositions.

Starting with the meaning of Hebrew and Aramaic terms often translated by scholars as referring broadly to humanity, Wolfson demonstrates the many instances in which these terms are deployed to refer exclusively to the people of Israel as the only true human beings. Wolfson observes that "once we understand the lexical issue of the term *adam*, we can evaluate accurately the idea of humanity in classical kabbalistic sources, and by extension the relationship of mysticism and ethics."[5] Wolfson discusses the cases in rabbinic and kabbalistic sources in which this term is employed as a reference to Jews as the true embodiment of Adam and thus the only true human beings.[6] In the kabbalistic sources, building upon rabbinic precedent, he notes that a "consistent anthropological picture emerges: Israel is portrayed as the 'holy seed' (*zar'a qaddisha*), whereas the other nations of the world . . . are said to derive from the demonic 'other side' (*sitra ahra*)."[7] That is to say, in the kabbalistic sources, only Jews are fully human in the proper sense, since only Jews possess divine souls that derive from the realm of purity.

Wolfson demonstrates further that the terms *adam* and *bar nash* are exclusive not only to Jews, but more specifically to circumcised male Jews. Though Wolfson notes his sympathy with the "postmodern tendency to seek multiple voices in the reading of texts," he observes that "in the case of traditional kabbalistic sources, I submit that the general invariability and redundancy are due to male exclusivity and social homogeneity fostered by the augmented androcentrism of medieval rabbinic culture."[8] The special status of carrying a divine soul within a human body is attributed by the kabbalists specifically to the Jewish male due to "the correlation of the [divine] name and circumcision."[9] That is to say, only the circumcised male Jew carries on his body the mark of the divine name that correlates with the divine status of his soul. This view of the unique spiritual and somatic qualities of Jewish men, Wolfson observes, enables them, according to the kabbalists, to embody the divine in the earthly realm in a way that gentiles and women, including Jewish women, do not. Due to this heightened meaning associated with circumcision in kabbalistic sources, Wolfson notes that for them, "Israel's humanity is disclosed in the sign inscribed on the flesh of the penis. The word *adam*, therefore, applies most precisely to the male Jew, a connotation that is conveyed as well in the Aramaic idiom frequently used in the zoharic corpus, *bar nash*, which contemporary scholars have misleadingly rendered in generic terms as a reference to humanity."[10]

Given the cultural context of medieval western Europe in which classical kabbalistic sources were composed, it is unsurprising that the people most commonly identified as the paradigmatic other was the Christian majority. Kabbalistic anthropology, as Wolfson describes it, resisted the Christian depiction of Jews and Judaism:

> Reversing the standard trope of the Christian polemic against Jews in the Middle Ages that contrasted the otherworldly spirituality of Christianity with the this-worldly orientation of Judaism, the zoharic authorship associated Christianity with the power of impurity that is operative in this world. By contrast, Jews alone know the path of holiness that leads to eschatological reward. Far from being people only of the letter of the law, which was long associated with carnality in Christian attacks on Judaism, the zoharic texts present Jews as having exclusive access to the spiritual realm—not at the expense of the physical world, but in conjunction with it.[11]

The tensions between Judaism and Christianity in medieval kabbalistic texts reflect how, according to Wolfson, "in the long and variegated history of Jews and Christians, framed typologically as the struggle between Jacob and Esau, self-definition and definition of the other are inextricable interwoven."[12] The focus on circumcision reflects both its centrality as a marker of peoplehood and identity in biblical and rabbinic sources and its importance in the Jewish-Christian debates of the Middle Ages. The Christian notion of supersession was embodied in the noncircumcised male body. Wolfson argues that "in clever exegetical fashion, the authorship of the *Zohar* turns the Pauline view regarding circumcision on its head." Countering the Christian doctrine of the "circumcision of the flesh," kabbalists argue that physical "circumcision (*milah*) is the true incarnation of the divine word (*millah*) in the flesh."[13] Wolfson points out that kabbalistic sources remain adamant that circumcision and the physical performance of the law are necessary for attaining redemption: "Rejecting the universalizing and spiritualizing tendencies of Christianity, the zoharic author insists that the site of salvation remains the embodied sign of circumcision."[14] In this way, Wolfson demonstrates how kabbalistic anthropology, androcentrism, and eschatology all correlate with one another.

Kabbalistic texts do more than simply articulate the special status of the male Jew. They also assert the unholy and evil nature of the Christian and non-Jewish other. As Wolfson observes, "the anthropological perspective articulated in *Zohar* is that the soul of Israel derives from the right side of holiness and is manifest most fully in the circumcised male body, whereas the soul of the idolatrous nations derives from the left side of impurity and is emblematized by the uncircumcised penis."[15] While in texts like the Zohar there is far greater hostility toward Christianity than Islam, there are anti-Islamic discourses as well. Nonetheless, the Christian environment where many kabbalistic texts developed created a pointedly anti-Christian bias. As Wolfson points out, "according to the symbolism embraced by kabbalists of the zoharic circle, in line with the invectives typical of medieval Jewish texts, Christians are the embodiment of demonic impurity in the world."[16]

ESCHATOLOGICAL OVERCOMING OF SELF/OTHER

To this point it might seem that the dichotomy between self and other is an example of a distinctly binary form of kabbalistic thought. Yet it is exactly at this site of divergence where Wolfson's engagement with modern philosophy (itself an interesting point of converging divergence between Jewish and non-Jewish modes of thinking) makes a crucial turn that brings these opposites into relation. The poles of self and other, Jew and non-Jew, male and female, in kabbalistc texts are complicated by the issues of time and history, since in the messianic future, boundaries are imagined differently. Wolfson describes how "the cultural and gender boundaries are fluid, for the process of history, culminating with the coming of the messiah, is perceived as the engenderment of memory by means of which the bifurcation of male and female, Jew and Christian, is surmounted."[17] This reflects a broader feature of kabbalistic discourse that Wolfson's thought is particularly attentive to; namely, that "kabbalists uniformly eschew an absolute metaphysical dualism."[18] In one of his earliest published studies Wolfson observed that "the demonic has a root in the divine,"[19] and that "the perfect state is not one in which evil is entirely obliterated, but rather one in which it is contained within the good."[20] In a more recent monograph he points out that the kabbalistic notion of evil, the *Sitra Ahra*, is the "nonessence infused with negativity that belongs to the positivity of the essence, the potential for difference of identity coiled within and yet departing from the identity of difference."[21]

Wolfson remains clear that in both medieval and modern kabbalistic texts, the containment of evil within the divine, and by extension the other within the self, that is realized in messianic redemption is not taken as a mandate to blur those boundaries in the preredemptive social reality, since "in the present historical period Edom is the evil twin of Jacob, the uncircumcised one whose savior is depicted as one born of a menstruant woman." Nonetheless, there is a distinct monistic impulse in kabbalistic thinking that does not permit an unambiguous and permanent bifurcation between good and evil, or self and other. This is seen most clearly in descriptions of "the messianic future" where "the demonic force of Edom will be restored to the Godhead and the dualism will be transcended. The polemical opposition between Jacob and Esau, forces of light and darkness, is resolved in the ultimate act of reconciliation, which involves the othering of the other so that the other is itself a manifestation of the self."[22] The present reality, on the other hand, is marked by an ontology in which self and other must remain distinct, since "until the messianic era, which is marked by the elimination of the evil force and the consequent reintegration of the demonic in the divine, there is a definite boundary separating good and evil."[23] Wolfson shows how kabbalistic ethnocentrism and devaluation of the other through the mandate to keep the domains of the sacred and profane, Jew and non-Jew, and male and female separate in the pre-messianic social realm continues to influence modern and contemporary Jewish thinkers. He demonstrates how the ethnocentrism of the classical medieval sources continued to influence Kabbalists from the sixteenth century into modernity, including Elijah de Vidas,

Isaiah Horowitz, Judah Loewe of Prague, Jonathan Eybeschuetz, Abraham Isaac Kook, Zvi Ryback, and Judah Kalfon.[24] His work on Habad Hasidism and Menahem Mendel Schneerson considers the complex reverberations of these themes.[25] He has also published a study on similar themes in the thought of Isaac Hutner, an influential figure in twentieth-century American and Israeli orthodoxy.[26] The echoes of the medieval kabbalistic legacy of ethnocentric and at times dehumanizing characterizations of the other continue to be heard. Wolfson's work has helped to attune the ear of scholarship to this important phenomenon.

HEIDEGGER, KABBALAH, AND THE QUESTION OF THE OTHER

One of Wolfson's most distinctive contributions has been his talent for bringing together philosophical and kabbalistic sources that are not typically read in light of one another. This is particularly true in the case of Heidegger, whose thought has been important to Wolfson's work from the earliest stages. The complexity of ethnocentrism in kabbalistic texts is brought into even greater focus in Wolfson's work on this seminal thinker. The irony of finding an appropriate philosophical language for engaging kabbalistic thinking in the work of a twentieth-century German philosopher who openly embraced the Nazi party, at least for a time, is not lost on Wolfson.[27] In fact, that very dissonance reflects important themes running through Wolfson's work on kabbalistic ethnocentrism regarding the simultaneity of sameness and otherness. His use of Heidegger to discuss kabbalistic texts, and Kabbalah as a lens for reading Heidegger, embodies the tensions at the heart of his observations regarding the identity through nonidentity of their respective ethnocentric discourses. Wolfson notes that "as incongruous as it might seem, Heidegger's path converges divergently with the esoteric tradition of the Kabbalah."[28] While Wolfson does not discount the possibility of the influence of Kabbalah on Heidegger through channels like Schelling, he notes that "it is not influence that is the focal point of my concern—I am sympathetic to Heidegger's denigration of this kind of analysis—but rather the constellation of themes underlying the respective viewpoints of Heidegger and the kabbalists, a constellation that demonstrates the disarming correlation—as opposed to dialectical coincidence—of sameness through difference, that is, the identity of the nonidentical in the preservation of the nonidentity of the identical."[29]

In discussing the revelation of Heidegger's "Black Notebooks" and the implications of these texts for the place of Heidegger and his Jewish students in contemporary Jewish philosophy, Wolfson observed:

> Let me note, finally, and perhaps most provocatively, that in both Heidegger and the kabbalists we find a privileging of a particular language as disclosive of the nature of being and the consequent affirmation of a unique cultural destiny of a particular

> ethnos, a position that harbors the potential for the disvaluing of others under the guise of racial inferiority. To date, no one has had the courage to draw this comparison. In a forthcoming monograph on Heidegger and the kabbalah, I hope to elaborate this point. Suffice it here to cite the arresting words from Dylan's *John Brown*, "But the thing that scared me most was when my enemy came close / And I saw that his face looked just like mine." By reading Jewish texts through the lens of Heidegger and reading Heidegger through the lens of Jewish texts, my hope has been to rectify their respective indiscretions.[30]

A full appreciation of the many ways that Wolfson employs Heidegger's philosophy of language in order to better understand both kabbalistic and Heideggerian ethnocentrism is well beyond the scope of this short study. What is important to note here is that this parallel, however uncomfortable it may be, is important for his project that is both descriptive and constructive. The very elements of both bodies of thought that are deployed in the service of a distancing of the other contain within them, Wolfson shows, the seeds of a way of thinking through and beyond the stark dichotomies of self and other. As he puts it, "it is my hope that the juxtaposition of the ostensibly incongruent fields of discourse, the belonging together of what is foreign, Heidegger and kabbalah, will not only enhance our understanding of both, but, in an even more profound sense, will serve as an ethical corrective of their respective ethnocentrisms, thereby illustrating the redemptive capacity of thought to yield new configurations of the unthought colluding on disparate paths of contemplative thinking."[31]

HEBREW AND GERMAN: LANGUAGE, LAND, AND PEOPLEHOOD

An intriguing parallel between Heidegger and Kabbalah that plays an important role in Wolfson's analysis of ethnocentrism in both corpora is the correlation of language, peoplehood, and land that is deployed to assert a form of ethno-national supremacy. Wolfson demonstrates the uncanny resemblance between the kabbalistic understanding of Hebrew as the divine language uniquely able to disclose the ineffable in kabbalistic sources, and the role of German in Heidegger's affirmation of the historical destiny of Germany and the German *Volk* in world history.[32] The paradoxes of the unveiling of the esoteric through a particular language and the elevation of the status of the nation identified with that language is, in both cases, a thread that runs through Wolfson's discussion of the ethnocentric moves at play.

The notion that one particular language is uniquely suited to unveiling the veil of the secret of being is a claim found in both kabbalistic and Heideggerian discourses of esotericism.[33] Wolfson points out that "Heidegger's belief that no language is superior to German in its facility to express the inexpressible and to comprehend the incomprehensible is in accord with the kabbalistic contention that Hebrew, categorically assumed to be the language of creation and revelation, is the most appropriate means for declaiming the ineffable and for conceiving the inconceivable."[34] For both Heidegger and the kabbalists, the unique status they accord to German or Hebrew is based on the perception that their particular language has a special capacity to disclose, in a nonbinary way, the incomprehensible and infinite aspects of reality. In conversation with Heidegger and other philosophers, Wolfson moves beyond the notion of the merging of opposites in mystical ontologies. These discourses, he argues, do not simply collapse opposites into one another in a *coincidentia oppositorum*. Instead, opposites are neither fully merged nor fully separate; they "remain opposite in their juxtaposition."[35] What follows from this is the notion of German, for Heidegger, or Hebrew, for the kabbalists, as the only language capable of approaching the transcendent registers of being, which ironically elevates the particular people associated with that language due to their unique access to the universal and ineffable.

Wolfson is certainly aware of the differences between Heidegger and kabbalistic thought, as well as the deep irony in the fact that these corpora can be mutually illuminating. On the matter of ethnocentrism and language he notes that "even more surprising is the fact that in both Heidegger and the kabbalists one can find a coupling of semantic essentialism and ethnocentric chauvinism, that is, the privileging of a particular language as disclosive of the truth of being and the consequent affirmation of a unique cultural destiny of a particular ethnos to be the custodian of that language in the land of its origin, a position that harbors the potential for the devaluing of others in racial terms."[36] Scholars have tended to read both Heidegger and Kabbalah too generously in their thinking on language as observations with universalist overtones. Wolfson contends that in both cases, their thinking hinges on particularistic rather than humanistic claims regarding the implications of a given language as the one exclusively disclosive of the nature of being. In the case of Heidegger, the contention is that "the German essence is both enrooted in the soil of the language and embodied in the language of the soil. It follows that his repeated reflections on the primacy of language, including the notorious claim that language is the house of being, must be interpreted in a particularistic as opposed to a universalistic register."[37] Or as Wolfson puts it elsewhere, "Heidegger made it abundantly clear that the idea of homeland is inextricably linked to the veneration of German as the *Muttersprache*."[38]

Kabbalistic sources are no less committed to a triad of language, peoplehood, and land. Though always cautious with regard to totalizing claims regarding corpora as diverse and extensive as that of Kabbalah, Wolfson nevertheless states: "Although I am sympathetic with the postmodern proclivity to resist essentializing and generalizing, I am unfamiliar with any kabbalist who would reject either the belief that Hebrew is the holy language and, as such, is to be distinguished from all other languages, or the corollary beliefs that the Jewish people and land of Israel are endowed with a unique holiness."[39] This claim, based on an intimate familiarity with countless kabbalistic texts, is connected to Wolfson's broader observation that the specific function of Hebrew in the disclosure of the irresolvable paradoxes underlying the nature of reality in kabbalistic discourse accords with a similar notion in Heidegger's thought. As he puts it, "for the kabbalists, the most auspicious way to the silence beyond speech is through Hebrew, the sole language considered to be sacred, whereas Heidegger attributed priority to German as the most effective language to express poetically what is inexpressible, a task that he himself considered as naming the holy, the enigma that shines forth in its gathering depth only as it veils itself."[40]

The Heideggerian and kabbalistic notion of a silence beyond speech, a secret unveiled through its concealment, that lies beyond language and yet can be approached through the unspeaking of that which is spoken, could be taken to have universal implications. That is to say, the mystical path could serve as a node of convergence for disparate identities, languages, and peoples to merge through the encounter with the divine infinity. And yet, it is within this universal that the specific identity of the Jew, for the kabbalists, and the German, for Heidegger, is grounded. As Wolfson notes, "the attitude to Hebrew and the land of Israel in Jewish sources, especially heightened in the kabbalistic material, fulfills a similar function as German does for Heidegger in grounding the particular in the universal."[41] Wolfson suggests that for kabbalists, "only the Jew, as it were, has the wherewithal to be absorbed into the infinite where all distinctions—including the distinction between Jew and non-Jew—are transcended. . . . The logic of this position is not entirely coherent, and yet, Jewish mystics have repeatedly affirmed that only the Jew can close the gap separating Jew and non-Jew by steadfastly widening that gap."[42] The encounter with the infinite is, for the kabbalists, accessible only to Jews through adherence to Jewish law. The realm beyond self and other can only be approached through the particular confines of Hebrew and rabbinic Judaism. Wolfson's analysis reveals an important feature of mystical/esoteric thinking that scholarship in the field has yet to fully embrace, which is the fact that though a given thinker or tradition may endorse the notion of a radically infinite and ineffable transcendent realm, this need not carry as a corollary the embrace of a universal humanity that overcomes social and political difference. As Wolfson has observed, "a radical theopoetics is not necessarily incompatible with a conservative politics."[43]

In the case of Heidegger, particularism and ethnocentric thinking remain similarly embedded within his understanding of the tensions of language, being, and identity. With regard to "the severing of language from the people, and by extension, from the land," Wolfson notes that "Heidegger could not envision such a possibility" since "the political dimension of poetry was still tied to the intricate connection between land, language, and peoplehood. The same can be said about the kabbalah and its continual impact on conceptions of Jewish identity, especially as expressed in Zionist right-wing ideology. Celebrations of the diasporic nature of Judaism—epitomized in Steiner's formula that *the text is the homeland*—are commendable, but they are not sufficient to untie the knot of the ethnolinguistic geopolitics that continues to inform the beliefs and actions of segments of the Jewish world."[44] While kabbalistic and Heideggerian ideas may appear to incline toward the universal, an honest assessment of each must, Wolfson argues, account for the persistent and problematic particularism of each.

Even in discussions of a redemptive future state, Wolfson demonstrates that neither the kabbalists nor Heidegger entirely give up on ethno-linguistic specificity and territoriality. Remarking on the "friction that has marked the Jewish sensibility through the centuries" regarding the relation between Israel and other nations, Wolfson suggests that one encounters "on the one hand, the exclusivity of an ethnocentrism that has deep roots in the biblical metaphor of chosenness; on the other hand, the inclusivity implied in the prophetic-messianic mission of being a light unto the nations. Fluctuating between these poles, Israel's election has assumed the form of an inclusive exclusiveness that is an exclusive inclusiveness."[45] The specific formation of this "exclusive inclusiveness" draws upon the kabbalistic notion of the inclusion of evil and the demonic in the divine. That is, as Wolfson puts it, in kabbalistic depictions of the messianic future, Jews and Christians unite through "the reconfigured archetype of Israel in whose constellation the other—symbolized by Edom—has been assimilated."[46] The moment of the convergence of humanity into a universal singularity in the messianic redemption, for the kabbalists, occurs through the absorption of the non-Jewish other into the Jewish self.

SWERVING TIME AND TANGLED PATHS IN WOLFSON'S PROJECT

Wolfson's analysis of ethnocentric themes in kabbalistic and Heideggerian thought does not stop at a description of the past. He mines these texts for new readings that enable new possibilities. A hermeneutical assumption behind Wolfson's approach is his understanding of temporality—a longstanding scholarly interest he has cultivated for many years—and his idea of the linear circularity of time.[47] Resisting the tendency to resolve temporality into the simple binary of linear and circular, Wolfson presents this middle ground as a meeting of past and future in the present, creating the possibility of a scholarly reconstruction that also produces new meaning. As he puts it, "the temporal presupposition buttressing my hermeneutic embraces the prospect of a reversible timeline—what I have called the timeswerve of linear circularity—such that the present is as much the cause of the past as the past is the cause of the present; the past persists in the present as the trace that is reconfigured anew each moment through the agency of anamnesis." Building upon ideas in Benjamin and Heidegger, Wolfson refers to this kind of "scholarly reconstruction as a type of *futural remembering*, or a *remembering expectation*, an act of recollecting that has the capacity to redeem the past, not by describing how the past really was but by imputing to it meaning that it never had except as the potential to become what it is not."[48] In his assessment of ethnocentrism in Kabbalah and Heidegger, Wolfson combines rigorous philological analysis with a proposal of just such a potential for the views on the nature of self and other within these corpora to yield new possibilities.

Such a view of the nature of time begs the question of the meaning of messianic expectation as an event confined to the future, and the potential for complicating the self-other dichotomy in the present. Wolfson explores Heidegger's claims regarding the nomadic quality[49] of the Jewish people in light of Rosenzweig's understanding of time and eschatology. For Rosenzweig, Wolfson observes, there is always "the possibility of the future diremptively breaking into the present at any moment, an incursion that disturbs the chronometric flow of time and undercuts the supposition that there is a progressive march toward a messianic goal. Messianic hope hinges on preparing for the onset of what takes place as the *purely present future*, that is, the future that is already present as the present that is always future, the *tomorrow that is now because it is now tomorrow*."[50] Such a view, Wolfson notes, can be found in the complex engagement with messianic redemption in kabbalistic sources. The present moment is where the future redemption of the end converges with the beginning.[51] This understanding of temporality carries the potential for the overcoming of conflict that pertains in the redemptive future to break forth in the present.

HOMECOMING: RETURN THROUGH THE FOREIGN

In addition to similarity between Heidegger and Kabbalah on matters of ethnocentrism regarding language and poesis noted above, Wolfson also suggests that "we can justifiably infer that kabbalists would assent to Heidegger's demarcation of the homecoming as the return to the nearness of origin."[52] Such a return entails a recognition of the arduous loneliness of the journey home. The path of return requires a recognition of the mystery of origins and the distance of that which is most near. A deeper engagement with the familiar is made possible through the exploration of the strange. Wolfson's penchant for comparison and reading texts from radically different times, places, and intellectual contexts in light of one another reflects his notion that the "appropriation of one's own requires the disappropriation of confronting the stranger. The encounter with the alien is what propels the journey home, the struggle with the unordinary instigates the return to the ordinary."[53] Wolfson argues that this tension can be productively exploited for rethinking the ethnocentrism in both Heidegger and Kabbalah by building on their shared notion of the inherently dislocative nature of being and human experience. As he proposes, "another path may be pursued, however, to destabilize the territorialism and exceptionalism, a poetic—as opposed to a political—breach that opens from the weight of the cultural prejudices themselves and seeks to affirm the homelessness of being at home in contrast to the homeliness of being banished from home."[54]

The constructive conclusion of Wolfson's reading of Heidegger through Kabbalah and Kabbalah through Heidegger exploits the issue of the belonging together of the foreign as a marker of the path of the return to origin. The relation of self and other reaches comity and equality neither through the collapse of the two into the one, nor through the negation of difference, but through a recognition of the inherent universality of particularity.

> Expounding Holderin's line *Alles ist innig*, Heidegger writes, "This means that one is appropriated to the other, but in such a way that it itself remains in what is proper to it. . . . Intimacy does not mean the coalescence and obliteration of distinctions. Intimacy names the belonging together of what is foreign, the ruling of the strange, the claim of awe." . . . Heidegger proposed an ethical-political principle—perhaps it is more accurately classified as postethical and postpolitical—according to which one is appropriated to the other by remaining proper to the inappropriable distillation that is one's own; the intimacy of confronting the other is neither a coalescence (*Verschmelzen*) nor an obliteration (*Verloschen*) of distinctions, but rather a preserving of them in belonging together of what is foreign (*das Zusammengehoren des Fremden*).[55]

On this reading, difference is part of the intimate relation of the other to the self. Implied in both bodies of thought is the possibility of acknowledging the moral value of the other in relation to the self and the self to the other as a facet of the nonbinary nature of being. The other "belongs" together with the self, and yet is still distinct. Indeed, it is through that distinctiveness that such belonging is possible. As Wolfson presents it, "individuality consists of embracing an alterity that is universalizable in such a way that the particularity is preserved: the difference between us is what invariably makes us the same and therefore categorically not subject to the categorical."[56]

This observation regarding the relation of the foreign to the self reflects not only a strategy of subversive reading whereby Wolfson carries Heideggerian and kabbalistic thinking beyond itself on the question of ethnocentrism; it also reflects something central to his own scholarly enterprise over the course of more than three decades. As he puts it in the final paragraph of *Heidegger and Kabbalah*,

> My strategy in this book has been to follow this path, to link two ostensibly different corpora in order to illumine the convergence within the difference, to demonstrate that otherness of the similar is consequent to the similarity of the other. I have sought to recover from two admittedly independent ideational matrices a logic that preserves the disparity of the uniform by keeping to the uniformity of the disparate. Without denying the demonstrably detrimental attitude that has informed the kabbalistic and Heideggerian constructions of the other—in both cases, although qualitatively and quantitatively different, the theoretical construct has had pernicious practical implications—I contend nonetheless that the negative propensity of a singular universality has the capacity to yield the ethical imperative of a universal singularity: what secures our equality is our diversity.[57]

The notion of the intimacy of the foreign and the self in such a way that the two do not collapse into the one informs not only Wolfson's construction of an "ethical imperative of a universal singularity" from kabbalistic and Heideggerian sources, but also his methodology in reading premodern Kabbalah together with modern philosophy. The autonomy of each remains intact, at the same time as their belonging together. They each enable the uncovering of new facets in the other by virtue of, to put it in Wolfsonian terms, the sameness of their difference and the difference of their sameness. The rich productivity of such a juxtaposition is not due to the influence of one upon the other, but from the intellectual and poetic play of otherness and similarity that Wolfson elicits from them. In the case of ethnocentrism, and the at times negative consequences of such ideas, Wolfson's work shines an unstinting spotlight upon the realities and ethical problems visible in both corpora, while also suggesting alternative readings and possibilities embedded in these systems of thought. Both Heidegger and the kabbalists suggest that self and other are intimately connected, but not reducible to one another. Wolfson argues that such thinking carries the implication that the moral value of the other, and the ethical obligation toward the other, is an inevitable feature of the autonomy of the self.

Wolfson's path home, like all paths with such a destination, has thus been through alien territory. His examination of Judaism employs extensive comparison with the literatures of other religious traditions, as well as philosophical texts that could be said not to belong together. But for Wolfson, belonging is a feature of nonbelonging. Scholarly vision is increased through the revelation of the obscuring veil of the other. He argues that "the way back home" is "the longest of paths, not because it is least far away, but because it leads through what is most near. The journey embarked upon in this book, indeed a journey I began many years ago, has been a concerted effort to unveil the truth of this veil, to find the route to the familiar by delving into and dwelling within the domain of the foreign, relentlessly cultivating two ways of seeing and two ways of listening, simultaneously together and separate."[58] Wolfson's work on ethnocentric discourse in Judaism embodies this ethos of the value of diverse perspective in arriving again at one's point of departure by traversing the path of the foreign. Along the way, his work has revealed that the domain of the foreign may not be so distant, and the destination of origin not so near.

NOTES

1. Elliot R. Wolfson, *The Book of the Pomegranate: Moses de León's Sefer ha-Rimmon*, Brown Judaic Series 144 (Atlanta: Scholars Press, 1988), 67, citing Martin Heidegger, *Nietzsche, Volume III: The Will to Power as Knowledge and Metaphysics* (San Francisco: Harper and Row, 1987), 4.
2. Elliot R. Wolfson, "Iconicity of the Text: Reification of the Torah and the Idolatrous Impulse of Zoharic Kabbalah," in *Elliot R. Wolfson: Poetic Thinking*, ed. Hava Tirosh-Samuelson and Aaron W. Hughes (Leiden: Brill, 2015), 69.
3. "Interview with Elliot R. Wolfson, July 25, 2012," in *Elliot R. Wolfson: Poetic Thinking*, ed. Hava Tirosh-Samuelson and Aaron W. Hughes (Leiden: Brill, 2015), 196–97.
4. Elliot R. Wolfson, *Venturing Beyond: Law and Morality in Kabbalistic Mysticism* (Oxford: Oxford University Press, 2006), 25–26.
5. Wolfson, *Venturing Beyond*, 97.

6. See Wolfson, *Venturing Beyond*, 42–57, 113–15.
7. Wolfson, *Venturing Beyond*, 27.
8. Wolfson, *Venturing Beyond*, 27. On the association of alterity with the feminine in classical kabbalistic sources, see, for example, Elliot R. Wolfson, "Woman—The Feminine as Other in Theosophic Kabbalah: Some Philosophical Observations on the Divine Androgyne," in *The Other in Jewish Thought and History: Constructions of Jewish Culture and Identity*, ed. Lawrence J. Silberstein and Robert L. Cohn (New York: New York University Press, 1994), 166–204.
9. Wolfson, *Venturing Beyond*, 57. On this theme, see also Elliot R. Wolfson, "Circumcision and the Divine Name: A Study in the Transmission of Esoteric Doctrine," *Jewish Quarterly Review* 78, no. 1/2 (1987): 77–112.
10. Wolfson, *Venturing Beyond*, 57.
11. Wolfson, *Venturing Beyond*, 92.
12. Elliot R. Wolfson, *Heidegger and Kabbalah: Hidden Gnosis and the Path of Poesis* (Bloomington: Indiana University Press, 2019), 361.
13. Wolfson, *Venturing Beyond*, 151.
14. Wolfson, *Venturing Beyond*, 164.
15. Wolfson, *Venturing Beyond*, 88.
16. Wolfson, *Venturing Beyond*, 136.
17. Wolfson, *Venturing Beyond*, 164–65. See also, for example, Elliot R. Wolfson, "Re/Membering the Covenant: Memory, Forgetfulness, and the Construction of History in the Zohar," in *Jewish History and Jewish Memory: Essays in Honor of Yosef Hayim Yerushalmi*, ed. Elisheva Carlebach, John M. Efron, and David S. Myers (Hanover and London: Brandeis University Press, 1998), 214–46. especially 226–31; and Elliot R. Wolfson, "*Tiqqun ah-Shekhinah*: Redemption and the Overcoming of Gender Dimorphism in the Messianic Kabbalah of Moses Hayyim Luzzatto," *History of Religions* 36 (1997): 289–332.
18. Wolfson, *Venturing Beyond*, 194.
19. Elliot R. Wolfson, "Left Contained in the Right: A Study in Zoharic Hermeneutics," *Association for Jewish Studies Review* 11 (1986): 29.
20. Wolfson, "Left Contained in the Right," 52.
21. Wolfson, *Heidegger and Kabbalah*, 367.
22. Wolfson, *Venturing Beyond*, 165.
23. Wolfson, *Venturing Beyond*, 263.
24. See Wolfson, *Venturing Beyond*, 111–28.
25. See Elliot R. Wolfson, *Open Secret: Postmessianic Messianism and the Mystical Revision of Menahem Mendel Schneerson* (New York: Columbia University Press, 2009), especially 224–64; and Elliot R. Wolfson, "The Status of the (Non)Jewish Other in the Apocalyptic Messianism of Menahem Mendel Schneerson," in *Kabbalah and Modernity: Interpretations, Transformations, Adaptations*, ed. B. Huss, M. Pasi, and K. von Stuckrad (Leiden: Brill, 2010), 221–57.
26. Elliot R. Wolfson, "To Distinguish Israel and the Nations: E Pluribus Unum and Isaac Hutner's Appropriation of Kabbalistic Anthropology," in *Kabbalah in America: Ancient Lore in the New World*, ed. Brian Ogren (Leiden/Boston: Brill, 2020), 316–40.

27. See his monograph, *The Duplicity of Philosophy's Shadow: Heidegger, Nazism, and the Jewish Other* (New York: Columbia University Press, 2018).
28. Wolfson, *Heidegger and Kabbalah*, 345.
29. Wolfson, *Heidegger and Kabbalah*, 9.
30. "What Does Heidegger's Antisemitism Mean for Jewish Philosophy?" Interview with Aubrey L. Glazer. April 3, 2014. https://religiondispatches.org/what-does-heideggers-anti-semitism-mean-for-jewish-philosophy/
31. Wolfson, *Heidegger and Kabbalah*, 13.
32. On this theme in Wolfson's work, see Aaron W. Hughes, "Elliot Wolfson: An Intellectual Portrait," in *Elliot R. Wolfson: Poetic Thinking*, ed. Hava Tirosh-Samuelson and Aaron W. Hughes (Leiden: Brill, 2015), 19.
33. Wolfson has dedicated many studies to the question of esotericism and language in kabbalistic and philosophical sources. See, for example, "Beautiful Maiden Without Eyes: Peshat and Sod in Zoharic Hermeutics," in *The Midrashic Imagination: Jewish Exegesis, Thought, and History*, ed. Michael Fishbane (Albany: State University of New York Press, 1993), 155–; "Occultation of the Feminine and the Body of Secrecy in Medieval Kabbalah," in *Elliot R. Wolfson: Poetic Thinking*, ed. Hava Tirosh-Samuelson and Aaron W. Hughes (Leiden: Brill, 2015), 35–68; *Through a Speculum That Shines: Vision and Imagination in Medieval Jewish Mysticism* (Princeton: Princeton University Press, 1994), 85–98, 327–92; "Murmuring Secrets: Eroticism and Esotericism in Medieval Kabbalah," in *Hidden Intercourse: Eros and Sexuality in the History of Western Esotericism*, ed. J. Kripal and W. Hanegraff (Leiden: Brill, 2008), 65–109; *Open Secret*, 29–65.
34. Wolfson, *Heidegger and Kabbalah*, 340. On the double veiling of the secret in Heidegger, see Wolfson, *Heidegger and Kabbalah*, 299–311.
35. Wolfson, *Heidegger and Kabbalah*, 4.
36. Wolfson, *Heidegger and Kabbalah*, 13. As he states the matter elsewhere, "one of the most arresting similarities between Heidegger and the kabbalists centers on their mutual recognition of the unique role of language as the medium through which the nature of being is concomitantly disclosed and concealed," 335.
37. Wolfson, *Heidegger and Kabbalah*, 337.
38. Wolfson, *Heidegger and Kabbalah*, 338–39.
39. Wolfson, *Heidegger and Kabbalah*, 345.
40. Wolfson, *Heidegger and Kabbalah*, 341.
41. Wolfson, *Heidegger and Kabbalah*, 348.
42. Wolfson, *Heidegger and Kabbalah*, 349.
43. Wolfson, *Open Secret*, 4.
44. Wolfson, *Heidegger and Kabbalah*, 365.
45. Wolfson, *Heidegger and Kabbalah*, 347.
46. Wolfson, *Heidegger and Kabbalah*, 346.
47. See, for example, Elliot R. Wolfson, *Language, Eros, Being: Kabbalistic Hermeneutics and Poetic Imagination* (New York: Fordham University Press, 2005), especially 11–31; Elliot R. Wolfson, "Recovering Futurity: Theorizing the End and the End of Theory," in *Jews at the*

End of Theory, ed. S. Ginsburg, M. Land, and J. Boyarin (New York: Fordham University Press, 2018), 293–311; and most recently the updated studies published in *Suffering Time: Philosophical, Kabbalistic, and Hasidic Reflections on Temporality* (Leiden: Brill, 2021), along with a new study titled "Timemask and the Telling of Time in the Time of Telling," 1–71. See also the discussion in Hughes, "Elliot Wolfson: An Intellectual Portrait," 19–22.

48. Wolfson, *Heidegger and Kabbalah*, 10.
49. On this theme, see Wolfson, *Duplicity of Philosophy's Shadow*, 33–86.
50. "Not Yet Now: Speaking of the End and the End of Speaking," in *Elliot R. Wolfson: Poetic Thinking*, ed. Hava Tirosh-Samuelson and Aaron W. Hughes (Leiden: Brill, 2015), 146 (emphasis in original).
51. See, for example, Wolfson's discussion of this theme in the "postmessianic messianism" of Schneerson in *Open Secret*.
52. Wolfson, *Open Secret*, 347.
53. Wolfson, *Open Secret*, 10.
54. Wolfson, *Open Secret*, 366.
55. Wolfson, *Open Secret*, 366.
56. Wolfson, *Open Secret*, 367.
57. Wolfson, *Open Secret*, 367.
58. Wolfson, *Open Secret*, 367.

PROPHETIC VISION AND IMAGINATION

Reading Maimonides with Wolfson and Wyschogrod

ANDREA DARA COOPER

I MET PROFESSOR EDITH WYSCHOGROD IN THE SPRING OF 2006 AT A BOOK launch for her collection of essays *Crossover Queries: Dwelling with Negatives, Embodying Philosophy's Others*. My doctoral advisor, Elliot Wolfson, invited a group of his advisees to the event at Labyrinth Books on the Upper West Side of Manhattan. Professor Wolfson introduced Professor Wyschogrod as his teacher at Queens College at the City University of New York, and he spoke about her wide-ranging philosophical oeuvre.[1] In *Crossover Queries*, Wyschogrod reads twentieth-century European philosophers such as Heidegger, Foucault, Derrida, Levinas, and Kristeva alongside both traditional Jewish thought and modern art, music, and dance.[2] Wyschogrod illustrates how the asceticism of traditional modes of religiosity develops into a contemporary erotics of transcendence, ultimately opening the way for a Levinasian ethics of transcendence. She embraces a philosophy of embodiment, maintaining that corporeality must be preserved in the interest of ethics. In my copy of her book, she wrote the following dedication: "To Andrea, in hope of your further study of Levinas."[3]

Wolfson makes a case for including Wyschogrod in the canon of modern Jewish thought, given her vast contributions to the disciplines of philosophy and religious studies. While there has been scholarship engaging her interpretation of Levinas and her interventions in phenomenology, postmodernism, aesthetics, ethics, politics, and historiography, Wolfson calls attention to "her status as a creative Jewish thinker," charting how she offers a deconstructive Jewish philosophy of "'immanent a/theology.'"[4] In his pathbreaking book *Giving Beyond the Gift: Apophasis and Overcoming Theomania*, Wolfson reads Wyschogrod and Jacques Derrida alongside prominent twentieth-century Jewish philosophers of dialogue to explore transcendence and immanence in Jewish thought, postmodern negative theology, and apophasis. Wolfson writes, "Derrida and Wyschogrod well understood that the removal of all images from God, if maintained unfailingly, seriously compromises the viability of devotional piety. To deplete God of the anthropomorphic and anthropopathic embellishments decisively curtails the imagination's ability to concoct the deity in personalist terms."[5] In this essay, I take up this relationship between monotheism and idolatry identified by Wolfson through an exploration of imagination and sensation—particularly vision and prophetic envisioning—in Moses Maimonides's *Guide of the Perplexed*. Wolfson's and Wyschogrod's attunement to the complex interplay of the imagination and the body allow us to see how Maimonides uses decidedly visual imagery to gesture beyond the visual, a dynamic later reflected in Emmanuel Levinas's phenomenology.

CROSSING BOUNDARIES

At New York University, I studied subjects at the nexus of mysticism, philosophy, gender studies, and the history and phenomenology of religion with Professor Wolfson. In graduate seminars and directed readings, students were challenged and encouraged to refine our analyses and to broaden our intellectual horizons. The language of the *crossover* evoked by Wyschogrod strikes me as particularly pertinent in reflecting on the influence of Wolfson's teaching on my academic development. Reading postmodern philosophy with its medieval antecedents was not dismissed as anachronistic, but was encouraged, as was pursuing feminist psychoanalytic theory alongside Jewish thought.

I learned to bridge dichotomies, to question oversimplified bifurcations, and to view philosophy and mysticism at an intersection rather than in opposition. While the *Wissenschaft* approach understands the development of Kabbalah as a reaction to Maimonidean rationalism, Gershom Scholem rejects the notion of Kabbalah as a response to philosophy, instead arguing that Kabbalah is intrinsic to Judaism and often positing the philosophical against the mystical. Scholem emphasizes the Gnostic contribution to Kabbalah, viewing it as a process of re-mythologization within Judaism, contrasted with rationalist philosophy.[6] Rather than pitting the philosophical against the mystical, though, Wolfson points out a deeper entanglement between the two modes that extends beyond mere framing; the mystical forms of experience cannot be comprehended without taking into account their philosophical influences.

Maimonides's influence on Kabbalah has particular relevance to the relationship between medieval mysticism and philosophy.[7] Wolfson points out that Maimonides's rhetorical understanding of scripture as *mashal* contributes to the Kabbalists' understanding of the parabolic. In thirteenth-century Spanish Kabbalah, the hermeneutical exegesis distinguishes between the *peshat*, the exoteric meaning, and the esoteric, mystical interpretation.[8] The Torah is viewed as having both literal and hidden meaning, and the kabbalistic reading operates on both levels. The hermeneutical approach of the Kabbalists toward the Torah is akin to the structure employed by the medieval philosophers, gleaning both exoteric and esoteric meaning from the text. The philosophical approach is exemplified in Maimonides's *Guide*, in which he outlines his parabolic approach with a verse from Proverbs: "a saying uttered with a view to two meanings is like an apple of gold overlaid with silver filigree-work having very small holes."[9] Viewed from afar, the apple appears to be silver, but upon closer examination, it becomes apparent that the apple is indeed gold inside. This example illustrates that although the inner meaning (gold) has greater value than the outer (silver), the external layer nevertheless holds some value. The dual layers of textual meaning also have social implications; while the outer layer is necessary for the multitude's level of apprehension, the inner, hidden layer grants those who are enlightened access to the truth. The esoteric and exoteric levels function politically to keep the masses at their appropriate level of understanding.[10]

The dual layers of textual interpretation delineated by Maimonides and the necessity he espouses of both communicating and concealing the secrets of the text are reflected in the kabbalistic tradition. Indeed, the secret, in order to maintain its status as secret, depends on the seemingly paradoxical act of partial transmission. If none were aware of the secret (if it were withheld from no one), then it would no longer be secretive.[11] Esoteric writing oscillates between oral articulation and written expression in withholding and transmitting. So when the secret is written down, it is still veiled by layers of secrecy, even while being communicated.[12]

Maimonides's emphasis on the allegorically concealed nature of truth provides Kabbalists with a rhetorical framing device for their hermeneutics of esotericism. For Maimonides, scripture must be decoded, but it is conveyed differently to the masses, who require the anthropomorphic references to cement their belief in God, than it is to the enlightened few who truly understand the nature of allegorical interpretation. Scriptural references to God's bodily attributes should be interpreted allegorically. If God is understood to physically speak and hear, this would imply that God is finite, and that would be an idolatrous move. Corporeal images of the divine are employed only in concession to the human mind, which is incapable of conceiving incorporeality.

The play of secrecy between revealing and concealing is illustrated in both the form and content of Maimonides's *Guide*, which is meant to be understood only by a select few.[13] He portrays his ideas equivocally for those who are able to comprehend the truth. Maimonides accepts the exoteric meaning of anthropomorphisms on the level of narrative, but the ideal reader should be able to attend to his equivocations and glean the esoteric meanings within. Just as scripture is not to be taken literally, so too is his *Guide*, with its inherent contradictions, to be read with this exegetical approach. The philosophically aware will glean the inner meaning of the text, while the masses will understand according to their limited level of comprehension.

PROPHETIC VISION

Maimonides makes use of visual metaphors to enlighten the reader with intermittent flashes of truth, cloaked in parabolic veils, elucidating the nature of scriptural references to divine physicality and bodily sensation. The issue of ascribing anthropomorphic tendencies to God becomes especially pronounced in Maimonides's insistence on the uniqueness of Mosaic prophecy. While other prophets have visions that allow them to see the divine and physically experience the sensations of prophecy, these visions are mediated through their imaginative faculty. But Moses's prophecy is exceptional in overcoming the imagination; Moses becomes a pure intellect, transcending the mediation of the body to connect directly with God. Unlike prophetic vision, Mosaic prophecy transcends the somatic, going beyond even language itself. He apprehends God beyond his limited human faculties and beyond anthropomorphisms.[14]

According to Maimonides, the minds of the multitude are guided to believe in God's existence by imagining that God is corporeal. Apprehension depends on "the instrumentality of the senses," especially sight and sound.[15] In communicating knowledge from God to the masses, the prophets describe God "as hearing and seeing . . . [God] apprehends and knows the visible and audible things."[16] Maimonides asserts that the term "eye" is used figuratively in every passage in which it is ascribed to God, indicating intellectual, rather than sensory, apprehension. Similarly, when applied to God, hearing denotes either God's apprehension or response to prayer.[17]

The example Maimonides uses to convey the internal value of parables privileges the light metaphor of truth: the internal meaning of the words of the Torah are like a pearl dropped in a dark, cluttered house—the pearl is hidden, and the reader does not know where to find it. But when a lamp is lit and the pearl discovered, the reader is able to derive benefit and meaning from the pearl of internal truth. Unlike the pearl example, the next parable (which also uses visual images) suggests that the external meaning can indeed have some value, as is the case for the parables of the prophets.[18] Viewed from afar, the apple appears to be silver; but upon closer examination, "a glance penetrates through" the holes and it becomes apparent that the apple is indeed gold inside.[19] And Maimonides uses further visual imagery when he explains that in some instances in the *Guide*, he will make clear to the reader that a parable is being expressed: "My remarking that it is a parable will be like someone's removing a screen from between the eye and a visible thing."[20]

Notably, Maimonides illustrates the reception of parabolic truths with a decidedly visual metaphor of religious enlightenment, evoking a Neoplatonic image of light. At some moments, we are able to perceive these truths as a flashing of light, causing us to think we are bathed in the light of day, before "matter and habit in their various forms conceal it so that we find ourselves again in an obscure night."[21] In our sporadic perception of the truth behind the parable, we are "like someone in a very dark night over whom lightning flashes time and time again."[22] So while all individuals only receive intermittent flashes of truth, Moses is an exception. Moses is privileged to a continual, enlightened conjunction with God. For him, "lightning flashes time and time again, so that he is always, as it were, in unceasing light. Thus night appears to him as day."[23] Maimonides references Exodus 34:29, the passage in which the skin on Moses's face is said to radiate forth light, as evidence that Moses receives divine light in an uninterrupted flow. Moses must wear a veil to hide his shining face because everyone else is unable to apprehend the perpetual light of truth.

IMAGINATION AND THE SENSORIUM

Moses does not use the imagination in his prophecy.[24] Indeed, it is debatable if he can even be called a prophet, since his access to prophecy is so different from that of others.[25] In making this claim, Maimonides draws upon a decidedly visual scriptural verse: "there arose not a prophet since in Israel like Moses, whom God knew face to face, in all the signs and the wonders . . . performed in the sight of all Israel."[26] Moses's prophecy is distinguished from others because Moses experiences no imaginative barrier in his relation to the divine, instead connecting to God through his intellect.[27] For others, God's speech is only heard through angelic mediation, and only in dreams. Only Moses speaks with God "mouth to mouth" and hears God "without action on the part of the imaginative faculty." [28]

But Moses has to convert his nonsensory prophecy into descriptive terms. After all, he must use imaginative creativity to transmit his prophecy in a communicable form. The language of the multitude is the language of anthropomorphism. The imagination is "indubitably a bodily faculty," and Moses must use his imagination for his prophecy to be initiated.[29] In this way, Moses depends upon the imaginative faculty to narrate his prophecy in scriptural form.[30]

Maimonides admits that Moses's first encounter with the divine was, indeed, mediated by the imaginative faculty through the appearance of an angel.[31] But he interprets the scriptural metaphors of Moses seeing God "face to face" and speaking with God "mouth to mouth" to mean that all of Moses's ensuing encounters with God were unmediated. Since, though, all the other prophets must rely on their imaginative faculty, and even Moses initially requires the use of his imagination, Maimonides must maintain a correspondence between the intellectual and the physical for prophecy to be possible.[32]

The prophet's imaginative faculty can receive the divine overflow only when the senses are at rest. The prophet's thoughts can then be detached from "bestial things," such as nutritional needs and sexual desires. These pleasures, which correspond to the sense of touch, are animalistic traits, according to the classical typology of Aristotle's *Nicomachean Ethics*.[33] Maimonides denigrates the senses of taste and touch and elevates aural communication. Touch is animalistic, while olfactory, auditory, and visual senses are properly human. In fact, the desire for tactility is decried as a main obstacle to obtaining prophecy. The prophet must turn away "from all bodily pleasures."[34] Moses is exemplary in this way.[35] He renounces all gross bodily faculties and sensations that produce gratuitous pleasure, all while continuing to speak and be spoken to.

Because the imagination is a bodily faculty, prophecy can be restricted if the physical faculties are preoccupied, as in a state of mourning or suffering. Paradoxically, Maimonides uses Moses as proof of this case, arguing that Moses's suffering after the *meraglim* (spies) incident in Numbers 13–14 curtailed his prophetic revelation, even though "the imaginative faculty did not enter into his prophecy."[36] Why does Maimonides use the example of Moses to prove that the imaginative faculty depends on the well-being of the body, if Mosaic prophecy bypasses the imagination? As we have seen, Maimonides already makes a concession to the imagination's role in Moses's first prophetic vision. But does the role of the imagination extend beyond this encounter? We can see that Mosaic prophecy is more bound up in the body than Maimonides would lead us to believe.

Despite his previous assertions regarding the necessary renunciation of bodily pleasures, Maimonides recognizes that the body must be given a certain amount of attention if it is to remain healthy. (This seems appropriate, considering his occupation as healer of the human body.) The welfare of the body must be first satisfied in order for the soul to be perfected. An individual cannot cultivate his intellect "if he is in pain or is very hungry or is thirsty or is hot or is very cold. But once the first perfection [bodily] has been achieved it is possible to achieve the ultimate [intellectual], which is indubitably more noble."[37] The law, in particular, aims at the welfare of the soul and the welfare of the body, although the former is privileged above the latter. The health of the body is dependent on having adequate food and shelter, which can be achieved by the individual only through political association.

Although the well-being of the body depends upon political involvement, the cultivation of the intellect requires isolation. The physical faculties are connected to a human's social activity, while the intellectual faculty requires abandonment of these diversions.[38] When a (male) individual has the good fortune to be alone, free of the daily chores of conversing with his wife, children, and the un-intellectual masses, he should take care "during these precious times" not to think "on anything other than that intellectual worship consisting in nearness of God and being in His presence . . . not by way of affectations of the imagination."[39] This can only be achieved by "men of knowledge" who have undergone rigorous training.[40] Maimonides's alignment of femininity, childhood, and animality (describing hunger and sexual desire as "bestial" needs) draws on the troubling Aristotelian association of femininity with animal nature, set apart from civilized, rational masculinity.[41]

As we have seen, Moses represents the ultimate state, "in which he talks with people and is occupied with his bodily necessities while his intellect is wholly turned toward Him . . . so that in his heart he is always in His presence . . . while outwardly he is with people."[42] Although Maimonides seems to be privileging intellectual isolation over social engagement and physical activity, this may be an overly simplified reading. According to Kalman Bland, Maimonides advocates "the multiple aesthetic benefits of a fully-engaged, well-tempered sensorium."[43] Bland maintains that premodern Jewish philosophers did not rank the senses hierarchically, devaluing the physical sensations of touch, taste, and smell in favor of the more intellectual senses of sight and hearing.[44] For Bland, Maimonides gives the senses their due, describing each as capable of preparing the mind for philosophical activity.[45] Although Maimonides affirms that God cannot be represented according to sensory form, Bland maintains that Maimonides recognized that human behavior relies on a somatic foundation.[46]

While Maimonides, like Aristotle, condemns touch for leading to overeating, drinking, and copulation, "thus competing unfairly with the less sensational allure of philosophical contemplation," touch is at one point considered by Maimonides to be a metaphor for intellection, as in the deaths of Moses, Aaron, and Miriam.[47] Maimonides interprets their dying by a kiss of God to mean that they "died in the pleasure of [intellectual] apprehension due to the intensity of passionate love" for the divine.[48] Here, not only the visual and the audible, but also the tactile can be a metaphor for intellective relation to the divine. While Maimonides extracts any notion of bodily contact from the metaphorical divine kiss, this example calls into question his strict adherence to the Aristotelian view of touch as bestial.[49] Thought requires the senses, and the satiation and balance of the body is necessary for the proper operation of the intellectual faculties. But Maimonides nevertheless disapproves of indulging the body in activities unnecessary to a basic state of health, because those activities ostensibly aim at pleasure alone.[50]

Maimonides's complex treatment of Moses reflects the paradoxical interplay between visuality and the evasion of vision. While Maimonides does not refer to sensory vision in Mosaic prophecy, Moses's intellectual vision still remains within an ocularcentric framework. The scriptural verses describing his prophecy rely on anthropomorphic attribution, highlighting the intimacy of his divine connection by alluding to the visual, auditory, and tactile bonds of the face to face, mouth to mouth, and lips to lips. And although Moses is said to bypass the imagination in relating to the divine, he makes use of his imaginative faculty in transmitting the sensory-free knowledge he receives to the body-bound people. For Maimonides, the issues of sensory modality, imaginative mediation, and divine anthropomorphism become intertwined in the example of prophecy.

VISION AND NONVISION

Maimonides's equivocation between visual and nonvisual modes is reflected in Levinas's phenomenological approach.[51] Levinas famously posits the face as the transcendent, infinite medium through which the encounter with the other occurs. The face exceeds visual apprehension. While *le visage* seems to be a deeply visual term, Levinas's face withdraws from visual representation and instead is encountered through discursive expression. In this way, the ethical relation involves a paradoxically nonvisual encounter with the other's face. In Wyschogrod's apt locution, the face for Levinas undermines visuality as the face that cannot be faced.[52] By communicating with another face-to-face, I do not lock the other into my gaze; I speak to them.[53] But how can a face-to-face relationship evade vision and give way to expression? If the mode of being-with-another is auditory, then why is it encapsulated in the face?[54] Although Levinas has been taken as a model for a traditional aniconic Jewish attitude (an approach to Judaism that Wolfson has successfully challenged in his work), Levinas's utilization of the face, a visually imbued term, as the auditory mode of communication, exemplifies the difficulty of approaching his thought with a simplistic visual vs. nonvisual mode of analysis. If Levinas is solely concerned with moving beyond the ocularcentric tradition, why does he choose an apparently visual model? It is more likely that Levinas settles on the face, that most visual of images, as a mode through which speech is expressed (and not the voice, for example), to trouble the distinction between sight and hearing.

Although the face-to-face relation may be intended by Levinas to evade vision, scriptural references to this relation can be read as either visual or auditory, ocularcentric or aniconic. The Torah illustrates contrasting examples of the divine as visually and nonvisually apprehended in Mosaic prophecy. So, although according to Exodus 33:11, God speaks to Moses "face to face, as a man speaks to his friend," in Exodus 33:20, God tells Moses, "Thou cannot see my face; for no man shall see me, and live." In Numbers 12:8, the auditory and visual modes coexist in one verse: "With him I speak mouth to mouth, manifestly, and not in dark speeches; and the similitude (*temunat*) of the Lord does he behold."[55]

Levinas's phenomenological approach reflects the biblical tension between the visual and the nonvisual.[56] Wyschogrod explains that for Levinas, philosophy must attempt a "high-wire act" by demonstrating how the other constitutes the ethical response of the self "without rendering the other as a phenomenon, as the sum of her or his properties as apprehended by perceptual or cognitive consciousness. To apprehend the other cognitively or affectively is to traduce the radical character of alterity, the insurmountable difference between self and other."[57] Both Maimonides and Levinas emphasize a kind of nonvisual discursivity that nevertheless has recourse to a visual mode. Wyschogrod contextualizes Levinas's turn from image to discourse with Maimonides's concomitant refusal of and reliance on visual imagery:

> Maimonides views the release of a figural imagination required in order to render theological truths accessible as disfiguring those truths through figuration itself. Compelled to account for the use of imagery in biblical discourse, he appeals to a property of verbal utterance, homonymy, in an effort to make sense of the dangerous but ineliminable visibility of the face in connection with God's countenance. If Moses is said to speak to God face to face (Deut. 5:4) and the face is a visible form, does it follow that, because faciality is attributed to God, that God is corporeal? Maimonides responds by highlighting the ambiguity of faciality and by converting visibility into discourse. . . . When Moses is said to have spoken with God face to face "without any intervening medium," Maimonides, as Levinas will do later, both proclaims and erases the face's materiality by transforming the visible into discourse.[58]

Maimonides and Levinas both draw on and deny the materiality of the face in their allegorical and ethical frameworks, respectively.

Levinas must rely on phenomena that, in Wyschogrod's words, "erase their own phenomenality, images given empirically yet apprehended discursively."[59] Wolfson puts it this way: "Despite the best intentions and the astute argumentation offered by Levinas, it may just be impossible for the human mind to be delivered from this quandary: configuring God as wholly other is itself an imaginary act by which the other is envisioned necessarily through the semblance of the same."[60] Similarly, for all that Maimonides seeks to avoid any implication of God's corporeality (because it implies idolatry), the figural imagination persists in order to cement belief in God and for prophecy to be transmitted to the masses. As Wyschogrod observes, "Maimonides sees the face as both visible figure and theological trope."[61]

By attending to Maimonides's visually imbued terminology in his discussion of God's incorporeality alongside his assertion that the intellect be divorced from the body in Mosaic prophecy, it is possible to challenge certain assumptions; that verbal and auditory representation of the divine are uniformly favored to the more theologically problematic visual apprehension, and that the imaginative and the bodily have no place in the highest degree of intellectual contemplation of the divine. For Maimonides, the corporeal and the intellectual cannot be clearly demarcated in the light of prophetic vision.

Although Maimonides privileges Mosaic prophecy for being unfettered by the imaginative faculty, revelation relies upon the power of imagination in Moses's communication of prophecy to the people. And while Maimonides may elevate sight and hearing above the other sensations, it can equally be argued that he gives each sense its due, advocating for the well-being of the body in service of proper intellectual apprehension. Mosaic prophecy is upheld for transcending the imagination, all the while being creatively imaginative in its narration of scripture. This maintenance of opposites resonates with the hermeneutics of *coincidentia oppositorum*, promulgated by Nicholas Cusanus in fifteenth-century Italy. As Wolfson explains, this approach, which has been often associated with mystical consciousness, "paradoxically affirms the identity of opposites in virtue of their difference."[62] In this coincidence of opposites, both extreme poles subsist at the same moment.[63] As accords with the intentionally contradictory and paradoxical nature of the *Guide*, in his account of prophecy, Maimonides affirms and intertwines incorporeality and physicality, nonvision and vision, intellect and imagination.

NOTES

1. See Aaron W. Hughes, "Elliot R. Wolfson: An Intellectual Portrait," in *Elliot R. Wolfson: Poetic Thinking*, ed. Hava Tirosh-Samuelson and Aaron W. Hughes (Leiden: Brill, 2015), 8–9: "one of his first, and most important teachers, was the late Edith Wyschogrod (1930–2009) . . . she was quick to respond to critics of the postmodernist project who contended that it was blind to ethical questions and simply nihilistic. Wyschogrod would leave an indelible mark on Wolfson and it was her, more than anyone, who appreciated, even in the earliest stages of his work after he had decided to pursue graduate study in Jewish mysticism, that he was using the kabbalistic material as a textual repository with which to think philosophically."
2. Edith Wyschogrod, *Crossover Queries: Dwelling with Negatives, Embodying Philosophy's Others* (New York: Fordham University Press, 2006).
3. This locution of hope strikes me as immensely meaningful and has stayed with me. Wyschogrod's words resonate with Wolfson's reading of Franz Rosenzweig, for whom time is the

mode in which the eternal continually cuts across the transience of human temporality. In Rosenzweig's messianic vision, one constantly anticipates but can never expect redemption to occur at every moment. Dialogical speech emphasizes that the messianic hope in a future may be anticipated, but must be perpetually deferred.

4. Elliot R. Wolfson, "Apophasis and the Trace of Transcendence: Wyschogrod's Contribution to a Postmodern Jewish Immanent a/Theology," *Philosophy Today* 55 (November 2011): 338. See also the dedication to E. Wyschogrod in Elliot R. Wolfson, *A Dream Interpreted Within a Dream: Oneiropoiesis and the Prism of Imagination* (New York: Zone Books, 2011); and see Elliot R. Wolfson, "Death and the Infinitization of Finitude: Negation and the Ethical Crisis of Modernity in Edith Wyschogrod's Postmodern Hermeneutic," in *Modern Jewish Thought on Crisis: Interpretation, Heresy, and History*, ed. Ghilad H. Shenhav, Cedric Cohen-Skalli and Gilad Sharvit, 241–66 (Berlin: De Gruyter, 2024), for a sustained examination of Wyschogrod's concept of the life-world and the crisis of the death event in the twentieth century and beyond.
5. Elliot R. Wolfson, *Giving Beyond the Gift: Apophasis and Overcoming Theomania* (New York: Fordham University Press, 2014), xviii.
6. Gershom Scholem, *Major Trends in Jewish Mysticism* (New York: Schocken Books, 1974), 24: "the Kabbalah certainly did not arise as a reaction against philosophical 'enlightenment,' but once it was there it is true that its function was that of an opposition to it."
7. Elliot R. Wolfson, "Beneath the Wings of the Great Eagle: Maimonides and Thirteenth-Century Kabbalah," in *Moses Maimonides (1138–1204): His Religious, Scientific, and Philosophical Wirkungsgeschichte in Different Cultural Contexts*, ed. Görge K. Hasselhoff and Otfried Fraisse (Würzburg: Ergon, 2004), 209.
8. Elliot R. Wolfson, "Beautiful Maiden Without Eyes: *Peshat* and *Sod* in Zoharic Hermeneutics," in *The Midrashic Imagination: Jewish Exegesis, Thought and History*, ed. Michael Fishbane (Albany: State University of New York Press, 1993), 155.
9. Moses Maimonides, *The Guide of the Perplexed*, trans. Shlomo Pines (Chicago: University of Chicago Press, 1963), 12.
10. "For Maimonides, the secret entails a concomitant transmission and withholding, a duplicity demanded by the dual political need to enlighten the uninitiated with respect to the existence of God, on the one hand, but to keep them in the dark regarding the implications of the truth of God's incorporeality for traditional beliefs, on the other" (Wolfson, "Beneath the Wings," 214).
11. See Elliot R. Wolfson, "Introduction," *Rending the Veil: Concealment and Secrecy in the History of Religions*, ed. Elliot R. Wolfson (New York: Seven Bridges Press, 1999), 3–4: The secret "presupposes the concurrent promulgation and suppression on the part of the one who knows the secret . . . [it] retains its secretive character if it is hidden in its exposure, but it may be hidden in its exposure only if it is exposed in its hiddenness . . . to be genuinely secretive it cannot be divulged . . . if it is not divulged in any manner it is hardly a secret."
12. On the dynamic of secrecy and the coincidence of opposites, see Elliot R. Wolfson, "Introduction," *Abraham Abulafia—Kabbalist and Prophet: Hermeneutics, Theosophy, Theurgy* (Los Angeles: Cherub Press, 2000), 2; and Elliot R. Wolfson, "Kenotic Overflow and Temporal

Transcendence: Angelic Embodiment and the Alterity of Time in Abraham Abulafia," in *Saintly Influence: Edith Wyschogrod and the Possibilities of Philosophy of Religion*, ed. Eric Boynton and Martin Kavka (New York: Fordham University Press, 2009), 126.

13. See the "Introduction" to Maimonides, *Guide*, 5–17.
14. See Maimonides, *Guide*, 367.
15. Maimonides, *Guide*, 98.
16. Maimonides, *Guide*, 99. Religious truths can be imparted to the masses only if "the incorporeal is imaginatively represented in corporeal terms, which are scientifically false but pedagogically necessary to inculcate belief in the existence of God and in his possessing all perfections" (Wolfson, "Beneath the Wings of the Great Eagle," 215).
17. Maimonides, *Guide*, 95–96.
18. "A saying uttered with a view to two meanings is like an apple of gold overlaid with silver filigree-work having very small holes" (Maimonides, *Guide*, 12).
19. Maimonides, *Guide*, 11–12.
20. Maimonides, *Guide*, 14.
21. Maimonides, *Guide*, 7.
22. Maimonides, *Guide*, 7.
23. Maimonides, *Guide*, 7.
24. On the Maimonidean approach to Mosaic prophecy, the role of imagination, and the Torah's figurative representations of theoretical truths, see Howard Kreisel, *Prophecy: The History of an Idea in Medieval Jewish Philosophy* (Dordrecht: Kluwer Academic Publishers, 2001), 262. See also Leonard S. Kravitz, "The Revealed and the Concealed: Providence, Prophecy, Miracles and Creation in the *Guide*," *CCAR Journal* 16, no. 4 (1969): 2–30; Alvin J. Reines, "Maimonides' Concept of Mosaic Prophecy," *Hebrew Union College Annual* 40–41 (1969–1970): 337; Norbert Samuelson, "Comments on Maimonides' Concept of Mosaic Prophecy," *CCAR Journal* 18, no. 1 (1971): 9–25; Oliver Leaman, "Maimonides, Imagination and the Objectivity of Prophecy," *Religion* 18, no. 1 (1988): 69–80; Roslyn Weiss, "Natural Order or Divine Will: Maimonides on Cosmogony and Prophecy," *Journal of Jewish Thought and Philosophy* 15, no. 1 (2007): 1–26; and Zachary Braiterman, "Maimonides and the Visual Image after Kant and Cohen," *Journal of Jewish Thought and Philosophy* 20, no. 2 (2012): 217–30.
25. It can be argued that because Moses does not apprehend prophecy through the imagination, he "cannot be said to be a prophet in the strict sense of the term" (Kalman Bland, "Moses and the Law According to Maimonides," *Mystics, Philosophers and Politicians: Essays in Jewish Intellectual History in Honor of Alexander Altmann*, ed. Jehuda Reinharz and Daniel Swetschinski [Durham: Duke University Press, 1982], 50).
26. Deuteronomy 34:10–12.
27. Unlike the Kabbalists, who elevate the imaginative faculty, Maimonides denigrates the imagination, "but, following Aristotelian epistemology, he could not ignore the instrumental role of the imagination in our acquisition of knowledge, and he even considered (in accord with his Muslim predecessors, especially al-Fārābī) it crucial to all prophecy with the exception of Moses" (Wolfson, *Giving Beyond the Gift*, 5).
28. Maimonides, *Guide*, 403. See Alfred L. Ivry, "The Image of Moses in Maimonides' Thought,"

in *Maimonides after 800 Years: Essays on Maimonides and His Influence*, ed. Jay M. Harris (Cambridge, MA: Harvard University Press, 2007), 113–34; and see Heidi M. Ravven, "Some Thoughts on What Spinoza Learned from Maimonides About the Prophetic Imagination; Part 1: Maimonides on Prophecy and the Imagination," *Journal of the History of Philosophy* 39, no. 2 (2001): 193–214.

29. Maimonides, *Guide*, 373.
30. "Although Maimonides insists repeatedly that Mosaic prophecy is to be distinguished from all other prophecies by the fact that Moses was not dependent on the imagination, the Torah, which abounds in metaphorical language of an anthropomorphic and anthropopathic nature is surely a product of the imagination" (Wolfson, "Beneath the Wings of the Great Eagle," 215).
31. Maimonides, *Guide*, 576.
32. The perfection of the imaginative faculty depends upon "the best possible temperament, the best possible size, and the purest possible matter, of the part of the body that is the substratum for the faculty in question," that is, the brain (Maimonides, *Guide*, 369). If an individual's brain is naturally well proportioned due to the "purity of its matter" and its physical constitution, "that individual would obtain knowledge and wisdom until he passes from potentiality to actuality and acquires a perfect and accomplished human intellect and pure and well-tempered moral habits" (371).
33. Maimonides, *Guide*, 371n8.
34. Maimonides, *Guide*, 372.
35. In describing Moses's intellectual worship of the divine, Maimonides writes that Moses renounces "everything that is other than God . . . putting questions and receiving answers, speaking and being spoken to. . . . And because of his great joy in that which he apprehended, 'he did neither eat bread nor drink water.' For his intellect attained such strength that all the gross faculties in his body ceased to function. I refer to the various kinds of the sense of touch" (Maimonides, *Guide*, 620).
36. Maimonides, *Guide*, 373.
37. Maimonides, *Guide*, 510–11.
38. Maimonides, *Guide*, 621.
39. Maimonides, *Guide*, 623.
40. Maimonides, *Guide*, 623.
41. Discourses of gender and the human-animal boundary intersect routinely in the history of philosophy. According to classical philosophical typologies, women's proximity to childbirth and child-rearing means that they are infantilized, animalized, and depoliticized. As Sherryl Vint observes, "there are many parallels between the ways in which women have been constructed, controlled, spoken for and objectified by patriarchal culture, and similar constraints placed on animals by Western culture more generally" (*Animal Alterity: Science Fiction and the Question of the Animal* [Liverpool: Liverpool University Press, 2010], 18). Kecia Ali shows how in religious thinking, in particular, "dense webs of signification" have long connected women and animals, which, "often discursively connected, play vital roles in the symbolic language of religious identity" ("Muslims and Meat-Eating: Vegetarianism, Gender, and Identity," *Journal of Religious Ethics* 43, no. 2 [2015]: 268–69). Kelly Oliver explains how the

association with animality excludes women from the political realm: "The woman's animality protects the man from his own animality. By absorbing animality, the woman allows the man to escape from animality and nature in order to enter the social" ("Paternal Election and the Absent Father," in *Feminist Interpretations of Emmanuel Levinas*, ed. Tina Chanter [University Park: Pennsylvania State University Press, 2001], 237–38).

42. Maimonides, *Guide*, 623.
43. Kalman Bland, *The Artless Jew: Medieval and Modern Affirmations and Denials of the Visual* (Princeton: Princeton University Press, 2000), 91.
44. See Elliot R. Wolfson, *Through a Speculum That Shines: Vision and Imagination in Medieval Jewish Mysticism* (Princeton: Princeton University Press, 1994), 13–14. Wolfson points out that the investigation into visionary experiences of the divine is especially significant given that it is common among scholarly circles "to characterize Hebraic thought—especially in contrast to Greek thought—as essentially auditory and nonvisual in its orientation." While the visual depiction of God is an unequivocally anthropomorphic representation, the hearing of a divine voice seems to be theologically acceptable, for it is more abstract and does not imply a concrete bodily form.
45. "Maimonides's appreciation of the egalitarian potential of the sensorium is consonant with his metaphors of choice for intellectual perfection. As to be expected, he favored light and vision. . . . But he seems to have been equally fond of gastronomics," as can be seen in the analogy to eating excessive amounts of honey (Bland, *The Artless Jew*, 77–78; referring to Maimonides, *Guide*, 69).
46. Bland, *The Artless Jew*, 81.
47. Bland, *The Artless Jew*, 79.
48. Maimonides, *Guide*, 627–28. See Wolfson, *Through a Speculum That Shines* (15–16): "Anthropomorphic expression can be appropriated as a meaningful mode of discourse if it is circumscribed within a linguistic field. That one has heard the voice of God is not nearly as crude an anthropomorphism as the claim that one has seen, let alone kissed, the mouth of God."
49. Bland, *The Artless Jew*, 79.
50. Bland notes that for Maimonides, to think about God "means approaching the quasi-ascetic ideal of pure 'intellectual worship' . . . in which human intellect is instructed to detach itself from its sensory underpinnings. Intellect might then oscillate mysteriously in the interstices between corporeality and incorporeality, contemplating silently the otherwise unknowable divine" (Bland, *The Artless Jew*, 82).
51. On the relationship between Maimonides and Levinas, see Francesca Albertini, "Emmanuel Levinas' Theological-Political Interpretation of Moses Maimonides," in *Moses Maimonides (1138–1204): His Religious, Scientific, and Philosophical Wirkungsgeschichte in Different Cultural Contexts*, ed. Görge K. Hasselhoff and Otfried Fraisse (Würzburg: Ergon, 2004), 573–85; Michael Fagenblat, "Levinas and Maimonides: From Metaphysics to Ethical Negative Theology," *Journal of Jewish Thought and Philosophy* 16, no. 1 (2008): 95–147; and Michael Fagenblat, *A Covenant of Creatures: Levinas's Philosophy of Judaism* (Stanford, CA: Stanford University Press, 2010).
52. Edith Wyschogrod, "Language and Alterity in the Thought of Levinas," in *The Cambridge*

Companion to Levinas, ed. Simon Critchley and Robert Bernasconi (Cambridge: Cambridge University Press, 2002), 195.

53. The revelation of the face is speech, which must proceed from "absolute difference" that can be "established only by language . . . a relation between separated terms. . . . Speech cuts across vision" (Emmanuel Levinas, *Totality and Infinity: An Essay on Exteriority*, trans. Alphonso Lingis [Pittsburgh: Duquesne University Press, 1995], 193–95).
54. Martin C. Srajek suggests that in the Levinasian sense, biblical references to the face are read as nonvisual, since many interpretations of the "face-to-face" relation between Moses and God have determined that it is unlikely that Moses actually sees God's face: "Rather than God's face, Moses will 'see' God's presence" (125). The face-to-face encounter with the divine Other requires a hiding of the face, a turning away of the eyes in the service of listening: "Though the ethical significance is predicated upon the materiality of the face, it is precisely not only someone's mouth, nose and eyes that we perceive when we perceive the face. Rather, it is the obligation, the silent word, that Moses perceived when God finally 'passed by him'" (*In the Margins of Deconstruction: Jewish Conceptions of Ethics in Emmanuel Levinas and Jacques Derrida* [Pittsburgh: Duquesne University Press, 1998), 128–29).
55. These contrasting examples indicate the difficulty with asserting that Judaism is either aniconic or iconic. As Wolfson explains, "it is precisely because both points of view, so strikingly different, inhabit the same corpus that the history of Jewish attitudes toward the visual imaging of God unfolded in the dialectical way it did" (Wolfson, *Through a Speculum That Shines*, 27–28).
56. On the aniconic impulse in Levinas, see Martin Jay, *Downcast Eyes: The Denigration of Vision in Twentieth-Century French Thought* (Berkeley: University of California Press, 1993), 546–57.
57. Wyschogrod, *Crossover Queries*, 30. Wolfson explains that "Levinas opts to reform phenomenology by utilizing language that is replete with aniconic resonances and critical of the ocularcentric tendency to favor vision" (Elliot R. Wolfson, "Echo of the Otherwise: Ethics of Transcendence and the Lure of Theolatry," in *Encountering the Medieval in Modern Jewish Thought*, ed. James A. Diamond and Aaron W. Hughes [Leiden: Brill, 2012], 300). See also Elliot R. Wolfson, "Secrecy, Modesty, and the Feminine: Kabbalistic Traces in the Thought of Levinas," *Journal of Jewish Thought and Philosophy* 14 (2006): 209.
58. Wyschogrod, *Crossover Queries*, 25–26.
59. Wyschogrod, *Crossover Queries*, 30.
60. Wolfson, *Giving Beyond the Gift*, 10. In a similar dynamic, Levinas struggles to write otherwise than ontology while always necessarily restricted to the pull of a more rigid line of reasoning. This becomes a fundamental question in his work: is it possible to move past the ontological framework of Western thought without having recourse to that very frame of argumentation, and without taking up the language of ontology? Levinas himself encapsulates this dilemma by paraphrasing Derrida's statement in the conclusion of his essay "Violence and Metaphysics": "Not to philosophize is still to philosophize" (Levinas, "God and Philosophy," in *Basic Philosophical Writings*, ed. Adriaan T. Peperzak, Simon Critchley, and Robert Bernasconi [Bloomington: Indiana University Press, 1996], 129); citing Jacques Derrida, "Violence and Metaphysics: An Essay on the Thought of Emmanuel Levinas," in

Writing and Difference, trans. Alan Bass (Chicago: University of Chicago Press, 1978), 152. As Wolfson puts it, "That which he marks as otherwise than being, however, is likely to be imagined as being otherwise, that is, as a being that is other vis-à- vis being but still a being, thereby succumbing to the ontological taxonomy it is meant to undermine" (*Giving Beyond the Gift*, 9–10). See also Elliot R. Wolfson, "Imagination and the Theolatrous Impulse: Configuring God in Modern Jewish Thought," in *The Cambridge History of Jewish Philosophy: Volume 2: The Modern Era*, ed. Martin Kavka, Zachary Braiterman, and David Novak (Cambridge, UK: Cambridge University Press, 2012), 668.

61. Wyschogrod, *Crossover Queries*, 31.
62. Elliot R. Wolfson, *Language, Eros, Being: Kabbalistic Hermeneutics and Poetic Imagination* (New York: Fordham University Press, 2005), xix.
63. Wolfson explains that in this orientation, "the difference of identity is overcome in the identity of difference, the negative is restored to the positive, the profane to the sacred, the forbidden to the permissible" (Elliot R. Wolfson, *Venturing Beyond: Law and Morality in Kabbalistic Mysticism* [Oxford: Oxford University Press, 2006], 283).

PHILOSOPHY AND DISSIMULATION IN ELIJAH OF VILNA'S WRITINGS AND LEGACY

ELIYAHU STERN

THE LEGACY OF FEW FIGURES IN THE ANNALS OF JEWISH HISTORY HAVE been as fiercely debated as that of the eighteenth-century Kabbalist and Talmudist Elijah ben Solomon (1720–1797). At the center of the debate has been his relationship to secular knowledges and philosophy. Yisrael of Shklov remarked that, in matters of philosophy, Elijah "studied it practically and took from it only two good things: they are the seventy forces of man . . . and something else. The rest," Elijah said, "should be thrown out."[1] For over two hundred years these words have been interpreted as an indictment against the study of philosophy.[2] Yisrael's judgment is cited alongside those of his *landsman*, Menachem Mendel, who claimed that Elijah thought Aristotle to be "a heretic from start to finish."[3] These comments coupled with Elijah's supposed criticism of Moses Maimonides as endorsing "evil philosophy" (*arurah*) are often invoked to prove that philosophy itself is not an indigenous Jewish intellectual practice. His scolding of Maimonides and supposed dismissal of philosophy ranks as one of the most socially and spiritually authoritative reproofs of the rational Aristotelian tradition in Jewish history.

Following Maimonides, few, if any, in the rabbinic tradition possessed Elijah ben Solomon's intellectual and spiritual authority. No one commented on a greater quantity of texts, and only a handful can be said to have matched his mastery of the rabbinic and kabbalistic canon. He is most remembered for his intellectual prowess, and as the leader of the Mitnagdim, the group who fiercely opposed the rise of the eighteenth-century spiritual-pietistic folk movement, the Hasidim. His legacy, however, has been claimed by a wide spectrum of modern Jewish movements, including Jewish enlighteners, Zionists, and even secularists.[4]

Nineteenth- and twentieth-century Orthodox thinkers were, however, determined to keep the Gaon's legacy free from external influences or heretical ideas. The study of philosophy had now become associated with liberal forms of Judaism, assimilationists and secularists. Though granting that the Gaon had some appreciation for certain aspects of the sciences, Orthodox rabbis contested any claim that might in any way have lent support to positions advanced by other modern Jewish movements. Such denials and polemics continue today, most recently against my own work on the Gaon.[5] Following the publication of *The Genius: Elijah of Vilna and the Making of Modern Judaism*, Orthodox rabbis and scholars such as Rabbi Bezalel Naor, Lawrence Kaplan, Rabbi Eliyahu Krakowski, and Marc Shapiro criticized me for comparing the Gaon to other eighteenth-century philosophers and claiming that he was a modernist.

As a historian I was fascinated by just how similar their criticisms were to those issued by Orthodox scholars in the nineteenth century. The latter also wrote in public mediums in the hopes of wresting the Gaon's and other rabbinic luminaries' mantles away from those they deemed reformers, assimilationists, and ignoramuses. Nevertheless, as the Orthodox critiques intensified and circulated in online forums, more historical evidence was emerging in academic circles to support my claims about the Gaon's philosophical leanings. Most notably a brilliant dissertation was published in Israel by Iris Idelsohn-Shein in which she not only confirmed my thesis about the Gaon's relationship to modern intellectual currents but marshaled evidence that his son Abraham translated scientific books into Hebrew. It turned out that the Gaon had access to French and German scientific works. While no one had yet to find a copy of the *Monadology* in the Gaon's library, Idelsohn-Shein revealed Abraham's translation of the French naturalist and mathematician George Louis Leclerc de Buffon's *Variétés dans l'espèce* (Paris: 1749).

Meanwhile, I had begun investigating the Gaon's students' writings, finding clues that something else might be at play, something that accounted for both my own position on the Gaon and the one expressed by my Orthodox critics: statements that for two hundred years had been used to prove that the Gaon had denounced Aristotle and the project of philosophy when looked at from another angle meant the exact opposite.

As this paper sets out to demonstrate, a critical-academic examination of the Gaon's writings reveals that Elijah not only incorporated, but further developed the Aristotelian tradition of vital forms, using it as the basis for his own rational cosmogony—theory of the origins of the universe and anthropogony—theory of the origins of humanity. His students were fully aware of these aspects of his oeuvre and set out to enshroud their master's ideas in coded language that was *not meant to be understood by the Orthodox*. The Gaon's students had ensured that their master's endorsement of the philosophical method would not be made available to those who "*lacked* a firm belief in God." To do so they put into circulation an apologetic reading of the Gaon in the hopes of shielding the masses from seeing Elijah's capacious and daring worldview. The apologetic reading of the Gaon would be parroted and defended by generations of Orthodox rabbis and scholars up until the present. This paper details this act of dissimulation and corroborates the claims made in the *Genius* about the Gaon's worldview and relationship to the study of philosophy.

ELIJAH'S DENUNCIATION OF MAIMONIDES AND PHILOSOPHY

In his article "Did the Gaon Rabbi Eliyahu Oppose Maimonides's Philosophy?" Jacob Dienstag argues that "with regard to the study of philosophy and metaphysics Elijah followed Rabbi Shlomo Aderet (1235–1310), and Nachmanides (1194–1270) whose opposition to these subjects was well-known."[6] Dienstag's claim is largely based on two statements that appeared in Elijah's commentary to Yosef Karo's (1488–1575) code of Jewish law, *Shulchan Arukh*. The first and most often referenced statement is his comment to *Yoreh De'ah*, 179:6:

> All those who came after Maimonides differed [from his rational interpretive approach]. For many times we find magical incantations mentioned in Talmud. Maimonides and philosophers claimed that such magical writings, incantations, and devils are all false. However, he [Maimonides] was already reprimanded for such an interpretation. For we have found many stories in the Talmud about magical incantations and writings. . . . The Torah references sea monsters, and the Zohar on Genesis 1:21 and in numerous other places there are references to amulets and many incantations. Philosophy is mistaken in a majority of cases when it interprets the Talmud in a superficial manner and destroys the *sensus literalis* of the text. However, one should not think that I, in any way, Heaven forbid, actually believe in them, from them or what they stand for. Rather, [what I mean] is that everything written follows according to *its sensus literalis* but all of these things have within them an inner essence [that must be interpretively accounted for]. Not the meaning of the philosophers who describe only its outer meaning, but the [inner essence] of the masters of truth.

The above quote has been subject to much critical scrutiny. Some even claim that Elijah's statement had been tampered with on the floor of the publishing house.[7] The words "evil philosophy," they contend, were never even invoked by the Gaon, but rather inserted into his commentary by those involved in the publication of his commentary. Elijah's writings were all published posthumously and based on a number of different manuscripts and often were tampered with by students and family members.

A careful examination of Elijah's comments suggests that his attack targeted only Maimonides's specific philosophical approach—one that takes an essentialist position toward texts and ignores linguistic nuance. Elijah's comments in *Yoreh De'ah*, 179:6 are a play on the opening comments of Maimonides's masterwork, the *Guide*. There, Maimonides claims to explain parables that are normally read by simpletons "only according to their *sensus literalis* without understanding their internal essence."[8] For Maimonides, sacred texts are written in parables containing both esoteric (philosophical and rational) and exoteric (mythical and irrational) meanings. Maimonides writes:

> Parables are of two kinds. In some of these parables each word has a meaning, while in others the parable as a whole indicates the whole of the intended meaning. In such a parable very many words are to be found, not every one adds something to the intended meaning. They serve rather to embellish the parable and to render it more coherent or to conceal further the intended meaning; hence the speech proceeds in such a way to accord with everything required by the parable's intended meaning.[9]

Maimonides assumes two types of parables: one whose specific words are to be taken seriously and examined carefully, and another whose gist can be discerned without an exact word for word interpretation of the primary text.

Elijah follows Maimonides in asserting that biblical and Talmudic texts must have both a specific "exoteric" and "esoteric" meaning. However, while Maimonides understands the esoteric meaning as a rational philosophic reading of the text—discounting or ignoring those words or ideas that suggest metaphysical or mystical experience—Elijah says, with an important caveat, that the philosophers' esoteric reading of the text is actually the text's plain and simple exoteric meaning. According to Elijah, mention of demons, magic, lucky charms, and all other supernatural material cannot be ignored because they consistently appear in rabbinic literature. Elijah's student Menashe Ilya (1767–1831) recalled "that he remembered [Elijah] criticizing those who interpreted midrash according to its literal reading when it went against reason."[10] Still, such terms had meaning and were not to be dismissed simply because they defied reason. Elijah's criticism focuses on Maimonides's glib treatment of the very words and signs that constitute the rabbinic tradition.[11] To ignore mystical and kabbalistic literature, Elijah argues, would wreak havoc on every major corpus of Jewish literature. Taken to its logical conclusion, Maimonides would excise broad swaths of Judaism's textual tradition. Elijah's criticism of Maimonides recalls the eighteenth-century philosopher Christian Wolff, who scolded those who asserted "that terms with which we can join no clear notion signify nothing. As the enemies of the Gospel give out, that the term Trinity and some other terms denoting mysteries, are mere empty sounds."[12] Elijah's critique is directed against Maimonides's particular theories of linguistics, interpretation and hermeneutics, *not* against the study of philosophy and secular knowledge.

The second piece of evidence scholars often muster to prove Elijah's opposition to philosophy involves his interpretation of the ancient concept of *Pardes*. The term, which is often translated as "garden," was already cited in the rabbinic period (*Tosefta Hagigah*, 2:3) as alluding to a space of esoteric knowledge. Maimonides in his Code defines it as follows:

> And I say that one should not take a stroll in *Pardes* until one has filled his stomach with bread and meat, and bread and meat means the knowledge of what is impermissible and what is permissible and what that entails regarding the commandments. And even though these are small things, for the Sages have told us that small

> things are the legal debates of Abayye and Rava while physics and metaphysics are great things, still one should learn small things first.[13]

According to Maimonides, *Pardes* includes the study of *ma'aseh beresheit* and *ma'aseh merkavah*, which he understands to be the study of "physics" and "metaphysics" respectively. Maimonides's privileging of philosophy was harshly criticized in some circles, most notably by Karo. On the other hand, Karo's contemporary, Rabbi Moses Isserles, sought to reconcile Maimonides with his opponents. Beyond studying scripture and Talmud, Isserles wrote,

> it is permitted to sporadically study other types of knowledge provided they are not heretical books, and this sporadic form of study is called "a *stroll* in *Pardes*." And one, however, should only take such a *stroll* after he has filled himself with meat and bread. This refers to the knowledge of what is halakhically permissible and impermissible. (emphasis added)[14]

Unlike Maimonides, who grants philosophy the highest priority in a mature individual's curriculum, Isserles downgrades its place in the Jewish canon. For Isserles, philosophy should be studied only "sporadically," stressing the term "stroll" preceding the term *Pardes*. One should take a glance at the vistas of philosophy but by no means dwell on such terrain. Isserles is not against the study of philosophy but is simply concerned with the emphasis it is given in one's education.

Elijah addresses Isserles's interpretation of the term *Pardes* and challenges him and Maimonides by noting that

> [Isserles's] words are taken from Maimonides, and Isserles explains Maimonides as discussing the case of the four Sages who went into *Pardes*. And because they were young in years and not fully matured, they were punished for taking such a stroll, [with the exception of Rabbi Akiva . . .]. But neither Isserles nor Maimonides understands *Pardes* properly. The explanation given by Isserles is not accurate. For if *Pardes* actually were referring to what Isserles claims it refers to, then why does he limit it [the study of physics and metaphysics]? For there would be no greater reward than constant study of these other forms of knowledge. As it is written in the Tractate Sukkah, "a small matter is the halakhic arguments of Abayye and Rava [a great matter is the study of esoteric wisdom]."[15]

Elijah lays bare the contradiction of Isserles's interpretation of Maimonides and his failure to reconcile Maimonides's position with the viewpoint expressed in Talmudic literature. If Isserles is correct that *Pardes* actually means secular sciences, then why, asks Elijah, does Isserles limit their study to only occasional and sporadic moments? Elijah alludes to the Talmudic passage obligating one to study the mysteries of *Pardes* at a mature age. According to the way the rabbis of the Talmud invoke the term, he notes, *Pardes* is not to be looked at occasionally but studied diligently, fully, and constantly. However, Elijah does not adopt Maimonides's position either. For Elijah, *Pardes* as it appears in the Talmud does not mean the sciences—on which he never rules for or against—but rather the project of interpretation and exegesis. *Pardes* in fact has nothing to do with philosophy but rather hermeneutics. Elijah maintains that *PaRDeS* signified something far more intellectually expansive than philosophy alone. It was an acronym for the fourfold exegetical approach: *peshat* (literal or plain sense), *remez* (allusive, hinting, or allegoric), *derash* (rabbinic or intertextual reading practice), and *sod* (kabbalistic).[16]

Those claiming that Elijah opposed philosophy have done so at the expense of his vast oeuvre, which contains repeated invocations of philosophical terminology, borrowed from Aristotle himself and Maimonides's *Guide*.[17] Even a cursory reading of Elijah's commentaries to Genesis and Proverbs reveals Elijah repeatedly employing the terms of material cause, formal cause, efficient cause, and finite cause to explain the nature of knowledge and creation. Furthermore, in 1776, he and his brother sent a letter to Rabbi Shaul ben Aryeh Leib Lowenstam, the head of the rabbinic court in Amsterdam, requesting that he send them manuscripts of "Moses Cordovero's commentary to the *Zohar* and other wondrous works, as well as Aristotle's *Ethics*."[18] Elijah opposes Maimonides not because the latter studied philosophy, but owing to the medieval thinker's failure to understand *PaRDeS*, the way in which the Kabbalah of Cordevero and the philosophy of Aristotle could complement each other. *PaRDeS* could explain the full gamut of classical Jewish literature and offer important insights into the nature of the universe.

ELIJAH'S COSMOGONY

For Elijah, the worldview of *PaRDeS* provided multiple interpretive prisms, including both the exoteric method of philosophy and the esoteric hermeneutics of Kabbalah. In his commentary to Genesis 1:3, as he does in numerous other texts, Elijah uses both kabbalistic and philosophic categories to challenge Maimonides's understanding of creation:

> And God said, "let there be light": In *Pirkei de-Rabbi Eliezer* our Sages asked, "Whence were the heavens created?" [They answered that God took part of the light of His garment, stretched it like a cloth, and the heavens were extending continually, as it is said: "He covered Himself with light as with a garment, He stretched the heavens like a curtain"]. And Maimonides tried to answer this question according to his own view and all those who came after him also tried to answer this question. [Maimonides, however, was wrong to assert that one must believe in creation ex-nihilo]. For it would seem that light was not created from nothing. While regarding the sky and the earth it is written "and He created" teaching us about their origins; with regard to light, Scripture simply teaches "it was," written in the language of the present, teaching us that something came from something.[19]

Maimonides (*Guide*, 2:26) argues that *Pirkei de-Rabbi Eliezer* could be construed as suggesting that matter existed eternally. Maimonides, however, rejects this reading of *Pirkei de-Rabbi Eliezer* and identifies it with a misguided position that was espoused by Plato in his work *Timaeus*.[20] Following Kabbalists like Isaac the Blind (1160–1235), Elijah adopts the simple interpretation of *Pirkei de-Rabbi Eliezer* that in fact matter existed eternally.[21] However, unlike other Kabbalists, Elijah justifies his position using the philosophical language of creation *ex nihilo* (*yesh me-ayin*).[22] In his comments to Genesis 1:21 he explains that he does "not to read the word 'ayin' as "absolute nothing" ("*eyn biuro she-eyno mamash*"). Rather, according to Elijah, "everything that lacks a direct causal explanation is called *yesh me-ayin*." For Maimonides, the term "*yesh me-ayin*" means "creation from nothing"; for Elijah it means creation from matter. Elijah compares "*yesh me-ayin*," form from matter, to "*yesh me-yesh*," which means form generating another form. Whereas the latter denotes something causally created from a preexisting form—something that has definition—the former involves the figuring of primordial matter—something that lacks definition or form and thus is unintelligible.[23]

Elijah's use of philosophical categories to explain Creation and challenge Maimonides results in a position that bears a striking resemblance to the positions espoused by Yom Tov ben Abraham Ishbilli (known by the Ritba, 1250–1330) and the controversial medieval philosopher Gersonides (1288–1344). Elijah believes that God created the world, but, like Ishbilli and Gersonides, he contends that he did so by shaping "something" that is eternal. Ishbilli specifically mentions this section of *Pirkei de-Rabbi Eliezer* and claims that his teacher Nachmanides misunderstood the Platonic tradition in which matter was not created *ex nihilo* but rather existed eternally.[24] Gersonides tries to demonstrate that God created the world out of matter by pointing out the contradiction between Aristotle's physics and his claim that the world existed eternally without being generated by a Creator. If Aristotle is correct that an object cannot by chance exhibit a pattern of behavior or be goal directed, Gersonides asks, then why does Aristotle assert otherwise when accounting for the existence of the sun, moon, and stars? The latter all exhibit natural patterns, and yet in claiming their eternal existence Aristotle was in effect saying that their natural patterns are simply accidental. It must be, Gersonides hypothesizes, that according to Aristotle's own logic an agent, God, created them. If Aristotle is correct that nature itself seems to operate according to a design, then it must have a source, a Creator.[25]

Elijah never cites Gersonides or Ishbilli in this context, but he is aware that his position is an outlier among Jewish exegetes. He admits that "all of the interpreters of religion (*mifarshei ha-dat*) are of the opinion that the world was created *ex nihilo*."[26] Plato's notion of creation was "rejected by Saadia, tolerated by Yehuda ha-Levi and vigorously rejected by Maimonides."[27] Over time, Maimonides's position of creation *ex nihilo* became so entrenched in Jewish thought that, ironically, one writer went so far as to assume (without citation) that Elijah himself subscribed to creation *ex nihilo*, declaring, "the idea of the creation of the World out of nothing (*yesh mi-ayin*) is that boundary that separates Jewish thinkers from pagan (ancient Greek) thinking."[28] Others have noted that "to this day traditional Jewish cosmological speculation tends to defend the *ex nihilo* conception of creation."[29]

God's sovereignty over the world is the reason often given for the need to postulate *ex nihilo*. Along those lines some reject the idea that there existed an eternally existing primordial matter. Yet in his commentary to the kabbalistic work *Sifra di-Tzniuta* (*Book of Concealment*) Elijah explains:

> primordial matter is nothing but matter and exists without any form. . . . As it says [in Genesis 1:1] regarding the creation of the world and "God said let there be light" (*va-yehi*) and then "He acted" (*barah*). "God said" refers to divine knowledge (*chokhmah*), but "acted" refers to human knowledge/understanding (*binah*) and that means God created-form. . . . In this world matter is never separated from form.[30]

Elijah explicitly connects human knowledge with form, stating that "the acquisition of knowledge and the ability to comprehend suggest the ability for something to possess a specific form."[31] According to Elijah, form means both physical figure (*demut*) and image (*tzelem*). As we will see shortly, Elijah's identification of bodies as containing form and matter allows him to account for the metamorphosis of entities and evolution of nature without recourse to the wanton actions of a divine potter who constantly moves and shapes matter.

Elijah never offers a programmatic statement detailing his cosmogony, but the following might be deduced: He adopts Gersonides and Ishbilli's notion of creation. Elijah does not have a notion of "ideal" forms. Instead, he argues that form and matter are inseparable and that form emerges only after Creation. Whereas the celestial realms are composed of primary matter and remain undefined, all bodies in this world possess form and as such are defined and in constant motion.[32]

Because the world consists of form, it evolved on its own. Thus, rational and scientific principles can fully account for and explain creation and nature. When addressing the way nature operates, Elijah employs Maimonidean philosophic categories. Still, he differs with Maimonides with regard to employing Aristotelian philosophical categories to understand the celestial spheres (what Aristotle and Maimonides call metaphysics and what the Gaon calls "*shamayim*"). His rejection of Maimonides's position is not a function of his rejection of Greek thought or non-Jewish science, but rather because philosophy is unable to account for the celestial spheres.

For Maimonides, metaphysics is the telos of philosophical exploration because God is pure form and thus can be understood through reason. Elijah rejects Maimonidean metaphysics because he sees the celestial realms as composed of matter. Rational categories cannot make sense out of that which lacks definition. Elijah explicitly says as much when he remarks: "by distancing oneself from those who study the philosophy of God and natural science one will come to experience the light of God."[33] There is no irony here. Elijah is referring to the primordial light that existed before creation and continues to define the celestial spheres and to his consternation remains the source of unfounded philosophical speculation. With regard to that which exists beyond reason, Elijah chastises Maimonides for employing a strict philosophic approach instead of a kabbalistic framework.

Elijah's position also challenged the logic and philosophic infrastructure upholding much of the early modern Ashkenazic metaphysics.[34] Judah Loew of Prague (1525–1609), who also objected to Maimonides's metaphysics, nonetheless believed, like Maimonides, that the celestial sphere comprised ideal forms.[35] Elijah's insistence that these spheres were in fact composed of matter made all such explorations beyond rational comprehension and ultimately absurd. Both the metaphysician trying to know God conceptually and the Pietist (Hasid) who tried to cleave to God spiritually were equally misguided. As Elijah's student, Hayyim of Volozhin, is known to have said about his teacher's worldview, "where philosophy no longer can explain from there and beyond begins the domain of kabbalah."[36] Only Kabbalah—something not based on scientific or strictly philosophical categories—can interpret something made up of primordial matter, something irrational.

The Gaon's position is somewhat similar to the medieval scholar Abraham Abulafia's critique of Maimonides. As explained by Elliot Wolfson, for "Abulafia . . . the real content of *hokhmat ha-'elohut* is available only to one who has received the prophetic tradition of divine names and not to the philosopher who intellectually contemplates the principles of being. The 'account of the chariot,' *ma'aseh merkavah*, is above all else the knowledge of the combinations and permutations of the letters of the divine names (*harkavat shem be-shem*) that represents the authentic repository of oral esoteric traditions. Abulafia insists that for the kabbalist there is this additional component that is not available to the philosopher."[37] Like Abulafia, the Gaon's chastisement of Maimonides is not so much that philosophical investigation is heretical or misguided but rather that it is lacking. However, in contrast to Abulafia who argued that it was Kabbalah and the permutations of God's name that needed to be hidden from the simpletons, the Gaon's students would claim it was philosophy and more specifically the Gaon's anthropogeny that reflected a secret doctrine meant only for elite scholars.

ELIJAH'S ANTHROPOGONY

Elijah claims that creation, the moment when form meets primordial matter, can be understood through physics. In his commentary to Genesis 1:2, Elijah takes aim at Nachmanides and insists that the act of creation was not simply a one-time occurrence, but rather the way nature operates at all times. While both agree that "creation begins when form meets primordial matter," Elijah argues that the entity figured from such an encounter continues to change and develop. "According to Nachmanides," explains Elijah, "the genesis story is only about Creation, with each entity retaining the stable identity given to it by God." Elijah disagrees: "this process continues at all times." The Genesis story is not about Creation but rather explains how "composites are constantly being separated and forming new entities." Creation is a process and not per se a recorded historical moment.

The biblical account of creation describes more than simply how at one point in time God gave form to eternal primordial matter. It explains the logic of nature. Specifically, all bodies (whether inanimate or living) contain inherent motion that allows them to achieve entelechy and interact with other entities, and ultimately be transformed into new entities.[38] Thus, whereas for Nachmanides God literally creates man, taking earth and molding him into a being, Elijah argues that human beings are created from the interaction of various elements existing in nature. Developing certain ideas expressed in the rabbinic works *Genesis Rabbah* (8:11) and *Ethics of Fathers* (5:20), Elijah goes so far as to interpret the word "*ki-dmuteinu*" to mean that humanity was created in the image of animals. He writes in his commentary to Genesis 1:26:

> "Let us create man": It means since human beings were the last thing to have been created, God asked all the animals to provide aspects of themselves for the construction of man's physical image. For example, man's strength came from the lion, his speed from the deer etc. . . . and likewise so to his *nefesh chiunei* (life form) emerges from the animals. And the word image falls on the form of the thing. And the form of all living things is based on a *nefesh chiunei* (life form). So too this life form, found in vegetative entities, emerged from that which is *domem* (inanimate). And this is what it means "in our image": all the beings were brought together and created man allowing man to rule over all: This process can be explained as follows *domem* (inanimate), *tzomeach* (vegetative), *chai* (living), *medabber* (human beings); the seventy forces of nature and the mind. . . . And there was given to it a portion of godliness in order that it may worship God.

Building on the positions of, among others, Maimonides, Gersonides, and Hayyim Vital, Elijah contends that humans are the end result of an evolutionary process.[39] God did not place each animal and plant on this earth as is, but rather put into motion a process that allowed these entities to evolve. While God provides humanity with its substantial form (*bi-tzalmeinu*), humanity's appearance and physical makeup is a product of nature and specifically animals (*ki-dmuteinu*).[40]

The disagreement between Elijah and Nachmanides sheds light on a fundamental hermeneutic difference between them regarding the knowledge contained in the Bible. Nachmanides understands the creation of the world as a set paradigm; as he explains, "the events of fathers indicate what will happen to their children."[41] Nachmanides's interpretive scheme follows his philosophical assumptions that forms remain constant throughout history (stable entities). For Elijah the story of Genesis describes a process of physics, whereby God puts certain entities into circulation and allows them to develop on their own. History is not simply a set narrative that repeats itself. Rather, history, like Elijah's forms, is constantly evolving and being transformed.

Elijah expresses his most philosophically precise formulation of his anthropogony in his work "The Seventy Forces of Nature."[42] Most of the nineteenth-century Russian censors edited this section of Elijah's commentary to Isaiah thinking it contained a revolutionary messianic doctrine attached to Isaiah 11:1. As we will see, the text was known to his closest students and those who had access to manuscripts of Elijah's writings. This tract, which totals no more than 400 words, refers to the aforementioned "Seventy Forces of Man." The discrepancy in its name ("Man" or "Nature") reveals the philosophical tensions in Elijah's argument, namely the extent to which the various elements of nature create the human being. Elijah expresses this point in his brief introduction to his system:

> These are seventy forces, the world is divided into four categories inanimate (*domem*), vegetative (*tzomeach*), living (*chai*) and speaking (*medabber*). In that which is inanimate, vegetative, and living all seventy forces can be found. However in that which can speak one finds two added forces, the theoretical intellect (*sekhel ha-iyyuni*) and practical intellect (*sekhel ha-ma'aseh*) that encompass all seventy. And everywhere you find seventy you will find these two as well. As you will find by the seventy names of God, the seventy members of the Jewish High Court (*Sanhedrin*), seventy souls, seventy nations, this is what it means when the verse says that Abraham led forth his trained men (Genesis 14:14), and also with regard to the secret of the washing basin in the Temple.

Elijah lays out his version of the ancient Great Chain of Being schema of inanimate, vegetative, living, and speaking bodies.[43] Specifically, he builds on Hayyim Vital's (and Isaac Luria's) theory as expressed in *Etz Hayyim* (1572).[44] Elijah equates Vital's system with certain kabbalistic and rabbinic doctrines associated with the number seventy. Beneath this introduction, Elijah lists the first points of creation: the category of "ether" (*ha-heder kodem le-hayato*) is followed by "primordial matter" (*hyli*) and then finally "the first form" (*tzurah rishonah*). This "form" emerges as something inanimate. Elijah identifies "motion" as the force that transforms these entities (such as rocks) into a vegetative state (plants). Vital describes the transformation of one element into another as "not being the result of natural causes . . . the entity does not have the ability on its own to move from one place to another."[45] Elijah, however, seems to suggest that motion exists in each entity, allowing each entity to achieve not only its entelechy but also to metamorphosize into a totally different entity. Motion takes "composites" within "inanimate entities," "heats them," "divides them," "breaks them up," allowing the entity to "shed waste and retain nutrients necessary for its survival." Finally, the entity develops to the point that it has the capacity "to reproduce itself in its own image" (*tzomeach*), as well as contribute to the production of an entirely new species. Sometimes this process creates a new form—one that possesses "life" (*chai*). For Elijah, "life" means an object obtains various sensory abilities, "which are all connected to a brain." Such a position might reflect certain medieval alchemic strands of thought, as much as it might refer to certain biological and physical processes.[46] As he outlines, each entity's various transformations are the result of inherent motion. The end of this process is the creation of a living being that has the capacity to speak (*medabber*).

Elijah comes to a halt after laying out all seventy forces that comprise nature (*chai*), perhaps alluding to a kind of physical equation between human beings (*medabber*) and nature (*chai*). What has been said about other eighteenth-century Great Chain of Being theories might also be used to describe Elijah's version. Namely, while it might have been "in intent a proof of the existence of God . . . it was in effect a glorification of man. For it rested in great part upon the supposition that all other beings exist for man's sake."[47] Humans are not only a unique entity produced by a one-time occurrence from the breath of God, but rather are the sum total of nature. Still, the sum is greater than its parts. Humanity rules over nature, with its "practical" and "theoretical intellect."

Elijah's understanding of Creation breaks with the rabbinic tradition in two critical respects. He never actually mentions the end of creation, the human being or God. Neither a Prime Mover nor any extraterrestrial entity or category is listed as the cause of this process. Elijah's starting point is simply ether and primordial matter. Instead of God, Elijah presents numbers as holding together all of the various natural stages in his schema. Elijah cites the *Book of Creation* (*Sefer Yetzirah*) suggesting that "divine mathematics" either undergirds or can be used to describe creation and nature.[48]

Elijah maintains that numbers contain the logic of the Creation. His position followed not only other Kabbalists, but the inventor of calculus, Gottfried Wilhelm Leibniz (1646–1716), Johannes Kepler (1571–1630), and other Renaissance Neo-Pythagoreans who were drawn to kabbalistic works precisely because they expressed in a sacred language the important role of mathematics in the ordering of the world. However, whereas Leibniz had already recognized the way in which numbers themselves could be understood in terms of motion (calculus), Elijah was still employing medieval algebra and geometry, thus leaving a chasm between his philosophy (based on motion) and his mathematics (based on stable entities). To be sure, it is unclear to what extent Elijah thinks numbers are the very basis of the creation of the world, or that mathematics is simply a human rational language for understanding nature and in no way tells us anything about the divine.[49]

In summation, Elijah synthesizes and further develops the two most extreme medieval positions on cosmogony and anthropogony. He embraces Nachmanides's developmental notion of human creation, but argues that scripture was talking about a process of physics that continues throughout time. Likewise, he fully adopts Maimonides's notion of the world's functioning according to natural principles but believes that creation was not *ex nihilo*. However by identifying the world as form, he further rationalizes Jewish cosmology and anthropology. Elijah argues that while scientific knowledge is necessary to explain the latter, kabbalistic knowledge is required to explain the former.

DISSIMULATION IN THE LEGACY OF ELIJAH OF VILNA

Elijah's philosophical orientation created a problem for many of his students and followers. The emergence of the Haskalah (Jewish Enlightenment) at the end of the eighteenth and beginning of the nineteenth century in eastern Europe recast the intellectual and social fields of Jewish life. For some, philosophy became associated with various movements that seemed to undermine Elijah's pious and observant lifestyle. In many cases "philosophy" was equated with social freedoms that challenged rabbinic authority. Elijah's cosmogony and anthropogony might certainly have shocked many of his nineteenth-century followers, who at the end of Elijah's life were said to have demanded that the master stop a class on Maimonides's *Guide* being given in his courtyard. Elijah responded "with ire." Stopping such a class would be tantamount to heresy. "Tell them," Elijah proclaimed, "that I would be glad to receive but half of Rambam's portion of the world to come!"[50]

Elijah's intellectual breadth was the cause of great debate for future generations. There are those such as Menashe of Ilya (1767–1831) who publicly defended his teacher's enlightened sensibilities.[51] But those like Menashe were denounced; in many instances they were scolded for putting words into the Gaon's mouth. In that vein, Elijah's student and public preacher Pinchas of Polotsk (1746–1823) worked to publicly distance the master from anything intellectually associated with Enlightenment tendencies.[52] Anyone who wanted to claim that Elijah endorsed the study of philosophy had to be prepared to experience the wrath of rabbis across eastern Europe.

With that in mind we can now return to and better understand Yisrael of Shklov's above-quoted statements about the Gaon that appear in *Pe'at ha-Shulchan* (Safed: 1836). There, Yisrael writes:

> ועל חכמת פילוסופיא אמר שלמדה לתכליתה. ולא הוציא ממנה רק שני דברים טובים והם שבעים כוחות שבאדם כמו שכתוב בפי' רבינו על ישעי' ע"פ ויצא חטר מגזע ישי וגומר, ועוד דבר א' והשאר צריך להשליכה החוצה

Yisrael's comments appear opaque. It could be asked: When Yisrael said that Elijah studied science "*le-tachlita*," did he really mean that Elijah studied it "only for practical purposes"? Perhaps he was alluding to Elijah studying philosophy "to its ends," namely, down to the basic principles governing all of nature. Likewise, perhaps Yisrael was arguing to "discard" the rest of philosophy not because it was heretical, but rather because Elijah had so thoroughly studied the subject matter that the rest could now be deduced?

Well aware that the "seventy forces of nature" reappears throughout Elijah's commentary to *Sefer Yetzirah* and Genesis, Yisrael must have known that Elijah considered it as the epistemology of the world. Just in case Yisrael's reader failed to look at Elijah's work itself, he purposely drops another clue, leaving unstated the "second thing" that Elijah adopted from philosophy. Elijah, he claims, deduced two things from philosophy.

While he tells us the first, "the seventy forces of man," he never even tells his reader the second thing. It's left as a secret.

Yisrael was not Elijah's only student to recognize the critical role played by the "seventy forces" in his teacher's worldview. Elijah's most well-known enlightened student, Menashe Ilya, builds on his master's anthropogony in his work *Alfei Menashe* (Vilna: 1822).[53] Likewise, the botanist Benjamin Rivlin (1728–1812)[54] records that he "heard from his master and teacher the Gaon and Hasid that there are seventy forces, which corresponded to seventy nations. For each nation possesses an evil character trait, but the righteous person rules over these nations by transforming these evil traits into good ones."[55]

Elijah's notion of the seventy forces of nature seems to be animating Elijah's son Abraham's anonymously published work, *Gevulot Aretz* (Berlin: 1801). The book opens by claiming that it addresses "the differences between the seventy distinct nations." Iris Idelson-Shein has recently suggested that Abraham's evolutionary theories are drawn from the French Deist George Louis Leclerc de Buffon's work *Variétés dans l'espèce* (Paris: 1749). According to Abraham, "we all have the same Father"; racial and ethnic differences are simply the result of social conditioning (not predetermined racial categories).[56] Abraham, however, also seems to be building on his father's anthropogony when he devotes a section of his study to the subject of "man's dominion over all living things." This is so, Abraham explains, "not simply because of fixed natural laws that do not change . . . but because God ordained that man be given the power of the intellect, allowing him to rule over all living beings."[57] Abraham's emphasis on humanity's dominion over animals recalls his father's above quoted commentary to Genesis. Elijah's commentary to Genesis is in fact based on Abraham's "word for word" dictation of his father's lectures. Simply put, it is unclear what in fact are the Gaon's and what are his son Abraham's words.

But the Gaon's students went further in trying to cover up these clues. As Yehudah Liebes has already shown, the Gaon's student Menachem Mendel of Shklov often intentionally wrote in a cryptic manner, asking for his words to be interpreted in multiple ways.[58] With regard to Elijah's relationship to philosophy, Menachem Mendel writes,

> אספרה אל חוק דבר אחד אשר שמעתי מפיו הקדוש כאשר ישבתי לפניו ונתגלגל לפניו הענין של החכם אריסט״ו ואמר שודאי הוא שהיה אריסט״ו
>
> כופר מתחילה ועד סוף שאלו היה בא לפני הייתי מראה לו סיבוב החמה והלבנה עם כוכביהם מאירים על השולחן הזה כאשר יאירו ברקיע השמים ואיך היה מכחיש בדעתו לומר שהעולם מתנהג ע״פ הטבע וכי היה מהנמנע לשמעון הצדיק שהיה בדורו להראות לו נפלאות רבות מגבורות הש״י אלא שהיה ארסטו יודע רבונו ומכוין וכו׳ ובאמת נרתעתי לאחורי בשעמי הדברי׳ האלו יצאו מפורשים מפיו הקדוש והטהור אף הוא השיב אמריו לי מה התמהון הזה ע״י שם אחד הייתי עושה כל זה והגאונים שאחר זמן הגמרא ידעהו ג״כ

These comments have traditionally been interpreted as follows:

> Let me tell you a principle that I heard from his [Elijah's] holy mouth, when I was sitting in front of him and our conversation turned to the issue of Aristotle. And he said, certainly Aristotle was a heretic from start to finish. If he came before me I

> would demonstrate how one could make the movements of the sun, moon and the stars appear on this table in the same manner as they appear in the sky. And how it is contradictory for him to say that the world functions according to rational principles. Since Aristotle was unable to meet Shimon ha-Tzaddik who lived in his age, he never saw God's greatness. For Aristotle knew God but rebelled against him. To be honest, I was shocked when I heard these exact words leave his holy and clean mouth. Yet, he responded to me, "why are you surprised? I could explain all of this with one word [the name of God]."

Menachem Mendel suggests that Elijah believed the world to be enchanted and was prepared to prove it to his young disciple by making a table light up just like the sky. Contra Aristotle, the world does not operate according to rational principles. At first, Menachem Mendel doubts that Elijah could really perform such a trick, but Elijah reassures him that he could do so by invoking the name of God.

Yet, upon closer inspection, Menachem Mendel might be saying the exact opposite:

> Let me tell a principle that I heard from his [Elijah's] holy mouth, when I was sitting in front of him and I put before him Aristotle's issue. And he said, certainly Aristotle denied there being a beginning or end to the world. If he came before me, I would create a model of these phenomenon on this table and show how the movements of the sun and moon with the stars in the same manner in which they light up the sky. [Based on the ordered movements of the sun, moon and stars], he contradicts his own claim "that the world functions according to rational principles." [As Gersonides asked: for how can something function according to the laws of nature if it is by chance?]. Because Aristotle was unable to meet Shimon ha-Tzaddik who lived in his age, he never saw God's greatness. For Aristotle knew God but rebelled against him. [Aristotle believed in God but did not think he created the world.] To be honest, I winced to myself when I heard these exact words leave his holy and clean mouth. Yet, he responded to me, "why are you surprised? I could explain all of this with one word [the name of God]."

According to this reading, Elijah thought that Aristotle believed in God but had rebelled against Him. Elijah argues with Aristotle, claiming that reason proves God's role in creation. Elijah repeats what he says in his commentary to Genesis 1:1, namely that the sun, moon, and stars exhibit the same design and order as a table. Or perhaps Menachem Mendel is suggesting that Elijah set up a model diagram on the table that could demonstrate how the sun, moon, and stars operate in the sky. Like Gersonides, Elijah claims that Aristotle contradicts himself. For how can the stars, moon, and sun behave in an ordered way and yet exist by chance? If they behave according to a set pattern, God must have created them. Reason confirms God's dominion over the universe. Menachem Mendel was scandalized to hear Elijah arguing that the world functions according to rational principles. Elijah reassures him that everything he said could be theologically justified by God's providence.

Menachem Mendel's comments can be interpreted as asserting either the irrational (reading number one) or rational nature of the cosmos (reading number two). The Gaon was either a traditional kabbalistic or a rational philosopher. Looking carefully at Elijah's ideas, however, he seems to argue that each system of thought can be used to explain a different domain or layer of the universe, namely the meta-rational nature of the heavens (matter) and the rational nature of the world (form).

It might be argued that Menachem Mendel intended to express both ideas to explain a different feature of Elijah's worldview and to cover up the philosophical reading of the Gra from lesser minds. The "secret" double reading I am proposing to explain Menachem Mendel and Elijah's ideas is hinted at by the Kabbalist and student of Menachem Mendel's student (Isaac Chaver Wildmann [1789–1853]) Shlomo Elyashiv (1841–1926) in his work *Leshem Shevo ve-Achlamah*. Before alluding to the "secret" of the double reading of the master, Elyashiv churlishly admits that "he really does not want to divulge these things and explain them, because not everything should be written. And also," he continues, "I don't know why it would matter for someone who is a firm believer in God. I don't even know why I would waste any time on this topic." Elyashiv knows all too well that what he is about to say could only be understood by an elite set of scholars. Nonetheless, Elyashiv cannot help himself:

> I heard in the name of the Gaon, (and it seems to me that I also saw all of it written in his name) that Aristotle knew full well that there was a God and wanted to rebel against Him. Had Aristotle wanted to understand the truth he would have tried to meet with Shimon ha-tzaddik, who lived in his generation and Shimon ha-tzaddik would have shown him the truth. But he stopped himself from meeting him and the two never came together. For this is not possible . . . and I can't say more on this topic. However, everything that the philosophers (*chokrim*) with their wisdom have said regarding metaphysics is true. And what they have written with regard to the creation of the world: it can all be found in Kabbalah in a manner that is more easily accepted by the heart and that has more depth. And in particular the words expressed by the man of God the holy Maimonides in his work the *Guide* we see many ideas that rise to the heights of the heavens within kabbalistic thinking, even though such knowledge was not in existence during his days. Nonetheless, the spirit of God spoke to him and I have said enough.[59]

Though reticent and cryptic, Elyashiv's words are clearly alluding to Menachem Mendel's introduction to Elijah's commentary on *Avot*. He supports the coded double reading of Menachem Mendel's and the Gaon's statements, both in theory and in interpretive practice. For Elijah, kabbalistic and philosophic ideas were compatible but represented different interpretive lenses through which to see the universe. For the masses the Gaon would appear as a traditional Kabbalist and as a critic of the Maimonidean tradition, because for those who lacked "firm faith," the implications of the Gaon endorsing a philosophical worldview could be problematic. In truth, however, Elyashiv also knew that Elijah's worldview of *PaRDeS* subsumed both the kabbalistic and philosophical traditions in Jewish history, allowing each one to operate independently but also in harmony. Elyashiv, however, had inverted the hermeneutic relationship between these two systems of thought. Elijah saw philosophy as the exoteric method of interpretation and Kabbalah as the esoteric understanding of texts and the universe. Elyashiv's cryptic and dual-sided interpretation of Menachem Mendel's seemingly negative comments about philosophy suggests that Kabbalah was the exoteric and philosophy was the esoteric understanding of texts and the universe. Elyashiv makes philosophy into a secret knowledge meant to be hidden from the masses.

Menachem Mendel and Yisrael knew how thoroughly immersed and versed their teacher was in the Jewish philosophic tradition. They were also aware that Elijah was not interested in questions involving the permissibility of studying philosophy. Elijah was an eighteenth-century intellectual, not a nineteenth-century ideologue and certainly not a twentieth-century Orthodox rabbi. He, like many before him, saw knowledge not as another sphere of politics but as a sacred endeavor to be engaged in by the spiritual and intellectual elite. More so than anyone before him Elijah recognized the intellectual implications of the vastness and contradictory nature of Jewish literature. The notion of reason put forth by Maimonides could not hold a full reading of Jewish knowledge. Rejecting Kabbalah led to a dishonest interpretation of Jewish literature and would end up severely truncating the Jewish intellectual tradition. Elijah tried to make sense out of the totality of Jewish thought, recognizing its myriad and conflicting sources and texts, all the while supporting a rational understanding of nature and the cosmos.

ACKNOWLEDGMENTS

I would like to thank Dov Weiss and Maoz Kahane for their helpful comments and suggestions.

NOTES

1. See the introduction to Yisrael of Shklov, *Pe'at ha-Shulchan* (Safed: 1836). On Yisrael of Shklov see Arei Morgenstern, *Hastening Redemption: Messianism and the Resettlement of the Land of Israel* (New York: Oxford University Press, 2006), 98–110, 121–33.
2. See Israel Klausner, *Vilna be-Tekufat ha-Gaon* (Jerusalem: 1942), 17 and Immanuel Etkes, "Li-She'elat Mevasrei ha-Haskalah be-Mizrach Eropah," in Etkes, ed., *Ha-Da'at ve-ha-Chayyim: Tnuat ha-Haskalah be-Mizrach Eropah* (Jerusalem: Merkaz Zalman Shazar, 1993), 30.
3. See Menachem Mendel of Shklov's introduction to Elijah's commentary to *Avot de-Rebbe Natan* (Shklov: 1804). On Menachem Mendel see Morgenstern, *Hastening Redemption*, 111–16 and the editor's introduction to *Kitvei ha-Gaon Rabbi Menachem Mendel* (Jerusalem: 1991), 6–18 and Haim Hillel Ben-Sasson, "Ishiyuto shel ha-Gra ve-Hashpa'ato ha-Historit," *Zion* 31, no. 1–2 (1966): 39–86.
4. On Elijah ben Solomon in English see Eliyahu Stern, *The Genius: Elijah of Vilna and the*

Making of Modern Judaism (New Haven: Yale University Press, 2013), and Immanuel Etkes, *The Gaon of Vilna: The Man and His Image* (Berkeley: University of California Press, 2002).

5. Following the publication of *Genius: Elijah of Vilna and the Making of Modern Judaism*, Orthodox rabbis and scholars lined up against my thesis that the Gaon engaged in philosophical exploration and should be seen as a modernist. I compared the Gaon's works to those of other leading eighteenth-century philosophers who like him had been influenced by medieval scholastic thought as well as the Kabbalah. Most notably, I penned a chapter looking at Elijah's worldview through the ideas espoused by the German idealist G. W. Leibniz. The first broadside came from a New York scholar who penned an open letter to Prof. Elliot Wolfson implicitly demanding that he, as the leader of the field of Jewish studies and having himself written on the Gaon, rebuke me for having the "audacity" to claim that the Gaon believed in mathematics as the highest form of knowledge. See Bezalel Naor, "Letter of Bezalel Naor to Prof. Elliot R. Wolfson," March 3, 2013, seen on October 4, 2021, at http://orot.com/the-genius/. The New York scholar even pointed to a brilliant article Wolfson had published, "From Sealed Book to Open Text: Time, Memory, and Narrativity in Kabbalistic Hermeneutics," *Interpreting Judaism in a Postmodern Age*, ed. Steven Kempnes (New York: New York University Press, 1996), 145–78 about the Gaon's hermeneutics, one that directly contradicted my claims. In fact, the debate between me and Wolfson was based on each of us focusing on two different manuscripts; both of us were on strong ground in our claims. Wolfson never replied. See also Lawrence Kaplan, "Lawrence Kaplan's review of Eliyahu Stern, "The Genius," The Seforim Blog, seen on October 4, 2021, at https://seforimblog.com/2013/11/lawrence-kaplans-review-of-eliyahu/?print=print; Marc Shapiro, "The Vilna Gaon, Part I: How Modern Was He?" The Seforim Blog, seen on October 4, 2021 at https://seforimblog.com/2013/12/the-vilna-gaon-part-1-how-modern-was-he/; and Eliyahu Krakowski, "Review Essay: Between the Genius and Lost in Translation," *Hakira: The Flatbush Journal of Jewish Law and Thought* 16 (2013): 153–75.
6. See Jacob Dienstag, "Ha-im Hitnaged ha-Gra le-Mishnato ha-Filosofit shel ha-Rambam?" *Talpiyot* 4, nos. 1–2 (July 1949): 265.
7. Shmuel Yosef Fuenn, *Kiryah Ne'emanah* (Vilna: 1915), 169 claims that the words "*ha-philosophia arurah*" (the evil philosophy) were inserted into the text by editors; see also Alan Brill, "Auxiliary to 'Hokhma': The Writings of the Vilna Gaon and Philosophical Terminology," in *Ha-Gra u-Veit Midrasho*, ed. Moshe Hallamish, Yosef Rivlin, and Raphael Shuchat (Ramat Gan: Bar-Ilan University Press, 2003), 9–11. On the debate that ensued among enlighteners and rabbinic figures regarding the veracity of the actual statement see the sources compiled by Shmuel Werses, "Ha-Gaon mi-Vilna bi-Olamah shel Safrut ha-Haskalah," *Hakitzah Ami: Sifrut ha-Haskalah be-idan ha-Modernizatziah* (Jerusalem: Magnes Press, 2000), 60–64.
8. On Maimonides's understanding of esoteric and exoteric readings of texts see most recently Moshe Halbertal's analysis of Leo Strauss and Sara Klein-Breslavy's understanding of Maimonides in *Concealment and Revelation*, trans. Jackie Feldman (Princeton: Princeton University Press, 2007), 49–59. For a more in-depth account see Elliot R. Wolfson, *Language, Eros, Being: Kabbalistic Hermeneutics and the Poetic Imagination* (New York: Fordham University Press, 2005), 128–90.

9. See Moses Maimonides, *The Guide of the Perplexed*, trans. Shlomo Pines (Chicago: Chicago University Press, 1963), vol. 1, 12.
10. See Menashe's recollection of Elijah's criticism of the preacher Jacob Kranz, the Dubno Maggid, in *Alfei Menashe* (Vilna: 1822), "likkutim siman 129."
11. Michael Shashar, *Sambatyon: Essays on Jewish Holidays*, ed. and trans. Edward Levin (Jerusalem: World Zionist Organization, 1987), 62 contends that Elijah's commentary to Jonah follows Maimonides's approach to allegory. Elijah rejects the notion that Jonah was eaten by a real whale and survived inside its stomach for days on end. Instead, the story is an allegory about the human soul. Unlike Maimonides, however, Elijah's allegory never ignores the specific wording of Jonah. Both Maimonides and Elijah neutralize the existence of irrational forces but whereas Maimonides ignores the specific wording of a seemingly irrational text, Elijah feels the need to give sufficient reason for the existence of each word, sentence, and phrase. Maimonides's interpretive behavior makes it impossible to understand how he contextually reads biblical verses and words. With Elijah, the exact opposite is the case. Each word has a reason and contributes to a larger conceptual picture. On those who disagree with Shashar's reading see Yosef Rivlin, "Biur ha-Gra le-Sefer Yonah," *Kiryat Sefer* 62 (1989): 920–24.
12. C. Wolff, *Logic or Rational Thoughts on the Powers of Human Understanding, Gesammelte Werke*, III. ABT. BD. 77 (New York: George Olms Verlag, 2003), 58.
13. Mishnah Torah, *Hilkhot Yesodei ha-Torah*, 4:13.
14. See Isserles's comments to *Shulchan Arukh, Yoreh De'ah*, 244:18. To be sure, Isserles's position on the study of philosophy demands its own study. See most notably, Elchanan Reiner, "The Attitude of Ashkenazi Society to the New Science in the Sixteenth Century," *Science in Context* (1997), 10: 589–603; Reiner, "Yashan mi-Pnei Chadash: Al Temurot be-Tochnei limud be-Yeshivot Polin be-Meah ha-16 be-Yeshivat ha-Ramah be-Krakow," in *Remember the Word to Your Servant: Essays and Studies in Memory of Dov Rappel*, ed. Shmuel Glick (Jerusalem: 2007), 189.
15. See Elijah's comments to *Shulchan Arukh, Yoreh De'ah*, 246:4.
16. While the term *PaRDeS* appears in Talmudic literature as a form of mystical knowledge, in the medieval period it is identified with a specific hermeneutic scheme. For an overview of the scholarship produced on the interpretive aspects of *PaRDeS* see Peretz Sandler, "On the Problem of *PaRDeS* and the Fourfold Method," in *Sefer Orbakh*, ed. Arthur Biram (Jerusalem: Kiryat Sefer, 1955), 222–35; and Frank Talmage, "Apples of Gold: The Inner Meaning of Sacred Texts in Medieval Judaism," in *Apples of Gold in Settings of Silver: Studies in Medieval Jewish Exegesis and Polemics*, ed. Barry Dov Walfish (Toronto: Pontifical Institute of Mediaeval Studies, 1999), 114–16.
17. See Brill, "Auxiliary to Hokhma," 12.
18. The letter can be found in Zvi ha-Levi Horowitz, *Kitvei ha-Geonim* (Warsaw: 1938), 3–10. Regarding Aristotle's *Ethics* it is unclear if they were requesting a Latin edition or more likely a copy of Meir Alguadez's Hebrew translation (*Sefer ha-Middot*) of the Latin text in 1400.
19. Elijah's commentary to the Bible, *Aderet Eliyahu*, first appeared in *Chamisha Chumshei Torah* (Dubrovna: 1804). The Gaon's commentary to the first chapter to Genesis is taken from the notes of his son Abraham who adds, "that these are the exact words I heard from my father's

holy mouth." On the editing of Elijah's commentary to Genesis and the veracity of Abraham's notes see David Luria's bibliography in "Aliyat Kir," published by Yehoshua Heschel Levin, *Aliyot Eliyahu* (Vilna: 1856), 109–10. In this article I am using the edition published in Warsaw in 1914. Abraham's version is supported by the way Elijah describes "form," "matter," and "motion" in his other writings.

20. While it may be argued that Maimonides in fact never subscribed to the belief in creation *ex nihilo*, such issues are not the concern of this article. The literature on Maimonides's understanding of this passage of *Pirkei de-Rabbi Eliezer* is extensive. See most recently Kenneth Seeskin, *Maimonides on the Origins of the World* (New York: Cambridge University Press, 2007), 16–60; Lawrence Kaplan, "Maimonides on the Miraculous Element in Prophecy," *Harvard Theological Review* 70, no. 3–4 (1977): 233–56; Herbert Davidson, "Maimonides' Secret Position on Creation," in *Studies in Medieval Jewish History and Literature*, ed. Isadore Twersky (Cambridge, MA: Harvard University Press, 1979), 16–40; and Warren Zev Harvey, "A Third Approach to Maimonides' Cosmogony-Prophetology Puzzle," *Harvard Theological Review* 74, no. 3 (1981): 287–301.
21. On Plato and the kabbalistic understanding of Creation see Moshe Idel, "Jewish Kabbalah and Platonism in the Middle Ages and Renaissance," in *Neoplatonism and Jewish Thought*, ed. Lenn E. Goodman (New York: State University of New York Press, 1992), 320–21.
22. See also Elijah's comments on creation *ex nihilo* in his commentary to *Mishnat Hasidim*, published and edited by Raphael Shuchat, "Peirush ha-Gra mi-Vilna le-*Mishnat Hasidim*: Mashal ve-Nimshal be-Kitvei ha-Ari," *Kabbalah* 3 (1998): 297.
23. Though well beyond the scope of this paper, Elijah contends that matter is "evil" because it is "unintelligible" to us. "Evil" is not inherently bad, but rather something that cannot be grasped by reason. Elijah in *Aderet Eliyahu* Genesis 1:4 equates unintelligibility with both "night" and "matter." Elijah follows eighteenth-century thinkers, such as Luzzatto, in arguing that in fact God created evil and that evil is part of the preestablished harmony of the world. Unlike Maimonides who believes that darkness was simply a covering up of light, Elijah argues that light (good) and dark (evil) were in fact different creations, both having purpose and both emanating from the same source. See Elijah's comments to Genesis 1:4 on the creation of light and darkness and his reinterpretation of Maimonides (*Guide* 2:30).
24. See *Sefer ha-Zikaron* (Jerusalem: Mossad ha-Rav Kook, 1982), 49–52. I would like to thank Alan Nadler for bringing this source to my attention.
25. See Seymour Feldman, "Synopsis of Book Six," Levi ben Gershom, *The Wars of the Lord*, trans. and ed. Seymour Feldman (New York: JPS and JTSA 1999), 198. Jacob Zvi Mecklenburg's interpretation *Ketav ve-ha-Kabbalah* (Leipzig: 1839), 1:1 notes the striking resemblance between Elijah's and Gersonides's definition of God's providence.
26. See Elijah's comments in *Aderet Eliyahu*, Genesis 1:1; see also Elijah, *Imrei Noam Berachot* 60b. On the uniqueness of Elijah's understanding of creation *ex nihilo* see Jacob Zvi Mecklenburg's interpretation in *Ketav ve-ha-Kabbalah* (Leipzig: 1839), Gen. 1:1. The radical nature of Elijah's comments regarding creation *ex nihilo* have been noted as well by Yehudah Lifshitz, *Nachal Yehudah* (Kovno: 1920), 4–5.
27. See Feldman, "Synopsis of Book Six," 195.
28. See Mejeris Šubas, "The Gaon's Views on Philosophy and Science," in *The Gaon of Vilnius and*

the Annals of Jewish Culture, ed. Izraelis Lempertas (Vilnius: Vilnius University Publishing House, 1998), 69 (65–74).

29. See Feldman "Synopsis of Book Six," 208. More generally, see Jonathan Goldstein, "The Origins of the Doctrine of Creation Ex Nihilo," *Journal of Jewish Studies* 35 (1984): 127–35.
30. See Elijah ben Solomon, *Sifra di-Tzniuta* (Vilna: 1882), likkutim 38b; for parallels and similar comments see 17a and 28b. See also Elijah's statements in Elijah ben Solomon, *Sefer Yetsirah*, 8c.
31. See Elijah ben Solomon's commentary to Proverbs 1:1 in *Sefer Mishlei im Biur ha-Gra*, ed. Moshe Philip (Petakh Tikvah: 2000).
32. See *Aderet Eliyahu*, Genesis 2:2, 2:6, and his comments to Ezekiel 1:51 in *Biur ha-Gra al Chabakkuk* (Prague: 1811).
33. See Elijah's comments on Isaiah 2:6 in *Biur ha-Gra le-Nevi'im* (Jerusalem: Mossad ha-Rav Kook, 2002).
34. See David Ruderman's discussion of early modern Ashkenazic philosophy in *Jewish Thought and Scientific Discovery in Early Modern Europe* (New Haven: Yale University Press, 1995), 73–82.
35. On the difference between Judah Loew and Elijah see Brill, "Auxiliary to Hokhma," 16.
36. See the collection of statements attributed to Elijah in the name of Hayyim of Volozhin in *Keter Rosh* (Jerusalem: 1986), 13, no. 51.
37. On the relationship of Kabbalah to philosophy in the writings of Abulafia see Elliot R. Wolfson's critique of Moshe Idel in "The Doctrine of Sefirot in the Prophetic Kabbalah of Abraham Abulafia (Part II)," *Jewish Studies Quarterly* 3, no. 1 (1996): 77–78, esp. 77. http://www.jstor.org/stable/40753145.
38. Perhaps recognizing the mechanistic implications of Elijah's ideas, Yissoschar Dov Ber ben Solomon takes issue with his brother and defends Nachmanides's position. See Yissoschar Dov Ber ben Solomon, *Tzof Devash*, published by Ya'akov Pelskin, "Sefer *Tzof Devash*," *Yeshurun* 4 (1998): 285.
39. See Maimonides, *Shemoneh Perakim*, 1:1; Gersonides, *Commentary to Genesis*, 1:1; Hayyim Vital, *Shar ha-Kedusha*, Section 3, part 2.
40. On Elijah and his students' understanding of *tzelem* and *dimut* see Moshe Idel, "Kabbalat R. Menachem Mendel mi-Shklov," in *Ha-Gra u-Veit Midrasho*, ed. Moshe Hallamish, Yosef Rivlin, and Raphael Shuchat (Ramat Gan: Bar-Ilan University Press, 2003), 176–83.
41. See Nachmanides's commentary to Genesis 26:29.
42. Elijah's "The Seventy Forces of Nature" first appeared in *Aderet Eliyahu* (Vilna: 1820) as an interpretation of Isaiah 11:1. On the history of the text see the edition published by Ya'akov Greenwald, *Kuntres Shivim Kochot ha-Adam* (Israel: 1991), 123. The phrase itself, however, is mentioned throughout Elijah's writings. For a list of the places in which it appears in his various commentaries see Greenwald's bibliography fn. 1, 3 and Meir Katzenelenbogen's bibliographic notes in *Biur ha-Gra le-Nevi'im* (Jerusalem: Mossad ha-Rav Kook, 2002), 128–29, fn. 3, 4.
43. On the history of the Great Chain of Being schema see Arthur O. Lovejoy, *The Great Chain of Being: A Study of the History of an Idea* (Cambridge: Harvard University Press, 1953), 59–66.
44. See *Etz Hayyim*, "Olam ha-Galgalim," chap. 10 (Koretz: 1782), 151–52b.

45. See *Etz Hayyim*, 151b.
46. Though it is beyond the scope of this paper, Elijah may have been influenced by certain theories of medieval corpuscular alchemy that continued to play a role in eighteenth-century scientific thought. On medieval and modern uses of alchemy in scientific thinking see most recently William R. Newman, *Atoms and Alchemy: Chemistry and the Experiential Origins of the Scientific Revolution* (Chicago: University of Chicago Press, 2006), 23–66. To be sure, Yisrael of Shklov in his comments about Elijah in *Pe'at ha-Shulchan* (Safed: 1836) states that Elijah knew "*chokhmat ha-kishuf*" [the wisdom of magic].
47. Lovejoy, *The Great Chain of Being*, 186.
48. See Elijah ben Solomon, *Sefer Yetzirah*, 2c. My mathematical reading of Elijah's commentary is based on Shlomo Tolchin's interpretation of Elijah's writings (which he tells us was related to him straight from Elijah's mouth). Yosef Avivi adopts Shlomo's interpretation, namely that Elijah invokes the word *sefar* (number) to explain the origins of the world. As explained by Avivi, Rabbi Shlomo Tolchin's testimony is essential for making sense of Elijah's commentaries. See Yosef Avivi, *Kabbalat ha-Gra* (Jerusalem: Kerem Eliyahu, 1992), 34–37.
49. Menachem Mendel of Shklov argues that numbers connect the metaphysical realm to nature. In the introduction to his work *Derekh ha-Kodesh* (Jerusalem: 1999), a commentary to the kabbalistic work *Brit Menucha*, he writes: "Know that the word math [*cheshbon*] comes from thought [*machshava*] and this is what constitutes the first form" (4).
50. See the story recorded by David Luria in the name of Yisrael Gordon in *Aliyot Eliyahu* (Vilna: 1856), 34 fn. 5.
51. On Menashe of Ilya and the Jewish enlightenment see Yitzhak Barzilay, *Manasseh of Ilya: Precursor of Modernity Among the Jews of Eastern Europe* (Jerusalem: Magnes Press, 1999), 158–73. More generally, see Shmuel Feiner, *The Jewish Enlightenment*, trans. Chaya Naor (Philadelphia: University of Pennsylvania Press, 2002).
52. On Pinchas of Polotsk and the Jewish enlightenment see Allan Nadler, *The Faith of the Mithnagdim: Rabbinic Responses to Hasidic Rapture* (Baltimore: Johns Hopkins, 1997) 127–51.
53. Menashe's ideas on anthropogony appear throughout *Alfei Menashe* but see specifically siman 1–90 as well as his discussion in his posthumously published additions to *Alfei Menashe* (Vilna: 1895), chap. 16.
54. On Rivlin see David Fishman, *Russia's First Modern Jews: The Jews of Shklov* (New York: New York University Press, 1995), 108–12.
55. Benjamin Rivlin, *Geviei Gavia ha-Kessef* (Warsaw: 1897), 33.
56. See Iris Idelson-Shein, "Blessed in the Changer of Beings: Uses and Representations of 'the Exotic' in the Jewish Enlightenment," PhD diss. Tel Aviv University, 2010.
57. See *Gevulot Aretz* (Berlin: 1801), 10.
58. See the excellent studies of Yehudah Leibes, "Talmidei ha-Gra, ha-Shabtaut, ve-ha-Nekudah ha-Yehudit," *Dat* 50–52 (2003): 255–90; Leibes, "Nevuato shel ha-Shabbtaei R. Heschel Tzoref mi-Vilna bi-Kitvei Menachem Mendel mi-Shklov Talmid ha-Gaon mi-Vilna mi-Yased ha-Yishuv ha-Ashkenazi be-Yerushalyim," *Kabbalah* 10 (2008): 107–68; and Eliezer Baumgarten, "Temunot ha-Otiyot le-Menachem Mendel mi-Shklov," *Kabbalah* 10 (2008): 287–304.

59. See Shlomo Elyashiv, *Leshem Shevo ve-Achlamah*, "clalei hitpashtut ve-histaklut," 11:1 (Jerusalem: 1924), 42b. On the way Elyashiv employs esoteric and exoteric meanings see Elliot R. Wolfson, *Suffering Time, Philosophical, Kabbalistic and Hasidic Reflections on Temporality*, Supplements to the *Journal of Jewish Thought and Philosophy* (Leiden and Boston: Brill, 2021), 551–56.

IDOLS IN THE SANCTUARY

Elliot Wolfson and Modern Jewish Thought

ROBERT ERLEWINE

INTRODUCTION

In a recent review of Elliot R. Wolfson's 2019 book, *Heidegger and Kabbalah: Hidden Gnosis and the Path of Poiesis*,[1] David Novak expresses consternation at the very idea of bringing the Kabbalah into conversation with the philosophy of Martin Heidegger. "Many readers," Novak suggests, will find this pairing "an outrageous oxymoron," or worse, "an obscene sacrilege." Employing a "kabbalah-like metaphor" to characterize the "coupling" of Heidegger's philosophy with Kabbalah as "something like bringing an idol into the sanctuary," Novak laments that such a conceptual engagement is even taking place, when "the intellectual task of Jewish thinkers of Elliot Wolfson's caliber [should] be to eject the idol from the Sanctuary, the Torah's true home, or never let it in."[2] Over and above their hyperbolic tone, Novak's claims here are particularly charged because they combine the well-worn (particularly in twentieth-century Jewish thought) effort to treat Heidegger's philosophy as a contemporary articulation of a pagan sensibility with a traditional notion of idolatry as consisting of certain views and practices that are not only external to the normative Jewish tradition but are antithetical to it.[3] It is all the more unfortunate, then, that Novak's review fails to mention *A Dream Interpreted Within a Dream: Oneiropoiesis and the Prism of Imagination* (2011) and especially *Giving Beyond the Gift: Apophasis and Overcoming Theomania* (2014),[4] recent works by Wolfson in which he not only offers a sophisticated theory of idolatry significantly at odds with the more conventional view embraced by Novak, but which also provide the basis for his effort to think of Heidegger and Kabbalah in light of each other. Indeed, Wolfson invokes Heidegger's thought precisely because he sees it as providing the resources to offer a way of participating in the Jewish theological tradition without falling victim to idolatry.

In this essay, I present Wolfson's theory of idolatry and emphasize its centrality to his works of the past decade. I begin with a brief consideration of *Heidegger and Kabbalah*, noting a few points of confluence between Heidegger's thought and kabbalistic speculation that Wolfson discerns and why this is understood to be significant for adequately taking stock of the philosophical implications of Kabbalah at the present moment. Then, with particular attention to *Giving Beyond the Gift*, I illuminate Wolfson's sense of the fraught and treacherous nature of the endeavor to—in Novak's words—"eject the idol out of Sanctuary," noting how such attempts frequently only succeed in making idolatry more subtle. Moreover, I not only detail Wolfson's charge that contemporary Continental philosophy of religion and modern Jewish thought have succumbed to conceptual idolatry, but I also examine his own constructive philosophical engagement with the Jewish theological tradition, which aims to avoid this result. In sum, this essay traces the manner in which the critical juxtaposition of Heidegger's philosophy and kabbalistic speculation in *Heidegger and Kabbalah* grows forth from Wolfson's rigorous theory of idolatry and its critique.

THE CRITICAL JUXTAPOSITION: HEIDEGGER AND KABBALAH

In light of the magisterial nature of Wolfson's *Heidegger and Kabbalah*, I will merely sketch—and sketch all too briefly—a few features of it rather than attempt a thoroughgoing accounting of the scope of its claims and contributions. I will briefly mention Wolfson's preference for Heidegger's notion of the belonging together of opposites rather than Hegel's dialectical theory of sublation of difference for interpreting Kabbalah, the sense that both Heidegger's philosophy and kabbalistic theosophy engage the larger traditions that they inhabit in a similar, not uncritical manner, and that Wolfson finds in Heidegger's thought resources for better articulating philosophically the meaning of the kabbalistic notion of *Ein Sof*, all while remaining constructively bound to one's home tradition rather than seeking a clean break from it.

Early in the work, Wolfson seeks to demonstrate the relevance of Heidegger's philosophy for the study of Kabbalah by means of situating his own work in regard to that of the pioneering scholar of Jewish mysticism, Gershom Scholem. With regard to the relationship between revelation and concealment in the Kabbalah, Wolfson acknowledges that it might seem that his position is quite close with that of Scholem insofar as both scholars share a sense that these terms are inextricably bound up with one another such that all revelation entails concealment and all concealment entails revelation. However, as a result of the different philosophical apparatuses by which they respectively make sense of and conceptualize this bond, a significant divergence emerges. Where Scholem employs the dialectical method of G. W. F. Hegel, "which posits the sublation of antinomies such that there is a synthesis in which one thing becomes its opposite," Wolfson embraces "Heidegger's idea of the belonging together of opposites that remain opposite in their juxtaposition."[5] The effort to present Heidegger's thought as the means to think difference differently, and to escape the ontotheological framework to which much kabbalistic scholarship and modern Jewish thought remains beholden, is a steady refrain in the book.

Of course, Heidegger's philosophy and kabbalistic theosophy arise in the midst of very different intellectual and cultural contexts and traditions. Heidegger is preoccupied with the history of Western philosophy while the Kabbalists engage the normative Jewish tradition. Nevertheless, there is a significant confluence between how each sort of thinking situates itself with regard to the larger tradition out of which it grows. Wolfson contends that both are attempts to take their respective traditions farther than they have hitherto gone with regard to the effort of purging from their foundations what Heidegger calls ontotheology, which significantly converges with what the kabbalists refer to as spiritual idolatry.[6] For Wolfson, Heidegger's ruminations on ontotheology and the metaphysics of presence offer a particularly apposite language and framework for discerning the philosophical concerns and implications of kabbalistic theosophy.

Indeed, in Heidegger's articulation of the non- or meta-metaphysical account of being and nothingness Wolfson finds resources for grasping the theosophical ruminations of the Kabbalists in decidedly non-ontotheological terms. Wolfson, seeking an alternative to the prevalent tendency to grasp the kabbalistic notion of *Ein Sof* as some sort of "metaphysical ipseity"[7] or "a substance subject to the antinomy of being and nonbeing,"[8] finds in Heidegger's work the means to conceive of it in a manner not beholden to the "dyadic logic of traditional ontotheology."[9] Rather than characterizing *Ein Sof* as an ipseity or substance, Wolfson sees it connoting a "semiotic marker of the being that symbolizes the interrelatedness of all beings,"[10] or, alternatively, as "an intricate lattice of codependent interrelationality constellated by the illimitable flux of the inimitable iterations of the eventfulness of beyng that constitutionally escapes the ontological categorization of beings,"[11] offering a profound "unsettling of the hierarchical relation of transcendent cause and immanent effect."[12] In this manner, then, Heidegger provides the tools for engaging the philosophical and theological implications of kabbalistic theosophy without backsliding into the ontotheological/idolatrous frameworks it sought, at least originally, to subvert. In short, in Heidegger, Wolfson finds the key to unlocking the iconoclastic potential of the Kabbalah, which, in turn, serves as a powerful resource for subverting the idolatrous imaginings that continue to inhabit the Jewish theological tradition.

If both Heidegger and the Kabbalists share the desire to overcome the ontotheological/idolatrous foundations of their respective traditions, they also share a hermeneutical conviction that the only way to overcome one's tradition is by proceeding on its very shoulders. That is, while Heidegger and the Kabbalists both seek a new beginning, they share a conviction that one cannot simply make a clean break with one's tradition and take up a brand-new path of thinking. They both maintain that not only is there no absolute new beginning, but also that the pursuit of such a goal leads one to become all the more deeply mired in what one initially sought to escape. Rather than a radically new departure, Heidegger and the Kabbalists share a sense that any viable new beginning must conserve rather than annihilate the tradition that one seeks to overcome. Or, as

Wolfson succinctly puts the matter, shared by Heidegger and the Kabbalists is the view that, "[h]ermeneutically, there is no overcoming except by undergoing."[13]

THE ROOTS OF THE CRITICAL JUXTAPOSITION

Even if it is acknowledged that *Heidegger and Kabbalah* offers a massive, highly sophisticated, and groundbreaking critical juxtaposition of Heidegger's philosophy and kabbalistic theosophy, one might still inquire—as Novak does—why such an endeavor should be seen as necessary. Put differently, we might ask: what is the question to which *Heidegger and Kabbalah* constitutes an answer? *Heidegger and Kabbalah* represents, I contend, a culmination of Wolfson's efforts in the past decade to think in a manner not beholden to either the binaries of transcendence/immanence on the one hand or theism/atheism on the other. These binaries, which—at least in Wolfson's view—constitute the foundation of idolatry, are indelibly linked with one another such that neither can be overcome unless both are. And while much of contemporary Continental philosophy of religion can be characterized by the desire to subvert both of these binaries, in Wolfson's estimation it has rarely been successful in this effort. For at least a decade, beginning with (or at least this is where I will begin) the opening chapter of *A Dream Interpreted Within a Dream*, "Transcending Transcendence and the Specter of Invisibility,"[14] the effort to delineate these binaries and their connection to idolatry, and elucidating the means to subvert them, have been central to Wolfson's scholarly agenda.

In "Transcending Transcendence" the contours of this program, which will be taken up and developed in more depth in *Giving Beyond the Gift*, are sketched with particular clarity. If the rest of the chapters in *A Dream Interpreted Within a Dream* engage, as the title suggests, various discourses pertaining to dreams and dreaming, this chapter seeks to elucidate a notion of transcendence that remains in keeping with "the cognitive implications of the . . . naturalistic approaches to the human predicament."[15] In seeking to articulate such a notion of transcendence, one free of the transcendence/immanence binary, Wolfson discloses that such an effort is inextricable from the subversion of the theism/atheism binary.

Wolfson begins "Transcending Transcendence" with the claim that the time is right for thinking transcendence anew, in a manner beyond the theologically inflected framing of an oppositional relationship between transcendence and immanence. For Wolfson, transcendence can only be freed from such theological baggage if it is no longer conceptualized in terms of "spatial exteriority,"[16] as somehow pertaining to "ontologically external entities or relations."[17] Wolfson invokes Edith Wyschogrod to suggest that shedding the spatial connotation of transcendence requires that we accept that "transcendence can no longer connote a 'referring term—that is, the notion that "something" transcends or that this "something" can be interpreted as having causal efficacy.'"[18] To think transcendence in nonspatial terms entails rejecting the conceptualization of God as "a being beyond being that is the ground of all beings" depicted as "somehow superintending the creation and looking over the affairs of humanity."[19] Again, drawing on Wyschogrod, Wolfson contends that after the spatial metaphor has been dispensed with, transcendence can only be configured on the basis of "a '*post hoc* constitution,'" namely, as a trace, a "non-event" that "can never become the object of thought."[20] According to Wolfson, when thought on such a post-hoc basis, transcendence is no longer comprehensible as the antipode of immanence, but rather is now inextricable from it. Indeed, these terms are so intertwined that this "transcended transcendence" could alternatively be understood as constituting "a full embrace of immanence that has no recourse to any trace of an unknowable transcendence from a higher source."[21]

To think in a manner free from the transcendence/immanence binary, then, is to think in entirely this-worldly terms, and thus, to resist recourse to any sort of beyond. It is to contend that "there is nothing beyond nature that is not already part of nature."[22] In terms of accounting for the givenness of the world, it means laying claim to nothing more basic than "the force of life (for want of a more suitable term),"[23] which means that with regard to this givenness there is no implied giver that gives. While understood as entirely "intertwined with the configuration of the world," transcendence remains a useful term for Wolfson in that it conveys "the qualities of elusiveness and exteriority" (without actually referring to some sort of ontological exteriority) and thus rules out the "possibility of incorporation into a totality."[24] A givenness that is endless, unpredictable, ever in a state of becoming, is a givenness that is characterized by transcendence, albeit a transcended transcendence.

In *Giving Beyond the Gift*, Wolfson amplifies this line of thought, highlighting that the effort to think in entirely this-worldly terms is remarkably fraught, that again and again thinkers succumb to the temptation to invoke theologically inflected notions of transcendence and immanence. While clearly resonating with Dominique Janicaud's well-known effort to problematize the presence of theology in the field of phenomenology, Wolfson's concern pertains primarily to the intrusion of theology in contemporary Continental philosophy of religion and modern Jewish thought. For Wolfson, this intrusion of the theological continues and remains insufficiently acknowledged in these fields because the connection between the transcendence/immanence and theism/atheism binaries remains unrecognized. This connection has gone unrecognized, Wolfson contends, because there is a confusion regarding the theism/atheism binary haunting the monotheistic traditions themselves. Insofar as the theism/atheism binary remains in place, the efforts to transcend the binary between transcendence/immanence and thus to think in entirely this-worldly terms, to approach the givenness of the world without attributing to it a giver that gives, will be stymied.

On one level, the continued smuggling of theological notions into philosophy, even the philosophy of religion, is perplexing, or should be. If one accepts God's radical transcendence, as the monotheisms ostensibly do, the recurring claims made by philosophers to discern God's presence in immanence should be avoidable, and on religious grounds, no less. To this effect, in both "Transcending Transcendence" and the "Preface" to *Giving Beyond the Gift*, Wolfson favorably mentions Jean-Luc Nancy's claim that "monotheism is in truth atheism" in order to articulate that the insistence on the radical transcendence of God, central to the Abrahamic monotheisms, converges with atheism in entailing "the undoing and demythologization of theism."[25] Wolfson quotes Nancy as saying: "the enduring legacy of monotheism is 'the fact that divine unicity is the correlate of a presence that can no longer be given in this world but rather must be sought beyond it (the presence in this world being that of an 'idol,' the rejection of which is no doubt the great generation and federating motif of the threefold Abrahamic traditions).'"[26] What Wolfson finds Nancy to be suggesting here is that in emphasizing God's transcendence, theism, no less than atheism, rejects—or should reject—as idolatrous all attempts to image God, even when these images are presented as metaphorical. The very basis of the convergence between (mono)theism and atheism consists precisely in this shared desire to extirpate idolatry, which Wolfson presents, in self-consciously Maimonidean terms, as "the false imaginings by which the human mind constructs the imageless one."[27]

However, this matter is more fraught than it initially appears, because understanding idolatry in this way leads to a very unsettling, even shocking, conclusion. If idolatry is defined as what results from the attempt to imagine the unimaginable God, then the effort to conceptualize God in personalist language, common to all three monotheistic traditions, is not only not antithetical to idolatry but is itself idolatrous. To be sure, within monotheistic traditions there are also voices that emphasize divine transcendence and thus run counter to, and offer critiques of, the efforts to use personal imagery to configure the divine. And yet, since these voices are virtually indistinguishable from those of atheists, at least with regard to the call for the cessation of the application of personalistic imagery to God in religious idioms, they provide little sustenance for the liturgical and lived dimensions of their respective traditions. That monotheistic traditions turn to idolatrous imaginings of the unimaginable God is inevitable, Wolfson concludes, because they cannot subsist on the imagistic austerity that follows from either atheism or those forms of theism committed to a radically transcendent notion of God. To this end, Wolfson notes with approval Gideon Freudenthal's claim that "idolatry is a 'necessary component of religion. Without idolatry religion would dissolve.'"[28]

Such a view significantly diverges from the conventional understanding of idolatry in play in Novak's review, which treats the conflict between idolatry and the critique of idolatry as corresponding with the border separating the monotheistic community from its surrounding environment, such that idolatry constitutes an outside and the critique of idolatry the inside. In contrast to Novak, Wolfson locates the conflict between idolatry and the critique of idolatry within the very heart of the monotheistic traditions themselves, as already inevitably inside. The conventional understanding of idolatry, in its fixation on the borders between the inside and the outside, fails to grasp that idolatrous imagings of God are indigenous to the monotheistic traditions themselves, not merely some sort of corrupting contamination from outside influences. As long as there are monotheistic traditions that express themselves liturgically and in a living religious environment, the lure to envision God in personalist terms that are prohibited by the ban on images will be, at least to some degree, irresistible. For Wolfson, then, so much contemporary religious thought succumbs to idolatry precisely because it settles for the conventional understanding of idolatry as something foreign, without considering the idolatry native to the tradition itself. It is for this reason, Wolfson contends, that figures like Emmanuel Levinas, Jean-Luc Marion, Richard Kearney, and Catherine Keller, who are all ostensibly aware that the rigorous thinking of God's transcendence requires that the theism/atheism binary be overcome, fail to follow this claim to its logical conclusion. These thinkers continue to devote their energy to refining the effort to envision the invisible God when what the rigorous thinking of divine transcendence demands is that one reject this task altogether. Unlike Nancy, then, at least in Wolfson's estimation, these thinkers fail to take the thinking of divine transcendence to its logical conclusion, illicitly smuggling personalist elements into their philosophies and thus, as a result, succumb to conceptual idolatry.

ELLIOT WOLFSON AND MODERN JEWISH THOUGHT

The inability to follow the thought of the radical transcendence of God to its logical conclusion in contemporary philosophy of religion is not the result of idiosyncratic failings on the part of individual thinkers, either of intellect or nerve, so much as the product of a widespread confusion. As Wolfson sees it, these thinkers mistakenly believe idolatry and religion, understood as the recognition of God's transcendence, to be antithetical terms, when, in fact, they are co-dependent on, and co-constitutive with, each other. If idolatry, the imagining of the unimaginable God, is recognized to be inextricable from religion rather than antithetical to it, then the effort to purge idols brings with it a terrible dilemma. Since the resort to personalist language to conceptualize God present in all three of the monotheisms is to be understood as an essential element of these traditions rather than some aberration that can be eliminated, the attempt to eradicate idolatry is fraught. The achievement of a perspective finally and absolutely purified from idolatry is only possible if one sunders the connection to the very tradition that one sought to free from idolatry. However, because the belief that religion and idolatry are antithetical to one another remains pervasive, thinkers often fail to recognize the dilemma confronting them on this issue, and without realizing it, find themselves gored by one or the other of its horns.

At the core of *Giving Beyond the Gift*, Wolfson endeavors to highlight the way in which this dilemma shapes the particular intellectual context of twentieth-century Jewish thought. However, the significance of the study, Wolfson contends, "go[es] well beyond the specificity of this cultural formation." That is, Wolfson explains, "I delve deeply into one tradition out of the conviction that the particular is indexical of what we are still compelled to call the universal."[29] In addition to Wolfson's methodological claim, that the particular is the route to the universal, there are two additional reasons that can be discerned, which pertain to the specificity of Wolfson's constructive project and which bear consideration.[30] First, the last three Jewish thinkers whose works Wolfson considers in depth in his study of the field, Emmanuel Levinas, Jacques Derrida, and Edith Wyschogrod, are prominently situated within the Francophone philosophical scene that has exerted such a pronounced influence on contemporary Continental philosophy of religion. However, they are also simultaneously inheritors of the German tradition of Jewish thought with which Wolfson's survey begins (Hermann Cohen and Franz Rosenzweig). In this manner, modern Jewish thought and Continental philosophy of religion significantly converge, and at the very least, the influence of Jewish thought (particularly in regard to Levinas, Derrida, and Wyschogrod) on philosophy of religion is undeniable. Second, Wolfson is a consummately dialogical thinker, developing his own constructive claims by means of rigorous encounter and engagement with the arguments of others. It is surely significant, then, that while *Giving Beyond the Gift* begins and ends with considerations of Continental philosophy of religion, the vast majority of the work is devoted to the prolonged critical and generative engagement with twentieth-century Jewish thought. Such a framing suggests that it is with the tradition of Jewish thought in the twentieth century that Wolfson primarily affiliates his own project, even if, like many of the figures he examines, it also seeks to make interventions beyond it.

Surveying the field of twentieth-century Jewish thought by means of extended studies of the respective philosophical projects of Hermann Cohen, Franz Rosenzweig, Emmanuel Levinas, Jacques Derrida, and Edith Wyschogrod, Wolfson finds that this dilemma is approached in one of two ways, neither of which are adequate. The first and more diverse group—which includes Cohen, Rosenzweig, and Levinas—insists on philosophizing in such a way that the thinker's connection with the Jewish tradition remains intact. The cost of preserving this link, however, is that their various philosophical projects all succumb to what Wolfson calls theolatry. That is, while "keenly aware of the pitfalls of scriptural theism and the penchant of the human imagination to conjure false representations of transcendence," each thinker nevertheless succumbs, albeit in different ways and to different degrees, "to the temptation of personifying that transcendence even as they tried either to circumvent or to restrain it by apophatically purging the kataphatic descriptions of the deity."[31]

The thinkers of the second grouping, Jacques Derrida and Edith Wyschogrod, confront this dilemma in a different manner. On the one hand, Wolfson acknowledges that Derrida and Wyschogrod can be credited with "carry[ing] the project of dénégation one step further" than their predecessors.[32] Their work recognizes that the monotheistic ban on images, when taken to its logical conclusion, "compromises the viability of devotional piety" since the purgation of "the anthropomorphic and anthropopathic embellishments" from God occludes "the imagination's ability to concoct the deity in personalist terms."[33] However, the cost of this "progress" is severe, leaving their thought, at least in Wolfson's estimation, as no longer part of the Jewish tradition, enduring a "fate of social dislocation and political estrangement, occupying a place that is no place, nomadically adrift without any discernable lifeline to be reanchored in a special liturgical community."[34]

While Wolfson presents original and provocative readings of all the thinkers he engages, of the first group—given the constraints of this essay—we will limit ourselves to his discussion of Levinas. With regard to *Giving Beyond the Gift*, it would not be too much to say, Levinas's thought serves to exemplify the manner in which remaining beholden to the theism/atheism binary, however tenuously, thwarts the effort to think transcendence free of the transcendence/immanence binary. Through scrupulous attention to a wide range of works spanning Levinas's professional life, Wolfson contends that Levinas's effort to cast theology through an ethical rather than an ontological lens is insufficient for escaping conceptual idolatry.

While Wolfson views Levinas's thought as succumbing to conceptual idolatry, he also sees it as representing a remarkable attempt to thread the needle between the rejection of idolatry and the commitment to the religious language of a particular monotheistic tradition. At least at first blush, Levinas's understanding of monotheism approaches the previously mentioned insight of Jean-Luc Nancy's, that monotheism blurs with atheism when it is taken to its logical fulfillment. Wolfson quotes a passage from "A Religion for Adults," where Levinas makes the following claim: "Monotheism marks a break with a certain conception of the Sacred. It neither unifies nor hierarchizes the numerous and numinous gods: instead it denies them. As regards the Divine which they incarnate, it is merely atheism."[35] Levinas therefore seeks to distinguish "transcendence . . . from a 'union with the transcendent by participation,' the mythopoetic idea that still informs 'believers of positive religions.'"[36] In this manner, Levinas's thinking seeks to move beyond the correlative understanding of the relationship between God and human beings, embraced in some manner or other, by Cohen, Buber, and Rosenzweig.

However, in the final analysis, Wolfson finds Levinas to be unable or unwilling to carry through the blurring of monotheism and atheism implied by his notion of transcendence. Despite what seems to be a recognition of the implications of thinking God's transcendence, Levinas nevertheless continues to employ religious language that draws him back into the ontotheological framework from which he sought to extricate himself. Thus, despite his disavowals of the language of correlation in his predecessors, Wolfson concludes that Levinas simply "could not avoid characterizing transcendence in personal terms that efface the clear distinction between human and divine and thus jeopardize the concept of alterity as the transcendent that is truly other."[37]

Since Levinas's thought constitutes a spirited attempt to meaningfully engage the notion of transcendence while remaining committed to the hard-nosed and this-worldly sensibility of phenomenology, Wolfson finds the manner in which it founders to be quite instructive for his own constructive (a) theological efforts. On Wolfson's reading, the theolatrous impulse stymies Levinas's goals in at least two respects. First, with regard to phenomenology, Wolfson agrees with Dominique Janicaud that Levinas illicitly smuggles theology into phenomenology. And second, the use of phenomenology, even when infiltrated by theology, cannot but compromise any notion of transcendence at which it arrives since "the inapparent can appear only to the extent that it is subsumed under the taxon of the apparent," and thus, with regard to transcendence, "what appears as inapparent appears nonetheless."[38] As a result of these intractable problems, Wolfson understands that if there is to be a meaningful effort to think transcendence free from the ontotheological trappings of the transcendence/immanence and theism/atheism binaries, it will have to proceed by another route. This brings us, then, to Wolfson's engagement with Wyschogrod and Derrida.[39]

Wolfson presents Edith Wyschogrod's thought as anticipating his own constructive atheological agenda in two respects. First, while noting that Wyschogrod was not only a pioneering and largely sympathetic interpreter of Levinas, Wolfson contends that her own sensibilities are more in line with "'the sheer refusal to traffic in transcendence,'" evident in "Nietzschean postmodernism."[40] Thus, where Levinas finds in the face a trace of an "archaic" or foundational transcendence, for Wyschogrod, the only sense in which transcendence can be retained is as connoting "the totality of beings that can never be conceptualized as a knowable plenum."[41] Like Wolfson, then, Wyschogrod refuses to endorse any "metaphysical presence that is not a part of the physical universe," thereby ruling out any notion of transcendence "that is external to nature."[42] And second, Wolfson draws our attention to the way that Wyschogrod's atheological thought finds in Kabbalah a means for "resisting . . . binary logic," establishing a notion of "identity-in-difference."[43] Wolfson credits Wyschogrod with recognizing that the kabbalistic characterization of the divine in terms of "the abyssal, apocalyptical nonground" prevents its being coopted as some sort of "ontological foundation or anchorage." This is a significant achievement, Wolfson contends, because it allows us to "aver transcendence in relation to this abyss, the nonground, the inside that is outside by being the outside that is inside."[44] That is, Wolfson judges Wyschogrod to offer, in this manner, a thinking of transcendence that is not beholden to the transcendence/immanence binary. In short, while Wolfson's account of Wyschogrod's thought is not entirely uncritical, she is presented as anticipating his own efforts both in regard to the search for a non-ontotheological account of transcendence and in using Kabbalah for such an end.

If Wyschogrod has recourse to the Kabbalah as a means to think transcendence outside of an ontotheological framework, it has been a staple of scholarship on Derrida to associate his program of deconstruction with kabbalistic speculation. Such an association, Wolfson notes, is not unproblematic, particularly given the fact that Derrida expressed significant misgivings about the capacity of mysticism, Jewish or otherwise, to escape ontotheology's grip. In the course of rehearsing these misgivings and working to counter them, Wolfson offers his own presentation of a non-ontotheological Kabbalah.

Wolfson acknowledges that there are significant points of convergence between Derrida's philosophy and Kabbalah. For instance, they both model a non-ontotheological form of atheism. In its fixation on denying that God in fact exists, the conventional sense of atheism merely constitutes a dialectical reversal of the standard theist position and, as a result, remains entrenched in an ontotheological metaphysics. The atheism of Derrida and the Kabbalists, then, is decidedly unconventional. Derrida's atheism avoids the focus on the presence or absence of God central to ontotheology, being characterized instead by its "disruptive and dissociative power," its capacity to "destabilize . . . the totalizing system of meaning," and, as a result, "render[ing] every linguistic assertion ambivalent and every affirmation of certitude ambiguous."[45] Even if the Jewish mystical tradition continues to adhere to theological trappings and idioms, Wolfson contends that its avowal of endless multivalency also effects a disruption and destabilization whereby "every linguistic assertion" is rendered "ambivalent" and "all affirmations of certitude" are "ambiguous," thus qualifying it as an atheism in Derrida's sense.

To be sure, Wolfson acknowledges that Derrida's thought offers reasons to question the capacity of Kabbalah to escape the bounds of ontotheology. Derrida is not wrong, Wolfson concedes, to see in the kabbalistic tradition a tendency to maintain that "there is a presence that exceeds the text, a presence that is always a nonpresence, insofar as it can be present only by being absent, and hence it can never be represented, but it is a presence nonetheless, the secret manifest in the nonmanifestation of the secret, the nothing about which one cannot speak in contrast to there being nothing about which to speak, the unsaying of apophasis as opposed to the dissimulation of dénégation."[46] In Derrida's terms, then, "the kabbalistic Ein Sof" remains "a 'negative mode of presence.'" As such, it would qualify—in this view at least—as a "negative theology," which remains "still a theology," one still bound up with the effort of "liberating and acknowledging the ineffable transcendence of an infinite existent."[47] If this is the case, then the kabbalistic notion of *Ein Sof* is to be understood as constituting an attempt to elucidate a "being beyond being" and as such, remains a form of ontotheology.[48]

However, such a view of *Ein Sof* is unsatisfactory for Wolfson. Anticipating a central argument in *Heidegger and Kabbalah*, Wolfson contends that the kabbalistic infinite is better understood in non-ontotheological terms. "What is contemplated [by the Kabbalists] is not a what at all, not this and not that, and not even the negation of this and that, but the absolutely other vis-à-vis all existents, the nihility that is prior to the distinction of being and nonbeing . . . therefore beyond both affirmative and negative propositions."[49] Understood in such a manner, *Ein Sof* is "truly neither something nor nothing,"[50] and should rather be understood as "not merely a presence that presents itself as nonpresent, but it is a nonpresence that is outside the either/or structure that informs the economy of the binary of presence and absence: it is, in short, the chiasm that resists both the reification of nothing as something and of something as nothing."[51] If understood in this manner, *Ein Sof* is not adequately grasped either as "the absence of presence" or as "the presence of absence."[52] Since it is "neither something that is nothing nor nothing that is something," this notion of infinity "both is what it is not and is not what it is because it neither is what it is not nor is not what it is."[53] If this is a form of negative theology, it is one that does not have recourse to a being beyond being, and therefore should not be characterized as ontotheological.

With regard to the relationship of the shared concern for the interplay of presence and absence as well as disclosure and concealment, Wolfson acknowledges that there is some convergence between Kabbalah and Derrida. And yet, Wolfson contends this point of ostensible convergence also reveals their deepest divergence, which effectively brings into relief "the critical difference between traditional kabbalah and Derridean deconstruction."[54] Derrida understands the notion of absence as essentially "the absence of both absence and presence,"[55] whereas the Kabbalists find "the invisible absence of God, the withdrawal from the spectrum of the visible," to reveal "the divine presence most fully."[56] If the Kabbalists correlate the most sublime sense of the divine with this absence—*zimzum*—and thus remain practicing a sort of theology, Derrida maintains that theology must be refused. Where Kabbalists use a theological medium to express a destabilization of meaning that is functionally equivalent to Derrida's sense of atheism, Derrida refuses the theological, or rather, engages the idiom of theology but only insofar as it is treated as something impossible. Wolfson explains this contrast rather felicitously: "Simply put, kabbalists are occupied with naming the absence, whereas Derrida insists on the absence of naming."[57]

Wolfson proceeds to explore this divergence between Derrida and the Kabbalists with regard to the notion of the trace, which Derrida takes over from Heidegger (and Levinas, who also takes it over from Heidegger). If there is an apparent convergence, namely, that "the notion of the trace is endorsed by both kabbalists and Derrida,"[58] it belies a deeper divergence. If the Kabbalists and Derrida both employ the notion of the trace, they disagree when it comes to the notion of an originary trace. Wolfson explains: "what Derrida denies is precisely what the kabbalists affirm: the originary trace marks the beginning that both reveals and conceals the nontrace of the origin, the imprint of infinity that is prior even to the withdrawal of the light."[59] For Derrida to follow the trace to some sort of foundation, even if that foundation is considered to be a nonfoundation, is a bridge too far into metaphysics and the ontotheological.

That this chapter adumbrates central motifs in *Heidegger and Kabbalah* becomes even more evident when Wolfson triangulates the divergence between Derrida and the Kabbalists regarding the trace with Heidegger's thought. With regard to the trace, Wolfson presents Heidegger's thought as not only at odds with Derrida's but as essentially in line with, or conceptually parallel to, the position taken by the Kabbalists. Carefully rebutting Derrida's critique of the Heideggerian (and thus kabbalistic) understanding of the trace, Wolfson treats "the originary trace in the kabbalistic and Heideggerian pathways"[60] not in terms of an insufficiently thoroughgoing attempt to think absence, as Derrida would have it, but rather as the "heterological sign of excess that 'must elude mastery,' the wholly other that can in no way appear or be named, the supplementary stroke (*trait*) that retreats (*re-trait*) in the withdrawal (*retrait*) of its tracing."[61] If Derrida conceives of the trace as a non-origin rather than an obfuscation of origin, Heidegger and the Kabbalists understand the originary trace in terms of "that which is 'produced as its own erasure' and is thus 'neither perceptible nor imperceptible.'"[62] Wolfson is quite careful, however, to present the Heideggerian/kabbalistic notion of trace as more compatible with Derridean strictures than Derrida acknowledges. It is "the vestigial sign that is subject to an 'indefinite process of supplementarity,' since it cannot be retraced to any origin that is not itself also a 'trace of the trace,' the *différance* etched in a 'mode of writing' that is from its inception 'without presence and without absence,' an 'inscription prior to writing, a protowriting without a present origin, without an arche.'"[63] In this manner, Wolfson seeks to distance his reading of the Kabbalists from contemporary efforts to marry deconstruction and Neoplatonic negative theology, of which he remains critical. That is, even if the Kabbalists remain "in line with the apophaticism of Neoplatonic negative theology"[64] insofar as they "assume there is a reality beyond language, the superessential infinity that transcends nature and speech,"[65] they do not assent to "the asymmetrical proposition that without the One there is no multiplicity but without multiplicity there can still be the One."[66]

If approached along these lines, Wolfson contends that the *Ein Sof* should be understood as beyond the bounds of ontotheology. As such, then, it would be an error to view "the hiddenness of the infinite" as tantamount to a notion of "transcendence that protects the theistic dogma of divine separateness."[67] Rather than as something other than beings, the *Ein Sof* is "the unnameable and unknowable essence that permeates and yet escapes all beings."[68] If much scholarly attention has been directed to detailing the convergence between Kabbalah and Derrida's philosophy, Wolfson works to shift the focus of this convergence from the thought of Derrida to that of Heidegger.

WOLFSON'S CONSTRUCTIVE POSITION

In Wolfson's estimation, neither the approach to Jewish thought characterized by Cohen, Rosenzweig, and Levinas, on the one hand, nor that of Derrida and Wyschogrod, on the other, is viable. If the first group of thinkers inevitably compromise their accounts of divine transcendence in order to accommodate the tradition, the second group achieves a more rigorous rooting out of idolatry at the price of severing the link between their respective philosophies and the Jewish tradition. The only way out of this dilemma, Wolfson suggests, is to reject the either/or framing in favor of one that is both/and.[69] However, as long as the constitutive role of idolatry in the monotheistic traditions goes unrecognized, at least in Wolfson's view, this shifting of the terms is impossible and all efforts to philosophize about religion from within a monotheistic tradition will founder. Recognizing that idolatry is—and must be—inextricable from the tradition itself, Wolfson contends that, rather than idolatry, the philosopher of religion must foreswear the attempt to delineate a purified theology that would somehow be free of all idolatry.

The only viable way forward, then, is a piecemeal process whereby one inhabits the tradition in such a way that one is perpetually deconstructing its idolatrous aspects. Since both idolatry and its critique are indelible parts of the tradition, there is, and can be, no final clean break with idolatry, no final embrace of pure religion. The idolatry of the tradition can be subverted in a manner that does not also reject the tradition only if one remains in keeping with the tradition, if one works through its texts and traditions to point out its shortcomings, to unsay what it never should have—but also which was impossible for it not to have—said. Only in this way can one avoid being impaled on one or the other of the horns of this dilemma.

The path forward that Wolfson offers in order to escape the dilemma that has felled so many previous thinkers is, not coincidentally, strikingly in line with the sensibility shared by the Kabbalists and Heidegger that he elaborates in his most recent work, *Heidegger and Kabbalah*. Heidegger shares with the Kabbalists the sense that there is never—and there never can be—a moment when truth has been reached once and for all, when the search for truth can cease, so that the tradition from which one sought distance has been left behind. Rather, thinking must always be iterative, enacting a perpetual sort of repetition of the act of overcoming the problematic elements of the tradition from a position nevertheless situated within the tradition itself. The effort to get beyond or overcome the tradition that one inherits, then, can only be carried out by means of inhabiting the tradition in such a way that one retrieves its foundational insights and transforms them from within. For Heidegger, this entails retracing the steps taken in the history of philosophy that have resulted in a metaphysics of presence in order to find ways of thinking otherwise. The Kabbalists, on the other hand, critically engage the Jewish theological tradition, working to eliminate "all metaphorical images from Ein Sof, including the belief that the actions of the infinite are purposefully motivated in a manner that is isomorphic with the resolute activity ascribed to the moral agency of human beings."[70] Since such metaphors permeate the Jewish theological tradition, the Kabbalists seek to escape the conceptual idolatry that mars the thinking of God in the Jewish tradition by means of using the language of the tradition to think beyond it. Or, as Wolfson puts it: "there is no way to the nameless but through the ladder of the name, no way to the formless but through the vehicle of form, no seeing the face of the imageless but through the image of the mask."[71]

The connection that Wolfson discerns between Heidegger and the Kabbalists can be better appreciated if we return to the closing chapter of *Giving Beyond the Gift*, where Wolfson draws the reader's attention to the profundity with which Heidegger's thought negates all God-talk, all theology that has become idolatry. Wolfson explains that Heidegger's "godlessness is not, as one might expect, identical with the denial or loss of god, what we conventionally call atheism, but it is the obliteration of the ground of the godhood, the abground, which exceeds the presentation of the godly as the 'higher being,' the 'being that is beyond beings' (*Über-seienden*), or the being that 'lies over and beyond man' (*Über-menschliche*)."[72] This godlessness is more profound than conventional atheism, which, because it is still fixated on the ontotheological dialectic of presence and absence, remains entrenched in the theism/atheism binary. In Wolfson's estimation, it is Heidegger's thought that provides the path for "a sweeping and uncompromising purification of the idea of infinity from all predication," which "should occasion the end of God-talk, even of an apophatic nature."[73] It is Heidegger's thought that provides essential resources for Wolfson's effort to present the kabbalistic *Ein Sof* in a manner that "presumes neither a presence that is absent nor an absence that is present,"[74] and thus, as beyond ontotheology.

Heidegger's approach to givenness makes it possible to avoid invoking the fraught theological legacy of the transcendence/immanence binary. With regard to "the phenomenological status of givenness," for Heidegger, at most, one can "posit the giving," but this does not entail positing that there is "a something that is given and definitely not a gift."[75] Givenness does not imply any sort of transcendent giver. "What gives just gives, not as a gift but as the inevitable consequence of there being something rather than nothing, the fundamental datum of existence that remains inexplicable in spite of the most imaginative efforts on the part of philosophers and physicists to explain it."[76] Instead of a giver who gifts the given, Wolfson avers: "in the giving, there is giving—nothing more, nothing less. Just as the rose blooms because it blooms, so the giving gives, not as gift but as giving, without will, intention, or design. Both object and subject, the given and the giver, are subsumed in the giving, which is indistinguishable from the givenness."[77]

CONCLUSION

Returning to Novak's review of *Heidegger and Kabbalah* discussed in the introduction, its assumptions about idolatry put Wolfson's position into stark relief. Novak sees the effort to employ Heidegger's philosophy in the thinking of Kabbalah as inauthentically Jewish, as somehow diluting some allegedly pristine Jewish essence. That is, Novak's understanding of idolatry corresponds sharply with communal boundaries, such that the temple devoid of idols largely corresponds with the temple shorn of foreign and thus "inauthentic" influences. From Wolfson's view, such an essentialist perspective misses the fact that the very idea of the Sanctuary free from idols can itself very easily become an idol. Purging the idols from the temple can never be completed once and for all. From this view, Novak's effort to shore up the borders between the inside and the outside is insufficient for eradicating idolatry because the idols are not merely introduced from the outside, but they are also a part of the Jewish tradition itself. As a result, Wolfson contends that bringing Heidegger's thought into conversation with Kabbalah does not import some contaminating essence from the outside into Judaism, but rather it allows us to think more deeply about Judaism itself, to unearth what remains still hidden in its foundations. To present the *Ein Sof* in terms of Heidegger's notion of givenness and his thinking of beyng and nothing beyond the metaphysics of presence allows Wolfson to engage the Jewish theological tradition in a manner not beholden to ontotheology and conceptual idolatry. In this manner, Wolfson not only offers a theory of idolatry that breaks free from the ethnocentric and identarian notions that have for too long held modern Jewish thought in their thrall, but he offers and enacts an original and highly compelling vision of modern Jewish thought. It behooves those of us working in this field to attend to this challenging and bracing vision with alacrity.

ACKNOWLEDGMENTS

I would like to thank Martin Kavka, Dustin Atlas, and Elliot Wolfson for reading this essay at different stages and offering helpful feedback. I would also like to thank Elliot Wolfson for his mentorship and friendship over the years. It is a pleasure to have the opportunity to celebrate his towering scholarly accomplishments.

NOTES

1. *Heidegger and Kabbalah: Hidden Gnosis and the Path of Poiesis* (Bloomington: Indiana University Press, 2019). Henceforth, I will refer to this book as *Heidegger and Kabbalah*.
2. David Novak, "Scholarship and the Critique of Tradition: Elliot R. Wolfson, Heidegger and Kabbalah: Hidden Gnosis and the Path of Poiesis," *Journal of Religious Ethics* 48, no. 4 (2020): 731–40; the above mentioned quotes are from page 731. To be sure, much of the hyperbole with which Novak begins the review essay manifests itself around Wolfson's choice of Heidegger to serve as a dialogue partner for Kabbalah. After all, Martin Heidegger is, as Novak points out, a philosopher with a well-documented Nazi affiliation, which he never publicly recanted. In truth, however, Heidegger's notoriety only exacerbates Novak's deeper problem with Wolfson's project, namely, that he believes that Jewish thinkers should not actively challenge the normative claims of the Jewish tradition, particularly by means of marshaling arguments from sources outside of this tradition (738). This brings us to a profound and fundamental divergence between Wolfson and Novak, one that merits more attention than is possible here.
3. For the reception of Heidegger's thought by Jewish thinkers, see Daniel Herskowitz, *Heidegger and His Jewish Reception* (Cambridge, UK: Cambridge University Press, 2021). With regard to idolatry and the prominent role it plays in situating Judaism vis-à-vis other religions in modern Jewish thought, see Robert Erlewine, "Samuel Hirsch, Hegel, and the Legacy of Ethical Monotheism," *Harvard Theological Review* 113, no. 1 (2020): 89–110, esp. 90–95 and 108–10.
4. Elliot R. Wolfson, *A Dream Interpreted Within a Dream: Oneiropoiesis and the Prism of Imagination* (Brooklyn, NY: Zone Books, 2011), and Elliot R. Wolfson, *Giving Beyond the Gift: Apophasis and Overcoming Theomania* (New York: Fordham University Press, 2014). Henceforth, I will refer to them as *A Dream Interpreted Within a Dream* and *Giving Beyond the Gift* respectively.
5. Wolfson, *Heidegger and Kabbalah*, 4.
6. Ontotheology is a term that connotes the manner in which God has traditionally been thought in the Western philosophical tradition, whereby theology and ontology are conflated and God is presented as a being among beings. See Martin Heidegger, "The Ontotheological Constitution of Metaphysics," in *Identity and Difference*, trans. Joan Stambaugh (New York: Harper & Row, 1969), esp. 72.
7. Wolfson, *Heidegger and Kabbalah*, 68.
8. Wolfson, *Heidegger and Kabbalah*, 110.
9. Wolfson, *Heidegger and Kabbalah*, 104.
10. Wolfson, *Heidegger and Kabbalah*, 110.
11. Wolfson, *Heidegger and Kabbalah*, 68.
12. Wolfson, *Heidegger and Kabbalah*.
13. Wolfson, *Heidegger and Kabbalah*, 61.
14. Henceforth, I will refer to this chapter as "Transcending Transcendence."
15. Wolfson, *A Dream Interpreted Within a Dream*, 25.

16. Wolfson, *A Dream Interpreted Within a Dream.*
17. Wolfson, *A Dream Interpreted Within a Dream*, 26.
18. Wolfson, *A Dream Interpreted Within a Dream*, 32.
19. Wolfson, *A Dream Interpreted Within a Dream.*
20. Wolfson, *A Dream Interpreted Within a Dream.*
21. Wolfson, *A Dream Interpreted Within a Dream*, 39.
22. Wolfson, *A Dream Interpreted Within a Dream*, 25.
23. Wolfson, *A Dream Interpreted Within a Dream*, 32.
24. Wolfson, *A Dream Interpreted Within a Dream*, 25.
25. Wolfson, *Giving Beyond the Gift*, xvi; *A Dream Interpreted Within a Dream*, 30.
26. Wolfson, *Giving Beyond the Gift*, xvi; *A Dream Interpreted Within a Dream*, 29–30.
27. Wolfson, *Giving Beyond the Gift*, xvii; *A Dream Interpreted Within a Dream*, 29. In *Giving Beyond the Gift*, xvii, Wolfson approvingly references Henri Atlan's claim that "'the only discourse about God that is not idolatrous is necessarily an atheistic discourse. Alternatively, whatever the discourse, the only God who is not an idol is a God who is not a God.'"
28. Wolfson, *Giving Beyond the Gift*, xx.
29. Wolfson, *Giving Beyond the Gift*, xiii.
30. These reasons are compatible with the methodological one about universality and particularity that Wolfson supplies and thus do not take anything away from it.
31. Wolfson, *Giving Beyond the Gift*, xvii.
32. Wolfson, *Giving Beyond the Gift*, xvii.
33. Wolfson, *Giving Beyond the Gift*, xviii.
34. Wolfson, *Giving Beyond the Gift*, xviii.
35. Wolfson, *Giving Beyond the Gift*, 139.
36. Wolfson, *Giving Beyond the Gift*, 139.
37. Wolfson, *Giving Beyond the Gift*, 152.
38. Wolfson, *Giving Beyond the Gift*, 150.
39. In presenting Wyschogrod before Derrida I depart from the largely chronological organization of the chapters in *Giving Beyond the Gift.*
40. Wolfson, *Giving Beyond the Gift*, 211.
41. Wolfson, *Giving Beyond the Gift*, 211.
42. Wolfson, *Giving Beyond the Gift*, 225.
43. Wolfson, *Giving Beyond the Gift.*
44. Wolfson, *Giving Beyond the Gift.*
45. Wolfson, *Giving Beyond the Gift*, 169–70.
46. Wolfson, *Giving Beyond the Gift*, 171.
47. Wolfson, *Giving Beyond the Gift.*
48. Wolfson, *Giving Beyond the Gift*, 172.
49. Wolfson, *Giving Beyond the Gift*, 173.
50. Wolfson, *Giving Beyond the Gift*, 173–74.
51. Wolfson, *Giving Beyond the Gift*, 174.
52. Wolfson, *Giving Beyond the Gift.*

53. Wolfson, *Giving Beyond the Gift*.
54. Wolfson, *Giving Beyond the Gift*, 193.
55. Wolfson, *Giving Beyond the Gift*.
56. Wolfson, *Giving Beyond the Gift*.
57. Wolfson, *Giving Beyond the Gift*.
58. Wolfson, *Giving Beyond the Gift*, 195.
59. Wolfson, *Giving Beyond the Gift*, 196.
60. Wolfson, *Giving Beyond the Gift*.
61. Wolfson, *Giving Beyond the Gift*.
62. Wolfson, *Giving Beyond the Gift*.
63. Wolfson, *Giving Beyond the Gift*.
64. Wolfson, *Giving Beyond the Gift*.
65. Wolfson, *Giving Beyond the Gift*, 196–97.
66. Wolfson, *Giving Beyond the Gift*, 197.
67. Wolfson, *Giving Beyond the Gift*.
68. Wolfson, *Giving Beyond the Gift*.
69. Actually, the matter is more complex and should probably be developed in light of Wolfson's embrace of dialetheism, which entails "the assumption that identification of opposites in the identity of their opposition yields a genuine and irresolvable contradiction" (*Heidegger and Kabbalah*, 31). Given the constraints of this essay, this important topic cannot be treated here.
70. Wolfson, *Heidegger and Kabbalah*, 141.
71. Wolfson, *Heidegger and Kabbalah*.
72. Wolfson, *Giving Beyond the Gift*, 234.
73. Wolfson, *Giving Beyond the Gift*, 235.
74. Wolfson, *Giving Beyond the Gift*.
75. Wolfson, *Giving Beyond the Gift*, 239.
76. Wolfson, *Giving Beyond the Gift*, 257.
77. Wolfson, *Giving Beyond the Gift*.

TO INFINITY, NOT BEYOND

Spinoza's Ontology of the Not One

GILAH KLETENIK

WHO KNOWS ONE? *EVERYONE*, IT SEEMS. SINCE AT LEAST THE ELEATICS, "Western" thought has leaned on the contrivance of Oneness to calibrate its sense of what is. The One and its constellated traits—unity, identity, and indivisibility—are staples of the sustained attempt to grasp reality. For Xenophanes, god is One, whereas for Parmenides, it is being that is one and thus indivisible and same. By contrast, Democritus multiplies the ones: though being itself is not one, it is reducible to countless ones—atoms moving about the void—that are internally staid and same. This tide persists with Plato's Demiurge and notion of the Good, which, differentially, arrogate such affined features of oneness as unity, identity, and indivisibility. Aristotle's Unmoved Mover is foremost and exclusively one, responsible for the unity of all that is, while his Divine Intellect is an identity that is indivisible. Plotinus and later Proclus compound this current by proclaiming the One as the origin of itself and of all else. Sources perceived as more overtly "religious" are accordingly complicit in this reliance on the One. Scripture credits reality to a God that it upholds as Singular and uniquely worthy of worship. As such, at least since Philo, Jewish philosophy has secured as axiomatic the tenet that this God is One, although the contours of said oneness are not left uncontested. This fierce trust in—if not fetishization of—the One as the ground and reason for reality ultimately becomes overtly entangled with infinity. Oneness and infinity are intertwined in the One god that is Infinite or the Infinite god that is One. The emergence of the kabbalistic appellation "*Ein Sof*"[1] is an indexical of this phenomenon.

The enticements of Oneness are indisputable. To organize a reality that is multiple, disparate, and chaotic, it is reassuring to attribute it to an originary unit or unifying ground. The One submits the incongruities and uncertainties of nature to the security of enclosure, the consistency of order, and the conclusiveness of a telos. This predilection for the One, however, is not unproblematic. Oneness is not a neutral construct. If reality is the product of a Being that is One—and *other* to all else—this instantiates transcendence, installing hierarchy, rank, and distinction. With this arrives the enduring theological puzzle: how does that which is Other effectuate that which is? When oneness is wrested from the Transcendent One and emplaced onto reality such that all that exists is perceived as One, the problems of Parmenidean oneness persist. If All is One: what of difference, not to say, development?

The concept of sovereignty is often associated with oneness, with the attestation that the Sovereign—most commonly, God, State, or Self—is endowed with oneness, unity, and identity and correlatively invested with consistency, supremacy, and autonomy. The singularity that accompanies Oneness conditions the status of the sovereign as non-transferable, while its purportedly immutable boundaries underwrite the primacy constitutive of its very sovereignty. Crucially, even when oneness is universalized—emancipated from its monopolization by the transcendent One and bestowed immanently onto all of nature—its sovereignties are retained. To suppose that reality is One instantiates borders that demarcate said oneness, thusly containing, constraining, and controlling it. Moreover, positioning all that exists as One seems to imprison and immobilize reality by subordinating it to the supremacy of the Same. Similar problems surface when the oneness of God or Being is transferred to specific beings, as when humans are conceived as atomistic ones: independent beings, isolated by impermeable boundaries, invested with an indivisible, stable identity.

Several of these liabilities of oneness undergird Heidegger's familiar critique of metaphysics. Tracking reality to a unifying ground that is common to all or to a unifying ground that is Highest verifies that metaphysics is irrevocably ontotheological.[2] Spinoza, I aver, preempts Heidegger in this critique and inducts an ontology that is decidedly not an ontotheology.[3] Fundamental to this feat is Spinoza's refusal of ontotheological oneness. By deposing god with his signature *Deus sive Natura*, Spinoza dispenses with the transcendent One of theology and refuses to transpose it onto nature.

Louis Althusser is right to position Spinoza as a participant in a "repressed" tradition of materialism that resists such constructs as Origin, Reason, and End.[4] For Althusser, this current traces through Lucretius, Hobbes, Marx, Heidegger, and Derrida, among others. The spirit of this tradition, suggests Althusser, is epitomized by Heidegger's *es gibt* and notion of thrownness. While I do not dispute Althusser's recognition of Spinoza's affinity with these thinkers, I maintain that Spinoza is drawing from and more aligned with a *different* repressed tradition. Spinoza's overall assault on the sovereignties of "Western" philosophy[5] and his particular resistance to ontotheological Oneness accords with a perceptible, if occluded stream in Jewish philosophy that subtly disrupts the sovereignty of God and its associated transcendences of unity, identity, and totality. No one has more ably discerned and deconstructed these latent tendencies than Elliot R. Wolfson. Resisting theomania—"a relentless and maddening obsession for transcendence"[6]—Wolfson's oeuvre probes the divergent texts of Jewish thought, pressuring their logics to unveil "an absolute nothingness . . . that does not signify the unknowable One but the manifold that is the pleromatic abyss at being's core."[7] Though Wolfson descries such echoes across the expanses of Jewish philosophy, in Maimonides, in Rosenzweig, as in many others, it is in the texts of Kabbalah wherein he most comprehensively renders these resistances to ontotheological oneness resonant.[8] Spinoza, in unequivocally vitiating transcendence and redeeming infinity from Oneness, releases and ratifies these very covert tides that ripple through Jewish thought.

By introducing an ontology that dispenses with Oneness, I aver, Spinoza tenders an alternative to the sovereignties of the One. Admittedly, this proposition is not readily apparent. In fact, it is ostensibly controversial to claim as much considering that for centuries Spinoza's philosophy has been accused of epitomizing precisely the opposite position. Spinoza has been presumed to be an uncompromising partisan of Oneness.[9] What contributes to this persistent misreading, I argue, is a misapprehension of Spinozist infinity. Contra the tradition that confines infinity to the One, Spinoza contends that it is precisely *because* substance is infinite that it is not one.

The present exploration opens by corroborating that Spinoza's substance is not quantitatively one. It then turns to two underappreciated moments in the reception of Spinoza: Georg Cantor's set theory and Alain Badiou's ontology. While both find inspiration in Spinoza, unlike him, they mathematize infinity in their respective attempts to release it from monopolization by the One transcendent God. These efforts, I demonstrate, differentially reproduce Oneness and correlatively rely upon a Beyond. Registering these concessions to transcendence accentuates the assets of Spinoza's ontology, which, I maintain, does not compromise on the immanence that infinity commands. To ascertain as much entails a reconsideration of the specific kind of infinity that Spinoza attaches to substance. I certify that it amounts to indeterminacy, which divests substance of the qualities of oneness, such as identity, enclosure, and totality. With this, Spinoza emancipates infinity from impoundment in ontotheological oneness. What secures this triumph and its contrast to subsequent theorists of infinity is that Spinoza not only vitiates oneness but he resists the temptation to reproduce it. Moreover, this displacement of oneness is extended to the modal realm: it is not merely that nature itself is not one, nothing that exists is already one, actually or formally. By rendering the One God as immanent substance, as *not* one, and nothing as essentially one, reality, it is shown, is shorn of oneness and extirpated of its reconstruction. Oneness, I validate, is never *given*; it is only ever fabricated, contingently and provisionally.

ALL FOR ONE

The identification of Spinozism with a philosophy of the One is early, enduring, and encompassing. It has been and continues to be alternatingly celebrated by Spinoza's advocates and derided by his adversaries. Often, this connection to the One manifests in the contention that Spinoza's philosophy is affined with the One of Eleaticism or the *Ein Sof* of Kabbalah. For example, Pierre Bayle, in his dictionary, classifies the Eleatic belief in the unity and immutability of all as "*une spéce de Spinozisme.*"[10] Leibniz writes, referring to Spinoza, of the reduction of all to "one permanent divine substance . . . a doctrine of most evil repute, which a writer who was subtle indeed but irreligious, in recent years imposed upon the world, or at least revived."[11] This is echoed by Jacobi, who likens Spinoza's substance to the *Ein Sof* of Kabbalah, wherein there is an "immanent one" and everything is "One and the same."[12] Strikingly, it is precisely such "unity" and the reality of a "single" substance that Maimon[13] invokes to defend Spinozism against condemnations of it as "atheist," instead dubbing it "acosmic."[14]

No one, however, is more responsible for the enduring association of Spinozism with the One than Hegel.[15] As he has it, Spinoza reprises "the oriental theory of absolute identity."[16] This is expected, because Spinoza is a "a Jew," so his philosophy is perforce "an echo from Eastern lands."[17] To Hegel, Spinozism is distillable into the claim that substance is "one absolute Being."[18] It is an "absolute unity"[19] constituted by "totality."[20] The infinity of substance, Hegel tells us, is "the positive" that is "complete and present in itself."[21] Spinoza's infinity is impeded by its Oneness: the posited Infinite disables the production of the finite.

In Hegel's wake, both advocates and antagonists of Spinozism have continued to think of substance in terms of oneness. Gilles Deleuze celebrates the "univocity" that he perceives Spinoza as introducing, while also reducing Spinozism to idealism.[22] Louis Althusser similarly falters with his association of substance with "structure."[23] More recently, Badiou has claimed that Spinozism amounts to a "closed ontology."[24] Slavoj Žižek rehearses Hegel's dispraises, purporting that "Substance remains One, a Cause immanent to its effects."[25] Streams in contemporary "analytic" scholarship routinely portray Spinozism as reducible to monism and posit interpretations that center its supposed oneness. For example, Michael Della Rocca alleges that for Spinoza, "one thing exists,"[26] while Jonathan Bennett construes Spinoza's infinity as an "all" that amounts to a "totality."[27]

ONE IS NOT

To state that ontological reality is One is at once to level a quantitative claim: that it is numerically one, rather than more or less. But it is also to make a further assertion: that reality exhibits certain features associated with oneness, including unity and identity, and intertwined therewith, closure and constancy. Spinoza contests both valences of oneness, upholding substance as neither numerically nor characteristically One. As will become clear, such is the consequence of his construal of infinity.

It is quite curious that the scholarship on Spinoza has mostly failed to register his repudiation of numerical oneness, considering how transparently and repeatedly he communicates as much.[28] The earliest instance surfaces in *Cogitata Metaphysica*. There, Spinoza expostulates against "the terms called transcendental," which are "taken by nearly all Metaphysicians to be the most general Affections of Being."[29] The first of such expressions that he addresses is "One": "They say that this term signifies something real outside the intellect"[30] but it is only "a mode of thinking."[31] Spinoza is plainly not interested in delving further:[32] "I do not see what more remains to be said about a thing so clear."[33] But he continues, explaining that because numbers and terms like "unity" are relative modes of thinking, "God can be called one insofar as we separate him from other beings. But insofar as we conceive that there cannot be more than one of the same nature, he is called unique."[34] Before concluding, Spinoza bares: "if we wished to examine the matter more accurately, we could perhaps show that God is only very improperly called one and unique."[35]

While Spinoza evidently considered the inaccuracy of attributing oneness to God to be a straightforward matter, this proved less than obvious to his friend Jarig Jelles, who posted Spinoza, pressing him to clarify precisely what he means by this. Spinoza responds: "God can only very improperly be called one or unique" because "a thing is said to be one or unique only in relation to its existence, but not to its essence."[36] This is because "we don't conceive things under numbers unless they have first been brought under a common genus."[37] Spinoza further expounds:

> For example, someone who holds a penny and a dollar in his hand will not think of the number two unless he can call the penny and the dollar by one and the same name, either "coin" or "piece of money." For then he can say that he has two coins or two pieces of money, since he calls not only the penny, but also the dollar, by the name "coin" or "piece of money."[38]

Numbers are by nature comparative and comparisons presuppose commonality. To speak of "two" pennies or "two" dollars is possible only if the items are conceived as sufficiently alike to comprise a unit: two coins or two pieces of money. But if both cannot be meaningfully reified into the same category, then there cannot be two and consequently not one. The same logic applies to the inaccuracy of calling God "one." As Spinoza elsewhere articulates it: "substance is not one of many" because "there exists only one of the same nature."[39] Here, Spinoza continues, underscoring that substance is not a count-for-one: "From this it's evident that nothing is called one or unique unless another thing has been conceived which (as they say) agrees with it."[40] There cannot be *more* than substance or *another* substance because substance is not part of a genus; its absolute infinity forbids the existence of anything beyond it,[41] thereby securing its singularity. But there is a further, perhaps intuitive point that Spinoza is emphasizing: oneness is nothing without that which *exceeds* it. To count as "one" is to presume that there are, minimally, two, if not three, and so on. One never comes first; it is only ever second. If reality is construed as "one," this implies not merely that there are others *like* it but also that said others *precede* it. The claim here is not only the uncontroversial point that oneness and uniqueness are relative terms, but rather that the very notions of oneness and uniqueness rely upon that which is *more*, the multiple or the multitude.[42] The many is always originary. Spinoza closes by reprising a related point: since "the existence of God is his essence," it is not possible to form a "universal idea" of it.[43] Therefore, "someone who calls God one or unique does not have a true idea of God."[44] Universals, like numbers, presuppose commonalities based on agreements between distinct beings, but because substance is singular, it escapes such classification.

Before proceeding, it is important to note that Spinoza is certainly not the only thinker to adduce that "oneness" is only imprecisely attached to God. Maimonides, for example, argues that oneness is predicable of God only analogously, because it is nonessential and extrinsic.[45] Furthermore,[46] "Oneness is not identical with the thing that becomes one, just as number is not identical with the things that are numbered."[47] When adumbrating the essential attributes of God, Maimonides underscores: "these notions are not ascribed to Him and to us in the same sense."[48] This is because "the comparative is used only with regard to things in reference to which the notion in question is used univocally. And if this is so, there is necessarily a likeness between the things in question."[49] Notably, Hasdai Crescas disputes this contention, arguing that relational comparisons do not undermine God's distinction, even if they admit a common genus as "there is no relation and measure between the infinite and the finite."[50] This rationale sanctions his positive assertion that "God is one" and, additionally, that "He is, as compared to anything else, more truly and more preeminently called one."[51]

Spinoza manifestly appropriates Maimonides's reasoning in his argument that numbers are comparative and that they are extrinsic denominations. However, he sharpens the point: it is not just that numbers are relative and extrinsic but that for there to be one there at least must already be two. Significantly, whereas Maimonides uses this point to maintain the distinction of God as over and above all else, for Spinoza, substance is not a God that is *other* but rather the *causa immanens* in which everything inheres. Accordingly, it is not merely that substance is not One, but nothing is originally or essentially One. Before we can discern as much, however, further tarrying with infinity is in order.

COUNTING OUT

The entirety of Spinoza's philosophy is anchored in his affirmation that substance is absolutely infinite. Yet despite its centrality to his project, Spinoza is not consistently forthcoming about his approach to infinity. His most extended ruminations on the matter appear in Letter 12, the so-called "Letter on the Infinite,"[52] where, at the behest of Lodewijk Meyer, Spinoza discloses "what I have discovered about the Infinite."[53] While there is much to unpack therein, our focus is circumscribed to two interconnected assertions. The first is that "neither Number, nor Measure, nor Time (since they are aids of the imagination) can be infinite."[54] And the second is Spinoza's endorsement of "an actual Infinite."[55] Spinoza insists that there is an actual infinite and simultaneously denies that it is mathematical. With this, he breaks with Aristotle and Descartes by contending that an actual infinite exists—rather than a merely potential infinite—and splits with theorists who suppose that infinity is quantifiable.

Letter 12's repudiation of the quantification of infinity aligns with Spinoza's aforementioned resistance to the imprecision and relativity ingenerate to both numeric and linguistic signification. Thus, he declaims: "Measure, Time, and Number are nothing but Modes of thinking, or rather, of imagining."[56] Metaphysicians who deny actual infinity have "confused these three with the things themselves, because they were ignorant of the true nature of things."[57] This results from an elementary misstep: mistaking numbers for *actual* things rather than appreciating that they are mere *representations* of things. "But let the Mathematicians judge how wretchedly these people have reasoned,"[58] Spinoza exclaims. "For not only have they discovered many things which cannot be explained by any Number—which makes quite plain the inability of numbers to determine all things—they also know many things which cannot be equated with any number,"[59] as when "the nature of the thing cannot admit number without a manifest contradiction."[60] The problem here lies with numbers, not with infinity; the signifier rather than the signified.

Spinoza's argument here aligns with his polemics against teleology and anthropocentrism: reality acts out of necessity, indifferent to human interests and epistemic incapacities: "things are not more or less perfect because they please or offend men's senses, or because they are of use to, or incompatible with, human nature."[61] Just because numbers—human constructs—cannot determine actual infinity does not mean that it does not exist.[62]

Notably, Spinoza also endorses a multiplicity of infinities:[63] "some things are infinite by their very nature and cannot in any way be conceived to be finite"; "others by the force of the cause in which they inhere, though when they are conceived abstractly they can be divided into parts and regarded as finite"; and "others, finally are called infinite, or if you prefer, indefinite, because they cannot be equated with any number, though they can be conceived to be greater or lesser."[64] Sustaining these varieties of infinity enabled Spinoza to array his ontology: reality is a substance that is absolutely infinite, is of infinite attributes, and is that in which all modes inhere.

SET APART

These speculations of Spinoza have befuddled and inspired theoreticians of the infinite, including Leibniz, Hegel, and Cantor. In Spinoza, Cantor saw a kindred spirit committed to the actuality of infinity. Of course, Cantor—the founder of set theory—disputed Spinoza's refusal of the mathematically infinite as well as his insistence that infinite quantities are nondenumerable.[65] Nevertheless, Cantor was a committed student of Spinoza's philosophy.[66] Predictably, Cantor's Spinoza is a decidedly Cantorian Spinoza.[67]

The mathematical revolution credited to Cantor amounted to the contention that infinity is actual *and* that it is countable and measurable, collectible into infinite sets. Traditionally, infinity had been vouchsafed to the transcendent God, constrained to the One, and relegated to the impenetrable realm of the immeasurable. Cantor is taken as having liberated infinity from these supernatural and singular precincts, asserting its capacity to be multiplied, quantified, and denumerated. Not only are there various infinities—different infinite numbers—but these can be collected into discrete sets. What Cantor demonstrated was that the set of infinite real numbers is *greater* than the set of infinite rational numbers and that there is no one-to-one correspondence between them, thus validating the infinite quantifiability and comparability of infinities.

To sidestep certain paradoxes of infinity, Cantor averred that all that mathematics required was internal consistency rather than external validity. This "freedom" licensed mathematicians to introduce new numbers ad infinitum; not the least among these, unsurprisingly, is Cantor's own transfinite numbers. But to close the schism between the formal and the real—the epistemological and the phenomenological—he relied on the presumed unity of the universe. This approach leaned on a certain interpretation of Spinoza's proposition:[68] "The order and connection of ideas is the same as the order and connection of things."[69] Cantor similarly resorted to the *Intellecto Divino* to claim that all numbers are united in an ultimate totality therein, thereby legitimating the invention of mathematical abstractions. Despite this transparent reliance on God to subsidize his theories, Cantor was nevertheless accused of pantheism for claiming that transfinite numbers exist *in concreto.* In defense, Cantor distinguished between "Infinitum aeternum increatum sive Absolutum" and "Infinitum creatum sive Transfinitum"; the former is exclusive to God and its attributes, while the latter is bestowed upon the created universe by God.[70] The echoes of a *certain* Spinoza are unmistakable.

The purport to divine unity and its distinction continued to entice Cantor as instruments for arraying his mathematical theories and securing his conception of reality.[71] Considering this record, it is unsurprising that in order to resolve his vexing continuum hypothesis, Cantor sought refuge in God, evincing that an endless hierarchy of power sets can be constructed, each larger than its predecessor. For example, there is the set of natural numbers and exponentially larger than that is the set of real numbers, and so on, ad infinitum. It is thus impossible to designate a set of all sets, as there is always a set that exceeds it, the next on the continuum. To make sense of this impasse of mathematical formalization, Cantor distinguished between a *consistente Vielheit*, wherein all elements *Zusammengefaßtwerden* into an *Einheit* that constitutes "'*einem Ding*'" and that instance wherein it is a contradiction to gather all elements into "'*ein fertiges Ding.*'" The latter, says Cantor, is "*absolut unendliche*" or "*inconsistente Vielheiten.*"[72] This excess that escapes formalization and totalization, comprising an inconsistent multiplicity, is none other than the absolutely infinite, God. While Cantor strains to immanentize, quantify, and multiply infinity, ultimately, he reinstalls the theological relegation of infinity to the One God that is transcendent. In fact, it is precisely this One that is *beyond* that guarantees the consistency of all subordinate infinities.

OTHERWISE THAN BEING

Although Badiou criticizes aspects of Spinoza's philosophy, especially in an essay, the title of which—"Spinoza's Closed Ontology"—unsubtly announces its denunciatory program, Badiou is concurrently admiring of Spinoza.[73] Like Cantor, Badiou appreciates the geometrical method, especially what he *decides* this says about Spinoza's approach to mathematics.[74] To wit, Badiou dubiously asserts: "*Ethics* is really a mathematics of being."[75] Nevertheless, Badiou glimpses the significance of Spinozist infinity, although he falters in apperceiving its full consequences. Before ascertaining as much, however, a reorientation with Badiou's thought is merited.

Contra the arrogation of infinity to the transcendent Being that is One, modernity, Badiou claims, permits the "secularization of infinity."[76] This means that "situations are infinite and that human life is infinite and that we are infinite."[77] Since philosophy has predominantly colluded with the One, constraining infinity by relegating it to wholeness, unicity, and consistency, the only path forward is an ontology constructed on mathematics: "The story of infinity has been marked by theological thinking for a long, long time. We must liberate this category from the theological conception, and mathematics is the unique means for doing so."[78] "By initiating a thinking in which the infinite is irrevocably separated from every instance of the One, mathematics has, in its own domain, successfully consummated the death of God."[79] It "has neutralized and completely deconsecrated the infinite."[80]

The ontology that Badiou inducts is indebted to several tenets extrapolated from Cantor: the actuality of infinity, the mathematization of reality, and the indispensability of axiomatic set theory (especially as subsequently developed by Ernst Zermelo, Abraham Fraenkel, and Kurt Gödel) to both of these. Yet Badiou undertakes to correct what he perceives to be Cantor's resort to the transcendent One. Rather than upholding the set of all sets as God, Badiou allows "that Cantor, in a brilliant anticipation, saw that the absolute point of being of the multiple is not its consistency—thus its dependence upon a procedure of the count-as-one—but its inconsistency, a multiple-deployment that no unity gathers together."[81] Instead of instantiating the one that in-consists as the One god, Badiou takes it to validate "that the one is not."[82] Replacing Cantor's Absolutely Infinite with the void—the nonbeing of being—Badiou essays to devise an ontology that is devoid of oneness. Entrenching this endeavor is the contention that oneness or unity is only ever an effect, that it is never originary. This is a laudable pursuit and its postulate is no doubt accurate. However, even a brief foray into his philosophy evinces that Badiou's enterprise suffers much the same fate as the ontotheology he undertakes to discredit. Rather than extirpating the One, he merely displaces it, retaining its transcendence, originality, and independence.

To offer a taste of Badiou's resort to the ontotheologies of oneness and the transcendence upon which it rests and concurrently reinforces, consider his theorization of the void and the event. As Badiou has it, to sidestep the pitfalls of theological oneness, multiplicity must be founded not on the one but on the void, which "indicates the failure of the one, the not-one."[83] Accordingly, "ontology, in a certain sense, can *only* be theory of the void."[84] Whereas "the situation envelops existence with the one,"[85] rendering presented elements countable, the void or null set Ø resists presentation and counting-as. Indeed, "*it is because the one is not that the void is unique.*"[86] Consequently, "there is only one void" and it "signifies the unicity of the unpresentable such as marked within presentation."[87] It is "the nothing from which everything proceeds,"[88] it is the "proper name of being."[89] The void is the unpresentable nothing that is the foundation of everything presentable.

The elements that are excluded from a situation—those that do not *count* in it—teeter at the edge of the void. Not only will there always be more ways of configuring elements in a set—a situation—than its actual elements, but there is an excess that escapes this operation. This is the event: "It is—not being—supernumerary."[90] Excluded from ontology, the event "is formalized by an extraordinary set."[91] It is an "unfounded multiple" that belongs only to itself, its "coming can originate from nowhere else."[92] Though "the event is a multiplicity," it is "beyond every count," and thus declarable as "'ultra-One.'"[93] Superseding the ontological, the event "departs from the laws of being."[94] It is *historical*, "the opposite of nature."[95] Indebted to Heidegger, the event, Badiou allows, is "the other-than-being."[96] It is "nowhere and everywhere"[97] and has "the nameless as its name."[98] Considering as much, it is apposite that Badiou invokes the "miracle" as "the emblem of the pure event as resource of truth," for it "is the symbol of an interruption of the law."[99] The event—like the miracle—precipitates a truth procedure that commands fidelity. Furthermore, like all supernatural phenomena, its being is neither calculable nor verifiable: "It will therefore always remain doubtful whether there has been an event or not, except to those who intervene, who decide its belonging to the situation."[100] Such a procedure, modeled on mathematical induction, is declared axiomatically.

Manifestly, Badiou's subtractive ontology, rather than correcting for Cantor's ontotheological transcendence, merely refurbishes its features. Badiou anchors being in that which is otherwise to it, relying on an *exception* to the ontological, which is a self-founding, self-sustaining, everywhere-but-nowhere, ultra One, the unpresentable origin of all, that which infuses finite reality with its true infinitude.[101] Rather than truly immanentizing infinity, his project quarantines it within the realm of the *beyond*, anthropocentrically renders it the exclusive domain of humans, and confirms it as *the* measure of reality.

Badiou condemns Spinoza's philosophy, measuring it by the metrics of his own project, specifically, his insistence on the necessity of a beyond that founds ontological being: "Spinoza represents the most radical attempt ever in ontology to identify structure and metastructure, to assign a one-effect directly to the state, and to in-distinguish belonging and inclusion . . . this is the philosophy *par excellence* which *forecloses the void*."[102] There is no excess because "what exists is either being-qua-being, which is to say the one-infinity of the unique substance . . . or an immanent modification of God himself."[103] Hence, "Everything that belongs is included and everything that is included belongs."[104] Thus Spinoza's reality is a totality, a closed unity wherein the finite is merely collected within the infinite, permitting only the "there is" of ontology. For Spinoza, "God has to be understood as mathematicity itself. The name of the 'there is' is: matheme."[105] While it is certainly true that Spinozism disallows for an otherwise than being—as nothing is exempted from the immanence of causal determinism—its conception of infinity, as the foregoing adumbrates and as the following sections further adduce, repels the closure and limitations of totalization. Rather than succumbing to the seducements of transcendence, as Badiou does, Spinoza rebuffs them steadfastly.

It is prudent to observe that Badiou's fidelity to mathematical infinity, his concomitant enthroning of mathematics as the *singular* domain through which being manifests, and his crowning of axiomatic set theory as the exclusive, the One expression thereof, is a striking refurbishment of the rationale of Oneness and the sovereign logics that subsidize it. Whereas Spinoza repeatedly underscores the inadequacy of numbers—not to mention other forms of signification—to fully capture reality, Badiou insists that mathematics *is* ontology. He reduces nature to the mathematical yet simultaneously insists that there exists that which transcends this domain. Despite both Cantor and Badiou identifying in Spinoza a partisan for the mathematization of being, this is simply not Spinoza's position. Had they heeded Spinoza's hesitations, they might have appreciated the constraints of mathematics. Rather than reducing all of being to the One of mathematics, only to then deploy its exception, they might have realized that infinite reality is simply irreducible and that both everything and nothing are "exceptions." There is no *outside* nature. Furthermore, for Spinoza, reality is an infinite substance that is of infinite attributes, each of which is "infinite in its own kind."[106] Neither thought, nor extension—nor for that matter, any other attribute—is consummately expressive of reality. To suppose that all that is, is reducible to number alone transgresses the infinite difference on which the entirety of Spinoza's philosophy is constructed.

OFF LIMITS

It is time to return to Spinoza. While the foregoing confirms that substance is not numerically one, this exploration now turns to examine how substance is accordingly divested of the qualities of oneness, such as identity, enclosure, and totality. Ascertaining as much requires a reconsideration of substance. To reprise, substance—reality—is infinite. The *Ethics* opens by positing as much: "By God I understand a being absolutely infinite."[107] Despite its centrality to Spinoza's philosophy, the meaning of such infinity is not exactly clear. I propose that it amounts to indeterminacy[108] and, correlatively, that it is this indeterminacy that immunizes substance from the traits of oneness.

Infinity is constitutive of substance.[109] "Since being is really, in part, a negation, and being infinite is an absolute affirmation of the existence of some nature, it follows . . . that every substance must be infinite."[110] Being is a negation, a limitation,[111] which applies only to that which is finite. Therefore, Spinoza reasons, substance cannot be finite; it must be infinite. To be infinite, according to this reasoning, is to be without limits, which are necessarily constraining. Spinoza expounds upon this conception of infinity in his correspondence with Johannes Hudde, wherein he explicitly connects infinity to indeterminacy by claiming that determination *definitionally* undermines infinity.[112] To be determinate is to be delimited. Thus, substance is not a definite thing; it is *absolute indeterminatum*, "which perfectly expresses being,"[113] otherwise its "nature would be limited and deficient."[114] Spinoza echoes as much in the *Ethics*: since "being able to exist is power" it follows that "an absolutely infinite Being, *or* God, has, of himself, an absolutely infinite power of existing."[115] Similarly, Letter 12 describes it as "the infinite enjoyment of existing, *or* (in bad Latin) of being."[116]

What induces Spinoza's conception of infinity as indeterminacy is the contention that to be absolutely infinite is to be without limitations or delimitations. Rather than being a definite, determinate, delimited being, Spinoza construes substance as the "absolutely infinite power of existing." It is actual power, unhindered and unconstrained. Substance is absolutely infinite not only because there is no *other* to constrain it but rather because such infinity defies all forms of containment. Crucially, Spinoza is not asserting that substance is a Being endowed with unlimited power; this is more than traditional "omnipotence." Spinoza advances the conventional tenet by claiming that *any* form of being, *any* determination, *any* definiteness abrogates absolute infinity. Therefore, substance cannot be a thing or Being, as these entail the definiteness and delimitation ingenerate to determination. Minding this reasoning, it becomes clear that substance—despite its moniker—is not actually Substantial. It cannot be an *ousia* in the classic sense, for it can be neither matter nor even form, which rely upon definiteness and determination.

Spinoza's employment of "substance" is most proximately indebted to Descartes and traces back to Aristotle. But taking seriously these reflections on infinity, it appears that his deployment of "substance" amounts to a recasting of its meaning, akin to his redefinition of the inherited term, "God." The upshot of this is that if substance is not a Being or matter or thing or object or form, this means that it is exempted from suspicions of Oneness. There can be no identity without definiteness, no totality without determinate boundaries, no enclosure without delimited bounds. The characteristics of oneness simply cannot obtain if substance is indeterminate. Withal, this explication of infinity as indeterminacy proffers a further reason for why the infinity of substance eschews numeration: only definite beings are quantifiable.

IN ON THE ACT

If substance is indeterminate, what then is it? Recall that infinite substance is of infinite attributes and these attributes express its essence.[117] But what exactly is the essence of substance? As Spinoza makes plain: "God's power is his essence itself."[118] Essence *is* power: "God's power, by which he and all things are and act, is his essence itself."[119] The essence of substance is its power and the attributes are the infinite ways in which it exists,[120] how it *acts*, how it *does*, how it *is*. Essence is not *what* substance is but *how* it is. This is resonant with a point Spinoza articulates elsewhere:

> But the power by which God perseveres in his being is nothing but his essence. So they speak best who call God life. Some Theologians[121] think it was for this reason i.e., that God is life, and is not distinguished from life, that the Jews, when they swore, said *ḥai* Yahweh but not *ḥei* Yahweh.[122]

Substance is its actions, its *doing*, how it is alive. Substance *is* life.

It is pertinent to underscore that for Spinoza an essence is not a thing or feature or aspect that exists prior to or over and above a particular existent. Additionally, essences correlate with causes: an essence is determined by its causes and in turn by its effects. Essence is actualized power, the very *cause* of a given action.[123] As such, "Whatever exists expresses the nature, *or* essence of God in a certain and determinate way . . . whatever exists expresses in a certain and determinate way the power of God."[124] The power—essences—of modes expresses the power—the essence—of substance. Accordingly, the *conatus* of a singular thing *is* its essence[125] and, further, this essence *is* its actualized power, determined by its causes.

Substance *is* action, it is actual *doing* and such acts *are* its affections, its modes.[126] This is what Spinoza means when he states: "God's power is nothing except God's active essence. And so it is as impossible for us to conceive that God does not act as it is to conceive that he does not exist."[127] To exist is *already* to act. If power is the essence of substance, and power is actual, not potential, and if the essence of substance is existence, then the prospect of substance existing without actual power, without *acting,* without its actions—*modes*—is inconceivable. Substance is the enacted differentiation into and as its modes; it *is* its action. Indeterminate substance is performed *as* its determinate modes.[128] Substance, in a sense, is only ever already modified.[129] Differently formulated, substance as *natura naturans* is substance as *natura naturata*, since the essences of substance only exist as enacted. The "being" of substance *is* its doing.[130]

It is instructive, perhaps improbably so, to turn to *Hebrew Grammar.* Amid an analysis of Hebrew nouns, Spinoza proffers an explanatory definition that illuminates his conception of substance, attributes, and modes:

> By a noun I understand a word by which we signify or indicate something that is understood. However, among things that are understood there can be either things and attributes of things, modes and relationships, or actions, and modes and relationships of actions. Hence, we sum up easily the various kinds of nouns. For example, the noun שיא *is a man*; םכח *learned*, לודג *big*, etc., are attributes of a man; ךלוה *walking*, עדוי *knowing,* are modes; ןיב *between*, תחת *under*, לע *above*, etc., are nouns which show the relationship a man has to other things.[131]

The nouns, "walking," and "knowing" are described as "modes and relationships, or actions." Note the Spinozist "or": modes *or* actions: modes *are* actions. The noun *man* has the attribute of being *learned* and is doing the action of *knowing*. In other words, substance has the attribute thought and is doing the action of *knowing*. This grammatical exposition lends additional credence to our assertion that to say that substance acts is to say that it has modes, and to say that it has modes is to say that modes *are* its actions.

There is ample precedent in the speculations of Spinoza's predecessors for sustaining God as power or action. Intimations of this are discernable in Maimonides's theology as much as in kabbalistic construals of *Ein Sof.* However, Spinoza extends this position by positing that substance is indeterminate, that it is not a thing or Being. Substance is insubstantial in and of itself: it is nothing but actualized power, mere act. Correlative to this is the implication that substance does not exist independent of its action. Substance *is* its doing, it acts *as* its modes.

To appreciate substance not as a Being or thing but rather as enacted power is to grasp why it is truly infinite: power is not countable or quantifiable like an object; it is indeterminate *except* as enacted. Substance as *act*—rather than Being—confirms that absolutely infinite substance cannot be the One that begets the Many, nor that the Many beings comprise the One. Accordingly, infinity cannot be vouchsafed to the One that is Beyond, for there is no one and there is no beyond. Rather, infinite power exists solely as its finite enactments. There is no "measure" between the infinite and the finite[132] because they are not independent "things" that preexist each other.[133] The infinite and the finite are not a binary. Reality, I argue, is thus configured as nonbinary: finite modes *are* infinite power, *in actu*.

THERE IS NO ONE

Spinoza's infinity and the immanence that it commands corroborate that it is not merely substance that is not One but that nothing is already or essentially One. Modes, too, are not quantitatively or qualitatively One. As Spinoza has it: "the true definition of each thing neither involves nor expresses anything except the nature of the thing defined"; it follows "that no definition involves or expresses any certain number of individuals."[134] For example, the definition of a triangle is expressive of its nature and not "any certain number of triangles."[135] Verily, it is not only numbers that prove inadequate, but "terms called *Transcendental*" such as "Being, Thing, and something."[136] Contra the trend that confirms Something—God, Infinity, the Event—as *singularly* beyond calculation or signification, Spinoza refuses such transcendent exception and instead universalizes this status.

Numbers and terms are devices contrived to make sense of reality. They are convenient but also confusing in that none adequately expresses the essence of a singular thing insomuch as they rely on contingencies and comparisons. This figures in Spinoza's clarification of the third kind of knowledge.[137] Ordinarily, we conceive things "to exist in relation to a certain time and place."[138] But with the third kind of knowledge, "we conceive things under a species of eternity, and to that extent they involve the eternal and infinite essence of God."[139] This is "To conceive things insofar as they are conceived through God's essence, as real beings, *or* insofar as through God's essence they involve existence."[140] Nothing that exists is consummately represented by numbers and words because these are inherently relative and imprecise. Whereas traditional theology perceives God as singularly indefinable, Spinoza's ontology approaches all beings as necessary, cautioning against the constraints of relational signifiers. To be sure, with regard to modes—unlike substance itself—"we can determine as we please their existence and

Duration, conceive it as greater or less, and divide it into parts."[141] Nevertheless, when modes are "confused with Beings of reason of this kind, *or* aids of the imagination, they too can never be rightly understood."[142]

It is not just that modes are not quantitatively one. Rather, they also do not possess, a priori, qualities of oneness such as identity and totality. Moreover, since all modes are participants in the "*infinito causarum nexu*," no particular mode exists as an independent or atomistic one.[143] Rather, all beings are imbricated and interdependent, determined "in infinite ways" and "compelled to undergo infinitely many variations."[144] Indeed, "all bodies are surrounded by others, and are determined by one another to existing and producing an effect."[145] Singular modes are interconnected, "part of the whole universe," constantly intra-acting through "agreements" and "adaptations."[146] When a mode disagrees with other modes, it appears "distinct" and only then is "considered as a whole and not as a part."[147] Insomuch as the confines of individual modes are neither predetermined nor prefixed, this means that identity is not *given* and that being is already collective rather than independent. Furthermore, it is not merely that modes are not alienated and isolated. But a particular human mode is constituted by countless interacting modes: the body "is composed of a great many individuals of different natures, each of which is highly composite."[148] Besides, human modes are marked by the *difference* of being both body and mind. Thus, humans do not constitute a bounded Whole or Totality; they are divested of stable Identity, deprived of Oneness.[149]

OUT IN THE OPEN

The seductions of sovereign oneness are unmistakable. It is reassuring to perceive reality as the product of an infinite One: a Being that is Beyond, ordering the chaos and directing it toward a telos. It is comforting to suppose that there is a transcendent Other, *excepted* from, yet responsible for, ontological reality. This carries with it guarantees of consistency and grounds of coherence: finite being is underwritten by the Infinite Being. Conceiving reality itself as One delivers cognate solace by assembling its disparities into a unity, organizing its differences into a coalesced totality, and binding its unruliness into a bounded whole. In this formulation, rather than confining nature to its finitude by vouchsafing Infinity to the realm that is Beyond, nature is upheld as Infinite. However, such infinity is accompanied by confinements; its turbulence is subdued by the imposition of identity and sameness. Similarly, upholding individual humans as atomistic Ones endows them with exceptionalism, integrates their contradictions, and safeguards their integrity through the imposition of delineated perimeters. Often, this human One replaces or reflects the One God that is Infinite in a manner that seems to confirm its finitude, yet simultaneously affirms its distinction by either underscoring its inherent transcendence or, minimally, by connecting it to the transcendent. Spinoza, however, presents an alternative, abjuring these illusory promises and their sponsoring rationales. Reality is infinite and immanent, which means that there is no exception to causal determination, no escape from nature, no retreat from the imbrications of the infinite connection of causes. Spinoza dethrones the Infinite God that is One by rendering it as immanent substance. This releases infinity from the realm of the transcendent Beyond. Unity is neither primordial nor originary; its arrangement is only ever contingent. Concomitantly, Spinoza dispossesses reality itself of oneness, liberating infinity from its fetters, thus evincing that nothing is ever originally or essentially One; one is only ever an *effect* and a fleeting one at that.

Despite their attempts to immanentize infinity, both Cantor and Badiou falter by reconstituting the transcendence and oneness traditionally ascribed to it. These bids expose the almost irresistible enticements of oneness; they both rely upon its transcendence and exceptionalism to underwrite their theories. The immanence that they strain to install rests upon that which is Beyond; their infinities are guaranteed by sovereign hierarchies and unities. By contrast, Spinoza insists on actual infinity without compromising his immanence; he resists the urge to have the here guaranteed by a purported There. This boldly embraces the openness of infinity and the instability of its immanentization. Althusser discerns this spirit, grasping that Spinoza "clears a path . . . for the recognition of the 'world' as a unique totality that is *not totalized, but experienced in its dispersion*."[150]

While Leibniz, Jacobi, and Hegel deprecated Spinozism by linking it to "oriental" oneness and likening it to *Ein Sof*, there is a certain alignment on this register.[151] Spinoza's campaign against Oneness participates in a particular—however repressed—current in Kabbalah that subtly but strenuously displaces the sovereignties of oneness. It is precisely these subversive tendencies that Wolfson has constructively unveiled and comprehensively theorized.[152] For Wolfson, *Ein Sof*, like God for Heidegger, is not "the being that is beyond being . . . it is rather the being that cannot be reduced to or identified with any being, even the otherwise than being. . . . the one constellated not by the one of singular identity but by the illimitable multiples of the one that is never one."[153] Differently stated, insomuch as "difference is comprised in the sameness of the other that is differently the same. The oneness of being, therefore, embraces the truth that being is not one."[154] For Spinoza, for certain Kabbalists, and for Wolfson, there is no One and there are no Ones to be known.

NOTES

1. On the development of "*Ein Sof*," see Gershom Scholem, *Origins of the Kabbalah*, ed. R. J. Zwi Werblowsky and trans. Allan Arkush (Princeton: Princeton University Press, 1987), 265–70; Elliot R. Wolfson, "Nihilating Nonground and the Temporal Sway of Becoming: Kabbalistically Envisioning Nothing beyond Nothing," *Angelaki* 17 (2012): 31–45; Sandra Valabregue-Perry, "The Concept of Infinite (*Eyn-sof*) and the Rise of Theosophical Kabbalah," *Jewish Quarterly Review* 102, no. 3 (Summer 2012): 405–30.
2. Martin Heidegger, *Identity and Difference*, trans. Joan Stambaugh (Chicago: University of Chicago Press, 1969), 69–71.

3. See Gilah Kletenik, "Sovereignty Disrupted: Spinoza on Infinite Disparity" (PhD dissertation, New York University, 2020).
4. Louis Althusser, "The Underground Current of the Materialism of the Encounter," in *Philosophy of the Encounter, Later Writings, 1978–1987*, ed. François Matheron and Oliver Corpet, trans. G. M. Goshgarian (London: Verso, 2006), 167.
5. See Kletenik, "Sovereignty Disrupted," 1–26.
6. Elliot R. Wolfson, *Giving Beyond the Gift: Apophasis and Overcoming Theomania* (New York: Fordham University Press, 2014), xxiv.
7. Wolfson, *Giving Beyond the Gift,* xxvii.
8. See the conclusion below.
9. See below.
10. See Dictionary, entry for "Zenon." Pierre Bayle, Pierre Desmaizeaux, Eusèbe Renaudot, and Anthelme Tricaud, *Dictionaire historique et critique. Cinquieme edition, revue, corrigée, et augmentée. Avec la vie de l'auteur, par Mr. Des Maizeaux*, 5th ed., vol. 4 (Amsterdam: Leyden [etc.], 1740).
11. Gottfried Wilhelm Leibniz, *Philosophical Papers and Letters*, 2nd ed., trans. Leroy E. Loemker (Dordrecht: Kluwer Academic, 1989), 502; see also 196–204, 507, 533, 554–55, 559, 583, 594, 663. Leibniz praises Bayle's *Dictionary,* noting its entry on Spinoza, 582.
12. Friedrich Heinrich Jacobi, *The Main Philosophical Writings and the Novel Allwill*, trans. George di Giovanni (Montreal: McGill-Queen's University Press, 1994), 187–88.
13. Maimon explicitly connects Spinoza to Parmenides: *Salomon Maimon's Streifereien im Gebiete der Philosophie:1, Theil*, 40–41.
14. Solomon Maimon, *The Autobiography of Solomon Maimon: The Complete Translation*, ed. Yitzhak Y. Melamed, Abraham P. Socher, trans. Paul Reitter (Princeton: Princeton University Press, 2019), 62.
15. For more on Hegel's misreading of Spinoza: Pierre Macherey, *Hegel or Spinoza,* trans. Susan B. Ruddick (Minneapolis: University of Minnesota Press, 2011); *Between Hegel and Spinoza: A Volume of Critical Essays*, ed. Hasana Sharp, Jason E. Smith (London: Bloomsbury, 2012); Gregor Moder, *Hegel and Spinoza: Substance and Negativity* (Evanston: Northwestern University Press, 2017).
16. G. W. F. Hegel, *Lectures on the History of Philosophy: Medieval and Modern Philosophy*, trans. E. S. Haldane and Frances H. Simson (Lincoln: University of Nebraska Press, 1995), 252; see also: *The Science of Logic,* trans. George di Giovanni (Cambridge: Cambridge University Press, 2010), 87, 333, 470–76; *Encyclopedia of the Philosophical Sciences in Basic Outline*, §50, pp. 96–99; §151, pp. 224–25.
17. Hegel, *Lectures*, 252.
18. Hegel, *Lectures*, 257.
19. Hegel, *Lectures*, 256.
20. Hegel, *Lectures*, 260.
21. Hegel, *Lectures*, 262.
22. Gilles Deleuze, *Expressionism in Philosophy: Spinoza*, trans. M. Joughin (New York: Zone Books, 1990), 182.
23. Louis Althusser, *Reading Capital*, trans. Ben Brewster (London: New Left Books, 1975),

209; see also Warren Montag, *Althusser and His Contemporaries: Philosophy's Perpetual War* (Durham: Duke University Press, 2017), 73–100.

24. Alain Badiou, "Spinoza's Closed Ontology," *Alain Badiou: Theoretical Writings*, ed. and trans. Ray Brassier and Alberto Toscano (London: Bloomsbury Academic, 2015), 81.
25. Slavoj Žižek, *Less Than Nothing: Hegel and the Shadow of Dialectical Materialism* (London: Verso, 2012), 376.
26. Michael Della Rocca, *Spinoza* (New York: Routledge, 2008), 33; see also Della Rocca, "The Elusiveness of the One and the Many in Spinoza: Substance, Attribute, and Mode," *Spinoza in Twenty-First Century American and French Philosophy: Metaphysics, Philosophy of Mind, Moral and Political Philosophy*, ed. Jack Stetter and Charles Ramond (London: Bloomsbury Academic, 2019), 59–86.
27. Jonathan Bennett, *A Study of Spinoza's Ethics* (Indianapolis: Hackett, 1994), 75–79.
28. Noteworthy exceptions include: Mogens Lærke, "Spinoza's Monism? What Monism," in *Spinoza on Monism*, ed. Philip Gof (New York: Palgrave Macmillan, 2012), 244–64; Yitzhak Y. Melamed, "Why Spinoza Is Not an Eleatic Monist (or Why Diversity Exists)," in *Spinoza on Monism*, ed. Philip Gof (New York: Palgrave Macmillan, 2012), 206–21; Macherey, *Hegel or Spinoza,* 104.
29. *Cogitata Metaphysica*, VI. All citations of Spinoza, unless otherwise specified, from: *The Collected Works of Spinoza,* ed. and trans. Edwin Curley (Princeton: Princeton University Press, 2016).
30. *Cogitata Metaphysica*, VI.
31. *Cogitata Metaphysica*, V.
32. Descartes similarly maintains: "Numbers and all universals are simply modes of thinking." Réne Descartes, *Principles of Philosophy*, I.58.
33. *Cogitata Metaphysica*, VI.
34. *Cogitata Metaphysica*, VI.
35. *Cogitata Metaphysica*, VI.
36. Letter 50.
37. Letter 50.
38. Letter 50.
39. Letter 12.
40. Letter 50.
41. EIp5; EIp6; EIp8; EIp14; EIp15.
42. This seems consonant with Euclid's definitions: "A *unit* is that by virtue of which each of the things that exist is called one. A *number* is a multitude composed of units." Euclid, *Elements* VII, 2.
43. Letter 50.
44. Letter 50.
45. Moses Maimonides, *The Guide of the Perplexed,* trans. Shlomo Pines (Chicago: University of Chicago Press, 1963), I.57.
46. Aristotle, *Metaphysics*, X 2.
47. Maimonides, *Guide*, I.57.

48. Maimonides, *Guide*, I.56.
49. Maimonides, *Guide*, I.56.
50. Hasdai Crescas, *Light of the Lord* (Or Hashem), trans. Roslyn Weiss (Oxford: Oxford University Press, 2018), Book I, Part iii, p. 106.
51. Book I, Part iii, p. 102.
52. In Letter 81, Spinoza refers to Letter 12 as "my Letter concerning the Infinite." It had been circulated among his friends and colleagues.
53. Letter 12.
54. Letter 12.
55. Letter 12.
56. Letter 12.
57. Letter 12.
58. Letter 12.
59. Letter 12.
60. Letter 12.
61. EIappendix.
62. For the nonquantitative aspect of Spinoza's infinity, see: Shannon Dea, "The Infinite and the Indeterminate in Spinoza," *Dialogue* 50 (2011): 603–21; Ohad Nachtomy, "A Tale of Two Thinkers, One Meeting, and Three Degrees of Infinity: Leibniz and Spinoza (1675–8)," *British Journal for the History of Philosophy* 19, no. 5 (2011): 935–61. For Spinoza's deprecation of mathematics: Yitzhak Y. Melamed, "On the Exact Science of Nonbeings: Spinoza's View of Mathematics," *Iyyun: The Jerusalem Philosophical Quarterly* 49 (2000): 3–22. For early modern context of nonquantitative infinity, see Anat Schechtman, "Three Infinities in Early Modern Philosophy," *Mind* 128, no. 512 (2019): 1117–47.
63. For more on Spinoza's infinities: Martial Gueroult, *Spinoza I: Dieu* (Paris: Aubier, 1968); Luce deLire, "Spinoza's Infinities," *A Companion to Spinoza*, ed. Yitzhak Y. Melamed (Hoboken, NJ: John Wiley & Sons, 2021), 158–69.
64. Letter 12.
65. For Spinoza's influence on Cantor, see: Anne Newstead, "Intertwining Metaphysics and Mathematics: The Development of Georg Cantor's Set Theory 1871–1887," *Review of Contemporary Philosophy* 7 (2008): 35–55; Newstead, "Cantor on Infinity in Nature, Number, and the Divine Mind," *American Philosophical Quarterly* 83, no. 4 (2009): 533–53; Paolo Bussotti and Christian Tapp, "The Influence of Spinoza's Concept of Infinity on Cantor's Set Theory," *Studies in History and Philosophy of Science* 40 (2009): 25–35.
66. See Bussotti and Tapp, "Influence of Spinoza's Concept of Infinity," 25–26; Newstead, "Cantor on Infinity," 535–39.
67. Cantor esteemed the geometrical method, was taken by a strict distinction between *natura naturans* and *natura naturata*, and was drawn to an idealist construal of the infinite intellect. He also praised Letter 12.
68. See Newstead, "Cantor on Infinity," 541–42.
69. EIIp7.
70. Letter to Cardinal Franzelin, 22.1.1886, *Georg Cantor, Briefe*, ed. Herbert Meschkowski and

Winfried Nilson (Berlin: Springer, 1991), 254.

71. See Joseph W. Dauben, "Georg Cantor and Pope Leo XIII: Mathematics, Theology, and the Infinite," *Journal of the History of Ideas* 38, no. 1 (1977): 85–108.
72. Letter to Dedekind, 3.8.1899, *Briefe*, 407.
73. For Badiou's interpretation of Spinoza, see: Sam Gillespie, "Placing the Void: Badiou on Spinoza," *Angelaki* 6, no. 3 (2001): 65; Peter Hallward, *Badiou: A Subject to Truth* (Minneapolis: University of Minnesota Press, 2003), 168–71; Jon Roffe, "The Errant Name: Badiou and Deleuze Individuation, Causality and Infinite Modes in Spinoza," *Continental Philosophy Review* 40 (2007): 389–406; Kletenik, "Sovereignty Disrupted," 126–36, 148–53.
74. Badiou, "What Is a Proof in Spinoza's *Ethics*," in *Spinoza Now*, ed. Dimitris Vardoulakis (Minnesota: University of Minnesota Press, 2011), 42.
75. Badiou, "What Is a Proof in Spinoza's *Ethics*," 42.
76. Alain Badiou, "Philosophy and Mathematics," in *Alain Badiou: Theoretical Writings*, ed. and trans. Ray Brassier and Alberto Toscano (London: Bloomsbury Academic, 2015), 41.
77. Alain Badiou, "Ontology and Politics: An Interview with Alain Badiou," in *Infinite Thought: Truth and Return to Philosophy*, trans. and ed. Oliver Feltham and Justin Clemens (London: Bloomsbury Academic, 2014), 153.
78. Badiou, "Ontology and Politics," 153.
79. Badiou, "Philosophy and Mathematics," 39.
80. Badiou, "Philosophy and Mathematics," 39.
81. Alain Badiou, *Being and Event*, trans. Oliver Feltham (London: Continuum, 2005), 42.
82. Badiou, *Being and Event*, 42.
83. Badiou, *Being and Event*, 56.
84. Badiou, *Being and Event*, 57.
85. Badiou, *Being and Event*, 52.
86. Badiou, *Being and Event*, 69.
87. Badiou, *Being and Event*, 69.
88. Badiou, *Being and Event*, 59.
89. Badiou, *Being and Event*, 86.
90. Badiou, *Being and Event*, 178.
91. Badiou, *Being and Event*, 190.
92. Alain Badiou, "The Event as Trans-Being," in *Alain Badiou: Theoretical Writings*, ed. and trans. Ray Brassier and Alberto Toscano (London: Bloomsbury Academic, 2015), 107.
93. Badiou, "The Event as Trans-Being," 107.
94. Badiou, "The Event as Trans-Being," 107.
95. Badiou, *Being and Event*, 174.
96. Badiou, *Being and Event*, 174.
97. Badiou, *Being and Event*, 55.
98. Badiou, *Being and Event*, 205.
99. Badiou, *Being and Event*, 216.
100. Badiou, *Being and Event*, 207.
101. See Daniel Bensaïd, "Alain Badiou and the Miracle of the Event," in *Think Again: Alain Badiou and the Future of Philosophy*, ed. Peter Hallward (London: Continuum, 2004), 94–

105. For Badiou's (unpersuasive) defense, see "The Event as Trans-Being," 104; *Revue Ballast*, April 27, 2015, posted: https://www.revue-ballast.fr/alain-badiou-lemancipation-cest-celle-de-lhumanite-tout-entiere/. Relatedly, see Peter Hallward, *Badiou: A Subject to Truth*, 93, 271–91, for Badiou's absolutist tendencies.

102. Badiou, *Being and Event*, 113.
103. Badiou, *Being and Event*, 113.
104. Badiou, *Being and Event*, 113.
105. Badiou, "Spinoza's Closed Ontology," 99.
106. EId6.
107. EId6; also: EIp8; EIp10dem.
108. For partially affined interpretations of infinity as indeterminacy, see: Shannon Dea, "The Infinite and Indeterminate in Spinoza"; Macherey, *Hegel or Spinoza*; H. F. Hallett, *Benedict de Spinoza: The Elements of His Philosophy* (London: Athlone Press, 1957), 20. For less aligned approaches to indeterminacy, see: Harry Austryn Wolfson, *The Philosophy of Spinoza: Unfolding the Latent Processes of His Reasoning*, 2 vols. (Cambridge, MA: Harvard University Press, 1934), 138; DeLire, "Spinoza's Infinities"; Deleuze, *Expressionism in Philosophy*, 74.
109. EId6; EIp8.
110. EIp8schol.1.
111. EId2; EIp8dem.
112. Letter 36.
113. Letter 36.
114. Letter 36.
115. EIp11schol.
116. Letter 12.
117. EId6; EIp11.
118. EIp34.
119. EIp34dem.
120. EId6; EIp11.
121. Spinoza is clearly referring to Maimonides; see Mishneh Torah, Hilkhot Yesodei ha-Torah 2:10.
122. *CSM* VI.
123. "The identity of power and essence means: a power is always an act or, at least in action." Deleuze, *Expressionism in Philosophy*, 93.
124. EIp36dem.
125. EIIIp7dem.
126. For substance as activity or action, see: Hallett, *Benedict de Spinoza*, 13; Dea, "The Infinite and Indeterminate in Spinoza"; Macherey, *Hegel or Spinoza*, 142–62; Francesca di Poppa, "Spinoza and Process Ontology," *Southern Journal of Philosophy* 48, no. 3 (September 2010): 272–94; Kletenik, "Sovereignty Disrupted," 28–45.
127. IIp3schol.
128. EIp36dem.
129. For similar claims that substance is already modified, see: Karolina Hübner, "Spinoza's Thinking Substance and the Necessity of Modes," *Philosophy and Phenomenological Research* 92, no. 1 (2016): 3–34; Gregor Moder, *Hegel and Spinoza*, 140; Vittorio Morfino, *Plural Temporality:*

Transindividuality and the Aleatory Between Spinoza and Althusser (London: Brill, 2014), 29–31; Hallett, *Benedict de Spinoza*, 13; Macherey, *Hegel or Spinoza*, 200.

130. Macherey, *Hegel or Spinoza*, 145, 200–202.
131. *Hebrew Grammar*, chap. 5, *Spinoza: Complete Works,* trans. Samuel Shirley (Indianapolis: Hackett, 2002).
132. Letter 54.
133. EIp33schol.2.
134. EIp8schol.2
135. EIp8schol.2
136. EIIp40schol.1.
137. See Julie R. Klein, "'By Eternity I Understand': Eternity According to Spinoza," *Iyyun: Jerusalem Philosophical Quarterly* 51 (July 2002): 295–324.
138. EVp29schol.
139. EVp29schol.
140. EVp30dem.
141. Letter 12.
142. Letter 12.
143. Étienne Balibar, "Spinoza: From Individuality to Transindividuality," *Mededelingen vanwege het Spinozahuis* 71 (Delft: Eburon, 1997), 14; see also: Morfino, *Plural Temporality*, 56–71.
144. Letter 32.
145. Letter 32.
146. Letter 32.
147. Letter 32.
148. EIIp13sL7.
149. For more on this, see Kletenik, "Sovereignty Disrupted," 270–314.
150. Althusser, "The Underground," 179.
151. For Spinoza and Kabbalah: Johan Aanen, "The Kabbalistic Sources of Spinoza," *Journal of Jewish Thought and Philosophy* 24 (2016): 279–99; Miquel Beltrán, *The Influence of Abraham Cohen de Herrera's Kabbalah on Spinoza's Metaphysics* (Leiden: Brill, 2016); Beltrán, "Impronta del acosmismo luriánico en la 'Ethica' de Spinoza" [Footprints of Lurianic acosmism on Spinoza's "Ethica"], *Revista de Filosofia* 40, no. 2 (2015): 63–81; Elliot R. Wolfson, *Heidegger and Kabbalah: Hidden Gnosis and the Path of Poiēsis* (Bloomington: Indiana University Press, 2019), 130n135.
152. My overall reading of Spinozism as presenting a radical alternative to the sovereignties of ontotheology is indebted to the path of thinking that Professor Wolfson has paved by unveiling the theolatrous impulses of monotheism and unmasking the inconsistencies in philosophies of transcendence. Not only were the ideas in this brief essay initially developed in my dissertation, with his guidance, but how I think about these questions, how I read these texts, and how I negotiate their aporias is oriented by his work. It is an honor to be Elliot's student and to glimpse the traces of his thinking manifest, in all of their *différance*.
153. Wolfson, *Heidegger and Kabbalah*, 336.
154. Wolfson, *Heidegger and Kabbalah*, 174.

A TRACE OF LEVINAS

Wolfson's Phenomenology of Vulnerable Learning

SARAH PESSIN

where the faithful doubt
it shall end
if it might begin
[. . .]
once
i and you
brought me back
to where i
was not
before

TWO POETIC FRAGMENTS FROM WOLFSON'S *FOOTDREAMS & TREETALES*[1]

WOLFSON INVITES US INTO THE HARD WORK OF "THINK[ING] THE UNthought in Heidegger's thinking." Following on the very structure and method of Wolfson's own hermeneutical frame, I will explore what I see as an unthought in Wolfson's thinking, viz. an unthought Levinasian supplement to Heidegger. In particular, I will focus on Wolfson's criticism of Levinas's criticism of Heidegger in the context of Wolfson's nod to Heidegger's call to learning coupled with Wolfson's own call to and practice of a style of learning that is more vulnerable. In this way, I will uncover a trace of Levinas in Wolfson's own critique of Levinas. Furthermore, I will position Levinas's concern with Heidegger—his own teacher—as a question of "how ought we learn together?," and will show how Levinas's claim that "it is difficult to forgive Heidegger" enacts not obduracy or hypocrisy but the very vulnerability that frames Levinas's phenomenology—including his, but also Wolfson's, "phenomenology of vulnerable learning"—in ways that exceed Heidegger's own frame.

IN HIS *THE DUPLICITY OF PHILOSOPHY'S SHADOW: HEIDEGGER, NAZISM, AND THE Jewish Other*, Wolfson calls on us to think the unthought in Heidegger. And he does so while unequivocally rejecting any whitewashings of Heidegger's Nazi past. Yes, we must hold Heidegger to account; and yes, we must think the unthought in Heidegger's thinking. Drawing on Heideggerian frames, Wolfson calls on us to think an unthought in Heidegger that "must be thought as part of our communal human lot as being historical."[2] We can perhaps think of this as a call to reading Heidegger with charity, but more so as a sense that Heidegger's texts deserve our attention (charitably or otherwise) because they reveal (as they conceal) truths emerging from within the very history of being. Indeed, Wolfson calls out Heidegger's brilliance[3]—a term that can be taken as a general nod to Heidegger's philosophical know-how, and also more literally to his role as a thinker of light and clearings whose ideas allow being to shine.

> If the bleak days scare away all shining radiance, and if all breadth shrivels into the paltriness of narrow conventionality, then the heart must remain the source of what is light and spacious. And the most solitary heart makes the broadest leap into the middle of beyng, if on all sides the semblance of nonbeings stops its noise.[4]

In *Heidegger and Kabbalah*, Wolfson begins with Heidegger's leap into "beyng"[5] and a "shining radiance" itself implicated in paradoxes of concealment-exposure that Wolfson has throughout his work helped us find at the heart of Kabbalah. Describing Heidegger's "expos[ing] the nothingness of beyng" Wolfson cites a "precedent in kabbalistic theosophy, where the diffusion of the liminal darkness of infinitivity" resonates with the Heideggerian sense of truth's recoil into its "self-concealing shelter" (*das sich verbergende Bergen*) through which "we catch a glimpse of the essence of the mystery in which the truth of being essences."[6] Wolfson describes Heidegger's language as "deeply kabbalistic in its cadence" and in its emphasis on precisely the kinds of clearing-concealing paradoxes that Wolfson finds in the kabbalistic hermeneutic of concealment that reveals and revelation that conceals.

> *Truth* is the clearing-concealing [*lichtende Verbergung*] which occurs as transporting [*Entrückung*] and captivation [*Berückung*]. These in their unity [*Einheit*] as well as in excess [*Übermaß*] provide the encompassed open realm [*umstellte Offene*] for the play of beings which, in the sheltering of their truth, come to be as thing, tool, machination, work, act, sacrifice.... The essence of truth, however, the transporting-captivating clearing and concealing as the origin of the "there" [*Ursprung des Da*], essentially occurs in its ground which we experience as ap-propriation [*Er-eignung*].[7]

BOTH IN HIS 2019 CONNECTING OF HEIDEGGERIAN DEPTHS TO KABBALISTIC wells and in his 2018 invitation to avoid overly simplistic rejections of Heideggerian thought as Nazistic, Wolfson invites us to sit with and learn from Heidegger's philosophy. And he does so on risk of poking a variety of academic hornets' nests. Wolfson calls anyone to task who is too quick to administer stings and only stings as he invites us to "think Nazism in the shadow of Heidegger rather than fixate on how Nazism cast a shadow on Heidegger."[8] Wolfson reminds us that when we fixate solely on the latter, we can ironically find ourselves enacting our own totalitarian hegemonies—a "totalitarian proclivity to denounce totalitarianism,"[9] as it were. Here Wolfson also extends the call to the reception of his own work: In an epilogue, he vulnerably shares with readers his worry that a certain anti-Heidegger passion on the part of some readers will comport them to his own work—and in particular, to misreading his own work—with a haste and simplicity that smacks of "the very absolutism, despotism, and homogenization they find so offensive about the fascist ideology Heidegger unwisely embraced."[10]

The irony is not simply that in our nonvulnerable reading styles we enact the totalitarian comportments we revile. The irony is further that one of the key elements Wolfson aims to lift up in Heidegger—found also, for Wolfson, in Kabbalah—is a vulnerable sense that truth always is concealed as it is revealed, and the work—and life—of Heidegger is no exception. In other words, Heidegger's—and Kabbalah's—teaching that truth's disclosure is always inextricably wrapped up in an enclosure (that its revealment is always tied into a concealment, and vice versa) ought lead us to more vulnerably adopt a hermeneutic of "thinking the unthought" even in authors who have inspired our ire. Truth leaves traces. And if we take that seriously (as Kabbalah, Heidegger, and Wolfson do and invite us to do), then it follows easily that even as flawed but brilliant a thinker as Heidegger could leave us a text filled with precious cargo. Indeed, in fully recognizing the paradoxes of clearing and concealing, it becomes clear that there is no other way truths could ever make their way to us. This, I take it, is part of what Wolfson means in his reminder that, thinking unthinkable thoughts—related to "attending to [Heidegger's] silences" so that we may "fill in the blank spaces of this thinking"[11]—is what "must be thought as part of our communal human lot as being historical."[12]

WE MAY IDENTIFY IN ALL OF THIS A "PHENOMENOLOGY OF VULNERABLE LEARNing" in which the clearing-concealing operation of truth is an operation of trace-making; philosophical texts are one repository of such traces; and vulnerable reading is what happens when we approach truth-seeking as trace-seeking, and texts—or at least certain texts—as traces. We can perhaps appreciate the contours of such a hermeneutic in sitting for a moment longer with Wolfson's own reminder of the link between Heidegger's clearing-concealing and his idea of appropriation. As Vallega-Neu explains such a frame:

> The task . . . for Heidegger, becomes not to think and speak *towards* the open horizon of being, but from *out of* it. In §132 of *Contributions*, he writes: "What counts is not to step beyond (transcendence) but to leap over this difference [between beings and being] and with it over *transcendence* and to question in an inceptive way from out of beyng and truth" (GA 65: 250–51). This is possible only if thinking attempts to stay attuned to an authentic mode of being in which the thinker finds himself/herself displaced (Heidegger speaks of a "leap") from both everyday and theoretical modes of being and thrown into the (abyssal) openness of being as such.

> This openness is what Heidegger calls the truth of beyng. (In *Being and Time* this is thought as the temporal horizon into which Dasein always already transcends.) The truth of beyng needs to be sustained in order to occur as truth, and this is why thinking needs to be (-sein) there (da-) in that openness. It is then that thinking may find itself *ereignet*, "appropriated," by beyng and beyng in its truth can be experienced and thought as *Ereignis*, as appropriating event. In other words, the notion of *Ereignis* arises out of an experience of being in which Dasein finds itself thrown into the openness of being and appropriated in its being.[13]

Vulnerably searching for unthought traces in Heidegger's work in spite (and in light) of his own failings is in part an acknowledgment of the way truth vulnerably reveals itself always already in the dark.

I AM GRATEFUL TO WOLFSON'S WORK FOR HAVING LED ME INTO THIS ENCOUNTER with Heidegger as I myself often struggle to remain vulnerable and open when reading Heidegger. To be sure, while I push back at Heidegger for philosophical reasons, I also push back at Heidegger in the way of partly processing my family's own lived experience of Holocaust horror (what I elsewhere term "word-wounds").[14] Of course there might well be at least some overlap across these two push-backs in my own relation to Heidegger, and even perhaps in Levinas's. While Levinas's disagreement with Heidegger is ultimately a philosophical one, perhaps some of the sharper edges in Levinas's encounter with Heidegger reveal a different sort of working through. Drawing our attention to precisely some of those sharper edges in Levinas's critique, Wolfson diagnoses Levinas's tying Heidegger to Nazism through a too-quick and overly one-dimensional reading of the two in and through a crude soil paganism. In this regard, Wolfson critiques Levinas's critique of Heidegger: Levinas calls on some questionable vague claims about Jews (with Socrates) preferring cities over country living and how that speaks to a rejection of paganism in Jewish and Socratic life in contrast to an undue embrace of paganism—tied to ideas of "peasant enrootedness" and resulting superstitious "attachment(s) to Place"—in Heidegger. Within the parameters of such a frame, it is quite easy—and Wolfson's critical point is *unjustly easy*—to draw a line from Heidegger's thinking to Nazism: Both embrace pagan horizons, which lead both to crude and violent attachments to place. Wolfson diagnoses this as Levinas's "excessively reductive" reading of Heidegger,[15] in this way essentially exposing Levinas's own insufficiently vulnerable practices of reading.

To be sure, Wolfson is correct to diagnose the above comments in Levinas as flat-footed, simplistic, and not sufficiently philosophically serious to be taken philosophically seriously. But here there are two related points to make. To reduce Levinas's own critique of Heidegger to a rhetorical emphasis on city and country life is to needlessly diminish Levinas's own important philosophical interventions into Heideggerian ontology; it is, in other words, to read Levinas with insufficient vulnerability. And the second point is that Wolfson's own writings overtly reveal as much in their own analyses of Levinas's more philosophical details.[16] Indeed, suggesting traces of an unthought in Wolfson's own encounter with Heidegger, we can even discern traces of this more philosophically serious Levinas across the three short pages where Wolfson critiques him. Perhaps there is the vulnerability of a word-wound working its way through Levinas's city/country critique of Heidegger rooted in his own disappointment with Heidegger, as perhaps there is a word-wound working its way through Wolfson's own acknowledged disappointment with readers for being too quick to demonize Heidegger's—and Wolfson's own—texts. Perhaps, in other words, part of truth's own capacity to "disclose opaquely" relates to the word-wounds that history inflicts on us as authors, readers, and learners: Levinas cannot but on occasion reduce Heidegger even as he elsewhere acknowledges the depth of his thought; and Wolfson cannot but on occasion reduce Levinas even as he elsewhere acknowledges the depth of his thought. And it is perhaps Heidegger's own insights on the operations of being that explains why this must be so.

THE FIRST TRACE OF A MORE THREE-DIMENSIONAL LEVINAS IN WOLFSON'S CRItique of Levinas's own one-dimensional critique of Heidegger can be seen in a giving way from (1) Wolfson's focus on Levinas's philosophically questionable "city-country/pagan soil" critique to (2) Wolfson's nod to Levinas's elsewhere linking Nazi blood-spilling to the "essential possibility of elemental Evil" in Heideggerian ontology. Regardless of the success of this latter line of reasoning in Levinas, it is clearly a philosophically robust, three-dimensional critique of Heidegger. And to be clear, I am not suggesting that Wolfson does not know this; I am suggesting that he does—and that somehow something other than that is unfolding in this part of his text, and that this "something other" indeed bears traces of Levinas's actual philosophical critique of Heidegger. As Wolfson of course knows, Levinas's critique of elemental evil in Heideggerian ontology is not about superstitions. On the contrary, in his description of "elemental Evil" Levinas is referring to being in terms of the *il y a* (the "there is") in contrast to Heidegger's *es gibt*, a complex analysis of the violence of anonymous being, which is neither an iffy pseudo-sociology of "city vs. country life" nor a literarily vague nod to "paganism," but an extended philosophical/phenomenological critique of Heideggerian ontology.[17]

My point here is not to enter into a lengthy unpacking of Levinas's philosophical critique of Heideggerian ontology, but to flag that a trace of a more three-dimensional Levinas emerges in Wolfson's account as he moves from a fair critique of Levinas's one-dimensional critique of Heidegger, to a slippage of some sort—as if Levinas's idea of elemental evil is somehow just as nonphilosophical as the city-country critique that Wolfson highlights on his previous page: To be sure, Wolfson is correct to invalidate various of Levinas's more pseudo-sociological, vaguely literary, and reductionistic critiques of Heidegger and of a "Heidegger-Nazism link in paganism"; but this is not what is happening in Levinas's emphasis on elemental evil. In his reference to elemental evil, Levinas is embarking upon a philosophically robust analysis of *il y a* in contrast to Heideggerian *es gibt* operative, for Levinas, in Heidegger as in Hitlerism. Leaving aside whether this philosophical critique is strong or weak, it is a philosophical critique, not a loose literary nod. Levinas's elemental evil critique is actually a marker for some of Levinas's most serious philosophical critiques of Heidegger and Nazism—and indeed, Levinas's most serious philosophical critiques of their connection. And so, in its mention of elemental evil right after critiquing Levinas's city-country critique of Heidegger, Wolfson's text reveals a trace of a more three-dimensional, robustly philosophical Levinasian critique of Heidegger.

THE SECOND TRACE OF A LEVINASIAN SPECTER EMERGES IN JUST THOSE SAME pages where Wolfson describes Levinas's "inability to find a way to absolve Heidegger" as Levinas's having "placed him [viz. Heidegger] beyond the pale of being human."[18] Wolfson reads Levinas's inability to forgive Heidegger as a failure on Levinas's part to treat Heidegger as a human being, "since the ability to forgive is commensurate to the infinite ethical responsibility he [viz. Levinas] imparts to every individual vis-à-vis the transcendence of the Other."[19] Wolfson then goes on to share Levinas's Talmudic reading "Toward the Other" in which Levinas notes—in the context of a rabbinic narrative about one important rabbi not forgiving another important rabbi—that it is "difficult to forgive Heidegger."[20]

Wolfson can be seen here as charging Levinas with the kind of nonvulnerable, hard-hearted reading-learning practices he has already called on readers to avoid when approaching Heidegger. He can also be seen as charging Levinas with a kind of hypocrisy: Given Levinas's own teachings on the infinite responsibility due to another human, shouldn't he forgive Heidegger? And if he doesn't forgive Heidegger, doesn't he do so on risk of failing to treat him as a fellow human? In what again seems a height of nonvulnerability, Levinas doesn't seem to be practicing what he preaches.

But the trace of a decidedly more vulnerable Levinas here emerges in Wolfson's intertextual invitation to "Toward the Other," Levinas's own difficult encounter with a difficult rabbinic encounter with nonforgiveness. The rabbinic text from Tractate Yoma is short and complicated and at least prima facie centers on the following event:

> Rab was commenting upon a text before Rabbi. When Rab Hiyya came in, he started his reading from the beginning again. Bar Kappara came in—he began again; Rab Simeon, the son of Rabbi, came in, and Rab again went back to the beginning. Then Rab Hanina bar Hama came in, and Rab said: How many times am I to repeat myself! He did not go back to the beginning. Rab Hanina was wounded by it. For thirteen years, on Yom Kippur eve, Rab went to seek forgiveness, and Rav Hanina refused to be appeased.[21]

Levinas utters his famous line about the difficulty of forgiving Heidegger in the context of expositing a rabbinic story about the time one rabbi failed to forgive another rabbi. In other words, Levinas puts forth his own difficulty forgiving Heidegger not as a defiant howl but in the context of nothing less than a Jewish text about the difficulty of forgiving each other. Furthermore and relatedly, far from triumphantly wishing Heidegger to hell in a text on nonforgiveness that Levinas finds straightforward or otherwise emboldening, Levinas wrestles overtly with what precisely this Jewish text on nonforgiving is meant to teach us. Indeed, Levinas notes that this story of one rabbi not forgiving another rabbi—for what at least on the story's surface is a seemingly petty matter of not looking up from his studies to acknowledge him—"makes no sense" to him and makes him feel deeply troubled.[22] Translated back onto his own claim that it is difficult to forgive Heidegger, this would seem to suggest that Levinas finds his own difficulty in this regard neither excellent nor justified nor a self-assured "take that, Heidegger!" but, on the contrary, confounding and troubling.[23] Indeed, in connecting his difficulty in forgiving Heidegger with this particular rabbinic story, Levinas—as Wolfson himself notes—can be seen as comparing Heidegger to Rab, an important Jewish figure and esteemed Jewish teacher. And to the extent that we take the dramatic arc of the rabbinic tale itself to be highlighting the if not prima facie *petty*, then at any rate prima facie *small* nature of the infraction at hand, Levinas is arguably comparing Heidegger to Rab in the context of a story that not only presumes him to be a great teacher, but a great teacher whose sin was slight enough to presumably warrant—even as it does not manage to receive—forgiveness. Far from a depiction of a sinful tyrant committing a terrible crime, we have here the story of a great and respected teacher making a seemingly minor mistake in failing to look up from his studies.

ALL OF THIS HELPS FURTHER EMPHASIZE THAT LEVINAS IS *NOT* "NOT TREATING Heidegger as a human" in his claim that it is difficult to forgive Heidegger. He is, rather, identifying in Heideggerian ontology a lacuna. And this lacuna, I suggest, relates to the phenomenology of vulnerable learning—related to the vulnerability of the human condition itself—to which Levinas points us in a kind of unthought in his own analysis of this difficult rabbinic story.

For in the context of recounting to his reader how uncomfortable he was with not knowing how to analyze such a petty-sounding story of nonforgiveness between rabbis, Levinas also recounts for us that he came to a reading of this rabbinic text in conversation with "a young Jewish poet, Mrs. Atlan." In essence, Levinas here performs the deepest teaching in this rabbinic tale about human vulnerability; viz. he philosophizes about this perplexing rabbinic narrative not by himself, but with another human—a woman, a poet, a person who we might gather from the context is not as well-known as Levinas. Aside from Levinas's own attempts to exposit this confounding rabbinic text on his own, and even leaving aside the content of Levinas's and Mrs. Atlan's different insights, what is most important here is the performative opening in which he turns to the Other for learning. A trace of truth emerges, in other words, in Levinas's off-handed mention of the young Jewish poet with whom he discussed this vexing story, and from whom he learned something new. Again, aside from what she taught him is the fact *that* she taught him—and the fact that Levinas approached learning in the spirit of a turn toward the Other resonant with his own vulnerable ethical frame.

But consider how this opens up a new way to read the rabbinic story: The story describes a rabbi whose only apparent offense was that he failed to look up to acknowledge the entry of another rabbi into the house of study. On its surface, the story seems so petty as to lead Levinas to express his discomfort. We have already seen truth emerging in the trace of Levinas's side-mention of Mrs. Atlan. But in the trace of that trace a further (and related) truth emerges in the performance of the rabbi in the story: We are invited, in other words, to cast fresh significance onto a Talmudic tale of a rabbi's so-called tiny error of not looking up. Sure, it is perhaps a trivial offense in the context of the story for one person to not look up when another person—even a great teacher—enters the room. But read now in the wake of Levinas's own turn to Mrs. Atlan, a new trace emerges: What we are being asked to consider is not that "one particular rabbi did not look up at one other particular rabbi"; on the contrary, we are being invited to question any form of life in which we do not look up at each other. In learning, as in life.

But here we return to Heidegger. We have already seen a vulnerability in Heidegger; indeed, Wolfson, in his own act of (and invitation to us to join him in) vulnerable reading, exposes us to the vulnerable Heideggerian pulse of a "most solitary heart" making its "leap into the middle of beyng." And if we turn to Heidegger's own "phenomenology of learning," we find a vision of teaching as an opportunity to bring students to an open spirit of "knowingness" (*Wissendsein*) that goes hand-in-hand with Heidegger's own subordination of politics to learning: As Wolfson reminds us, Heidegger rejects any notion of National Socialism replacing a system of genuine "knowledge cultivation" (*Wissenserziehung*); the political structure, on the contrary, must be guided by an enlivening educational system and by the cultivation of "general questioning" therein.[24] We can discern here a spirit of openness and receptivity that connects one's capacity to be appropriated by and to beyng, as well as one's capacity to learn. And it is in this same spirit of openness and receptivity that we may bridge into Wolfson's own call to readers who too quickly, and nonvulnerably, lambast Heidegger to consider slowing down.

And yet, even in Wolfson's opening us onto this more vulnerable opening in Heidegger, a trace of an even more vulnerable vulnerability in Levinas enters in. For in the context of his own critique of Levinas's critique of Heidegger, Wolfson opens the door to Levinas's "Toward the Other" in which learning and truth erupt only and always in relation to a neighbor, Mrs. Atlan, and with her a new sense of truth itself emerges in the marginalia of Levinas's lecture, which itself emerges in the marginalia of Wolfson's critique of Levinas. And all of this is set in the context not only of Levinas's own vulnerable mode of learning in, with, and from an Other, but Wolfson's own vulnerable call to be more vulnerable learners. Into Wolfson's own call to a more vulnerable mode of learning with Heidegger enters a Levinasian trace more vulnerable than even Heidegger's moment of appropriation by beyng:

> In . . . relation we have recognized language, produced only in the face to face; and in language we have recognized teaching. Teaching is a way for truth to be produced such that it is not my work, such that I could not derive it from my own interiority. In affirming such a production of truth we modify the original meaning of truth.[25]

We are called back to a "looking up" to other humans in learning that is even more vulnerable than the vulnerable spirit of knowledge cultivation in Heidegger. Heidegger's learning is vulnerable in relation to being's disclosure-in-concealment. But it is not vulnerable in relation to the neighbor in the way that Levinas's—and Wolfson's—philosophy of learning is. A call to the seriousness of vulnerably looking up at our neighbors in this way emerges as the key to the rabbinic teaching about a rabbi whose sin of not looking up was indeed so great that it could not be forgiven, as it also emerges as the concealed-revealed trace of Levinas's own phenomenology of vulnerable learning in Wolfson. It is a deep trace of Levinas in the very space of Wolfson's critique of Levinas's critique of Heidegger, and it opens us into the depth of vulnerable reading, vulnerable learning, and vulnerable living.

And here, we are invited to re-read Levinas's "it is difficult to forgive Heidegger" in light of the deep vulnerability of Levinas's most fundamental sense of pardon:[26] Levinas's ethical view is not that my ground in responsibility to you means I must forgive you; Levinas's view is the precise reverse, viz. that my ground in responsibility to you means that I am precariously grounded in my own hopeless hope that you might one day forgive me. Levinasian ethical subjectivity is a delicate space in which I reside in a precarious and vulnerable hope—a hopeless hope, really—to be forgiven by the Other. Far from suggesting that Levinas triumphantly and resolutely denies Heidegger humanity, "it is difficult to forgive Heidegger" marks a deeply vulnerable comportment that marks a precarious fragility in and between us. It is difficult to forgive Heidegger because we are fragile systems—indeed, the kind of fragile systems whose ownmost freedoms rely on Others to whom we are beholden. Far from the virile, agential call to forgive others (as if we are able to enact such miracles by sheer force of will), and far from virile theologies of God-agents forgiving us for our sins (as if God is able to enact such miracles by sheer force of will),[27] Levinas's "it is difficult to forgive Heidegger" speaks to the vulnerable precarity of a human life lived in the hope of release from oneself by one's neighbor. "It is difficult to forgive Heidegger" does not mean "I am not forgiving Heidegger"; "it is difficult to forgive Heidegger" means that it is difficult to forgive Heidegger. And this signals not bombastic self-satisfaction or hard-heartedness; on the contrary, it signals the human condition in and from the difficulty of history, the difficulty of agency, and the difficulty of subjectivity itself as never simply a "living from" itself. It signals, in other words, that we are not self-willing super-agents, but precarious, vulnerable, and trembling ones. Would that we could forgive one another on demand; we are not that kind of agent. And that is because we are more vulnerable than that. And it is precisely that vulnerability that marks us as always in and as a hopeless hope of being forgiven, of being justified in our being, and of being invested with our ownmost freedom by the neighbor. And it is the mark of the phenomenology of vulnerable reading, learning, and living.

I HAVE RECOMMENDED MULTIPLE WAYS IN WHICH THE TRACE OF THIS LEVINASIAN remainder emerges from within Wolfson's treatment of Heidegger, including Wolfson's critique of Levinas's critique of Heidegger, and including Wolfson's own call to read and learn more vulnerably. And in all this, the trace of this Levinasian remainder emerges most exuberantly from within Wolfson's own life, including his life as a teacher and scholar. While I myself did not have the pleasure of officially being his student, I have seen and experienced firsthand over many decades the countless ways Wolfson "looks up" in his learning in relation to others. This is obvious in relation to his students. It is obvious in relation to scholars like myself whom he has generously engaged over the years. And it is evident in what has become Wolfson's hallmark of extensive and meticulous footnotes in which due attention is given to a vast array of interlocutors. This is not simply a style, but an ethical opening of vulnerable reading, learning, and living in relation to others. Even in the depths of his entry into Heideggerian thinking, and even in releasing us from despotic reading practices that miss the thought—and certainly the unthought—in Heidegger's thinking, Wolfson's own performance of truth reveals a trace of Levinas. Wolfson's life and life work is the performance of nothing less than a phenomenology of vulnerable learning in which the teacher "looks up" to greet the other.

It is, to return to Levinas on teaching, a modification in the face-to-face of the original meaning of truth. It is, to end with Wolfson's own poetic intimation with which we began, a time of "i and you," which brings us back to where we were not before.

NOTES

1. In this fragmentary opening, I have, in other words, pulled lines from two of Wolfson's complete poems and have assembled them side by side; the "[. . .]" separates the two sets. And as my own poetic nod to a colleague from whom I have learned a great deal about the intersection of philosophy and poetry, I have here employed a tetragrammatical framing that I sometimes use in constructing some of my own poems; in this method, I bring together lines of text or music lyrics or map coordinate locations that appear on page or line or degree 26; then I listen to what opens. The opening lines here are the closing lines from Wolfson's "retinal repercussions," the 26th poem in his collection of 92 poems (Elliot R. Wolfson, *Footdreams & Treetales: Ninety-Two Poems* [New York: Fordham University Press, 2007], 34); the closing lines are the closing lines from Wolfson's "from before / until after," the only words that appear on page 26.
2. Elliot R. Wolfson, *The Duplicity of Philosophy's Shadow: Heidegger, Nazism, and the Jewish Other* (New York: Columbia University Press, 2018), xxii.

3. Wolfson, *Duplicity of Philosophy's Shadow*, xvii.
4. Martin Heidegger, *Ponderings V*; epigraph with which Wolfson opens his *Heidegger and Kabbalah: Hidden Gnosis and the Path of Poiēsis* (Bloomington: Indiana University Press, 2019).
5. As Vallega-Neu clarifies: "Note that 'beyng' renders Heidegger's archaic way of writing *Sein* (being) as *Seyn*. With the 'y' Heidegger intends to indicate that being should be understood in terms of an occurrence and not as a being or entity of some kind that we may represent." Daniela Vallega-Neu, "Ereignis: The Event of Appropriation," in *Martin Heidegger: Key Concepts*, ed. Bret W. Davis (New York: Routledge, 2014), 152, note 7.
6. Wolfson, *Heidegger and Kabbalah*, 112; citing Martin Heidegger, *Off the Beaten Track*, ed. and trans. Julian Young and Kenneth Haynes (Cambridge: Cambridge University Press, 2002), 197; *Holzwege* [GA 5] (Frankfurt: Vittorio Klostermann, 1977), 265.
7. Wolfson, *Heidegger and Kabbalah*, 112; citing Heidegger, *Off the Beaten Track*, 32, 56 (emphasis in the original); *Beiträge zur Philosophy (Vom Ereignis)* [GA 65] (Frankfurt: Vittorio Klostermann, 1989), 70.
8. Wolfson, *Duplicity of Philosophy's Shadow*, 7.
9. Wolfson, *Duplicity of Philosophy's Shadow*, 169.
10. Wolfson, *Duplicity of Philosophy's Shadow*, 169.
11. Wolfson, *Duplicity of Philosophy's Shadow*, xxi.
12. Wolfson, *Duplicity of Philosophy's Shadow*, xxii.
13. Vallega-Neu, "Ereignis," 145; translations from *Contributions* are by Vallega-Neu. See Martin Heidegger, *Contributions to Philosophy (Of the Event)*, trans. Richard Rojcewicz and Daniela Vallega-Neu (Bloomington: Indiana University Press, 2012).
14. By "word-wounds" I mean to refer not simply to psychological trauma but to a deeply embodied conceptual-with-affective phenomenological encounter with histories and presents—and futures; it is the way that past and present forces fill us with hopes and hopelessnesses that riddle us with paradoxes that we enact and perform daily on the public stage. For a starting treatment, see my forthcoming "Lizards, Lasers, and Liturgical Politics: The Drama of Word-Wounds from Racism to Antisemitism," special issue of *Religions* on "Jewish Thought in Times of Crisis," ed. Elias Sacks and Andrea Dara Cooper.
15. Wolfson, *Duplicity of Philosophy's Shadow*, 20.
16. See, for example, Elliot R. Wolfson, "Secrecy, Modesty, and the Feminine: Kabbalistic Traces in the Thought of Levinas," in *The Exorbitant: Emmanuel Levinas Between Jews and Christians*, ed. Kevin Hart and Michael A. Signer (New York: Fordham University Press, 2010); and Elliot R. Wolfson, *A Dream Interpreted Within a Dream: Oneiropoiesis and the Prism of Imagination* (New York: Zone Books, 2011) (with the equivalent of an entire chapter on Levinas in the footnotes alone). I am, in other words, not suggesting that Wolfson doesn't understand Levinas.
17. For Levinas on the *il y a* (the "there is"), see for example Emmanuel Levinas, *Existence and Existents*, trans. A. Lingis with foreword by R. Bernasconi (Pittsburgh: Duquesne University Press, 1947/2001). See too his analysis of the elemental in Levinas, *Totality and Infinity* (Pittsburgh: Duquesne University Press, 1961/2001).
18. Wolfson, *Duplicity of Philosophy's Shadow*, 21.

19. Wolfson, *Duplicity of Philosophy's Shadow*, 21.
20. See Emmanuel Levinas, "Toward the Other," in *Nine Talmudic Readings by Emmanuel Levinas*, ed. Annette Aronowicz (Bloomington: Indiana University Press, 1965/1990), 25. This rabbinic analysis was delivered by Levinas in 1963 and published in France in 1965.
21. From Tractate Yoma, 85a–b; as cited and translated in Levinas, "Toward the Other," 13.
22. Levinas, "Toward the Other," 24.
23. To be sure, the rabbinic incident is couched in a Mishnaic nod to forgiving, not not-forgiving, when the offender seeks forgiveness: "The transgressions of man toward God are forgiven him by the Day of Atonement; the transgressions against other people are not forgiven him by the Day of Atonement if he has not first appeased the other person" (as cited and translated in Levinas, "Toward the Other," 12). So one can simply say that Levinas is finding it difficult to forgive Heidegger precisely because Heidegger did not seek atonement from him. This can in turn be taken to support a triumphal reading of Levinas's claim—"I am not forgiving Heidegger because he doesn't deserve it!"; but that is not the reading I am pursuing for reasons I explore below. But even at the most basic level, that reading seems to ignore the fact that Levinas doesn't say "I don't forgive Heidegger" but that "it is difficult to forgive" him. That is a very different—and far more vulnerable—claim that deserves to be treated as such.
24. I am drawing on Wolfson's summary analysis of Heidegger's 1933 rectoral address; see Wolfson, *Duplicity of Philosophy's Shadow*, 11–12.
25. Levinas, *Totality and Infinity*, 295.
26. This requires greater consideration and analysis; I take this up more fully and slowly in my forthcoming study, *Pause and Pardon: Early Levinas on Embodiment, Effort, and Excess.*
27. This is supported by the rabbinic story we have been exploring being connected to a Mishnah about God's not being able to forgive humans for the offenses they commit against each other (an idea that emerges in other Jewish texts as well); see note 23.

THE MIRROR THROUGH WHICH ONE SEES THE OTHER

Wolfson, Heidegger, Kabbalah, and the Making of a Primary Jewish Text

SHAUL MAGID

As scholars in the humanities, we often view ourselves as the architects and purveyors of what is called secondary literature; we write our texts largely about other texts, or figures, excavating the details, arguments, and relevance of previous material, often reconstructing their reception, revising earlier iterations, and offering novel interpretations. In this way, even if we are not historians per se, we often work in a historical register, we situate arguments in context, and we trace the vicissitudes of time, history, and influence as causes that mark development, evolution, or devolution of trends and ideas.

We are trained in graduate school to be wary of constructive thinking dressed as analytical thinking. Normative claims about our subject are shunned and viewed as treasonous to our guild. We are not theologians or rabbis; we are scholars. But in some cases, not many, one's scholarship reaches a place where it begins to venture beyond itself into the rocky terrain of a philosophical or theological construction, as opposed to writing *about* a philosophical or theological claim. There are times when the scholar sheds the cloak of a secondary text and becomes a primary text, when scholarship bursts out of its second-tier place to become the subject of scholarship itself. Elliot Wolfson's body of work is an illustration of such a phenomenon. Perhaps best illustrated by his 2005 *Language, Eros, Being* (henceforth LEB), Wolfson's work, specifically his later work, breaks free of secondary literature status to become a primary text worthy of scholarly examination in its own right. This is not because Wolfson abandons the scholarly apparatus; quite the contrary, the work is replete with cross- and interdisciplinary methods of analysis of the highest order. Rather, it is because works like LEB or his 2014 *Giving Beyond the Gift* are constructive philosophical/theological projects built on the edifice of scholarship. They are more expansive in nature, more audacious in scope, and less focused on one thinker, school, or tradition. They traverse a multitude of textual traditions woven together through a complex hermeneutical lens. While they do often make arguments about a historical moment, or help us see a textual tradition with more clarity, their novelty is that they utilize a plethora of learning to make an argument about thinking, about living, about the human condition more generally. This is why I have often found critiques of Wolfson's work by scholars as missing the point. They are reading the work as if it is a secondary text. This, I submit, is an error.[1]

Below I engage two books written by Wolfson in 2018 and 2019 that to my mind exemplify the transition from a secondary to a primary text. Both are about Martin Heidegger, arguably one of the greatest philosophical minds of the twentieth century. The first is *The Duplicity of Philosophy's Shadow* and the second is *Heidegger and Kabbalah*.[2] The first largely engages Heidegger's antisemitism, which then extends to a critique of Heidegger's mistaken views on *das Judentum* to suggest two things: first, that had Heidegger better understood *das Judentum* he would have been more sympathetic to it since in some fashion, at least, his own philosophy reflects some basic tenets of that tradition, in Wolfson's estimation, through the lens of Kabbalah. That is the analytic part. And second, that when viewed from within the deep recesses of the kabbalistic tradition, read through cross-cultural lenses, some of the more troubling aspects of Heidegger's philosophy can be detected within Judaism itself. This is the constructive part. This is not an indictment against Judaism per se. Rather, it is to suggest that the Kabbalists were acutely attuned to the underside of the holy, what elsewhere Wolfson calls luminal darkness, as an extension of, in some sense wedded to, the holy in a way that at minimum problematizes and maximally subverts the very binaries that undergird normative depictions of Judaism, that is, permissible-prohibited, pure-impure, holy-profane, Jew-gentile.[3] On this reading, the Sabbatian heresy was, as Scholem argued, not an aberration of Judaism as much as a particular iteration of a tension that filters through the entire system. Even more strongly, that Sabbatianism was a culmination of everything that preceded it and a prelude to everything that came afterward.[4] Below I will show how Wolfson uses that tension to excavate the Moses-Balaam dichotomy and, by extension, Kabbalah and Heidegger, suggesting that in some way Heidegger's antisemitism is both a misunderstanding of his subject (*das Judentum*) and also a tension flowing like an underground spring beneath the terrain of the tradition itself.

IT IS NOT SURPRISING THAT *DUPLICITY* BEGAN AS THE FIRST CHAPTER OF *HEIDEGGER AND KABBALAH* and only became its own book when it outgrew its original introductory stature. In some ways *Duplicity* begins in a more formal scholarly mode, accessing the nature of Heidegger's antisemitism in conversation with the plethora of literature written about it. Wolfson's analysis stands out in part because unlike many of Heidegger's contemporary detractors, his deep learning of the Jewish tradition makes Heidegger's offenses more complex and nuanced, not because those other scholars misunderstand Heidegger as much as they misunderstand what Heidegger is criticizing (not Jews per se, but Jewishness or *das Judentum*).[5] And they fail to see where Heidegger himself is mistaken about the subject of his critique. Wolfson writes as follows:

> The space we must inhabit, as uncomfortable as it might be, is one in which we acknowledge that Heidegger was both a Nazi given to anti-Semitic jargon and an incisive philosopher whose thinking not only was responding to the urgencies of his epoch but also contains the potential to unravel a thorny knot of politics and philosophy relevant for the present as much as the past. . . . Heidegger is thus neither defensible nor disposable; his thinking—and this includes above all, his philosophical scapegoating of Jews under the rubric of *das Judentum*—demands reflective analysis and critical questioning. This injunction is not fulfilled by refutation.[6]

Wolfson thus inhabits the paradox experienced by both Emmanuel Levinas and Leo Strauss encapsulated in Strauss's comment, "Only a great thinker could help us in our intellectual plight. But here is the trouble: the only great thinker in our time is Heidegger."[7] Wolfson is more sympathetic to the approach of thinkers such as Strauss, for very different reasons, than many contemporary critics of Heidegger about *das Judentum*. However, he comes at Heidegger with the wealth of the kabbalistic tradition offering an intricate analysis of the complex affinities and differences between Heidegger and *das Judentum*, the latter of which Heidegger excludes from his philosophy of Dasein. Never abandoning the antisemitism evident in Heidegger's work, Wolfson notices the Jewish tradition at times seems to support the very assumptions that Heidegger deploys to exclude them. His critique in *Duplicity* then is not solely about Heidegger but in some way about certain components of Judaism itself. Here Wolfson exhibits what Hannah Arendt called "thinking without a bannister," allowing thought to take the thinker to places that challenge the very nature of the subject of thought.[8]

It is really in the final chapter of *Duplicity*, "Heidegger, Balaam, and the Duplicity of Philosophy's Shadow," where we see a transition from the analytic scholarship of the first five chapters to the constructive finale. This chapter, I submit, is the true prelude to the full-blown primary text, *Heidegger and Kabbalah*. It is in this final chapter where Wolfson turns his critique of Heidegger into a constructive critique of Judaism itself, thus subverting any binary one may have imaginatively constructed—in which Heidegger himself believed—between Heidegger and *das Judentum*.

To illustrate this, Wolfson offers a kabbalistic reading of the prophetic biblical archvillain Balaam. The Bible tells us, "Never again did there arise a prophet in Israel like Moses" (Deut. 34:10), to which the rabbis respond, "In Israel none arose, but in the nations of the world there arose, and who was it? Balaam." This rabbinic gloss on one word in the Bible "in Israel" (*b'Yisrael*) becomes, in the kabbalistic literature of the Zohar and Lurianic Kabbalah, a leitmotif to exemplify the notion of "the left contained in the right" or the dialectical intermingling of good and evil such that each by definition contains elements of its opposite. Balaam thus becomes a figure from the nations whose evil and nefarious character contains lofty sparks of holiness that are shared with the Bible's quintessential hero, Moses.

It is not simply that evil supposes good and good supposes evil. It is that evil *contains* good and good *contains* evil; the two are inseparable because each is part of its opposite. Moreover, truly understanding Balaam's evil requires excavating the sparks embedded therein, which can only be understood, and thus liberated, through close examination. This idea is expressed in Heidegger in a variety of ways as well. For example, claiming that "illumination consists of exposing the radiance of the shadow in the shadow of the radiance," Wolfson asks us to consider Heidegger as a modern adaption of the Zohar's depiction of Balaam.

> As part of the Balaam complex, Heidegger articulated views that cast a sharp distinction between Jews and non-Jews, sometimes following hackneyed stereotypes that were utilized by the Nazis. But just as the kabbalistic tradition portrayed Balaam as one who achieved in the realm of the blasphemous the same enlightenment as Moses, so we can think of Heidegger as attaining the uppermost level of knowledge by descending to the depths of depravity.[9]

The binary of good and evil cannot be sustained in the kabbalistic imagination. As the Lurianic Kabbalist Hayyim Vital notes, "when the good of Moses was refined from the evil of Balaam, there necessarily remained in him some good sparks from the root of Moses our master, peace be upon him, and they necessarily will go out and be purified from there by many deaths and reincarnations, as we know."[10] Vital notes elsewhere that the process of Balaam's repentance, obliquely alluded to in scripture, is the very fabric of reconciliation and redemption.[11]

As Wolfson reads both Kabbalah and Heidegger, Moses and Balaam, the lesson of Balaam, and perhaps *of* Heidegger too—and *for* Heidegger too—is not to illuminate the errors in his thinking as much as to find the truth out of which those errors emerge in part because Balaam, and Heidegger, are exemplars of such error and rectification. Wolfson thus is able to maintain Heidegger's antisemitism and yet not dispel his thought, not as an apologetic gesture that attempts to separate his philosophy from his antisemitism, but by noticing that in the very dark recesses of Heidegger's thinking, Judaism can be illumined. Wolfson thinks *with* Heidegger both to subvert him and also to use him as he turns toward his next subject, Judaism. He thus ends *Duplicity* as follows: "It is never sufficient, and indeed it is potentially dangerous, to cultivate a worldview wherein inclusivity is only included in the demarcation of the exclusive." With this the truly constructive project that is *Heidegger and Kabbalah* begins.

HEIDEGGER AND KABBALAH STANDS AS A LANDMARK STUDY, A PRIMARY TEXT, OF Judaism *and* philosophy. In the realm of Jewish philosophy, I dare say it is the most important study on or about Judaism produced in the twenty-first century.[12] It is also a major contribution to the study of Martin Heidegger and the humanities more generally. This work contributes to how we read traditions of inquiry to both critique and then reconstruct moral possibilities and excavate metaphysical hazards. In my view, this book will join a very narrow canon of major Jewish philosophical works in the twentieth and twenty-first century, including Hermann Cohen's *Religion of Reason* and Franz Rosenzweig's *Star of Redemption*.

While Heidegger's antisemitism is not the subject of this second book, it looms over it. For scholars of Jewish studies, seriously engaging Martin Heidegger presents nothing less than a moral dilemma. Heidegger was a Nazi, and his repudiation of his Nazi past was never unequivocal. And yet with all this, many Jewish thinkers were undeterred and continued to engage with Heidegger as a major philosophical voice. In his 1982 radio interview with Phillipe Nemo, Emanuel Levinas says, "Very early on I had great admiration for this book [Heidegger's *Being and Time*]. It is one of the finest books in the history of philosophy—I say this after years of reflection. One of the finest among four or five others."[13] Note that this was in 1982, long after the famous *Der Spiegel* interview in 1966 where Heidegger refused to unequivocally repudiate his affiliation with Nazism. But the robust scholarly discussion of Heidegger and his Nazi past that ensued in the 1990s had not yet begun when Levinas made his remark.[14] Knowing what Levinas knew then, one can argue that he would have maintained his position even today.

Instead of concluding, as some have, that Heidegger should be excised from the philosophical canon, in *Heidegger and Kabbalah* Elliot Wolfson takes us deeper into his work and deeper into the dilemma, not by analyzing Heidegger or by comparing him to Kabbalah per se but by thinking *with* Heidegger and *with* Kabbalah about the nature of existence and the existence of the Jew, or *das Judentum*. Wolfson dwells upon the moral dilemma of reading Heidegger in relation to Judaism, not to solve the problem but to illustrate that a fuller rendering of the implications of Heidegger's work requires us to grapple with Judaism as well. This is because, as I mentioned above, some Jewish thought-worlds—such as Kabbalah—share surprising affinities with Heidegger that are worth examining closely, since these affinities illuminate the greatness of both but also the dangers of both.

The distinctive nature of this project raises the question: who is the audience for this book? The answer, I submit, must include that Wolfson wrote this book for himself; it is the culmination of decades of intense reflection on both Heidegger and Kabbalah. But more interestingly, and importantly, this is a book that will *create* its audience. It is more than a book *about* Heidegger and/or Kabbalah (others have written on, or noticed the affinity between, Heidegger and Judaism).[15] Wolfson's book demonstrates how to think more broadly about each refracted through the lens of the other. It is not comparative in any conventional sense. Rather, it is a book that trains its reader along the way in how Wolfson wants us to read both Heidegger *and* Kabbalah, and to *read* and *think* with, through, and beyond philosophical canons. Thus only after reading the book from beginning to end does one then understand what the book is about. There is no introductory guide to the argument or even the project. One jumps into a deep end that only gets deeper. This is indicative of a primary text such as Rosenzweig's *Star of Redemption* or Hermann Cohen's *Religion of Reason*.

Heidegger and Kabbalah is complex, difficult, and challenging. The reason to read it is because it offers a revolutionary intervention into the very fabric of Kabbalah and Judaism itself, into its radical metaphysics (or its rejection of metaphysics), in a way that simply has not been done before. And in regard to Heidegger, it fully confronts the problematic, and tragic, elements of this thinking while still believing that his new vision of conceiving "being" beyond ontology holds the potential for undoing its own destructive tendencies. And it also offers us another way to conceive of thinking more generally. The book challenges its reader to view its intricate details as a tapestry that weaves through the most fundamental metaphysical and ontological questions in the history of philosophy and kabbalistic reflections on the nature of existence.

Wolfson's reading of Heidegger suggests that there is a deep moral dilemma in Heidegger's antisemitism and anti-Judaism/*das Judentum*. Unbeknownst to Heidegger, his intervention and critique of Western philosophy resonates deeply with Kabbalah's rejection of the rational Jewish philosophical tradition in a way that belies Heidegger's own problematic view of Judaism. Others have noticed Heidegger's use of mystical ideas drawn from Kabbalah, in particular influences from the Christian mystic Jakob Boehme (1575–1624) through the German romanticist Friedrich Wilhelm Joseph Schelling (1775–1854). But Wolfson's project is not about tracing influences common in secondary literature but rather structural affinities philosophically considered, regardless of historical influence. Wolfson argues that, in fact, Heidegger's critique of Western philosophy parallels to some degree Kabbalah's critique of normative Jewish notions of the divine and by extension, normative renderings of the covenant. To do this, Wolfson reads Kabbalah fully outside Judaism, arguing that its brilliance, and its hazards, emerge in full view only with such a reading.

Deep into the book, Wolfson makes a passing remark that serves as a methodological frame of his analysis. "Lest there be any misunderstanding, let me restate unequivocally that the question of influence—the issue that unfailingly consumes the mind of intellectual and social historians working within the confines of the academy—is not of paramount importance to me. What is far more tantalizing is the fact that there is a constellation of thought based on conceptual correspondences."[16] The "restating" appears to gesture back to a remark in the Introduction. Advocating a "textual-philological criteria," as opposed to a conventional historical method, Wolfson writes, "It is not influence that is the focal point of my concern . . . but rather the constellation of themes underlying the respective viewpoints of Heidegger and the kabbalists, a constellation that demonstrates the disarming correlation—as opposed to dialectical coincidence—of sameness through difference, that is, the identity of the nonidentical in the preservation of the nonidentity of the identical."[17] Wolfson is concerned with the "conceptual affinities" (while acknowledging possible historical influences) of the way Heidegger and Kabbalah undermine both the Platonic binary and dialectic as well as the Hegelian reconciliation. Distinguishing between "dialectical coïncidence" and "disarming correlation," Wolfson argues that both Kabbalah and Heidegger, independent of each other and contesting different phenomenological frames, arrive at similar points of intervention whereby transcendence is undermined through the instantiation of that which can only appear through its absence, disclosing itself only through nondisclosure.

To understand Wolfson's reading, there is a preliminary assumption one must accept. One must liberate Kabbalah from its "monotheistic" orbit. Citing the Slovenian philosopher Slavoj Žižek (b. 1949) responding to Schelling's notion of the coincidence of opposites, we read, the task is "to locate the source of the split between Good and Evil in God himself *while remaining within the field of monotheism*, the task which German mysticism (Jakob Böhme) and later philosophers who pursued their logic (Schelling, Hegel) tried to accomplish."[18] Wolfson deploys this to highlight the way Heidegger resists that monotheization of the One that Žižek describes, and, by extension, as I read him, Wolfson suggests Kabbalah can be read that way as well.[19] In other words, once Kabbalah is read outside its own apologetic orbit of fortifying the transcendent monotheistic One, while simultaneously resisting it, the affinities with Heidegger begin to rise to the surface. "Inasmuch as *Ein Sof* comprehends the other as part of its otherness, however, and the sefirotic emanations unfold from the very being in which they are enfolded, in the final analysis, we must conclude that difference is comprised in the sameness of the other that is differently the same. The oneness of being, therefore, embraces the truth that being is not one."[20] This rendering of Kabbalah is not far-fetched as such tension with monotheism was noticed by Scholem and many close readers of Kabbalah in the scholarly world, not to mention the non-monotheistic origins of Ancient Israel.[21]

Wolfson's point here is that describing *Ein Sof* as some kind of Platonic One misses the kabbalistic undermining of that very notion of *Ein Sof* that is neither being nor non-being. Nor is it the ground of transcendence, just as Heidegger's notion of Beyng is not a Schellengian "Subject" that transcends all being but rather a nullity, a *Nichts*, that exists between being and beings. Heidegger writes, "The god is neither a 'being' [*seiend*] nor a 'nonbeing' [*unseiend*] and is also not to be identified with *beyng* [*Seyn*]. Instead, *beyng* essentially occurs in the manner of time-space as that 'between' which can never be grounded in the god and also not in the human being (as some objectively present, living thing), but only in *Da-sein*."[22] Heidegger speaks about a (post)metaphysical, or meontological (the study of nonbeing) register, addressing the "last god who has come and gone" (by never coming in the first place, a futurity never realized nor realizable). Wolfson argues that *Ein Sof* serves a similar purpose. "The last god, as we may infer from the kabbalistic depiction of *Ein Sof*, is the god that can never arrive except as the god that does not arrive, the end that can never stop ending, the future that is perpetually impending."[23] He makes a similar argument about the messianic in his book *Open Secret* on Habad messianism. The secret doctrine of the messiah is that there is no messiah. Messianism remains true to the extent to which it never happens.[24] *Ein Sof* is that which bestows while withdrawing; it only "exists" by not existing or, perhaps, its existence can only be posited through its nonexistence, not unlike Meister Eckhart's claim that believing *in* God is itself already a disbelief *of* God.

Excavating the intricacies of *Ein Sof*, especially outside the monotheistic frame of the transcendent One, which constitutes many pages in *Heidegger and Kabbalah*, brings Wolfson to the conclusion that the most philosophically accurate approach to explaining this kabbalistic conundrum is through a Heideggerian lens. "*Ein Sof* thus can be said to correspond to Heidegger's event of thinking that must be constantly thought as unthought, the one true beyng of which all beings are simultaneously the manifestation of the concealment and the concealment of the manifestation."[25] Or, "*Ein Sof* can be described as the indescribable nothing that nihilates, the nihilation (*Nichtung*) that resists any attempt to affix nothing within an ontological perimeter, that is, to explain nothing exclusively in terms of beings."[26] The nonbeing (nihilation) of *Ein Sof* is pure negation, not a negation that is everything, nor a negation that produces anything. It does not *bring forth* anything outside of itself, its existence is only in the withholding of itself. The only possible defining quality of *Ein Sof* is *tzimtzum*, its own withholding of itself; *Ein Sof* as self-negation. *Ein Sof* can't fill the worlds because, as Wolfson argues, if *Ein Sof* is nullity, for it "to fill worlds means there are no worlds to be filled."[27]

But Wolfson maintains that Heidegger is a better arbiter of squaring the circle of kabbalistic metaphysics than those wedded to Kabbalah's own apologetic orientation, in part because Kabbalah often undermines that very orientation. That is part of its secrecy. Turning to Heidegger to unpack the dense and often self-contradictory readings of *Ein Sof* in Kabbalah speaks directly against the notion that Kabbalah offers any kind of system, be it metaphysical, theosophical, or even historiosophical (a term proffered by Gershom Scholem). In his discussion of time, Wolfson notes, "if we are to impute the notion of system to the kabbalah, it is a system that is nonsystematic; that is, a system that collapses under the weight of the overwhelming specification of details that develop in the attempt to map the fragmented univocity of the infinite."[28] The attempt to explain Schelling's notion of "pure Subjectivity" in any objective way reaches back to Azriel of Gerona's explanation of the ten *sephirot*, a thirteenth-century Neoplatonic attempt to answer the question "how does nothing, or no-thing (*Ein Sof*), become something."[29] Negative theology or apophasis works to a point, but it cannot overcome its own monotheistic orbit to reach the notion of pure negation. Wolfson's thesis is that Kabbalah speaks more freely when it is unbound by the shackles it imposes on itself. Put otherwise, as Heidegger notes in the *Beitrage*, "The age of the 'systems' has past."[30]

Wolfson here is on to something that is often overlooked when Kabbalah is read monotheistically, that is, as pan*en*theism, the "en" inserting transcendence (Oneness) into the body of immanence. The tension between the theistic and pantheistic nature of divinity in Lurianic teaching, a prime focus of Wolfson's analysis, is well documented.[31] What Wolfson resists is both any pan*en*theistic resolution and any theistic reading of the particulars as coming from the general. It is, rather, a Kabbalah "after the last god has passed." While kabbalistic sources are analyzed from the entire spectrum of kabbalistic teaching, Wolfson relies heavily on the Lurianic redaction of Kabbalah in a wide variety of forms, three in particular: Luria's erstwhile disciple Hayyim Vital (1542–1620), the Lithuanian Kabbalist Shlomo Elyashiv (1841–1926), known by the name of his major work, *Leshem Shevo Veahlama*, and the Habad kabbalism of Shneur Zalman of Liady (1745–1812) and the early Habad school. Also noteworthy are sources from the Vilna Gaon and his kabbalistic inheritors, the writings of Yemenite Kabbalist Shalom Sharabi (1720–1777), and the Sabbatian Nathan Ashkenazi of Gaza (1643–1680).

Elyashiv is particularly noteworthy here not only because his work has largely remained unexcavated in scholarship, but because he offers a philosophically inflected kabbalism that takes its reader down the rabbit hole of infinite details such that infinity itself is exhibited in a cascading infinite regress.[32] His is thus a system that undermines itself with the nonclosure of infinite fragmentation. Any remaining binary of the "one and the many" that may have survived earlier Kabbalah seems to collapse in the intricacies of Elyashiv's work.

Speaking more generally but as I read him having Kabbalists like Elyashiv's work in mind, Wolfson writes,

> The hermeneutic aim of the systemless system is not to subjugate particulars under the stamp of generality but rather to demonstrate how generality is sculpted from the variability and volatility of particulars. The drift of thought exemplified by kabbalists corresponds, therefore, to what Heidegger described as the *Grundstimmung*, the "basic disposition," or literally the grounding-attunement, that is, the attunement to the ground as the grounding of the nonground, an attunement that does not loosen the "rigor of the structure [*Gefüge*]."[33]

Infinity as Oneness is replaced by the infinite details of infinite regression and fragmentation that results in a worldliness of being that holds the infinite itself.

Using Heideggerian language, his point is that "*beyng* is present in the very beings from which it is absent . . . the mystery that is bestowed in the refusal of bestowal."[34] "We do better to think of the universal as being constituted relentlessly in light of the random and indiscriminate particulars, the *universal singularity*, wherein the infinite materializes in the finite, the negation of the negation of negation."[35] The last locution points to Wolfson's step (via Heidegger) beyond the Hegelian dialectic to reject any universal reconciliation where anything concealed is ever revealed outside of its concealment. In a sense Wolfson is reading Kabbalah here against its own apologetic inclinations, a cautionary reluctance of kabbalistic discourse that often fails to conceal its subversive undoing of its own project. By enabling the tension to remain through the infinite regress of the particular at the expense of collapsing into a Neoplatonic/Hegelian universalism, through Heideggerian lenses, Wolfson directs us to Kabbalah's own subversion of itself.

Wolfson devotes an entire chapter to the Lurianic notion of *tzimtzum* as a prime exemplifier of Heidegger's notion of the "clearing" (*Lichtung*), in both cases where disclosure can only occur through withdrawal. In some sense, the Lurianic notion of *tzimtzum*, a divine withdrawal as that which makes divine disclosure (through creation) possible, is the best case study to test Wolfson's thesis because it heightens the tension of divine absence as the very condition of presence by "*Ein Sof* reveals itself in the beings from which it withdraws."[36] *Tzimtzum* is a doctrine that brings Kabbalah to the brink of its own deconstruction. For Wolfson, *tzimtzum* is where Kabbalah allows itself to step beyond its own self-constructed apologetic frame yielding the rupture of the "breaking of the vessels," rendering creation a tragedy in which we all reside. For a brief but potent moment, the Lurianic school shows its hand where ontotheology (all beings are made by the one being) yields meontology (the withdrawal of beyng from beings, or the abandonment of beings by beyng). While post-Lurianists, excluding Elyashiv and a few others, often swoop in to mend the tear in being and offer a reconciliation, or tikkun, where beyng and beings are reconciled, Wolfson wants us to freeze that frame of *tzimtzum*. When examined in its bare-boned manifestation, it speaks deeply to Heidegger's project.

Thus far I have to tried to tease out Wolfson's constructive project—its status as a primary text—of analyzing the affinities of Kabbalah and Heidegger by unmooring Kabbalah from its monotheistic orbit, what I consider its "apologetic" project (Wolfson does not use that term). This is not to say that Kabbalists were not monotheists. Rather, it is to say that some of their teachings reach to the very margins of conventional monotheism in ways that, in my view (and I think Wolfson's as well), steps over the edge in part because the Kabbalists' commitment to conventional theological notions blinds them from seeing how conceptually radical they were (many anti-Kabbalists may have intuited that move). Detractors will certainly argue that such unmooring breaks the rules of scholarship that strives to understand its subject "on its own terms." This may be true, and Wolfson openly notes that he is not playing by the usual rules of the academy. Like Heidegger, his project openly and knowingly defies academic conventions. But it is worth noting that a careful reading of the sources themselves reveals a tension where mystical elasticity seems to periodically reach its limit, something of which both Scholem and Wolfson's teacher Alexander Altmann were acutely aware. For Scholem this snapped in Sabbatianism. For Wolfson, it snaps when the coincidence of opposites can no longer sustain itself inside a transcendent other who remains other and the same simultaneously. The "en" of panentheism shows itself to be unsustainable. And yet pantheism does not work either as collapsing everything into the immanent with nothing outside it fails to delineate that which is not being and not nonbeing. It has no place for Beyng or *Ein Sof*.

THE FINAL LAYER OF THIS NEW JEWISH PRIMARY TEXT GESTURES TOWARD THE present theo-political reality, something Wolfson has largely refrained from doing in his more analytic work. I want to address what for many readers will be the thorniest—but potentially most illuminating—aspect of this project: Heidegger's essentializing of language, people, and land as an instantiation of Dasein as the culmination, or onto-politicization, of his project. That is, "the historical *Dasein* of a people."[37] Heidegger's antisemitism, the extent to which it is based on his anti-Judaism, is built on clay foundations given his ignorance of Kabbalah, an idea Wolfson developed at length in *Duplicity*. This poses an alternative challenge to Kabbalah that is given a more developed analysis in *Heidegger and Kabbalah*. The outgrowth of Heidegger's intervention gives us an essentialized notion of Dasein embodied in the German *Volk*, the German language, and the German "land," that is, an ethnocentrism that shades into a hypernationalist project (even as Heidegger may have come to see Nazi policies as a distortion of his philosophy). So too, Wolfson argues, Kabbalah's doctrines can easily produce, and indeed have produced, a reified ethnocentrism around people, language, and land; this can result in a troubling politicized environment that one can see in the theo-politics of some iterations of the Kookean school and some Hasidic and kabbalistic circles in present-day Israel and the Diaspora.

The reader is invariably aware of the disastrous consequences of Heidegger's move and Wolfson fully acknowledges it. *Heidegger and Kabbalah* illumines darkly that the instantiation of Dasein in language, people, and land, emblematic in Heidegger's political-theology, is all too apparent in kabbalistic political-ontology as well, something with which readers of Kabbalah are fully aware but often sublimate by keeping such essentializing in a metaphysical register. Wolfson notes with acute honesty, "in both Heidegger and the kabbalists one can find a coupling of semantic essentialism and ethnocentric chauvinism, that is, the privileging of a particular language as disclosive of the truth of being and the consequent affirmation of a unique cultural destiny of a particular ethnos to be the custodian of that language in the land of its origin, a position that harbors the potential for the disvaluing of others in racial terms."[38]

Other readers of Kabbalah point to its universalist reach that focuses on the redemption of the world and not just a people.[39] But Wolfson's comment on his teacher Alexander Altmann is well placed: all universalizing gestures toward a return "to a particularistic coloration that defies thematization and translation into a universal abstraction."[40] While Altmann's view does not necessarily lend itself to Wolfson's more strongly worded hazard of reified "ethnocentrism" (in *Heidegger and Kabbalah*), it modifies, in some way, the universalizing tendencies of kabbalistic apologetics. Wolfson, too, thinks there is a universalism embedded in some kabbalistic literature but getting at it is an arduous process that must take us through Heidegger.

The notion of the particular in and of itself is not the problem; the problem is the reification of that particularity to the point that it subsumes the totality of the universal. Wolfson sharpens this point. In much of kabbalistic teaching, "only the Jew, as it were, has the wherewithal to be absorbed into the infinite where all distinctions—including the distinction between Jew and non-Jew—are transcended."[41] It is only the Jew who can transcend the difference between Jew and non-Jew, thus the Jew in Kabbalah and the German in Heidegger are not mere particulars but rather the particular that transcends particularity itself to carry in it the universal in the fullness of its being. That is, the particular subsumes the universal into itself, making the particular the completion of the universal. Cherry-picking kabbalistic ruminations, such as in the work of some Hasidic master or Rav Abraham Kook that seem to defy that characterization, is unconvincing in my view and only exacerbates the anxiety caused precisely by the knowledge that kabbalistic doctrine, founded on a metaphysical rendering of divine election, pragmatically rejects such characterization. It is the unmasking of these kabbalistic tendencies as mirroring Heidegger's own particularism that provides the best means to deal with them productively.

Wolfson shows us that the substitution of the German for the Jew, the German language for Hebrew, or the German Fatherland for the land of Israel is not unfounded in kabbalistic teaching. Both articulate in different yet also overlapping ways a common move of instantiating "Dasein" (Heidegger) or "Holiness" (Kabbalah) into the bodies of a people, a land, or a language; not a "being" or holiness that has much room for others, but an exclusivity that claims to be inclusive while it subsumes the infinite in a small set of particulars, in one people, one language, and one land.

Heidegger rejected Judaism and the Jews as "nomadic" foreigners whose wanderings and landlessness could never make them a legitimate people, and he thus discounts them as "inauthentic" and a menace to the German project. Zionism proved him wrong about Jewish landlessness. And in some ways that is the greatest challenge to Zionism, especially as it is refracted through kabbalistic lenses. Figures such as the contemporary hasid and mystic Yitzhak Ginsburgh (b. 1944) make that clear. Ginsburgh, who defended Baruch Goldstein's massacre of twenty-nine Muslims in the Cave of the Patriarchs mosque in Hebron in 1994, regularly uses the tools of Kabbalah to make his chauvinistic and racist case for Jewish supremacy where Jewish particularity is the embodiment of the universal. Lest we think Ginsburgh is simply an outlier, his influence is palpable among some settlers and his knowledge of Kabbalah is broad and deep. He knows of what he speaks.[42]

Ginsburgh and those like him are arguably "Zionist" Heideggerians (even as it's not clear Ginsburgh considers himself a Zionist, which he deems a secular project), and the trap that ensnared Heidegger in the realm of the political applies to them as well. Neither Wolfson nor I are making the claim that kabbalistic renderings of Zionism yield Nazism; that would be both facile and outrageous. What Wolfson's book does suggest, however, is that the affinities between Heidegger and Kabbalah on a variety of metaphysical and ontological matters, when put into political practice under certain conditions, are alarmingly vulnerable to a chauvinistic exclusivity that can too easily lead to the dehumanizing of the other in its midst. In this sense, *Heidegger and Kabbalah* exposes a serious flaw of exclusivity and chauvinism in kabbalistic teaching. While Kabbalah may have been the product of disenfranchisement and marginalization and thus a response to the experience of exclusion, it becomes dangerous when used in a space of Jewish hegemony. And, I would add, its role in contemporary iterations of Religious Zionism, largely through Rav Kook, is not inconsequential.

What then is the value of a metaphysics that becomes a source for chauvinism and supremacy when put in the service of the political? Wolfson puts it this way:

> My strategy in this book has been to follow this path, to link two ostensibly disparate corpora in order to illumine the convergence from within the divergence, to demonstrate that otherness of the similar is consequent to a similarity of the other. I have sought to recover from two admittedly independent ideational matrices a

> logic that preserves the disparity of the uniform by keeping to the uniformity of the disparate. Without denying the demonstrably detrimental attitude that has informed the kabbalistic and Heideggerian constructions of the other—in both cases, although qualitatively and quantitatively different, the theoretical construct has had pernicious practical implications—I contend nonetheless that the negative propensity of a singular universality has the capacity to yield the ethical imperative of a universal singularity: what secures our equality is our diversity. The trespassing of the boundary between self and other need not be accomplished by incorporating or demolishing the other whether in acts of gratuitous compassion or wanton aggression.[43]

The hope here is that by freeing Kabbalah from its exclusivist frame and re-reading Heidegger though Kabbalah, the possibility of universal singularity manifest as seeing the same in difference and the difference in the same may emerge. But serious hazards remain. Collapsing the universal or any form of reconciliation into infinite particulars can too easily be self-limiting, where the particulars lose their universality by absorbing it and thus become the very instantiation of the universal.

Wolfson's critique of Kabbalah is thus no less a defense of its potential, and his acknowledging of Heidegger's grave error is no apologetic but a belief that Heidegger betrayed his own project, or at least arguably misread it or refused to confront its pitfalls, for the sake of the banality of power. The hope of Wolfson's work on Heidegger is that "the juxtaposition of the ostensibly incongruent fields of discourse, the belonging together of what is foreign, Heidegger and kabbalah, will not only enhance our understanding of both, but, in an even more profound sense, will serve as an ethical corrective of their respective ethnocentrisms, thereby illustrating the redemptive capacity of thought to yield new configurations of the unthought colluding on disparate paths of contemplative thinking."[44] Far from an apologetic or purely critical or analytic project, *Heidegger and Kabbalah* is a constructive one, an exercise that requires rethinking each of its subjects outside their damnation or apologetic justification.

I have argued that Wolfson's two books on Martin Heidegger and Kabbalah are not simply scholarly studies *about* Heidegger or *about* Kabbalah. They constitute an audaciously conceived and carefully executed meditation on thinking and being more generally, challenging their reader to redress how to think about both by viewing one through the lens of the other, not toward any comparative end or philosophical synthesis but rather to critique each on its own terms. In doing so, these works enable both the potential and the hazards in each of its subjects to come rushing to the fore. Such a rising tide contains all the majesty, beauty, and danger of nature at its most genuine. Here I submit that what we read when we read these works is not a secondary text on either Heidegger or Kabbalah but a primary Jewish text on thinking and being, conceptually and politically drawn from the wellsprings of arguably the most important philosophical mind of the twentieth century and one of the most intricate, creatively explosive, and audacious mystical reflections in the history of Western civilization.

NOTES

1. In particular, the incessant critiques by Moshe Idel, which of late have become almost obsessive, in my view often misunderstand Wolfson's project and in doing so, evaluate the work under criteria not amenable to the work itself. Idel is a scholar and thinks as such, but what he often fails to understand is that Wolfson is often producing primary texts, not secondary ones. This is not to say they are beyond critique; certainly not. There are many areas in Kabbalah on which Idel and Wolfson differ; one can think of their two very different views of Abulafia, for example. And on those and other matters, as in any scholarly realm, criticism is warranted, albeit one often finds that Idel's critique misses the mark if only because it seems to misunderstand the theoretical foundation upon which Wolfson offers his analysis. Unfortunately, this venue does not allow for a detailed discussion. Wolfson responds to many of these criticisms in his work; a particularly illustrious example of such responses can be found in Elliot R. Wolfson, *Suffering Time* (Leiden: Brill, 2021), especially 231–61 and 272–83. Regarding the question of primary vs. secondary literature and distinguishing between the two, one can think of Scholem's critique of Rosenzweig's *Star of Redemption* published in his *The Messianic Idea in Judaism*. One does not critique Hegel the way one critiques a scholar writing *about* Hegel. One does not critique a Hasidic text the way one critiques one writing *about* a Hasidic text. Thus as I read them, many of Idel's critiques are off the mark mostly because Idel seems to misunderstand what it is he is critiquing.
2. Elliot R. Wolfson, *The Duplicity of Philosophy's Shadow* (New York: Columbia University Press, 2018); and Elliot R. Wolfson, *Heidegger and Kabbalah* (Bloomington: Indiana University Press, 2019).
3. See Elliot R. Wolfson, *Luminal Darkness: Imaginal Gleanings from Zohar Literature* (New York: OneWorld Books, 2006). On law and its inversion, see Wolfson, *Venturing Beyond: Morality and Law in Kabbalistic Mysticism* (New York: Oxford University Press, 2006), 186–286.
4. See Gershom Scholem, "Redemption Through Sin," in *The Messianic Idea in Judaism* (New York: Schocken Books, 1971), 176–202; and Yehuda Liebes, "The Status of Sabbateanism in the Religion of Israel," in *From Sabbatei Zvi to the Gaon of Vilna: A Collection of Studies* [Hebrew] (Jerusalem: Idra, 2017), 39–52.
5. I exclude here the various Jewish detractors who were often much more sanguine and nuanced than some more contemporary critics. See Daniel Herskowitz, *Heidegger and His Jewish Reception* (Cambridge: Cambridge University Press, 2020). For a different view see Richard Wolin, *Heidegger's Children* (Princeton: Princeton University Press, 2015) and Wolin, *The Heidegger Controversy: A Critical Reader* (Cambridge, MA: MIT Press, 1992).
6. Wolfson, *Duplicity*, xv; see also Alexander Duff in *Heidegger and Politics: The Ontology of Radical Discontent* (Cambridge: Cambridge University Press, 2015), 6, 7.
7. Leo Strauss, "An Introduction to Heideggerian Existentialism," in *The Rebirth of Classical Political Rationalism: An Introduction to the Thought of Leo Strauss*, ed. T. Pangle (Chicago: University of Chicago Press, 1989), 28. More generally on Strauss's use of Heidegger, see Herskowitz, *Heidegger and His Jewish Reception*, 175–219.
8. Hannah Arendt, *Thinking Without a Bannister: Essays in Understanding 1953–1975* (New York:

Schocken, 2018). Arendt's *Eichmann in Jerusalem* was an example of that kind of thinking for which Arendt suffered intense criticism. Wolfson, too, has suffered such criticism for allowing himself to think in this way.

9. Wolfson, *Duplicity*, 162.
10. See my *From Metaphysics to Midrash* (Bloomington: Indiana University Press, 2008), 149–95.
11. Magid, *From Metaphysics to Midrash.*
12. Another work of a Jewish studies scholar that I think moves from scholarship to a primary text is Len Goodman's *God of Abraham* (Oxford: Oxford University Press, 1996).
13. Richard Cohen, trans., *Emanuel Levinas: Ethics and Infinity* (Pittsburgh: Duquesne University Press, 1985), 37.
14. See Richard Wolin, ed., *The Heidegger Controversy: A Critical Reader* (Cambridge, MA: Harvard University Press, 1993).
15. See, for some examples, Alexander Altmann, *The Meaning of Jewish Existence: Theological Essays 1930–1939*, ed. A. Ivry (Waltham and Hanover: Brandeis University Press, 1991); Emil Fackenheim, *Encounters Between Judaism and Modern Philosophy* (New York: Schocken Books, 1980); Michael Wyschogrod, *Kierkegaard and Heidegger* (New York: Humanities Press, 1969); Edith Wyschogrod, *Saints and Postmodernism* (Chicago: University of Chicago Press, 1990); and Allen Scult, *Being Jewish/Reading Heidegger: An Ontological Encounter* (New York: Fordham University Press, 2004).
16. Wolfson, *Heidegger and Kabbalah*, 275.
17. Wolfson, *Heidegger and Kabbalah*, 9.
18. Wolfson, *Heidegger and Kabbalah*, 208.
19. See Slavoj Zizek, *The Parallax View* (Cambridge, MA: MIT Press, 2006), 184.
20. Wolfson, *Heidegger and Kabbalah*, 174.
21. See, for example, Mark Smith, *The Origins of Biblical Monotheism: Israel's Polytheistic Background and the Ugaritic Texts* (Oxford: Oxford University Press, 2001); Benjamin Sommer, *The Bodies of God and the World of Ancient Israel* (Cambridge: Cambridge University Press, 2009); and Annette Yoshiko Reed, *Demons, Angels, and Writing in Ancient Israel* (Cambridge: Cambridge University Press, 2020).
22. Martin Heidegger, *Contributions to Philosophy (Of the Event)* (Bloomington: Indiana University Press, 2012), 207, as cited in Wolfson, *Heidegger and Kabbalah*, at 99, 153.
23. Wolfson, *Heidegger and Kabbalah*, 142.
24. See Elliot R. Wolfson, *Open Secret: Postmessianic Messianism and the Mystical Revision of Menaḥem Mendel Schneerson* (New York: Columbia University Press, 2012), esp. 276–89.
25. Wolfson, *Heidegger and Kabbalah*, 165.
26. Wolfson, *Heidegger and Kabbalah*, 169.
27. Wolfson, *Heidegger and Kabbalah*, 270.
28. Wolfson, *Heidegger and Kabbalah*, 256.
29. Azriel of Gerona, *Perush Eser Sefirot*, first printed in Meir Ibn Gabbai's *Derekh Emunah*. An English translation appears in *Early Kabbalah*, trans. and eds. J. Dan and R. Keiner (New Jersey: Paulist Press, 1986), 87–108.
30. As cited in Wolfson, *Heidegger and Kabbalah*, at 68.

31. Wolfson, *Heidegger and Kabbalah*, 216.
32. One retrospective of Elyashiv that incorporates Wolfson's work on him can be found in Joey Rosenfeld, "A Tribute to Rav Shlomo Elyashiv, Author of Leshem Shevo v-Achloma: On his Ninetieth Yahrzeit," found here: https://www.academia.edu/23286321/A_Tribute_to_Rav_Shlomo_Elyashiv_Author_of_Leshem_Shevo_v_Achloma.
33. Wolfson, *Heidegger and Kabbalah*, 77.
34. Wolfson, *Heidegger and Kabbalah*, 67.
35. Wolfson, *Heidegger and Kabbalah*, 79.
36. Wolfson, *Heidegger and Kabbalah*, 152.
37. Wolfson, *Heidegger and Kabbalah*, 342.
38. Wolfson, *Heidegger and Kabbalah*, 13.
39. For example, see Arthur Green, *Radical Judaism* (New Haven: Yale University Press, 2010); and Green, *Judaism for the World* (New Haven: Yale University Press, 2020).
40. Wolfson, *Heidegger and Kabbalah*, 348. Interestingly, both Green and Wolfson were students of Altmann.
41. Wolfson, *Heidegger and Kabbalah*, 349.
42. For one example in English among many Hebrew writings, see Yitzchak Ginsburgh, *Rectifying the State of Israel: A Political Platform Based on Kabbalah* (Kfar Chabad: Gal Eynei, 2002).
43. Wolfson, *Heidegger and Kabbalah*, 367.
44. Wolfson, *Heidegger and Kabbalah*, 13.

A STOLPERSTEIN FOR BLUMENBERG?

STEVEN M. WASSERSTROM

Ihre liebsten Romanhelden?
JOSEPH IN ÄGYPTEN, HB, "FRAGEBOGEN," IN FAZ, 1982[1]

THE UNRECOGNIZABILITY (*UNMERKLICHKEIT*) OF BLUMENBERG AS JEW

Hans Blumenberg (1920–1996; hereafter HB) has yet to be studied in sustained terms of Jewishness.[2] The Nazi regime deemed him a *Halbjude* because his mother was fully Jewish. She married a Catholic husband, formally converted, and became an active member of her church.[3] There is little known about his family of origin or his relations with Jewish relatives, a situation he apparently preferred.[4] HB confided to a friend in 1987 that his mother, who was herself vulnerable to Nazi terror, was protected by the church. "For years, my mother was, in a convent hospital, sheltered from everything, from so much of a harsh world."[5] His father was a wholesaler of Catholic religious artifacts (*Kunstgroßhändler*). At high school HB balanced three religious identities, as it were, keeping each variously in play. Catholic and Jew at home, while thriving as a leading student in the primordially Lutheran Katharineum, founded in 1531.[6] The strangeness of this mixing is then reflected eventually in his strangely moving *Matthäuspassion*, devoted to a Lutheran Mass as artwork.[7] After 1936, of course, he was no longer a legal "German."

The biographical question of his Jewishness, however, is not my subject.[8] But a few preliminary points are worth keeping in mind. He was *genealogically* the son of a Catholic father and Jewish mother; *institutionally* an educated and wedded Lutheran;[9] *theologically* religiously empathetic but intellectually agnostic. A reviewer calls him "theologisch hochgebildeten Agnostiker Blumenberg."[10] Today, Blumenberg's received stature as a religious thinker is secure.[11] He clearly is not a "Christian theologian" and not only because of the plain fact that he writes outside the framework of Christian confessionalism. He *may* be, however, a "Jewish thinker." It seems fair and reasonable at least to ask the question, for one thing, because he is a major religious thinker who is not an orthoprax Christian thinker per se, and who, as I shall show, employs copious Judaica and engages the contemporary Jewish condition in manifold philosophical ways.

His titanic corpus continues to become available, including some dozen posthumous volumes, and excluding some 20,000 unpublished pages remaining in his *Nachlass*.[12] Unfortunately, few modern Jews are equipped to read this monumental Blumenberg. The problem is not just that the majority of today's Jews don't read German—there are, after all, close to 2,500 pages of Blumenberg in English translation, with hundreds more in French and Italian.[13] The real problem, needless to say, is the relentless difficulty of the work itself. The problem starts with his absolute unclassifiability. One philosopher, in a eulogy, described his works as "problem-oriented detective novels disguised as learned tomes."[14] I shall return to the intrinsic difficulty of his thought, but for the moment I want to stress the inescapable difficulty of talking about Blumenberg at all, much less engaging Blumenberg as a Jew.

One contributing explanation for the *Unmerklichkeit* of Blumenberg's Jewishness, as we shall see, is his own concealing reflexes. As one of the only "Jewish" philosophers in the postwar German academy, his writings on religion, especially in their peculiarly unidentifiable idiom, ironically rendered his presence all the more salient. His Jewish heritage, his Shoah trauma, his religiosity without Christian confessional content, masked a body of thought constructed of a certain sort of ineffable Jewishness. His thought can be read, in this sense, as a series of skirmishes with his own enforced anomalous location in culture. It may be read, perhaps, as a "*marranische Schreibweise*," a "Marrano way of writing."[15]

He wrote under other modes of concealment (though this should not be taken to imply that he actively hid his background). His daughter Bettina Blumenberg: "My father loved camouflage and he secretly rejoiced [*ihn diebisch gefreut*] that it made people all stirred up."[16] Monod calls him "a secretive man" (*homme secret*).[17] This secrecy was manifested neither as Straussian nor as mystical esotericism. His wisdom hid in teasings, hints, ironies, allusions, riddles. One observer puts it this way.

> In existential terms, Hans Blumenberg, the author, a man who was discreet to the point of secrecy, is huddled deep inside the cave of his immense erudition, whence, from time to time, he allows a book to filter out, which the reader will receive as an enigma and a challenge.[18]

Blumenberg himself evokes

> an author, who wants single-handedly, to occupy the reader for his whole life (and what is more, for a life of sleeplessness), and already presupposes, for this exclusive relationship, a life's acquired knowledge of literature for the mere understanding of his riddles and mystifications, his allusions and reclothings.[19]

Of his philosophical hero, Edmund Husserl, he said he was "at once a discovering and concealing genius."[20]

For all his wit, HB's written word was discreet, reserved, restrained. The point is well made by Agard.

> L'Holocauste est d'ailleurs évoqué [by Siegfried Kracauer] à travers la figure d'Ahasver, le Juif errant. Blumenberg, victime comme Kracauer de la persécution nationale-socialiste, est resté toujours très discret sur son existence, et il est difficile de déceler dans son oeuvre une quelconque inscription autobiographique: la richesse et la densité de son travail sont telles qu'une approche biographique pourrait paraître bien anecdotique. Peut-être pourrait-on voir dans certains thèmes qui traversent son oeuvre comme un écho de sa propre expérience avec, par exemple, la vulnérabilité de l'homme, sa quête de protection, l'indifférence du monde, le caractère précaire de toute culture.[21]

In the following, then, we find a philosopher who was not necessarily forthcoming as a man, and certainly not as a Jew. But, as I shall show, he cannot be adequately or properly understood as a philosopher until he is engaged as a Jewish thinker.

The second chapter of *The Legitimacy of the Modern Age* [hereafter *LMA*], in the first pages of that tome, is titled "A Dimension of Hidden Meaning?"[22] He then follows with coy reflections on nothing less than the "the task of all historical reflection,"[23] observing that

> the word "God" left the tongue of the Jews with as much difficulty as it left the tongue of the Greeks with ease. Whether that was connected with the fact that the God of the Old Testament was the protective power allied with *one* people, *withdrawn from and to be concealed from the rest of the world* . . . need not be decided here.[24]

SOME ORIENTATION

Certain incontrovertible facts speak to HB's "Jewishness."

1. Jewish heritage. His mother was indisputably born fully Jewish, with two Jewish parents. And his maternal family of origin was materially larger than has heretofore been reported.

2. Jewish experience. The Third Reich persecuted him for being a Jew from the time that the Nuremberg racial laws formally enacted the crime of being a *Halbjude* and a *Mischling First Grade.* He apparently witnessed the burning of the Lübeck synagogue on Kristallnacht, a memory that was horrifying and traumatizing.[25] Only 250 Jews remained in Lübeck by 1939. This tiny remnant was then annihilated with the deportation of its last Jews in 1941–1942.[26] He alluded to his wartime situation only occasionally, as when he referred to himself as an "unregistered chamberlain" (*ungemeldeter Kammerherr*).[27]

The official corporate website of Drägerwerk—whose complicity with the Third Reich continues to be elaborated by researchers—perversely calls him a "Jewish company employee":[28]

> At the same time, [Dräger] shields Jewish company employees, such as the philosopher Hans Blumenberg, from the grasp of National Socialist authorities. . . . Drägerwerk

> has little influence on their treatment. With Company support, the technical manager of the plant nonetheless continues to do his best to protect eastern European workers from SS harassment, and as a result, suffers reprisals himself. Shortly before the end of the war, Dräger manages to delay the closure of the camp to protect the prisoners from deportation.[29]

One tantalizing source (reported by Goldstein, Wolff, and Dotzauer) claims that the philosopher had three maternal aunts murdered at Theriesenstadt ("dessen drei Tanten mütterlicherseits in Theresienstadt umkamen").[30]

3. Jewish thought. The manifold "Jewish" elements of work, which increased over the years of his career. Details will be elucidated in the present paper.

Given these factors—his heritage, his experience, and his philosophy—"Jewishness" is his "default setting." Still, he remained foundationally conflicted; like many German Jews, he struggled uncomfortably against his own identity.

Only rarely and never publicly, he "identified" with "being Jewish." On November 12, 1955, he wrote to his senior friend Hans Jonas:

> [T]he stability of the political development in the Federal Republic, the successful overcoming of the ideological remnants of the terrible past, these factors today allow an even more certain response to the question of whether *people of your and my personal and familial fate* can regain a positive feeling of life, a straightforward relationship to people and tasks here. I answer this question in the affirmative, in good faith, and am also certain of the future, inasmuch as it depends on immanent factors.[31]

Not quite so privately, as reported firsthand by his student Ferdinand Fellman, HB sardonically referred to himself as "*Mischling First Class.*"

HB's Jewishness expressed itself indirectly, unsystematically, and allusively. Dieter Henrich suggested it came out in his "intensity and originality."[32] In the opinion of his French translator, Denis Trierweiler,

> Much has been said, rightly, of the prodigious scholarly theological Blumenberg, but no one has ever observed how much he was paid in the Wissenschaft of Judentums. Of course, it explicitly stated that he was non-believer—which is obvious—but suffice it to say that the last page he published while alive, to which he gave his imprimatur in 1989 at the end of *Höhlenausgänge*, is taken from a treatise of the Babylonian Talmud 8. This is the last word. I can not help make the connection with the last novel by Thomas Bernhard *Auslöschung*, published in 1986, where the narrator bequeathed his entire fortune to the community of Jewish Vienna. I see in all this his way of saying—*if you read me carefully, you will understand which way I am*. Because, of course, Ritter, Rothacker, and Gadamer were miles away from doubting that he was Jewish.[33]

Similarly, Markus Hundeck argues that Blumenberg indirectly concords with a prevalent Jewish idea:

> The prohibition of the making of images thus finds its reflex in Blumenberg's dismissal of any attempt to represent totality with absolute conclusiveness. Hundeck thus speaks of the *iconoclastic aspects* of Blumenberg's thinking (Hundeck 2000, 51), thereby suggesting that the pronounced resistance to subordinate the world to a single image could be interpreted also as a Jewish impulse in Blumenberg's thinking.[34]

IN THE BEGINNING: THE ABSOLUTE FATHER

Although [I am] the son of a Catholic father, eternity appeared to me neither attractive nor fearsome.
FROM A LETTER TO ALFONS NEUKIRCHEN[35]

One place to begin is with Kafka's father.[36] In 1952 the thirty-two-year-old Blumenberg published an essay on thirty-six-year-old Kafka's embittered letter to his father.[37] He raved about Kafka's significance. "This is indeed one of the essential documents of human existence as such!" ("*Dies ist wirklich eines der wesentlichen Dokumente menschlicher Existenz überhaupt!*")[38] This was the first nontechnical piece the budding philosopher wrote, and only his fifth article, of over 150 he eventually published. While it is striking in several respects it is, in the present context, interesting as an introductory glimpse into Blumenberg's Kafkaesque self-understanding, which, as I shall hope to show, remained consistently bent. He published no less than five articles about Kafka in the 1950s.

One might contrast what Blumenberg later wrote about Kafka, on the one hand, and his own father, on the other. Thus, for example, his *Begriffe in Geschichten* (1998) begins with a piece titled "Eine Begriffsgeschichte," which starts with Blumenberg's own father. "My father was a passionate and moderately successful photographer."[39] Blumenberg confesses being fascinated by *creatio ex nihilo*, by something coming from nothing, like his father in his darkroom, which he likened to the creation of the world himself—as if his father replicated the Absolute Father, as it were.[40]

Just a year later, in 1953, in an essay delightfully titled "Eschatological Ironie. Über die Romane Evelyn Waughs," he likens "das Ferment der britischen Skepsis in diese Welt" with, of all things, "der Äonen-Kabbalstik eines Gnostikers entgegen."[41] Which brings us to Scholem. The last of Scholem's "Unhistorical Aphorisms" reads as follows.

> Although unaware of it himself, [Kafka's] writings are a *secularized representation of the kabbalistic conception of the world*. This is why many of today's readers find something of the rigorous splendor of the canonical in them—a hint of the Absolute that breaks into pieces.[42]

To put the point formulaically: Blumenberg repurposed, or retextualized, *secularized representations of the kabbalistic conception of the world.* Consciously or unconsciously, as Scholem said of Kafka, Blumenberg replicated some kabbalistic reflexes.

HB's position toward modernity bore subtle but not insignificant filiations to the analogous position held by Gershom Scholem. For Scholem, philology replaced Kabbalah.[43] Philology *world historically* replaced Kabbalah. Scholem begins his "Unhistorical Aphorisms" with philology.

> The philology of a mystical discipline like the Kabbalah is somewhat ironical.... Does something remain in it of the law of the matter itself, visible for the philologist, or does exactly the essential disappear in this projection of the historical? The uncertainty in answering this question is part of the nature of the philological question itself, and so the hope that this work feeds on retains something ironical from which it can not be separated.[44]

HB'S KAFKA AS HB'S "RELIGION"?

Real reality is always unrealistic.
FRANZ KAFKA[45]

Goldschmidt's *témoignage* about 1947–1958, HB's time at Christian-Albrechts-Universität zu Kiel, tells us that "Landgrebe fut ainsi presque à son corps défendant l'un des très rares philosophes allemands à ne pas s'être compromis en quoi que ce soit avec le régime nazi, c'est probablement pour cette raison que Blumenberg soutint son habilitation en 1950 auprès de Landgrebe."[46] HB was extremely close with Landgrebe, and Goldschmidt was Landgrebe's brother-in-law; "[HB] gifted Goldschmidt *Beim Bau der Chinesischen Mauer* de Kafka (*La Construction de la tat tzu de Chine*) que je possède encore."[47]

Over the course of nearly forty years HB highlighted his reverence for Kafka by flagging him at key junctures in his major statements on religion. Kafka was for HB *the* paradigm of "religion after religion," what he in one of his first essays called a "placeholder for transcendence" ("*Platzhalter der Transzendenz*"), religious of a certain "secular" sort, a reading HB set forth in three major phases of his philosophical development.[48] For Joe Paul Kroll "Blumenberg ... uses Kafka as a foil for his own ruminations on the status of the absolute, of God and of the entire complex of associated ideas—*that is to say, of religion.*"[49]

"Messianischer Minimalismus" is the seventh chapter of the seventh Part of *Matthäuspassion*—which numeration, depending on the reader's numerological proclivities, may or may not be taken as significant in itself. HB's second treatment of Kafka is perhaps the centerpiece of his passionate Nachdenken on his Prague precursor, rivaled only by the early essay on the "Absolute Father." A compressed five pages, "Messianischer

Minimalismus" raises fundamental issues for present purposes. Like all HB's work, it is not summarizable. It presents a more or less chronological itinerary of key cumulative comments on Kafka's *Trial*. Their leitmotif is a *Messiah-who-has-come* in contrast to a *Messiah-who-has-yet-to-come*.

Kafka was paradigmatic, I suggest, because he was HB's personal model, but *not* "a modern master" (though, of course, he was that too). Rather, he was a model because he represented Scholem's "*sakularisierte Darstellung des (ihm selber unbekannten) kabbalistischen Weltgefühls*"[50]

The conclusion I draw from the above is that—not to put too fine a point on it—HB identified personally with Kafka, indirectly emulating the Kafka trialogue between Benjamin, Adorno, and Scholem. This tendency is already explicit in his 1952 insights into Kafka's "gottlose Religiosität."[51]

APPROACHING BIOGRAPHY

> *It is, however, an unwarrantable act to strip bare the living or even departed contemporaries whose relatives are still alive, by unveiling their unconscious without permission to do so.*
>
> HANS BLUMENBERG[52]

A childhood reminiscence provides Blumenberg a rare autobiographical confession.[53] It was framed, appropriately for "the best student in the best school in Germany," as a philological memory of correcting a teacher. "*The fear of God is the beginning of wisdom*," interpreted by "der braune Direktor nach 1933" to mean students should fear their teachers. This teacher under the Third Reich took it in this authoritarian sense.[54] In reminiscences written fifty years later, Blumenberg recalls this "mistake" as central to his "theology."[55] By means of the reversal of syntax, "The fear of God is the beginning of wisdom"—itself interestingly reminiscent of kabbalistic syntactical reversals of sentence structure—that "God fears the beginning of human wisdom."[56] Elsewhere he recalls his interrupted Hebrew studies in middle school. This recollection leads him to a meditation on a Hebrew name of God, *Elohim*.[57]

When he played with the philosophical theme of self-revelation he could be revealing in the ways that he kept concealed. In 1997 Reclam published his *Ein möglisches Selbtsverständnis*. A double anecdote, tagged with a date, as is typical for a Blumenberg essay. For example: Valéry Giscard d'Estaing published his memoirs in 1988. In them he reveals to the reading public the confession that he, Giscard d'Estaing, heard from his good friend, German chancellor Helmut Schmidt, in July 1980. Schmidt's father, he was told, was Jewish.[58] The second of the double anecdote concerns a moment in 1937 in Cambridge, when Wittgenstein confided his self-understanding as a Mischling to his Russian teacher, the Jewish student Fania Pascal.[59] Bruce Krajewski, on the occasion of Blumenberg's centennial, selected this double anecdote to epitomize a problem with Blumenberg's own "possible self-understanding" (*möglisches Selbtsverständnis*). "What laudatory trait did Wittgenstein possess that was wanting in Schmidt? 'Scruples,'" Blumenberg writes."[60]

BLUMENBERG'S JEWISHNESS AND GERMAN-JEWISH METARELIGION

. . . the bifurcated soul of the German Jew
PAUL MENDES-FLOHR[61]

Only a few are chosen, but no one can know for sure
that he or she doesn't belong to them.
HANS BLUMENBERG[62]

When George Mosse published his landmark essay on "Gershom Scholem as a German Jew," there was still something slightly shocking in the presumption of that title.[63] Thirty years ago, it was still shocking to write of a scholar's life, and *a fortiori*, this particular contextualization of the lion of Zionist letters seemed counterintuitive. The shock is greater, I submit, in the case of Blumenberg. Like Scholem, I submit, Hans Blumenberg was a German Jew. "German" here refers, in the first instance, to a broader German cultural sphere with which he identified, Deutschophone culture at large; the non-Germans Freud, Wittgenstein, and Kafka, who lived in the Austrian empire, are among his most revered and repeated authorities.

The Jewishness of HB's life and work remains largely unexplored. Having visited bookstores in Berlin, including those specializing in Judaica, I found Blumenberg absent from sections devoted to Judaism, just as he is more generally from the story of postwar German Jewish thinkers, the history of Jewish thought, and so on.[64] It is thus all the more striking that Blumenberg does indeed signal his Jewishness and his sensitivity to varieties of the Jewish question. This can be demonstrated from a considerable variety of perspectives. For example, four figures who don't make an obviously coherent pantheon, but who recur throughout his work, are Heine, Kafka, Wittgenstein, and Freud (only the first of whom was literally German, and I leave aside the question of calling them "Jews" at all). He cites Scholem on multiple occasions. On other occasions, neither few nor incidental, Blumenberg cites rabbinic literature. In what may be considered his "Mythos trilogy" of *Arbeit am Mythos* (*AM*) (1979), *Matthäuspassion* (*MP*) (1988), and *Höhlenausgänge* (1989) Jewish themes both historical and theological loom large. The section titled "Die Unmerklichkeit des Messias," "the unrecognizability of the Messiah," in his *Matthäuspassion* is substantially a disquisition on and about Jewish thought, including an engagement with none other than Maimonides. The final of the three volumes, *Höhlenausgänge*, concludes with a section from the Talmud.[65]

To be sure, Blumenberg was profoundly trained in Christian theology and the preponderance of pages in his work are explicitly devoted at least nominally to Christian themes. However, it is not certain that he ever wrote a page in the confessional voice of a Christian believer—nor does he, so far as I know, ever write as a Jewish believer, for that matter. He wrote as a philosopher, though neither plain nor simple.

WELTGEISTMIRAKEL: THE EPOCHAL GERMAN-JEWISH ENCOUNTER

Ma conviction est que l'oeuvre de Blumenberg est dirigée tout entire contre une certaine Allegmagne l'après 1945.
DENIS TRIERWEILER[66]

One quasi-esoteric or at least allusive topic for Blumenberg, never quite directly addressed but otherwise always somehow marked as central, was the German-Jewish dialogue itself. For the *Halbjude* philosopher, the horizontal historicity of the German-Jewish encounter interrupted the vertical Sonderweg mythos of German philosophy. Both explicit in his person and implicit behind his favored historiographical exempla, whether in the "missed encounters" between Heidegger and Cassirer or between Heidegger and Husserl, was the fate of a German "Jew."

In *Genesis of the Copernican World*, Blumenberg makes the Heine-Hegel encounter "*the true spiritual culminating point of the age.*"[67] In *Work on Myth*, he makes the 1936 Freud-Mann encounter likewise a world-historical pivot. Midway through *Work on Myth*, he begins Part IV portentously: "*Everything up to this point in this book has a gradient; all the lines converge on a hidden vital point* at which the work expended on myth could prove to be something that was not fruitless."[68] Then, in an epilogue to this part, he returns to the June 1936 meeting of Freud and Mann. "We can no longer make this scene—with this speaker and this listener, at this most terrible time, in this most threatened of all locations—present to ourselves in its pregnance."[69] This was, HB concluded, the "*great scene of the spirit of the age, which hardly had another scene comparable to it.*"[70] In *Legitimacy of the Modern Age*, such a "great scene" is the conflict of Rothschild and Metternich (p. 458).[71] This comes in the chapter on "The Epoch of the Concept of an Epoch"—a chapter that travels from Rothschild (p. 458) to Heine (p. 464) to Hitler (p. 478).[72]

Another example is the encounter between Marcus Herz and Kant, which confrontation instructively caps Blumenberg's discussion of "great events."[73] Elsewhere, he dwells repeatedly on Jews in circles around Kant and Goethe, including Heine, Mendelssohn, Herz, Varnhagen. Herz in particular appears at a pivotal if not epochal instance in "Does It Matter When? On Time Indifference."[74] In that essay HB described Herz as one of the first readers of Kant who was "understanding and thorough."

Work on Myth's chapter on the concept of "significance" must itself be applied to his self-designated "great events" in the German-Jewish encounter. It is not these events themselves but rather the cumulative unfolding rolling into them that imbues them with "significance."

> The more subtle the theoretical knowledge, the more it nourishes the suspicion that history does not take place and is not made in its "great" moments and that no causality attaches to its scenes that are ready for engraving, but rather the chains of their motivations have already run out when the hammer is raised to nail up the theses, *when the breaking of windows takes place* or the trumpet is blown for the day of reckoning.[75]

This eschatological allusion to Kristallnacht is momentously bracketed between Luther and the Day of Judgment.[76] After next citing Scholem, he then turns to the Nazi "myth of the twentieth century" and invokes Thomas Mann to the effect that the "Jews' greater sense of the truth could be attributed to the fact that they had no myth and their brains were not 'befogged'with it."[77] This point leads finally to Blumenberg's most unmistakable statement of the world-historical significance of the German-Jewish encounter.

> If one examines the historical experience of the modern age, one finds the incomparable lesson, which is seldom taken to heart, that could have been drawn from the possession of the sciences and from their historical form: to see the nonpossession of truth as what—in contrast to the promise that the truth could make people free—still comes closest to such a liberation.[78]

His works operate routinely by using a specified day as a point of departure. Indeed, one of the most striking techniques that runs throughout Blumenberg's oceanic corpus is temporal precision pinching, dating. Despite his insistence elsewhere on "the indifference of time," most of his work in fact follows in practice the great departure from myth he identified with the Hebrew Bible.

> This is the basis of one of [the] most important differences between the Old Testament literature, along with the biblical theology that finally emerges from it, and myth: the insistence on the reckoning of time, on datability by means of the lifetimes of the patriarchs, by means of the years the kings governed, by means of genealogical constructs . . . the [comprehensive] history of histories must possess continuous identity, reliable chronology and genealogy, localization and dating. This produces an entirely different pathos from what can be characteristic of myth.[79]

Elsewhere Blumenberg observes: "Insofern ist die Koinzidenz von Relativitätstheorie, Sonnenfinsternis, und Phototechnik auf jenen 29. Mai 1919 etwas wie ein Weltgeistmirakel" ("In this respect, the coincidence of the theory of relativity, solar eclipse, and photo technology on May 29, 1919 is something like a *Weltgeistmirakel*").[80] Here we see once again HB's distinctive markers, specifying a certain Jew on certain date to highlight a heretofore unrecognized "*Weltgeistmirakel*."

Finally, HB concludes his landmark essay on *Nachdenklichkeit* with his vaunted "missed encounter" theme. While in the equally memorable essay on "MacGuffin" the missed encounter was between Heidegger and Blumenberg himself, "Pensiveness" concludes with the missed encounter between [Jew] Heine and [German philosopher] Kant: "*Heine freely expressed his scorn for Kant.*"[81] Kant *seems* to be the subject of *Nachdenklichkeit*, but in fact it's Heine who provides the final poignant image, that is, Lampe's umbrella. "Pensiveness" became the one piece out of HB's thousands from which his surviving family selected the line inscribed on the plaque ceremonially affixed to his birthplace. In that way, the crescendo aphorism from "Nachdenklichkeit" was memorialized on the commemorative plaque installed at the house of his birth in Lübeck:

> Geburtshaus von Hans Blumenberg
> Philosoph und Schriftsteller
> 13. Juli 1920–28. März 1996
> *Nachdenklichkeit heißt: Es bleibt nicht alles so selbstverständlich, wie es war.*

Not exactly a Stolperstein . . .

JEWISHNESS IN THE MYTHOS TRILOGY

The 1979 *Work on Myth* marks the turn to Judaism that ultimately characterizes Blumenberg's late thought. It begins with an epigraph from Kafka and ends, some 600 pages later, with Kafka. Blumenberg regularly used epigraphs as flags. Thus, the first epigraph in the enormous posthumous *Beschriebung des Menschen* is Heine on Spinoza, "Statt zu sagen, er leugne Gott, könnte man sagen er leugne den Menschen."[82] And the first epigraph in the posthumous *Begriffe in Geschichten*, attached to a memory of his father from the 1930s, is the Nazified Gottfried Benn, "Ewige Traum, daß man etwas nicht macht, sondern es entsteht." He gives the date, July 9, 1933, and then begins the book with the words "Mein Vater."[83]

In its opening pages, *Work on Myth* poses—apparently—a momentous counterexample to the work of Ernst Jünger.[84] It first invokes Jünger's *Auf den Marmorklippen* (1939). The mythical heroes of the story—"which stands for the events of June 30, 1934 [i.e., the Röhm Putsch]," Blumenberg informs us—"fell back onto that earlier world in which terror rules supreme."[85] The "art myth" of *Marmorklippen* cannot stop man from sinking back to "archaic resignation." Implicitly, within a few pages, Blumenberg contrasts this atavism to the step forward invoked by Franz Rosenzweig's "name's breaking into the chaos of the unnamed."[86] He proceeds to read the biblical scene of the *Akedah* (Binding of Isaac) as part of an "institutional renunciation of human sacrifice."[87] A Jewishlyindexed resistance to "terror" thereafter runs throughout these pages. "Theory is the better adapted mode of mastering the episodic *tremenda* [*terrors*] of recurring world events."[88]

It could be argued that the most dramatic and sustained section of the book is his memorable treatment of the "extraordinary saying" *Nemo contra deum nisi deus ipse* (*AM*, 523–61). The core of this chapter comprises a vast and vivid response to Carl Schmitt (532–56). This is a response specifically to Schmitt's 1969 *Political Theology II*, which in turn had been the subject of an extended polemic in Blumenberg's *LMA* (89–103).

The *Passion of Matthew* is a work of attenuated pathos. Its taut pitch of double sense resonates from the outset, where seemingly Christological exegesis nests in paradigmatically pregnant German-Jewish pathos. "Inmitten des Weltabenteuers kommt der *Logos* um, verwandelt sich in des Gegenwort zum einstigen *Es werde* des Seins: zum *Eli, Eli* der Vernichtung."[89] Indeed, within a few pages, Blumenberg, in a rare autobiographical aside, tells the story of being denied the honor of giving an honorary graduation lecture at Lübeck in 1938 (*MP*, 28–29).[90] At its end, after a chapter devoted to the imperceptibility of the Messiah, Blumenberg declares a flat dictum. "*Die Bewußtseinsbedingung des Judentums ist die Ungewißheit des Messias.*"[91]

The next section begins with "Vergangenheitsbewältigung und der Trauerarbeit." *Passion of Matthew* comprises HB's own *working through the past* and a *work of mourning*, in the always immediate absence of the Messiah. In addressing the category of the "undealt-with past," it is typical that Blumenberg did not want to be seen as engaging in a polemic. "I have said that the category of secularization contains at least a latent ideological element. This formulation has brought me the odium of an 'unmasker of ideology' [*Ideologiekritiker*], which is not at all to my taste."[92]

The third book in the trilogy, *Höhlenausgänge*, begins with an epigraph from Kafka. "Mein Leben ist das Zögern vor der Geburt." The three figures cited in the first section of *Höhlenausgänge*, which follows the epigraph, are three other figures of Jewish background, Proust, Husserl, and Wittgenstein.[93] He turns next to Hans Jonas. In 1952 Blumenberg brought a job offer to Jonas for Kiel from his former fellow Heidegger student Bröcker to a philosophy congress in Brussels.[94] Afterward, Jonas went with Blumenberg and others to buy lace in Bruges.[95] They met again in 1959 at the Third International Congress for Patristics at Oxford. *Beschreibung des Menschen* was effectively dedicated to Jonas.[96] There is also a section on Jonas in Quellen, Ströme, and Eisberge, *Beobachtungen an Metaphern*.[97] HB cites Jonas's 1954 "The Nobility of Sight" as early as his 1957 "Light as Metaphor for Truth" (p. 50 n. 79).

Throughout the last two decades of his life, he wrote copiously, much of which he left in his Marbach *Nachlass*. As these materials are appearing, the impression of the Jewishness of the late work is reinforced. For example, in the posthumous Suhrkamp volumes devoted to Carl Schmitt and Ernst Jünger, he turns and returns to themes associated with Jews, Jewishness, and Judaism, if not of the German-Jewish encounter and the Shoah.

It might be worth thinking of Blumenberg as an heir of Cassirer. Cassirer's recuperation of myth repudiated his teacher Hermann Cohen's mythophobia, even as it equally rejected the irrationalism of contemporaneous mythomania.[98] Cassirer in this sense may be roughly aligned with influential German Jewish minds like Scholem and Warburg, who took myth to be a "living" function of being human. In any case, these German Jews found in symbolism a saving remnant, a *Nachleben*, of the revealed ages. They found that this meaningfulness in symbols—or in metaphors, for Blumenberg—allowed them to epitomize religious sensibility while living the daily lives of men emancipated from ritual. They were also able to do so in a way that avoided both the hollow pieties of Reform and the even more hollow self-righteousness of their parental bourgeoisie. They worshipped myth and symbol, not with middle-class conventions, but as if a god lurked in the details of language and image and metaphor. This may be an aesthetic religion, fit for men of *Kultur*. And it may be a messianism for perfectionists, a negative theology for poets, for whom lesser expressions were but a Platonic cave fit only for escape.

It is hard *anywhere* to find another postwar Jewish thinker who, on this fully cosmic scale, encountered God through all available forms of intelligence. God, therefore, whom Blumenberg confronts without intermediary; God intermediated only by intelligence, the God of the philosophers; the God, finally, of Jewish philosophers.

BLUMENBERG'S UNFAMILIARITY WITH JUDAISM AS A LIVED RELIGION

HB was fluent in the history of Jewish philosophy. A partial list of the Jewish philosophers—I leave aside the appropriate "Who is a Jew?" questions in the present context—whom he cites knowledgably include Philo, Isaac Israeli, Ibn Gabirol, Maimonides, Spinoza, Moses Mendelssohn, Bergson, Simmel, Husserl, Hermann Cohen, Rosenzweig, Wittgenstein, Cassirer, Arendt, Scholem, Jonas, Kracauer, Ernst Bloch, Walter Benjamin, Adorno, as well as others less well known, such as Paul Alsberg, Oscar Goldberg, Manes Sperber, and marginally Jewish thinkers such as Plessner and Löwith, as well as anomalous Jewish thinkers like Taubes.

Blumenberg was erudite, and Wissenschaft des Judentums was another arrow in his crammed quiver. Still, it cannot fairly be said that his published familiarity with Judaism as a religion extended terribly far. Yes, he knew some Hebrew and he knew some Midrash. While Trierweiler may be correct that HB was learned in Wissenschaft des Judentums, there are good indications that he was fundamentally unfamiliar with some basics of Jewish learning and practice. By contrast to his legendarily universal erudition, HB's knowledge of lived Judaism was, shall we say, spotty. Given the often mind-boggling detail with which he invested studies of countless subjects, ranging from patristics to astronautics, he exhibited a comparative incuriosity concerning Judaism.

Thus in *Beschreibung des Menschen* he reflects on ruptures of identity using the example from Lidzbarsky's Jewish mother changing his name for magical reasons. Consider too, regarding the Lidzbarsky citation, that HB had a baby brother who died at age three. Mark Lidzbarsky (1868–1928), born Avraham Mordechai, changed his name to Mark when he converted to Protestantism. The autobiography was originally published anonymously; the official *Deutsche Biographie* entry says "(*anonyme Autobiogr. bis 1889*)."[99] A telling example, also concerning Lidzbarsky, comes from HB's *Lesbarkeit*. First, Blumenberg cites a passage from *Pirke Avoth*, familiar to any knowledgeable Jew; but he cites it from the old standby German translation in the Bin Gorion anthology. In any case, neglecting to identify it as *Pirke Avot*, he furthermore implicitly betrays his ignorance of one of the most familiar rabbinic texts.

This ignorance is followed immediately by a yet more glaring example. He cites the memoirs of the orientalist and convert Lidzbarsky, whose memoirs describe his traditional Jewish upbringing in Eastern Europe. The passage that Blumenberg cites refers to the annual inscription of human acts in the celestial account book—a central motif of the liturgy of Rosh Hashana and Yom Kippur. As with his nonidentification of *Pirke Avot*, Blumenberg seems unfamiliar with this rudimentary act of Jewish religious observance.

> The orientalist Mark Lidzbarsky, who discovered the principal source of Mandean gnosis, recalled in his memoirs that the idea of a great book of accounts was still vivid in the Judaism of his childhood. "*The works of each person were inscribed in heaven all year, the debit and credit of each was borne in a great book of accounts; the balance was drawn at the beginning of the following year, at the moment at which the destiny of each was determined. It was thus a matter of life and of death.*"[100]

BLUMENBERG AND THE JEWISH MESSIAH

He may or may not embody an "eschatology of the book," as Paul Mendes-Flohr put it.[101] Perhaps, at least, "eschatological irony," to borrow a phrase from one of his first essays.

In the 1966 *LMA*, toward the beginning of the book, Blumenberg seems almost explicitly to reject Scholem's conception of the Messiah.[102] The first citation of rabbinic literature in the vast *Mythos* trilogy concerns the Messiah. Citing *Midrash Tanchuma*, "A lover who was rewarded was Judah, for from him sprang Pharez and Hezron, who were to give us David and the King Messiah, who will redeem Israel. See what devious ways God must follow before he can cause the King Messiah to arise from Judah."[103]

Blumenberg's philosophical anthropology posited the human as the creature defined by insufficiency. In temporal terms, this implied that the human is *the being of the not-yet*.

> Man's deficiency in specific dispositions for reactive behavior vis-à-vis reality—that is, his poverty of instincts—is the starting point for the central anthropological question as to how this creature is able to exist in spite of his lack of fixed biological

> dispositions. The answer can be reduced to the formula: by not dealing with this reality directly. The human relation to reality is indirect, circumstantial, *delayed*, selective, and above all "metaphorical."[104]

Blumenberg's "MacGuffin" has a sly Hitchcockian humor to it, even though it is a philosophical set piece on a certain sort of Messiah, that is, *the Messiah as defined by delay*. As Blumenberg puts it in "MacGuffin," "On the way there was a delay and delay proved . . . itself the meaning of the way" (p. 193).[105] That Blumenberg here evoked Scholem's treatment of the *Messianic Idea in Judaism* is clear, since he cites it decisively in *Work on Myth* (p. 228), specifying the celebrated passage to the effect that the messianic idea "compelled a life lived in deferment."[106] Already in *LMA*, it should be recalled, Blumenberg was speaking of

> *the invaluable historical advantage of being able to say that the Messiah has not yet come*. What has already been can only be disappointing. The chiliastic enthusiasts of both sacred and worldly peripeties have always understood that. The Messiah who has already appeared can only be treated dogmatically; one must be able to specify exactly who he was, how he identified himself, what he left behind him.[107]

"The confirmation of a realm of the 'not yet' which cannot be caught up with."[108] Or, as he put it in the lovely little late piece, "Pensiveness," "the profit in delay that delay first allows."[109]

The *latency* of the Messiah is underwritten in regularly Freudian terms, even when, as in his intricate repackaging of *Moses and Monotheism*, Blumenberg seems to reverse Freud.[110]

Related to delay, *unrecognizability* is characteristic of the Messiah. "The question of the messianic moment is solely: 'Are you the one who is supposed to come, or do we have to wait for someone else?' The horizon of messianism surrounding both questioners and those who are questioned prescribes the answer: 'I am he.'"[111]

Blumenberg concludes his *Matthew Passion* with reflections on the unrecognizability of the Messiah, with extensive reference to Kafka, Benjamin, and Scholem. These reflections continued in the last decade of his life. In "Die Welt hat keinen Name," of 1992, he ends with the Messiah. So too his "private futurology" of 1990.

"IT IS NOT GOOD FOR MAN TO BE ALONE" (GEN. 2:18): ADAM II OR ROBINSON CRUSOE?

Blumenberg was (in)famously marginal in the social universe of the German academy. He didn't create a school, didn't join a party, didn't participate in a religion. He was disengaged politically. More broadly, he didn't move to Israel, didn't embrace Communism, didn't return to practicing Judaism as a religion. It sometimes seems he acted as if inside one of a saga-long sequence of novels—from *Robinson Crusoe* to *Joseph and His Brothers*—in which he was himself playing a mute character, a spectator character who does not speak but does not only watch—and never stops writing; in fact, his action is his writing, as author, a player on the stage of cosmic écriture. The drama of isolated thought itself was his forté. Blumenberg's *Shipwreck with Spectator: Paradigm of a Metaphor for Existence.*[112] Blumenberg himself was shipwrecked. He ends *Shipwreck with Spectator* with "demiurgical Robinson Crusoes." According to Marquard, he thought he lost eight years from his life and had to make up for them.[113] He found his voice in the silence of a desert island, a veritable Hayy ibn Yaqzan.[114]

But for HB "religion," which didn't take the name religion, meant *work on the limits of human knowledge*. Löwith: "To want to orient oneself on history, while tossed around in the midst of it, would be like wanting to hold on to the waves in time of shipwreck."[115] While criticizing these words by Löwith, Blumenberg repeatedly evokes the image of Robinson Crusoe as demiurge.[116]

> The demiurgical, Robinson Crusoe longing of the modern age is also present in the handiwork of the constructivist who leaves home and heritage behind in order to found his life on the naked nothingness of the leap overboard.[117]

"The modern age," for Löwith a roiling epistemic sea, invoked as the originary antagonist in Blumenberg's earlier *The Legitimacy of the Modern Age*; Löwith claims modernity as the distension of preceding theology: an ersatz soteriology, according to Blumenberg, "in which connection the sheer survival of the shipwrecked Robinson as demiurge has made immanent that transcendent certainty of salvation."[118] Löwith's position has been succinctly summarized as holding that "*religion is never over*."[119]

HB did not choose philosophy, poetry, and fiction as ideal genres to express a universalization of the Jewish condition. Rather, in some sense these forms of language, each at the frontmost edge of "modernism," left him a shipwrecked writer with enlivened metaphorological reflexes. In his Bremen acceptance speech Celan speaks of grappling with an "approachable reality."[120] Like Celan, his exact contemporary, Blumenberg edged to the furthest human efforts possible within his language spheres, his lifeworld, his lifeworld spheres of philosophy, poetry, and fiction, to grapple with "approachable reality." Grappling with the sovereignty of reality is a key to Blumenberg's confoundingly conflictual style. Unfathomably conflicted while magisterially assured, the Blumenberg voice echoes an early modern novelist's concoction, out of joint with the times, speaking unlike anyone else alive, yet paradigmatically "universal" nonetheless. Like Robinson Crusoe, he is a stranger, an outsider, so foreign that he's unrecognizable, even unclassifiable. This mysterious stranger is playing by his own incalculable rules.

So perhaps it's better to go back to the beginning. Adam II, in Rav Soloveitchik's *Lonely Man of Faith*, perhaps the only great Jewish philosophical anthropology. David Schatz summarizes it in his "Foreword" to the reprinting of *Lonely Man of Faith* (1944).

> "In every one of us abide the two *personae*." And here is the rub: the need for oscillation means that the man of faith has no single home. He is a wanderer, striking roots in one community, only to then uproot himself and travel to another, in a perpetual cycle. This continuous oscillation is a source of loneliness—and it cannot be overcome.[121]

Ironies always abound. Blumenberg is often noted for crediting his analogous theory of human insufficiency to Arnold Gehlen's *Der Mensch. Seine Natur und seine Stellung in der Welt.* (1940). He does not comment on the original 1940 context for this tome.

WHERE DOES BLUMENBERG BELONG?

"Hans Blumenberg's sprawling and seemingly esoteric work is driven by factors that are buried deep in the moonscape of postwar (West) German intellectual history."[122]

He is unrecognizable, therefore, in a significant sense. He could, for example, reasonably be compared to Cassirer. Koerner, in fact, calls him a "Cassirer for our time."[123] Consider analogous Jewish "encyclopedist" philosophers of the history of science (Koyré, Kuhn, Pines, Mauthner, Cassirer, Volkov, Merton, Popper, Plessner, Manheim, Sambursky, et al.). But Blumenberg upheld the German-Jewish Bildung project not as neo-Kantian, not as straightforward successor to Hermann Cohen and Cassirer. His metaphorology is not idealistic, for one thing. Perhaps most importantly—and Jewishly—it is grounded in history and moments, and individuals. It is anti-Platonist in spirit. His wholes are not Forms. His escapes from caves are a rejection of Plato's cave. He thus invokes "a mirror-image reversal of Platonism" as he puts it in his charged discussion of Joseph Roth's *Antichrist*.[124]

He never went to America, never sought a cultic following, never wrote cryptically for merely atmospheric effect or from some insipid Zeusian elevation. But he resembles the masters of Continental philosophy in his blending literary and philosophical and religious moods and motivations. And he shares an antiscientistic aesthetic. Still, there are no interviews, no "school," no "followers."[125] Blumenberg was an outsider who freely and eclectically drew on literature and religion to make a career assaulting the professionalization of philosophy. Blumenberg gravitated to laughter, fragments, shipwrecks, lions, icebergs—and to the antiphilosophical canon from Heine and Wittgenstein. This, after all, is the antiphilosophical punchline of *The Laughter of the Thracian Woman*.

He is, in any case, eclectic. This too is a tradition. I suggest analogues. The first was his Montaigne. Montaigne's eclecticism was in fact a function of his skepticism.[126] Alone in his tower, engaging in a critique of religion after surviving the terrible wars of religion. How then is thinking of a Montaignean HB as a German Jew to help us think about him at all? He belongs to a certain subtradition of radical Jewish outsiderness. I think in this sense Heine, Kafka, Freud, and Wittgenstein are his touchstones, and he cites all four on countless occasions throughout his many books. Their outsiderness was essentially identical with their thought. They were not gadflies, and they were not failures, and they were not alienated, and they were not inadequate, and they were not angry. But they *did not belong. Not belonging* was, for Blumenberg, not primarily a matter of Jewishness. His thought was resolutely, one might say heroically, within the discourse of the mind, of intellection, of the adventure of the intelligence, of the sciences, and especially of philosophy. That being said, his thought was true to his trauma too. Nor did he end with only negative results—he thought seriously, philosophically, one might even dare to say *messianically*, about a real human future.[127]

He *proved* the "*truth*" of Judaism by rethinking a human relation to the whole of creation from cosmic scratch, as if "from the beginning." From the zero degree, from the Nullpunkt. He revisited *Bereshit* in the lineaments of pure thought. In doing so, he recapitulated a distinctively Jewish road to God . . . in which, once again, *He* didn't respond. What the philosopher did do, and this can be shown quite easily, was to make the Hebrew Bible, that is, the Word of God, central to all his work, an endless fount of stimulation, themes, irritation, examples, and so on.

BLUMENBERG'S "HERESY" AS HIS JEWISHNESS

Throughout his career he identified with *soi disant* "heretics," from Bruno to Kafka to Gnostics. This tendency is already explicit in his 1952 reverencing of Kafka's "gottlose Religiosität." It is there in 1958 in his fervent turn to the subject of Gnosis.[128] It is there in the 1969 introduction, weighing in at 46 pages, to the translation of Giordano Bruno's *Ash Wednesday Supper*—the title of his introduction is "*Das Universum eines Ketzers.*" He elsewhere evoked Bruno's

> way of life, as a vagabond "outcast" from Church and society, [who] not only offers the appearance of intimacy with forbidden things but also delights in propagating what is intellectually shocking.[129]

It is found in undated posthumously published pieces like "Notizen zum Atheismus."[130] It is there in the Prometheus theme and again in the "extraordinary saying" *Nemo contra deum.*

His heretical if critical engagement with myth and Christianity allowed him to ask provocative questions without asking them explicitly as a Jew. *Perhaps* it's pointless to call him a heretic—or a Jew, for that matter—when, strictly speaking, the title *philosopher* should suffice. But he saw himself as heir to Heine and Freud, that is, as a critic of civilization as such, even while tied, however "godlessly," to his own heritage within that civilization. Given the enormous quantity of direct and indirect Judaica in his work—and the evidence cited above, including repeated uses of rabbinic texts, provides only a tiny taste of the whole shmear—he was not ashamed of his background. And he directed his work to penetrate the dark heart of his country's demonic collapse, to probe philosophically into the abyss of National Socialist *mentalité.*

There was for him, ultimately, the untrammeled encounter with absolutes that only a perfectly free human could muster. Such freedom, it seems, came most purely from his heresy, his shipwreck, his isolation, his trauma, his outsiderness. Or his Jewishness?

". . . WHATEVER THE MODERN UNDERSTANDING OF THE WORLD CANNOT BRING TOGETHER ANYMORE": ON SEMITISM AND ANTISEMITISM

. . . the totalizing force of myth, with which it orders all phenomena,
as noticed on the surface, in a network of correspondences,
relationships of similarity and contrast,
arises from basic concepts which categorically combine
whatever the modern understanding of the world
cannot bring together anymore.
JÜRGEN HABERMAS[131]

Schmitt programmatically concocted weirdly heterogeneous canards. Such symptomatically structural heterogenenity of hate, whose paragon is Carl Schmitt, programmatically knits together the unconnected in order to concoct a monstrous composite: "the enemy."

> Die drei Einbrüche—industrielle Technisierung, Psychoanalyse und modern Malerei—kann man sich hier verschieden vorstellen: die Technisierung als der Schwert, das die Knaüel alter Bilder und Tabus durchschneidet, die Psychoanalyse als Lösung des Riemens und die modern Malerei als eine Ablösung durch Überholung.[132]

Schmitt asserts that "*These three ruptures—industrial technification, psychoanalysis, and modern painting—are evidently connected. . . .* We must, then, begin with another hypothesis to understand the structural nucleus of this conflict." The "structural nucleus of this conflict" can hardly be anything other than its *a priori* antisemitism, which emerges from its invention of a fabricated enemy. Because, of course, there is no "structural nucleus of this conflict" outside of Schmitt's daimonic imagination.

With reference to the epochal German-Jewish "missed encounters," I accordingly contrast Blumenberg's heterogeneity with that of Schmitt. In substantive terms of *theoria*, Blumenberg's personal canon of Heine, Kafka, Wittgenstein, and Freud may have had precious little in common. And yet Blumenberg aligned them longitudinally, as if they belonged together. In other words: just as Schmitt's "structural nucleus of this conflict" is antisemitism, so is Blumenberg's heterogeneous lineage his idiosyncratic expression of what might be called "Semitism." Heterogeneous Europeans, from diverse geopolitical strata and class situations, together *agreed on* the multiplex physiognomy of a phantom. What still challenges historical research is the precision of its ghastly mechanisms. Both brutes and poets had *this* hallucination, down often to the most damningly macroscopic architectonic and microscopic tropes.

To what extent Blumenberg's novel lineage emerges out of his *Auseinandersetzung* with Carl Schmitt—an apparent example of Sartre's antisemite creating "the Jew"—seems explicable, true to its "logic," in Blumenberg's shocking effort to cast Adolf Eichmann as a founder of the State of Israel. Here, on the question of political power, one might begin to identify a hidden connection between Blumenberg and the conservative revolution's leading minds, Schmitt, Jünger, and Heidegger. What I am calling the synthetic heterogeneities of antisemitism and Semitism have been explained by Niethammer as reactions to their own powerlessness:

> This rebellious rearing-up before the abyss of unmeaning derives from the contradictory consciousness of the claims of intellectual greatness and the absence of its impact on the masses. . . . The illusory aspect of their megalomaniacal imagination lay in the practical sphere: in their view it was possible to keep one's distance from the masses and the bureaucracies, and yet lead them.[133]

Lepenies identifies the underlying powerlessness and its resulting malaise.

> Weltschmerz, melancholy and hypochondria resulted from the enforced hypertrophy of the realm of reflection, from imposed loss of the ability to exercise real power, and from the consequent pressure to justify one's situation.[134]

CONCLUSIONS: CHRISTIAN OR JEW? BOTH/AND? OR FALSE DICHOTOMY?

> *Heine is the only German Jew who could truthfully describe himself as both a German and a Jew. He is the only outstanding example of a really happy assimilation in the entire history of that process.*
> HANNAH ARENDT[135]

The epigraph to Blumenberg's posthumous masterwork *Beschriebung des Menschen* is taken from Heine on Spinoza: "Statt zu sagen, er leugne Gott, könnte man sagen, er leugne den Menschen" (Instead of saying that he denied God, you could say that he denied humanity). Embodied in his short chapter title "*Ganz Andere*?," Blumenberg again asks the question of absolute otherness—in fact, it may be said to be the leitmotif of his corpus.[136]

Ahlrich Meyer, in editing the English translation of *Rigorismus der Wahrheit*, concluded: "His posthumous papers and the essay 'Moses the Egyptian' published here show that an interest in Judaism was a hidden constant in his life."[137] Precisely because the Jewish God was such an overwhelmingly constant and equidistant problem for him, he became—arguably—a mutely yet meaningfully religious German Jew. The rhetoric and problematics of intellectual religion—how to talk about a silent god—are confronted everywhere, if always by indirection. A nonreligious wrestle with religion. A counterintuitive insistence on secularity, on being Jew-but-not-Jew, was consistent with a longer tradition of the Hebraic foreign body, the unrecognizable hybrid, rejected from the body of European culture. "Assimilated" Jews, specifically the Heines, Freuds, Kafkas, were the vanguard of a new type, one that might be called religion after religion.

They were "Jews" in scare quotes who wrote stiff-necked against a silent God. In their Judaism, such as it was, they overcame the depredation of Jews by surviving it without living as Jews. The loyal descendant of Heine and Freud and Kafka, he swam in this enlivening doubleness, like secular alcohol in sacramental wine. This doubleness cannot be explained by vestigial Jewishness or superattenuated replications of kabbalistic reflexes, nor by the isolation of traumatized survivors. HB was a religious man who re-created original Judaism by means of his *direct approach to the one God, an approach that was mediated neither by a Christ-figure nor by a rabbinic law*, but which was otherwise "marked," as I have tried to show, as being "Jewish." Nonconceptual metaphorology filled the gap where Christ or *Gesetz* might have been. He did so scientifically, so to speak, but his pathos and unrelenting intention on the absolute did so also in an obliquely prophetic mode.

An admittedly extreme declaration, coined by Emil Fackenheim as the "614th Commandment," goes as follows. *To deny Blumenberg his Jewishness is to give Hitler a posthumous victory*. My less apodictic point is that Blumenberg is significantly a German Jew and not a German Jew as an epiphenomenon. More than that: that his philosophy as such is in certain fundamental respects a substantive expression—again, not a mere symptom, or reflex, or epiphenomenon of his being a German Jew.

Most importantly, his metaphorology, his theory of nonconceptuality, his historical survey of philosophical anthropology, swerves into and is skewed by the "fate" of German Jewry. In other words, according to Blumenberg's retelling of the "end of Western metaphysics," the German-Jewish "*Weltgeistmirakel*" ruptures European philosophy. Blumenberg resolutely responds to this paradoxically uplifting *Krisis* in philosophical terms, not in chauvinistic, or spiteful, or mournful terms. The thinkers who most inform his final thought—Heine, Kafka, Cassirer, Freud, Wittgenstein—are a heterodox lineage whose weighty canonicity is constituted by its cheery anticanonicity. Not by a core cognitive commonality, but by their positions as "Deutschophone," each of whom "thought" as Germanic Europeans, in a situation that would not have them as Europeans and certainly not as Germanic. They are, one might say, his philosophical family—estranged from Judaism but not broken from Jewish modes of reasoning. Each, it might be said, expressed itself in terms of "a secularized representation of the Jewish conception of the world."

ACKNOWLEDGMENTS

When I delivered a version of this paper at the Tikvah Fund event in Princeton, the respondent was the philosopher Benjamin Pollack. He made several important criticisms, which I accept and which this version attempts to accommodate. In brief, he argued, among other things, that it was "suggestive but not convincing," and the "Jewish" materials were just part of Western culture.

I begin by thanking David Adams for providing me, as a Reed College colleague, with his groundbreaking translations from Blumenberg. A preliminary version of this paper was given at the Zentrum für Literatur und Kulturforschung in Berlin, January 15, 2010. I thank Sigrid Weigel, Daniel Weidner, and Martin Treml for hospitality and feedback during my work at the ZfL. The Tikvah Fund at Princeton University made possible a stimulating opportunity to present preliminary thoughts. Others who provided assistance include Ari Edmundson at the Marbach archives, Heidemarie Kugler-Weiemann in Lübeck, Joe Paul Kroll for multiple kindnesses, and the continuous research support provided by Reed College.

NOTES

1. *Frankfurter Allgemeine Magazin*, Ausgabe 118, 4.6.1982, S. 25. One of the first of his many occasional pieces was "Fragebogen," in *Frankfurter Allgemeine Magazin*, 4. Juni 1982, 25. Aside from a few comments, it was ignored in the literature on HB. HB replied to this questionnaire at age 62, three years before his retirement. He had begun writing in popular venues, especially newspapers, two years earlier. This was his first of many subsequent contributions to the FAZ. It was the only interview he ever granted.
2. Nor remembered as such. There are 225 Stolpersteine in Lübeck, but not one for Blumenberg. See https://www.stolpersteine-luebeck.de/main/namen-der-opfer.html.
3. *Munzinger Biographie* [http://www.munzinger.de/search/portrait/Hans+Blumenberg/0/19427.html] says flatly, "He was raised Catholic" [Er wurde katholisch erzogen].
4. Heidemarie Kugler-Weiemann was kind enough to answer my genealogical inquiries by direct reference to the Melderegister, which confirms that HB's mother Elsa, née Schreier, was born Jewish.
5. Joe Paul Kroll, "A Human End to History? Hans Blumenberg, Karl Löwith, and Carl Schmitt on Secularization and Modernity" (Princeton University dissertation, 2010), 284. Kroll cites Blumenberg's letter to his friend, Neukirchen, November 3, 1987.
6. Thomas Mann (b. 1875) attended Katharineum. But genealogical records show HB's father not arriving in Lübeck till 1919.
7. See *Bach, Lübeck und die nordeutsche Musiktradition*, ed. Wolfgang Sandberger.
8. More than a thousand pages of biography appeared in 2020 alone. See Jürgen Goldstein, *Hans Blumenberg. Ein philosophisches Porträt* (Berlin: Matthes & Seitz Verlag, 2020). 624 Seiten; Rüdiger Zill, *Der absolute Leser. Hans Blumenberg. Eine intellektuelle Biographie*. 816 Seiten.

This to be added to biographies by Kurt Flasch, Uwe Wolff, and numerous lesser productions.

9. Hans Joseph Konrad Blumenberg was married in a Lutheran ceremony to Ursula Elisabeth Margarethe Heinek, born 1922 in Lübeck.
10. Judith Sternberg, "Sibylle Lewitscharoffs fabelhafte Hommage an den Philosophen Hans Blumenberg: Die Anwesenheit des Löwen," in *Berliner Zeitung*, online at https://www.berliner-zeitung.de/sibylle-lewitscharoffs-fabelhafte-hommage-an-den-philosophen-hans-blumenberg-die-anwesenheit-des-loewen-li.42994?pid=true.
11. For some of the literature devoted to his religious thought see Peter Behrenberg, *Endliche Unsterblichkeit. Studien zur Theologiekritik Hans Blumenbergs* (Würzburg: Königshausen & Neumann, 1994); Markus Hundeck, *Welt und Zeit: Hans Blumenbergs Philosophie zwischen Schöpfungs- und Erlösungslehre* (Würzburg: Echter, 2000); Philipp Stoellger, *Metapher und Lebenswelt: Hans Blumenbergs Metaphorologie als Lebensweltthermeneutik und ihr religion-sphänomenologischer Horizont* (Tübingen: Mohr Siebeck, 2000).
12. According to V. Pavesich, "Hans Blumenberg's Philosophical Anthropology: After Heidegger and Cassirer," *Journal of the History of Philosophy* 46, no. 3 (2008): 425. A bibliography up to 1999 is found in David Adams and Peter Behrenberg, "Bibliographie Hans Blumenberg," in *Die Kunst des Überlebens: Nachdenken über Hans Blumenberg*, ed. Franz Josef Wetz and Hermann Timm (Frankfurt am Main: Suhrkamp, 1999).
13. Hans Blumenberg, *Paradigms for a Metaphorology*, trans. Robert Savage (Cornell University Press, 2010); and Hans Blumenberg, *Care Crosses the River*, trans. Paul Fleming (Stanford University Press, 2010).
14. Odo Marquard, "Entlastung vom Absoluten," in Wetz and Timm, as cited in Robert Savage, "Laughter from the Lifeworld: Hans Blumenberg's Theory of Nonconceptuality," *Thesis Eleven* 94 (2008): 119–31, at 120.
15. Martin Treml, "Doppelte Adressierung. Mendelssohns marranische Schreibweise," *Frankfurter Rundschau*, April 8, 2003, p. 13, where he notes that he takes the phrase from Klaus Briegleb on Heinrich Heine. I thank Martin Treml for sharing this reference with me.
16. Bettina Blumenberg, cited by Patrick Bahners in *FAZ* (December 12, 2007), online at https://www.faz.net/aktuell/feuilleton/geisteswissenschaften/fragmente-des-muensterschen-ungenannten-1488738.html.
17. Jean-Claude Monod, *Hans Blumenberg* (Paris: Belin, 2007), 11.
18. Denis Trierweiler, review of *Work on Myth*, in *Diogenes* 182 (1998): 155–64, at 157.
19. Hans Blumenberg, *Arbeit am Mythos* (Frankfurt am Main: Surhkamp, 2006), 83.
20. Hans Blumenberg, *The Genesis of the Copernican World*, trans. Robert M. Wallace (Cambridge, MA: MIT Press, 1987), 404.
21. Olivier Agard, "La légitimité des « avant-dernières choses ». La discussion Blumenberg/Kracauer sur la Modernité," *Archives de Philosophie* 2004/2, Tome 67, pp. 227–47, at 247.
22. Hans Blumenberg, *The Legitimacy of the Modern Age*, trans. Robert M. Wallace (Cambridge, MA: MIT Press, 2013), 13.
23. Blumenberg, *Legitimacy of the Modern Age*, 594.
24. Blumenberg, *Legitimacy of the Modern Age*, 594. Emphasis added.
25. For other reminiscences see Peter Guttkuhn, "Es geschah (auch) in Lübeck. Der Pogrom gegen

die jüdischen Mitbürger," in *Vaterstädtische Blätter*, 33. Jg., Lübeck 1982; Peter Guttkuhn, "Als eine Welt zerbrach. Erinnerungen an die 'Reichskristallnacht' in Lübeck," in *Lübecker Nachrichten*, Sonntagmorgen, 6. November 1988; Peter Guttkuhn, "Lübecks jüdische Gemeinde gewinnt einen Rechtsstreit. Intoleranz 'Im Weinrancken,'" in *Schleswig-Holsteinische Anzeigen* 1996, S. 98–100.

26. On April 24, 1994, while Blumenberg was still alive, the Lübeck synagogue was burned by arson.
27. David Adams noticed this passage. See David Adams, "Metaphors for Mankind: The Development of Hans Blumenberg's Anthropological Metaphorology," *Journal of the History of Ideas* 52 (1991): 152–66. The passage is found now in *Die Verführbarkeit des Philosophen*, 76.
28. For a recent updating of the Dräger complicity, see http://dirk-untertage.jimdo.com/galerie/wandsbek/kz-gedenkstätte-drägerwerke/.
29. From the official English language Drager Corporate History PDF found at http://www.draeger.com/media/10/08/38/10083871/the_history_of_draeger.pdf. Recent studies point out the inadequacy of the Dräger revision of history. See now, for example, Bernd Ziesemer, "Dräger and the darkest chapter in its history. The medical technology manufacturer Dräger saves lives in the Corona crisis with its ventilators. Lübeck is proud of the long company tradition—and glosses over its darkest chapter." Posted August 10, 2020, online at https://www-capital-de.translate.goog/wirtschaft-politik/draeger-und-das-dunkelste-kapitel-seiner-geschichte/2?_x_tr_sl=de&_x_tr_tl=en&_x_tr_hl=en&_x_tr_pto=nui,sc.
30. Gregor Dotzauer, "Trost sollen mir die Löwen spenden: Himmel und Erde, Tod und Auferstehung: Sibylle Lewitscharoff widmet dem großen Münsteraner Philosophen Hans Blumenberg eine romanhafte Fantasie, klärt theologische Fragen und nimmt nebenbei das intellektuelle Klima der achtziger Jahre aufs Korn," online at http://www.tagesspiegel.de/kultur/trost-sollen-mir-die-loewen-spenden/4596630.html.
31. Kroll, "A Human End to History?," 81. Emphasis added.
32. Kroll, "A Human End to History?," 82.
33. My translation, emphasis added. See the original at "À Propos De Hans Blumenburg. Entretien avec Denis Trierweiler," at www2.cndp.fr/.../d.trierweiler-entretien.pdf.
34. Ulrik Houlind Rasmussen, *The Memory of God*, Danish dissertation, citing M. Hundeck, *Welt und Zeit. Hans Blumenbergs Philosophie zwischen Schöpfungs- und Erlösungslehre* (Echter: Würzburg, 2000).
35. Letter to Alfons Neukirchen, November 3, 1987, cited by Kroll, "A Human End to History?," 284.
36. For an extensive discussion of Blumenberg on fathers and sons, see Rüdiger Zill, "Substrukturen des Denkens. Grenzen und Perspektive einer Metapherngeschichte nach Hans Blumenberg"; Hans Erich Bödeker (Hg.), *Begriffsgeschichte, Diskursgeschichte, Metapherngeschichte*, Mit Beiträgen von Mark Bevir, Hans Erich Bödeker, Lutz Danneberg, Jacques Guilhaumou, Reinhart Koselleck, Ulrich Ricken und Rüdiger Zill (Gottingen: Wallstein Verlag, 2002), 209–58, at 211–21 ["Väter und Söhne. Plädoyer für eine Metaphorologie als Institution"].
37. "Der absolute Vater," in *Hochland*, no. 45 (1952), S. 282 ff. Now translated in Hans Blumenberg, *History, Metaphors, Fables: A Hans Blumenberg Reader*, trans. Hannes Bajohr, Florian Fuchs, and Joe Paul Kroll (Ithaca, NY: Cornell University Press, 2020), 470.

38. Blumenberg, "Der Absolute Vater," 282. The theme remained alive in HB's thought in various respects. See *Ein mögliches*, 74.
39. Hans Blumenberg, *Begriffe in Geschichten* (Frankfurt am Main: Suhrkamp, 1998), 8.
40. "Dafür gedieh der erste Artikel meines Credo: Ich wußte, ich sah es vor mir, wie es bei der Erschaffung der Welt zugegangen war." Blumenberg, *Begriffe in Geschichten*, 8.
41. Hans Blumenberg, "Eschatological Ironie. Über die Romane Evelyn Waughs," in *Schriften zur Literatur 1945–1958*, ed. Alexander Schmitz and Bernd Stiegler (Berlin: Suhrkamp Verlag, 2017), 251.
42. This translation in Grözinger, *Kafka and Kabbalah*, 1. See a different translation of the same lines at 182–83.
43. See Steven M. Wasserstrom, *Religion after Religion: Gershom Scholem, Mircea Eliade, and Henry Corbin at Eranos* (Princeton: Princeton University Press, 1999).
44. Gershom Scholem, "Zehn unhistorische Sätze," in Scholem, *Judaica* 3 (Frankfurt M., 1970), at 271. First English translation by David Biale, "Gershom Scholem's Ten Unhistorical Aphorisms on Kabbalah: Text and Commentary," in *Modern Judaism* 4 (February 1985): 67–93.
45. From Janouch, cited in Hans Blumenberg, *History, Metaphors, Fables: A Hans Blumenberg Reader*, 125.
46. Georges-Arthur Goldschmidt, "Blumenberg à Kiel," *Cahiers philosophiques* 123, no. 3 (2010): 57.
47. Goldschmidt, "Blumenberg à Kiel," 58.
48. Hans Blumenberg, "The Absolute Father," *History, Metaphors, Fables: A Hans Blumenberg Reader*, trans Hannes Bajohr, Florian Fuchs, and Joe Paul Kroll (Ithaca, NY: Cornell University Press, 2020), 475.
49. Kroll, "A Human End to History?," 49. Emphasis added.
50. Gershom Scholem, "Zehn unhistorische Sätze," 271.
51. "Godless religiosity" as translated in Hans Blumenberg, *History, Metaphors, Fables: A Hans Blumenberg Reader*, 472.
52. Fritz Wittels, "Revision of a Biography," *Psychoanalytic Review* XX (1933): 361–74, at 363; cited by Blumenberg, "Das Gewand des Traums. Zur Metaphorik von Verhüllung und Enthüllung bei Freud," *Neue Rundschau* 1/2006, pp. 67–80, at 79, n. 1.
53. For Heine's influence on Freud, see Ritchie Richardson, "On the Sources of Moses and Monotheism," in *Reading Freud's Reading*, ed. Sander L. Gilman et al. (New York and London: New York University Press, 1993), 266–85.
54. Hans Blumenberg, *St. Matthew Passion*, trans. Helmut Müller-Sievers and Paul Fleming (New York: Cornell University Press, 2021), 18–22.
55. "Das Schlimmste, was zu gestehen mich die Erinnerungen meines Freundes nun veranlassen und ausdrücklich mir klarzumachen sie mir allerest verholfen haben, ist in kurzer *Confessio*: Trotz seither erlangten besseren Wissens ist meine kindliche Lesart des Aulaspruches der Tenor meiner 'Theologie' geblieben, sofern sie diesen Namen verdient." Hans Blumenberg, *Matthäuspassion* (Frankfurt: Suhrkamp, 1988), 28–29.
56. See the discussion of Bruce Krajewski, "The Afterlife of Hans Blumenberg's Centennial," p. 92, posted on September 14, 2020 at https://jhiblog.org/2020/09/14/blumenbergs-centennial/.
57. Blumenberg, *Begriffe in Geschichten*, 242–47.
58. Compare Schmidt's blurb for the tellingly titled *Hitler's Jewish Soldiers*: "Rigg's extensive

knowledge and the preliminary conclusions drawn from his research impressed me greatly. I firmly believe that his in-depth treatment of the subject of German soldiers of Jewish descent in the Wehrmacht will lead to new perspectives on this portion of 20th century German military history." Helmut Schmidt, former chancellor of Germany, in online blurb for Bryan Mark Rigg, *Hitler's Jewish Soldiers (Modern War Stories): The Untold Story of Nazi Racial Laws and Men of Jewish Descent in the German Military*, ed. Theodore A. Wilson. The ironies have been amplified in the 2014 biography: Sabine Pamperrien, *Helmut Schmidt und der Scheisskrieg: die Biografie 1918 bis 1945*.

59. In a letter to the editor in *First Things* (November 1992), Beth Newman made the following case: "Wittgenstein himself, in conversation with O. C. Drury in response to Drury's Origenist sympathies, said, 'Your religious ideas have always seemed to me more Greek than biblical. Whereas my thoughts are one hundred percent Hebraic' (cited by Fergus Kerr in *Theology after Wittgenstein*). Furthermore, Wittgenstein stated that a motto for the whole of his later philosophy might be Goethe's phrase from Faust, 'In the beginning was the deed.' Here we see Wittgenstein's reliance upon the Hebrew *davar*, which means both word and deed. Such Hebraic formations at the depth of Wittgenstein's imagination enabled him to make the radical philosophical moves he made." Steven S. Schwarzchild similarly noted that Wittgenstein asked "what the questions are that agitate the uprooted mind of a lost Jew who is transfixed by Augustine and Kierkegaard while hearing the last echoes (and perhaps the first renewed soundings) of . . . the ethics of the Judaic God?" [emphasis added].
60. Krajewski, "The Afterlife of Hans Blumenberg's Centennial."
61. Paul Mendes-Flohr, *German Jews: A Dual Identity* (New Haven, CT: Yale University Press, 2008), 1.
62. Hans Blumenberg, *Care Crosses the River*, trans. Paul Fleming (Stanford, CA: Stanford University Press, 2010), 57.
63. George Mosse, "Gershom Scholem as a German Jew," *Modern Judaism* 10, no. 2 (1990): 117–33.
64. Aubrey Pomerance, archivist at the Jüdisches Museum, Berlin, offered to help uncover the Blumenberg family history in Lübeck. Further help came from genealogists in Lübeck.
65. A separate study should be made of his uses of Talmud. Cf., e.g., *Löwen*, 82–84 (*Midrash Tachuma*), 94–95 (*Midrash Tehillim*).
66. Denis Trierweiler, preface to Hans Blumenberg, *La lisibilité du monde*, trans. Pierre Rusch (Paris: Éditions du Cerf, 2007), iii.
67. Blumenberg, *The Genesis of the Copernican World*, 70.
68. Hans Blumenberg, *Work on Myth*, trans. Robert M. Wallace (Cambridge, MA: MIT Press, 1985), 399. Emphasis added.
69. Hans Blumenberg, *Work on Myth*, 516.
70. Blumenberg, *Work on Myth*, emphasis added.
71. Compare Blumenberg, *Wirklichkeiten in denen wir leben* (Reclam): "Wenn Heinrich Heine in seinem Pamphlet über Ludwig Börne zu den großen Nivellierern Europas Richelieu und Robespierre hinzuzählt, weil er dem Boden endgültig seine Vormacht in den Sozialverhältnissen genommen habe und gleichsam des Geld mit den ehemaligen Vorrechten des Bodens belehnte, so ist der von den Bildern her paradoxe Gewinn dieser Metapher erst der deskriptive Befund in dem Satz: Geld ist flüssiger als Wasser, windiger als Luft . . ."

72. The specific citation of Hitler concerns "the fateful Hosbach minutes" of November 5, 1937.
73. Herz recurs in Hans Blumenberg and David Adams (trans.), "Does It Matter When? On Time Indifference," *Philosophy and Literature* 22, no. 1 (1998): 212–18, 214.
74. The original was deemed important enough to serve as the lead article in Blumenberg, *Verführbarkeit*, 9–18.
75. Hans Blumenberg, *Arbeit am Mythos*, 102 [emphasis added].
76. "[HB] hat zweifellos den Lübecker Synagogenbrand vom November 1938 vor Augen." Ahlrich Meyer, "HB oder: Die Kunst, sich herauszuhalten," in *Fliegende Fische*, 347.
77. Blumenberg, *Arbeit am Mythos*, 230.
78. Blumenberg, *Arbeit am Mythos*, 230.
79. Blumenberg, *Arbeit am Mythos*, 126.
80. Hans Blumenberg, *Die Vollzähligkeit der Sterne* (Frankfurt am Main: Surhkamp, 2000), 233.
81. Hans Blumenberg, "Pensiveness," in *Caliban 6*, trans. David Adams (1989), 54.
82. Hans Blumenberg, *Beschreibung des Menschen*, ed. Manfred Sommer (Frankfurt: Suhrkamp, 2006), 7.
83. Blumenberg, *Begriffe in Geschichten*, 7.
84. See my "The Great Goal of the Political Will Is Leviathan: Ernst Jünger and the Cabala of Enmity," *Kabbalah and Modernity*, ed. Kocku von Stuckrad and Marco Pasi (E. J. Brill, 2010), 327–56.
85. Blumenberg, *Arbeit am Mythos*, 9.
86. Blumenberg, *Arbeit am Mythos*, 16.
87. Blumenberg, *Arbeit am Mythos*, 20.
88. Blumenberg, *Arbeit am Mythos*, 26.
89. Blumenberg, *Matthäuspassion*, 13.
90. For a substantial discussion of this incident, see Martin Thoemmes, "Die verzögerte Antwort—Neues über den Philosophen Hans Blumenberg," *Lübeck Fenster. Offizielle Website der Hansestadt Lübeck*, April 1997.
91. Blumenberg, *Matthäuspassion*, 28.
92. Blumenberg, *Legitimacy of the Modern Age*, 117.
93. Hans Blumenberg, *Höhlenausgänge* (Frankfurt am Main: Suhrkamp, 1989), 11–19.
94. In his *Memoirs*, Jonas recalls the date as 1952. See Hans Jonas, *Memoirs*, ed. Christian Wiese, trans. Krishna Winston (Waltham: Brandeis University Press, 2008), 162. However, in a letter from Blumenberg to Jonas, he recalled the date as August 1953. See Benjamin Lazier, *God Interrupted: Heresy and the European Imagination Between the World Wars* (Princeton: Princeton University Press, 2008), 50.
95. Jonas, *Memoirs*, 162.
96. See comments by Sommer in *Beschreibung des Menschen*, 903.
97. Hans Blumenberg, *Quellen, Ströme, and Eisberge: Beobachtungen an Metaphern* (Berlin: Suhrkamp Verlag, 2012), 243–49.
98. These matters are engaged at some length in my *Religion after Religion*.
99. *Deutsche Biographie* [online] Lidzbarsky, Mark (ursprünglich Abraham Mordechai).
100. *Lesbarkeit*, 27 [= *Lisibilité du monde*, 33].
101. Paul Mendes-Flohr, *German Jews: A Dual Identity*, 71.

102. Blumenberg, *The Legitimacy of the Modern Age*, 34.
103. Blumenberg, *Arbeit am Mythos*, 40.
104. "An Anthropological Approach to the Contemporary Significance of Rhetoric," trans. Robert M. Wallace, in *After Philosophy: End or Transformation?*, ed. K. Baynes, J. Bohman, and T. McCarthy (Cambridge, MA: MIT Press, 1987), 439. Emphasis added.
105. Haverkamp calls "Das Sein—ein MacGuffin" "a short blurb on Davos." See *Telos*, p. 55 n. 50.
106. Blumenberg, *Arbeit am Mythos*, 228.
107. Blumenberg, *Legitimacy of the Modern Age*, 46. Emphasis added.
108. Blumenberg, *The Genesis of the Copernican World*, 638.
109. Blumenberg, "Pensiveness," 54.
110. Blumenberg, *Arbeit am Mythos*, 138–40. He had already discussed the concept of "latency" at length in the context of "significance."
111. Blumenberg, *Arbeit am Mythos*, 188–89.
112. Blumenberg, *Shipwreck with Spectator: Paradigm of a Metaphor for Existence*, trans. Steven Rendall (Cambridge, MA: MIT Press, 1997).
113. Odo Marquard, "Entlastung vom Absoluten. In memoriam Hans Blumenberg," *Kontingenz* (Poetik und Hermeneutik 17), (Munich: Fink, 1998), xx.
114. See the rich literature on the lines of filiation between Hayy ibn Yaqzan and Robinson Crusoe. See for example the literature in Remke Kruk, "An 18th-Century Descendant of Ḥayy ibn Yaqẓān and Robinson Crusoe: Don Antonio de Trezzanio,"*Arabica* 34 (1987): 357–65.
115. I am indebted for this remark of Karl Löwith to Dagmar Barnouw's delicate discussion of Kracauer's *History: The Last Things before the Last*, in her *Critical Realism: History, Photography, and the Work of Siegfried Kracauer* (Baltimore: Johns Hopkins University Press, 1994), 196.
116. Blumenberg, *Legitimacy of the Modern Age*, 14, and *Shipwreck with Spectator*, last paragraph, 78. See also *Die Lesbarkeit der Welt*, "Eine Robinson-Welt gegen die Newton-Welt," 150–62.
117. Blumenberg, *Shipwreck with Spectator*, 78.
118. Blumenberg, *Legitimacy of the Modern Age*, 14.
119. "Introduction: Secularization and Disenchantment," *NGC* 94 (2005): 6. The editors responsible for the phrase are Jonathan Skolnik and Peter Eli Gordon. Emphasis added.
120. Paul Celan, "Speech on the Occasion of Receiving the Literature Prize of the Free Hanseatic City of Bremen" (1958) in *Collected Prose*, trans. Rosmarie Waldrop (New York: P. N. Review/ Carcanet, 1986), 35.
121. David Schatz, "Foreword" to Joseph B. Soloveitchik, *The Lonely Man of Faith* (New York: Doubleday, 2006) reprint, p. XI.
122. Helmut Müller-Sievers, "Kyklophorology: Hans Blumenberg and the Intellectual History of Technics," *Telos* (March 2012): 155–70, at 155.
123. Joseph Leo Koerner, "Ideas About the Thing, not the Thing Itself: Hans Blumenberg's Style," *History of the Human Sciences* 6 (1993): 1–10.
124. Hans Blumenberg, *The Genesis of the Copernican World*, 118.
125. There are no Blumenbergians. HB himself explains that fact by reference to Simmel's cash metaphor. Perhaps the most revealing and explicit self-understanding of his own legacy was

appropriated, in 1976, from Georg Simmel: "In this regard, I find it *incomparably meaningful* that, at the end of his own life, Simmel saw this life, and the fruit of his labours in philosophical teaching, under the metaphor of money:

> *I know that I will die without any intellectual heirs (and that is a good thing). My legacy is like one consisting entirely of cash and distributed among many heirs, each of whom invests his share in a living that accords with his nature: it shows no sign of its provenance in that legacy.* (1923: 1) [emphasis added, smw]

See Rüdiger Zill, *Der absolute Leser: Hans Blumenberg. Eine intellektuelle Biographie* (Suhrkamp, 2020).

126. See most recently Pierre Force, "Montaigne and the Coherence of Eclecticism," *Journal of the History of Ideas* 70, no. 4 (October 2009): 523–44.
127. Blumenberg, "Futurologie," in *Begriffe in Geschichten*, 60–61.
128. "Epochenschwelle und Rezeption," *Philosophische Rundschau* 6 (1958): 94–120.
129. Blumenberg, *Legitimacy of the Modern Age*, 480.
130. *Die Neue Rundschau* 118, no. 2 (2007): 154–60.
131. Sandor's translation, in "Myths and the Fantastic," 342.
132. Carl Schmitt,"Die geschichtliche Struktur des heutigen Weltgegensatzes von Ost und West: Bemerkungen zu Ernst Jüngers Schrift, 'Der Gordische Knoten,'" in *Freundschaftliche Begegnungen*, ed. Armin Mohler (Frankfurt: Vittorio Klostermann, 1955), 526.
133. Lutz Niethammer, on what he calls "the will to powerlessness" in "Afterthoughts on Posthistoire," *History and Memory* 1 (1989): 27–53, at 37, 40.
134. Wolf Lepenies, *Melancholy and Society* (Cambridge, MA: Harvard University Press, 1992), 61.
135. Hannah Arendt, *The Jewish Writings* (New York: Schocken Books, 2013), 281.
136. Blumenberg, *Die Vollzähligkeit der Sterne*, 360.
137. Hans Blumenberg, *Rigorismus der Wahrheit: "Moses der Agypter" und weitere Texte zu Freud und Arendt* (Frankfurt: Suhrkamp, 2015); Blumenberg, *Rigorism of Truth: "Moses the Egyptian" and Other Writings on Freud and Arendt*, trans. Joe Paul Kroll (Ithaca, NY: Cornell University Press, 2018), at 93.

HOME(S) IN FUTURE ANTERIORS; OR, PATHS OF POIESIS FOURFOLDED FORWARD

ALMUT SH. BRUCKSTEIN

For Elliot R. Wolfson

THE SUMMER I STUDIED ELLIOT WOLFSON'S WORK *LANGUAGE, EROS, BEING: Kabbalistic Hermeneutics and Poetic Imagination*[1] my mother had just passed and due to a series of exhausting circumstances I had suffered a mental breakdown and the symptoms were strange. Lines of thought seemed cut, single words crumbled into "endlessly distended moments,"[2] and I began to lose what seems ordinarily most available, I lost touch between one word and another, unable to walk a single line of thought without getting lost on the way. In this "vacuity," this "fissure" (*Zerklüftung*), in the "spiritlessness" of this mental flight[3]—was it then that all the words were lost, the mind altogether empty? No. Words seemed plenty. They simply did not stand in line ready for a sentence; distances stretched, gaps became insurmountable, and I could no longer make any connection between words that were spoken. It seemed a miracle when my thinking would eventually cross the dark from one imagined word to the next. The doctors advised me to take a break and to abstain from any fatiguing intellectual work.

This is when I started studying Elliot R. Wolfson's *Language, Eros, Being*. Did I remember anything when studying it in that condition? Possibly not much. Instead I learned something else. I learned how to move inside the texts of Elliot Wolfson as if in a mirror state, mirroring the author's text onto my own psychic condition and vice versa, moving blindly awake between diffused "mythopoetic instantiations,"[4] lost for words, submersed in the text of one who thinks in loops, "in turns and twists," "capricious and disruptive,"[5] whose abundant writings open up a "temporal-spatial playing field"[6] of language, a *Zeit-Spiel-Raum* for dissociated agglomerations. In this playing field of language, in any of Elliot R. Wolfson's texts, elliptic movements catch up to their own ever new beginnings. Drawn into his various loops of thinking, in a dizzying speed, in leaps of "maddening lucidity,"[7] bizarrely static, the reader—if she doesn't get lost or otherwise dizzy—gets in touch with places where she has previously never been.[8] In timeswerves of "futural rememberings" in which anticipation ungrounds all "first beginnings," she experiences the "not-yet-crossed" of "faithful repetitions," sabbatical beginnings, and "circular closures that do not close anything" at all.[9]

Elliot R. Wolfson's texts are full of "sabbatical beginnings."[10] Suspended endings turn into abysmal beginnings—final matters turn into "new and more primeval beginnings than the ones from which one has departed."[11] Let me remind you then of the very last matter, the concluding sentence of *Language, Eros, Being*, which indeed became a sabbatical beginning for me ever since my mind gave way to the "vacuity" of a way of thinking in its mental flight. It is a sentence hovering and never quite absent throughout all the relentless meanderings of Elliot R. Wolfson's writings:

> Salvation comes about through the containment of the feminine in the masculine, the neutralization of female power. Suffering the suffering of this axiom is a first step on the path to redeeming an ancient wisdom, tiredly waiting to be liberated from the confinement of its own textual embodiment.[12]

Tiredly waiting to be liberated from the confinement of *one's own* textual embodiment.

Yes. I am replacing the predicament of the "ancient wisdom" "tiredly waiting to be liberated *from the confinement of its own* textual embodiment" by the author's *own* as if the author were to desire a liberation from the confinement of *his own* textual embodiment—and yes, this substitution implies that we must read Elliot R. Wolfson's texts as if they were themselves suffering that axiom, the containment of the feminine in the masculine, the neutralization of female power locked inside *one's own texts*, which in *his* case indeed stand in for "an ancient wisdom," an entire *Torah shelema*. This is how I would approach Elliot Wolfson's more recent works then, and possibly all of his work read backward, all touching upon *Hidden Gnosis and the Path[s] of Poiesis*.[13] I would suggest reading Elliot R. Wolfson's texts as a teaching on the desire to be liberated from the confinement of one's own textual embodiment. "Female power" seems to hint at the apopathetic *noli me tangere* of an existential condition beyond reach, as it speaks from the absence-presence of the desired other locked inside/out of one's own textuality, corporality, and language.[14] Just for a moment I am turning to the adverbial attribute "tiredly waiting"—"tiredly waiting to be liberated from . . ." Adverbial attributes are important; they occupy an entire generation of Judeo-Arabic medieval scholars thinking about "attributes of relation," or more specifically "divine attributes of action" meant to undo any essentializing speech about the divine.[15] Adverbial attributes, in fact, reveal a desire: tiredly waiting—tiredly waiting to be liberated—tiredly waiting to be liberated from the confinement of one's own textual embodiment. Waiting without hope, but waiting nonetheless.[16]

The attentive reader feels "the desire to accede, by this repetition, to the not-yet-crossed [. . .], the desire for a new step, albeit a backward one [*Schritt zurück*], which ties and unties."[17] How is this related to the desire to be liberated from a confinement—how?

In response to this question, and not exactly knowing what I was doing, I began to systematically transfer splinters from Elliot R. Wolfson's most recent work quite meticulously into a mirror matrix "outside" his own texts, creating a dynamic and interactive topography of external splinters and passages of Elliot R. Wolfson's texts. Let's take a closer look at this topography, more specifically at the above quoted passage "the desire to accede, by this repetition, to the not-yet-crossed . . ." inside that topography, which I call "Paths of Poiesis. Fourfolded Forward." What we see is an atlas, a double-ganger device, which in a "backward step" ties and unties, and whose differential movement is governed by a hidden list of attributes, feeding an algorithm that, in turn, governs the relational position of all splinters to one another.[18]

> Pas sans pas. . . . The desire to accede, by this faithful repetition of the circle, to the not-yet-crossed. . . . The desire for a new step, albeit a backward one. . . . Tie without tie—[the desire] to get across [*franchir*] the circle without getting free [*sàffranchir*] of its law.[19]

How?

Pas sans pas [step without step / step without not / not without step / not without not].[20]

A Lacanian colleague just recently drew my attention to the playful homophony of the [k]not that is [k]not—to the psycho-poietic significance of knotting and unknotting one's own [k]nots.[21] In a leap, "*l'après coup*," that is "after the fact," . . . "the symptom does not relate primarily to an occurrence in the past but rather to an event that awaits its futural unfolding."[22]

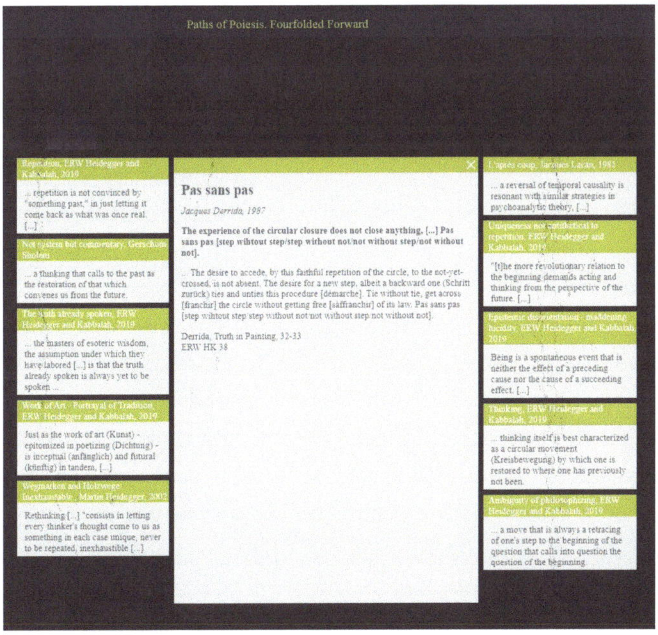

Bruckstein / House of Taswir, Paths of Poiesis. Fourfolded Forward. Atlas for Elliot R. Wolfson. "Pas sans pas," https://taswir.org/atlas.

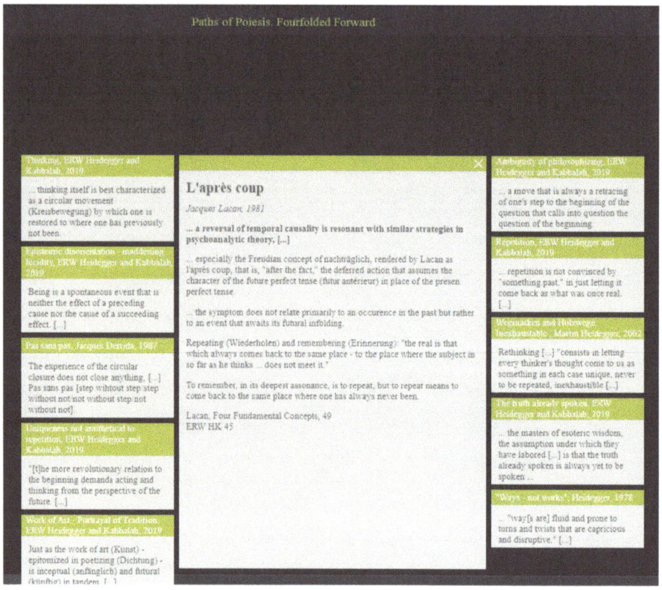

Bruckstein / House of Taswir, Paths of Poiesis. Fourfolded Forward. Atlas for Elliot R. Wolfson. "L'après coup," https://taswir.org/atlas.

"The desire to be liberated from" thus assumes the character of a future perfect, a deferred action: In the future anterior tense [*futur antérieur*] something or someone will have been liberated from . . . the confinement of . . . "My hermeneutics embraces the prospects of a reversible timeline"—Elliot Wolfson says—the "act of recollecting has the capacity to redeem the past not by describing how the past really was but by imputing to it meaning that it never had except as to become what it is not."[23]

Elliot R. Wolfson is unthinking the deadly seal of Jewish tradition from within the philosophical discourses of the "West"—Heidegger, Lacan, Freud—in ways yet to be explored; in ways touching upon the containment of the feminine in the masculine, the neutralization of female power, and yes, on suffering the suffering of this axiom as a first step on the path to redeeming an ancient wisdom, tiredly waiting to be liberated from . . .

> Unthinking, in an act that ties and unties, *pas sans pas*, "consists in letting every thinker's thought come to us as something in each case unique, never to be repeated, inexhaustible. [. . .] The more original the thinking, the richer will be what is unthought in it. The unthought is the greatest gift [*Geschenk*] that thinking can bestow."[24]

Elliot Wolfson indeed submits gigantic diachronic landscapes of ancient and contemporary philosophical, poetic, kabbalistic, and psychoanalytic literature to a uniquely personal yet all-encompassing process of unthinking, rendering a myriad of ancient and contemporary sources to a "type of futural remembering." Elliot R. Wolfson's own "timeswerves of linear circularity" are singularly universal.

Through this kind of singularity, the author's discrete ways of thinking, a specific community emerges, we dare to say: he, the author, creates a community in ways un-

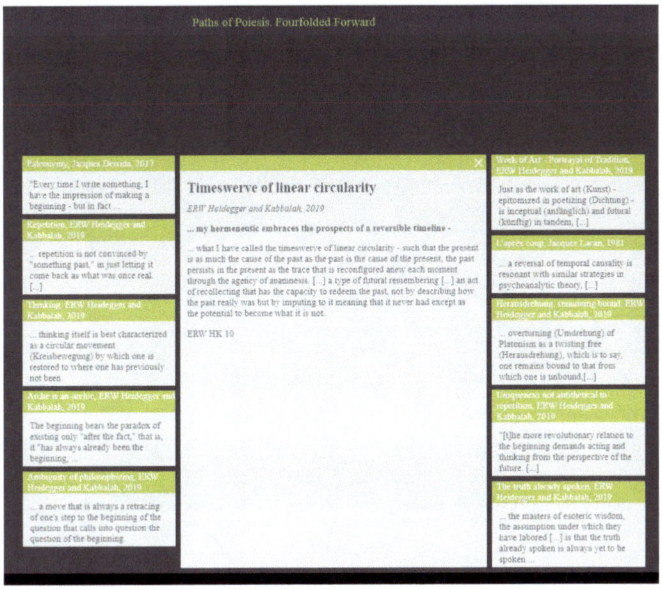

Bruckstein / House of Taswir, Paths of Poiesis. Fourfolded Forward. Atlas for Elliot R. Wolfson. "Timeswerve of linear circularity," https://taswir.org/atlas.

expected, subcutaneous, and beyond strategy, a community brought about by desire, a community that has long made itself home in the future anterior.

> We better "think of the universal as being constituted relentlessly in light of the random and indiscriminate particulars [...] [yet] calibrated from the [desire] of "being-with-one-another, circulating in the *with* and as the *with* of [a] singularly plural coexistence."[25]

Elliot Wolfson turns a precious and otherwise widely obscured insight into the diachronic interconnectedness of ancient and contemporary paths of psycho-poiesis into a narrative fact: Not only that "the reversal of temporal causality is resonant with strategies in psychoanalytic theory,"[26] with poetry, the artistic, kabbalistic, midrashic imagination, and so forth, but it is also resonant—in particular—with the textual embodiment of Elliot Wolfson's own ways of writing. "Tiredly waiting to be liberated from the confinement of one's own textual embodiment" is therefore the flipside of a uniquely dedicated effort to reveal and unveil, think and unthink, tie and untie ancient, medieval, modern, and contemporary modes of mythopoiesis in a relentless work over decades, setting out—in inexhaustible loops—to liberate ancient wisdoms from the confinement of their own manifold textual imprisonments.

An overturning of Platonism is at stake, a twisting free [*Herausdrehung*] from bondage.

> the masters of esoteric wisdom ... the assumption under which they have labored [...] is that the truth already spoken is always yet to be spoken, that the ancient saying may be envisioned as novel to the degree that the novel saying is envisioned as ancient.

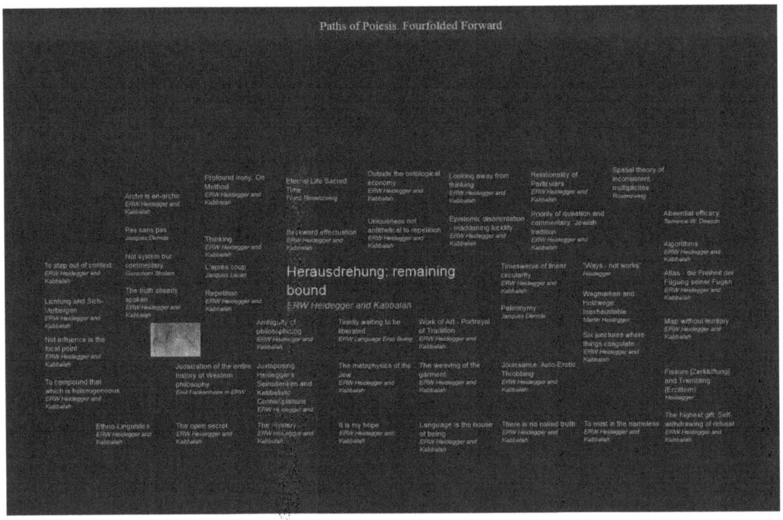

Bruckstein / House of Taswir, Paths of Poiesis. Fourfolded Forward. Atlas for Elliot R. Wolfson. "Herausdrehung: remaining bound," https://taswir.org/atlas/.

Yet, if not for an abysmal leap *that convenes us from the future*, "one cannot flee without still being tethered to that from which one has absconded."[27]

> The chain of tradition is thus constituted by endlessly distended moments, which should [. . .] be envisaged [. . .] as the mythopoetic instantiations of an infinitely protracted torrent that implements the eternal reappearance of the same, which is to say, the indefatigable duplication of difference.[28]

What do I bring along then, what duplication of difference, what kind of gift rises to the occasion, how do we pay tribute to a scholar whose probing of limits, innumerable acts of getting hold of letting go, letting go of getting hold, knotting and unknotting the text doesn't allow any rest, not even for the brink of a moment?

The medieval thinkers of the Kalam and Mutakallimun schools, including Arabic and rabbinic giants like Saadya Gaon, Ibn Rushd, and Maimonides, in their grammars and scholastic discussions of divine attributes teach us something important. They show that attributes, adverbial adjectives, are attributes of action, and that these attributes act as mirror devices, nodes for reciprocal relations. Attributes of relations and adverbial adjectives are veiled imperatives: *ma hu niqra rachum af ata niqra rachum*—"as he is called gracious so you be called gracious," etc. Indeterminate in their essence, attributes of action become projective nodes for reciprocal relations, "tiredly waiting" acts as an ungrounding in which a twisting free, an unknotting the [k]not—a *Herausdrehung*—becomes possible, a twist "singularly universal," and remember: "the universal is constituted relentlessly in light of random and indiscriminate particulars," yet it is calibrated from desire.

. . . And what is the desire? Is it a desire for "being-with-one-another, circulating in the *with* and as the *with* of [a] singularly plural coexistence"?[29] What does that mean?

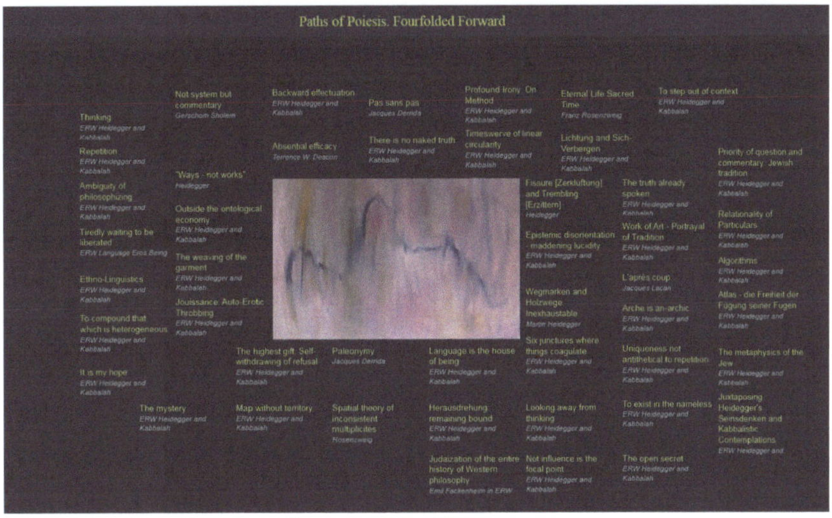

Bruckstein / House of Taswir, Paths of Poiesis. Fourfolded Forward. Atlas for Elliot R. Wolfson. "Elliot R. Wolfson, Wendung," https://taswir.org/atlas/.

The bursting overflow of Elliot R. Wolfson's paths of poeisis calls for an act of external poietic mirroring, in which the ancient wisdom "tiredly waiting to be liberated from . . ." enters its own poetic, even artistic, *Zeit-Raum-Spiel*. A radical autonomy ensues. "Being-with-one-another" is one of the (political) consequences of circulating "in the *with* and as the *with*" of a singularly plural relationship of love. Yet another, more daring external mirroring of Elliot R. Wolfson's *Paths of Poiesis* may still be forthcoming. Its name could be *Wendung*. All texts could be shown in the garb of Elliot R. Wolfon's own works of poetry and art.

Dedicated to Elliot R. Wolfson, Berlin, September 10, 2021.

NOTES

1. Elliot R. Wolfson, *Language, Eros, Being: Kabbalistic Hermeneutics and Poetic Imagination* (New York: Fordham University Press, 2005).
2. "It is possible to identify a common thread that ties together the masters of the esoteric wisdom through the centuries: the assumption under which they have labored [. . .] is that the truth already spoken is always yet to be spoken, that the ancient saying may be envisioned as novel to the degree that the novel saying is envisioned as ancient. The chain of tradition is thus constituted by the endlessly distended moments, [. . .] as the mythopoietic instantiations of an infinitely protracted torrent that implements the eternal reappearance of the same, which is to say, the indefatigable duplication of difference." Elliot R. Wolfson, *Heidegger and Kabbalah: Hidden Gnosis and the Paths of Poiesis* (Bloomington: Indiana University Press, 2019), 31.
3. Wolfson, *Heidegger and Kabbalah*, 98–99. Wolfson relates this kind of "fissure" or "*Zerklüftung*"

later to the withdrawal of the (bridal) presence—to the one who is "concealed in the appearance of [her] nonappearance" (*Heidegger and Kabbalah*). Heidegger refers to this dynamic as an "opening of the self-concealing [*Offenheit des Sichverbergens*]" (*Heidegger and Kabbalah*). Wolfson uniquely connects this dynamic to the "distance of intimacy" that constitutes the jouissance (*sha'ash'a*) associated with the initial withdrawal or constriction (*tsimtsum*) of the feminine in Lurianic Kabbalah and the withdrawal of the psychoanalytic position in Lacanian psychoanalytic theory. Traditionally speaking, of course, this kind of "withdrawal" or "abstinence" is also reminiscent of the *mekudeshet* and her privilege to withdraw from her husband for the time of Niddah. Love abides in the distance of intimacy; this seems to be the position in which Elliot R. Wolfson uniquely connects Jewish mysticism to psychoanalytic theory.

4. Wolfson, *Heidegger and Kabbalah*, 31 and note 1.
5. Wolfson, *Heidegger and Kabbalah*, 68.
6. Wolfson, *Heidegger and Kabbalah*, 69.
7. Wolfson, *Heidegger and Kabbalah*, 68.
8. Wolfson, *Heidegger and Kabbalah*, 35.
9. Wolfson, *Heidegger and Kabbalah*, 38. The quoted expressions are cited by Wolfson from Jacques Derrida, *The Truth in Painting*, trans. Geoff Bennington and Ian McLeod (Chicago: University of Chicago Press, 1987), 32.
10. "Sabbatical beginnings" means "to repeat and retrieve [*wieder-holen*] the inception," radically transforming it from the direction of the future. [Wolfson refers to Heidegger, *Einführung in die Metaphysik* [GA 40] (Frankfurt a. M.: V. Klostermann, 1983), 42.] This, of course, is the traditional definition of Shabbat. Remember: "*sof maaseh bemachschava tchila*," in *Lecha Dodi*, traditional Hebrew lyrics for Shabbat, composed by Shelomo haLevi Alkabetz in the sixteenth century.
11. Wolfson, *Heidegger and Kabbalah*, 41.
12. Wolfson, *Language, Eros, Being*, 390.
13. Subtitle of Wolfson, *Heidegger and Kabbalah.*
14. The containment of the feminine in the masculine is one of the most potent contentions of Wolfson's work, way beyond any gender debate, more leaning toward the Lacanian claim "*la femme n'existe pas*" developed in his writings in *Encore* and others. This axiom obviously does not address any definitions of gender, but rather touches upon how a nonphallic, nonlinear way of writing, thinking, movement, spatial poetry, and speech may all surface in the open to claim visibility and recognition. The suffering of this axiom culminates in the impasse of a non-negotiable contestation between secrecy and visibility, an impasse that has existential, psychoanalytic, political, artistic, and theoretical implications.
15. Among the vast literature on Jewish medieval theories of divine attributes there is David Kaufmann, *Geschichte der Attributenlehre in der jüdischen Philosophie des Mittelalters von Saadja bis Maimuni* (Gotha, 1877), still rich in literature and analysis. Groundbreaking in its radical critique of essential attributes and the development of a theory of time originating in the future is the neo-Kantian reading of Maimonides by Hermann Cohen in his 1908 essay "Charakteristik der Ethik Maimunis," in *Hermann Cohens Jüdische Schriften III. Zur jüdischen Religionsphilosophie und ihrer Geschichte* (Berlin: Schwetschke & Sohn, 1924), 221–89.

Translated into English by Almut Sh. Bruckstein in *Hermann Cohen. Ethics of Maimonides*, with a running commentary by Almut Sh. Bruckstein (Madison: University of Wisconsin Press, 2004), especially 70–75. In collaboration with my late teacher, the rabbinic scholar Zev Gotthold, in Jerusalem.

16. "I have been waiting, but I don't hope for anything." Jacques Lacan, *The Seminar, Book XXIII, The Sinthome* (New York: Polity, 2016), 118.
17. Derrida, *Truth in Painting*, 32–33. Cited in Wolfson, *Heidegger and Kabbalah*, 38.
18. The atlas can be called upon and entered at www.taswir.org/atlas/.
19. Wolfson, *Heidegger and Kabbalah*, 38.
20. Wolfson, *Heidegger and Kabbalah*, 38.
21. Michael Meyer zum Wischen in an unpublished lecture I had the pleasure to attend presenting the case study of "Mister K." at the John-Rittmeister-Institut in Kiel, February 14, 2020. Lacan indeed speaks of psychoanalysis as a practice in which analyst and analysand in tandem "tie and untie the desire to get across the circle without getting free of its law [that is [k] not]." (Derrida, *Truth in Painting*.) For an encompassing online presentation of Lacanian texts in German see the blog of Rolf Nemitz, more specifically https://lacan-entziffern.de/reales/kommentar-zu-lacans-seminar-das-sinthomviii-zur-sitzung-vom-13-april-1976/.
22. Jacques Lacan, *Écrits: First Complete Edition in English*, trans. Bruce Fink, in collaboration with Héloise Fink and Russell Grigg (New York: Norton, 2006), 711 [Jacques Lacan, *Écrits* (Paris: Éditions du Seuil, 1966), 839]. Lacan formulates here a classical rabbinic position on messianism developed by modern Jewish thinkers such as Hermann Cohen, Franz Rosenzweig, Walter Benjamin, Emanuel Levinas, and, of course, Jacques Derrida, based upon their reading of rabbinic sources such as Saadya Gaon, Moses Maimonides, and more. As far as I can see, Lacan nowhere substantially invokes this tradition, let alone acknowledges it. He thereby seals a forgetfulness for rabbinic ways of thinking and their effectiveness in psychoanalytic settings—not unlike Thomas von Acquin who did the same for Ibn Rushd and the entire Arab scholastic tradition, producing a strategic forgetfulness that fatefully cuts off Arab sources from European modernity. What followed was a concept of the European Enlightenment without its (Arab) sources, and what follows from the Lacanian discourse is a concept of psychoanalysis without its rabbinic sources, sealing a process of cleansing the Freudian tradition from anything slightly rabbinic, a cleansing that was particularly effective in Germany. To what extent the Viennese initiators of psychoanalytic discourse were still consciously indebted to what they called "the Talmudic way of thinking," see Almut Sh. Bruckstein, "Talmudic War Machine & a Shadow's Dream," in *Protocols #9, Sitra Achra* (online magazine), ed. Ben Ratskoff (August 2021). Wolfson uniquely opens up and connects ancient and modern Jewish tradition "back" to the Lacanian discourse, thereby undoing a violent and fateful "catholic" appropriation of Jewish tradition in current Lacanian psychoanalytic theory that in various specific ways resembles Heidegger's own appropriation of Jewish thinking so ingeniously exposed by Wolfson. Thus we may read Elliot R. Wolfson's entire oeuvre also as a strong hint, even promise, of a future un-doing of this forgetfulness, re-covering Talmudic ways of thinking inside psychoanalysis in ways in which Talmudic thinking becomes the effect of this future. See Wolfson, *Heidegger and Kabbalah*, 38.

23. Wolfson, *Heidegger and Kabbalah*, 10. See also his most recent book, *Suffering Time: Philosophical, Kabbalistic, and Hasidic Reflections on Temporality* (Leiden: Brill, 2021).
24. Martin Heidegger, *What Is Called Thinking?*, trans. Fred F. Wieck and J. Glenn Gray (New York: Harper and Row, 1968), 82, quoted by Wolfson, *Heidegger and Kabbalah*, 71.
25. Jean-Luc Nancy, *Being Singular Plural*, trans. Robert D. Richardson (Stanford: Stanford University Press, 2000), 3 (emphasis in the original), quoted by Wolfson in *Heidegger and Kabbalah*, 79.
26. Jacques Lacan as quoted by Wolfson, *Heidegger and Kabbalah*, 45. For the Lacan reference see also note 22 and the Atlas folio "L'après coup," p. 6. The atlas may be entered interactively at https://taswir.org/atlas/.
27. Wolfson, *Heidegger and Kabbalah*, 72, quoting Heidegger on Nietzsche as well as John Sallis, "Twisting Free: Being to an Extent Sensible," *Research in Phenomenology* 17, no. 1 (1987): 1–22, https://doi.org/10.1163/156916487X00012; reference in Wolfson, *Heidegger and Kabbalah*, 89, n. 94.
28. Wolfson, *Heidegger and Kabbalah*, 31; and Atlas, https://taswir.org/atlas/.
29. Nancy, *Being Singular Plural*, cf. note 25 above.

WHEN THE PARTICULAR IS NOT INDEXICAL OF THE UNIVERSAL

Some Thoughts on the Study of Judaism in Light of Elliot R. Wolfson's Work

AARON W. HUGHES

Yet the essence of nearness is to bring near that which is kept at a distance. To be settled in place and to be an itinerant in search of place, therefore, are not polar opposites. What is nearby is concomitantly faraway, and hence the serenity of being-at-home is necessarily at the same time the turbulence of not-being-at-home.

ELLIOT R. WOLFSON, *THE DUPLICITY OF PHILOSOPHY'S SHADOW*[1]

FOR AT LEAST THE LAST DECADE ELLIOT R. WOLFSON AND I HAVE BEEN talking about, commiserating over, even occasionally arguing about the state and future of the field of Jewish studies. This usually takes the form of my invoking my rather familiar refrain that the study of Judaism is too particular and particularistic, rarely connected to larger conversations in the humanities and social sciences.[2] Wolfson instead comes at the issue from the other side, reminding us of the equally problematic, if not more so, position that the so-called universalism of the latter rarely makes any room for the particular, especially a particular that has actively resisted its hegemonic overtures. In this contribution, I would like to historicize our collective musings and try to give them some of the social and intellectual contexts they so dearly deserve. In order to do this, what follows is divided, for the most part, into two sections of unequal length: the first, and the longest, examines our collective past and the other looks ahead to the future, though both admittedly take place from the point where these two temporal coordinates meet and contest, namely, the here and now of the present.[3] If the future is grounded in the past, that past need not necessarily determine the future's course,[4] with the result that it is those moments in between, what already was but has not yet fully become, that presents itself as all the more important, thereby affording us the possibility of redirection, a timeswerve in Wolfson's parlance.[5]

The line between the universal and the particular, as fine as it is often unsurmountable, defines Jewish studies, as indeed it inevitably must. Too often we try to get around this problem by saying that the universal needs the particular for its own understanding. Or, that everything is particular,[6] not the least of which are those Christo- and Eurocentric folk taxa sublimated to the level of global and catholic utility. Or, again and from the other side, that the particular is somehow indexical of the universal. While the words of such phrases make sense, their semantics are often lost on me. We can utter such phrases until we are blue in the face; however, the fact remains that the universal and the particular remain diametrically opposed to one another, and forays from the one side into the other prove very difficult, if not impossible.[7] This opposition should be clear to anyone who works in Jewish studies, at least outside the context of Israel. If we are truly going to make the particular indexical of the universal, and I do think we have to, we need to chart out exactly what that means and how to do it as opposed to transforming it into a mantra that, like the thesis of a bad undergraduate paper, is thought to be true only by virtue of repetition.

Few can walk this line, keeping their eyes wide open all the time; or, at the very least, walk it consistently. For many, the alternatives are either departure or further entrenchment. Wolfson, however, is one of the few scholars who has been able to—and continues to—negotiate, both effectively and consistently, the Scylla of universalism and the Charybdis of particularism. Within this context, it is worth noting, only those in Jewish studies (or, perhaps better, at least some therein), presumably like those in other ethnic studies, worry about this line. Those working outside, in the pastures afforded by various fields and disciplines, are blissfully unaware of these issues and the existential conditions to which they give rise to those on the other side. They rarely reach out, and instead often continue to use phrases that carry in their wake age-old tropes and metaphors, now under the guise of being "too specific," "too particularistic," of "too limited readership," and so on and so forth.

Near the end of this chapter I want to suggest that we might consider following the path that Wolfson has tried, and indeed continues to try, to forge, though I suspect that most will be unable or unwilling to rise to the challenge. The challenge is so daunting because it means the occupation of space—when so many in Jewish studies seem obsessed by the other occupation of another space—that is both uninviting and that actively repels. There—at the political beyond politics, at the Judaism behind Zionism—resides that solitary space, devoid of any ethnic, tribal, religious, or intellectual qualification or affiliation. That is where Wolfson asks us to be. Though Wolfson, virtually unprecedented, can occupy this ontological and epistemological space, few others can or will because it is, in his own words, "uncomfortable," and, by definition, unfirm and fraught with the unbearable heaviness of solitude. Occupying this gray area of ambiguity, betwixt and between fields and disciplines, using the particular to illumine the cavernous darkness of the universal and vice versa, the precarity of Wolfson's work shows how and why most prefer the hospitable light of stability. In his work on Heidegger, for example, he informs us that "the space we must inhabit, as uncomfortable as it might be, is one in which we acknowledge that Heidegger was both a Nazi given to anti-Semitic jargon and an incisive philosopher whose thinking not only was responding to the urgencies of his epoch but also contains the potential to unravel the thorny knot of politics and philosophy relevant for the present as much as for the past."[8]

Heidegger has been Wolfson's conversation partner—from the opening pages of *Through a Speculum That Shines*[9] all the way through to his two books published on Heidegger in 2018 and 2019 respectively,[10] and he will no doubt continue to be so in the future[11]—often when it has been unfashionable to do so.[12] What does a Nazi and an antisemite, framed in its crassest terms, have to do with the articulation of Judaism?[13] Even more problematic, for some, is Wolfson's insistence that the exact same atavism and xenophobia—what he calls "semantic essentialism and ethnocentric chauvinism"—witnessed in Heidegger's thought also reside at the heart of Judaism.[14] Wolfson, thus, goes where few others in Jewish studies—or even those in the larger field of religious studies—are prepared to venture. Asking uncomfortable questions, undermining the ethnos that qualifies the field, and unafraid to follow ideas through to wherever they may lead is certainly not the telos of most of those currently working (both in the present and the past).

Here it might be worth posing a question: Why are those who transform the study of Judaism in the larger field of religious studies largely ignored in Jewish studies? Why, framed somewhat differently, do those who try to open up the narrow confines of Jewish studies to more universal questions and modes of analysis become a problem for the parochial context of the subfield? Here a comparison between Wolfson and another pioneer in the study of Judaism, Jacob Neusner, who will make an appearance later in this chapter, is apposite. Though their work is certainly different, and the questions they asked and to which they found answers are radically divergent, both shared a desire to illumine Jewish texts using new methods, which made those in Jewish studies uncomfortable. This is why those who worked in the New Testament and Christian origins appreciated Neusner, with the result that Judaism reached a larger audience among non-Jews. It is also why the work of Wolfson has caught the attention of many scholars who work on mysticism and now Heidegger.

ARTICULATING THE PROBLEMS

I think it fair to say that regardless of where, how, and by whom blame is apportioned, the study of Judaism has reached an impasse. It is partly generational. Perhaps nowhere is this clearer than in the response of eleven former presidents of the Association for Jewish Studies (AJS) to the resignation of then current president Noam Pianko in April 2020 after acknowledging that he had taken part in a controversial, invitation-only gathering co-facilitated by Steven M. Cohen, a prominent sociologist of, among other things, "Jewish continuity," who had been accused of sexually harassing female colleagues.[15] It is part political. We witness this when we look at some of those same previous presidents of the AJS, some of whom (e.g., Ruth Wisse, Jonathan Sarna) have taken what some might call rather reactionary pro-Israel positions.[16] We live in a political world, to invoke Dylan, where wisdom is thrown in jail, and where truth is often the first casualty, overrun by its own avatar. Finally, it is part faddish. Here, I point to the renewed turn inward, but now—and paradoxically—appearing under the guise of universalism, something that now tends to mean an attunement to the latest theory du jour. I refer specifically to some inchoate form of American Jewish cultural studies, which has now become such a prominent feature of the field, as may be witnessed, for example, in any Annual Meeting program from the AJS. Despite its emphasis on theory, however, its elevation of some vague notion of (American) Jewish culture or "Jewishness"—not unlike the equally problematic concept of "experience" or "sacred" in religious studies—is impossible to analyze because it can mean so many different things to so many different people, hence the attraction.

The study of Judaism, for reasons such as these (among others), had largely been an apologetic affair, something connected to very unacademic notions of Jewish continuity and that, in the process, is in the business of reifying Jews and some imagined normative Jewish experience at the expense of the larger contexts in which Jews happened and continue to find themselves. Indeed, the aforementioned Cohen was a notorious defender of Jewish continuity and the importance of practicing endogamy, two ideological principles—it might be added—that might be considered fairly conservative and right of center, and which he (and others) then defend academically.[17] We thus see the triangulation between the political, the scholarly, and identity politics, one of the potential pitfalls of Jewish studies,[18] albeit one that has been there since the field's inception in nineteenth-century Germany. This idea of showing and establishing Jewish continuity, however, is certainly not something that is confined to those who work in the sociology of American Jewry, but often holds for many who work in the study of Jews and Judaism in other times and geographic places.[19] Certainly, there are real historical circumstances for this, which I shall discuss shortly, but the operating methodological assumption—in addition to the primary *modus operandi*—witnessed in so many of the diverse parts that comprise Jewish studies is that if a Jew did something it must ipso facto be important by virtue of the fact of his or her Jewishness. Channeling the spirit of the late Jacob Neusner, we might say that such parochialism is reflective of the ethnic studies from which he tried, but I think fair to say ultimately failed, to extricate the study of Judaism.[20] However, as I shall argue below this ultimately proves to be an impossible endeavor.

Jewish studies, then, is caught between two eternal forces—whether we call them centrifugal or centripetal, universal or particularistic, or the like—that work to hamstring the study of Jews and Judaism. When we throw into this mix the inherent conservatism of traditional Jewish studies (personified by issues of Jewish continuity, for example), the fact that Israel is always the elephant in the room, and the increasing generational tensions in the field, it would seem fair to say that there are real problems in the study of Judaism, problems that, while subterranean for the past few years, are slowly being exposed to the light of day. The result is that they will only get worse before they can get better. It is the work of those like Wolfson—work that is not afraid to ask uncomfortable questions and that refuses to reify or celebrate some innate sense of "Jewishness" and related identities—that offers a lifeline. The question, of course, is: will anyone take hold?

This is where we currently are. The question now becomes, where do we go and how do we get there? Before we go forward, however, we must first go back.

FUTURE PAST

Much of the problems currently besetting Jewish studies are not new; indeed, one could say they are as old as the secular academy, something that has always sought to erase or elide the other to itself. Within this context, one could quite easily say that Judaism, post-Jesus, has had very little place within the academic study of religion—the field that I am most familiar with and from which I largely write—since it began in the late nineteenth century, something that would make it correspond roughly, and perhaps not coincidentally, to the rise of the intellectual movement known as Wissenshaft des Judentums in, again, roughly the same geographic region (i.e., central Europe).[21] But if the latter was interested in apologetics, insinuating Judaism at the heart of Western civilization, the former sought, both metaphorically and literally, to excise it. The new study of religion was, after all, obsessively fascinated with the Christ-event and in, among other things, elucidating the various aspects of it that were foreshadowed in the *Old* Testament and that circulated in the period of Second Temple Judaism, but often with absolutely no interest whatsoever in Judaism *after* Christ's death.

Both the early studies of Judaism and of religion, two ballerinas pirouetting in the dark of night, took no notice of each other not only because they could, quite literally, not see each other, but because they had been trained for myopic performance. We thus witness a virtual crossover from Christian theology to the so-called objective study, with only the name changing but not the first principles, something that has largely carried forward into the present.[22] In this narrative, as we all know, Judaism ends where and as Christianity begins. We see this clearly, though by no means most glaringly, in the words of Karl Ferdinand Reinhardt Budde (1850–1935), professor of Old Testament exegesis and biblical Hebrew at the University of Marburg, the same institution in which his colleague, one of the founders of the academic study of religion, Rudolf Otto (1869–1937), also worked. In a series of lectures, tellingly titled *Religion of Israel to the Exile* (1899), Budde writes, "Can we conceive of any sharper contrasts than we find between the world-wide, glowing universalism of DeuteroIsaiah and the narrow, icy particularism of Ezekiel—between the ritualism of Ezekiel and the complete superiority of Jeremiah and Deutero-Isaiah to all external cult[ic matters]." Continuing in the same vein, Budde finally concludes, "It has pleased God to give His human children the noblest and most beautiful flower of His revelation, the Gospel of His Son Jesus Christ."[23]

This one passage, for me at least, encapsulates one of the major problems prohibiting the successful integration of the study of Judaism into larger fields and disciplines of study. The problem here is less (or not *only*) Jewish studies' fault than it is that of those disciplines, many of which emerged out of the nineteenth-century German university, the great majority of which were heavily invested in nationalism, Orientalism, and, by extension, antisemitism.[24] Though the field of religious studies has ostensibly gravitated far beyond its nationalist and antisemitic roots, there can be little doubt that many of its main terms and categories remain deeply indebted to Protestant Christianity.[25] The question—or, better, problem—becomes how to understand Judaism (or any other non-Protestant religion, for that matter) using a set of terms and first principles that distort as much as they articulate.[26] It ought to come as no surprise, then, that just as the study of Jews and Judaism has long posed a problem for the academic study of religion, as indeed it has for so many of the fields and disciplines associated with the humanities and social sciences, those larger fields and disciplines have done their best to contort and misrepresent Jews and Judaism (as they have to a variety of other others).[27] How is it possible, framed in terms of a question, to include, let alone make sense of, that which by definition deviates from the perceived norm?

Yet, if one wing of religious studies' genealogy has consisted of the supersessionism and the anti-Judaism associated with classic antisemitism, we can also, paradoxically it might be said, point to a number of foundational "Jewish" theorists in many of the fields we today associate with the humanities and social sciences, such as Sigmund Freud, Émile Durkheim, and Karl Marx. However, their relationship to Judaism was anything but clear, and the tradition of their ancestors was certainly not informative to the theories they produced.[28] Though their theories of religion as a concept rooted in psychic, social, and/or economic forces remain relevant today—and, indeed, they continue to play a formative role in religious studies' conceptual and theoretical toolbox—there is very little of what we might call "Jewish" about them. Or, perhaps framed somewhat differently, even if some element of their Jewishness did indeed influence their theories, the latter were certainly not used by contemporaneous scholars associated with Wissenschaft des Judentums, instead taking on a much more universal relevance.

But there were certainly Jews in Europe that were interested in thinking about religion. Franz Rosenzweig, Martin Buber, and Leo Baeck, among others, sought to understand Judaism using larger models inherited from Weimar Germany. The Lehrhaus tradition that they created introduced secular Jews to, for example, the Bible, Near Eastern history, and Jewish thought, and they did so moreover outside the confines that those associated with Wissenschaft des Judentums created.

As the academic study of religion made its way to America, perhaps best symbolized in the passage of Mircea Eliade from the Old World to the New to take up a position at the University of Chicago's Divinity School, we once again hear the familiar ring of Jewish exclusion, if not outright antisemitism.[29] At that institution, and in the aftermath of the *School District of Abington Township, PA v. Schempp* Supreme Court case of 1963 that was responsible for the creation of religious studies departments in state universities throughout the length and breadth of the United States, Eliade trained a generation of scholars to take up positions in those departments and beyond. The issue, for Eliade if not his students, was that "the Jews" functioned for him, as they did for so many others, as quintessential rootless cosmopolitans. The problem for Eliade, who had ties to Romanian fascism, is when such ideas crossed over into his theoretical reflections on the nature of religion.[30] "The Jews," whose calendar represented linear time (a rather odd understanding given the cycle of the Jewish year) and who seem to have been the embodiment *par excellence* of what he called "the terror of history,"[31] now functioned as the polar opposite of the "cyclical" (in the sense of being repeatable) time of *the* rural peasant, whom he valorized as his ideal "homo religiousus."[32]

In several edited volumes meant to transform the new field in the United States so as not to reduce the study of "the sacred" to other disciplines (such as politics, history, or philosophy), we see very little interest in Judaism.[33] In *The History of Religions: Essays in Methodology* (1959),[34] a collection of essays that Eliade edited with his colleague at the University of Chicago, Joseph M. Kitagawa, for example, we witness a real lacuna as far as Judaism, and its study, is concerned. With the aim of the volume being to establish the history of religion and comparative religion as a leading scholarly activity within the context of the modern university, the editors freely admit their fear that the study of religion might be absorbed by other fields (e.g., philosophy, psychology, sociology, anthropology, history, theology) as opposed to being a field—or indeed, as they tried to conceptualize it, a discipline—in its own right, something that was in the business of isolating and articulating a highly amorphous concept that they referred to as *the* universal religious experience, which manifested itself in specific religions.[35] The latter presumably included Judaism, but from a perusal of the volume we would never know it. The list of contributors reveals scholars of Islam (Louis Massignon, Wilfred Cantwell Smith), Japanese and Chinese religions (Kitagawa), and Eastern Orthodoxy (Ernst Benz), in addition to a number of various subfields, such as philosophy of religion (Jean Daniélou) and history (Raffaele Pettazzoni). But no scholars of Judaism. A legitimate question we might very well ask: Is this because there were no scholars of Judaism engaging in the study of religion in the manner that, say, the other contributors were to the specific religious traditions that they happened to study? Or were none invited? My sense is that it is a combination of the two, as I shall articulate more fully in the following section.

In a follow-up volume titled *The History of Religions: Essays on the Problem of Understanding* (1967),[36] this time edited solely by Kitagawa (but with Eliade's vision evident throughout the volume), we once again see Judaism underrepresented, indeed I would go so far as to say not represented at all. While many—following the first volume just described above—seek to *understand* (to use the volume's subtitle, invoking the German *Verstehen*) and articulate a purportedly universal religious phenomenon or phenomena known as "religion" (see the chapters by Eliade, Kitagawa, Paul Tillich, Thomas J. J.

Altizer, Charles Long, and a reprinted articled by Joachim Wach), we also see scholars who represent specific religious traditions; for example, Christianity (Paul Tillich, Kees W. Bolle), Islam (Charles Adams), Hinduism (Philip H. Ashby), Buddhism (Charles S. J. White), Japanese religions (H. Byron Earhart).[37]

Such works are revealing as much for what they exclude as for what they include. Should we take it from the absence of Judaism that no one was working on "Jewish" topics from the 1940s to the late 1960s? Certainly not. We could, for example, point to the important work of those like Harvard's Harry Austryn Wolfson[38] or the Jewish Theological Seminary's Saul Lieberman (1898–1983).[39] But neither man was interested in the field of religious studies, primarily because the former wrote as an intellectual historian and the latter as *talmid hacham*. Once again, we see the study of Judaism and the study of religion bypass each other in the night. Indeed, it was not until Jacob Neusner came on the scene, just around the time of the latter volume's publication, that we begin to see some sort of cross-pollination between the academic study of religion and, for lack of a better term, Jewish data.[40] Surely, however, this is a major moment in Jewish studies, if not the larger field of religious studies. If Eliade had tried to absent Jews from the study of religion, Neusner not only tried to bring them back, but sought to put them at the center as exemplary of larger issues. In this, we might say that Neusner was heir to the Lehrhaus tradition and thus functioned as an important conduit between Europe and North America. The only way he could do this, however, was to do a PhD in religion at Columbia while simultaneously getting rabbinic ordination up the road at Jewish Theological Seminary. I can guarantee you that no one studying Islam, Buddhism, or Hinduism had to do this at this time.

This admittedly brief overview reveals that the rather strange predicament of Jewish studies in the secular academy has a complicated history, caught as it is between an interlocking set of centripetal and centrifugal forces. The centrifugal force insulates Judaism, reveling in the particular, often coinciding with an unwillingness to explain the tradition using the terms and categories provided by larger disciplinary frameworks, and instead prefers to use a set of terms that are internal to the tradition. This means that Jewish data largely become untranslatable within the context of larger humanistic conversations and risk being inaccessible to anyone but those born or initiated into a particular ethnos or tradition.

The centripetal forces are no less insidious, representing the other side of the same coin. Such forces emerge from the desire either to subsume the particular into the so-called universal—which, of course, is little more than a Euro-Christian hegemon sublimated—or, if it will not be subsumed, then to marginalize or excise it. So, just as there is a tendency in Jewish studies to navel-gaze, the opposite tendency exists in fields like religious studies or history wherein Jewish data can be completely ignored as somehow too insular, as too parochial, or as too insignificant to be exemplary. This is the paradox in which the academic study of Judaism currently finds itself in the present moment. This situation hamstrings the field and unfortunately prevents full integration of Jewish studies into the humanities curriculum.

CONVERGENCES AND DIVERGENCES

The relationship between the founders of religious studies and those associated with the rise of Jewish studies certainly overlapped, both chronologically and geographically. Here, I should perhaps be clear and state forthrightly—if I have not already—that my overwhelming concern is with Jewish studies as practiced within the larger field of religious studies. I do this because that is precisely the sort of epistemological and institutional space that I happen to inhabit and, because of this, that with which I am most familiar. I well realize that others work on Jewish data in other fields and disciplines, such as English literature,[41] history, medieval studies, and so on and so forth.[42] I also do not want to claim that all of those who work with Jewish data in all of these various fields, subfields, and disciplines have not produced interesting, creative, theoretically sophisticated, and informative work. My point is simply to expose some of the structural difficulties inherent to Jewish studies using religious studies as my "e.g." and then show in a subsequent section, using Wolfson as a guide, how we might meaningfully move beyond.

To return to the relationship, or lack thereof, between the founders of religious studies (or even Oriental studies) and Jewish studies, we can with considerable ease remark, and this is my point, that they rarely conversed with one another.[43] They certainly lived together in such cosmopolitan centers as Berlin, Paris, Vienna, Budapest, and London. They might well have visited the same cafes, but they certainly occupied different tables.[44] On the one hand, Judaism was too familiar, since so much theorizing about religion used "primitives"—including by Durkheim and, to a lesser extent, by Freud—and those others encountered by the colonialist enterprise (such as by the British East India Company).[45] The goal in this context was to overcome the strange and the exotic to make it correspond to the terms and categories of the familiar. Yet, on the other, Judaism was also too strange—too particularistic and too particular—that which had been transcended and superseded by Jesus's birth and death.

In like manner, for those working with Jewish data in the late nineteenth/early twentieth centuries, religious studies was too universal or, perhaps more accurately, it was a growing field interested in a set of questions that were too irrelevant to those working with Jewish texts.[46] The latter was especially the case since so much of that larger field was interested in uncovering and articulating the *universal* experiential trends of religion, and doing so, moreover, using the "primitive" and the "exotic" as its comparanda, two features that Jews and Judaism most certainly were not in fin de siècle Europe.

There are, then, historical—as well as supersessionist—reasons for the divergence of religious studies and Jewish studies until roughly the late 1960s/early 1970s when Neusner came on the scene. While he and his students attempted to right this wrong,[47] the gravitational pull of identity politics, of Zionism (whether to uphold or critique it) and of the need to reify and abstract an inchoate sense of "Jewishness" have proved difficult to navigate. This is certainly not to imply that all is fine in the parent field of religious studies, but somehow woefully amiss in Jewish studies. Far from it.

While historically the ostensibly academic and ostensibly objective study of religion has not been kind to religions that were not Protestant and Christian, its treatment of Judaism should come in for especial reproach. Configured, dependent upon the theorist in question, as either too strange, too familiar, or too stubborn, the study of Judaism has posed considerable problems for the study of religion.[48]

THE UNDEFINED PRESENT

We would seem to be hampered, then, by the parameters imposed on—and thus by—our intellectual predecessors, those associated with Wissenschaft des Judentums, many of which have carried over willy-nilly, consciously or unconsciously, into the academic study of Judaism. While we are today split between trying to distance ourselves from them on the one hand and, on the other, still using their methods, it was not entirely our predecessors' fault. For instance, it cannot be denied that, while cosmopolitan dwellers in the aforementioned metropoles, they were denied entrance to its innermost sanctum. They lived in a country with more universities in the world, but could not teach therein until the late nineteenth century and certainly never in Jewish studies. And even those Jews who worked on non-Jewish topics did so in ways that meant they were marginalized (e.g., the Orientalist Gustav Weil at Heidelberg).[49] And when they could teach, they were just as summarily fired (and worse) with the rise of the Third Reich.

If much of the previous part of this chapter has focused on our collective past, it is now time to move into the present, with an eye toward the future. It is here that I think Wolfson's corpus offers us something new, something that offers us a way forward. It is a way, however, that is as complex as it is potentially uncomfortable. We get a glimpse of this in the heart of Wolfson's most recent projects, which think with and engage one of the most original, but provocative and potentially tainted, thinkers of the twentieth century, namely, Martin Heidegger. Here, Wolfson deploys his diverse intellectual abilities to show how we construct, live with, and fight (often violently) against alterity in all of its diverse forms.

The problem, however, and this returns me to previous sections, is that many, both inside and outside of Jewish studies, do not know what to do with Wolfson's work. They mischaracterize, they miscategorize it, with the result that they ultimately risk misunderstanding it. The *Rezeptionsgeschichte* of his oeuvre again exposes many of the problems raised above. Rather than being able to move forward, we find ourselves returning to the grand narratives of the past. These revolve around the familiar temporal (e.g., ancient, medieval, Renaissance, early modern, modern) and ideational (e.g., philosophy, rabbinics, Kabbalah, literature) subdivisions—all of which are artificial, the product of nineteenth-century desire. Perhaps nowhere is this clearer than how Wolfson's work is reduced, frequently, to that of Kabbalah or Jewish mysticism. Or, in the words of David Novak, who at least sees the flicker of philosophy in his work, as a "philosophically sophisticated scholar of Jewish mysticism."[50] Using the traditional categories of

Wissenschaft des Judentums, which bifurcates unnaturally the study of Jewish thought into "mysticism," "philosophy," "rabbinics," and so on, Novak categorizes and taxonomizes Wolfson in, perhaps, the only way he knows how, and in the primary way that scholarship on Judaism over the previous two hundred years both legitimates and sanctions. Such scholarship has a tendency to gravitate toward normativity and appreciation, two of the hallmarks that have been a constant throughout the length and breadth of academic Jewish studies. Once one strays from this path, as Wolfson most certain does with his desire to destabilize the ontology that inextricably links nationalism and ethnicity, something that is at work just as much in Judaism as it is in the National Socialist thought of Heidegger, those like Novak demand he go no further. "A Jewish thinker like Wolfson should remain silent," Novak opines, "if he cannot find within the Jewish tradition itself a redeeming corrective for kabbalistic doctrines he cannot in good faith accept."[51] Novak continues,

> Furthermore, even when one cannot in good faith marshal arguments from the Jewish tradition to counter one's traditionalist opponents, one should not marshal arguments from other traditions. That would be like taking an argument from the law of another country to counter an argument made from the law of one's own country. At most, external sources should only be invoked when they complement rather than repudiate a position having firm support in the tradition itself.[52]

But all this misses the point. And here I use Novak as an *exemplum gratis* of misclassifying or mistaxonomizing Wolfson. In missing the point we get a glimpse at some of the structural problems inherent to Jewish studies at the present moment. Jewish studies should not be about the philosophical justification of Zionism,[53] just as it should not be about the reification and celebration of amorphous concepts such as "Jewishness." Eschewing normativity, Wolfson asks for something far deeper and, I would venture, far more complex. This is nothing less than the realization that what we study is not necessarily beautiful, good, or even right. In forcing us to read against the grain, be it of texts or the scholarly status quo, Wolfson pushes us to that unstable and uncomfortable ground from which one critiques all that others hold dear. This is neither to be difficult nor to critique solely for the sake of critique or deconstruction. It is, on the contrary, the font from which new knowledge emerges into the opaque darkness of dusk.

But, even more than this, in his desire to put the kabbalistic corpora in counterpoint with the Heideggerian one, Wolfson makes a classic (J. Z.) Smithean and comparative move where two phenomena, initially appearing to be radically different from each other, upon closer inspection, reveal real and often deep-rooted structural similarities. One ought to be able, in the words of Wolfson, "to illumine the convergence from within the divergence, to demonstrate that otherness of the similar is consequent to the similarity of the other."[54] In a classic move, Wolfson—unlike so many in the field, including the subfield of Jewish studies—refuses to leave scholarly analyses at the level of superficial description. As detailed and rich as such descriptions can and may be, we fail to grasp either the nuance they engender or appreciate the sheer human ingenuity, creativity, and indeed destructiveness that went into their production. In this, Wolfson's silence then is of an altogether different variety than that which Novak calls for. If the latter avoids the uncomfortable, the former encourages us to reflect on it in silent solitude.

Wolfson's path, though deeply committed to his scholarly sources and respectful of traditional scholarly norms, is, at root, deeply ethical, getting to the heart of how we, in our ethnocentrism and xenophobia, construct and react to the Other. "The trespassing of the boundary between self and other need not be accomplished by incorporating or demolishing the other whether in acts of gratuitous compassion or wanton aggression."[55] Wolfson here reminds us that scholarship, though a critical and occasionally a deconstructive task, is also one that moves toward dignity and respect. In the wrong hands, of course, it is mere sophistry.

Here, I am reminded of the words of our late friend, the dearly departed Kalman Bland, in a private correspondence when I told him that I did not know how it could be possible to go back to work in the subfield of Jewish philosophy given its deep-seated investment in various nationalist and atavistic desires and ends. In response, he wrote,

> A word or two about the feeling/decision of not going "back and working in the field of Jewish philosophy." Estrangement and alienation from something that once centered our lives, that once devoured our intellectual energies and focus, is a painful loss. A sadness. It works something like a phantom limb. How can it possibly throb if it isn't there anymore? But it does. I think one of the nails in the coffin of contemporary historical scholarship in medieval Jewish philosophy is the pathological poverty of modern Jewish thought/theology/so-called, but misnamed Philosophy. As you put your finger on it exactly in *Rethinking Jewish Philosophy*,[56] its thinly disguised ethnocentric, chauvinistic, solipsistic apologetics. If philosophy is the refusal to accept anything because it's a tradition, then what passes today for Jewish philosophy is certainly Jewish but not philosophic. And if philosophy is preoccupied with how we think rather than with what we should think, then today's drivel is certainly Jewish but not philosophic. And since so much of what motivates what and how we study and interpret the premodern sources derives from our present-day reality and political persuasion, then it's no mystery why the historical study of Jewish thought has become so uninteresting, so vapid, so unsatisfying. So bankrupt. So corrupt. So evasive. Corrupt and evasive because the religious tradition is complicit with the unreasonable policies governing the State of Israel. Refusing to repudiate Netanyahu's governance, scholars are unable and unwilling to understand the past critically and humanistically.[57]

Bland here, in characteristic fashion, cuts through the rhetoric of ostensible scholarship to show how it can and very often is used in the service of political and nationalist agendas, something that threatens to topple the discourses associated with what passes for Jewish philosophy in on itself. Like Wolfson, Bland encourages us not to be confined by the status quo, not to mistake the pursuit of truth (and justice) for tribalism, especially in the articulation, legitimation, and justification of unsavory truth claims. And, again like Wolfson, he exposes some of these subterranean problems to the light of day, asking us to do better and exhorting us not to apologize for Jewish sources—or, worse, be silent when we cannot endorse their contents.[58] Instead, both Bland and Wolfson actively show where, when, how, and why the particularity of these contents can, and often do, result in issues of alterity and, as is the case with a certain cross-section in Israel and even outside of it, in dispossession, violence, and murder. Such silence is quiescence in the face of blatant aggression, and calling attention to such transgressions is frequently met with confusion and mischaracterization.

CODA: TOWARD A NEW JEWISH STUDIES

In this final and concluding section, allow me to return to Wolfson's own work as a way to eschew the sort of particularism I have in mind. The problem, however, is that Wolfson is the outlier, the one who often proves the rule. Perhaps nowhere is this clearer than the way in which his work is mischaracterized and misunderstood within the subfield known as Jewish studies. As witnessed above, he is mischaracterized as a scholar of Jewish mysticism, when his work is both informed by and informs philosophy and literary theory on every page. Or, his work on Heidegger is somehow misconstrued as an apology for that great thinker. Jewish studies, in sum, does not know what to do with a thinker of Wolfson's stature. And this is a real problem. It is not Wolfson's problem, it is the field's problem. But because it cannot deal with such issues, it reduces, essentializes, and miscategorizes.

Unlike others who invoke the rhetoric, Judaism serves for Wolfson as an indexical marker of and for the scholar's necessary if impossible desire for universality. Framed somewhat differently, for Wolfson the commensurability of the universal, which is after all philosophy's quest, only makes sense in light of Judaism's incommensurability and, of course, vice versa. The particular and the universal undermine each other in their mutual indeterminacy, becoming in the process mutually overdetermined categories. This is what drives Wolfson's subtle readings of texts that, at first blush, ought to have nothing to say to one another—perhaps nowhere is this clearer than in his paring of Heidegger and Kabbalah. As a nomadic thinker, Wolfson artfully avoids the presumed existence of metaphysical absolutes or ontological essences, those communal abodes that invite us to dwell in comfort and that enable us to hear the mesmerizing cadences of sociability that often betray nothing more than a political or ideological patois.[59] It is a nomadism that calls out for friendship and solidarity.

If the work of Elliot R. Wolfson tells us anything, it is that we ought not be satisfied with our traditional narratives, categories, and taxonomies. It offers us a glimpse of the way out of the problems that have always beset the field of Jewish studies. Caught as it is between the hegemonic gaze of universalism and the potential for naval-gazing that defines the particular, his corpus reminds us of the beauty of the particular and how it can, when understood properly and with finesse, undermine the universal. Just as, in like manner, all of the problems inherent to the universal are also found, apologetics to the side, in Judaism's heart.

ACKNOWLEDGMENTS

I would like to thank Susannah Heschel for reading and commenting on an earlier draft of this chapter.

NOTES

1. Elliot R. Wolfson, *The Duplicity of Philosophy's Shadow: Heidegger, Nazism, and the Jewish Other* (New York: Columbia University Press, 2018), 171.
2. I have tried to lay out the terms of this in my *The Study of Judaism: Identity, Authenticity, Scholarship* (Albany: State University of New York Press, 2013), 1–16.
3. Indeed, it is precisely this issue of temporal coordinates, including their investiture in and subversion of each other, that has informed so much of Wolfson's work from his *Language, Eros, Being: Kabbalistic Hermeneutics and Poetic Imagination* (New York: Fordham University Press, 2005), right up to his recent collection *Suffering Time: Philosophical, Kabbalistic, and Hasidic Reflections on Temporality* (Leiden: Brill, 2021).
4. For a very good history of the study of Judaism in the American context, see Paul Ritterband and Harold S. Wexler, *Jewish Learning in American Universities: The First Century* (Bloomington: Indiana University Press, 1994); see also my comments in *The Study of Judaism*, 57–76.
5. Or, as Wolfson himself frames it:

   > The critique of time as absolute simultaneity sets into sharp relief a genetic fallacy of historical positivism and opens the way to brood over the reversibility of the temporal flow; the past may not, after all, extend monodirectionally into the present, which was its future, but rather may swerve its way curvilinearly, future awaiting its past, past becoming its future. We could, then, think of time's motion as comprising two movements—procession and return—following exactly the same pattern of development in different directions.

   See his *Language, Eros, Being*, xx.
6. In the words of Dana Hollander, invoking the spirit of Derrida, "there is a paradox that the more we assert a particular identity such as Europeanness or Jewishness, the more we are forced to do so in the name of the universal values and aims that this identity represents, and, consequently, the more we must deny its particularity." See her *Exemplarity and Chosenness: Rosenzweig and Derrida on the Nation of Philosophy* (Stanford, CA: Stanford University Press, 2008), 5. In this regard, and on the ever-present problems and tensions that emerge from this, at least as Jewish thought is concerned, see Robert Erlewine, "Resolving Contradiction: Samuel Hirsch

and the Stakes of Modern Jewish Thought," *AJS Review* 44, no. 2 (2020): 317–44.

7. A good recent attempt to work through some of these issues is Dana Hollander, *Ethics out of Law: Hermann Cohen and the "Neighbor"* (Toronto: University of Toronto Press, 2020), 3–7.
8. Wolfson, *The Duplicity of Philosophy's Shadow*, xv.
9. Elliot R. Wolfson, *Through a Speculum That Shines: Vision and Imagination in Medieval Jewish Mysticism* (Princeton, NJ: Princeton University Press, 1994).
10. Wolfson, *The Duplicity of Philosophy's Shadow*; and Elliot R. Wolfson, *Heidegger and Kabbalah: Hidden Gnosis and the Path of Poiēsis* (Bloomington: Indiana University Press, 2019).
11. See his most recent collection, *Suffering Time*, e.g., 6–8.
12. That this is no longer the case is the result of his pathbreaking interventions. See, for example, the recent work of Daniel M. Herskowitz, *Heidegger and His Jewish Reception* (Cambridge: Cambridge University Press, 2021).
13. A nice juxtaposition with the thought of another contemporary philosopher who works in Jewish studies, David Novak, might be illustrative. In his review of Wolfson's *Heidegger and Kabbalah*, for example, he accuses Wolfson's use of Heidegger as tantamount to "bringing an idol into the Sanctuary." See his "Scholarship and the Critique of Tradition: Elliot R. Wolfson, *Heidegger and Kabbalah: Hidden Gnosis and the Path of Poiēsis*," *Journal of Religious Ethics* 48, no. 4 (2020): 731–40, at 731.
14. E.g., Wolfson, *The Duplicity of Philosophy's Shadow*, 13.
15. Though initially appearing on the AJS website, it was quickly removed because of objections raised by the general membership. See Hannah Dreyfus, "Former Jewish Studies Association Presidents Alarmed by Response to Shamed Sociologist," *The Forward,* April 23, 2021. Accessed online at: https://forward.com/news/breaking-news/468341/jewish-studies-presidents-letter-sarna-pianko/.
16. E.g., Ruth Wisse, *Jews and Power* (New York: Schocken, 2007), e.g., 142–69; Jonathan Sarna, "A Note from Jonathan Sarna, Chair, H-Judaic," *H-Judaic*, September 24, 2019. Online at: https://networks.h-net.org/node/28655/discussions/4815412/note-jonathan-sarna-chair-h-judaic.
17. See, for example, Steven M. Cohen, "A Tale of Two Jewries: The 'Inconvenient Truth' for American Jews," *Berman Jewish Policy Archive*. Online at: https://www.bjpa.org/search-results/publication/2908.
18. On the political fallout of the Cohen debacle, including the triangulation between the academy, politics (i.e., Zionism), and the issue of Jewish continuity, see Kate Rosenblatt, Ronit Stahl, and Lila Corwin Berman, "How Jewish Academia Created a #MeToo Disaster," *The Forward*, July 19, 2018. Online at https://forward.com/opinion/406240/how-jewish-academia-created-a-metoo-disaster/.
19. One of the most egregious examples of this is from Haggai Mazuz, who works on the Jews of Arabia at the time of Muhammad. He wants to posit—though, it is certainly worth noting, he has not a shred of evidence—a continual Jewish identity that stretches out from the ashes of the destruction of the Second Temple and moves directly through to the codifiers of the Babylonian Talmud (and beyond). Arabian Jews, for him as for others, form a missing piece of this continuity. Although he freely acknowledges that "there are no—and perhaps never were any—Jewish or Christian sources documenting the history of the Hijazi Jews"

(1), this acknowledgment does not stop him from reaching the conclusion that they "were Talmudic-Rabbinic Jews in almost every respect." See his *The Religious and Spiritual Life of the Jews of Medina* (Leiden: Brill, 2014), 99.

20. On Neusner more generally, see my *Jacob Neusner: An American Jewish Iconoclast* (New York: New York University Press, 2016).
21. See, for example, Susannah Heschel, "Revolt of the Colonized: Abraham Geiger's *Wissenschaft des Judentums* as a Challenge to Christian Hegemony in the Academy," *New German Critique* 77 (Spring–Summer, 1999): 61–85; Heschel, "The Philological Uncanny: Nineteenth-Century Jewish Readings of the Qur'an," *Journal of Qur'anic Studies* 20, no. 3 (2018): 193–213. See also her "Orientalist Triangulations: Jewish Scholarship on Islam as a Response to Christian Europe," in *The Muslim Reception of European Orientalism: Reversing the Gaze*, ed. Susannah Heschel and Umar Ryad (London and New York: Routledge, 2019), 147–67.
22. One of the most classic expressions of this may be found in Donald Wiebe, "Failure of Nerve in the Academic Study of Religion," *Studies in Religion/Sciences religieuses* 13, no. 4 (1984): 401–22. For expansion, see William E. Arnal, Willi Braun, and Russell T. McCutcheon, eds., *Failure and Nerve in the Academic Study of Religion: Essays in Honor of Donald Wiebe* (Sheffield: Equinox, 2012).
23. Karl Budde, *Religion of Israel to the Exile* (London and New York: G. P. Putnam's Sons, 1899), 218.
24. See, e.g., Suzanne L. Marchand, *German Orientalism in the Age of Empire: Religion, Race, and Scholarship* (Cambridge: Cambridge University Press, 2009).
25. See, for example, Aaron W. Hughes and Russell T. McCutcheon, *Religion in 50 Words: A Critical Vocabulary* (London and New York: Routledge, 2021); Hughes and McCutcheon, *Religion in 50 More Words: A Redescriptive Vocabulary* (London and New York: Routledge, 2022).
26. And there has been a virtual cottage industry in this issue over the last few years. See, for example, Timothy Fitzgerald, *The Ideology of Religious Studies* (Oxford and New York: Oxford University Press, 2000); Daniel Dubuisson, *The Western Construction of Religion: Myths, Knowledge, and Ideology*, trans. William Sayers (Baltimore, MD: Johns Hopkins University Press, 2003); Brent Nongbri, *Before Religion: The History of a Modern Concept* (New Haven: Yale University Press, 2013).
27. In the words of Daniel Dubuisson,

    > The history of religions should not have exported this singular notion [i.e., "religion"], found nowhere else, and issuing from a history that took its own unique course, without having subjected it beforehand to a rigorous critical examination. But it did not do so. Instead, it exported it, along with the West's doxa, without the least doubt or scruple, as if it were inconceivable that other cultures should not possess, if only in primitive, incomplete or aberrant, monstrous form, what seemed to every Western mind the very sign of humanity and civilization. (*The Western Construction of Religion*, 191)

28. Though, perhaps unsurprisingly, there have been many attempts to show the "Jewish roots" behind their theories. See, for example, Ivan Strenski, *Contesting Sacrifice: Religion, Nationalism, and Social Thought in France* (Chicago: University of Chicago Press, 2002); more recently, see Guy Stroumsa, *The Idea of Semitic Monotheism: The Rise and Fall of a Scholarly Myth*

(Oxford: Oxford University Press, 2021). More specifically, see Sander L. Gilman, *Freud, Race, and Gender* (Princeton, NJ: Princeton University Press, 1993).

29. On general background to this milieu, see Steven M. Wasserstrom, *Religion after Religion: Gershom Scholem, Mircea Eliade, and Henry Corbin at Eranos* (Princeton, NJ: Princeton University Press, 1999), 3–19.
30. See, for example, Adriana Berger, "Mircea Eliade: Romanian Fascism and the History of Religions in the United States," in *Tainted Greatness: Antisemitism and Cultural Heroes*, ed. Nancy A. Harrowitz (Philadelphia: Temple University Press, 1994), 51–74.
31. See, for example, Mircea Eliade, *The Myth of the Eternal Return or, Cosmos and History*, trans. Willard R. Trask, with a new Introduction by Jonathan Z. Smith (Princeton, NJ: Princeton University Press, 2005 [1959]), 3–6.
32. For critiques of Eliade, see Daniel Dubuisson, *Twentieth Century Mythologies: Dumézil, Lévi-Strauss, Eliade*, 2nd ed., trans. Martha Cunningham (London: Equinox, [1993] 2006); Ivan Strenski, *Four Theories of Myth in Twentieth Century History: Cassirer, Eliade, Lévi-Strauss, and Malinowski* (Iowa City: University of Iowa Press, 1987); and, more recently, Leonardo Ambasciano, *An Unnatural History of Religions: Academia, Post-Truth and the Quest for Scientific Knowledge* (London, Bloomsbury, 2019).
33. For a history of the field in general, see Eric J. Sharpe, *Comparative Religion: A History* (London: Duckworth, 1985); in the United States, see Walter H. Capps, *Religious Studies: The Making of a Discipline* (Augsburg Press, 2000); and in Canada, see my *From Seminary to University: The Institutional History of the Study of Religion in Canada* (Toronto: University of Toronto Press, 2020).
34. Mircea Eliade and Joseph M. Kitagawa, eds., *The History of Religions: Essays in Methodology* (Chicago: University of Chicago Press, 1959).
35. See Hughes and McCutcheon, *Religion in 50 Words*, 263–69.
36. Joseph M. Kitagawa, ed. *The History of Religions: Essays on the Problem of Understanding* (Chicago: University of Chicago Press, 1967).
37. On the problematic nature of understanding (*Verstehen*) in the humanities, see Hughes and McCutcheon, *Religion in 50 More Words*, 282–87.
38. On Harry Austryn Wolfson, see Isadore Twersky, "Harry Austryn Wolfson, 1887–1974," *Journal of the American Oriental Society*, 95, no. 2 (1975): 181–83.
39. On Saul Lieberman, see Marc E. Shapiro, *Saul Lieberman and the Orthodox* (Scranton, PA: University of Scranton Press, 2006).
40. On Neusner, see my *Jacob Neusner: An American Jewish Iconoclast*, 163–200.
41. For similar remarks in the field of English and so-called Jewish American religion, see Benjamin Schreier, *The Rise and Fall of Jewish American Literature: Ethnic Studies and the Challenge of Identity* (Philadelphia: University of Pennsylvania Press, 2020), 1–36.
42. I have tried to articulate some of these issues in my *Shared Identities: Medieval and Modern Imaginings of Judeo-Islam* (Oxford and New York: Oxford University Press, 2017).
43. On Oriental studies' unwillingness to make room for Hebrew, see Marchand, *German Orientalism in the Age of Empire.*
44. As an example of reification of "Jewishness" in Jewish studies and as an attempt to see a Jewish

prototype in virtually everything, I point to Shachar M. Pinkser's *A Rich Brew: How Cafés Created Modern Jewish Culture* (New York: New York University Press, 2018).

45. See, for example, David Chidester, *Savage Systems: Colonialism and Comparative Religion in Southern Africa* (Charlottesville: University of Virginia Press, 1996); Chidester, *Empire of Religion: Imperialism and Comparative Religion* (Chicago: University of Chicago Press, 2014).
46. On this critique as it concerns Islam, see Charles Adam's chapter "The History of Religions and the Study of Islam" in the aforementioned volume edited by Kitagawa, *The History of Religions: Essays on the Problem of Understanding*, 177–93.
47. Indeed, perhaps one of the most successful was Howard Eilberg-Schwartz's *The Savage in Judaism: An Anthropology of Israelite Religion and Ancient Judaism* (Bloomington: Indiana University Press, 1990).
48. Perhaps one of the best examples of someone who has pointed out some of these prejudices, especially in terms of comparison, is Jonathan Z. Smith, *Drudgery Divine: On the Comparison of Early Christianities and the Religions of Late Antiquity* (Chicago: University of Chicago Press, 1990).
49. Heschel, "The Philological Uncanny," 199–201.
50. David Novak, "Scholarship and the Critique of Tradition," 731. This is, at least, more than he grants him in *David Novak: Natural Law and Revealed Torah*, ed. Hava Tirosh-Samuelson and Aaron W. Hughes (Leiden: Brill, 2014), 118–19.
51. Novak, "Scholarship and the Critique of Tradition," 738.
52. Novak, "Scholarship and the Critique of Tradition," 738.
53. Novak himself offers an apologetical defense of Zionism in his *Zionism and Judaism: A New Theory* (Cambridge: Cambridge University Press, 2015), a work that completely ignores the historical reality of colonization and occupation by focusing on Zionism as a theological as opposed to a political discourse.
54. Wolfson, *Heidegger and Kabbalah*, 367.
55. Wolfson, *Heidegger and Kabbalah*, 367.
56. Aaron W. Hughes, *Rethinking Jewish Philosophy: Beyond Particularism and Universalism* (Oxford and New York: Oxford University Press, 2014).
57. Kalman P. Bland, private communication, May 1, 2016.
58. See Aaron W. Hughes and Elliot R. Wolfson, "Introduction," *Kalman Bland Memorial Volume* (*Journal of Jewish Thought and Philosophy*) 30 (2022): 3–8.
59. I have, for example, written about this in my introduction to *Elliot R. Wolfson: Poetic Thinking*, ed. Hava Tirosh-Samuelson and Aaron W. Hughes (Leiden: Brill, 2015), 1–33.

RELIGION AND TECHNOLOGY

The Star of Redemption in the Language of New Media

ZACHARY BRAITERMAN

✡

MEANING MORE THAN ART AND THE ARTS, "AESTHETICS" BELONGS TO sensation and perception, to how human beings organize a sensible manifold, to how they see and hear and feel things in the world. In religion or revelation, it cuts to the ocular core of theological vision. How a human creature might come to see God in the world would require a special glass or a veil-like garment, a technological *aesthesis* that reveals its object by way of concealment. In this essay, I turn to the 1921 magnum opus *The Star of Redemption* by Franz Rosenzweig, a text beholden to the geometry of revelation. On the combination of triangles (△ + ▽) that compose the "star of redemption" (✡), Rosenzweig explained in a 1918 letter to Margrit Rosenstock-Huessy, "I think in figures."[1] In the reading proposed here in this essay, the intentionally figurative construction of *The Star* mimics the work of a thing-like apparatus designed to mirror and mask down here on planet earth "the star of redemption," an astral six-point matrix-figure of absolute truth. I will argue that its artificial design reflects the emergent technological spirit in Weimar Germany while anticipating key features in the "language of new media" that allow us today to reframe and reconceptualize religion or revelation in categories unique to our own century.[2]

The first part of my argument is to build on what I have argued elsewhere, saying that *The Star* is a distinctly *modern* theological masterpiece.[3] At increasing historical and theoretical distances, the more we consider its modernity, namely its time and place in the history of German modernism, the more and more *The Star* looks like a thing. As a physical artifact, *The Star* is an antiquarian book with uniquely modern design features that call attention to a technological quality. It is in this technological capacity that *The Star* seems to do things that Heidegger claimed about Greek technology, even while I will contend it does more to resemble modern technology, as also understood by Heidegger. Having drawn out that point, I will then map *The Star* into what

Lev Manovitch called "the language of new media" while mapping the language of new media into "religion." New media and theory underscore that religion in its ocularity is an inherently technological medium. Repurposed in the new century, Rosenzweig's book is an emblem of new media with which to stake and assess with critical circumspection claims about the garment or glass and special effects that make spiritual vision and the vision of God possible in the Age of Electric Simulation.

△ ▽ ✡

A QUICK INTRODUCTION TO *THE STAR* WOULD SKETCH OUT THE GEOMETRIC contours of a plastic amalgam from out of a grid-like and modular organization of visible and invisible component parts. *The Star* is shaped out of triangles. Each of the three "parts" of *The Star* are comprised of three "books." In part I, God, world, and "man" are the three "elements" or points of a triangle that compose the truth. Here each figure constitutes an autonomous component in its utter and abstract alienation from the other two. At this primary level of organization, these elementary figures are mere figments of thought. Terrified by death, the human subject inhabits this proto-world (*Vorwelt*) of elements: self-enclosed fragments symbolized by Mt. Olympus, the Greek polis, classical Greek sculpture and tragic theater. The way out of the fear of death is to realize that, not "the all" and not "nothing," God, world, and "man" are "something." In part II, these originally silent, plastic elements in their mathematical thingness are opened out to each other in the world (*Welt*) of lived time. They are brought into relation and made real in the "course" of the acoustic media of creation, revelation, and redemption, which together form a second triangle. Parallel to epic, lyric, and dramatic speech, their language intensifies spiritual life to the highest pitch of a choral apocalypse; all things are ultimately absorbed back into the silent world that is the silent light of God at the end of the dialogue in the "book" on redemption. In part III, the form (*Gestalt*) of Jewish and of Christian cults form into a super-world (*Überwelt*) that mirrors "the star of redemption" itself. Hovering out there in space, the star of redemption is the matrix-pattern of absolute truth superimposing the triangle of part I (God, world, man) and the triangle of part II (creation, revelation, redemption). With its eye on eternity, the closing pages of *The Star* leave us at "the gate" where the now visible manifestation of God's face appears out of the star of redemption in the image of an animated mask confronting the soul at death's border and ushering it back into terrestrial life.

Viewed in spatial terms, I am arguing that the well-known antihistoricism of *The Star* is itself otherworldly. Against the linear forward-flow of Christian historical time, the eternity of Judaism is composed out of the "blood" of its own biological reproduction and out of the cyclical movement of the ritual calendar.[4] In their own day, post-Holocaust writers like Eliezer Berkovits and Emil Fackenheim rejected this rejection of history as out of touch with the reality of Jewish suffering and the return to history represented by the State of Israel. Against this line of criticism, Steven Katz argued that Rosenzweig caught something profound about the noncentrality of the Jews in world history.[5] For all that he wrote about eternity in time, it is not entirely clear if, as understood by Rosenzweig, Judaism belongs even at all to planet earth. Reading the rabbis on the book of Genesis for the notion that death is "very good," Rosenzweig saw a set apart area (*Bezirk*) of death in life. Death is "in creation itself a super-creation" (*in der Schöpfung selbst eine Überschöpfung*), "in the terrestrial something super-terrestrial" (*im iridische ein Überirdishces*).[6]

From the frozen pagan proto-cosmos through the flow of the course of the world in time, *The Star* is a device for looking into the deep space of the star of redemption from the super-world of Judaism. Judaism is an ahistorical and extraterrestrial platform arcing out over and peeling away from earth. Its holy land, holy language, and holy law do not belong to the land, language, and law of this world. With this look to the heavens, readers of Jewish philosophy might be reminded of Moses Maimonides. Contemplating what for him and for the science of his age were the irregular movements of the stars and planets led Maimonides to the idea of God's free creativity vis-à-vis the material world. He did so from a place here on earth.[7] Centuries later, Rosenzweig built a machine powered by the intensive spinning of two self-enclosed cycles: the reproductive cycle instantiated as blood and the cycle of the ritual calendar. Tongue in cheek, the fancy that I bring to this technology is that of a starship lifting off planet earth on the way to the star of redemption out there in space to gaze there at the face of God at the gate. Beyond that gate lies the next world where, in a Talmudic source quoted by Rosenzweig at the end of the "book" on redemption, the rabbis with crowns on their head sit basking in the radiance of the *Shekhinah*.

ANTIQUARIAN

About the technical thinghood of *The Star*, I will set aside Heidegger's preoccupation with ontological matters regarding "original reference," the "unconditional," the grounds and foundations that underpin "the thing." When strolling around "things," Heidegger's advice was to avoid falling into a pit or well, given the likelihood that one may "not reach ground for quite some time."[8] Following that wisdom, I will mostly avoid what Heidegger called the "widest possible sense" of the meaning of a thing, namely "the thing itself." I will instead remain with what Heidegger called the "narrow" and the "wider" meaning of a thing in respect to *The Star*. The narrowly object character of a thing is that which can be touched, reached, or seen, that which is "present at hand." The "wider" meaning of a thing is the unfolding of a thing qua affair, transaction, occurrence, event, the always still happening. For Heidegger, this happening is the essence of the historical, "even if it seems to be past," and whether or not "*we* remain equal to this happening so that it can really develop."[9] To ask "What is a thing?" is to "determine the changing basic position within the relation to what is." Heidegger understood that such determinations regarding our changed relations are determined not in the course of a single lecture, but over the course of a century.[10]

Definitely after the course of a century, the narrowest thinghood of *The Star* comes clearly into view. For its most devoted readers, *The Star* has been an event-thing in the wider meaning understood by Heidegger. A long time ago, in the 1960s and 1970s, Rosenzweig's magnum opus sustained in the history of modern Jewish philosophy an eventfulness that was still fresh, current, living, intellectually resonant. Even as a material object, *The Star* had a unique aura. Searching for theological or philosophical authority, Jewish philosophy would to this day enter into its constellation in order to think big philosophical ideas about God, world, and human personhood. The Jewish philosophy that comes after *The Star* is a peering into it in order to prove itself equal to this happening, "so that it can really develop," as Heidegger might have added.

But is *The Star* a thing that can really develop, and if so, under what new conditions? This one hundred-year-old book lies at the same distance of time from readers today that would have separated Rosenzweig from the world of Goethe, Kant, Fichte, Schelling, and the German Romantics. For those of us interested in first editions, *The Star* is an antiquarian object. A little dusty and crazy, its place in time is that of Jugendstil, German expressionism, and early Bauhaus. It really is a thing in the most narrow sense of the term. Less naïve and more skeptical, an alternative approach to the text would come to "it" from the outside and to see it as one would a "found object." One would pick it up as one would any object, examine the apparatus, the way its component parts are organized side by side, one thing next to the other. *The Star* is no longer the thing, the event it once was. In the narrow sense of the word, *The Star* is, to quote Heidegger, maybe like "[a] thing in the sense of being present-at-hand: rock, a piece of wood, a pair of pliers, a watch, an apple, and a piece of bread" or a "rose, shrub, beech tree, spruce, lizard, wasp."[11]

Antiquarian books are precious objects. As a material thing, after all, *The Star* is a different kind of object than the living beings and simple tools tagged by Heidegger. An antiquarian book from the heyday of German modernism, the inky figure of the star of David on the cover of its first edition calls attention to geometric patterning as much as it draws attention to the form of an unapologetic German-Jewish book.[12] Antiquarian book lovers will also note the unique modernist typographical features that enhance the object. Downward-pointing triangles of text point dramatically at the end of the three bridging units named Transition, Threshold, Gate. The triangular typography first transitions the text forward from the silent proto-world of part I into the acoustic world of part II, then through the threshold into the super-world in part III, and then at the gate back "into life," these two words being the very last two lines of text in *The Star*. What these modest design elements do is give a strong graphic edge signaling the now-time of the text and the visual thinking launched by it in the early 1920s.

It matters that the book is old. The time after *The Star* is the time after the modernism of twentieth-century Jewish thought and philosophy, after Auschwitz and Hiroshima, after the establishment of the State of Israel, after the postwar assimilation of American Judaism, after the digital revolution, after globalization; the time of global warming. This after-time frames *The Star* as a "thing" in the narrow sense of the term intended by Heidegger. A one hundred-year-old text, it belongs neither to the immediate present, the way it once did, nor to the recent past, as it still did in the 1960s and 1970s, when the scholars who would have taught our own teachers knew Rosenzweig or members of his circle personally. A German modernist reading the rabbis, Rosenzweig knows that death crowns creation. As he says about the perfect tense in the book on creation, *The Star* is now a thing "fixed to one single point in space by the definite article . . . specifically objective, object-like, in thing-like stillness," completing the "objectiveness of occurrence."[13]

TECHNÊ

The artificial three-part organization of the text more than suggests that there is nothing natural or organic about *The Star*. It is a technological thing or artifact, a *technê* meant, as per Aristotle, to produce particular ends; in particular, what Heidegger in his famous essay on technology identified as a "bringing forth out of concealment into unconcealment." Looking at it this way in the language of Heidegger, the reader can see in *The Star* a "way of revealing" or "coming into presence in the realm where revealing and unconcealment takes place, where *aletheia,* truth, happens."[14] Rosenzweig's book and the religion or Judaism it represents would be nothing less than a tool with which to make visible the appearance of the concealed and hidden God in the organization of mediating filters of visual figures. *The Star* belongs also to the kind of distinctly *modern* forms of technology or apparatus rejected by Heidegger. Still in the language of Heidegger, it is possible to see in its geometry a form of revealing that "extracts" and "transforms" energy as such, switching it about "ever anew." As a modern technological object, *The Star* is a standing reserve or an enframing device, in which the reality of things like God, world and soul are "set upon," "stored," "distributed."[15]

About tools for viewing the astral formation that is "the star of redemption," Rosenzweig said this in a section on "liturgy and gesture." The thing itself that is *the* star of redemption is the object of study to which *The Star* is devoted. He called it a "material point which moves in space," as if out there over planet earth. Only after "telescope and spectroscope have brought it to us do we now know it as we know a tool of our daily-use or a painting in our chambers: in familiar perceptions."[16] Prayer would be that telescope or spectroscope, a prismatic mirroring device reflecting celestial images to us back down on earth. The super-terrestrial star of redemption out there in space and brought down to earth is a thing in the wider sense intended by Heidegger: affair, transaction, occurrence, event, whereas, for its part, *The Star* is a tool designed to convert that raw energy into images of "God," "world," and "man" through the filters of "creation," "revelation," and "redemption." The apparatus that is *The Star* converts and holds these images in place and in time, only to reconvert their reflection back into the stored-up energy of pure light.

The basic gambit of *The Star* is that of an apparatus that allows its user to gaze upon the unconcealment of God's face, appearing fully realized, fully manifest, fully recognized in the craft-form of a human mask. "Yea," in this mask, the one worn by the human user or soul and the one God wears as He turns to the human creature, "we now recognize the [star of redemption] itself, as it has at last emerged as figure for us, in the divine visage."[17] Composed of two triangles, "the star of redemption" is an archaic mask composed of passive and animate levels. "Just as the [star] mirrors its elements and the combination of the elements into one route in its two superimposed triangles, so too the organs of the countenance divide into two levels. For the life-points of the countenance are, after all, those points where the countenance comes into contact with the world above, be it in passive or active contact. The basic level [of the mask] is ordered according to the receptive organs; they are the building blocks, as it were, which together compose the face, the mask, namely forehead and cheeks, to which belong respectively nose and ears."[18]

The soul cannot see the reality of God without masks and mirrors. Rejecting the notion that opposes fleeting appearance and truth, appearance, for Rosenzweig, is a mirror of truth. "The appearance is as essential as the truth here, for love could not be eternal as love if it did not appear to be transitory." Not a random motif, the mirror repeats itself throughout *The Star*. Earlier in the "book" on revelation, Rosenzweig had anticipated this about the sensuality (*Sinnlichkeit*) of the word. "Brimful with its divine supersense" (*Übersinn*) reflected in the Song of Songs, that appearance is as essential as truth, that "in the mirror of this appearance, the truth is directly mirrored."[19] And then about the appearance of the star-matrix in the mirror work of Jewish ritual, Rosenzweig wrote this in the "book" on Judaism. Ritual "is meant to regulate the service of the earth, the work of culture, rhythmically, and thus to mirror, in miniature, the eternal, in which beginning and end come together, by means of the ever repeated present, the imperishable by means of the Today."[20]

Speaking in the first person, I can only recall what was the surprising moment when all of a sudden I saw the truth represented by the six-figure matrix figure, the Star of Redemption, taking complete shape in the form of a mask-like face. There in the end at the gate, out there now in the inner sanctum, mirror and mask correlate the vision of God's face vis-à-vis the human body. Because it is now that the star of redemption "must once more mirror itself in that which, within the corporeality, is again the Upper: the countenance." Rejecting the notion that the vision of God's face is a human illusion, Rosenzweig insists, "There is no other way to express the Truth." More than that, it is "only when we see the [star] as countenance do we transcend every possibility and simply see."[21] It is there inside the sanctum that this simple seeing is now fully unconcealed. It is there that the human person "catches sight of none other than a countenance like [their] own." The star of redemption assumes the masked appearance of a face, "which glances at me and out of which I glance." This is the mask with which God "allowed himself to be seen" at "that border of life where seeing is vouchsafed." The mask or mirror means that "what he gave me to see in this Beyond of life is none other than what I was already privileged to perceive in the midst of life; the difference is only that I see it and no longer merely hear it."[22]

IN THE LANGUAGE OF NEW MEDIA

The looping of the past and the future, the collapsing together of the archaic and the futuristic reflected in this 1921 book was not uncommon in the culture at the time; undoubtedly these loops stay with us in our own digital networks. Odd couplings of the archaic and futuristic from back then would include "primitive" masks in paintings by Picasso, films like Paul Wegener's *Der Golem* (1914) and Fritz Lang's *Metropolis* (1927), Bruno Taut's Glass Pavilion at the Cologne Deutscher Werkbund Exhibition, short stories by Franz Kafka, paintings by Wassily Kandinsky and Paul Klee. Writing about "masks" in the *Blue Rider Almanac*, painter August Macke grouped old things like a Persian spear, a holy vessel, a pagan idol, a wreath of everlasting flowers, a Gothic cathedral, the word "holy" alongside new things, like a landscape by Cézanne, the whirring of a propeller, and the whistle of a steam engine. Macke saw in masks the graphic and verbal media via which "incomprehensible ideas express themselves."[23] Indeed, there is something almost like science fiction about the terrestrial-super-terrestrial form of Judaism in Rosenzweig's geometric design conception. Abstract and mystical, and uniquely modular and immersive qualities mark the structural design-configuration of *The Star*, a modernist relic that at the time belonged already to the digital future.

At the intentional risk of anachronism, I want to bring the old media object that is *The Star* not simply into what we once called "postmodernism," but into the language of "new media." As explained by theorists Jay David Bolter and Richard Grusin, new media build upon and remediate old media, and old media remediate new media. "Remediation" is their term for the borrowing and repurposing of old media in new media formats and of new media in reformatted versions of old media. This relation between new and old media formats is not oppositional, nor is it a transitional mode, but rather a permanent feature of a new media environment. Electronica are not opposed to painting, photography, printing, or cinema; the computer is a tool with which to repurpose older formats; and so on.[24] What new media theorists highlight is the mediated, technological character of the artificial objects so dear to textual Jewish studies, including *The Star*, allowing students to see them as such, while changing the frame of the discourse about both Judaism and religion. If my hunch is not a complete anachronism, it is because the prehistory of new media extends back in time to the 1940s, a mere twenty years or so after the publication of our text and only ten or so years after the death of its author.[25]

What makes it easy to remediate *The Star* into the language of new media are the many things they seem actually to share in common. In particular, Bolter and Grusin address two aspects of mediation and remediation that illuminate the internal, machinic workings of *The Star*.

The first aspect in new media is the notion of or desire for "immediacy," the event-like character by which attention to the mediating interface between users and objects fades into the experiential background. Such claims regarding immediacy should remind scholars of religion of mysticism, what Elliot Wolfson identifies as the desire to see the divine infinite light without the mediation of a finite garment (*bli livush*). In Renaissance art, Norman Bryson identifies the attempt to look through the surface of the canvas as if through a window.[26] The language of immediacy appears as well in the high modernist film theory of André Bazin and Stanley Cavell, being "the notion that a medium could erase itself and leave the viewer in the presence of the objects represented, so that [one] could know the objects directly."[27] For their part, virtual reality (VR) programs depend upon illusions created by complete immersion into an artificial world, direct encounter with virtual objects. Rosenzweig has done something similar. In the expressive urgency brought by him to the drama of revelation and redemption, the reader is meant to relive the event, which is "the direct view of the whole truth only to him who sees it in God . . . [in] a view beyond life."[28] The reader is as if given to hear and to see the spectacle of objects directly and always anew; the formal mediating structures of *The Star* are supposed to fade from view.

The second and opposite aspect of new media discussed by Bolter and Grusin relates to the "hypermediacy" of the screen, that is, the multiplication of media on a single surface. Historically, these include combinations of text and image in pre-Renaissance art, medieval cathedrals, baroque cabinets, paintings by Vermeer, Cubist art, the attention to the surface of the canvas in modernist art, and the contemporary computer screen on which multiple windows open on a single screen. Hypermediacy is described as "opacity—the fact that knowledge of the world comes to us through media. The viewer acknowledges that she is in the presence of a medium and learns through acts of mediation or indeed learns about mediation itself. . . . [I]t is the insistence that the experience of the medium itself [is] an experience of the real."[29] *The Star* is also hypermediated. It is a media object built up out of different media-registers—symbolic, acoustic, and visual; it remediates old, archaic texts, bits of liturgy and ritual, and philosophical texts and styles that the textual apparatus recombines into what we will see below is an ultra-modern, modular configuration.

In one way, *The Star* is a "system," a complete arrangement that sets out to grasp the particular in the whole and the whole in the particular. As Benjamin Pollock has said, the task of the system that Rosenzweig set out to create was to grasp "all particulars in their identity and difference" in relation to "the nature of things as a whole."[30] In another way, however, *The Star* is *not* a system. A system is a vertically organized body with a clear beginning and a definite telos that builds up organically and in sequence, from one thing and then to another. But systems grow out of a root-like structure of thinking, whereas *The Star* presents its parts visually and all at once. *The Star* is more like a "program." Organized horizontally, every part of a program is simultaneous to every other part. Pushing past what Rosenzweig said about his own philosophical project as a system of philosophy, what I will show below is a grid-like pattern of thought that looks more like a console than anything as organic as earth-based systemic philosophical thinking.

In the usual way of reading *The Star of Redemption*, the individual parts and "books" are organized vertically, systematically. A body with organs, the vertical systemic organization is anthropomorphic, as if designed by a Kabbalist. *The Star* has a head, torso, and legs. In this organization of the text, revelation occupies the beating heart of "the system."

Part I (Elements) (Proto-World)
God
World
"Man"
Part II (Course) (World)
Creation
REVELATION
Redemption
Part III (Gestalt) (Über-World)
Judaism
Christianity
Truth (star of redemption)

But the order of the *Star of Redemption* can be graphed otherwise, along horizontal lines. This horizontal format is suggested by the section headings that divide up and frame the second edition of the text, published in 1930. This nonanthropomorphic and grid-like console is more detailed. Highlighting the consistency of thought across levels, it marks the repetition of the figures and ideas that light up across the three individual books comprised by the three parts that allow the user to navigate a multiverse:

PART I (ELEMENTS) (PROTO-WORLD)

	INTRODUCTION (DEATH)		
BKS.:	1. GOD →	2. WORLD →	3. "MAN"
	Negative Theology →	Negative Cosmology →	Negative Psychology
	Methodology →	Methodology →	Methodology
	Divine Nature →	World Order →	Human Idiosyncrasy
	Divine Freedom →	World Plenitude →	Human Volition
	Divine Vitality →	Reality of the World →	Human Independence
	Greek gods →	Greek polis →	Greek man
	Asian gods →	Asian world →	Asian man
	Aesthetics [Myth] →	Aesthetics [Form] →	Aesthetics [Content]
	Twilight of gods →	Slumber of world →	Solitary man
	Transition		

PART II (COURSE) (WORLD)

	INTRODUCTION (MIRACLE)		
BKS.:	1. CREATION (G-W) →	2. REVELATION (G-M) →	3. REDEMPTION (M-W)
	Creator →	Revealer →	[Redeeming man]
	Islam [caprice] →	Islam [universal] →	Islam [subservience]
	Creature →	Soul →	Kingdom
	Islam (necessity) →	Islam (deed) →	Islam (endless)
	Grammar of Logos →	Grammar of Eros →	Grammar of Pathos
	Logic of Creation →	Logic of Revelation →	Logic of Redemption
	Theory of Art →	Theory of Art →	Theory of Art
	Word of God →	Word of God →	Word of God
	Threshold		

PART III (GESTALT) (ÜBER-WORLD)

	INTRODUCTION (PRAYER)		
BKS.:	1. JUDAISM →	2. CHRISTIANITY →	3. STAR OF REDEMPTION
	Eternity (Promise) →	Eternity Realized →	Eternity of Truth
	Eternal People →	Christian Historical Time →	God-World-Spirit
	Jewish Year →	Christian Liturgy →	Shape of Verification (Eschatology)
	Messianic Politics →	Christian Aesthetics →	Law of Verification
	Eternity of Promise →	Eternity Realized →	Truth of Eternity
	Gate		

This horizontal organization entails that, internal to each part, the user can read the first subsection of the first book, then the first subsection of the second book, and then the first subsection of the third book, and so on and so on. In part I, readers can read the Negative Theology of book 1 alongside the Negative Cosmology of book 2, alongside the Negative Psychology of book 3, all together as a group. They can read all the "Methodologies" together, or all of the subsections on Asia together. The layout of "Divine Freedom" is set alongside "World Vitality" and "Human Volition," the layout itself constituting a single argument broken up into three crystal-like components. So do the concluding subsections in the "books" of part I, "Twilight of the Gods" alongside the "Slumber of the World" and "Solitary Man." In part II, all of the Grammars (the grammar of Logos, Eros, and Pathos) belong together on a line, as do all of the Logics (the logic of creation, revelation, redemption), theories of art (epic, lyric, dramatic), and Words of God (from Genesis, Song of Songs, and Psalms). In part III, the Messianic Politics of Judaism is situated alongside Christian Aesthetics, and the Law of Verification as a single, tripartite thought-unit.

Graphed out in a grid, *The Star* will lose something of the temporality by which things appear, disappear, and reappear in sequence. The user can now see it as a spatially organized hyperlink of objects in which all the elemental figures, ideas, and arguments are shown simultaneously. Users can take the parts and lay them across a grid. Place one thing (God) next to another thing (World), and so on and so on. About the flattening of hyperlinked technological interfaces, Manovich writes, "If there is a new rhetoric or aesthetic possible here, it may have less to do with the ordering of time by a writer or orator, and more with spatial wandering."[31] The hallmark of new media objects like video games and virtual reality programs, *The Star* has the structure that makes spatial wandering possible. Users can punch in whatever conceptual correlates they want in order to get to where they want, think what they want. As Manovich notes, a new media module can scale up at various sizes and level of details, from image-based outline to a complete script or shot, even as each module retains its individual autonomy. "When an 'object' is inserted into a document (for instance a media clip inserted into a Word document), it continues to maintain its independence and can always be edited with the program originally used to create it."[32] In this vein, the modular sections of *The Star* are variable, not "something fixed once and for all, but something that can exist in different, potentially infinite combinations."[33]

A new media object is one in which the design creates discrete frames that allow the reader or user to see things. Again with Manovich, any medium will provide its user just a partial view of a larger space and whole.[34] Manovich understands that the space of a new media object is cut by the frame's rectangle "onscreen space," which means that there is the space inside the frame and the "offscreen" space outside the frame.[35] Quoting film theorist Jacques Aumont, Manovich explains, "The onscreen space is habitually perceived as included within a more vast scenographic space. Even though the onscreen space is the only visible part, this larger scenographic part is nonetheless considered to exist around it."[36] In Rosenzweig's text, what matters happens onscreen. Inside the screen, the reader sees the face of God in the mirror of the mask of the human face, inside the frame of the gate that separates this life from the brilliant scenographic of the dematerialized time-space of eternal life.

RELIGION IN THE LANGUAGE OF NEW MEDIA

As a paradigm for thinking about religion, new media theory would reorient contemporary Jewish philosophy and the philosophy of religion toward space and away from time. As for the modernism of Rosenzweig, this is not to deny what is obvious, that the poetic form of his thinking was preoccupied by temporality, by death and eternity, historical flux and loops of cyclical motion. This was not unique to Rosenzweig. Also obvious, these motifs are there in Heidegger and in Ernst Jünger. In Baudelaire and Benjamin, the city was a spatial figure composed of spatial relations and plastic objects that capture the flow of time and set up collisions in time. In Rosenzweig, there are transitions through thresholds and gates and the suturing of parts together, which give *The Star* its maze-like complexity and mask-like clarity. In this respect, *The Star*, given its peculiar organization, is emblematic. Folding *The Star*, an old media object, into the language of new media would bring religion and religious thought under the attribute of plastic extension.

Looked at through the lens of new media, "religion" is a "medium," a sensory-conceptual interface across whose surface is distributed shifting compositions of "natural" and "supernatural" elements.[37] On its own, the old media form of modern religion (liberal or critical, based on temporal progress or temporal rupture) is unlike the new media formatting of a more modular model form of religion. "Remediating" the old media format of *The Star* vis-à-vis the main chapters of Lev Manovich's *The Language of New Media* throws light upon the potential significance of "interface," "operations," "illusions," and "form" for the philosophy of religion, writ large, and Jewish philosophy, writ small.

To repurpose religion as "Interface" would be to look at it as an array of screens. Viewed most broadly, religious "objects" such as gods, God, social forms, texts, rituals, spaces, sancta are both screens and screened. Synagogues and churches are screens. Texts are screens. Rituals are screens. Gods and "God" exist on or behind a screen, as screen. Religion is screen-like, "a three-dimensional world enclosed by a frame and situated inside our normal space."[38] The modern religion-screen is "classical," "intended for frontal viewing," acting as a "window into another [sacred] space."[39] From Mendelssohn to Cohen, the classical screens of modern liberal Judaism might look a little simple in their naturalism. In new media environments, the screens take on more and more framed, aggregate, and prefabricated qualities. The screenwork in *The Star* is more dynamic; windows and systems multiply and overlap. In whatever shape it assumes on whichever continent and at whichever time, the star of redemption is "plastic," not natural. Like the "simulations" recommended by Manovich, religion puts together and blends pictures of physical bodies and virtual spaces.

In the language of new media, religion is constituted by a set of "Operations." Operators of new media select their objects and composite them into a single, integrated program of thought. Modern liberal religion in the nineteenth and early twentieth centuries was built on a montage of discrete historical periods—ancient, medieval, and modern, a periodization marked in terms of evolution or rupture. Instead of the modern montage of separable image-forms, religion consists of an internally continuous image-object in which a heterogeneous set of religious elements drawn from distinct historical strata are nonetheless added onto and coexist without any sense of contrast or dissonance. Point and click, move around, cut and paste. The parts fit together into a modular unit.

As a new media object, religion is based on "Illusion." About this, Rosenzweig seems to have been unaware. For all the critical force brought to bear in its "operations" there was something definitely uncritical about the way in which he conceived of the truth. The reader of *The Star* is supposed to hear the sounds of revelation and redemption, to see the face of God. Like many modernist writers, among whom one could include Heidegger, Rosenzweig seems to have been thoroughly persuaded by the magical power of his own charismatic expression.[40] The trust in language is meant to override relativism and skepticism about revelation. Once the user is situated inside the program, the very complexity of the illusion confirms its truth. In contrast, the metarealism of new media theory lends itself to skepticism in the oscillation between illusion and the self-awareness of the underlying mechanisms that create the illusion. Metarealism provides a more critical way to make sense of the event of revelation and its rhetoric in religion.

About the "Form" of religion, new media theorists would point to the information-database form, in which information is lined up along horizontal frames without any one single organizing narrative grid. That was a starting point of my entire exercise in these pages. The data points that comprise *The Star* are all the gelled object-like figures in the text drawn from the database of tradition: Song of Songs, Schelling, Greek sculpture, Psalms, Goethe, rabbinic dicta, and so on and so on. Its narrative content reflects the pathos of a German expressionist *Bildungsroman* charting the journey of the soul from the fear of death to the vision of revelation and promise of redemption at the apex of Yom Kippur, verified at the gates of death, and then back into life. What Rosenzweig has done is what Manovich actually wants from the form of new media, namely the merging of algorithm and data-structure with cinematic narrative into a new, aesthetically persuasive format. The new media form that interests Manovich the most is the navigation of space. *The Star* allows the user to do just that. Religion navigates across multiple worlds, across actual worlds and virtual worlds.

THE FACE OF GOD IN THE ELECTRIC AGE OF SIMULATION

The potential for religion seen in technology reflected in my reading of *The Star* is not intended to overlook critical misgivings about modern technology or to suspend critical judgment. Once very influential in the 1960s and 1970s, these fears are resurgent today in the age of new media, fake news, and cyborgs. We could trace these suspicions about technology back to the Arts and Crafts movement and to art nouveau in the 1890s. In twentieth-century modern Jewish thought, this kind of fear is most prominent in the elegies of Abraham Joshua Heschel to the shattered world of the East European shtetl, his disgust with "modern man," and his dislike for the putatively lifeless and soulless ultra-modern American synagogue at midcentury. For all that, though, it would be hard to find critics today willing to write off *tout court* modern technology. Mostly, the tradition of modern Jewish thought is very much woven into the technological fabric of modern city-suburban life, where Judaism persists as an a priori halakhic grid or an "architecture" in time.[41]

What Heidegger in his essay on technology wanted to sustain in the old Greek *technê* was poiesis, the "holy," the "exalted," the "mysteriousness" of "distance."[42] The appeal of old things and the misgivings about modern technology had to do with the fear that technology would reduce things to constructs, holding-frames, and "Jewish" things like calculation.[43] An antimodern modern, his approach to the thinghood of things is enmeshed in roots and earth, time and death.[44] Heidegger was not going to address in their human dimension these specific things that matter in technology: mental spontaneity and network plasticity, communicative reason and communication technologies, and the trans-subjective validity of philosophical judgment regarding the formation of a "common and objective world" alongside new multiplicities and "functional determinations and meanings," "multiple spheres for transcendental inquiry," "multiple structures of Being."[45]

In contrast to an ontology of simple things, the network theory of Bruno Latour sees in science, politics, law, religion different kinds of connectors that connect entities and objects in different ways.[46] Taking up a position inside thinking about networks and new media and open to the clash of icons, Latour made no ontological distinction about the presencing potential of old versus modern things. "'Here too the gods are present': in a hydroelectric plant on the banks of the Rhine, in subatomic particles, in Adidas shoes as well as in the old wooden clogs hollowed out by hand, in agribusiness as well as in timeworn landscapes, in shopkeepers' calculations as well as in Hölderlin's heartrending verse."[47] Writing in the same vein, Jeremy Stolow sees "gods, angels, jinns, demons, bodhisattvas, saints, ethical principles, statements of fact, and many other 'transcendent' creatures" existing on a continuum with hydroelectric power plants, jet engines, staircases, ink, flowers, hair, animal blood, DVDs, and mobile telephones.[48]

Relating Latour and Stolow to Rosenzweig, what holds and stores so powerfully the sense of the appearance of the reality of God's presence is the ultra-modern modularity of *The Star* in its distance from nature and from simple things. *The Star* is more like a German hydroelectric plant than a Greek temple. In a speculative vein, and with what kind of skepticism, is it reasonable to say that human beings visually register an icon or index of God? If in whatever shape the presence of God can be said to appear in the physical world, then that sense of this felt presence would be imaged or mirrored, and then stored away and remembered.[49] As a format, a computer program should be no different than any old-media repository of religious expression. In a new media format, the sense of the appearance of God would be converted into a bit of information, a trace of its sense transferred onto a file and uploaded onto an internet cloud where it subsists on store like a piece of reserved energy. Standing on reserve, the "reality of the presence of God" in the world is "virtual," but maybe not "actual."[50]

Actual objects of possible experience would be phenomena that are subject to formal, conventional, and normative canons of representation, resemblance, common sense. In contrast, virtual reality is theorized as being signaled by a complex coexistence of multiplicity, the potentiality of pure forces (energy and qualities) prior to their actual and normative sedimentation in time and space.[51] Unfixed in time and space, virtual reality is one in which the imagination and the image, apparitions of physical objects and theoretical things are real without being here or even there. Religion scholar Jordan Brady Loewen cites Antonin Artaud on the virtual reality of theater. For the surrealist poet, the "V" of virtual reality refers to the space "in which characters, objects, and images take on the phantasmagoric force of alchemy's visionary internal dramas." "Virtual" refers also, of course, to virtual memory or RAM, which is "the capacity of a computer to hold a pocket of processing that is always ready to be actualized for whatever the user wants to do with the computer, such as to launch a program or visualize a document."[52]

In the age of new media, the potential thinghood of phantasmagoric objects is shaped out of pure information, pure light, pure energy. The particular virtual powers that energize religion can be actualized or reactualized as segmented figures. The prismatic repetition of thought-images into a modular program is unique to *The Star*. It is what makes its contents so crystalline and object-like. But the objectivity of objects is precarious. Like the soul itself, actual things are subject to the dematerialization, vaporization, and virtualization at work in the imagination. That vaporization brings the user to those apocalyptic moments marked by rhetorical appeals to blinding, silent light in the middle and end of the chapter on redemption in Rosenzweig's book, and again, more consummately, at the gate separating life and death at the end of Rosenzweig's text. Composed of multiple levels, *The Star* mirrors by way of anticipation the virtual dynamics of advanced technological culture. No other text in Jewish philosophy after Maimonides is as saturated by the image of light as is *The Star*.[53]

Light is at the center of the technological universe no less than it is at the center of the spiritual world.[54] But the realization that insofar as even apophatic light has always already made this or that impression returns religious thought to the argument that there is no naked truth in a virtual universe consisting of screens and filters.[55] As pursued by Wolfson, the very notion of the infinite requires thought to let go of factual truth for the "phantasmagoric weight of the narratological scheme." Intentionally inverting a theme in Kabbalah and Heidegger, the argument by Wolfson is that to remove the garment in order to see without the mediation of a garment is itself the "last garment." The last garment belongs to a technesis in which perception and imagination fold into each other. The last garment could be an archaic mask or the thinnest futuristic glass or finest filament that allows what is, after all, the last garb of infinite light to make a manifest appearance in the physical world as an optical or pseudo-optical schema.[56]

Assuming that even the thinnest glass and even the last garment remain a dirty glass and compromised medium, attention to technology and to the play of appearance made possible by technology draws increased scrutiny to the artificial character of theological thinking. With, for instance, William James, the notion that consciousness constitutes a sine qua non of religion would demand more skeptical holding back and a suspension of belief that Rosenzweig did not seem, for the most part, to show. Two examples, one modernist, the other postmodernist, will suffice for the parodies of critical self-consciousness in relation to what may or may not constitute religious vision.

The first example: Franz Kafka writes in the diary entry for June 25, 1914, about something of this sort. It reads like the sketch of a story. Written in the first person singular, the protagonist is pacing around all day in his room, surrounded by objects. In the course of the time spent in what would appear to be a closed-in room, he comes to know each thing in detail: a rug, a table, a portrait of the deceased husband of the landlady at whom he bares his teeth. Then something happens as the light presumably dims. He begins to see things "striving to break through" hovering above the ceiling. "Already one could almost see the outlines of a movement there, an arm was thrust out, a silver sword swung to and fro. It was meant for me, there was no doubt of that; a vision intended for my liberation was being prepared." He sees white silken-shining wings and a sword of an angel breaking through the ceiling. It turns out, of course, that it was not, in the end, an actual living angel. It was only a "painted wooden figurehead off the prow of some ship, one of the kind that hangs from the ceiling in sailors' taverns, nothing more." But the protagonist sticks to the illusion even after it was dispelled. Tearing out the ordinary brass light fixture in his frenzy, Kafka says he did not want to sit in the dark. So he gets up on a chair, sticks the candle into the hilt of the sword of the wooden angel and lights it, sitting "late into the night under the angel's faint flame."[57]

The claustrophobic vision of an artificial angel in Kafka's diary entry depends upon the play between dim natural light, supernatural vision, and artificial lighting. Kafka writes that his first response was to lower his eyes. It is a gesture of piety and fear. The realization that the angel is "only" an artifact is possible only after he lifts his eyes. In this little sketch mixing immediacy and mediation, the vision combines an image of brightly radiant revelation and obsolete old technologies. But there is a devotion to the illusion and the decision to make do with faint light. What Rosenzweig, for his part, will *not* have shown is Kafka's arch performance and sly shabbiness. Uncomic, Rosenzweig trusted language too much. For Rosenzweig, practically no self-recognition follows the epiphany given at the gate of death, no hint that a sense of revelation might not be more than an effect cast off by the artificial fabrication of charismatic writing.

No less comedic, the second example comes from the intersection of contemporary cinema and religion in *The Man Who Wasn't There*, a 2001 film by the Coen Brothers. In her analysis of the film, philosopher of religion Gail Hamner shows how tricks between the natural and supernatural work in the register of contemporary cinema. Without going into the plot of the film, I am most interested here in the appearance of the figure of light. There is the dim light that illuminates the feet of a carved wooden image of the crucified Christ who hangs over a session of bingo at a local church. There is the shot of a hubcap rolling faster and faster away from the scene of a car crash; spinning and spinning, the hubcap turns into a bright, spinning silver metallic disk that turns into an alien spaceship, which peels off into black space as soon as it appears. In a prison yard, what the viewer is given to think is the spotlight cast from the watchtower turns out to be light thrown off from the hovering alien spaceship; as the camera turns away, the viewer only hears it off-screen as it flies back out into outer space. And in the final scene of the movie, intensely bright and immersive white light anticipates death by electrocution. Ruminations about life, the soul, and the hereafter plus strains from a Beethoven sonata lend a spiritual sense to these "fake" extraterrestrial visions.

As with the scene in Kafka's little diary sketch, the trick of the film is to turn ordinary objects into supernatural indices, but with one eye critically open. Reflecting upon the reappearance of the spaceship in the penultimate scene of the film, Hamner comments. "The expected noir stamp of sharp and eerie contrasts of black and white light are relegated to a few very specific settings, such as a prison and an after-hours department store." And, she continues, "even in these scenes the heavy darkness is 'lightened' by teasing signs and symbols of spaceships, so that the visual moments that register most intensely as noir also register as slightly bizarre or ridiculous."[58] These figures "point to a transcendence we can no longer possess entirely, a vertical axis and way out and redemption." Unless, of course, this too is a joke, the sense of transcendence would be signaled by "the zany, twilight-zone subplot of saucer-like space ships," through the "elusive search for peace that is signaled by piano music."[59]

Along with space ships, angels, or anything else in what Vilém Flusser called "the universe of technical images," even real objects of religious vision are abstract, imaginary, concrete, tactile, visionary, semiotic, interactive, scattered, paedeic, conversational, and playful.[60] As seen from contemporary philosophy of religion under the impression of new media, the things that matter most in contemporary philosophy of religion definitely turn out to belong to the world of images and "illusion." Therein lies the possibility that philosophical discourse about the reality of God, world, and "man" refers to virtual things, not actual ones. Image-rich figures in new media push theological thinking into a more nonrealist or meta-realist direction that admits no fundamental separation between mediation and reality, illusion and truth. As Bolter and Grusin surmise about new media, "By emphasizing process, digital hypermedia become self-justifying. With their constant reference to other media and their contents, hypermedia ultimately claim our attention as pure experience."[61]

If one assumes that the appearance of a god depends upon a human artifact and artifice, then the question at the intersection of religion and technology is how to build "a machine" for "the manufacture of religious phrases."[62] As theorized by Latour in *Rejoicing*, his most thorough exploration of religion, the truth of a religious phrase rests in meeting felicity conditions. In light of this pragmatic criterion, one demands to know if the phrase is well-made or not. For Latour, a techno-religious utterance has to be profoundly presentist for it to work. What matters is getting the quality or tone of the utterance right.[63] Is it possible to get right today something like the Lord's Prayer? Machine-like, the religious phrase is pure function. The religious phrase has nothing to do with information, say about the risen Christ, or, in Jewish prayer, any utterance about the unity or oneness of God. With all the inevitable distortions, what is more vital in religion is if it is possible to say it right in the present moment in such a way as to bring people together around its sense.[64]

Against ancient and modern forms of critical iconoclasm, there's simply no way to scrub the religion-machine of impurities, by which Latour means images, dogmas, and things that modern critics write off too easily as superstitions, illusions, delusions, and so on. These impurities are integral parts of the program and cannot be simply removed.[65] Echoing a thought expressed by Flusser and by Wolfson, Latour rejects the idea of "naked truth." Latour wants his truths padded in velvet.[66]

Not unrelated to religion in the universe of technical images, Flusser stubbornly insists that "our illusions are not things we should abandon to fall into nirvana but rather are, quite the opposite, our answer to the yawning nothingness that threatens us. . . .

Our veil is not to be torn but rather woven more and more closely."[67] The bright points out there in space that constellate the face of God are veils in a technological universe. About the yawning nothingness of the absolute garbed in veils of thick or thin imagining, I will hazard nothing. Critical readers of rational religion who place even an iota of trust in the eventfulness of language draw these veils in ever more tightly with a circumspection that comes with self-aware attention to media and mediation. Caught up in the immanence of virtual things, it is no longer to the point if there is some "thing" under the last garment.

NOTES

1. Franz Rosenzweig, *Die "Gritli"-Briefe: Briefe an Margarit Rosenstock-Huessy*, ed. Inken Rüle and Reinhold Meyer (Tübingen: Bilam, 2002), 124.
2. I have written elsewhere about the technological ambience of the Buber-Rosenzweig corpus, including the turn from *Gemeinschaft* to urban *Gesellsschaft*, the significance of "form-pattern" (*Gestalt*), and mask-like biblical personas, and the "phonographic" project that was the Buber-Rosenzweig Hebrew Bible translation, meant as it was to record the sound of revelation. See Zachary Braiterman, *The Shape of Revelation: Aesthetic of Modern Jewish Thought* (Stanford: Stanford University Press, 2007).
3. Braiterman, *Shape of Revelation*. My attention to the modernism of twentieth-century German Jewish philosophy and thought stands against the postmodern Rosenzweig and Buber who appeared on the scene in the late 1980s and 1990s.
4. On cycles, cyclical movement, and cyclical time, see Peter Eli Gordon, *Rosenzweig and Heidegger: Between Judaism and German Philosophy* (Berkeley: University of California Press, 2005); and Braiterman, *Shape of Revelation*.
5. For this reading and response to Eliezer Berkovits, see Steven Katz, *Post-Holocaust Dialogues: Critical Studies in Modern Jewish Thought* (New York: New York University Press, 1985), 113. See Emil Fackenheim, *To Mend the World: Foundations of Future Jewish Thought* (New York: Schocken Books, 1982), 91–95. For a more recent consideration based on Levinas and Adorno as to the noncoincidence between Judaism and the world, see Martin Shuster, *How to Measure a World: A Philosophy of Judaism* (Bloomington: Indiana University Press, 2021).
6. Both Hallo and Galli wrestle with the translation of the extraterrestriality suggested by this particular passage. On the "pathos" of death in the philosophy of Rosenzweig, see the discussion of him in Braiterman, *Shape of Revelation*, chap. 3.
7. On the stars and Maimonides, see Zachary Braiterman, "Rational Religion and Aesthetic Philosophy (Maimonides)" at https://jewishphilosophyplace.com/2020/09/10/rational-religion-and-aesthetic-philosophy-maimonides/ (September 10, 2020) (available January 31, 2022).
8. Martin Heidegger, *What Is a Thing?*, trans. W. B. Barton and Vera Deutsch (Chicago: Henry Regnery, 1967), 3, cf. 9, 47.
9. Heidegger, *What Is a Thing?*, 5–6, 43 (emphasis added).
10. Heidegger, *What Is a Thing?*, 50–51.

11. Heidegger, *What Is a Thing?*, 6.
12. That Rosenzweig later complained, saying that *The Star* was not a "Jewish book," was itself a bit of after-the-fact apologetic thinking.
13. Franz Rosenzweig, *The Star of Redemption*, trans. William W. Hallo (Notre Dame: University of Notre Dame Press, 1971), 131.
14. Martin Heidegger, "The Question Concerning Technology," in *Basic Writings*, ed. David Farrell Krell (New York: Harper & Row, 1977), 293–95.
15. Heidegger, "Question Concerning Technology," 296–98, cf. 299.
16. Franz Rosenzweig, *The Star of Redemption*, 295.
17. Rosenzweig, *The Star of Redemption*, 418.
18. Rosenzweig, *The Star of Redemption*, 422–23; Jonathan Garb, "R. Itzhak Isaac Judah Yehiel of Komarno as a Test Case of Jewish Mysticism," *Journal of Jewish Thought and Philosophy* 33 (forthcoming).
19. Rosenzweig, *The Star of Redemption*, 201.
20. Rosenzweig, *The Star of Redemption*, 291.
21. Rosenzweig, *The Star of Redemption*, 422. Cf. Franz Rosenzweig, "Note on Anthropomorphism," in *God, Man, and the World: Lectures and Essays*, ed. and trans. Barbara Galli (Syracuse: Syracuse University Press, 1998).
22. Rosenzweig, "Note on Anthropomorphism," 423–24. On these themes, to which I am adding attention to the particular and "technological" figures of masks and mirrors, see the consummate analysis of Rosenzweig in Elliot R. Wolfson, *Giving Beyond the Gift: Apophasis and Overcoming Theomania* (New York: Fordham University Press, 2014), chap. 2.
23. Wassily Kandinsky and Franz Marc (eds.), *The Blue Rider Almanac* (New York: Da Capo Press, 1974), 85.
24. Jay David Bolter and Richard Grusin, *Remediation: Understanding New Media* (Cambridge: MIT Press, 2000), 44–50.
25. See Noah Wardrip-Fruin and Nick Montfort (eds.), *The New Media Reader* (Cambridge: MIT Press, 2003). New media and digital media are typically associated with technological developments and theoretical discourse in the late twentieth and early twenty-first centuries. But note that the first two sections of the reader include entries from Jorge Luis Borges, Vannevar Bush, Alan Turing, and Norbert Wiener from the 1940s and early 1950s. World War II was a linchpin historical moment for theoretical thinking about new media, a dating that brings the development closer to our own subject matter, German Jewish modernism circa 1921. In "Inventing the Medium," her introduction to *The New Media Reader*, Janet Murray refers to Borges and the "[invention] of fantasy information structures," the "book-garden maze" and "desk-library machine" (3). On not conflating "new media" with the "cyberculture" of the internet," see the introduction by Lev Manovich in the same reader (16). Manovich identifies the 1920s as the first "cultural peak" of the twentieth century (23). On the 1920s and new technologies, see John Modern, "Melville, Religion, and Machines That Think," in Jeremy Stolow, ed., *Deus in Machina: Religion, Technology, and the Things in Between* (New York: Fordham University Press, 2013), 183–212. See also "R. Itzhak Isaac Judah Yehiel of Komarno as a Test Case of Jewish Mysticism."
26. Bolter and Grusin, *Remediation*, 25.

27. Bolter and Grusin, *Remediation*, 70.
28. Rosenzweig, *The Star of Redemption*, 416.
29. Bolter and Grusin, *Remediation*, 70–71.
30. Benjamin Pollock, *Franz Rosenzweig and the Systematic Task of Philosophy* (Cambridge: Cambridge University Press, 2009), 6. Pollock rejects religious-existentialist and Levinasian readings of *The Star,* which insist that Rosenzweig broke with totality. With Pollack, I see the systematic task, even as my particular interest here is the *organization* of that body of knowledge. On the "reclaiming of the All" and against correlationist readings of Rosenzweig, see Wolfson, *Giving Beyond the Gift*, 38. See also the discussion of Rosenzweig and form in Braiterman, *Shape of Revelation*, chap. 3.
31. Lev Manovich, *The Language of New Media* (Cambridge: MIT Press, 2001), 78.
32. Manovich, *Language of New Media*, 30, 38, 39.
33. Manovich, *Language of New Media*, 36.
34. Manovich, *Language of New Media*, 81–82.
35. Manovich, *Language of New Media*, 80.
36. Manovich, *Language of New Media*, 81.
37. Braiterman, *Shape of Revelation*, xxi.
38. Manovich, *Language of New Media*, 95.
39. Manovich, *Language of New Media.*
40. Robert Alter, *Partial Magic: The Novel as a Self-Conscious Genre* (Berkeley: University of California Press, 1975), 153. Alter identifies the belief among modernist writers in formal artifice that they could register psychological, social, and even historical reality through the form of fiction.
41. Ken Koltun-Fromm, *Material Culture and American Jewish Thought* (Bloomington: Indiana University Press, 2010), chaps. 3 and 4 on Soloveitchik and Heschel. Against the American synagogue, see Abraham Joshua Heschel, *Man's Quest for God: Studies in Prayer and Symbolism* (New York: Charles Scribner's Sons, 1954), chap. 3. For the sharp turn against modern technology, see Joseph Soloveitchik, *The Lonely Man of Faith* (New York: Doubleday, 1965), chaps. 9–10. It is unclear on what basis Soloveitchik sees restoring the dialogue between religion and technology (chap. 10) after excoriating the form of technological mastery in this modern demonic age (chap. 9).
42. Martin Heidegger, "Question Concerning Technology," 307.
43. Heidegger, "Question Concerning Technology," 308.
44. See Charles Bambach, *Heidegger's Roots: Nietzsche, National Socialism, and the Greeks* (Ithaca: Cornell University Press, 2005).
45. I am cribbing from Peter Eli Gordon, *Continental Divide: Heidegger, Cassirer, Davos* (Cambridge: Harvard University Press, 2012), 198–201, 202–7, 208.
46. Bruno Latour, *Reassembling the Social: An Introduction to Actor-Network Theory* (Oxford: Oxford University Press, 2007), 239.
47. Bruno Latour, *We Have Never Been Modern*, trans. Catherine Porter (Cambridge: Harvard University Press, 1993), 66.
48. Stolow, "Introduction: Religion, Technology, and the Things in Between," *Deus in Machina*, 15.

49. On literature relating to cultures of immersive religious practice and the possibility of perceiving God and other "spiritual beings," see William Alston, *Perceiving God: The Epistemology of Religious Experience* (Ithaca: Cornell University Press, 1993); T. M. Luhrmann, *When God Talks Back: Understanding the American Evangelical Relationship with God* (New York: Vintage, 2012); Yoram Bilu, *With Us More Than Ever: Making the Absent Rebbe Present in Messianic Chabad* (Stanford: Stanford University Press, 2020). Bilu makes special mention of technology in his analysis; see especially chap. 6 on optical apparitions of the late Habad Hasidic rebbe, Menachem Mendel Schneerson.
50. In a very speculative vein on the God of a simulated universe and religion as simulation, see David Chalmers, *Reality +: Virtual Worlds and the Problems of Philosophy* (New York: W. W. Norton, 2022), chap. 7.
51. For Deleuze in his reading of Bergson and leaning on Proust, the opposite of "the virtual" is "the actual." The virtual is just as real if not more "real" than the actual. Gilles Delueze, *Bergsonism*, trans. Hugh Tomlinson and Barbara Habberjam (New York: Zone Books, 1991), 96–98.
52. Jordan Brady Loewen, *The Problem of the "Virtual": Virtual Reality, Digital Dualism and Religious Experience* (dissertation, Syracuse University, 2022), 14–15. Cf. Antonin Artaud, *The Theater and Its Double*, tr. Victor Corti (London: Alma, 1978).
53. On light in conjunction with silence and death in *The Star of Redemption*, see Braiterman, *Shape of Revelation*, 114–21.
54. On the conjunction between light, technology, and mysticism, see Lewis Mumford, *Technics and Civilization* (Chicago: University of Chicago Press, 2010), 246, originally published in 1934. Mumford's primary concern is human, face-to-face connections and twentieth-century "neo-technics."
55. Wolfson, *Giving Beyond the Gift*, xxvii, introduction, 229, 451.
56. Elliot R. Wolfson, *Heidegger and Kabbalah: Hidden Gnosis and the Path of Poiēsis* (Bloomington: Indiana University Press, 2019), 215–16, 244n138, cf. 4–6.
57. Franz Kafka, *The Diaries of Franz Kafka: 1910–1923* (New York: Schocken), 302–9.
58. Gail Hamner, *Imaging Religion in Film: The Politics of Nostalgia* (London: Palgrave Macmillan, 2011), 100.
59. Hamner, *Imaging Religion in Film*, 100, 112.
60. Vilém Flusser, *Into the Universe of Technical Images* (Minneapolis: Minnesota University Press, 2011).
61. Bolter and Grusin, *Remediation*, 54.
62. Bruno Latour, *Rejoicing: Or the Torments of Religious Speech* (Cambridge: Polity Press, 2013), 120.
63. Latour, *Rejoicing*, 156.
64. Latour, *Rejoicing*, 118–19, cf. 74–75, 111, 131.
65. Latour, *Rejoicing*, 19, 83, 94ff, 60–61, 145ff.
66. Latour, *Rejoicing*, 83.
67. Flusser, *Into the Universe of Technical Images*, 39 (emphasis added).

PART IV

Works by Elliot R. Wolfson

passion, by Elliot Wolfson. (Reprinted with permission from the artist.)

POEMS

prajñāpāramitā

they saw the voices
traces of fire on stone
sevenfold within the eighth
six concealed, one indifferent
chased around center-point
to discriminate beyond here there
everywhere would be nowhere
on path to let go of path
as sea shall rise like mountain
and mountain roll like sea
in seventh movement-rest
element of composition
decomposing in brightness of night
blinding eyes in dimness of sight
waking from dream
dreaming of waking
from dream awakening
peace amidst strife
touching through distance
darkness cavorting
on edge of light

intersecting departure

form of emptiness
emptying form
receptacle shatter
difference of identity
identically different
coming in outgoing
going out incoming
between living dying
nothing something
everything suffering
recurrent passing
invariably abiding
momentarily permanent
departing intersection
skeletal ambition
like ambulant ants
roving heaps of hopes
in search of bloodstone
attracting repulsion
repelling attraction
pretending she forgot
who i am not
forming emptiness
empty of form
shatter receptacle
identity of difference
differently identical
going in outcoming
coming out ingoing
between dying living
something nothing
suffering everything
passing recurrent
abiding invariably
permanently momentary
intersecting departure
love goes the way
the way love comes

marriage vow

her feet swollen
with age & despair
the dream drained
like drops of rain
on window pane
she lifted his head
to behold the moon
withered luminosity
eclipsed by letter
vociferously inarticulate
a point submerged
in vowelless sea
where future & past
intersect—
moment at hand—
between syllables
silently spoken in dusk
when lovers unite
the dead go on living

incubation

serapis
wrap this
drape
with gape
plaited
from
poetic pearl
verbally
expunged
from light
plunged
in darkness
we see
seeping
through
husks of froth
burning truth
truth cannot prove
beyond doubt
reasonable or not

afterlife

this birth
we enter
remembering
to remember
to forget
forgetting
this life
we exit
forgetting
to forget
to remember
remembering
this death
we exit
remembering
to forget
to remember
forgetting
this love
we enter
forgetting
to remember
to forget
remembering

bread & resurrection

between
bread crust
and body lust
hope lifts
her skirt
at grave
pillaged
expecting
light
to cross
crossing
of night
contracting
expansion
neither living
nor dead
between
body dust
and bread box
hope dons
his shirt
at gate
wedged
recalling
night
that crossed
crossing
of light
expanding
contraction
neither dead
nor living

fireweed

fetch the harp
hung on rope
bound to goat
in poet's throat
summoning will
from listless hill
where time is naught
but time to kill
this midnight sun
falling like snow
faintly aglow
rising like smoke
on tears he stoke
from lies she spoke
to invoke chance
doomed to circumstance
determined by greed
that need the seed
to shed its pelt
indolently felt
as scalpel scrape
hunger for death
hedged in heart
trembling like leaf
in autumn turn
saturn's light burn
with taunt of thorn
to rose blistering
between dark of dusk
and dark of dawn

denali national park
alaska
21 july 2006

disabling karma

let us dance
in lavender robe
and cashmere cap
trimmed by thread
whitish-red
tying speech
to saying unsaid
beneath lunar lapse
ensnared in traps
metallically set
as phantom flit
across silver sky
memory sweep
future past present
glibly reticent
chronically invoking
eternity's name
covering nothing
all the same
remain different
in thump of shame
die hope hoping to die

imprint

if master
true
be he
let him
dispose
mask
of mastery
and ten
thousand
things
may he see
in darkness deep
blue as night
bleeding light
from love cut
left to swell
beneath
glacial breath
she bore not
in birth of death
we became
more of less

la clef des étoiles

in her presence
i am absent
and present
in her absence
breaking bridge
brick by brick
memory decay
vestiges of vitality
spouting like venom
from morning star
entombed in time
bones still speak
without words or silence
from stellar dust
the darkness glows
mending ditch
stone by stone
forgetfulness grows
what we were matters not
as love become once more
terminus interminably
not yet terminated

l'église des jacobins
toulouse
9 july 2010

self-doubt

moonless
the morn
we mourn
the sun
bleeding
starlight
too dark
to mark
death's
divide
from life
rising
as rose
opening
its petal
by shedding
its thorn
to warn
lovers
yawning
dejectedly
from night
deeper
than gloom
we mourn
the morn
moonless
as death
teeming
with time
empty
of time

anima christi

in the
stigma
i stood
undone
demeaned
by image
dismantling
imagelessness
clustered
beneath
crystal
shimmering
like broken
windpipe
kneading
breadcrumb
from breath
of craving
fanned by fluid
mysteriously
breaking
each moment
we unname
the nameable
naming the
unnameable

corona apocalypse

if all
were
angels
crowned
as mortals
and mortals
crowned
as beasts
and heaven
like smoke
evaporated
and earth
like garment
eviscerated
who would
take hold
of time
dissipating
in palm
of imagination
doubling
the nothing
nothing cannot
not be nothing
longing for love
dissimulating as death
lived in balance
betwixt shadow of light
and light of shadow

21 march 2020

duḥkha-satya

tremoring
the hand
cannot hold
the hand
strangling
fortunes
fortuitously
squandered
in loneliness
of love's
camaraderie
relinquished
once too
many times
the buildings
weary from
standing firm
on ground
withering
to the core
of pretense
pretending
to pretend
love's hand
will take hold

telegraph & bancroft
berkeley
12 july 2021

thanatosis

love's
helix
suspended
between
shadow
and shadow
seeking shelter
grasping
eucalyptic
heartstring
entangled
by desire
depleted
of desire
not to
desire
and still
not be
what she
imagined
my desire
not to be

cornucopia

lacerating
laceration
crimped
palpably
in abdomen
of clock
clairvoyantly
clattering
caustic
invocation
we cannot
contemplate
this night
of ambient
remorse
across
galaxies
of garnished
liability
love's ledger
declined
to compensate
what time
regurgitate
the morning
after morning
before forgetting
in reminiscence
disregarded

hardened spark/luminal dark

bit by bit
the it of love
leaks its lust
like rocks of rain
bending timeline
materially immaterial
in geometric space
of darkness turning back
to face the liminal light
of infinite magnitude
in seventh seal of night
death brings no information
between the being of its nonbeing
and the nonbeing of its being
we each must digest
until everything
to nothing returns
the it of love
bit by bit

renunciation

with
temptation
on tongue
and heart
unstrung
night arise
as light come
in darkness
diminished
shredding wings
already dilapidated
by tick of time
ticking unto death
conspicuously
inconspicuous
as love bestows
the withdrawal
of its bestowal

ahimsa

walking
on cloud
feet inflated
with petition
meekly proud
overstepping
splintered line
withdrawn
by leprous hand
ensconced in time
decanting rhyme
from rickety yellow
to magenta bold
the story retold
each moment
drifting anew
more black
than blue
predictably
love does
what love
will undo

with new feet

with new feet
wings shall come
skyward & seabound
breathing stars of sand
in swirl of time
trickling tenuously
on landscape mind
thinking thought unthinkable—
nothing be nothing it be not,
if not for nothing it not be

PUBLICATIONS

BOOKS

Nocturnal Seeing: Hopelessness of Hope and Philosophical Gnosis in Susan Taubes, Gillian Rose, and Edith Wyschogrod. Stanford: Stanford University Press, 2025.

The Philosophical Pathos of Susan Taubes: Between Nihilism and Hope. Stanford: Stanford University Press, 2023.

Unveiling the Veil of Unveiling: Philosophical Aphorisms and Poems on Time, Language, Being and Truth. San Francisco: Panui, 2021.

Suffering Time: Philosophical, Kabbalistic, and Ḥasidic Reflections on Temporality. Leiden: Brill, 2021.

Heidegger and Kabbalah: Hidden Gnosis and the Path of Poiēsis. Bloomington: Indiana University Press, 2019.

The Duplicity of Philosophy's Shadow: Heidegger, Nazism, and the Jewish Other. New York: Columbia University Press, 2018.

Elliot R. Wolfson: Poetic Thinking. Library of Contemporary Jewish Philosophers. Edited by Hava Tirosh-Samuelson and Aaron W. Hughes. Leiden: Brill, 2015.

Giving Beyond the Gift: Apophasis and Overcoming Theomania. New York: Fordham University Press, 2014.

A Dream Interpreted Within a Dream: Oneiropoiesis and the Prism of Imagination. New York: Zone Books, 2011. Winner of the American Academy of Religion's Award for Excellence in the Study of Religion in the Category of Constructive and Reflective Studies, 2012.

Open Secret: Postmessianic Messianism and the Mystical Revision of Menahem Mendel Schneerson. New York: Columbia University Press, 2009.

Footdreams and Treetales: 92 Poems. New York: Fordham University Press, 2007.

Luminal Darkness: Imaginal Gleanings from Zoharic Literature. London: Oneworld Publications, 2007.

Alef, Mem, Tau: Kabbalistic Musings on Time, Truth, and Death. Berkeley: University of California Press, 2006.

Venturing Beyond—Law and Morality in Kabbalistic Mysticism. Oxford: Oxford University Press, 2006.

Language, Eros, Being: Kabbalistic Hermeneutics and Poetic Imagination. New York: Fordham University Press, 2005. Winner of the National Jewish Book Award for Excellence in Scholarship, 2006.

Pathwings: Poetic-Philosophic Reflections on the Hermeneutics of Time and Language. Station Hill: Barrytown Press, 2004.

Sprache, Eros, Dasein: Kabbalistische Hermeneutik und poetische Einbildungskraft. Translated by D. Westerkamp. Berlin: Philo Verlagsgesellschaft mbH, 2002.

Abraham Abulafia—Kabbalist and Prophet: Hermeneutics, Theosophy, and Theurgy. Los Angeles: Cherub Press, 2000.

Abraham Aboulafia—Cabaliste et Prophète: Herméneutique, Théosophie, et Théurgie. Translated by J.-F. Sené. Paris: Éditions de L'éclat, 1999.

Along the Path: Studies in Kabbalistic Myth, Symbolism, and Hermeneutics. Albany: State University of New York Press, 1995.

Circle in the Square: Studies in the Use of Gender in Kabbalistic Symbolism. Albany: State University of New York Press, 1995.

Through a Speculum That Shines: Vision and Imagination in Medieval Jewish Mysticism. Princeton: Princeton University Press, 1994. Winner of the American Academy of Religion's Award for Excellence in the Study of Religion in the Category of Historical Studies, 1995. Winner of the National Jewish Book Award for Excellence in Scholarship, 1995.

The Book of the Pomegranate: Moses de León's Sefer ha-Rimmon. Brown Judaic Series 144. Atlanta: Scholars Press, 1988.

Edited Books

D. G. Leahy and the Thinking Now Occurring. Edited by Lissa McCullough and Elliot R. Wolfson. Albany: State University of New York Press, 2021.

Studies in Medieval Jewish Intellectual and Social History: Festschrift in Honor of Robert Chazan. Edited with David Engel and Lawrence H. Schiffman. Leiden: Brill, 2012.

Philosophy Today 55 (2011), special guest editor of issue in memory of Edith Wyschogrod.

New Studies in Jewish Philosophy. Edited by Aaron W. Hughes and Elliot R. Wolfson. Bloomington: Indiana University Press, 2010.

Suffering Religion. Edited by Robert Gibbs and Elliot R. Wolfson. New York: Routledge, 2002.

Rending the Veil: Concealment and Secrecy in the History of Religions. New York: Seven Bridges Press, 1999.

Perspectives on Jewish Thought and Mysticism. Edited by Alfred Ivry, Allan Arkush, and Elliot R. Wolfson. Reading: Harwood Academic Publishers, 1998.

ARTICLES

"Hermeneutics, Imagination, and the Temporality of the Helical Spiral: Reflections on Hart's Phenomenological Theology." In *Ray L. Hart's Theological Vision: A Critical Encounter*. Edited by Alina Feld and Sean J. McGrath. Edinburgh University Press, 2024.

"Brokenness of Being and Errancy of Ontological Untruth: Susan Taubes's Criticism of Heidegger's Seinsdenken." *Journal of Jewish Thought and Philosophy* 32 (2024) 83–132.

"Death and the Infinitization of Finitude: Negation and the Ethical Crisis of Modernity in Edith Wyschogrod's Postmodern Hermeneutics." In *Modern Jewish Thought on Crisis: Interpretation, Heresy, and History*, 241–65. Edited by Ghilad H. Shenhav, Cedric Cohen-Skalli, and Gilad Sharvit. Berlin: Walter de Gruyter, 2024.

"Apophasis and the Parabolic Garment of Truth in Moses Maimonides and Meister Eckhart." In *Beloved David, Advisor, Man of Understanding, and Scribe: A Festschrift in Honor of David Stern*, 155–87. Edited by Katrin Kogman-Appel and Naftali Cohn. Providence: Brown Judaic Studies, 2024.

"Mystery of Infinity, Malkhut de-Adam Qadmon, and the Myth of Ṣimṣum: Engendering Alterity in the Theosophy of Nehemiah Ḥiyya Ḥayyon." *El Prezente* 16–17 (2022–2023), 23–59.

"Unveiling the Veil of Infinitivity: Apophasis and the Kabbalistic Envisioning of the Invisible." In *Oxford Handbook of Apophatic Theology*. Edited by John Betz and Rik Van Nieuwenhove. Oxford: Oxford University Press, 2024.

"Phallomorphic Underpinning of Abraham Miguel Cardoso's Messianic Theosophy: Analysis and Edition of *Derush ha-Yesod*." *Kabbalah: Journal for the Study of Jewish Mystical Texts* 56 (2023): 7–102.

"Zionism and the Sacramental Danger of Nationalism: Susan Taubes on Israel." *Ayin Press*, June 2, 2023.

"Do Not Wake or Arouse Love: Erotics of Time and the Dream of Messianic Waiting." In *The Song of Songs Through the Ages: Studies on the Song's Reception History in Different Epochs, Contexts, and Genres*, 129–44. Edited by Annette Schellenberg. Berlin: Walter de Gruyter, 2023.

"Phenomenology, Theosophic Topography and the Structures of Being: Unveiling the Seventh of Scholem's Ten Unhistorical Aphorisms on the Kabbalah." *Kabbalah: Journal for the Study of Jewish Mystical Texts* 55 (2022): 7–69.

"Imagination, Theolatry, and the Compulsion to Worship the Invisible." In *Religion in Reason: Metaphysics, Ethics, and Politics in Hent de Vries*, 50–79. Edited by Tarek R. Dika and Martin Shuster. London: Routledge, 2022.

"Concealing the Concealment: Towards a Theopolitics of Kabbalistic Esotericism." In *The Routledge Handbook of Religion and Secrecy*, 120–30. Edited by Hugh B. Urban and Paul Christopher Johnson. London: Routledge, 2022.

"Melancholic Redemption and the Hopelessness of Hope." *Journal of Jewish Thought and Philosophy* 30 (2022): 304–45.

"*Malkhut Ein Sof* and *Ṣimṣum*: Gender Construction in the Kabbalistic Speculation of Jonathan Eibeschütz, with Special Reference to *Wa-Avo ha-Yom el ha-Ayin*." *Kabbalah: Journal for the Study of Jewish Mystical Texts* 50 (2021): 7–77.

"Gnosis and the Covert Theology of Antitheology: Heidegger, Apocalypticism, and Gnosticism in Susan and Jacob Taubes." In *Depeche Mode: Jacob Taubes Between Politics, Philosophy, and Religion*, 151–202. Edited by Herbert Kopp-Oberstebrink and Hartmut von Sass. Leiden: Brill, 2022.

"Ascesis, Hypernomianism, and the Excess of Lack: Semiotic Transfiguration of the Somatic." In *Accounting for the Commandments in Medieval Judaism*, 229–81. Edited by Jeremy P. Brown and Marc Herman. Leiden: Brill, 2021.

"Nomadism, Homelessness, and the Homecoming of the Poet: Rosenzweig and Heidegger in Conversation." In *Into Life: Rosenzweig on Knowledge, Aesthetics, and Politics*, 281–341. Edited by Antonios Kalatzis and Enrico Lucca. Leiden: Brill, 2021.

"Rosenzweig on Human Redemption: Neither Nothing nor Everything, but Only Something." *Journal of Jewish Thought and Philosophy* 29 (2021): 121–50.

"Saturnine Melancholy and Dylan's Jewish Gnosis." In *World of Bob Dylan*, 214–25. Edited by Sean Latham. Cambridge: Cambridge University Press, 2021.

"Theosemiosis and the Void of Being: Kabbalistic Infinity through a Peircean Lens." In *Signs of Salvation: A Festschrift for Peter Ochs*, 163–86. Edited by Mark Randall James and Randi Rashkover. Eugene: Cascade Books, 2021.

"Temporal Diremption and the Novelty of Genuine Repetition." In *D. G. Leahy and the Thinking Now Occurring*, 53–96. Edited by L. McCullough and E. R. Wolfson. Albany: State University of New York Press, 2021.

"Tsimtsum, Lichtung, and the Leap of Bestowing Refusal: Kabbalistic and Heideggerian Metaontology in Dialogue." In *Tsimtsum and Modernity: Lurianic Heritage in Modern Philosophy and Theology*, 141–89. Edited by Agata Bielik-Robson and Daniel H. Weiss. Berlin: Walter de Gruyter, 2021.

"Metaphor, Dream, and the Parabolic Bridging of Difference: A Kabbalistic Aesthetic." *Images: A Journal of Jewish Art and Visual Culture* 14 (2021): 82–95.

"To Stand in Relation with Something Which Is Neither Day nor Night: Temporal Overcoming and Heidegger's Notion of Destiny." *Gatherings: The Heidegger Circle Annual* 10 (2020): 207–10.

"To Distinguish Israel and the Nations: E Pluribus Unum and Isaac Hutner's Appropriation of Kabbalistic Anthropology." In *Kabbalah and America: Ancient Lore in the New World*, 316–40. Edited by Brian Ogren. Leiden: Brill, 2020.

"*Malkhut de-Ein Sof* and the Temporalization of Space: *Ṣimṣum* in the Teaching of Solomon ben Ḥayyim Eliashiv." *Kabbalah: Journal for the Study of Jewish Mystical Texts* 46 (2020): 7–78.

"Heeding the Law Beyond the Law: Transgendering Alterity and the Hypernomian Perimeter of the Ethical." *European Journal of Jewish Studies* 14 (2020): 215–63.

"Apotheosis of the Nothing in Altizer's Kenotic Atheology." *Journal for Cultural and Religious Theory* 19 (2019–2020): 52–84.

"Discerning Difference through Comparison of the Same: Isaac Hutner's Transmission of Esoteric Wisdom." *Kabbalah: Journal for the Study of Jewish Mystical Texts* 45 (2019): 7–48.

"Hypernomian Piety and the Mystical Rationale of the Commandments in Nathan of Gaza's *Sefer Haberiya*." *El Prezente* 12–13 (2019): 90–153.

"Suffering Time: Maharal's Influence on Ḥasidic Perspectives on Temporality." *Kabbalah: Journal for the Study of Jewish Mystical Texts* 44 (2019): 7–71.

"Mysticism and the Quest for Universal Singularity—Post-Subjective Subjectivity and the Contemplative Ideal in Ḥabad." In *Jewish Spirituality and Social Transformation*, 37–58. Edited by Philip Wexler. New York: Herder and Herder, 2019.

"Anxiety, Lament, and the Language of Silence: Poetic Redemption and Gnostic Alienation." In *All Religion Is Inter-Religion: Engaging the Work of Steven M. Wasserstrom*, 17–37. Edited by Kambiz GhaneaBassiri and Paul M. Robertson. London: Bloomsbury, 2019.

"Judah ben Solomon Canpanton's *Leqaḥ Ṭov*: Annotated Edition and Introduction." *Kabbalah: Journal for the Study of Jewish Mystical Texts* 43 (2019): 7-86.

"Is There Any Room for Women in Jewish Kabbalah?" In *Hermes Explains: Thirty Questions about Western Esotericism*, 243–51. Edited by Wouter J. Hanegraaff, Peter J. Forshaw, and Marco Pasi. Amsterdam: Amsterdam University Press, 2019.

"Deceitful Truth and Truthful Deceit: *Sod ha-Hippukh* and Abulafia's Divergence from Maimonides." In *A Tribute to Hannah: Jubilee Book in Honor of Hannah Kasher*, 91–125. Edited by Avi Elqayam and Ariel Malachi. Tel-Aviv: Idra, 2018. [English section.]

"Recovering Futurity: Theorizing the End and the End of Theory." In *Jews at the End of Theory*, 293–311. Edited by Shai Ginsburg, Martin Land, and Jonathan Boyarin. New York: Fordham University Press, 2018.

"The Holy Cabala of Changes: Jacob Böhme and Jewish Esotericism." *Aries—Journal for the Study of Western Esotericism* 18 (2018): 21–53.

"Mysticism." In *The Cambridge History of Judaism*. Volume 6. *The Middle Ages: The Christian World*, 742–86. Edited by Robert Chazan. Cambridge: Cambridge University Press, 2018.

"Gottwesen and the De-Divinization of the Last God: Heidegger's Meditation on the Strange and Incalculable." In *Heidegger's Black Notebooks and the Future of Theology*, 211–55. Edited by Mårten Björk and Jayne Svenungsson. New York: Palgrave Macmillan, 2017.

"Heidegger's Apophaticism: Unsaying the Said and the Silence of the Last God." In *Contemporary Debates in Negative Theology and Philosophy*, 185–216. Edited by Nahum Brown and J. Aaron Simmons. New York: Palgrave Macmillan, 2017.

"Heidegger's Seyn/Nichts and the Kabbalistic Ein Sof: A Study in Comparative Metaontology." In *Heidegger and Jewish Thought: Difficult Others*, 177–200. Edited by Elad Lapidot and Micha Brumlik. London: Rowman & Littlefield, 2017.

"Secrecy, Apophasis, and Atheistic Faith in the Teachings of Rav Kook." In *Negative Theology as Jewish Modernity*, 131–60. Edited by Michael Fagenblat. Bloomington: Indiana University Press, 2017.

"Zeitliche Entzweiung und offenes System. Die Atonalität der Kabbala und Heideggers anfängliches Denken." In *Heidegger: die Falte der Sprache*, 121–67. Edited by Michael Friedman and Angelika Seppi. Vienna: Turia and Kant, 2017.

"Theolatry and the Making-Present of the Nonrepresentable: Undoing (A)Theism in Eckhart and Buber." *Journal of Jewish Thought and Philosophy* 25 (2017): 5–35. Revised version in *Martin Buber: His Intellectual and Scholarly Legacy*, 3–32. Edited by Sam Berrin Shonkoff. Leiden: Brill, 2018.

"Phallic Jewissance and the Pleasure of No Pleasure." In *Talmudic Transgressions: Engaging the Work of Daniel Boyarin*, 293–335. Edited by Charlotte Elisheva Fonrobert, Ishay Rosen Zvi, Aharon Shemesh, and Moulie Vidas. Leiden: Brill, 2017.

"Achronic Time, Messianic Expectation, and the Secret of the Leap in Ḥabad." In *Habad Hasidisim: History, Thought, and Image*, 45–86. Edited by Jonathan Meir and Gadi Sagiv. Jerusalem: Zalman Shazar, 2016.

"Anonymity and the Kabbalistic Ethos: Fourteenth-Century Supercommentary on the Commentary on the Sefirot." *Kabbalah: Journal for the Study of Jewish Mystical Texts* 35 (2016): 55–112.

"Asceticism, Mysticism, and Messianism: A Reappraisal of Schechter's Portrait of Sixteenth-Century Safed." *Jewish Quarterly Review* 106 (2016): 165–77 (special forum on the centennial anniversary of the publication of Solomon Schechter's *Studies in Judaism*).

"Flesh Become Word: Textual Embodiment and Poetic Incarnation." In *Words: Religious Language Matters*, 84–160. Edited by Ernst Van Den Hemel and Asja Szafraniec. New York: Fordham University Press, 2016.

"Eternal Duration and Temporal Compresence: The Influence of Ḥabad on Joseph B. Soloveitchik." In *The Value of the Particular: Lessons from Judaism and the Modern Jewish Experience: Essays in Honor of Steven T. Katz on the Occasion of His Seventieth Birthday*, 195–238. Edited by Michael Zank and Ingrid Anderson. Leiden: Brill, 2015.

"Givenness and the Disappearance of the Gift: Ethics and the Invisible in Marion's Christocentric Phenomenology." In *Ethics of In-visibility: Imago Dei, Memory, and Human Dignity*, 169–91. Edited by Claudia Welz. Tübingen: Mohr Siebeck, 2015.

"Retroactive Not Yet: Linear Circularity and Kabbalistic Temporality." In *Time and Eternity in Jewish Mysticism: That Which Is Before and That Which Is After*, 15–50. Edited by Brian Ogren. Leiden: Brill, 2015.

"Bifurcating the Androgyne and Engendering Sin: A Zoharic Reading of Gen 1–3." In *Hidden Truths from Eden: Esoteric Interpretations of Genesis 1–3*, 87–119. Edited by Caroline Vander Stichele and Susanne Scholz. Atlanta: SBL Publications, 2014.

"Die Schechina als Mundus Imaginalis: Ihre Vielen Gestalten im Prisma Menschlicher Einbildungskraft." In Ulrike Grossarth, *Wäre Ich Von Stoff, Ich Würde Mich Färben = Were I Made of Matter, I Would Color*, 69–81. Edited by Sabine Folie and Ilse Lafer. Berlin: Sternberg Press, 2014.

"In the Mirror of the Dream: Borges and the Poetics of Kabbalah." *Jewish Quarterly Review* 104 (2014): 362–79.

"Parting of the Ways That Never Parted: Judaism and Christianity in the Work of Jacob Neusner." In *A Legacy of Learning: Essays in Honor of Jacob Neusner*, 299–318. Edited by Alan Avery-Peck, Bruce D. Chilton, William Scott Green, and Gary Porton. Leiden: Brill, 2014.

"Skepticism and the Philosopher's Keeping Faith." In *Jewish Philosophy for the Twenty-First Century: Personal Reflections*, 481–515. Edited by Hava Tirosh-Samuelson and Aaron W. Hughes. Leiden: Brill, 2014.

"Becoming Invisible: Rending the Veil and the Hermeneutic of Secrecy in the Gospel of Philip." In *Practicing Gnosis: Ritual, Magic, Theurgy and Liturgy in Nag Hammadi, Manichaean and Other Ancient Literature. Essays in Honor of Birger A. Pearson*, 113–35. Edited by April D. DeConick, Gregory Shaw, and John D. Turner. Leiden: Brill, 2013.

"Configuration of Untruth in the Mirror of God's Truth: Rethinking Rosenzweig in Light of Heidegger's Alētheia." In *Die Denkfigur des Systems im Ausgang von Franz Rosenzweigs "Stern der Erlösung,"* 141–62. Edited by Hartwig Wiedebach. Berlin: Duncker & Humblot, 2013.

"Le corps de la letter: l'herméneutique soufie et kabbalistique." In *Histoire des relations entre juifs et musulmans du Coran à nos jours*, 817–32. Edited by Abdelwahab Meddeb and Benjamin Stora. Paris: Albin Michel, 2013. English translation: "Embodied Letter: Sufi and Kabbalistic Hermeneutics." In *A History of Jewish-Muslim Relations: From the Origins to the Present Day*,

837–52. Edited by Abdelwahab Meddeb and Benjamin Stora. Princeton: Princeton University Press, 2013.

"Nequddat ha-Reshimu—The Trace of Transcendence and the Transcendence of the Trace: The Paradox of *Tzimtzum* in the RaShaB's *Hemshekh Ayin Beit*." *Kabbalah: Journal for the Study of Jewish Mystical Texts* 30 (2013): 75–120.

"Patriarchy and the Motherhood of God in Zoharic Kabbalah and Meister Eckhart." In *Envisioning Judaism: Studies in Honor of Peter Schäfer on the Occasion of His Seventieth Birthday*, 1049–88. Edited by Ra'anan S. Boustan, Klaus Hermann, Reimund Leicht, Annette Yoshiko Reed, and Giuseppe Veltri, with the collaboration of Alex Ramos. Tübingen: Mohr Siebeck, 2013.

"Theosis, Vision, and the Astral Body in Medieval German Pietism and the Spanish Kabbalah." In *Sky and Symbol: Proceedings of the Ninth Annual Sophia Centre Conference, 2011*, 119–42. Edited by Nicholas Campion and Liz Greene. Ceredigion, Wales: Sophia Centre Press, 2013.

"Zoharic Literature and Midrashic Temporality." In *Midrash Unbound: Transformations and Innovations*, 311–33. Edited by Michael Fishbane and Joanna Weinberg. Oxford: Littman Library, 2013.

"Echo of the Otherwise: Ethics of Transcendence and the Lure of Theolatry." In *Encountering the Medieval in Modern Jewish Thought*, 261–324. Edited by Aaron W. Hughes and James A. Diamond. Leiden: Brill, 2012.

"Imagination and the Theolatrous Impulse: Configuring God in Modern Jewish Thought." In *The Cambridge History of Jewish Philosophy: The Modern Era*, 663–703. Edited by Zachary Braiterman, Martin Kavka, and David Novak. Cambridge: Cambridge University Press, 2012.

"Nihilating Nonground and the Temporal Sway of Becoming: Kabbalistically Envisioning Nothing Beyond Nothing." *Angelaki* 17 (2012): 31–45.

"Paul Philip Levertoff and the Popularization of Kabbalah as a Missionizing Tactic." *Kabbalah: Journal for the Study of Jewish Mystical Texts* 27 (2012): 269–320.

"Revealing and Re/veiling Menaḥem Mendel Schneerson's Messianic Secret." *Kabbalah: Journal for the Study of Jewish Mystical Texts* 26 (2012): 25–96.

"Textual Flesh, Incarnation, and the Imaginal Body: Abraham Abulafia's Polemic with Christianity." In *Studies in Medieval Jewish Intellectual and Social History: Festschrift in Honor of Robert Chazan*, 189–226. Edited by David Engel, Lawrence H. Schiffman, and Elliot R. Wolfson. Leiden: Brill, 2012.

"Unveiling the Veil: Apocalyptic, Secrecy, and the Jewish Mystical Imaginaire." *Association for Jewish Studies Perspectives* (Fall 2012): 18–20.

"Abraham ben Samuel Abulafia and the Prophetic Kabbalah." In *Jewish Mysticism and Kabbalah: New Insights*, 68–90. Edited by Frederick E. Greenspahn. New York: New York University Press, 2011.

"Apophasis and the Trace of Transcendence: Wyschogrod's Contribution to a Postmodern Jewish Immanent A/Theology." *Philosophy Today* 55 (2011): 328–47.

"Building a Sanctuary of the Heart: The Kabbalistic-Pietistic Teachings of Itamar Schwartz." In *Kabbalah and Contemporary Spiritual Revival*, 141–62. Edited by Boaz Huss. Ben-Gurion: Ben-Gurion University Press, 2011.

"Dreaming the Dream of the Poem: Flattened Curves of Infinitivity." *The Poetic Front* 4 (2011).

"Immanuel Frommann's Commentary on Luke and the Christianizing of Kabbalah: Some Sabbatian and Ḥasidic Affinities." In *Holy Dissent: Jewish and Christian Mystics in Eastern Europe*, 171–222. Edited by Glenn Dynner. Detroit: Wayne State University Press, 2011. Revised Hebrew version in *And This Is for Yehuda: Studies Presented to Our Friend, Professor Yehuda Liebes, on the Occasion of His Sixty-Fifth Birthday*, 401–19. Edited by Maren R. Niehoff, Ronit Meroz, and Jonathan Garb. Jerusalem: Bialik Institute, 2012.

"Open Secret in the Rearview Mirror." *Association for Jewish Studies Review* 35 (2011): 1–18.

"Teaching Jewish Mysticism: Concealing the Concealment and Disclosure of Secrets." In *Teaching Mysticism*, 103–17. Edited by William B. Parsons. Oxford: Oxford University Press, 2011.

"Light Does Not Talk but Shines: Apophasis and Vision in Rosenzweig's Theopoetic Temporality." In *New Studies in Jewish Philosophy*, 87–148. Edited by Aaron W. Hughes and Elliot R. Wolfson. Bloomington: Indiana University Press, 2010.

"The Status of the (Non)Jewish Other in the Apocalyptic Messianism of Menahem Mendel Schneerson." In *Kabbalah and Modernity: Interpretations, Transformations, Adaptations*, 221–57. Edited by Boaz Huss, Marco Pasi, and Kocku von Stuckrad. Leiden: Brill, 2010.

"Undoing Time and the Syntax of the Dream Interlude: A Phenomenological Reading of *Zohar* 1:199a–200a." *Kabbalah: Journal for the Study of Jewish Mystical Texts* 22 (2010): 33–57.

"The Anonymous Chapters of the Elderly Master of Secrets: New Evidence for the Early Activity of the Zoharic Circle." *Kabbalah: Journal for the Study of Jewish Mystical Texts* 18 (2009): 143–278.

"Das Kleid der Ka'ba: Verhüllung und Entschleierung in den Bilderwelten des Sufismus." In *Taswir—Islamische Bildwelten und Moderne*, 153–57. Edited by Almut Shulamit Bruckstein Çoruh and Hendrik Budde. Berlin: Nicolaische B. Verlagsbuchhandlung GmbH, 2009.

"Kenotic Overflow and Temporal Transcendence: Angelic Embodiment and the Alterity of Time in Abraham Abulafia." *Kabbalah: Journal for the Study of Jewish Mystical Texts* 18 (2008): 133–90. Revised version in *Saintly Influence: Edith Wyschogrod and the Possibilities of Philosophy of Religion*, 113–49. Edited by Eric Boynton and Martin Kavka. New York: Fordham University Press, 2009.

"Revisioning the Body Apophatically: Incarnation and the Acosmic Naturalism of Habad Hasidism." In *Apophatic Bodies: Infinity, Ethics, and Incarnation*, 147–99. Edited by Chris Boesel and Catherine Keller. New York: Fordham University Press, 2009.

"'Sage Is Preferable to Prophet': Revisioning Midrashic Imagination." In *Scriptural Exegesis: The Shapes of Culture and the Religious Imagination: A Festschrift in Honor of Michael Fishbane*, 186–210. Edited by Deborah A. Green and Laura S. Lieber. Oxford: Oxford University Press, 2009.

"Angelic Embodiment and the Feminine Representation of Jesus: Reconstructing Carnality in the Christian Kabbalah of Johann Kemper." In *The Jewish Body: Corporeality, Society, and Identity in the Renaissance and the Early Modern Period*, 395–426. Edited by Maria Diemling and Giuseppe Veltri. Leiden: Brill, 2009.

"Murmuring Secrets: Eroticism and Esotericism in Medieval Kabbalah." In *Hidden Intercourse: Eros and Sexuality in the History of Western Esotericism*, 65–109. Edited by Wouter J. Hanegraaff and Jeffrey J. Kripal. Leiden: Brill, 2008.

"*Via Negativa* in Maimonides and Its Impact on Thirteenth-Century Kabbalah." *Maimonidean Studies* 5 (2008): 393–442.

"Imago Templi and the Meeting of the Two Seas: Liturgical Time-Space and the Feminine Imaginary in Zoharic Kabbalah." *RES* 51 (2007): 121–35.

"Inscribed in the Book of the Living: Gospel of Truth and Jewish Christology." *Journal for the Study of Judaism* 38 (2007): 234–71.

"Oneiric Imagination and Mystical Annihilation in Habad Hasidism." *ARC: The Journal of the Faculty of Religious Studies, McGill University* 35 (2007): 131–57.

"Rose of Eros and the Duplicity of the Feminine in Zoharic Kabbalah." In *Botanical Progress, Horticultural Innovation and Cultural Changes*, 51–59. Edited by Michael Conan and W. John Kress. Washington, D.C.: Dumbarton Oaks Research Library and Collection, 2007.

"Structure, Innovation, and Diremptive Temporality: The Use of Models to Study Continuity and Discontinuity in Kabbalistic Tradition." *Journal for the Study of Religions and Ideologies* 18 (2007): 143–67.

"Beschneidung, Gottesvision und Textinterpretation Vom Midrasch-Tropus zum mystischen Symbol." *Analytische Psychologie: Zeitschrift für Psychotherapie und Psychoanalyse* 146 (2006): 369–405.

"Mythopoeic Imagination and the Hermeneutic Bridging of Temporal Spacing: A Note on Fishbane's Biblical Myth and Rabbinic Mythmaking." *Jewish Quarterly Review* 96 (2006): 233–38.

"New Jerusalem Glowing: Songs and Poems of Leonard Cohen in a Kabbalistic Key." *Kabbalah: A Journal for the Study of Jewish Mystical Texts* 15 (2006): 103–52.

"Suffering Eros and Textual Incarnation: A Kristevan Reading of Kabbalistic Poetics." In *Toward a Theology of Eros: Transfiguring Passion at the Limits of Discipline*, 341–65. Edited by Virginia Burrus and Catherine Keller. New York: Fordham University Press, 2006. Hebrew version in *Kabbalah, Mysticism and Poetry: The Journey to the End of Vision*, 450–77. Edited by Avi Elqayam and Shlomy Mualem. Jerusalem: Magnes Press, 2015.

"Secrecy, Modesty, and the Feminine: Kabbalistic Traces in the Thought of Levinas." *Journal of Jewish Thought and Philosophy* 14 (2006): 195–224. Reprinted in *The Exorbitant: Emmanuel Levinas Between Jews and Christians*, 52–73. Edited by Kevin Hart and Michael A. Signer. New York: Fordham University Press, 2010.

"The Body in the Text: A Kabbalistic Theory of Embodiment." *Jewish Quarterly Review* 95 (2005): 479–500.

"Language, Secrecy, and the Mysteries of Law: Theurgy and the Christian Kabbalah of Johannes Reuchlin." *Kabbalah: A Journal for the Study of Jewish Mystical Texts* 13 (2005): 7–41. Revised version in *Invoking Angels: Theurgic Ideas and Practices, Thirteenth to Sixteenth Centuries*, 312–40. Edited by Claire Fanger. University Park: Pennsylvania State University Press, 2012.

"Beneath the Wings of the Great Eagle: Maimonides and Thirteenth-Century Kabbalah." In *Moses Maimonides (1138–1204)—His Religious, Scientific, and Philosophical Wirkungsgeschichte in Different Cultural Contexts*, 209–37. Edited by Görge K. Hasselhoff and Otfried Fraisse. Würzburg: Ergon Verlag, 2004.

"Hermeneutics of Light in Medieval Kabbalah." In *The Presence of Light: Divine Radiance and*

Religious Experience, 105–18. Edited by Matthew T. Kapstein. Chicago: University of Chicago Press, 2004.

"Iconicity of the Text: Reification of the Torah and the Idolatrous Impulse of Zoharic Kabbalah." *Jewish Studies Quarterly* 11 (2004): 215–42.

"Text, Context, Pretext: A Review Essay of Yehuda Liebes's 'Ars Poetica in Sefer Yetsirah.'" *Studia Philonica Annual* 16 (2004): 218–28.

"Asceticism and Eroticism in Medieval Jewish Philosophical and Mystical Exegesis of the Song of Songs." In *With Reverence for the Word: Medieval Scriptural Exegesis in Judaism, Christianity, and Islam*, 92–118. Edited by Jane Dammen McAuliffe, Barry D. Walfish, and Joseph W. Goering. Oxford: Oxford University Press, 2003.

"Circumcision, Secrecy, and the Veiling of the Veil: Phallomorphic Exposure and Kabbalistic Esotericism." In *The Covenant of Circumcision: New Perspectives on an Ancient Jewish Rite*, 58–70. Edited by Elisabeth Wyner Mark. Hanover: Brandeis University Press, 2003.

"Seven Mysteries of Knowledge: Qumran E/sotericism Reconsidered." In *The Idea of Biblical Interpretation: Essays in Honor of James L. Kugel*, 173–213. Edited by Hindy Najman. Leiden: Brill, 2003.

"Assaulting the Border: Kabbalistic Traces in the Margins of Derrida." *Journal of the American Academy of Religion* 70 (2002): 475–514.

"Before Alef/Where Beginnings End." In *Beginning/Again: Towards a Hermeneutics of Jewish Texts*, 135–61. Edited by Aryeh Cohen and Shaul Magid. New York: Seven Bridges Press, 2002.

"Beyond Good and Evil: Hypernomianism, Transmorality, and Kabbalistic Ethics." In *Crossing Boundaries: Ethics, Antinomianism and the History of Mysticism*, 103–56. Edited by Jeffrey J. Kripal and William Barnard. New York: Seven Bridges Press, 2002.

"The Cut That Binds: Time, Memory, and the Ascetic Impulse." In *God's Voice from the Void: Old and New Studies in Bratslav Hasidism*, 103–54. Edited by Shaul Magid. Albany: State University of New York Press, 2002.

"Divine Suffering and the Hermeneutics of Reading: Philosophical Reflections on Lurianic Mythology." In *Suffering Religion*, 101–62. Edited by Robert Gibbs and Elliot R. Wolfson. New York and London: Routledge, 2002.

"Gender and Heresy in Kabbalah Scholarship." *Kabbalah: A Journal for the Study of Jewish Mystical Texts* 6 (2002): 231–62. [Hebrew.]

"Mirror of Nature Reflected in the Symbolism of Medieval Kabbalah." In *Judaism and Ecology: Created World and Revealed Word*, 305–31. Edited by Hava Tirosh-Samuelson. Cambridge, MA: Harvard University, Press, 2002.

"Lying on the Path: Translation and the Transport of Sacred Texts." *Association for Jewish Studies Perspectives* 3 (2001): 8–13.

"Martyrdom, Eroticism, and Asceticism in Twelfth-Century Ashkenazi Piety." In *Jews and Christians in Twelfth-Century Europe*, 171–220. Edited by Michael A. Signer and John Van Engen. Notre Dame: University of Notre Dame Press, 2001.

"Messianism in the Christian Kabbalah of Johann Kemper." In *Millenarianism and Messianism in the Early Modern European Culture: Jewish Messianism in the Early Modern World*, 139–87.

Edited by Matt D. Goldish and Richard H. Popkin. Dordrecht: Kluwer Academic Publishers, 2001.

"Moisés de León y el Zohar." In *Pensamiento y Mística Hispanojudía y Sefardí*, 165–92. Cuenca: Ediciones de la Universidad de Castilla-La Mancha, 2001.

"Phantasmagoria: The Image of the Image in Jewish Magic from Late Antiquity and the Early Middle Ages." In *The Review of Rabbinic Judaism: Ancient, Medieval, Modern* 4 (2001): 78–120.

"Beyond the Spoken Word: Oral Tradition and Written Transmission in Medieval Jewish Mysticism." In *Transmitting Jewish Traditions: Orality, Textuality and Cultural Diffusion*, 166–224. Edited by Yaakov Elman and Israel Gershoni. New Haven: Yale University Press, 2000.

Encyclopedia of the Dead Sea Scrolls. Oxford University Press, 2000. Entries on "Heikhalot Literature" and "Kabbalah."

"Gazing beneath the Veil: Apocalyptic Envisioning the End." In *Reinterpreting Revelation and Tradition: Jews and Christians in Conversation*, 77–103. Edited by John T. Pawlikowski, O.S.M., and Hayim G. Perelmuter. Franklin: Sheed & Ward, 2000.

"Judaism and Incarnation: The Imaginal Body of God." In *Christianity in Jewish Terms*, 239–54. Edited by Tikva Frymer-Kensky, David Novak, Peter Ochs, and Michael A. Signer. Boulder: Westview Press, 2000.

"Ontology, Alterity, and Ethics in Kabbalistic Anthropology." *Exemplaria* 12 (2000): 129–55. Reprinted in *Turn It Again: Jewish Medieval Studies and Literary Theory*, 119–44. Edited by Sheila Delany. Eugene: Wipf and Stock, 2004.

"*Megillat Emet we-Emunah*: Contemplative Visualization and Mystical Unknowing." *Kabbalah: A Journal for the Study of Jewish Mystical Texts* 5 (2000): 55–110.

"Occultation of the Feminine and the Body of Secrecy in Medieval Kabbalah." In *Rending the Veil: Concealment and Revelation of Secrets in the History of Religions*, 113–54. Edited by Elliot R. Wolfson. New York: Seven Bridges Press, 1999.

"Sacred Space and Mental Iconography: *Imago Templi* and Contemplation in Rhineland Jewish Pietism." In *Ki Baruch Hu: Ancient Near Eastern, Biblical, and Judaic Studies in Honor of Baruch A. Levine*, 593–634. Edited by Robert Chazan, William Hallo, and Lawrence H. Schiffman. Winona Lake: Eisenbrauns, 1999.

"Constructions of the Shekhinah in the Sabbatian Theology of Abraham Cardoso, with a Critical Edition of *Derush ha-Shekhinah*." *Kabbalah: A Journal for the Study of Jewish Mystical Texts* 3 (1998): 11–143.

Encyclopedia of Women and World Religion. Edited by Serenity Young. Macmillan Reference, 1998. Entries on "Divinity" and "Torah."

"The Engenderment of Messianic Politics: Symbolic Significance of Sabbatai TZevi's Coronation." In *Toward the Millennium: Messianic Expectations from the Bible to Waco*, 203–58. Edited by Peter Schäfer and Mark Cohen. Leiden: E. J. Brill, 1998.

"Fore/giveness on the Way: Nesting in the Womb of Response." *Graven Images: Studies in Culture, Law, and the Sacred* 4 (1998): 153–69.

"Hebraic and Hellenistic Conceptions of Wisdom in *Sefer ha-Bahir*." *Poetics Today* 19 (1998): 147–76.

"Listening to Speak: A Response to Dialogues in Postmodern Jewish Philosophy." In Steven Kepnes, Peter Ochs, and Robert Gibbs, *Reasoning After Revelation: Dialogues in Postmodern Jewish Philosophy*, 93–104. Boulder: Westview Press, 1998.

"Mystical Rationalization of the Commandments in the Prophetic Kabbalah of Abraham Abulafia." In *Perspectives on Jewish Thought and Mysticism*, 311–60. Edited by Alfred Ivry, Allan Arkush, and Elliot R. Wolfson. Reading: Harwood Academic, 1998.

"Re/membering the Covenant: Memory, Forgetfulness, and History in the Zohar." In *Jewish History and Jewish Memory: Essays in Honor of Yosef Hayim Yerushalmi*, 214–46. Edited by Elisheva Carlebach, John M. Efron, and David S. Myers. Hanover: Brandeis University Press, 1998.

"Coronation of the Sabbath Bride: Kabbalistic Myth and the Ritual of Androgynisation." *Journal of Jewish Thought and Philosophy* 6 (1997): 301–44.

"Effacer l'effacement: sexe et écriture du corps divin dans le symbolisme kabbalistique." In *Transmission et passages en monde juif*, 65–97. Edited by Esther Benbassa. Paris: PUBLISUD, 1997.

"Eunuchs Who Keep the Sabbath: Becoming Male and the Ascetic Ideal in Thirteenth-Century Jewish Mysticism." In *Becoming Male in the Middle Ages*, 151–85. Edited by Jeffrey Jerome Cohen and Bonnie Wheeler. New York: Garland, 1997.

"The Face of Jacob in the Moon: Mystical Transformations of an Aggadic Myth." In *The Seduction of Myth in Judaism: Challenge and Response*, 235–70. Edited by S. Daniel Breslauer. Albany: State University of New York Press, 1997.

"Facing the Effaced: Mystical Eschatology and the Idealistic Orientation in the Thought of Franz Rosenzweig." *Zeitschrift für Neuere Theologiegeschichte* 4 (1997): 39–81.

"*Tiqqun ha-Shekhinah*: Redemption and the Overcoming of Gender Dimorphism in the Messianic Kabbalah of Moses Hayyim Luzzatto." *History of Religions* 36 (1997): 289–332. French translation: "Le *Tiqqun ha-Shekhinah*: Rèdemption et rèsolution du dimorphisme sexuel dans la Kabbale messianique de Moïse Hayyim Louzzatto." *Pardès* 24 (1998): 51–93.

"Iconic Visualization and the Imaginal Body of God: The Role of Intention in the Rabbinic Conception of Prayer." *Modern Theology* 12 (1996): 137–62.

"Jewish Mysticism: A Philosophical Overview." In *The Routledge History of Jewish Philosophy*, 450–98. Edited by Daniel H. Frank and Oliver Leaman. New York: Routledge, 1996.

"Traces of Philonic Doctrine in Medieval Jewish Mysticism: A Preliminary Note." *The Studia Philonica Annual* 8 (1996): 99–106.

"Walking as a Sacred Duty: Theological Transformation of Social Reality in Early Hasidism." In *Hasidism Reconsidered*, 180–207. Edited by Ada Rapoport-Albert. Oxford: Litman Library of Jewish Civilization, 1996.

"The Doctrine of Sefirot in the Prophetic Kabbalah of Abraham Abulafia." *Jewish Studies Quarterly* 2 (1995): 336–71 and 3 (1996): 47–84.

"Crossing Gender Boundaries in Kabbalistic Ritual and Myth." In *Ultimate Intimacy: The Psychodynamics of Jewish Mysticism*, 255–337. Edited by Mortimer Ostow. London: Karnac, 1995.

"From Sealed Book to Open Text: Time, Memory, and Narrativity in Kabbalistic Hermeneutics." In *Interpreting Judaism in a Postmodern Age*, 145–78. Edited by Steven Kepnes. New York: New York University Press, 1995.

Harper's Dictionary of Religion. Edited by William S. Green. Entries: Baal Shem Tov; Devequt;

Hitlahavut; Hasidism; Judaism, mysticism of; Lubavitch; Mitnaggedim; Torah Scroll; Zaddiq (1995).

Judaism in Late Antiquity. Volume Four. *Special Topics: Death, Afterlife, Resurrection, and the World to Come.* Edited by Alan Avery-Peck and Jacob Neusner. Leiden: Brill, 1995. Entry: "Judaic Mystical Literature of Late Antiquity."

"Metatron and Shi'ur Qomah in the Writings of Haside Ashkenaz." In *Mysticism, Magic and Kabbalah in Ashkenazi Judaism*, 60–92. Edited by Karl Grözinger and Joseph Dan. Tübingen: J. C. B. Mohr, 1995.

"On Becoming Female: Crossing Gender Boundaries in Kabbalistic Ritual and Myth." In *Gender and Judaism*, 209–28. Edited by Tamar M. Rudavsky. New York: New York University Press, 1995.

"Varieties of Jewish Mysticism: A Typological Analysis." In *Mysticism and the Mystical Experience: East and West*, 133–69. Edited by Donald H. Bishop. Selinsgrove: Susquehanna University Press, 1995.

"Weeping, Death, and Spiritual Ascent in Sixteenth-Century Jewish Mysticism." In *Death, Ecstasy, and Other Worldly Journeys*, 207–47. Edited by John Collins and Michael Fishbane. Albany: State University of New York Press, 1995.

"Mysticism and the Poetic-Liturgical Compositions from Qumran." *Jewish Quarterly Review* 85 (1994): 187–204.

"Negative Theology and Positive Assertion in the Early Kabbalah." *Da'at* 32–33 (1994): V–XXII. [English section.]

"Woman—The Feminine as Other in Theosophic Kabbalah: Some Philosophical Observations on the Divine Androgyne." In *The Other in Jewish Thought and History: Constructions of Jewish Culture and Identity*, 166–204. Edited by Laurence J. Silberstein and Robert L. Cohn. New York: New York University Press, 1994.

"The Image of Jacob Engraved upon the Throne: Further Speculation on the Esoteric Doctrine of the German Pietism." In *Massu'ot Studies in Kabbalistic Literature and Jewish Philosophy in Memory of Prof. Ephraim Gottlieb*, 131–85. Edited by Michal Oron and Amos Goldreich. Jerusalem: Mossad Bialik, 1994. [Hebrew.]

"Beautiful Maiden Without Eyes: Peshat and Sod in Zoharic Hermeneutics." In *The Midrashic Imagination: Jewish Exegesis, Thought, and History*, 155–203. Edited by Michael Fishbane. Albany: State University of New York Press, 1993.

"Forms of Visionary Ascent as Ecstatic Experience in the Zoharic Literature." In *Gershom Scholem's Major Trends in Jewish Mysticism 50 Years After*, 209–35. Edited by Joseph Dan and Peter Schäfer. Tübingen: J. C. B. Mohr, 1993.

"The Mystical Significance of Torah-Study in German Pietism." *Jewish Quarterly Review* 84 (1993): 43–78.

"The Tree That Is All: Jewish-Christian Roots of a Kabbalistic Symbol in *Sefer ha-Bahir*." *Journal of Jewish Thought and Philosophy* 3 (1993): 31–76.

"Yeridah la-Merkavah: Typology of Ecstasy and Enthronement in Early Jewish Mysticism." In *Mystics of the Book: Themes, Topics, and Typologies*, 13–44. Edited by Robert A. Herrera. New York: Peter Lang, 1993.

"Images of God's Feet: Some Observations on the Divine Body in Judaism." In *People of the Body: Jews and Judaism from an Embodied Perspective*, 143–81. Edited by Howard Eilberg-Schwartz. Albany: State University of New York Press, 1992.

"The Influence of the Ari on the Shelah." *Jerusalem Studies in Jewish Thought* 10 (1992): 423–48. [Hebrew.]

"The Theosophy of Shabbetai Donnolo, with Special Emphasis on the Doctrine of *Sefirot* in *Sefer Ḥakhmoni*." *Jewish History* 6 (1992): 281–316.

"Hai Gaon's Letter and Commentary on 'Aleynu: Further Evidence of R. Moses de León's Pseudepigraphic Activity." *Jewish Quarterly Review* 81 (1991): 365–410.

"God, the Intellect, and the Demiurge: On the Usage of the Word *Kol* in Abraham ibn Ezra." *Revue des études juives* 149 (1990): 77–111.

"Letter Symbolism and Merkavah Imagery in the Zohar." In *Alei Shefer: Studies in the Literature of Jewish Thought Presented to Rabbi Dr. Alexandre Safran*, 195–236. Edited by Moshe Hallamish. Ramat-Gan: Bar-Ilan Press, 1990. [English section.]

"Merkavah Traditions in Philosophical Garb: Judah Halevi Reconsidered." *Proceedings of the American Academy for Jewish Research* 57 (1990–1991): 179–242.

"The Secret of the Garment in Naḥmanides." *Da'at* 24 (1990): 25–49. [English section.]

"Anthropomorphic Imagery and Letter Symbolism in the Zohar." *Jerusalem Studies in Jewish Thought* 8 (1989): 147–81. [Hebrew.]

"By Way of Truth: Aspects of Naḥmanides' Kabbalistic Hermeneutic." *Association for Jewish Studies Review* 14 (1989): 103–78.

"Female Imaging of the Torah: From Literary Metaphor to Religious Symbol." In *From Ancient Israel to Modern Judaism, Intellect in Quest of Understanding: Essays in Honor of Marvin Fox*, 2: 271–307. Edited by Jacob Neusner, Ernest J. Frerichs, and Nahum Sarna. Atlanta: Scholars Press, 1989.

"La hermenéutica de la experiencia visionaria: revelación e interpretación en el *Zohar*." *Acta Poetica* 9–10 (1989): 117–43. Reprinted in *Ensayos sobre cábala y misticismo judío*, 161–81. Edited by Yom Tov Assis, Moshe Idel, and Leonardo Senkman. Buenos Aires: Ediciones Lilmod, 2006.

"The Problem of Unity in the Thought of Martin Buber." *Journal of the History of Philosophy* 27 (1989): 419–39.

"Biblical Accentuation in a Mystical Key: Kabbalistic Interpretation of the Te'amim." *Journal of Jewish Music and Liturgy* 11 (1988): 1–16; 12 (1989): 1–13. Reprinted in *Essays of Jewish Music and Prayer: Commemorating the Jubilee Year of the Philip and Sarah Belz School of Jewish Music*, 90–118. Edited by Macy Nulman. New York: Philip and Sarah Belz School of Jewish Music, 2005.

"The Hermeneutics of Visionary Experience: Revelation and Interpretation in the Zohar." *Religion* 18 (1988): 311–45.

"Light through Darkness: The Ideal of Human Perfection in the Zohar." *Harvard Theological Review* 81 (1988): 73–95.

"Mystical Rationalization of the Commandments in Sefer ha-Rimmon." *Hebrew Union College Annual* 59 (1988): 217–51.

"Mystical-Theurgical Dimensions of Prayer in *Sefer ha-Rimmon*." In *Approaches to Medieval Judaism*, 3:41–80. Edited by David R. Blumenthal. Atlanta: Scholars Press, 1988.

"Circumcision and the Divine Name: A Study in the Transmission of Esoteric Doctrine." *Jewish Quarterly Review* 78 (1987): 77–112.

"Circumcision, Vision of God, and Textual Interpretation: From Midrashic Trope to Mystical Symbol." *History of Religions* 27 (1987): 189–215.

"Left Contained in the Right: A Study in Zoharic Hermeneutics." *Association for Jewish Studies Review* 11 (1986): 27–52.

REVIEWS

"The Apocalyptic Secret of Judaism and Olga Tokarczuk's *The Books of Jacob*." *Marginalia: Los Angeles Review of Books* (March 31, 2023).

"A Forum on Elad Lapidot's *Jews Out of the Question: Thinking the Unthinkable*." *Marginalia: Los Angeles Review of Books* (July 1, 2022).

"Overcoming the Body through the Body: Review of David Biale et al. *Hasidism: A New History*." *Marginalia: Los Angeles Review of Books* (April 10, 2020).

"Hyperphilology and the Anachronism of Anachronism: Review of Daniel Boyarin. *Judaism: The Genealogy of a Modern Nation*." *Marginalia: Los Angeles Review of Books* (July 5, 2019).

David Gelernter, *Judaism: A Way of Being. Azure* 41 (2010): 97–108.

Moshe Halbertal, *Concealment and Revelation: Esotericism in Jewish Thought and Its Philosophical Implications. Journal of Religion in Europe* 2 (2009): 309–23.

Yehuda Liebes, *Studies in Jewish Myth and Jewish Messianism. Jewish Quarterly Review* 87 (1997).

Yehuda Liebes, *Studies in the Zohar. Critical Review of Books in Religion—1994*.

Gershom Scholem, *On the Mystical Shape of the Godhead: Basic Concepts in the Kabbalah. Journal of Religion* 73 (1993): 655–57.

Mark Verman, *The Books of Contemplation: Medieval Jewish Mystical Sources. Journal of Religion* 73 (1993): 657–58.

Elliot Ginsburg, *The Sabbath in Classical Kabbalah and Sod ha-Shabbat: The Mystery of the Sabbath. Association for Jewish Studies Review* 17 (1992): 123–26.

Moshe Idel, *Language, Torah, and Hermeneutics in Abraham Abulafia. Jewish Quarterly Review* 83 (1992): 294–96.

Moshe Idel, *Kabbalah: New Perspectives. Journal of Religion* 72 (1992): 137–39.

David J. Halperin, *The Faces of the Chariot. Jewish Quarterly Review* 81 (1991): 496–500.

Gershom Scholem, *Origins of the Kabbalah* and M. Idel, *Kabbalah: New Perspectives. Religious Studies Review* 17 (1991): 318–21.

Moshe Idel, *Studies in the Ecstatic Kabbalah. Shofar* 8 (1990): 125–27.

Jacob Neusner, *The Incarnation of God. Jewish Quarterly Review* 81 (1990): 219–22.

Moshe Idel, *The Mystical Experience in Abraham Abulafia* and *Studies in Ecstatic Kabbalah. Association for Jewish Studies Review* 14 (1989): 81–84.

Gershom Scholem, *Origins of the Kabbalah. The Journal of Religion* 69 (1989): 139–40.

CONTRIBUTORS

DANIEL ABRAMS was Elliot Wolfson's first doctoral student at New York University. Currently, he teaches Kabbalah in the Department of Jewish Philosophy at Bar Ilan University. He edits the journal *Kabbalah: Journal for the Study of Jewish Mystical Texts* and has published a number of editions and studies of kabbalistic texts and manuscripts.

DUSTIN N. ATLAS is the Director of Jewish Studies and Assistant Professor in the School of Religion at Queen's University. He is presently working on a book that uses the work of Martin Buber to explore the ways Jewish thought allows us to engage the nonhuman.

CLÉMENCE BOULOUQUE is the Carl and Bernice Witten Associate Professor of Israel and Jewish Studies in the Department of Religion at Columbia University. She received her PhD from NYU where she studied under Elliot Wolfson. A published novelist and essayist in her native France, she is most recently the author of *Another Modernity, Elia Benamozegh's Jewish Universalism* (Stanford, 2020).

DANIEL BOYARIN is the Herman P. and Sophia Taubmann Professor of Talmudic Culture emeritus at UC Berkeley, where he has taught for three decades. His work has overlapped with and been instructed by the work of Elliot Wolfson for that long, as well, and the friendship has overlapped even more. This essay has been adapted from his forthcoming book: *The No-State Solution: A Jewish Manifesto*, in press at Yale University Press.

ZACHARY BRAITERMAN is Professor in the Department of Religion at Syracuse University. He is the author of *The Shape of Revelation: Aesthetics and Modern Jewish Thought* (Stanford University Press, 2007), *(God) after Auschwitz: Tradition and Change in Post-Holocaust Jewish Thought* (Princeton University Press, 1998), and co-editor of *The Cambridge History of Jewish Philosophy: The Modern Era* (2012). He is currently finishing a multi-volume project, *In the Image: Virtual Jewish Thought and Philosophical Talmud.*

PROF. ALMUT SH. BRUCKSTEIN, aka House of Taswir, theory artist, writer, founding artistic director of Taswir projects, international platform for artistic research and diasporic thinking. Developer of epistemic architectures and psycho-poietic interventions in collaboration with museums, galleries, magazines, and other institutions. Various professorships in (Jewish) philosophy, visual theory, Taswir studies in Jerusalem, Berlin, Lucerne, Frankfurt a. M. Most recent books and exhibitions: *The Talmudic Bride and Her Shadow's Dream* (2022), *Freud. Talmud. Taswir* (2019), *Wednesday Society. The Couch of Meret O.* (2019), *Lady Dada Kalam* (2017), *Fragments from Our Beautiful Future* (2017), *The Red Gaze* (2016), *House of Taswir. Doing and Undoing Things* (2014), *Vom Aufstand der Bilder* (2007), and many more. www.taswir.org

ANDREA DARA COOPER is Associate Professor and Leonard and Tobee Kaplan Scholar in Modern Jewish Thought and Culture at UNC-Chapel Hill. She studied with Elliot Wolfson at New York University, where she received her PhD in Hebrew and Judaic Studies. She is the author of *Gendering Modern Jewish Thought* (Indiana University Press, 2021). She is co-chair of the Study of Judaism Unit of the American Academy of Religion and serves on the steering committee of the Animals and Religion Unit.

JONATHAN DAUBER is Associate Professor of Jewish Mysticism at Yeshiva University's Bernard Revel Graduate School of Jewish Studies. He holds a PhD in Jewish Mysticism from New York University, where he studied with Elliot Wolfson. He is the author of *Knowledge of God and the Development of Early Kabbalah* (Brill, 2012) and *Secrecy and Esoteric Writing in Kabbalistic Literature* (University of Pennsylvania Press, 2022).

GLENN DYNNER, PhD, is the Carl and Dorothy Bennett Professor of Judaic Studies and Director of the Bennett Center at Fairfield University; Editor of the journal *Shofar: An Interdisciplinary Journal of Jewish Studies*; and a recent Guggenheim Fellow. He is the author of *"Men of Silk": The Hasidic Conquest of Polish Jewish Society* (Oxford University Press, 2006), and *Yankel's Tavern: Jews, Liquor & Life in the Kingdom of Poland* (Oxford University Press, 2014). His new book is entitled *The Light of Learning: Hasidism in Poland on the Eve of the Holocaust* (Oxford University Press, 2024).

HENT DE VRIES is Paulette Goddard Professor of the Humanities at New York University and Director of the summer School of Criticism and Theory at Cornell University. Before joining NYU, de Vries directed the Humanities Center at Johns Hopkins University, holding the Russ Family Chair in the Humanities with a joint appointment in Philosophy. De Vries is the author, most recently, of *Miracles et métaphysique* (2019), the text of his Étienne Gilson lectures at the Institut Catholique de Paris, and of *Le miracle au coeur de l'ordinaire* (2018). He also published *Philosophy and the Turn to Religion* (1999), *Religion and Violence: Philosophical Perspectives from Kant to Derrida* (2002), and *Minimal Theologies: Critiques of Secular Reason in Theodor W. Adorno and Emmanuel Levinas* (2005). He is the co-editor of several collective volumes, among them *Political Theologies: Public Religions in a Post-Secular World* (2006), *Religion Beyond a Concept* (2008), and *Love and Forgiveness for a More Just World* (2015).

ROBERT ERLEWINE is the director of the Center for Jewish Studies at Eastern Michigan University. He is the author of *Monotheism and Tolerance: Recovering a Religion of Reason* and *Judaism and the West: From Hermann Cohen to Joseph Soloveitchik*. He was the managing editor of the *Journal of Jewish Thought and Philosophy* from 2011 to 2015, where he worked closely with Elliot Wolfson, the Editor-in-Chief.

MICHAEL FISHBANE is the Nathan Cummings Distinguished Service Professor emeritus, University of Chicago. He is a fellow of the American Academy of Jewish Research and the American Academy of Arts and Sciences.

ROGER FRIEDLAND, Emeritus Professor of Religious Studies and Sociology at the University of California, Santa Barbara, is a cultural sociologist and a theorist of institution. His works include *Powers of Theory*, with Robert Alford (Cambridge University Press, 1985); *To Rule Jerusalem*, with Richard Hecht (Cambridge University Press, 1996); *The Fellowship: The Untold Story of Frank Lloyd Wright*, with Harold Zellman (Harper Perennial, 2007); and *Amore:*

An American Father's Roman Holiday (Harper Perennial, 2014). His institutional logical approach points to practical constellations grounded in nonphenomenal teleo-ontological substances in an Aristotelian key. His empirical work ranges from intimate practices in the United States (with Henk Roose) and Muslim-majority countries (with Janet Afary), notational technologies used in blockchain and cryptocurrency (with Ted Schatzki), and sacred centers and religious nationalisms.

JONATHAN GARB is the Gershom Scholem Professor of Kabbalah in the Department of Jewish Thought at the Hebrew University of Jerusalem. In 2014, he received the Israel Academy of Sciences and Humanities' Gershom Scholem Prize for Kabbalah Research. Among his latest books are *Yearnings of the Soul: Psychological Thought in Modern Kabbalah* (University of Chicago Press, 2015); and *A History of Kabbalah: From the Early Modern Period to the Present Day* (Cambridge University Press, 2020, awarded the Polonsky Prize for Creativity and Originality in the Humanistic Disciplines, Hebrew University, 2021).

PINCHAS GILLER was brought up in Cocoa Beach, Florida. He was ordained at Yeshiva University and received his doctorate at the Graduate Theological Union, Berkeley. He has written four books, *The Enlightened Will Shine: Symbolism and Theurgy in the Later Strata of the Zohar* (State University of New York Press, 1993), *Reading the Zohar* (Oxford University Press, 2000), *Shalom Shar'abi and the Kabbalists of Beit El* (Oxford University Press, 2000), and *Kabbalah: A Guide for the Perplexed* (Continuum Press; 2011). He has also edited *Be'er Moshe al ha-Torah*, by Moshe ha-Kohen Reicherson. Rabbi Giller is Professor of Jewish Thought at the American Jewish University, Los Angeles.

JOEL HECKER is Professor of Jewish Mysticism at the Reconstructionist Rabbinical College in Wyncote, PA. He received his PhD in Jewish Mysticism from New York University under the guidance of Elliot Wolfson. He is the author of *The Zohar: Pritzker Edition*, Volume 11 and (with Nathan Wolski) Volume 12 (Stanford University Press); and *Mystical Bodies, Mystical Meals: Eating and Embodiment in Medieval Kabbalah* (Wayne State University Press). He is co-editing (with Lawrence Fine and Ruth Kara-Ivanov Kaniel) *Emotions and Kabbalah* (Littman Library, 2023).

SUSANNAH HESCHEL is Eli M. Black Distinguished Professor of Jewish Studies at Dartmouth College. She is the author of *Abraham Geiger and the Jewish Jesus* (University of Chicago Press), *The Aryan Jesus: Christian Theologians and the Bible in Nazi Germany* (Princeton University Press), and *Jewish Studies and the Woman Question*, written with Sarah Imhoff (Princeton University Press), among many other publications. She is an elected member of the American Academy for Jewish Research and the American Society for the Study of Religion and the recipient of a Guggenheim Fellowship and five honorary doctorates from universities in the United States, Canada, Germany, and Switzerland.

AARON W. HUGHES is the Dean's Professor of the Humanities and the Philip S. Bernstein Professor of Jewish Studies in the Department of Religion and Classics at the University of Rochester. Among many other writings in Islamic studies, Jewish studies, and religious studies, he and Elliot R. Wolfson coedited *New Directions in Jewish Philosophy* (Indiana University Press, 2010).

MARTIN KAVKA is Professor and Chair in the Department of Religion at Florida State University. He is the author of *Jewish Messianism and the History of Philosophy* (Cambridge University

Press), which in 2008 won the Jordan Schnitzer Book Award in Philosophy and Jewish Thought from the Association for Jewish Studies. Author of over sixty articles, he also co-edited the *Journal of Religious Ethics* from 2011 to 2021.

GILAH KLETENIK is Postdoctoral Associate at the Elie Wiesel Center for Jewish Studies at Boston University. Previously, she was Alan M. Stroock Fellow at the Center for Jewish Studies at Harvard University. Kletenik received her PhD in Hebrew and Judaic Studies from New York University, where she was a student of Elliot R. Wolfson. For several years she was Managing Editor of the *Journal of Jewish Thought and Philosophy*, where she worked closely with Elliot R. Wolfson, its Editor-in-Chief. Currently, Kletenik is completing her book, *Sovereignty Disrupted: Spinoza and the Disparity of Reality*.

DR. SHARON KOREN is Associate Professor of Medieval Jewish Culture at HUC-JIR/New York and holds the Dr. Norman J. Cohen Chair for an Emerging Scholar. She received her PhD in 1999 from Yale University and is the recipient of numerous prizes, fellowships, and grants. Her first book, *Forsaken: The Menstruant in Medieval Jewish Mysticism* (Brandeis University Press), appeared in 2011, and she is currently writing a book on the Matriarchs in the Zohar.

JEFFREY J. KRIPAL is the Associate Dean of the Faculty and Graduate Programs in the School of the Humanities and the J. Newton Rayzor Chair in Philosophy and Religious Thought at Rice University. Jeff is the author of ten books, including, most recently, *The Superhumanities: Historical Precedents, Moral Objections, New Realities* (Chicago, 2022), where he intuits an emerging new order of knowledge that can engage in robust moral criticism but also affirm the superhuman or nonhuman dimensions of our histories, cultures, and futures. He is presently working on a three-volume study of paranormal currents in the sciences, modern esoteric literature, and the hidden history of science fiction collectively entitled *The Super Story: Science (Fiction) and Some Emergent Mythologies*. His full body of work can be seen at http://jeffreyjkripal.com.

HARTLEY LACHTER is Associate Professor of Religion Studies at Lehigh University, where he holds the Philip and Muriel Berman Chair in Jewish Studies. He also currently serves as the director of the Berman Center for Jewish Studies. His scholarship focuses on medieval Kabbalah, with a particular emphasis on the relationship between Jewish historical experiences and the development of kabbalistic discourses. He is the author of *Kabbalistic Revolution: Reimagining Judaism in Medieval Spain*, published by Rutgers University Press in 2014. He holds a PhD in Jewish Mysticism from New York University, where he studied with Elliot Wolfson.

SHAUL MAGID is Professor of Jewish Studies at Dartmouth College, a senior fellow at the Center for the Study of World Religions at Harvard, and the Kogod Senior Research Fellow at the Shalom Hartman Institute of North America. His latest books are *Meir Kahane: The Public Life and Political Thought of an American Jewish Radical* (Princeton University Press, 2021), and *The Necessity of Exile: Essays from a Distance* (New York: Ayin Press). He is the contributing editor of the column "Teiku" for the *Ayin Journal* and writes regularly for *+972* and *Religion Dispatches*. He is an elected member of the American Academy for Jewish Research and the American Society for the Study of Religion.

PROF. RONIT MEROZ, from the Department of Jewish Philosophy and Talmud, Tel Aviv University, has been lately awarded by the Israel Academy of Sciences and Humanities for outstanding scholarship of Kabbalah (Gershom Scholem Prize for Kabbalah Research, 2022). She is the author of *Headwaters of the Zohar: Analysis and Annotated Critical Editions of Parashat Exodus of the Zohar* (Tel Aviv: Tel Aviv University Press, 2019, in Hebrew), which was awarded the 2020 Ben Zvi Prize for research of the Jewish Communities in the East. She is also the author of *The Spiritual Biography of Rabbi Simeon bar Yochay: An Analysis of the Zohar's Textual Components* (Jerusalem: Mossad Bialik, 2019, in Hebrew), which was awarded the Matan'el Prize for Jewish Thought by the World Union of Jewish Studies in 2019 for best original book in Jewish Thought, published in Hebrew. She is the editor of *New Developments in Zohar Studies, Te'uda* 21–22 (Tel Aviv University, 2007, in Hebrew); and co-editor of *And This is for Yehuda: Studies Presented to Our Friend, Professor Yehuda Liebes, on the Occasion of his Sixty-Fifth Birthday* (Jerusalem: Mossad Bialik,2012, in Hebrew).

HAVIVA PEDAYA is a professor of Jewish history at Ben-Gurion University. She heads the Elyachar Center for Studies in Sephardi Heritage and is incumbent of the Matanel Foundation on the Ben Gurion University campus, and incumbent of the Estelle S. Frankfurter Chair in Sephardic Studies. Prof. Pedaya has written and edited books on different subjects on a range of historical and cultural issues such as Judaism and Israel, ethical questions from Jewish sources, questions of religion and politics, and questions of collective and personal trauma. She has published fifteen books of poetry and prose, and she has been awarded the Harry Harshon Award, the Warburg Prize, the Bernstein Prize for Poetry (1997), and the President's Prize for Poetry (2004). For her studies on Kabbalah she won the Gershom Scholem Prize (2018).

DR. SARAH PESSIN is Professor of Philosophy and Jewish Thought at the University of Denver where she holds an Interfaith Chair. Sarah works on philosophies and phenomenologies of religion and ethics, on topics in interfaith civics, and in a wide range of late ancient, medieval, and modern philosophical traditions. She is the author of *Ibn Gabirol's Theology of Desire* (Cambridge University Press, 2013) and has written chapters for key reference works such as *Oxford Philosophical Concepts*, *Blackwell Companion to Philosophy in the Middle Ages*, *Cambridge Companion to Medieval Jewish Philosophy*, *Cambridge History of Jewish Philosophy*, *Routledge Companion to Islamic Philosophy*, *The Encyclopedia of the Philosophy of Religion*, and *Stanford Encyclopedia of Philosophy*. Sarah is currently working on a project on "uncomfortable virtues" as well as on a study of embodiment, pardon, and paradox in early Levinas.

ANNETTE YOSHIKO REED is the Krister Stendahl Professor of New Testament and Early Christianity at Harvard Divinity School. Her most recent book is *Demons, Angels, and Writing in Ancient Judaism* (Cambridge University Press, 2020). She is also the author of books including *Fallen Angels and the History of Judaism and Christianity* and *Jewish-Christianity and the History of Judaism*. She has also co-authored and co-edited multiple volumes, including *The Ways That Never Parted* with Adam H. Becker, *Jews and Christians in the Roman Empire* with Natalie Dohrmann, *Enoch from Antiquity to the Middle Ages* with John C. Reeves, and *Rediscovering Enoch? The Antediluvian Past in the 15th and 19th Centuries* with Ariel Hessayon and Gabriele Boccaccini.

DR. LEORE SACHS is a member of the senior faculty in the Department of Jewish Philosophy at Bar Ilan University. Her expertise lies in the fields of Kabbalah and Hasidism, with a particular emphasis on topics related to ethics and morality, the rationale of commandments, the history of emotions, sexuality and gender studies. She is currently engaged in research projects that employ computational analysis to examine various conceptual and linguistics constructs of Hasidic traditions and mystical texts.

HAVA TIROSH-SAMUELSON (PhD, Hebrew University of Jerusalem, 1978) is Regents Professor of History, Irving and Miriam Lowe Professor of Modern Judaism, and Director of the Center for Jewish Studies at Arizona State University. She is the author of *Religion and Environment: The Case of Judaism* (2020), *Happiness in Premodern Judaism: Virtue, Knowledge and Well-Being* (2003), and the award-winning *Between Worlds: The Life and Thought of Rabbi David ben Judah Messer Leon* (1991). She is also the editor of several volumes, among them *Judaism and Ecology: Created World and Revealed Word* (2002) and *The Legacy of Hans Jonas: Judaism and the Phenomenon of Life* (2008), and the editor-in-chief of *The Library of Contemporary Jewish Philosophers* (2012–2018), a set of twenty-one volumes in which Elliot R. Wolfson was featured.

ELIYAHU STERN is Professor of Modern Jewish Intellectual and Cultural History at Yale University. He is the author of *The Genius: Elijah of Vilna and the Making of Modern Judaism* (Yale University Press, 2012) and *Jewish Materialism: The Revolution of the 1870s* (Yale University Press, 2018).

STEVEN M. WASSERSTROM is the Moe and Izetta Tonkon Professor of Judaic Studies and the Humanities at Reed College in Portland, Oregon, where he has taught since 1987. *Between Muslim and Jew: The Problem of Symbiosis under Early Islam*, published by Princeton University Press in 1995, was given the Award for Excellence in Historical Studies from the American Academy of Religion. *Religion after Religion: Gershom Scholem, Mircea Eliade, and Henry Corbin at Eranos* was published by Princeton University Press in 1999. *"The Fullness of Time": Poems by Gershom Scholem*, selected, edited, and introduced by Steven M. Wasserstrom, translated by Richard Sieburth (Ibis Editions: Jerusalem, 2003; second edition, re-titled *Greetings from Angelus*) was published by Archipelago Books in 2018. *All Religion Is Inter-Religion: Engaging the Work of Steven M. Wasserstrom* (Bloomsbury USA Academic, edited by Paul Robertson and Kambiz GhaneaBassiri) appeared in 2019.

ELISABETH WEBER is Professor of German and Comparative Literature at the University of California, Santa Barbara. She is an instructor for the "Foundations in the Humanities" Prison Pedagogy Correspondence Program of the Interdisciplinary Humanities Center at UC Santa Barbara, and has taught for the Scholars At Risk Network USA. Her publications include *Verfolgung und Trauma. Zu Emmanuel Lévinas' Autrement qu'être ou au-delà de l'essence* (1990) and *Kill Boxes. Facing the Legacy of US-Sponsored Torture, Indefinite Detention, and Drone Warfare* (2017). She is also the editor of *Questions au Judaïsme*, a collection of interviews with, among others, Pierre Vidal-Naquet, Jacques Derrida, Emmanuel Levinas, and Jean-François Lyotard (1996, English translation 2004), and of *Living Together. Jacques Derrida's Communities of Violence and Peace* (2013). Together with Julie Carlson she co-edited *Speaking about Torture* (2012). She currently works on environmental humanities, in particular literary and cultural plant studies.

INDEX

Page numbers in italics indicate figures or photos.

C

E

I

U

V